A Stanley Gibbons checklist
of the stamps of Great Britain

# Collect **British** *Stamps*

66th Edition
2015

38
FDC

37 × 1912
AIR FORCE

1 × 2000
Guernsey

Stanley Gibbons Limited
London and Ringwood

BY APPOINTMENT TO
HER MAJESTY THE QUEEN
PHILATELISTS
STANLEY GIBBONS LTD
LONDON

1914 - 2014

Published by Stanley Gibbons Ltd
Editorial, Publications Sales Offices
and Distribution Centre:
7 Parkside, Christchurch Road, Ringwood,
Hants BH24 3SH

© Stanley Gibbons Ltd 2014

British Library Cataloguing in
Publication Data.
A catalogue record for this book is available
from the British Library.

Errors and omissions excepted. The colour
reproduction of stamps is only as accurate as
the printing process will allow.

ISBN-10: 0-85259-923-4
ISBN-13: 978-0-85259-923-5

Item No. R0289-15

Printed by Stephens & George, Wales

# Contents

# The 2015 Edition

COLLECT BRITISH STAMPS has been the standard guide for collectors of Great Britain ever since the first edition was published in September 1967.

It provides a straightforward, easy-to-use work of reference, with every stamp design illustrated in colour and clear, uncomplicated listings ideally suited to the newer collector, while at the same time providing a handy checklist for the more advanced philatelist – small wonder that over four million copies have been sold to collectors around the world.

*Collect British Stamps* appears in the autumn of each year: for a more detailed listing, the *Great Britain Concise Catalogue* is published in the spring incorporating many additional features and is ideal for the collector who needs more information about GB stamps.

## Scope. Collect British Stamps comprises:

◆ All stamps with different watermark (wmk) or perforation (perf).

◆ Visible plate numbers on Victorian issues.

◆ Graphite-lined and phosphor issues, including variations in the numbers of phosphor bands.

◆ First Day Covers for Definitives from 1936, Regionals and all Special Issues.

◆ Presentation, Gift and Souvenir Packs.

◆ Post Office Yearbooks and year packs.

◆ Regional issues and War Occupation stamps of Guernsey and Jersey.

◆ Postage Due and Official Stamps.

◆ Post Office Picture Cards (PHQ cards).

◆ Commemorative gutter pairs and 'Traffic Light' gutter pairs listed as mint sets.

◆ Royal Mail Postage Labels priced as sets and on P.O. First Day Cover.

◆ Royal Mail Post & Go Stamps

◆ The introduction includes a full design index for commemorative issues, a Great Britain collector's glossary and articles giving helpful advice on a range of collecting topics

Stamps of the independent postal administrations of Guernsey, Isle of Man and Jersey are contained in *Collect Channel Islands and Isle of Man Stamps*.

## New for this edition

◆ A thorough review of all prices has been carried out, with a number of increases since the 2014 edition

◆ Issues for 2014 have been added and the listings of earlier issues carefully checked and updated

◆ A quick-reference priced listing of the popular Royal Mail Prestige and Sponsored booklets has been added.

## Layout

Stamps are set out chronologically by date of issue. In the catalogue lists the first numeral is the Stanley Gibbons catalogue number; the black (boldface) numeral alongside is the type number referring to the respective illustration. A blank in this column implies that the number immediately

above is repeated. The denomination and colour of the stamp are then shown. Before February 1971 British currency was:

£1 = 20s  One pound = twenty shillings and

1s = 12d  One shilling = twelve pence.

Upon decimalisation this became:

£1 = 100p

One pound = one hundred (new) pence.

The catalogue list then shows two price columns. The left-hand is for unused stamps and the right-hand for used. Corresponding small boxes are provided in which collectors may wish to check off the items in their collection. Our method of indicating prices is: Numerals for pence, e.g. 10 denotes 10p (10 pence). Numerals for pounds and pence, e.g. 4·25 denotes £4·25 (4 pounds and 25 pence). For £100 and above, prices are in whole pounds and so include the £ sign and omit the zeros for pence.

## Colour illustrations

The colour illustrations of stamps are intended as a guide only; they may differ in shade from the originals.

## Size of illustrations

To comply with Post Office regulations stamp illustrations are three-quarters linear size. Separate illustrations of surcharges, overprints and watermarks are actual size.

## Prices

The prices quoted in this catalogue are the estimated selling prices of Stanley Gibbons Ltd at the time of publication. They are *unless it is specifically stated otherwise*, for examples in fine condition for the issue concerned. Superb examples are worth more; those of a lower quality considerably less. For more details on catalogue prices, see page xxxv

The unused prices for stamps of Queen Victoria to King George V are for lightly hinged examples. Unused prices for King Edward VIII to Queen Elizabeth II are for unmounted mint (though when not available unmounted, mounted stamps are often supplied at a lower price). Prices for used stamps refer to fine postally used copies. All prices are subject to change without prior notice and we give no guarantee to supply all stamps priced, since it is not possible to keep every catalogued item in stock. Commemorative issues may only be available in complete sets.

In the price columns:

† = Does not exist.

(—) or blank = Exists, or may exist, but price cannot be quoted.

* = Not normally issued (the so-called 'Abnormals' of 1862–80).

## Minimum price

The minimum price quoted is 10 pence. For individual stamps prices between 10 pence and 95 pence are provided as a guide for catalogue users. The lowest price *charged* for individual stamps or sets purchased from Stanley Gibbons is £1.

## Perforations

The 'perforation' is the number of holes in a length of 2 cm, as measured by the Gibbons Instanta gauge. The stamp is viewed against a dark background with the transparent gauge put on top of it. Perforations are quoted to the nearest half. Stamps without perforation are termed 'imperforate'. From 1992 certain stamps occur with a large elliptical (oval) hole inserted in each line of vertical perforations. The £10 definitive, No. 1658, is unique in having two such holes in the horizontal perforations.

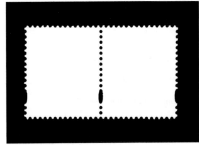

Elliptical perforations

## *Se-tenant* combinations

*Se-tenant* means 'joined together'. Some sets include stamps of different design arranged *se-tenant* as blocks or strips and these are often collected unsevered as issued. Where such combinations exist the stamps are priced both mint and used, as singles or complete sets. The set price refers to the unsevered combination plus singles of any other values in the set.

## First day covers

Prices for first day covers are for complete sets used on plain covers (Nos. 430/8, 453/60, 462/78b, 485/90, and 503/12) or on special covers (Nos. 461, 479/84, 491/502 and 513 onwards), the stamps of which are cancelled with ordinary operational postmarks (1924–1962) or by the standard 'First Day of Issue' postmarks (1963 onwards). The British Post Office did not provide 'First Day' treatment for every definitive issued after 1963. Where the stamps in a set were issued on different days, prices are for a cover from each day.

## Presentation Packs

Special packs comprising slip-in cards with printed information inside a protective covering, were introduced for the 1964 Shakespeare issue. Collectors packs, containing commemoratives from the preceding twelve months, were issued from 1967. Some packs with text in German from 1968–69, exist as does a Japanese version of the pack for Nos. 916/17. Yearbooks, hardbound and illustrated in colour within a slip cover, joined the product range in 1984.

It should be noted that prices given for presentation packs are for items as originally sold, including any additional inserts such as questionaire forms and publicity material.

## PHQ cards

Since 1973 the Post Office has produced a series of picture cards, which can be sent through the post as postcards. Each card shows an enlarged colour reproduction of a current British stamp, either of one or more values from a set or of all values. Cards are priced here in fine mint condition for sets complete as issued. The Post Office gives each card a 'PHQ' serial number, hence the term. The cards are usually on sale shortly before the date of issue of the stamps, but there is no officially designated 'first day'. Used prices are for cards franked with the stamp depicted, on the obverse or reverse; the stamp being cancelled with an official postmark for first day of issue. For 1973–76 issues cards with stamps on the obverse are worth about 25% more than the prices quoted.

Gutter pair

## Gutter pairs

Almost all modern Great Britain commemoratives are produced in sheets containing two panes of stamps separated by a blank horizontal or vertical margin known as a gutter. This feature first made its appearance on some supplies of the 1972 Royal Silver Wedding 3p, and marked the introduction of Harrison & Sons' new 'Jumelle' stamp-printing press. There are advantages for both the printer and the Post Office in such a layout which has now been used for nearly all commemorative issues since 1974. The term 'gutter pair' is used for a pair of stamps separated by part of the blank gutter margin. We do not list gutter pairs for self-adhesive stamps since, although the production format is the same, the stamps are separated by die-cutting.

Most printers include some form of colour check device on the sheet margins, in addition to the cylinder or plate numbers. Harrison & Sons used round 'dabs' or spots of colour, resembling traffic lights. For the period from the 1972 Royal Silver Wedding until the end of 1979 these colour dabs appeared in the gutter margin. Gutter pairs showing these 'traffic lights' are worth considerably more than the normal version. From the 2004 Entente Cordiale set, Walsall reintroduced traffic lights in the gutters of certain sets. Where these extend over more than one section of gutter margin on any stamp they are priced as blocks rather than pairs.

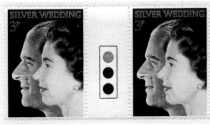

Traffic light gutter pair

## No Value Indicated Stamps

From 22 August 1989 various definitive and special stamps appeared inscribed "2nd", "1st" or "E" instead of a face value. These were sold at the current minimum rates for these services which were as follows:

| Inland Postage Rate | 2nd Class | 1st Class |
|---|---|---|
| 5 September 1988 | 14p. | 19p. |
| 2 October 1989 | 15p. | 20p. |
| 17 September 1990 | 17p. | 22p. |
| 16 September 1991 | 18p. | 24p. |
| 1 November 1993 | 19p. | 25p. |
| 8 July 1996 | 20p. | 26p. |
| 26 April 1999 | 19p. | 26p. |
| 17 April 2000 | 19p. | 27p. |
| 8 May 2003 | 20p. | 28p. |
| 1 April 2004 | 21p. | 28p. |
| 7 April 2005 | 21p. | 30p. |

| Inland Postage Rate | 2nd Class | 1st Class |
|---|---|---|
| 3 April 2006 | 23p. | 32p. |
| 2 April 2007 | 24p. | 34p. |
| 7 April 2008 | 27p. | 36p. |
| 6 April 2009 | 30p. | 39p. |
| 6 April 2010 | 32p. | 41p. |
| 4 April 2011 | 36p. | 46p. |
| 30 April 2012 | 50p. | 60p. |
| 31 March 2014 | 53p. | 62p. |

| European Airmail Rate | |
|---|---|
| 26 April 1999 | 30p. |
| 25 October 1999 | 34p. |
| 27 April 2000 | 36p. |
| 2 July 2001 | 37p. |
| 27 March 2003 | 38p. |
| 1 April 2004 | 40p. |

From June 2004, European Airmail rate stamps reverted to showing a face value.

From 21 August 2006 "Large" letters were charged at a higher rate following the introduction of "Pricing in Proportion". Rates as follows:

| Inland Postage Rate | 2nd Class Large | 1st Class Large |
|---|---|---|
| 21 August 2006 | 37p. | 44p. |
| 2 April 2007 | 40p. | 48p. |
| 7 April 2008 | 42p. | 52p. |
| 6 April 2009 | 47p. | 61p. |
| 6 April 2010 | 51p. | 66p. |
| 4 April 2011 | 58p. | 75p. |
| 30 April 2012 | 69p. | 90p. |
| 31 March 2014 | 73p. | 93p. |

## Catalogue numbers used

This checklist uses the same catalogue numbers as other current Stanley Gibbons catalogues.

Latest issue date for stamps recorded in this edition is 5 November 2013.

> **We regret we do not give opinions as to the genuineness of stamps, nor do we identify stamps or number them by our Catalogue**

# Commemorative Design Index

*This index gives an easy reference to the inscriptions and designs of the Special Stamps, 1953 to December 2013. Where a complete set shares an inscription or type of design, then only the catalogue number of the first stamp is given in addition to separate entries for stamps depicting popular thematic subjects. Paintings, inventions, etc., are indexed under the name of the artist or inventor, where this is shown on the stamp.*

## 1. £.s.d. ISSUES 1953–70

# Get the Best Deal!

## Thinking about selling your stamps?

Apex offers a FREE VALUATION SERVICE - with a full and immediate settlement - any currency, any amount, anywhere!

Apex is looking to buy quality single items and collections, from most countries. We especially need good quality Great Britain and Commonwealth. With tens of thousands of collectors on our books, we have the demand!

**Our offers are hard to beat!**

Send what you have for our immediate attention. Or our specialists will be delighted at meet you at our London offices – an appointment not always necessary. For properties of sufficient value, we can come to you if you prefer.

We'll provide an immediate appraisal of what your stamps are likely to fetch at auction and, based on that figure, an offer for private treaty purchase. You choose whether you prefer to consign at auction, or sell via private treaty at the full cash value – **we'll find the deal that's right for *you*.**

Get the best deal, by dealing with one of the UK's leading stamp dealers and auctioneers – Apex Philatelics.

Get in touch today!

Our Principle Philatelic Buyers and Specialists:

Tim Francis    + 44 (0) 7889 006 736
Rick Warren    + 44 (0) 1342 830 220
Colin Avery    + 44 (0) 207 495 9497

We look forward to hearing from you!

# APEX
## *The Name for Philatelics*

# The Stanley Gibbons Group plc

## 399 Strand

Our world famous stamp shop is a collector's paradise, with all of our latest catalogues, albums and accessories and, of course, our unrivalled stockholding of postage stamps.

www.stanleygibbons.com
shop@stanleygibbons.com
+44 (0)20 7836 8444

## Specialist Stamp Sales

For the collector that appreciates the value of collecting the highest quality examples, Stanley Gibbons is the only choice. Our extensive range is unrivalled in terms of quality and quantity, with specialist stamps available from all over the world.

www.stanleygibbons.com/stamps
shop@stanleygibbons.com
+44 (0)20 7836 8444

## Stanley Gibbons Great Britain Mail Order

Stanley Gibbons Mail Order Department provides the perfect support for those starting or furthering their collection, particularly for more modern issues. We produce regular brochures listing our available Great Britain, Channel Islands and Isle of Man material.

## Stanley Gibbons Auctions and Valuations

Sell your collection or individual rare items through our prestigious public auctions or our regular postal auctions and benefit from the excellent prices being realised at auction currently. We also provide an unparalleled valuation service.

www.stanleygibbons.com/auctions
auctions@stanleygibbons.com
+44 (0)20 7836 8444

## Stanley Gibbons Publications

Stanley Gibbons published one of the world's first stamp catalogues in 1865 and we haven't looked back since! Our catalogues are trusted worldwide as the industry standard and we print countless titles each year. We also publish consumer and trade magazines, *Gibbons Stamp Monthly* and *Philatelic Exporter* to bring you news, views and insights into all things philatelic. Never miss an issue by subscribing today and benefit from exclusive subscriber offers each month.

www.stanleygibbons.com
orders@stanleygibbons.com
+44 (0)1425 472 363

## Stanley Gibbons Investments

The Stanley Gibbons Investment Department offers a unique range of investment propositions that have consistently outperformed more traditional forms of investment, from structured portfolios in rare stamps and other premium collectibles designed to suit your needs to a longer-term investment product with regular monthly deposits and increased flexibility.

Investment.stanleygibbons.com
investment@stanleygibbons.com
+44 (0)1534 766 711

## Fraser's Autographs

Autographs, manuscripts and memorabilia from Henry VIII to current day. We have over 60,000 items in stock, including movie stars, musicians, sport stars, historical figures and royalty. Fraser's is the UK's market leading autograph dealer and has been dealing in high quality autographed material since 1978. Fraser's also has three specialist auctions per annum in conjunction with Dreweatts & Bloomsbury Auctions.

www.frasersautographs.com
sales@frasersautographs.com
+44 (0)20 7836 9325

## stanleygibbons.com

Our website offers the complete philatelic service. Whether you are looking to buy stamps, invest, read news articles, browse our online stamp catalogue or find new issues, you are just one click away from anything you desire in the world of stamp collecting at stanleygibbons.com. Happy browsing!

www.stanleygibbons.com

## Dreweatts & Bloomsbury Auctions

With a history that dates back over 250 years to 1759, Dreweatts & Bloomsbury Auctions are a UK 'Top 4' auctioneer of Fine and Contemporary Art, Antiques, Jewellery and Antiquarian Books. They have the broadest and most regular calendar of specialist catalogued sales in the industry and provide vendors and buyers alike access to market-leading specialist advice in any number of collecting fields.

www.dreweatts.com
info@dnfa.com
+44 (0) 1635 553 553

## Baldwin's

Founded in 1872, Baldwin's is one of the largest and longest established Numismatic dealers and auction houses in the world. The dedicated team of specialists have over 300 years combined experience covering all areas of numismatics including English, Ancient and Foreign coins, military and commemorative medals, tokens, books, banknotes, stamps and autographs.

www.baldwin.co.uk
coins@baldwin.co.uk
+44 (0)20 7930 6879

## Apex Philatelics

Whether you are buying or selling stamps, Apex prides itself on its personable staff, rapid turnaround and conscientious attention to detail. Acting as both a dealer and auctioneer, Apex handle pieces which range in value from 10p to £100,000 and our pricing has always been affordable when compared to the open market.

www.apexstamps.com
admin@apexstamps.com
+44 (0)20 7495 9497

## Benham Collectibles

Benham Collectibles is the leading producer of First Day Covers. In operation for over 35 years Benham offer a range of first day covers, stamps, autographs, & coins featuring royalty, military, sport, railways, aviation, entertainment, and much more.

www.benham.co.uk
benham@benham.co.uk
+44 (0)1303 762 050

## Murray Payne

Founded in 1990, Murray Payne is the world's leading dealer in British Commonwealth King George VI stamps and widely regarded as a leading expert in all aspects of British Commonwealth philately.

www.murraypayne.com
info@murraypayne.com
+44 (0) 1934 732511

## bidStart

bidStart is an online marketplace and community connecting buyers and sellers of collectibles; including stamps, coins, comics, sports cards and more; offering auction & store items.

www.bidstart.com

## Plastic Wax Records

Plastic Wax deal in vinyl, CD's and DVD's including rare and specialised items.

www.plasticwaxrecords.com
dave.kellard@plasticwaxrecords.com
+44(0)1179 427 368

# Collecting Stamps – the Basics

It seems reasonable to assume, since you are reading this, that you already collect British stamps – but of course there are many ways of building on any collection and, if you are relatively new to it, we hope that the following will be of some guidance.

Traditionally, stamp collectors were introduced to the hobby with a quantity of world stamps, some still on envelopes and cards, which were then sorted and mounted in an album. In due course, many would decide to concentrate on a single country or group of countries and "specialisation" would begin, based on the experience built up as a "world collector".

More recently, an alternative route has become prevalent, in which, often as a gift, collections may be built on a "standing order" from a philatelic bureau, with stamps or covers arriving automatically, as they are issued, to be mounted in an album or stockbook. Albums are conveniently designed to meet the needs of this type of collection, with an illustrated space in which to mount every stamp.

This type of collection has much to recommend it – but one big disadvantage – it will be exactly the same as thousands of others, built up in the same way.

For this reason, many collectors are now returning to the delights of general collecting while maintaining their existing collections, and finding that the fun they had as children is very easy to recapture!

If you came to the hobby via "the standing order" route and would like to start a second "general collection", here are a few tips and suggestions.

## Obtaining your stamps

Children were encouraged to buy – or persuade their parents to buy – the largest packet of stamps they could, as just sorting them into countries would prove enormously useful and interesting. Unfortunately large packets of world stamps are not as easy to obtain as they used to be, but you can still buy existing collections of all sorts at stamp fairs, shops or at auction, prices to suit every pocket. Just sorting and remounting such a collection will prove tremendously exciting.

Sooner or later, of course, you will identify gaps in your collection that you want to fill. It is useful to keep a note of these in a book that you can take with you when you visit a stamp shop or stamp fair – no one can remember everything and it is always annoying to discover that you have just bought a stamp you didn't need!

It is vitally important of course that you keep your "wants" book up-to-date and cross out items as you acquire them.

As well as visiting stamp fairs, you can check out the advertisements in the press; establish a good relationship with a dealer you like and, he will be happy to receive a "wants list" from you. He will then supply you with any items on it he has currently in stock and keep a record of anything else so that he can send it on to you if he gets one. All such items are usually "on approval", so that if you have found them somewhere else, you are not obliged to purchase them.

More expensive items can be purchased at auction. Many of the larger auction houses do not like to sell items of lower value and therefore, in the main, offer more expensive single stamps and covers or complete collections and accumulations.

Other auctions offer single items of lower value and these can be a great way of picking up items you need. Stanley Gibbons Postbid auctions fall into this category, but there are many others and, once again, it is good to identify an auction house which regularly offers the type of material you are looking for and provides a reliable service.

Another method of buying stamps is "kiloware". These are stamps sold by weight and generally assumed to be "unsorted" i.e. no one has been through them before and picked the good ones out. Many collectors enjoy this approach to stamp collecting and they will tell you of the wonderful "finds" they have made – but inevitably you will be left with a vast majority of stamps that you do not want because they duplicate items already in your collection. Charity shops will always be happy to receive them – and they will eventually finish up in someone else's "genuinely unsorted kiloware" – so once again, if this is your kind of collecting, establish a good relationship with a reliable supplier.

"Kiloware" is generally supplied in the form of stamps on paper, torn or cut from envelopes – so this is probably a good point at which to discuss one of the real basics of stamp collecting – soaking stamps off paper.

It is helpful to carry out some rudimentary sorting before you start. Soaking stamps is quite a time-consuming process, so you do not want to waste time on stamps you don't need or don't want, maybe because they are damaged.

Once you have sorted out the stamps you want to soak off, pour some clean water (warm but *not* hot) into a bowl; then float each stamp (face uppermost) on the surface of the water. You can float as many stamps at one time as you have room for.

Leave the stamps for 15 minutes or so to give the water time to soak the gum that is sticking the stamp to the paper. Most stamps can then be gently peeled away. If they do not come away easily do not try to tear them off the paper. Leave them for another five minutes or so and try again.

Providing your hands are clean it's better to handle the stamps with your fingers when peeling off the envelope paper. The paper of stamps is weakened when it is damp and picking them up with tweezers may damage them.

When you have peeled the stamps off the envelope there will probably be some damp gum still on the back of them.

Use a soft brush dipped in water to remove this, a paint brush is ideal. Alternatively let the stamp float on the water for a few minutes – the gum will dissolve away. However, do not immerse the stamp in water. For most stamps this would be safe enough but for some it would be dangerous as the ink may run.

Then shake off any excess water and place the stamps face upwards on a sheet of clean kitchen paper towel. This is why it is so important to clean all the gum off. If you do not, your stamps will stick to the paper and you will have to float them off all over again. When all the stamps are laid out cover them with more paper towel then make a kind of sandwich by putting a few sheets of ordinary paper on top.

Place a heavy book on this sandwich. This will flatten the stamps as they dry. After half an hour open up the sandwich and carefully remove the stamps. Spread them out on another piece of clean paper and leave to dry in the air for a little while. When completely dry they are ready for mounting in your album.

Or you can just lay the stamps face down on paper towel and allow them to dry out in the air. If you use this method do not try to speed up the drying by putting the stamps in the sun or close to a hot radiator as they will curl up and you may damage them when you flatten them out to put them in your album.

There are two things which you must be very careful about when floating stamps. Firstly, many old stamps were printed in special inks which run, change colour, or even disappear completely in water. Fewer modern stamps are affected in this way but even so it is best to be safe, so avoid letting water get on the surface of the stamp when you are floating-off. Be careful when floating stamps to keep separate stamps affixed to white and coloured envelopes. Take out any stamp which are stuck to bits of coloured paper and float these separately. Floating can easily make the ink run and so damage your stamps by staining them with unwanted colours.

These days, many countries produce "self-adhesive" stamps and these may not come away from their backing paper at all. If you believe that a stamp may be "self-adhesive', it would be better to leave it on the paper, carefully trimming round it with scissors, making sure you do not cut into the stamp.

Finally, always think twice before tearing a stamp off an envelope. Most old stamps and some modern ones too, if they have interesting postmarks, will be more valuable if left on the envelope. If in doubt always try to ask a more experienced collector's advice.

New Imperial album

## Choosing an Album and Mounting your stamps

These are two different topics but really need to be considered together, as the way you mount your stamps will depend on the album you choose and your choice of album may depend on the way you wish to mount your stamps. Here are some of the options:

### Printed Albums

You may be used to an album printed with a space for every stamp, and these may be obtained for larger groups of countries, such as the Stanley Gibbons New Imperial Album, with spaces for all Commonwealth and Empire stamps up to 1936. If this is the sort of collection you hope to build they are fine albums – but as they have a space for every stamp, filling one would be a time-consuming and expensive business!

### Blank albums

These are made up of blank pages, printed with a faint "quadrille" (tiny squares) which help you lay your stamps out neatly. These give you freedom to lay your collection out as you wish, leaving spaces for stamps you are hoping to obtain, or a neat display of the stamps you have. The former option may mean that you have a lot of gaps on the page, the latter may mean fairly regular rearrangement of your collection – the choice is yours.

Blank albums come in a wide range of prices and binding types, from inexpensive ring binders, through traditional "springbacks" to high quality "peg-fitting" types. Again, the choice is yours.

### Stockbooks

In the past, collectors used stockbooks to hold duplicates and stamps awaiting mounting in the main album, but due to their convenience and cost, many collectors are now using stockbooks to house their main collections.

They certainly make it easy to "mount" your stamps – you just slip them into the strips on the pages and you can move them around easily to accommodate new acquisitions too! You can even write notes regarding different stamps or sets and slip those into the strips.

### Stock albums

These are loose-leaf stockbooks, which have the added benefit of being able to insert extra pages in the book. Also, because the strips come in a number of formats, they look better than a stockbook layout which is a bit restricting and does not show larger items, such as covers, blocks and miniature sheets, very well.

### Mounting your stamps

Before we come on to cover albums, let's return to the matter of mounting your stamps. If you have chosen either the stockbook or stock album option, this is not really an issue as you can just slip your stamps into the strips on the page. If you have opted for a printed or blank album, on the other hand, the question of mounting is important.

The traditional stamp hinge is generally the preferred option for used stamps. Instructions for their use are generally given on the packet, so we will not repeat them here, but we must stress that the key points are to *lightly* moisten the hinge before attaching it to the stamp or album page and *not to try to remove it* until it's dry or you may damage the page – or even more important, the stamp.

For unused stamps that have been previously mounted, stamp hinges are also perfectly acceptable, but for stamps which still have "full original gum" and show no evidence of having been previously hinged, most collectors now favour "hingeless mounts", which allow you to attach the stamp to the page without disturbing the gum (keeping the stamp "unmounted").

For most of the most frequently encountered stamp sizes, cut-to-size mounts are available for immediate use. Less common sizes will have to be cut from bigger strips, but even large blocks and miniature sheets can be mounted in this way.

Although hingeless mounts are gummed, ready for use, many collectors prefer to use hinges to attach them to the album page as this makes them easier to move around when new stamps are added.

## Covers

Many collectors like to include covers in their collections – either "first day" or "souvenir" covers or simply envelopes that show examples of the stamps in use. This is especially desirable in the case of early covers, which might show unusual postmarks or other features.

Universal album

Covers can be mounted on blank pages using gummed photograph corners, but may also be accommodated in purpose-built cover albums. There are even albums, such as the Stanley Gibbons Universal, which are designed to hold stamp and cover pages together (and booklet pages too!).

## What else?

So, that's covered the choice of album and the mounting of stamps: What else do you need? This comes under two headings: equipment and information.

## Information

You can manage without background information, but it would be a bit like setting out on a journey to somewhere you've never been without a map.

The first thing is a catalogue to tell you what exists and will help you to identify what you have. The Stanley Gibbons catalogue range includes something for every collector from the beginner to the specialist.

Beyond that there are specialist handbooks on just about everything, but many are printed in quite small numbers and, once sold, are unlikely to be reprinted. However, specialist dealers and auction houses can be a useful source of out-of-print literature.

You should also try to keep up with what is going on in the philatelic world and, again, Stanley Gibbons is able to help, via its monthly magazine, *Gibbons Stamp Monthly*, recently described as "the best magazine for stamp collectors published anywhere". For a free sample copy and subscription details, please write to Stanley Gibbons Publications, *(the address is at the front of this checklist).*

Of course, as with everything else, much information may also be found on the internet and you will almost certainly find it worth joining the local society in your area, other stamp collectors are always happy to help a newcomer.

## Equipment

Again, what you need in the way of equipment will depend largely on what you are collecting, the degree of specialisation you intend to achieve and the type of album you use.

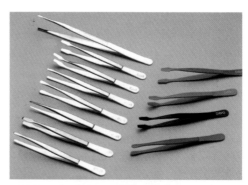

We have already discussed albums and stamp mounts, the only other item every stamp collector must have is a pair of tweezers. All stamps should be handled with tweezers; they ensure that the natural oils in our fingers do not get on to the stamps and, after a bit of practice, they are easier to use than fingers as well. They come in different lengths, with different points and made from different materials (generally stainless steel or gold-plated). Find a style that suits you and stick with it.

From then on the equipment you need is up to you. Most collectors like to have a magnifying glass so they can look at their stamps more closely. Again, they come in a wide range, from the fairly basic, offering 2 or 3× magnification to pocket microscopes giving 30× magnification, and digital microscopes that you can attach to your computer for really detailed examination of your stamps, such as the SG UM02 or UM05, or the pocket-size Pro 10 microscope with integrated digital camera which gives up to 200× magnification, stores up to 2000 images and is perfect for stamp shows.

Another useful type of magnifier is one that incorporates a millimetre scale – ideal for measuring overprints and other features.

Even a quick look in any catalogue will show that differences in perforation, watermark and colour can make an enormous difference to the price of a stamp. So most collectors like to have the necessary equipment to measure perforations, view watermarks and identify colours and shades.

Fortunately, as far as perforations are concerned, the perforation gauge used by most of the world's top collectors and dealers is accessible to all – it's the Stanley Gibbons Instanta – which measures perforations to a decimal point and is easy to use. There is an electronic perforation measurer which is even easier to use – but it is a bit more expensive than the Instanta.

Watermark detectors also come in a variety of types and a wide range of prices, all of which are effective in their different ways. If you are collecting older stamps, watermarks are generally clearer and can be identified simply by placing the stamps face down on a dark background or watermark tray and, if necessary, adding a few drops of lighter fluid or watermark fluid. The Morley Bright products are an excellent alternative if you do not like using fluids, which many collectors do not.

More modern stamps, especially mint ones are more difficult to sort and for these one of the electric watermark detectors will probably be the answer. The Stanley Gibbons Detectamark and other similar products take a bit of practice to get used to, but are very effective. Their drawback is that they can only handle single stamps and cannot accommodate blocks or sheets. If you are able to, visit a shop where you can see the different products demonstrated and make your choice.

Happily, the standard colour guide for stamp collectors, the Stanley Gibbons colour key, is another relatively inexpensive item which will provide years of use. It features 200 different colours and will allow you to tell the difference between "mauve", "purple", "lilac" and "violet" with ease.

Finally and especially if you are collecting the modern stamps of Great Britain at a more specialised level, you will probably want an ultraviolet lamp to identify different papers and phosphor types. Again, these come in a range of designs at different prices, so it is useful to seek the advice of an experienced collector before deciding on the one to buy. If you collect Great Britain stamps, you really need a "short wave" lamp to identify different phosphors, but some lamps incorporate both "long" and "short" wave bulbs, which give them wider potential use.

A lamp with a "hood" or viewing eyepiece is generally to be recommended, firstly because direct exposure to prolonged ultraviolet light is damaging to the eyes, so you should avoid lamps which cause you to see the bulb itself while you are using it. Also, such lamps are more effective in the dark, so anything which shields the stamp being examined from other light sources, including daylight, will improve the effectiveness of the lamp.

The new Stanley Gibbons Ultraviolet lamp, introduced in 2012, offers a broad spectrum light, suitable for detecting all phosphors, while the unique eyepiece makes it suitable for use wherever you are.

Philatelic accessories of all types are available from Stanley Gibbons Publications in Ringwood or at the SG shop in London. The current product guide is available on request. Alternatively, a host of useful information can be found here: www.stanleygibbons.com

# Stanley Gibbons Numbers

When Stanley Gibbons published his first stamp catalogue in 1865 the stamps in it were simply listed by country and description. It was not long, however, before there were just too many stamps to be listed in this way and in order to simplify the way in which stamps could be ordered by customers, each was given its unique and individual number.

Nowadays, as each stamp is added to the catalogue in the supplement published in *Gibbons Stamp Monthly*, it is assigned its number; sets being listed according to the date on which they were issued and then by face value within that set. If several stamps of the same value belong to one set, usually issued in the form of a sheet or sheetlet, the numbering starts at the top left-hand stamp and runs down to the stamp at bottom right.

Long definitive series are listed together for the convenience of collectors so this often involves adding new numbers to an existing series. It can also happen that a stamp or set of stamps are discovered which were unknown at the time of issue – these also have to be inserted in their correct chronological sequence.

## Easy identification

The Stanley Gibbons number appears in the left-hand column of the stamp listing and should not be confused with the bold number that often appears to its right and refers to its illustration. So, by using the country name and catalogue number, every stamp can be easily identified and, rather than having to order Great Britain 1924 10d. turquoise-blue on Block Cypher watermarked paper, all you have to do is order a Great Britain SG428 and state whether you want it used or unused.

In order to render them immediately identifiable, certain types of stamps are given a prefix to their catalogue number thus a number prefixed with a "D" is a postage due stamp, while an "O" means it's an official stamp. Some countries' stamps also have a prefix to allow them to be easily identified. Thus, in this catalogue, Scotland stamp numbers are prefixed with an "S" and those for Wales with a "W".

## Changes

Once a number has been assigned it is not changed unless absolutely necessary. The reason, for this is that collectors often maintain their "wants lists' using SG numbers, while auction houses around the world quote them in their descriptions, as do books and articles in the philatelic press.

Expertising bodies, including the expert committee of the Royal Philatelic Society London and the British Philatelic Association also quote SG numbers in their certificates, which generally identify scarcer or more valuable stamps, so regular changing of those numbers would render such certificates out-of-date.

Nevertheless, sometimes complete sections of the catalogue, occasionally even complete countries, have to be re-organised, and under such circumstances renumbering does take place – but this is infrequent.

Usually, new stamps added into the middle of listings have a letter suffix. This can occur in two forms. If the stamp is listable in its own right the suffix forms a part of the "main" number in the left-hand column of the listing. Thus, when the Wilding 4½d. and 5d. values with phosphor bands appeared, in 1961 and 1967 respectively, but the 4d. and 6d., both issued in 1960, had already been given the numbers 616 and 617, the 4½d. became 616a and the 5d. was listed as 616b.

Varieties of such "main" stamps, such as errors, booklet panes and watermark varieties are given letter suffixes in a different way, so that the phosphor version of the 1963 6d. Paris Postal Conference stamp (SG 636) has a "p" suffix which appears in the listing itself, to differentiate it from the normal, non-phosphor stamp – so to order one, all you need to ask for is SG 636p.

Sometimes, of course, so many stamps are subsequently added to a listing that the use of suffix letters would just become too complicated and, so far as Great Britain is concerned, this has happened with the decimal Machin series, which are prefixed "X" for the conventionally perforated series, first issued in 1971, and "Y" for the series with elliptical perforations at each side, first issued in 1993. In 2009 a new series with additional security features began to appear and these are listed with a "U" prefix.

## Adding new numbers

Thus when new stamps are added to such series – and several are appearing each year – adding new numbers does not have to mean changing those of subsequently issued commemorative issues.

Within the "U" series, new "main" values are initially added with a suffix letter, so the numbers of previously issued stamps do not have to be adjusted with each new catalogue, but every four or five years the complete listing is updated to eliminate the suffix letters and maintain a "clean" listing of numbers. When ordering stamps from these series it is as well to mention which edition of the catalogue you are using as, if your dealer is using a different one, you may not receive what you expect!

The Stanley Gibbons numbering system represents an easy-to-use and universally recognised system of stamp identification.

Collectors all over the world use it to keep their collections in order and dealers sort and classify their stocks by it, so its use makes life easier for everyone.

Stanley Gibbons numbers are fully protected by copyright and, while their use is encouraged, they may not be reproduced without the prior permission of Stanley Gibbons Limited.

# THE STAMP CENTRE

## 79 STRAND LONDON WC2R 0DE - WWW.THESTAMPCENTRE.CO.UK

### THE ONLY REMAINING INDEPENDENT STAMP DEALER ON THE STRAND

SHOP HOURS MON - SAT 9.30-5.00 - FREEPHONE HOTLINE 0800 975 4581
OVERSEAS CUSTOMERS PLEASE TELEPHONE 00 44 207 836 2341

## * COLLECT BRITISH STAMPS READER OFFERS *

### A. THE 1841 IMPERFORATE PENNY RED

We will supply 20 different three margin copies of this famous stamp, known the world over for just £39.90 post-free or 40 completely different for just £75 post-free.

### B. 1858/70 PENNY RED PLATE NUMBERS

We will supply 40 different stamps in sound used condition. Sort the plates to begin or build your collection & then start searching for the missing ones with this appealing offer for £39.90 post-free.

Welcome to The Stamp Centre, a collectors paradise here in the heart of London, established in 1985 and just twenty five yards across the road from our neighbours at Stanley Gibbons! We send out lists with offers similar to these every few weeks and if you would like to receive them, simply call or email mail@thestampcentre.co.uk

We also send out our Daily Offers email to an increasing number of customers and these feature a diverse array of recent acquisitions, collections and sundry items, many purchased that very day and offered direct to your 'Inbox'. These are hugely popular and you can subscribe to these completely free of charge by sending an email with the subject of 'join' to dailyoffers@thestampcentre.co.uk

### C. THE 1880/1 INDIGO SET

We offer this popular set of 5 different mid-reign Victorian stamps, SG 164/9 in sound used condition for just £57.50 post-free which represents superb value for money as all our offers.

### D. 1867/81 2½D BLUE

There's more plating fun to be had with these! We will supply four different collectable stamps, all with different plate numbers, with a minimum catalogue value of £150 for just £25 post-free.

### E. THE GEORGE V DOWNEY HEADS

This is an interesting set of the 10 basic values, SG 322/350. We offer these in sound used condition for £19.95 post-free.

### F. THE 1951 FESTIVAL HIGH VALUE SET

We offer this glorious set of 4, lightly mounted mint for just £39.90 post-free.

## YOU CAN ALSO CONTACT US AT ANY TIME BY EMAIL - MAIL@THESTAMPCENTRE.CO.UK

## G. COMMEMORATIVE COVER STARTER COLLECTION

This fantastic starter collection will provide you with 50 different clean illustrated commemorative FIRST DAY COVERS. What a bargain! Just £49.99 post-free.

## H. DEFINITIVE & REGIONAL COVER STARTER COLLECTION

This starter collection will provide you with 50 different clean illustrated Definitive & Regional First Day Covers. Another great offer for just £49.99 post-free.

### BUY ITEMS G AND H TOGETHER AND RECEIVE A FREE FIRST DAY COVER ALBUM

## I. 1970/81 MACHINS WITH PHOSPHOR BANDS

These stamps are from the complete basic set between SG x841/922. You will receive 83 different mint stamps (not including the ½p side band, available separately) for £75 post-free.

## J. 1980s MACHINS ON PHOSPHORISED PAPER

These stamps gradually replaced the banded stamps in offer I. They form a complete series ranging from SG x924/993, a total of 69 different mint stamps for just £39.90 post-free.

## K. PRE-DECIMAL REGIONALS COMPLETE MINT SET

This collection of 77 mint stamps includes ALL basic pre-decimal regionals. Save a fortune in show leather and purchase ALL 77 for just £39.90 post-free.

## L. DECIMAL REGIONALS COMPLETE MINT SET 1971-1983

The stamps above form part of the complete collection of 99 regional stamps issued between 1971 & 1983 for use in Scotland, Northern Ireland & Wales. The complete set just £39.90 post-free.

### TO PURCHASE ANY OF THESE OFFERS CALL FREEPHONE 0800 975 4581 MON-SAT 9-5

# PORTISHEAD STAMP AUCTIONS

During 2013, we acquired this popular public auction in the West Country.

Business continues to grow and we are seeing increasing numbers of bidders both postally and in the room with each sale. Material available depends on consignments but comprises both individual stamps, albums and collections plus the ever popular box lots. There is always a decent amount of material from Great Britain as well as the rest of the globe.

Our auction venue is Gordano School, St. Mary's Road, Portishead, North Somerset, BS20 7QR and catalogues for these sales are available free upon request.

Attend in person or bid postally, our 2015 Saturday auction dates are:

## 31 January - 28 March - 30 May
## 25 July -26 September - 28 November

# The Stanley Gibbons Guide to Stamp Pricing

Catalogue editor and lifelong collector, Hugh Jefferies, offers a few tips.

It is a common fallacy that the prices in this catalogue show what a stamp is "worth", should you wish to sell it.

They are, instead, the price at which Stanley Gibbons will sell a fine example of the stamp in question, but that price includes a lot of other factors, as well as the inherent "value" of the stamp itself. There are costs in running any business and these are built into the price of any stamp shown in the catalogue, although the proportion of the price that relates to the stamp and that which relates to "business overheads" will vary from stamp to stamp.

What is true is that the prices shown in this catalogue represent an accurate "guide" to the value of the stamps listed in it. Stanley Gibbons are now the only major philatelic publisher whose stamp catalogue is also their price list. Naturally, if the prices are set too high, no one will buy our stamps, if they are too low, we will have difficulty replacing our stocks. It is therefore vitally important to the future of the company that the prices in this catalogue are set as accurately as possible. As a result, a great deal of care is taken over those prices – which is why they are held in such authority by collectors, dealers and stamp auction houses throughout the world.

## A very accurate picture

Each year, every price in our annual catalogues is checked and amended if necessary, having regard to the prices being achieved at auction as well as the demands of our customers at 399 Strand and orders coming in via the post, email and our website. Prices are held, increased or reduced according to those factors, giving a very accurate picture of the state of the market for each and every stamp.

Can stamps be purchased for less than the prices quoted in this catalogue? Of course they can. Stanley Gibbons themselves will frequently have stamps in stock at prices lower than "full catalogue". Every business offers discounts and makes "special offers" from time to time and Stanley Gibbons is no different. That apart, however, it should always be remembered that the prices quoted in this catalogue are for stamps in fine condition. Stamps with minor defects, heavy postmarks, slight fading and other flaws will frequently be offered at lower prices, both by Stanley Gibbons and by other dealers and auction houses.

## Checking condition

It is very important that, when you are thinking of buying a stamp for your collection, you carefully consider the condition of the item in question. Does it match up to the Stanley Gibbons definition of "Fine"? If it doesn't, is the price at which it is being offered too high? If you believe that the price is higher that it should be, leave it alone – or if you are really desperate, haggle for a better deal.

The knowledge as to what is "fine" and therefore worthy of "full catalogue" is one that you will gain with experience and will vary from stamp to stamp. Any stamp less than 100 years old should really be perfect in every way, but one can be more forgiving with older issues.

Briefly, here are a few of the things to consider.

- **Gum** – for unused stamps issued after 1936 prices are for unmounted mint – stamps never previously hinged. Modern stamps with hinge marks should be substantially discounted. For earlier stamps, heavy mounts and multiple hinges will also detract from the value, while unused stamps with the gum removed are worth considerably less.

- **Margins** – for imperforate stamps these should be clear on all sides – the design should not be cut into or even touching the edge of the stamp.

- **Perforations** – check that these are complete, that none are missing or short, especially at the stamp corners. Ideally the margin between the stamp design and the perforations should be even and well balanced – known as "well-centred".

- **Paper** – Check that there are no tears or thins to the paper – on the front as well as the back – and that there are no bends or creases. Again, the greater the damage the further away from "full catalogue" the stamp is worth.

- **Postmarks** – these should be clear, clean and should not disfigure the stamp. **The prices for all British stamps issued after 1880 assume used stamps to be cancelled with a clean, clear circular datestamp. Heavy parcel, wavy line or slogan cancellations reduce stamp values significantly.** On the other hand, very lightly cancelled stamps should sometimes be viewed with suspicion. There needs to be enough of the postmark showing to prove that the stamp has really been used!

If the above notes seem complicated, don"t worry. You will soon become adept at viewing every stamp in the light of its condition and deciding what proportion of catalogue you are prepared to pay. If you are not certain, ask the dealer for a guarantee that he will refund your money if you"re not happy with your purchase. All good dealers will be happy to provide this.

So, buy carefully – but, above all, have fun!

It should always be remembered that the prices quoted in this catalogue are for stamps in fine condition.

**Adhesive** A gummed stamp

**Albino** A design impression without colour

**Aniline** A fugitive (water soluble) ink or dye

**Bisect** Part of a stamp that has been cut in two for separate use; usually during a shortage of stamps

**Blind perforation** A perforation which has not been punched out

**Block** A group of four or more unseparated stamps

**Bogus** A spurious, pretend stamp

**Booklet** A small book containing "panes" of stamps

**Booklet pane** A leaf or page of stamps from a booklet

**Cachet** A commemorative marking, usually applied by rubber stamp

**Cancellation** Any authorised defacing mark on a stamp

**Centre** The position of a stamp design within its perforations, e.g. "well-centred" or "off-centre"

**Chalk-surfaced paper** Stamp paper coated with a chalky solution for security purposes. Attempted removal of the postmark damages the surface of the stamp

**Charity stamp** One bearing a premium or surcharge for charitable purposes

**Classic** A country"s early stamp issues, mostly up to about 1875; a choice stamp

**Coil stamp** One from a roll of stamps used in vending machines

**Coil join** A tab uniting two sections of a roll of stamps

**Commemorative** A stamp issued to mark a special anniversary or event

**Country stamp** See Regional

**Cover** A postally used envelope, letter-sheet or wrapper

**Cylinder number** Letters/numerals in sheet margins identifying printing cylinders. Normally collected in "Cylinder block" of six stamps. Also see "Plate number"

**Die** An engraved plate for impressing design etc. on softer metal

**Doctor blade** A steel blade which removes surplus ink from the printing cylinder in the press – faulty wiping by this blade will cause a "Doctor blade" flaw

**Embossing** A form of printing in relief, now rarely used

**Error** A mistake in stamp design, printing or production

**Essay** A trial stamp design, sometimes differing from the issued stamps

**Face value** The denomination of a stamp, expressed on its face

**Fake** A genuine stamp doctored in some way to deceive collectors

**First Day Cover** A cover bearing stamps postmarked on their day of issue

**Flaw** A fortuitous blemish on a stamp; a printing fault

**Forgery** A fraudulent copy of a genuine postage stamp, overprint or postmark

**Frama stamps** See Machine label

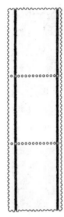

**Graphite lines** Black vertical lines printed on the back of GB definitives, 1957–1959, for use with automatic letter-sorting equipment. Also see "Phosphor" stamps

**Greetings stamp** Stamp intended for use on birthday or other greetings mail

**Gum** Mucilage on the back of adhesive stamps. Not "glue"

**Gutter** The narrow space between stamps in the sheet permitting perforation

**Gutter margin** The blank margins dividing a sheet of stamps into panes

**Handstamp** A postmark or overprint applied by hand

**Imperforate** Stamps printed and issued without perforations, deliberately or in error

**Imprint** The name of the printer or issuing authority inscribed on the stamps or in the sheet margins

**Imprinted stamps** Stamps other than adhesives, printed direct on postal stationery items (postcards, envelopes, etc)

**Jubilee line** Coloured line found in the sheet margin of British stamps

**"Local"** A stamp with geographical limits of postal use and validity. These are not normally listed in the Stanley Gibbons catalogues

**"Machin"** The name given to GB definitives, first issued in 1967, bearing the Queen's head designed by Arnold Machin

**Machine label** Postage stamp produced by a micro-processor machine after the insertion of coins of the required value, popularly known as Frama stamps

**Maltese cross** Name given to the cross-shaped cancellation used on the first British stamps

**Margin** The unprinted edging surrounding or dividing a sheet of stamps. See also "Gutter margin"

**Maximum card** A picture postcard bearing a stamp and cancellation relevant to the picture on the card

**Miniature sheet** A small sheet of one or several stamps, usually with decorative margins, issued as a souvenir for collectors

**Mint** A stamp in its original pristine state, with full gum (if so issued), when it is said to have its "original gum" ("O.G."). "Unmounted mint" stamps have not been hinged. Also see "Unused"

**Mulready** Envelopes and letter sheets issued by Britain in 1840 with a pictorial motif designed by William Mulready

**Non Value Indicator stamp (NVI)** A stamp which bears no monetary inscription, but shows the class of postage (1st, 2nd) instead

**Obsolete** A stamp no longer sold by a post office though it may still be valid for postage

**Overprint** A printed addition to a stamp. Also see "Surcharge"

**Pair** Two unseparated stamps, joined as originally issued

**Pane** A formation or group of stamps within the sheet. Also see "Booklet pane"

**Perforations** Holes punched between stamps in sheets to enable easy separation

**Personalised stamp** Stamp with an attached non-postal label bearing an image taken from a personal photograph

**Phosphor stamps** Stamps overprinted or coated with phosphorescent materials recognised by high technology letter sorting machinery

**Plate number** Letters/numerals in sheet margins identifying printing plates. Also see "Cylinder number"

**Postmark** Any mark, such as a cancellation, connected with the postal service and found on items transmitted by post

**Presentation pack** A philatelic souvenir containing a set of stamps and descriptive text

**Prestige booklet** Stamp booklet devoted to a particular subject or event and containing special panes of stamps with descriptive text printed alongside

**Proof** A trial impression taken from an original die or printing plate

**Regional** Name given by collectors to stamps issued by Royal Mail (who term them Country stamps) for use in England, Scotland, Wales or Northern Ireland. Issues were also made for Guernsey and Jersey (until 1969) and the Isle of Man (until 1973)

**Seahorse** Name given to the high value definitive stamps of King George V

**Self-adhesive** Gummed stamps (with protective backing) which do not require moistening

**Se-tenant** Stamps of different design or face value that are joined together

**Specimen** Sample stamp usually with "specimen" overprinted or perforated on it

**Strip** Three or more stamps joined in a row

**Tête-bêche** A stamp inverted in relation to the adjoining stamp in a pair

**Traffic lights** Collectors" term for the colour check dots found in sheet margins

**Unused** An uncancelled stamp, not necessarily "mint"

**Used** A stamp which has been postally used and appropriately postmarked

**Used abroad** Stamps of one country used and postmarked in another

**Used on piece** Stamp kept on part of the original cover to preserve the complete postmark

**Variety** A stamp differing in some detail from the normal issue

**Watermark** A distinctive device or emblem in stamps, formed by "thinning" of the paper during production. Watermarks illustrated in this catalogue are shown as if viewed through the front of the stamp

**"Wilding"** The name given to British definitive stamps, first issued in 1952, bearing the Queen"s head from a photographic portrait by Dorothy Wilding

**Wing margin** Wide margin on one side of a stamp caused by central perforation of the sheet gutter margin

For other and fuller definitions, see the Stanley Gibbons book *Philatelic Terms Illustrated* by James Mackay.

# How can Stanley Gibbons help you to build your collection?

## Our History

Stanley Gibbons started trading in 1856 and we have been at the forefront of stamp collecting for more than 150 years, making us the world's oldest philatelic company. We can help you build your collection in a wide variety of ways – all with the backing of our unrivalled expertise.

When building a collection it helps to know what you have. You can use Collect British Stamps as a checklist to highlight all the items you currently own. You can then easily see where the gaps are that you need to fill.

## Visit 399 Strand, London, UK

Our world famous stamp shop is a collector's paradise which aims to keep a full range of stock to sell at current catalogue price - so if there are any changes via a different catalogue, then prices will be adjusted accordingly. As well as stamps, the shop stocks albums, accessories and specialist philatelic books. Plan a visit now!

## GB Specialist Department

When purchasing high value items you should definitely contact our specialist department for advice and guarantees on the items purchased. You need to make sure you consult the experts to ensure they help you make the right purchase. With Stanley Gibbons this comes with over 150 years of experience. For example, when buying early Victorian stamps our specialists will guide you through the prices – so a penny red SG 43 has many plate numbers which vary in value. We can explain what to look for and where, and help you plan your future collection.

## Auctions and Valuations

You might find other ways of buying material to go into your collection, such as through auction – buying at auction can be great fun. You can buy collections and merge them with your own – not forgetting to check your Collect British Stamps checklist for gaps. Once again, you do need to make sure the condition of the collection you are buying is comparable to your own.

Stanley Gibbons Auctions have been running since the 1900's. They offer a range of auctions to suit all levels of collectors and dealers. You can of course also sell your collection or individual rare items through our public auctions and regular postal auctions. You can check out charges with the auction department directly (see contact details below).

## Stanley Gibbons Publications

Our catalogues are trusted worldwide as the industry standard (see page xlvi for more details).

To keep up to date with new issues you can follow the additions to this listing in our magazine Gibbons Stamp Monthly. This is a must-read for all collectors and dealers. It contains news, views and insights into all things philatelic, from beginner to specialist.

## Completing the set

When is it cheaper to complete your collection by buying a whole set rather than item by item? You can use the prices in Collect British Stamps, which lists single item values and a complete set value, to check if it is better to buy the odd items missing, or a complete set. Some of the definitive sets can be built up over time. The current definitive set is augmented by the Post Office regularly.

## Condition

Condition can make a big difference to the price you can pay for an item (see 'The Stanley Gibbons Guide to Stamp Pricing on p xxxv). The prices in this catalogue are for items in fine condition. When building your collection you do need to keep condition in mind and always buy the best condition you can find and afford. Collectors are reminded that for issues from 1936 to date, prices in the unused column are for unmounted mint. This means that the condition of the gum is the same as issued from the Post Office. If the gum is disturbed or has had an adhesion it can be classed as mounted. When buying issues prior to 1936 you should always look for the least amount of disturbance and adhesion. You do have to keep in mind the age of the issue when looking at the condition.

When buying philatelic items listed you need to make sure they are in the same condition as issued by the Post Office. This applies to Presentation packs, were the stamps are issued on a stock card with an information card and held together in a plastic wallet and also to Year Books, which should be in a slip case with a stock card of stamps. The prices quoted are for a complete item in good condition so make sure you check this - and of course that they are complete. You will find some items may appear in different formats (e.g. language cards, different bindings, etc) which will be listed under the normal listing within this catalogue.

## Ask the Experts

While you are building your collection, if you need help or guidance, you are welcome to come along to Stanley Gibbons in the Strand and ask for assistance. If you would like to have your collection appraised, you can arrange for a verbal evaluation Monday to Friday 9.00am – 4.30pm. We also provide insurance valuations should you require. Of course this up-to-date catalogue listing can assist with the valuation and may be presented to an insurance agent or company.

See the Stanley Gibbons Contact details: on page xxvii.

# Guide to Entries

(A) **Accession to the Throne**

(B) **Illustration** – Generally all stamps illustrated. To comply with Post Office regulations illustrations are reduced to 75%, with overprints shown actual size.

(C) **Illustration or Type Number** – These numbers are used to help identify stamps, in the type column.

(D) **Date of Issue** – When a set of definitive stamps have been issued over several years the Year Date given is for the earliest issue, commemorative sets are set in chronological order.

(E) **Phosphor Description** – Phosphorised paper is activated by ultraviolet light.

(F) **Perforations** – The "perforation" is the number of holes in a length of 2cm, as measured by the Stanley Gibbons *Instanta* gauge. From 1992 certain stamps occur with a large elliptical (oval) hole inserted in each line of vertical perforations. From 2009 certain stamps have U-shaped die-cut slits.

(G) **Stanley Gibbons Catalogue Number** – This is a unique number for each stamp to help the collector identify stamps in the listing. The Stanley Gibbons numbering system is universally recognized as definitive, where insufficient numbers have been left to provide for additional stamps listings, some stamps will have a suffix letter after the catalogue number.

(H) **Catalogue Value** – Mint/Unused. Prices quoted for pre-1945 stamps are for lightly hinged examples. Prices quoted of unused King Edward VIII to Queen Elizabeth issues are for unmounted mint.

(I) **Catalogue Value** – Used. Prices generally refer to fine postally used examples.

*Prices*

Before February 1971 British currency was:

£1 = 20s One pound = twenty shillings *and*
1s = 12d One Shilling = 12 pence

Under decimalisation this became:

£1 = 100p One pound = one hundred (new) pence

| Shown in Catalogue as | Explanation |
|---|---|
| 10 | 10 pence |
| 1.75 | £1.75 |
| 15.00 | £15 |
| £150 | £150 |
| £2300 | £2300 |

(J) **Face Value** – This refers to the value of the stamp and is sold at the Post Office when issued. Some modern stamps do not have their values in figures but instead shown as a letter.

(K) **Type Number** – Indicates a design type on which stamp is based. These are bold figures found below each illustration. The type numbers are also given in bold in the second column of figures alongside the stamp description to indicate the design of each stamp.

(L) **Colour** – Colour of stamps (if fewer than four colours, otherwise noted as "multicoloured").

(M) **Sets of Stamps** – Two or more stamps with a common theme or subject.

(N) **First Day Covers** – Prices for first day covers are for complete sets used on plain covers or on special covers.

(O) **Presentation Packs** – Special packs consisting of the issue and slip-in cards with printed information inside a protective covering.

(P) **PHQ Cards** – Each card shows a large reproduction of a current British stamp.

(Q) **Sets of Gutters** – The term is used for a pair of stamps separated by part of the blank gutter margin or with Traffic Lights on the gutter margin.

(R) **Footnote** – Further information on background or key facts on issues.

(S) **Other Types of Stamps** – Postage Dues, Officials and Regional Issues

(T) **Number Prefix** – Stamps other than definitives and commemoratives have a prefix letter before the catalogue number.

# QUEEN ELIZABETH II

**Ⓐ** Accession to the Throne — ●6 February, 1952

**Ⓑ** Illustration —

**Ⓒ** Illustration or Type Number — **1862** *The Very Hungry Caterpillar* (Eric Carle)

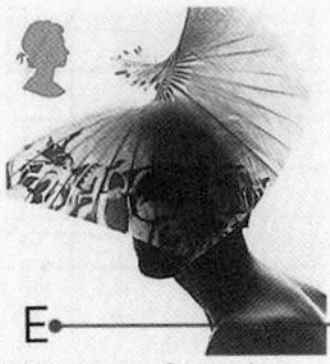

**1526** Butterfly Hat by Dai Rees

**Ⓔ** —

**Ⓙ** Face Value

Nos. 2589/90, 2591/2, 2593/4 and 2595/6 were printed together, *se-tenant*, as horizontal pairs in sheets of 60(2 panes 6 × 5).

**Animal Tales**

**Ⓓ** Date of Issue — ● 2006 (10 Jan.) One side phosphor band (2nd) or two● phosphor bands (others). Perf 14½●

**Ⓔ** Phosphor Description

**Ⓕ** Perforations

| Ⓖ | Ⓚ | Ⓙ | Ⓛ | Ⓗ | Ⓘ | | |
|------|------|--------------------|-------|-------|-------| --- | --- |
| 2589 | **1856** | (2nd) multicoloured | | 30 | 35 | ☐ | ☐ |
| | | a. Horiz pair. | | | | | |
| | | Nos. 2589/90 | | 70 | 70 | ☐ | ☐ |
| 2590 | **1857** | (2nd) multicoloured | | 30 | 35 | ☐ | ☐ |
| 2591 | **1858** | (1st) multicoloured | | 45 | 50 | ☐ | ☐ |
| | | a. Horiz pair. | | | | | |
| | | Nos. 2591/2 | | 1·50 | 1·50 | ☐ | ☐ |
| 2592 | **1859** | (1st) multicoloured | | 45 | 50 | ☐ | ☐ |
| 2593 | **1860** | 42p multicoloured | | 65 | 70 | ☐ | ☐ |
| | | a. Horiz pair. | | | | | |
| | | Nos. 2593/4 | | 3·75 | 3·75 | ☐ | ☐ |
| 2594 | **1861** | 42p multicoloured | | 65 | 70 | ☐ | ☐ |
| 2595 | **1862** | 68p multicoloured | | 1·00 | 1·10 | ☐ | ☐ |
| | | a. Horiz pair. | | | | | |
| | | Nos. 2595/6 | | 4·75 | 4·75 | ☐ | ☐ |
| 2596 | **1863** | 68p multicoloured ● | | 1·00 | 1·10 | ☐ | ☐ |

**Ⓖ** Stanley Gibbons Catalogue Number

**Ⓙ** Face Value

**Ⓚ** Type Number

**Ⓗ** Catalogue Value – Unused

**Ⓘ** Catalogue Value – Used

**Ⓛ** Colour

| | | | |
|---------------------------------|-------|-------|---|
| Set of 8 | 8·50 | 8·50 | ☐ |
| First Day Cover ● | | 8·00 | |
| Presentation Pack | 12·00 | | ☐ |
| PHQ Cards (*set of 8*) ● | 4·50 | 12·00 | ☐ ☐ |
| Set of 4 Gutter Blocks of 4 | 13·00 | | ☐ |
| Set of 4 Traffic Light Gutter Blocks of 8 | 28·00 | | ☐ |

**Ⓜ** Sets

**Ⓞ** Special Packs

**Ⓠ** Gutter Combinations

**Ⓝ** FDC for Complete Sets

**Ⓟ** PHQ Cards

No. 2595 contains two die-cut holes.

**Ⓡ** Footnotes — A design as No. 2592 but self-adhesive was also issued in sheets of 20 with each stamp accompanied by a *se-tenant* label.

**Ⓢ** Postage Due — D **1**

POSTAGE DUE STAMPS ●

**Ⓢ** Other Types of Stamps

| | | | | | | |
|------|------|---------|-------|-------|---|---|
| **1968–69** Design size 21½ × 17½ mm. No wmk | | | | | | |
| D75 | **D 1** | 4d blue | 7·00 | 6·75 | ☐ | ☐ |
| D76 | | 8d red | 50 | 1·00 | ☐ | ☐ |

**Ⓣ** Number Prefix

# QUEEN VICTORIA

1837 (20 June)–1901 (22 Jan.)

**5**　　　　**8**　　　　**6**

**9** Watermark extending over three stamps

**IDENTIFICATION.** In this checklist Victorian stamps are classified firstly according to which printing method was used –line-engraving, embossing or surface-printing.

**Corner letters.** Numerous stamps also have letters in all four, or just the lower corners. These were an anti-forgery device and the letters differ from stamp to stamp. If present in all four corners the upper pair are the reverse of the lower. Note the importance of these corner letters in the way the checklist is arranged.

**Watermarks.** Further classification depends on watermarks: these are illustrated in normal position, with stamps priced accordingly.

**Letters in all four corners**
**Plate numbers.** Stamps included a 'plate number' in their design and this affects valuation. The cheapest plates are priced here; see complete list of plate numbers overleaf.

**1858–70**

| | | | (i) Wmk Type **9** Perf 14 | | | | |
|---|---|---|---|---|---|---|---|
| 48 | **7** | ½d | red | £115 | 25·00 | ☐ | ☐ |
| | | | (ii) Wmk Large Crown Type **4** Perf 14 | | | | |
| 43 | **5** | 1d | red | 25·00 | 2·75 | ☐ | ☐ |
| 51 | **8** | 1½d | red | £500 | 75·00 | ☐ | ☐ |
| 45 | **6** | 2d | blue | £350 | 15·00 | ☐ | ☐ |

**Plate numbers on stamps 1858-70 having letters in all four corners**

## 1 Line-engraved Issues

**1**

**1a**

**1b**

Showing position of the plate number on the 1d. and 2d. values. (Plate 170 shown)

Showing the plate number (9)

Position of plate Number

**3** White lines added above and below head

**2** Small Crown watermark

**4** Large Crown watermark

**HALFPENNY VALUE (SG 48)**

| 48 | *Plate 1* | £325 | 90·00 | ☐ | ☐ |
|---|---|---|---|---|---|
| 48 | *Plate 3* | £240 | 50·00 | ☐ | ☐ |
| 48 | *Plate 4* | £150 | 42·00 | ☐ | ☐ |
| 48 | *Plate 5* | £115 | 25·00 | ☐ | ☐ |
| 48 | *Plate 6* | £120 | 25·00 | ☐ | ☐ |
| 48 | *Plate 8* | £600 | £120 | ☐ | ☐ |
| 48 | *Plate 9* | £6000 | £850 | ☐ | ☐ |
| 48 | *Plate 10* | £130 | 25·00 | ☐ | ☐ |
| 48 | *Plate 11* | £120 | 25·00 | ☐ | ☐ |
| 48 | *Plate 12* | £120 | 25·00 | ☐ | ☐ |
| 48 | *Plate 13* | £120 | 25·00 | ☐ | ☐ |
| 48 | *Plate 14* | £120 | 25·00 | ☐ | ☐ |
| 48 | *Plate 15* | £175 | 42·00 | ☐ | ☐ |
| 48 | *Plate 19* | £300 | 60·00 | ☐ | ☐ |
| 48 | *Plate 20* | £350 | 80·00 | ☐ | ☐ |

**Letters in lower corners**

**1840** Wmk Small Crown Type **2** Imperforate

| 2 | **1** | 1d | black | £12500 | £375 | ☐ | ☐ |
|---|---|---|---|---|---|---|---|
| 5 | **1a** | 2d | blue | £37000 | £900 | ☐ | ☐ |

**1841**

| 8 | **1b** | 1d | red-brown | £600 | 30·00 | ☐ | ☐ |
|---|---|---|---|---|---|---|---|
| 14 | **3** | 2d | blue | £6250 | 85·00 | ☐ | ☐ |

**1854–57**

| | | | (i) Wmk Small Crown Type **2** Perf 16 | | | | |
|---|---|---|---|---|---|---|---|
| 17 | **1b** | 1d | red-brown | £350 | 35·00 | ☐ | ☐ |
| 19 | **3** | 2d | blue | £4650 | £100 | ☐ | ☐ |
| | | | (ii) Wmk Small Crown Type **2** Perf 14 | | | | |
| 24 | **1b** | 1d | red-brown | £650 | 70·00 | ☐ | ☐ |
| 23 | **3** | 2d | blue | £12000 | £225 | ☐ | ☐ |
| | | | (iii) Wmk Large Crown Type **4** Perf 16 | | | | |
| 26 | **1b** | 1d | red | £2100 | £130 | ☐ | ☐ |
| 27 | **3** | 2d | blue | £16000 | £450 | ☐ | ☐ |
| | | | (iv) Wmk Large Crown Type **4** Perf 14 | | | | |
| 40 | **1b** | 1d | red | 50·00 | 12·00 | ☐ | ☐ |
| 34 | **3** | 2d | blue | £2850 | 70·00 | ☐ | ☐ |

**7**

**PENNY VALUE (SG 43)**

| 43 | *Plate 71* | 50·00 | 4·00 | ☐ | ☐ |
|---|---|---|---|---|---|
| 43 | *Plate 72* | 55·00 | 5·00 | ☐ | ☐ |
| 43 | *Plate 73* | 55·00 | 4·00 | ☐ | ☐ |
| 43 | *Plate 74* | 55·00 | 2·75 | ☐ | ☐ |
| 43 | *Plate 76* | 50·00 | 2·75 | ☐ | ☐ |
| 43 | *Plate 77* | — | £600000 | ☐ | ☐ |
| 43 | *Plate 78* | £120 | 2·75 | ☐ | ☐ |
| 43 | *Plate 79* | 45·00 | 2·75 | ☐ | ☐ |
| 43 | *Plate 80* | 60·00 | 2·75 | ☐ | ☐ |
| 43 | *Plate 81* | 60·00 | 3·00 | ☐ | ☐ |

| | | | |
|---|---|---|---|
| 43 | *Plate 82* | £120 | 5·00 |
| 43 | *Plate 83* | £145 | 9·00 |
| 43 | *Plate 84* | 75·00 | 3·00 |
| 43 | *Plate 85* | 55·00 | 4·00 |
| 43 | *Plate 86* | 65·00 | 5·00 |
| 43 | *Plate 87* | 45·00 | 2·75 |
| 43 | *Plate 88* | £175 | 9·50 |
| 43 | *Plate 89* | 55·00 | 2·75 |
| 43 | *Plate 90* | 55·00 | 2·75 |
| 43 | *Plate 91* | 70·00 | 7·00 |
| 43 | *Plate 92* | 50·00 | 2·75 |
| 43 | *Plate 93* | 65·00 | 2·75 |
| 43 | *Plate 94* | 60·00 | 6·00 |
| 43 | *Plate 95* | 55·00 | 2·75 |
| 43 | *Plate 96* | 60·00 | 2·75 |
| 43 | *Plate 97* | 55·00 | 4·50 |
| 43 | *Plate 98* | 65·00 | 7·00 |
| 43 | *Plate 99* | 70·00 | 6·00 |
| 43 | *Plate 100* | 75·00 | 3·00 |
| 43 | *Plate 101* | 75·00 | 11·00 |
| 43 | *Plate 102* | 60·00 | 2·75 |
| 43 | *Plate 103* | 65·00 | 4·50 |
| 43 | *Plate 104* | 95·00 | 6·00 |
| 43 | *Plate 105* | £120 | 9·00 |
| 43 | *Plate 106* | 70·00 | 2·75 |
| 43 | *Plate 107* | 75·00 | 9·00 |
| 43 | *Plate 108* | £100 | 3·00 |
| 43 | *Plate 109* | £110 | 4·50 |
| 43 | *Plate 110* | 75·00 | 11·00 |
| 43 | *Plate 111* | 65·00 | 3·00 |
| 43 | *Plate 112* | 85·00 | 3·00 |
| 43 | *Plate 113* | 65·00 | 15·00 |
| 43 | *Plate 114* | £300 | 15·00 |
| 43 | *Plate 115* | £120 | 3·00 |
| 43 | *Plate 116* | 95·00 | 11·00 |
| 43 | *Plate 117* | 60·00 | 2·75 |
| 43 | *Plate 118* | 65·00 | 2·75 |
| 43 | *Plate 119* | 60·00 | 2·75 |
| 43 | *Plate 120* | 25·00 | 2·75 |
| 43 | *Plate 121* | 55·00 | 11·00 |
| 43 | *Plate 122* | 25·00 | 2·75 |
| 43 | *Plate 123* | 55·00 | 2·75 |
| 43 | *Plate 124* | 40·00 | 2·75 |
| 43 | *Plate 125* | 55·00 | 2·75 |
| 43 | *Plate 127* | 70·00 | 3·00 |
| 43 | *Plate 129* | 55·00 | 10·00 |
| 43 | *Plate 130* | 70·00 | 3·00 |
| 43 | *Plate 131* | 80·00 | 20·00 |
| 43 | *Plate 132* | £175 | 27·00 |
| 43 | *Plate 133* | £150 | 11·00 |
| 43 | *Plate 134* | 25·00 | 2·75 |
| 43 | *Plate 135* | £120 | 30·00 |
| 43 | *Plate 136* | £120 | 24·00 |
| 43 | *Plate 137* | 40·00 | 3·00 |
| 43 | *Plate 138* | 30·00 | 2·75 |
| 43 | *Plate 139* | 75·00 | 20·00 |
| 43 | *Plate 140* | 30·00 | 2·75 |
| 43 | *Plate 141* | £150 | 11·00 |
| 43 | *Plate 142* | 90·00 | 30·00 |
| 43 | *Plate 143* | 75·00 | 17·00 |
| 43 | *Plate 144* | £120 | 25·00 |
| 43 | *Plate 145* | 45·00 | 3·00 |
| 43 | *Plate 146* | 55·00 | 7·00 |
| 43 | *Plate 147* | 65·00 | 4·00 |
| 43 | *Plate 148* | 55·00 | 4·00 |
| 43 | *Plate 149* | 55·00 | 7·00 |
| 43 | *Plate 150* | 25·00 | 2·75 |
| 43 | *Plate 151* | 75·00 | 11·00 |
| 43 | *Plate 152* | 75·00 | 7·50 |
| 43 | *Plate 153* | £130 | 11·00 |
| 43 | *Plate 154* | 65·00 | 2·75 |
| 43 | *Plate 155* | 65·00 | 3·00 |
| 43 | *Plate 156* | 60·00 | 2·75 |
| 43 | *Plate 157* | 65·00 | 2·75 |
| 43 | *Plate 158* | 45·00 | 2·75 |
| 43 | *Plate 159* | 45·00 | 2·75 |
| 43 | *Plate 160* | 45·00 | 2·75 |
| 43 | *Plate 161* | 75·00 | 9·00 |
| 43 | *Plate 162* | 65·00 | 9·00 |
| 43 | *Plate 163* | 65·00 | 4·00 |
| 43 | *Plate 164* | 65·00 | 4·00 |
| 43 | *Plate 165* | 60·00 | 2·75 |
| 43 | *Plate 166* | 60·00 | 7·00 |
| 43 | *Plate 167* | 60·00 | 2·75 |
| 43 | *Plate 168* | 65·00 | 10·00 |
| 43 | *Plate 169* | 75·00 | 9·00 |
| 43 | *Plate 170* | 50·00 | 2·75 |
| 43 | *Plate 171* | 25·00 | 2·75 |
| 43 | *Plate 172* | 45·00 | 2·75 |
| 43 | *Plate 173* | 90·00 | 11·00 |
| 43 | *Plate 174* | 45·00 | 2·75 |
| 43 | *Plate 175* | 75·00 | 4·50 |
| 43 | *Plate 176* | 75·00 | 3·00 |
| 43 | *Plate 177* | 55·00 | 2·75 |
| 43 | *Plate 178* | 75·00 | 4·50 |
| 43 | *Plate 179* | 65·00 | 3·00 |
| 43 | *Plate 180* | 75·00 | 6·50 |
| 43 | *Plate 181* | 60·00 | 2·75 |
| 43 | *Plate 182* | £120 | 6·50 |
| 43 | *Plate 183* | 70·00 | 4·00 |
| 43 | *Plate 184* | 45·00 | 3·00 |
| 43 | *Plate 185* | 65·00 | 4·00 |
| 43 | *Plate 186* | 85·00 | 3·00 |
| 43 | *Plate 187* | 65·00 | 2·75 |
| 43 | *Plate 188* | 90·00 | 12·00 |
| 43 | *Plate 189* | 90·00 | 8·50 |
| 43 | *Plate 190* | 65·00 | 7·00 |
| 43 | *Plate 191* | 45·00 | 9·00 |
| 43 | *Plate 192* | 65·00 | 2·75 |
| 43 | *Plate 193* | 45·00 | 2·75 |
| 43 | *Plate 194* | 65·00 | 10·00 |
| 43 | *Plate 195* | 65·00 | 10·00 |
| 43 | *Plate 196* | 65·00 | 6·50 |
| 43 | *Plate 197* | 70·00 | 11·00 |
| 43 | *Plate 198* | 55·00 | 7·00 |
| 43 | *Plate 199* | 70·00 | 7·00 |
| 43 | *Plate 200* | 75·00 | 2·75 |
| 43 | *Plate 201* | 45·00 | 6·00 |
| 43 | *Plate 202* | 75·00 | 10·00 |
| 43 | *Plate 203* | 45·00 | 20·00 |
| 43 | *Plate 204* | 70·00 | 3·00 |
| 43 | *Plate 205* | 70·00 | 4·00 |
| 43 | *Plate 206* | 70·00 | 11·00 |
| 43 | *Plate 207* | 75·00 | 11·00 |
| 43 | *Plate 208* | 70·00 | 18·00 |
| 43 | *Plate 209* | 60·00 | 10·00 |
| 43 | *Plate 210* | 85·00 | 15·00 |
| 43 | *Plate 211* | 90·00 | 25·00 |
| 43 | *Plate 212* | 75·00 | 13·00 |
| 43 | *Plate 213* | 75·00 | 13·00 |
| 43 | *Plate 214* | 85·00 | 23·00 |
| 43 | *Plate 215* | 85·00 | 23·00 |
| 43 | *Plate 216* | 90·00 | 23·00 |
| 43 | *Plate 217* | 90·00 | 9·00 |
| 43 | *Plate 218* | 85·00 | 10·00 |
| 43 | *Plate 219* | £120 | 85·00 |
| 43 | *Plate 220* | 55·00 | 9·00 |
| 43 | *Plate 221* | 90·00 | 20·00 |
| 43 | *Plate 222* | £100 | 50·00 |
| 43 | *Plate 223* | £120 | 75·00 |
| 43 | *Plate 224* | £150 | 65·00 |
| 43 | *Plate 225* | £3200 | £800 |

Plates 69, 70, 75, 77, 126 and 128 were prepared but rejected. No stamps therefore exist, except for a very few from Plate

77 which somehow reached the public. Plate 177 stamps, by accident or design, are sometimes passed off as the rare Plate 77.

**THREE-HALFPENNY VALUE (SG 52)**

| 52 | Plate (1) | £725 | £100 | | |
|----|-----------|------|------|--|--|
| 52 | Plate 3 | £500 | 75·00 | | |

Plate 1 did not have the plate number in the design. Plate 2 was not completed and no stamps exist.

**TWOPENNY VALUE (SG 45)**

| 45 | Plate 7 | £1900 | 65·00 | | |
|----|---------|-------|-------|--|--|
| 45 | Plate 8 | £1800 | 42·00 | | |
| 45 | Plate 9 | £350 | 15·00 | | |
| 45 | Plate 12 | £3000 | £140 | | |
| 46 | Plate 13 | £375 | 30·00 | | |
| 46 | Plate 14 | £500 | 38·00 | | |
| 46 | Plate 15 | £525 | 38·00 | | |

Plates 10 and 11 were prepared but rejected.

# 2 Embossed Issues

Prices are for stamps cut square and with average to fine embossing. Stamps with exceptionally clear embossing are worth more.

12

11

10

13

**1847–54** Wmk **13** (6d), no wmk (others) Imperforate

| 59 | 12 | 6d | lilac | £18000 | £1000 | | |
|----|----|----|-------|--------|-------|--|--|
| 57 | 11 | 10d | brown | £11000 | £1500 | | |
| 54 | 10 | 1s | green | £22000 | £1000 | | |

# 3 Surface-printed Issues

**IDENTIFICATION.** Check first whether the design includes corner letters or not, as mentioned for 'Line-engraved Issues'. The checklist is divided up according to whether any letters are small or large, also whether they are white (uncoloured) or printed in the colour of the stamp. Further identification then depends on watermark.

**PERFORATION.** Except for Nos. 126/9 all the following issues of Queen Victoria are perf 14.

14

15

16

17

18

19

20 Emblems

**No corner letters**

**1855–57**

| | | (i) Wmk Small Garter Type **15** | | | | |
|---|---|---|---|---|---|---|
| 62 | 14 | 4d | red | £8500 | £425 | |
| | | (ii) Wmk Medium Garter Type **16** | | | | |
| 65 | 14 | 4d | red | £10000 | £450 | |
| | | (iii) Wmk Large Garter Type **17** | | | | |
| 66a | 14 | 4d | red | £1700 | £140 | |
| | | (iv) Wmk Emblems Type **20** | | | | |
| 70 | 18 | 6d | lilac | £1350 | £120 | |
| 72 | 19 | 1s | green | £3000 | £325 | |

**Plate numbers.** Stamps Nos. 90/163 should be checked for the 'plate numbers' indicated, as this affects valuation (the cheapest plates are priced here). The mark 'Pl.' shows that several numbers exist, priced in separate list overleaf.

Plate numbers are the small numerals appearing in duplicate in some part of the frame design or adjacent to the lower corner letters (in the 5s value a single numeral above the lower inscription).

21

22

23

24

25

**Small white corner letters**

**1862–64** Wmk Emblems Type **20**, except 4d (Large Garter Type **17**)

| 76 | 21 | 3d | red | £2500 | £325 | | |
|----|----|----|------|-------|------|--|--|
| 80 | 22 | 4d | red | £1900 | £120 | | |
| 84 | 23 | 6d | lilac | £2200 | £125 | | |
| 87 | 24 | 9d | bistre | £3750 | £425 | | |
| 90 | 25 | 1s | green Pl. | £3000 | £275 | | |

26

27

28 Hyphen in SIX-PENCE

29

30

31

# Stanley Gibbons

## Great Britain Department

**Stanley Gibbons, a name synonymous with quality.**

Ever since the birth of our hobby Stanley Gibbons has been at the forefront of GB philately and we invite collectors access to one of the finest GB stocks in the world by registering for our renowned free monthly brochure. Whatever your budget or collecting interests you will find a range of the highest quality material for the discerning collector.

**Large white corner letters**

**1865–67** Wmk Emblems Type **20** except 4d (Large Garter Type **17**)

| | | | | | | | |
|---|---|---|---|---|---|---|---|
| 92 | **26** | 3d | red (Plate 4) | £2300 | £225 | ☐ | ☐ |
| 94 | **27** | 4d | vermilion Pl. | £575 | 75·00 | ☐ | ☐ |
| 97 | **28** | 6d | lilac Pl. | £1100 | £120 | ☐ | ☐ |
| 98 | **29** | 9d | straw Pl. | £4750 | £580 | ☐ | ☐ |
| 99 | **30** | 10d | brown (Plate 1) | * £52000 | | ☐ | ☐ |
| 101 | **31** | 1s | green (Plate 4) | £2800 | £250 | ☐ | ☐ |

**32**  **33** Spray of Rose  **34**

**1867–80** Wmk Spray of Rose Type **33**

| | | | | | | |
|---|---|---|---|---|---|---|
| 103 | **26** | 3d red Pl. | £525 | 60·00 | ☐ | ☐ |
| 105 | **28** | 6d lilac (with (hyphen) (Plate 6) | £1800 | £120 | ☐ | ☐ |
| 109 | | 6d mauve (without hyphen) Pl. | £675 | 90·00 | ☐ | ☐ |
| 111 | **29** | 9d pale straw (Plate 4) | £2300 | £300 | ☐ | ☐ |
| 112 | **30** | 10d brown Pl. | £3500 | £400 | ☐ | ☐ |
| 117 | **31** | 1s green Pl. | £800 | 45·00 | ☐ | ☐ |
| 118 | **32** | 2s blue Pl. | £3800 | £200 | ☐ | ☐ |
| 121 | | 2s brown (Plate 1) | £28000 | £4200 | ☐ | ☐ |

**1872–73** Wmk Spray of Rose Type **33**

| | | | | | | |
|---|---|---|---|---|---|---|
| 122b | **34** | 6d brown Pl. | £700 | 60·00 | ☐ | ☐ |
| 125 | | 6d grey (Plate 12) | £1850 | £275 | ☐ | ☐ |

## PLATE NUMBERS ON STAMPS OF 1862–83

**Small White Corner Letters (1862–64)**

| | | | | | | |
|---|---|---|---|---|---|---|
| 90 | *Plate 2* | 1s green | £3000 | £275 | ☐ | ☐ |
| 91 | *Plate 3* | | £32500 | | ☐ | ☐ |

Plate 2 is actually numbered as '1' and Plate 3 as '2' on the stamps.

**Large White Corner Letters (1865–83)**

| | | | | | | |
|---|---|---|---|---|---|---|
| 103 | *Plate 4* | 3d red | £1800 | £300 | ☐ | ☐ |
| 103 | *Plate 5* | | £525 | 70·00 | ☐ | ☐ |
| 103 | *Plate 6* | | £550 | 70·00 | ☐ | ☐ |
| 103 | *Plate 7* | | £650 | 70·00 | ☐ | ☐ |
| 103 | *Plate 8* | | £625 | 60·00 | ☐ | ☐ |
| 103 | *Plate 9* | | £625 | 70·00 | ☐ | ☐ |
| 103 | *Plate 10* | | £875 | £150 | ☐ | ☐ |
| 94 | *Plate 7* | 4d verm | £650 | £130 | ☐ | ☐ |
| 94 | *Plate 8* | | £600 | 90·00 | ☐ | ☐ |
| 94 | *Plate 9* | | £600 | 90·00 | ☐ | ☐ |
| 94 | *Plate 10* | | £825 | £150 | ☐ | ☐ |
| 94 | *Plate 11* | | £625 | 90·00 | ☐ | ☐ |
| 94 | *Plate 12* | | £575 | 75·00 | ☐ | ☐ |
| 94 | *Plate 13* | | £650 | 75·00 | ☐ | ☐ |
| 94 | *Plate 14* | | £775 | £110 | ☐ | ☐ |
| 97 | *Plate 5* | 6d lilac | £1100 | £120 | ☐ | ☐ |
| 97 | *Plate 6* | | £3750 | £225 | ☐ | ☐ |
| 109 | *Plate 8* | 6d mauve | £800 | £140 | ☐ | ☐ |
| 109 | *Plate 9* | | £675 | 90·00 | ☐ | ☐ |
| 109 | *Plate 10* | | * | £35000 | ☐ | ☐ |
| 123 | *Plate 11* | 6d buff | £1100 | £125 | ☐ | ☐ |
| 123 | *Plate 12* | | £3300 | £325 | ☐ | ☐ |
| 98 | *Plate 4* | 9d straw | £4750 | £580 | ☐ | ☐ |
| 98 | *Plate 5* | | £20000 | | ☐ | ☐ |
| 114 | *Plate 1* | 10d brown | £3500 | £375 | ☐ | ☐ |
| 114 | *Plate 2* | | £50000 | £15000 | ☐ | ☐ |
| 117 | *Plate 4* | 1s green | £975 | 65·00 | ☐ | ☐ |
| 117 | *Plate 5* | | £800 | 45·00 | ☐ | ☐ |

| | | | | | | |
|---|---|---|---|---|---|---|
| 117 | *Plate 6* | | £1200 | 45·00 | ☐ | ☐ |
| 117 | *Plate 7* | | £1400 | 90·00 | ☐ | ☐ |
| 119 | *Plate 1* | 2s blue | £3800 | £200 | ☐ | ☐ |
| 119 | *Plate 3* | | * | £15000 | ☐ | ☐ |
| 127 | *Plate 1* | 5s red | £11000 | £675 | ☐ | ☐ |
| 127 | *Plate 2* | | £18000 | £1500 | ☐ | ☐ |

**Large Coloured Corner Letters (1873–83)**

| | | | | | | |
|---|---|---|---|---|---|---|
| 139 | *Plate 1* | 2½d mauve | £625 | £115 | ☐ | ☐ |
| 139 | *Plate 2* | | £625 | £115 | ☐ | ☐ |
| 139 | *Plate 3* | | £950 | £160 | ☐ | ☐ |
| 141 | *Plate 3* | 2½d mauve | £1350 | £150 | ☐ | ☐ |
| 141 | *Plate 4* | | £525 | 80·00 | ☐ | ☐ |
| 141 | *Plate 5* | | £525 | 80·00 | ☐ | ☐ |
| 141 | *Plate 6* | | £525 | 80·00 | ☐ | ☐ |
| 141 | *Plate 7* | | £525 | 80·00 | ☐ | ☐ |
| 141 | *Plate 8* | | £525 | 80·00 | ☐ | ☐ |
| 141 | *Plate 9* | | £525 | 80·00 | ☐ | ☐ |
| 141 | *Plate 10* | | £550 | 95·00 | ☐ | ☐ |
| 141 | *Plate 11* | | £525 | 80·00 | ☐ | ☐ |
| 141 | *Plate 12* | | £525 | 80·00 | ☐ | ☐ |
| 141 | *Plate 13* | | £525 | 80·00 | ☐ | ☐ |
| 141 | *Plate 14* | | £525 | 80·00 | ☐ | ☐ |
| 141 | *Plate 15* | | £525 | 80·00 | ☐ | ☐ |
| 141 | *Plate 16* | | £525 | 80·00 | ☐ | ☐ |
| 141 | *Plate 17* | | £1700 | £300 | ☐ | ☐ |
| 142 | *Plate 17* | 2½d blue | £575 | 70·00 | ☐ | ☐ |
| 142 | *Plate 18* | | £575 | 55·00 | ☐ | ☐ |
| 142 | *Plate 19* | | £575 | 55·00 | ☐ | ☐ |
| 142 | *Plate 20* | | £575 | 55·00 | ☐ | ☐ |
| 157 | *Plate 21* | 2½d blue | £475 | 45·00 | ☐ | ☐ |
| 157 | *Plate 22* | | £425 | 45·00 | ☐ | ☐ |
| 157 | *Plate 23* | | £425 | 35·00 | ☐ | ☐ |
| 143 | *Plate 11* | 3d red | £450 | 80·00 | ☐ | ☐ |
| 143 | *Plate 12* | | £525 | 80·00 | ☐ | ☐ |
| 143 | *Plate 14* | | £525 | 80·00 | ☐ | ☐ |
| 143 | *Plate 15* | | £450 | 80·00 | ☐ | ☐ |
| 143 | *Plate 16* | | £450 | 80·00 | ☐ | ☐ |
| 143 | *Plate 17* | | £525 | 80·00 | ☐ | ☐ |
| 143 | *Plate 18* | | £525 | 80·00 | ☐ | ☐ |
| 143 | *Plate 19* | | £450 | 80·00 | ☐ | ☐ |
| 143 | *Plate 20* | | £850 | £140 | ☐ | ☐ |
| 158 | *Plate 20* | 3d red | £900 | £150 | ☐ | ☐ |
| 158 | *Plate 21* | | £500 | £100 | ☐ | ☐ |
| 152 | *Plate 15* | 4d verm | £3000 | £500 | ☐ | ☐ |
| 152 | *Plate 16* | | * | £34000 | ☐ | ☐ |
| 153 | *Plate 15* | 4d green | £1600 | £325 | ☐ | ☐ |
| 153 | *Plate 16* | | £1400 | £300 | ☐ | ☐ |
| 153 | *Plate 17* | | * | £20000 | ☐ | ☐ |
| 160 | *Plate 17* | 4d brown | £450 | 75·00 | ☐ | ☐ |
| 160 | *Plate 18* | | £400 | 75·00 | ☐ | ☐ |
| 147 | *Plate 13* | 6d grey | £500 | 85·00 | ☐ | ☐ |
| 147 | *Plate 14* | | £500 | 85·00 | ☐ | ☐ |
| 147 | *Plate 15* | | £500 | 85·00 | ☐ | ☐ |
| 147 | *Plate 16* | | £500 | 85·00 | ☐ | ☐ |
| 147 | *Plate 17* | | £950 | £180 | ☐ | ☐ |
| 161 | *Plate 17* | 6d grey | £450 | 75·00 | ☐ | ☐ |
| 161 | *Plate 18* | | £400 | 75·00 | ☐ | ☐ |
| 150 | *Plate 8* | 1s green | £800 | £165 | ☐ | ☐ |
| 150 | *Plate 9* | | £800 | £165 | ☐ | ☐ |
| 150 | *Plate 10* | | £750 | £200 | ☐ | ☐ |
| 150 | *Plate 11* | | £750 | £165 | ☐ | ☐ |
| 150 | *Plate 12* | | £625 | £150 | ☐ | ☐ |
| 150 | *Plate 13* | | £625 | £150 | ☐ | ☐ |
| 150 | *Plate 14* | | * | £40000 | ☐ | ☐ |
| 163 | *Plate 13* | 1s brown | £825 | £160 | ☐ | ☐ |
| 163 | *Plate 14* | | £700 | £160 | ☐ | ☐ |

**35**

**36**

**37**

**38**

**39** Maltese Cross

**40** Large Anchor

### 1867–83

|  |  | (i) Wmk Maltese Cross Type **39** Perf 15½ × 15 |  |  |  |  |
|---|---|---|---|---|---|---|
| 126 | **35** | 5s red Pl. | £11000 | £675 | ☐ | ☐ |
| 128 | **36** | 10s grey (Plate 1) | £60000 | £3200 | ☐ | ☐ |
| 129 | **37** | £1 brown (Plate 1) | £90000 | £4500 | ☐ | ☐ |
|  |  | (ii) Wmk Large Anchor Type **40** Perf 14 |  |  |  |  |
| 134 | **35** | 5s red (Plate 4) | £32000 | £4200 | ☐ | ☐ |
| 131 | **36** | 10s grey (Plate 1) | £130000 | £5200 | ☐ | ☐ |
| 132 | **37** | £1 brown (Plate 1) | £170000 | £10000 | ☐ | ☐ |
| 137 | **38** | £5 orange (Plate 1) | £14000 | £4750 | ☐ | ☐ |

**41**

**42**

**43**

**44**

**45**

**46**

**47** Small anchor

**48** Orb

**49** Imperial Crown

### Large coloured corner letters

### 1873–80

|  |  | (i) Wmk Small Anchor Type **47** |  |  |  |  |
|---|---|---|---|---|---|---|
| 139 | **41** | 2½d mauve Pl. | £625 | £115 | ☐ | ☐ |
|  |  | (ii) Wmk Orb Type **48** |  |  |  |  |
| 141 | **41** | 2½d mauve Pl. | £525 | 80·00 | ☐ | ☐ |
| 142 |  | 2½d blue Pl. | £575 | 55·00 | ☐ | ☐ |

|  |  | (iii) Wmk Spray of Rose Type **33** |  |  |  |  |
|---|---|---|---|---|---|---|
| 143 | **42** | 3d red Pl. | £450 | 75·00 | ☐ | ☐ |
| 145 | **43** | 6d pale buff (Plate 13) | *£25000 |  | ☐ | ☐ |
| 147 |  | 6d grey Pl. | £500 | 85·00 | ☐ | ☐ |
| 150 | **44** | 1s green Pl. | £625 | £150 | ☐ | ☐ |
| 151 |  | 1s brown (Plate 13) | £4750 | £700 | ☐ | ☐ |
|  |  | (iv) Wmk Large Garter Type **17** |  |  |  |  |
| 152 | **45** | 4d vermilion Pl. | £3000 | £500 | ☐ | ☐ |
| 153 |  | 4d green Pl. | £1400 | £300 | ☐ | ☐ |
| 154 |  | 4d brown (Plate 17) | £2800 | £525 | ☐ | ☐ |
| 156 | **46** | 8d orange (Plate 1) | £1800 | £350 | ☐ | ☐ |

$3^{\underline{d}}$
**(50)**

$6^{\underline{d}}$
**(51)**

Surcharges in red

**1880–83** Wmk Imperial Crown Type **49**

| 157 | **41** | 2½d blue Pl. | £425 | 35·00 | ☐ | ☐ |
|---|---|---|---|---|---|---|
| 158 | **42** | 3d red Pl. | £500 | £100 | ☐ | ☐ |
| 159 |  | 3d on 3d lilac (surch Type **50**) | £625 | £150 | ☐ | ☐ |
| 160 | **45** | 4d brown Pl. | £425 | 70·00 | ☐ | ☐ |
| 161 | **43** | 6d grey Pl. | £400 | 75·00 | ☐ | ☐ |
| 162 |  | 6d on 6d lilac (surchType **51**) | £675 | £150 | ☐ | ☐ |
| 163 | **44** | 1s brown Pl. | £700 | £160 | ☐ | ☐ |

**52**

**53**

**54**

**55**

**56**

**1880–81** Wmk Imperial Crown Type **49**

| 164 | **52** | ½d green | 55·00 | 20·00 | ☐ | ☐ |
|---|---|---|---|---|---|---|
| 166 | **53** | 1d brown | 35·00 | 15·00 | ☐ | ☐ |
| 167 | **54** | 1½d brown | £250 | 55·00 | ☐ | ☐ |
| 168 | **55** | 2d red | £320 | £110 | ☐ | ☐ |
| 169 | **56** | 5d indigo | £725 | £150 | ☐ | ☐ |

**57**

**Die** I

**Die** II

**1881** Wmk Imperial Crown Type **49**

|  |  | (a) 14 dots in each corner, Die I |  |  |  |  |
|---|---|---|---|---|---|---|
| 171 | **57** | 1d lilac | £225 | 35·00 | ☐ | ☐ |
|  |  | (b) 16 dots in each corner, Die II |  |  |  |  |
| 174 | **57** | 1d mauve | 2·75 | 1·70 | ☐ | ☐ |

58

59

60

74

75

76

77

78

79

80

81

82

### Coloured letters in the corners

**1883–84** Wmk Anchor Type **40**

| | | | | | | |
|---|---|---|---|---|---|---|
| 178 | **58** | 2s6d | lilac | £600 | £160 | ☐ ☐ |
| 181 | **59** | 5s | red | £975 | £250 | ☐ ☐ |
| 183 | **60** | 10s | blue | £2250 | £525 | ☐ ☐ |

61

**1884** Wmk 3 Imperial Crowns Type **49**

| | | | | | |
|---|---|---|---|---|---|
| 185 | **61** | £1 brown | £32000 | £2800 | ☐ ☐ |

**1888** Wmk 3 Orbs Type **48**

| | | | | | |
|---|---|---|---|---|---|
| 186 | **61** | £1 brown | £72000 | £4250 | ☐ ☐ |

**1891** Wmk 3 Imperial Crowns Type **49**

| | | | | | |
|---|---|---|---|---|---|
| 212 | **61** | £1 green | £4000 | £800 | ☐ ☐ |

62      63      64

65      66

## 'Jubilee' Issue

**1887–1900** The bicoloured stamps have the value tablets, or the frames including the value tablets, in the second colour.
Wmk Imperial Crown Type **49**

| | | | | | |
|---|---|---|---|---|---|
| 197 | **71** | ½d vermilion | 1·75 | 1·20 | ☐ ☐ |
| 213 | | ½d green* | 2·00 | 2·25 | ☐ ☐ |
| 198 | **72** | 1½d purple and green | 18·00 | 8·00 | ☐ ☐ |
| 200 | **73** | 2d green and red | 34·00 | 13·00 | ☐ ☐ |
| 201 | **74** | 2½d purple on blue | 25·00 | 3·50 | ☐ ☐ |
| 203 | **75** | 3d purple on yellow | 30·00 | 3·50 | ☐ ☐ |
| 205 | **76** | 4d green and brown | 40·00 | 15·00 | ☐ ☐ |
| 206 | **77** | 4½d green and red | 11·00 | 45·00 | ☐ ☐ |
| 207a | **78** | 5d purple and blue | 42·00 | 13·00 | ☐ ☐ |
| 208 | **79** | 6d purple on red | 40·00 | 12·00 | ☐ ☐ |
| 209 | **80** | 9d purple and blue | 75·00 | 45·00 | ☐ ☐ |
| 210 | **81** | 10d purple and red | 60·00 | 42·00 | ☐ ☐ |
| 211 | **82** | 1s green | £275 | 75·00 | ☐ ☐ |
| 214 | | 1s green and red | 65·00 | £140 | ☐ ☐ |
| *Set of* 14 | | | £650 | £375 | ☐ ☐ |

*The ½d No. 213 in blue is a colour changeling.

**1883–84** Wmk Imperial Crown Type **49** (sideways on horiz designs)

| | | | | | |
|---|---|---|---|---|---|
| 187 | **52** | ½d blue | 32·00 | 10·00 | ☐ ☐ |
| 188 | **62** | 1½d lilac | £125 | 45·00 | ☐ ☐ |
| 189 | **63** | 2d lilac | £230 | 80·00 | ☐ ☐ |
| 190 | **64** | 2½d lilac | 95·00 | 20·00 | ☐ ☐ |
| 191 | **65** | 3d lilac | £280 | £100 | ☐ ☐ |
| 192 | **66** | 4d dull green | £580 | £210 | ☐ ☐ |
| 193 | **62** | 5d dull green | £580 | £210 | ☐ ☐ |
| 194 | **63** | 6d dull green | £625 | £240 | ☐ ☐ |
| 195 | **64** | 9d dull green | £1250 | £480 | ☐ ☐ |
| 196 | **65** | 1s dull green | £1600 | £325 | ☐ ☐ |

The above prices are for stamps in the true dull green colour. Stamps which have been soaked, causing the colour to run are virtually worthless.

71

72

73

# KING EDWARD VII

1901 (22 Jan.)–1910 (6 May)

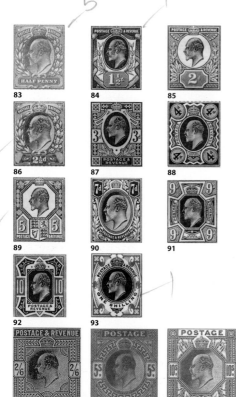

83    84    85

86    87    88

89    90    91

92    93

94    95    96

97

**1902–13** Wmks Imperial Crown Type **49** (½d to 1s), Anchor Type **40** (2s6d to 10s), Three Crowns Type **49** (£1)

### (a) Perf 14

| | | | | | | |
|---|---|---|---|---|---|---|
| 215 | **83** | ½d blue-green | 2·00 | 1·50 | ☐ | ☐ |
| 217 | | ½d yellow-green | 2·00 | 1·50 | ☐ | ☐ |
| 219 | | 1d red | 2·00 | 1·50 | ☐ | ☐ |
| 224 | **84** | 1½d purple and green | 45·00 | 22·00 | ☐ | ☐ |
| 291 | **85** | 2d green and red | 28·00 | 22·00 | ☐ | ☐ |
| 231 | **86** | 2½d blue | 20·00 | 12·00 | ☐ | ☐ |
| 232 | **87** | 3d purple on yellow | 50·00 | 18·00 | ☐ | ☐ |
| 238 | **88** | 4d green and brown | 40·00 | 20·00 | ☐ | ☐ |
| 240 | | 4d orange | 20·00 | 18·00 | ☐ | ☐ |
| 294 | **89** | 5d purple and blue | 30·00 | 22·00 | ☐ | ☐ |
| 297 | **83** | 6d purple | 30·00 | 22·00 | ☐ | ☐ |
| 249 | **90** | 7d grey | 15·00 | 22·00 | ☐ | ☐ |
| 307 | **91** | 9d purple and blue | 60·00 | 60·00 | ☐ | ☐ |
| 311 | **92** | 10d purple and red | 80·00 | 60·00 | ☐ | ☐ |
| 314 | **93** | 1s green and red | 60·00 | 35·00 | ☐ | ☐ |
| 260 | **94** | 2s6d purple | £280 | £220 | ☐ | ☐ |
| 263 | **95** | 5s red | £450 | £200 | ☐ | ☐ |
| 265 | **96** | 10s blue | £1000 | £500 | ☐ | ☐ |
| 266 | **97** | £1 green | £2000 | £825 | ☐ | ☐ |
| *Set of* 15 (to 1s) | | | £400 | £275 | ☐ | ☐ |

### (b) Perf 15 × 14

| | | | | | | |
|---|---|---|---|---|---|---|
| 279 | **83** | ½d green | 40·00 | 45·00 | ☐ | ☐ |
| 281 | | 1d red | 15·00 | 15·00 | ☐ | ☐ |
| 283 | **86** | 2½d blue | 22·00 | 15·00 | ☐ | ☐ |
| 285 | **87** | 3d purple on yellow | 45·00 | 15·00 | ☐ | ☐ |
| 286 | **88** | 4d orange | 30·00 | 15·00 | ☐ | ☐ |
| *Set of* 5 | | | £130 | 90·00 | ☐ | ☐ |

# KING GEORGE V

1910 (6 May)–1936 (20 January)

**PERFORATION.** All the following issues are Perf 15 × 14 except vertical commemorative stamps which are 14 × 15, unless otherwise stated.

98 (Hair dark)

99 (Lion unshaded)

100

**1911–12** Wmk Imperial Crown Type **49**

| | | | | | | |
|---|---|---|---|---|---|---|
| 322 | **98** | ½d green | 4·00 | 4·00 | ☐ | ☐ |
| 327 | **99** | 1d red | 4·50 | 2·50 | ☐ | ☐ |

**1912** Wmk Royal Cypher ('Simple') Type **100**

| | | | | | | |
|---|---|---|---|---|---|---|
| 335 | **98** | ½d green | 45·00 | 40·00 | ☐ | ☐ |
| 336 | **99** | 1d red | 30·00 | 30·00 | ☐ | ☐ |

101 (Hair light)

102 (Lion shaded)

103

**1912** Wmk Imperial Crown Type **49**

| | | | | | | |
|---|---|---|---|---|---|---|
| 339 | **101** | ½d green | 8·00 | 4·00 | ☐ | ☐ |
| 341 | **102** | 1d red | 5·00 | 2·00 | ☐ | ☐ |

**1912** Wmk Royal Cypher ('Simple') Type **100**

| | | | | | | |
|---|---|---|---|---|---|---|
| 344 | **101** | ½d green | 7·00 | 3·00 | ☐ | ☐ |
| 345 | **102** | 1d red | 8·00 | 4·50 | ☐ | ☐ |

**1912** Wmk Royal Cypher ('Multiple') Type **103**

| | | | | | | |
|---|---|---|---|---|---|---|
| 346 | **101** | ½d green | 12·00 | 8·00 | ☐ | ☐ |
| 350 | **102** | 1d red | 18·00 | 10·00 | ☐ | ☐ |

104

105

106

107

108

**1912–24** Wmk Royal Cypher Type **100**

| | | | | | | |
|---|---|---|---|---|---|---|
| 351 | **105** | ½d green | 1·00 | 1·00 | ☐ | ☐ |
| 357 | **104** | 1d red | 1·00 | 1·00 | ☐ | ☐ |
| 362 | **105** | 1½d brown | 4·00 | 1·50 | ☐ | ☐ |
| 368 | **106** | 2d orange | 4·00 | 3·00 | ☐ | ☐ |
| 371 | **104** | 2½d blue | 12·00 | 4·00 | ☐ | ☐ |
| 375 | **106** | 3d violet | 8·00 | 3·00 | ☐ | ☐ |
| 379 | | 4d grey-green | 15·00 | 2·00 | ☐ | ☐ |
| 381 | **107** | 5d brown | 15·00 | 5·00 | ☐ | ☐ |
| 385 | | 6d purple | 15·00 | 7·00 | ☐ | ☐ |
| | | a. Perf 14 | 90·00 | £110 | ☐ | ☐ |

| | | | | | | |
|---|---|---|---|---|---|---|
| 387 | | 7d olive-green | 20·00 | 10·00 | ☐ | ☐ |
| 390 | | 8d black on yellow | 32·00 | 11·00 | ☐ | ☐ |
| 392 | **108** | 9d black | 15·00 | 6·00 | ☐ | ☐ |
| 393a | | 9d olive-green | £110 | 30·00 | ☐ | ☐ |
| 394 | | 10d blue | 22·00 | 20·00 | ☐ | ☐ |
| 395 | | 1s brown | 20·00 | 4·00 | ☐ | ☐ |
| *Set of* 15 | | | £250 | 95·00 | ☐ | ☐ |

**1913** Wmk Royal Cypher ('Multiple') Type **103**

| | | | | | | |
|---|---|---|---|---|---|---|
| 397 | **105** | ½d green | £150 | £180 | ☐ | ☐ |
| 398 | **104** | 1d red | £225 | £225 | ☐ | ☐ |

See also Nos. 418/29.

109

110

**1913–18** Wmk Single Cypher Type **110** Perf 11 × 12

| | | | | | | |
|---|---|---|---|---|---|---|
| 413a | **109** | 2s6d brown | £190 | £100 | ☐ | ☐ |
| 416 | | 5s red | £325 | £125 | ☐ | ☐ |
| 417 | | 10s blue | £475 | £175 | ☐ | ☐ |
| 403 | | £1 green | £3500 | £1250 | ☐ | ☐ |
| *Set of* 4 | | | £4000 | £1500 | ☐ | ☐ |

T **109**. Background around portrait consists of horizontal lines. See also Nos. 450/2.

111

**1924–26** Wmk Block Cypher Type **111**

| | | | | | | |
|---|---|---|---|---|---|---|
| 418 | **105** | ½d green | 1·00 | 1·00 | ☐ | ☐ |
| 419 | **104** | 1d red | 1·00 | 1·00 | ☐ | ☐ |
| 420 | **105** | 1½d brown | 1·00 | 1·00 | ☐ | ☐ |
| 421 | **106** | 2d orange | 2·50 | 2·50 | ☐ | ☐ |
| 422 | **104** | 2½d blue | 5·00 | 3·00 | ☐ | ☐ |
| 423 | **106** | 3d violet | 10·00 | 2·50 | ☐ | ☐ |
| 424 | | 4d grey-green | 12·00 | 2·50 | ☐ | ☐ |
| 425 | **107** | 5d brown | 20·00 | 3·00 | ☐ | ☐ |
| 426a | | 6d purple | 3·00 | 1·50 | ☐ | ☐ |
| 427 | **108** | 9d olive-green | 12·00 | 3·50 | ☐ | ☐ |
| 428 | | 10d blue | 40·00 | 40·00 | ☐ | ☐ |
| 429 | | 1s brown | 22·00 | 3·00 | ☐ | ☐ |
| *Set of* 12 | | | £110 | 60·00 | ☐ | ☐ |

112

112a

**British Empire Exhibition**

**1924–25** Wmk **111** Perf 14

(a) 23.4.24. Dated '1924'

| | | | | | | |
|---|---|---|---|---|---|---|
| 430 | **112** | 1d red | 10·00 | 11·00 | ☐ | ☐ |
| 431 | **112a** | 1½d brown | 15·00 | 15·00 | ☐ | ☐ |
| First Day Cover | | | £450 | 1·00 | | |

(b) 9.5.25. Dated '1925'

| | | | | | | |
|---|---|---|---|---|---|---|
| 432 | **112** | 1d red | 15·00 | 30·00 | ☐ | ☐ |
| 433 | **112a** | 1½d brown | 40·00 | 70·00 | ☐ | ☐ |
| First Day Cover | | | | £1700 | | |

# BB STAMPS LTD

Est. 1988

## Retail Pricelist  of

# GREAT BRITAIN

## Postage Stamps  1840 - Date

### Autumn 2014

### List 25

PO Box 6277, Overton, Hampshire, RG25 3RN

www.bbstamps.co.uk

Tel: 01256 773269  Fax: 01256 771708

Email: Sales@bbstamps.co.uk

PROUD
MEMBER
OF THE

## PTS

PHILATELIC
TRADERS
SOCIETY

VISA  DELTA  EUROCARD MasterCard  Maestro

major credit cards accepted

OUT NOW!

113

114

115

116 St. George and the Dragon

117

**Ninth Universal Postal Union Congress**

**1929** (10 May)

(a) Wmk **111**

| | | | | | | |
|---|---|---|---|---|---|---|
| 434 | **113** | ½d green | 2·25 | 2·25 | ☐ | ☐ |
| 435 | **114** | 1d red | 2·25 | 2·25 | ☐ | ☐ |
| 436 | | 1½d brown | 2·25 | 1·75 | ☐ | ☐ |
| 437 | **115** | 2½d blue | 10·00 | 10·00 | ☐ | ☐ |

(b) Wmk **117** Perf 12

| | | | | | | |
|---|---|---|---|---|---|---|
| 438 | **116** | £1 black | £750 | £550 | ☐ | ☐ |
| 434/7 | *Set of* 4 | | 15·00 | 14·50 | ☐ | ☐ |
| 434/7 | First Day Cover (4 vals.) | | | £600 | ☐ | |
| 434/8 | First Day Cover (5 vals.) | | | £14000 | ☐ | |

118

119

120

121

122

**1934–36** Wmk **111**

| | | | | | | |
|---|---|---|---|---|---|---|
| 439 | **118** | ½d green | 50 | 50 | ☐ | ☐ |
| 440 | **119** | 1d red | 50 | 50 | ☐ | ☐ |
| 441 | **118** | 1½d brown | 50 | 50 | ☐ | ☐ |
| 442 | **120** | 2d orange | 75 | 75 | ☐ | ☐ |
| 443 | **119** | 2½d blue | 1·50 | 1·25 | ☐ | ☐ |
| 444 | **120** | 3d violet | 1·50 | 1·25 | ☐ | ☐ |
| 445 | | 4d grey-green | 2·00 | 1·25 | ☐ | ☐ |
| 446 | **121** | 5d brown | 6·50 | 2·75 | ☐ | ☐ |
| 447 | **122** | 9d olive-green | 12·00 | 2·25 | ☐ | ☐ |
| 448 | | 10d blue | 15·00 | 10·00 | ☐ | ☐ |
| 449 | | 1s brown | 15·00 | 1·25 | ☐ | ☐ |
| *Set of* 11 | | | 50·00 | 20·00 | ☐ | ☐ |

T **109** (re-engraved). Background around portrait consists of horizontal and diagonal lines

**1934** Wmk **110** Perf 11 × 12

| | | | | | | |
|---|---|---|---|---|---|---|
| 450 | **109** | 2s6d brown | 80·00 | 40·00 | ☐ | ☐ |
| 451 | | 5s red | £175 | 85·00 | ☐ | ☐ |
| 452 | | 10s blue | £350 | 80·00 | ☐ | ☐ |
| *Set of* 3 | | | £575 | £190 | ☐ | ☐ |

123

123a

123b

123c

**Silver Jubilee**

**1935** (7 May) Wmk **111**

| | | | | | | |
|---|---|---|---|---|---|---|
| 453 | **123** | ½d green | 1·00 | 1·00 | ☐ | ☐ |
| 454 | **123a** | 1d red | 1·50 | 2·00 | ☐ | ☐ |
| 455 | **123b** | 1½d brown | 1·00 | 1·00 | ☐ | ☐ |
| 456 | **123c** | 2½d blue | 5·00 | 6·50 | ☐ | ☐ |
| *Set of* 4 | | | 7·50 | 9·50 | ☐ | ☐ |
| First Day Cover | | | | £600 | | ☐ |

# SELLING YOUR STAMPS?

Warwick and Warwick have an expanding requirement for world collections, single country collections, single items, covers, proof material and specialised collections, with G.B. material being particularly in demand. Our customer base is increasing dramatically and we need an ever-larger supply of quality material to keep pace with demand. The market has never been stronger and if you are considering the sale of your collection, now is the time to act.

## FREE VALUATIONS

We will provide a free, professional and without obligation valuation of your collection. Either we will make you a fair, binding private treaty offer, or we will recommend inclusion of your property in our next specialist public auction.

## FREE TRANSPORTATION

We can arrange insured transportation of your collection to our Warwick offices completely free of charge. If you decline our offer, we ask you to cover the return carriage costs only.

## FREE VISITS

Visits by our valuers are possible anywhere in the country or abroad, usually within 48 hours, in order to value larger collections. Please telephone for details.

## ADVISORY DAYS

We are staging a series of advisory days across the country. Please visit our website or telephone for further details.

## EXCELLENT PRICES

Because of the strength of our customer base we are in a position to offer prices that we feel sure will exceed your expectations.

## ACT NOW

Telephone or email Ian Hunter today with details of your property.

Warwick & Warwick Ltd.
Auctioneers and Valuers
Chalon House, Scar Bank, Millers Road,
Warwick CV34 5DB
Tel: 01926 499031  Fax: 01926 491906
E-mail: ian.hunter@warwickandwarwick.com

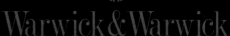

Warwick & Warwick

# KING EDWARD VIII

1936 (20 Jan.–10 Dec.)

**124**

**125**

**1936** Wmk **125**

| | | | | |
|---|---|---|---|---|
| 457 | **124** | ½d green | 30 | 30 |
| 458 | | 1d red | 60 | 50 |
| 459 | | 1½d brown | 30 | 30 |
| 460 | | 2½d blue | 30 | 85 |
| *Set of 4* | | | 1·25 | 1·75 |
| First Day Covers | | | | 3·25 |
| 1 Sept. 1936 Nos. 457, 459/60 | | | | £150 |
| 14 Sept. 1936 No. 458 | | | | £180 |

Collectors are reminded that for issues from 1936 to date, prices in the unused column are for unmounted mint.

# KING GEORGE VI

1936 (11 Dec.)–1952 (6 Feb.)

**126** King George VI and Queen Elizabeth

**127**

## Coronation

**1937** (13 May) Wmk **127**

| | | | | |
|---|---|---|---|---|
| 461 | **126** | 1½d brown | 30 | 30 |
| First Day Cover | | | 35·00 | |

**128**      **129**      **130**

### King George VI and National Emblems

**1937–47** Wmk **127**

| | | | | |
|---|---|---|---|---|
| 462 | **128** | ½d green | 30 | 25 |
| 463 | | 1d scarlet | 30 | 25 |
| 464 | | 1½d brown | 30 | 25 |
| 465 | | 2d orange | 1·20 | 50 |
| 466 | | 2½d blue | 40 | 25 |
| 467 | | 3d violet | 5·00 | 1·00 |
| 468 | **129** | 4d green | 60 | 75 |
| 469 | | 5d brown | 3·50 | 85 |
| 470 | | 6d purple | 1·50 | 60 |
| 471 | **130** | 7d green | 5·00 | 60 |
| 472 | | 8d red | 7·50 | 80 |
| 473 | | 9d deep green | 6·50 | 80 |
| 474 | | 10d blue | 7·00 | 80 |
| 474a | | 11d plum | 3·00 | 2·75 |
| 475 | | 1s brown | 9·00 | 75 |
| *Set of 15* | | | 45·00 | 10·00 |

First Day Covers

| | | |
|---|---|---|
| 10 May 1937 | Nos. 462/3, 466 | 45·00 |
| 30 July 1937 | No. 464 | 45·00 |
| 31 Jan. 1938 | Nos. 465, 467 | £100 |
| 21 Nov. 1938 | Nos. 468/9 | 65·00 |
| 30 Jan. 1939 | No. 470 | 60·00 |
| 27 Feb. 1939 | Nos. 471/2 | 85·00 |
| 1 May 1939 | Nos. 473/4, 475 | £500 |
| 29 Dec. 1947 | No. 474a | 55·00 |

For later printings of the lower values in apparently lighter shades and different colours, see Nos. 485/90 and 503/8.

**130a** King George VI      **131**      **132**

132a       133

**1939–48** Wmk **133** Perf 14

| | | | | | | |
|---|---|---|---|---|---|---|
| 476 | **130a** | 2s6d brown | 95·00 | 8·00 | ☐ | ☐ |
| 476b | | 2s6d green | 15·00 | 1·50 | | |
| 477 | **131** | 5s red | 20·00 | 2·00 | | |
| 478 | **132** | 10s dark blue | £260 | 22·00 | | |
| 478b | | 10s bright blue | 45·00 | 5·00 | | |
| 478c | **132a** | £1 brown | 25·00 | 26·00 | | |
| Set of 6 | | | £425 | 60·00 | ☐ | |
| First Day Covers | | | | | | |
| 21 Aug. 1939 | | No. 477 | | £800 | | |
| 4 Sept. 1939 | | No. 476 | | £1800 | | |
| 30 Oct. 1939 | | No. 478 | | £3250 | | |
| 9 Mar. 1942 | | No. 476b | | £1750 | | |
| 30 Nov. 1942 | | No. 478b | | £3750 | | |
| 1 Oct. 1948 | | No. 478c | | £325 | | |

**134** Queen Victoria and King George VI

**Centenary of**
**First Adhesive Postage Stamps**

**1940** (6 May) Wmk **127** Perf 14½ × 14

| | | | | | | |
|---|---|---|---|---|---|---|
| 479 | **134** | ½d green | 30 | 75 | ☐ | ☐ |
| 480 | | 1d red | 1·00 | 75 | | |
| 481 | | 1½d brown | 50 | 1·50 | | |
| 482 | | 2d orange | 1·00 | 75 | | |
| 483 | | 2½d blue | 2·25 | 50 | | |
| 484 | | 3d violet | 3·00 | 3·50 | | |
| Set of 6 | | | 8·75 | 5·25 | ☐ | |
| First Day Cover | | | | 55·00 | ☐ | |

Head as Nos. 462–7, but with lighter background

**1941–42** Wmk **127**

| | | | | | | |
|---|---|---|---|---|---|---|
| 485 | **128** | ½d pale green | 30 | 30 | ☐ | ☐ |
| 486 | | 1d pale red | 30 | 30 | | |
| 487 | | 1½d pale brown | 60 | 80 | | |
| 488 | | 2d pale orange | 50 | 50 | | |
| 489 | | 2½d light blue | 30 | 30 | | |
| 490 | | 3d pale violet | 2·50 | 1·00 | | |
| Set of 6 | | | 3·50 | 2·75 | ☐ | |
| First Day Covers | | | | | | |
| 21 July 1941 | | No. 489 | | 45·00 | | |
| 11 Aug. 1941 | | No. 486 | | 22·00 | | |
| 1 Sept. 1941 | | No. 485 | | 22·00 | | |
| 6 Oct. 1941 | | No. 488 | | 60·00 | | |
| 3 Nov. 1941 | | No. 490 | | £110 | | |
| 28 Sept. 1942 | | No. 487 | | 55·00 | | |

**135** Symbols of Peace and Reconstruction      **136** Symbols of Peace and Reconstruction

**Victory**

**1946** (11 June) Wmk **127**

| | | | | | | |
|---|---|---|---|---|---|---|
| 491 | **135** | 2½d blue | 20 | 20 | ☐ | ☐ |
| 492 | **136** | 3d violet | 20 | 50 | ☐ | ☐ |
| First Day Cover | | | | 65·00 | | ☐ |

**137** King George VI and Queen Elizabeth      **138** King George VI and Queen Elizabeth

**Royal Silver Wedding**

**1948** (26 Apr.) Wmk **127**

| | | | | | | |
|---|---|---|---|---|---|---|
| 493 | **137** | 2½d blue | 35 | 20 | ☐ | ☐ |
| 494 | **138** | £1 blue | 40·00 | 40·00 | ☐ | ☐ |
| First Day Cover | | | | £425 | | ☐ |

**1948** (10 May)
Stamps of 1d and 2½d showing seaweed-gathering were on sale at eight Head Post Offices elsewhere in Great Britain, but were primarily for use in the Channel Islands and are listed there (see after Regional Issues).

**139** Globe and Laurel Wreath      **140** Speed

**141** Olympic Symbol      **142** Winged Victory

**Olympic Games**

**1948** (29 July) Wmk **127**

| | | | | | | |
|---|---|---|---|---|---|---|
| 495 | **139** | 2½d blue | 50 | 10 | ☐ | ☐ |
| 496 | **140** | 3d violet | 50 | 50 | ☐ | ☐ |
| 497 | **141** | 6d purple | 3·25 | 75 | ☐ | ☐ |
| 498 | **142** | 1s brown | 4·50 | 2·00 | ☐ | ☐ |
| Set of 4 | | | 8·00 | 3·00 | ☐ | ☐ |
| First Day Cover | | | | 45·00 | | ☐ |

**143** Two Hemispheres

**144** U.P.U. Monument, Berne

**147** HMS *Victory*

**148** White Cliffs of Dover

**145** Goddess Concordia,
Globe and Points of Compass

**146** Posthorn and Globe

**149** St. George and the Dragon

**150** Royal Coat of Arms

### 75th Anniversary of Universal Postal Union

**1949** (10 Oct.) Wmk **127**

| | | | | | | |
|---|---|---|---|---|---|---|
| 499 | **143** | 2½d blue | 25 | 10 | ☐ | ☐ |
| 500 | **144** | 3d violet | 25 | 50 | ☐ | ☐ |
| 501 | **145** | 6d purple | 50 | 75 | ☐ | ☐ |
| 502 | **146** | 1s brown | 1·00 | 1·25 | ☐ | ☐ |
| Set of 4 | | | 1·50 | 2·50 | ☐ | ☐ |
| First Day Cover | | | | 80·00 | ☐ | |

4d as No. 468 and others as Nos. 485/9, but colours changed.

**1950–51** Wmk **127**

| | | | | | | |
|---|---|---|---|---|---|---|
| 503 | **128** | ½d pale orange | 30 | 30 | ☐ | ☐ |
| 504 | | 1d light blue | 30 | 30 | ☐ | ☐ |
| 505 | | 1½d pale green | 65 | 60 | ☐ | ☐ |
| 506 | | 2d pale brown | 75 | 40 | ☐ | ☐ |
| 507 | | 2½d pale red | 60 | 40 | ☐ | ☐ |
| 508 | **129** | 4d light blue | 2·00 | 1·75 | ☐ | ☐ |
| Set of 6 | | | 4·00 | 3·25 | ☐ | ☐ |
| First Day Covers | | | | | | |
| 2 Oct. 1950 No. 508 | | | | £120 | ☐ | |
| 3 May 1951 Nos. 503/7 | | | | 55·00 | ☐ | |

**1951** (3 May) Wmk **133** Perf 11 × 12

| | | | | | | |
|---|---|---|---|---|---|---|
| 509 | **147** | 2s6d green | 7·50 | 1·00 | ☐ | ☐ |
| 510 | **148** | 5s red | 35·00 | 1·00 | ☐ | ☐ |
| 511 | **149** | 10s blue | 15·00 | 7·50 | ☐ | ☐ |
| 512 | **150** | £1 brown | 45·00 | 18·00 | ☐ | ☐ |
| Set of 4 | | | £100 | 25·00 | ☐ | ☐ |
| First Day Cover | | | | £950 | | ☐ |

**151** Commerce and Prosperity

**152** Festival Symbol

### Festival of Britain

**1951** (3 May) Wmk **127**

| | | | | | | |
|---|---|---|---|---|---|---|
| 513 | **151** | 2½d red | 20 | 15 | ☐ | ☐ |
| 514 | **152** | 4d blue | 30 | 35 | ☐ | ☐ |
| Set of 2 | | | 40 | 40 | ☐ | ☐ |
| First Day Cover | | | | 38·00 | | ☐ |

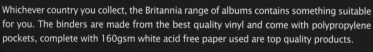

# QUEEN ELIZABETH II

6 February, 1952

**153** Tudor Crown

**154**

**155**

**156**

**157**

**158**

**159**

**160**

**163**

**164**

### Coronation

**1953** (3 June) Wmk **153**

| | | | | | | |
|---|---|---|---|---|---|---|
| 532 | **161** | 2½d | red | 20 | 25 | ☐ ☐ |
| 533 | **162** | 4d | blue | 1·10 | 1·90 | ☐ ☐ |
| 534 | **163** | 1s3d | green | 5·00 | 3·00 | ☐ ☐ |
| 535 | **164** | 1s6d | blue | 10·00 | 4·75 | ☐ ☐ |
| Set of 4 | | | | 16·00 | 9·00 | ☐ ☐ |
| First Day Cover | | | | | 75·00 | ☐ |

For £1 values as Type **163** see Nos. **MS**2147 and 2380.

**165** St. Edward's Crown

**166** Carrickfergus Castle

**167** Caernarvon Castle

**168** Edinburgh Castle

**169** Windsor Castle

**1955** (1–23 Sept.) Wmk **165** Perf 11 × 12

| | | | | | | |
|---|---|---|---|---|---|---|
| 536 | **166** | 2s6d | brown | 13·00 | 2·00 | ☐ ☐ |
| 537 | **167** | 5s | red | 35·00 | 4·00 | ☐ ☐ |
| 538 | **168** | 10s | blue | 85·00 | 14·00 | ☐ ☐ |
| 539 | **169** | £1 | black | £130 | 35·00 | ☐ ☐ |
| Set of 4 | | | | £225 | 50·00 | ☐ ☐ |
| First Day Cover | (Nos. 538/9) (1 Sept.) | | | | £850 | ☐ |
| First Day Cover | (Nos. 536/7) (23 Sept.) | | | | £650 | ☐ |

See also Nos. 595a/8a and 759/62.

**1952–54** Wmk **153**

| | | | | | | |
|---|---|---|---|---|---|---|
| 515 | **154** | ½d | orange | 10 | 15 | ☐ ☐ |
| 516 | | 1d | ultramarine | 20 | 20 | ☐ ☐ |
| 517 | | 1½d | green | 10 | 20 | ☐ ☐ |
| 518 | | 2d | red-brown | 20 | 20 | ☐ ☐ |
| 519 | **155** | 2½d | carmine-red | 15 | 15 | ☐ ☐ |
| 520 | | 3d | deep lilac | 1·50 | 90 | ☐ ☐ |
| 521 | **156** | 4d | ultramarine | 3·25 | 1·30 | ☐ ☐ |
| | | 4½d | (See Nos. 577, 594, 609 and 616b) | | | |
| 522 | **157** | 5d | brown | 75 | 3·50 | ☐ ☐ |
| 523 | | 6d | reddish purple | 4·00 | 1·00 | ☐ ☐ |
| 524 | | 7d | bright green | 9·50 | 5·50 | ☐ ☐ |
| 525 | **158** | 8d | magenta | 75 | 85 | ☐ ☐ |
| 526 | | 9d | bronze-green | 23·00 | 4·75 | ☐ ☐ |
| 527 | | 10d | Prussian blue | 18·00 | 4·75 | ☐ ☐ |
| 528 | | 11d | brown-purple | 35·00 | 15·00 | ☐ ☐ |
| 529 | **159** | 1s | bistre-brown | 80 | 50 | ☐ ☐ |
| 530 | **160** | 1s3d | green | 4·50 | 3·25 | ☐ ☐ |
| 531 | **159** | 1s6d | grey-blue | 14·00 | 3·75 | ☐ ☐ |
| Set of 17 | | | | £100 | 40·00 | ☐ ☐ |

**First Day Covers**

| | | | |
|---|---|---|---|
| 5 Dec. 1952 | Nos. 517, 519 | 25·00 | ☐ |
| 6 July 1953 | Nos. 522, 525, 529 | 50·00 | ☐ |
| 31 Aug. 1953 | Nos. 515/16, 518 | 50·00 | ☐ |
| 2 Nov. 1953 | Nos. 521, 530/1 | £170 | ☐ |
| 18 Jan. 1954 | Nos. 520, 523/4 | £110 | ☐ |
| 8 Feb. 1954 | Nos. 526/8 | £225 | ☐ |

See also Nos. 540/56, 561/6, 570/94 and 599/618a and for stamps as Types **154/60** with face values in decimal currency see Nos. 2031/3, 2258/9, **MS**2326, **MS**2367 and 2378/9.

**161**

**162**

**1955–58** Wmk **165**

| | | | | | | |
|---|---|---|---|---|---|---|
| 540 | **154** | ½d | orange | 15 | 15 | ☐ ☐ |
| 541 | | 1d | blue | 30 | 15 | ☐ ☐ |
| 542 | | 1½d | green | 25 | 30 | ☐ ☐ |
| 543 | | 2d | red-brown | 25 | 35 | ☐ ☐ |
| 543b | | 2d | light red-brown | 20 | 20 | ☐ ☐ |
| 544 | **155** | 2½d | red | 20 | 25 | ☐ ☐ |
| 545 | | 3d | lilac | 25 | 25 | ☐ ☐ |
| 546 | **156** | 4d | blue | 1·30 | 45 | ☐ ☐ |
| 547 | **157** | 5d | brown | 6·00 | 6·00 | ☐ ☐ |
| 548 | | 6d | purple | 4·50 | 1·20 | ☐ ☐ |
| 549 | | 7d | green | 50·00 | 10·00 | ☐ ☐ |
| 550 | **158** | 8d | magenta | 7·00 | 1·30 | ☐ ☐ |
| 551 | | 9d | bronze-green | 20·00 | 2·75 | ☐ ☐ |
| 552 | | 10d | blue | 20·00 | 2·75 | ☐ ☐ |
| 553 | | 11d | plum | 50 | 1·10 | ☐ ☐ |
| 554 | **159** | 1s | bistre | 22·00 | 65 | ☐ ☐ |
| 555 | **160** | 1s3d | green | 30·00 | 1·60 | ☐ ☐ |
| 556 | **159** | 1s6d | indigo | 23·00 | 1·60 | ☐ ☐ |
| Set of 18 | | | | £160 | 27·00 | ☐ ☐ |

**170** Scout Badge and 'Rolling Hitch'   **171** 'Scouts coming to Britain'

**172** Globe within a Compass   **173**

### World Scout Jubilee Jamboree

**1957** (1 Aug.) Wmk **165**

| | | | | | | | |
|---|---|---|---|---|---|---|---|
| 557 | **170** | 2½d | red | 50 | 50 | ☐ | ☐ |
| 558 | **171** | 4d | blue | 75 | 1·50 | ☐ | ☐ |
| 559 | **172** | 1s3d | green | 5·50 | 4·50 | ☐ | ☐ |
| Set of 3 | | | | 6·00 | 5·75 | ☐ | ☐ |
| First Day Cover | | | | | 25·00 | | ☐ |

### 46th Inter Parliamentary Union Conference

**1957** (12 Sept.) Wmk **165**

| | | | | | | | |
|---|---|---|---|---|---|---|---|
| 560 | **173** | 4d | blue | 1·00 | 1·00 | ☐ | ☐ |
| First Day Cover | | | | | £140 | | ☐ |

### Graphite-lined and Phosphor Issues

These are used in connection with automatic sorting machinery, originally experimentally at Southampton but now also operating elsewhere. In such areas these stamps were the normal issue, but from mid 1967 all low-value stamps bear phosphor markings.

The graphite lines were printed in black on the back, beneath the gum; two lines per stamp except for the 2d (see below).

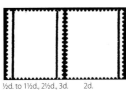

½d. to 1½d., 2½d., 3d.   2d.
Graphite-line arrangements
(Stamps viewed from back)

In November 1959, phosphor bands, printed on the front, replaced the graphite. They are wider than the graphite, not easy to see, but show as broad vertical bands at certain angles to the light.

Values representing the rate for printed papers (and second class mail from 1968) have one band and others have two, three or four bands according to size and format. From 1972 onwards some commemorative stamps were printed with 'all-over' phosphor.

In the small stamps the bands are on each side with the single band at left (except where otherwise stated). In the large-size commemorative stamps the single band may be at left, centre or right varying in different issues. The bands are vertical on both horizontal and vertical designs except where otherwise stated.

See also notes above No. 88.

### Graphite-lined issue

**1957** (19 Nov.) Two graphite lines on the back, except 2d value, which has one line. Wmk **165**

| | | | | | | | |
|---|---|---|---|---|---|---|---|
| 561 | **154** | ½d | orange | 25 | 25 | ☐ | ☐ |
| 562 | | 1d | blue | 40 | 40 | ☐ | ☐ |
| 563 | | 1½d | green | 1·20 | 1·40 | ☐ | ☐ |
| 564 | | 2d | light red-brown | 1·60 | 2·25 | ☐ | ☐ |
| 565 | **155** | 2½d | red | 8·50 | 7·00 | ☐ | ☐ |

| | | | | | | |
|---|---|---|---|---|---|---|
| 566 | | 3d | lilac | 80 | 50 | ☐ ☐ |
| Set of 6 | | | | 12·00 | 10·50 | ☐ ☐ |
| First Day Cover | | | | | 85·00 | ☐ |

See also Nos. 587/94.

**176** Welsh Dragon   **177** Flag and Games Emblem

**178** Welsh Dragon

### Sixth British Empire and Commonwealth Games, Cardiff

**1958** (18 July) Wmk **165**

| | | | | | | | |
|---|---|---|---|---|---|---|---|
| 567 | **176** | 3d | lilac | 20 | 20 | ☐ | ☐ |
| 568 | **177** | 6d | mauve | 40 | 45 | ☐ | ☐ |
| 569 | **178** | 1s3d | green | 2·25 | 2·40 | ☐ | ☐ |
| Set of 3 | | | | 2·50 | 2·75 | ☐ | ☐ |
| First Day Cover | | | | | 85·00 | | ☐ |

**179** Multiple Crowns

**WATERMARK.** All the following issues to No. 755 are Watermark **179** (sideways on the vertical commemorative stamps) unless otherwise stated.

**1958–65** Wmk **179**

| | | | | | | | |
|---|---|---|---|---|---|---|---|
| 570 | **154** | ½d | orange | 10 | 10 | ☐ | ☐ |
| 571 | | 1d | blue | 10 | 10 | ☐ | ☐ |
| 572 | | 1½d | green | 10 | 15 | ☐ | ☐ |
| 573 | | 2d | light red-brown | 10 | 10 | ☐ | ☐ |
| 574 | **155** | 2½d | red | 10 | 20 | ☐ | ☐ |
| 575 | | 3d | lilac | 10 | 20 | ☐ | ☐ |
| 576a | **156** | 4d | blue | 15 | 15 | ☐ | ☐ |
| 577 | | 4½d | brown | 10 | 25 | ☐ | ☐ |
| 578 | **157** | 5d | brown | 30 | 40 | ☐ | ☐ |
| 579 | | 6d | purple | 30 | 25 | ☐ | ☐ |
| 580 | | 7d | green | 50 | 45 | ☐ | ☐ |
| 581 | **158** | 8d | magenta | 60 | 40 | ☐ | ☐ |
| 582 | | 9d | bronze-green | 60 | 40 | ☐ | ☐ |
| 583 | | 10d | blue | 1·00 | 50 | ☐ | ☐ |
| 584 | **159** | 1s | bistre | 60 | 30 | ☐ | ☐ |
| 585 | **160** | 1s3d | green | 60 | 30 | ☐ | ☐ |
| 586 | **159** | 1s6d | indigo | 5·00 | 40 | ☐ | ☐ |
| Set of 17 | | | | 9·00 | 4·25 | ☐ | ☐ |
| First Day Cover (No. 577) (9 Feb. 1959) | | | | | £250 | | ☐ |

### Graphite-lined issue

**1958–59** Two graphite lines on the back, except 2d value, which has one line. Wmk **179**

| | | | | | | | |
|---|---|---|---|---|---|---|---|
| 587Wi | **154** | ½d | orange | 3·25 | 4·00 | ☐ | ☐ |
| 588 | | 1d | blue | 2·00 | 1·50 | ☐ | ☐ |
| 589Wi | | 1½d | green | 75·00 | 60·00 | ☐ | ☐ |
| 590 | | 2d | light red-brown | 9·00 | 3·50 | ☐ | ☐ |
| 591 | **155** | 2½d | red | 10·00 | 10·00 | ☐ | ☐ |
| 592 | | 3d | lilac | 50 | 65 | ☐ | ☐ |
| 593 | **156** | 4d | blue | 5·50 | 5·00 | ☐ | ☐ |
| 594 | | 4½d | brown | 6·50 | 5·00 | ☐ | ☐ |

# Did you miss the boat or did you take our advice?

In 1973 we recommended and sold the British definitive 1/2p (SGX842) with one phosphor band on side. We told our customers to buy them at 25p each. WE WERE RIGHT!! Today this stamp is catalogued at £55.00 each. If you had taken our advice, for an outlay of only £55 in 1973, the current catalogue value of your investment would be a staggering total of £11,000.00.

In 1999 we recommended our customers to buy the Princess Diana Welsh Language Presentation Packs. The catalogue value was only £2.50 each, but we were telling our customers to buy them for up to double catalogue value £5 each. Within only 6 years they had increased by 3,900%.

As everyone knows, investments can go down as well as up and the past in not necessarily a guide to the future. However, being selective and taking sound advice is the best way to make your hobby pay for itself.

In 2003 we recommended our customers to buy the Coronation £1 Green (SG 2380) which was catalogued by Stanley Gibbons at £1.50 per stamp. Within 1 year the catalogue value had increased to £50 per stamp, an increase of over 3,200%.

In 2004 we recommended our customers to buy the Nobel Prizes Presentation Pack, the SG catalogue value was £10 each. In the latest SG catalogue the price zoomed to a staggering £40 each.

In 2005 we recommended the 2003 Rugby Presentation Pack. The 2005 Stanley Gibbons concise catalogue listed this at £6 and, within 3 years, the catalogue value had soared. The 2008 Concise Catalogue value for the Rugby Presentation Pack was £30 each, a truly massive increase. We hope you took our advice.

In 2008 we recommended the 2002 Bridges of London Presentation pack (number 338). At the time the catalogue value was £8 each. Within 1 year of our recommendation the catalogue value of the Presentation Pack increased to £25 each. Now the catalogue value has doubled from £25 to £50 per pack.

In 2012 we recommended our customers to buy the complete year of 1967 Presentation Packs (4 pks). The catalogue value was £19, these are now catalogued at well over £70.

Our customers complemented us once again saying, **"Thank you again you were right"**.

| Set of 8 | | | | £110 | 70·00 | ☐ | ☐ |
|---|---|---|---|---|---|---|---|

The prices quoted for Nos. 587 and 589 are for examples with inverted watermark. Stamps with upright watermark are priced at: ½d £9 *mint*, £9 *used* and 1½d £90 *mint*, £80 *used*.

**1959–63** Wmk **179** Perf 11 × 12

| 595a | **166** | 2s6d brown | 35 | 40 | ☐ | ☐ |
|---|---|---|---|---|---|---|
| 596a | **167** | 5s red | 1·20 | 50 | ☐ | ☐ |
| 597a | **168** | 10s blue | 4·50 | 4·50 | ☐ | ☐ |
| 598a | **169** | £1 black | 13·00 | 8·00 | ☐ | ☐ |
| *Set of 4* | | | 15·00 | 11·00 | ☐ | ☐ |

### Phosphor-Graphite issue

**1959** (18 Nov.) Two phosphor bands on front and two graphite lines on back, except 2d value, which has one band on front and one line on back

| | | (a) Wmk **165** | | | | |
|---|---|---|---|---|---|---|
| 599 | **154** | ½d orange | 4·00 | 3·75 | ☐ | ☐ |
| 600 | | 1d blue | 11·00 | 11·00 | ☐ | ☐ |
| 601 | | 1½d green | 4·00 | 4·00 | ☐ | ☐ |
| | | (b) Wmk **179** | | | | |
| 605 | **154** | 2d light red-brown (1 band) | 5·00 | 4·25 | ☐ | ☐ |
| 606 | **155** | 2½d red | 22·00 | 18·00 | ☐ | ☐ |
| 607 | | 3d lilac | 10·00 | 8·00 | ☐ | ☐ |
| 608 | **156** | 4d blue | 20·00 | 16·00 | ☐ | ☐ |
| 609 | | 4½d brown | 30·00 | 20·00 | ☐ | ☐ |
| *Set of 8* | | | 85·00 | 70·00 | ☐ | ☐ |

### Phosphor issue

**1960–67** Two phosphor bands on front, except where otherwise stated. Wmk **179**

| 610 | **154** | ½d orange | 10 | 15 | ☐ | ☐ |
|---|---|---|---|---|---|---|
| 611 | | 1d blue | 10 | 10 | ☐ | ☐ |
| 612 | | 1½d green | 15 | 15 | ☐ | ☐ |
| 613 | | 2d light red-brown (1 band) | 18·00 | 18·00 | ☐ | ☐ |
| 613a | | 2d light red-brown (2 bands) | 10 | 15 | ☐ | ☐ |
| 614 | **155** | 2½d red (2 bands) | 40 | 30 | ☐ | ☐ |
| 614a | | 2½d red (1 band) | 60 | 75 | ☐ | ☐ |
| 615 | | 3d lilac (2 bands) | 60 | 55 | ☐ | ☐ |
| 615c | | 3d lilac (1 side band) | 60 | ·55 | ☐ | ☐ |
| 615e | | 3d lilac (1 centre band) | 40 | 45 | ☐ | ☐ |
| 616a | **156** | 4d blue | 25 | 25 | ☐ | ☐ |
| 616b | | 4½d brown | 55 | 30 | ☐ | ☐ |
| 616c | **157** | 5d brown | 55 | 35 | ☐ | ☐ |
| 617 | | 6d purple | 55 | 30 | ☐ | ☐ |
| 617a | | 7d green | 55 | 50 | ☐ | ☐ |
| 617b | **158** | 8d magenta | 70 | 45 | ☐ | ☐ |
| 617c | | 9d bronze-green | 70 | 55 | ☐ | ☐ |
| 617d | | 10d blue | 70 | 60 | ☐ | ☐ |
| 617e | **159** | 1s bistre | 70 | 35 | ☐ | ☐ |
| 618 | **160** | 1s3d green | 1·90 | 2·50 | ☐ | ☐ |
| 618a | **159** | 1s6d indigo | 2·00 | 2·00 | ☐ | ☐ |
| *Set of 17 (one of each value)* | | | 9·50 | 8·00 | ☐ | ☐ |

No. 615c exists with the phosphor band at the left or right of the stamp.

**180** Postboy of 1660

**181** Posthorn of 1660

### Tercentenary of Establishment of 'General Letter Office'

**1960** (7 July)

| 619 | **180** | 3d lilac | 50 | 50 | ☐ | ☐ |
|---|---|---|---|---|---|---|
| 620 | **181** | 1s3d green | 3·75 | 4·25 | ☐ | ☐ |
| *Set of 2* | | | 3·75 | 4·25 | ☐ | ☐ |
| First Day Cover | | | | 65·00 | | ☐ |

**182** Conference Emblem

### First Anniversary of European Postal and Telecommunications Conference

**1960** (19 Sept.)

| 621 | **182** | 6d green and purple | 2·00 | 50 | ☐ | ☐ |
|---|---|---|---|---|---|---|
| 622 | | 1s6d brown and blue | 9·50 | 5·00 | ☐ | ☐ |
| *Set of 2* | | | 11·00 | 5·50 | ☐ | ☐ |
| First Day Cover | | | | 65·00 | | ☐ |

**183** Thrift Plant

**184** 'Growth of Savings'   **185** Thrift Plant

### Centenary of Post Office Savings Bank

**1961** (28 Aug.)

| 623A | **183** | 2½d black and red | 25 | 25 | ☐ | ☐ |
|---|---|---|---|---|---|---|
| 624A | **184** | 3d orange-brown and violet | 20 | 20 | ☐ | ☐ |
| 625A | **185** | 1s6d red and blue | 2·50 | 2·25 | ☐ | ☐ |
| *Set of 3* | | | 2·75 | 2·50 | ☐ | ☐ |
| First Day Cover | | | | 75·00 | | ☐ |

**186** C.E.P.T. Emblem   **187** Doves and Emblem

**188** Doves and Emblem

# Mint G.B. Stamps Ltd

Unit 2 Lok 'n' Store, 1-4 Carousel Way, Riverside, Northampton, NN3 9HG
*Tel:* **01604 453427**   *Mobile:* **07851 576398**

The only retailer of just unmounted GB material from 1840-1970,
if you want perfection you should be talking to us.

We specialise in shades/ listed and unlisted varieties/ watermark
varieties and cylinder blocks and have comprehensive stocks of all
basic SG listed items from single stamps to full sheets.

SG 175 – Blued paper

SG 108 –
6d Mauve

344a – No cross on crown

N11(6) – scarlet
vermillion

SG 394 wi
10d R/c Inv

SG 405-413 De La Rue

N19(9) Intense

SG 264

SG 158 Plate 21

SG 161 Plate 17

## European Postal and Telecommunications (C.E.P.T.) Conference, Torquay

**1961** (18 Sept.)

| | | | | | | | |
|---|---|---|---|---|---|---|---|
| 626 | **186** | 2d | orange, pink and brown | 15 | 10 | ☐ | ☐ |
| 627 | **187** | 4d | buff, mauve and ultramarine | 15 | 15 | ☐ | ☐ |
| 628 | **188** | 10d | turquoise, green and blue | 15 | 50 | ☐ | ☐ |
| *Set of 3* | | | | 40 | 60 | ☐ | ☐ |
| First Day Cover | | | | | 6·00 | ☐ | |

**189** Hammer Beam Roof, Westminster Hall

**190** Palace of Westminster

## Seventh Commonwealth Parliamentary Conference

**1961** (25 Sept.)

| | | | | | | | |
|---|---|---|---|---|---|---|---|
| 629 | **189** | 6d | purple and gold | 25 | 25 | ☐ | ☐ |
| 630 | **190** | 1s3d | green and blue | 2·50 | 2·75 | ☐ | ☐ |
| *Set of 2* | | | | 2·75 | 3·00 | ☐ | ☐ |
| First Day Cover | | | | | 30·00 | ☐ | |

**191** 'Units of Productivity'

**192** 'National Productivity'

**193** 'Unified Productivity'

## National Productivity Year

**1962** (14 Nov.) Wmk **179** (inverted on 2½d and 3d)

| | | | | | | | |
|---|---|---|---|---|---|---|---|
| 631 | **191** | 2½d | green and red | 20 | 20 | ☐ | ☐ |
| | | p. | Phosphor | 60 | 50 | ☐ | ☐ |
| 632 | **192** | 3d | blue and violet | 50 | 25 | ☐ | ☐ |
| | | p. | Phosphor | 1·50 | 80 | ☐ | ☐ |
| 633 | **193** | 1s3d | red, blue and green | 1·50 | 1·75 | ☐ | ☐ |
| | | p. | Phosphor | 35·00 | 22·00 | ☐ | ☐ |
| *Set of 3 (Ordinary)* | | | | 2·00 | 1·90 | ☐ | ☐ |
| *Set of 3 (Phosphor)* | | | | 30·00 | 22·00 | ☐ | ☐ |
| First Day Cover (Ordinary) | | | | | 55·00 | ☐ | |
| First Day Cover (Phosphor) | | | | | £150 | ☐ | |

**194** Campaign Emblem and Family

**195** Children of Three Races

## Freedom from Hunger

**1963** (21 Mar.) Wmk **179** (inverted)

| | | | | | | | |
|---|---|---|---|---|---|---|---|
| 634 | **194** | 2½d | crimson and pink | 25 | 10 | ☐ | ☐ |
| | | p. | Phosphor | 3·00 | 1·20 | ☐ | ☐ |
| 635 | **195** | 1s3d | brown and yellow | 1·90 | 1·90 | ☐ | ☐ |
| | | p. | Phosphor | 30·00 | 23·00 | ☐ | ☐ |
| *Set of 2 (Ordinary)* | | | | 2·00 | 2·00 | ☐ | ☐ |
| *Set of 2 (Phosphor)* | | | | 30·00 | 23·00 | ☐ | ☐ |
| First Day Cover (Ordinary) | | | | | 35·00 | ☐ | |
| First Day Cover (Phosphor) | | | | | 50·00 | ☐ | |

**196** 'Paris Conference'

## Paris Postal Conference Centenary

**1963** (7 May) Wmk **179** (inverted)

| | | | | | | | |
|---|---|---|---|---|---|---|---|
| 636 | **196** | 6d | green and mauve | 50 | 50 | ☐ | ☐ |
| | | p. | Phosphor | 6·50 | 7·00 | ☐ | ☐ |
| First Day Cover (Ordinary) | | | | | 16·00 | ☐ | |
| First Day Cover (Phosphor) | | | | | 37·00 | ☐ | |

**197** Posy of Flowers

**198** Woodland Life

## National Nature Week

**1963** (16 May)

| | | | | | | | |
|---|---|---|---|---|---|---|---|
| 637 | **197** | 3d | multicoloured | 15 | 15 | ☐ | ☐ |
| | | p. | Phosphor | 60 | 60 | ☐ | ☐ |
| 638 | **198** | 4½d | multicoloured | 35 | 35 | ☐ | ☐ |
| | | p. | Phosphor | 3·25 | 3·25 | ☐ | ☐ |
| *Set of 2 (Ordinary)* | | | | 50 | 50 | ☐ | ☐ |
| *Set of 2 (Phosphor)* | | | | 3·50 | 3·50 | ☐ | ☐ |
| First Day Cover (Ordinary) | | | | | 22·00 | ☐ | |
| First Day Cover (Phosphor) | | | | | 40·00 | ☐ | |

**199** Rescue at Sea

**200** 19th-century Lifeboat

**201** Lifeboatmen

## Ninth International Lifeboat Conference, Edinburgh

**1963** (31 May)

| | | | | | | | |
|---|---|---|---|---|---|---|---|
| 639 | **199** | 2½d | blue, black and red | 25 | 25 | ☐ | ☐ |
| | | p. | Phosphor | 50 | 60 | ☐ | ☐ |
| 640 | **200** | 4d | multicoloured | 50 | 50 | ☐ | ☐ |
| | | p. | Phosphor | 50 | 60 | ☐ | ☐ |
| 641 | **201** | 1s6d | sepia, yellow and blue | 3·00 | 3·25 | ☐ | ☐ |
| | | p. | Phosphor | 48·00 | 28·00 | ☐ | ☐ |
| *Set of 3 (Ordinary)* | | | | 3·25 | 3·50 | ☐ | ☐ |
| *Set of 3 (Phosphor)* | | | | 48·00 | 28·00 | ☐ | ☐ |
| First Day Cover (Ordinary) | | | | | 35·00 | ☐ | |
| First Day Cover (Phosphor) | | | | | 55·00 | ☐ | |

**202** Red Cross

**203**

**204**

## Red Cross Centenary Congress

**1963** (15 Aug.)

| | | | | | | | |
|---|---|---|---|---|---|---|---|
| 642 | **202** | 3d | red and lilac | 25 | 25 | ☐ | ☐ |
| | | p. | Phosphor | 1·10 | 1·00 | ☐ | ☐ |
| 643 | **203** | 1s3d | red, blue and grey | 3·00 | 3·00 | ☐ | ☐ |
| | | p. | Phosphor | 35·00 | 30·00 | ☐ | ☐ |
| 644 | **204** | 1s6d | red, blue and bistre | 3·00 | 3·00 | ☐ | ☐ |
| | | p. | Phosphor | 35·00 | 27·00 | ☐ | ☐ |
| *Set of* 3 (Ordinary) | | | | 5·00 | 5·75 | ☐ | ☐ |
| *Set of* 3 (Phosphor) | | | | 65·00 | 55·00 | ☐ | ☐ |
| First Day Cover (Ordinary) | | | | | 40·00 | ☐ | |
| First Day Cover (Phosphor) | | | | | 90·00 | ☐ | |

**205** 'Commonwealth Cable'

## Opening of COMPAC (Trans-Pacific Telephone Cable)

**1963** (3 Dec.)

| | | | | | | | |
|---|---|---|---|---|---|---|---|
| 645 | **205** | 1s6d | blue and black | 2·75 | 2·50 | ☐ | ☐ |
| | | p. | Phosphor | 16·00 | 15·50 | ☐ | ☐ |
| First Day Cover (Ordinary) | | | | | 28·00 | ☐ | |
| First Day Cover (Phosphor) | | | | | 40·00 | ☐ | |

**206** Puck and Bottom
(*A Midsummer Nights Dream*)

**207** Feste
(*Twelfth Night*)

**208** Balcony Scene
(*Romeo and Juliet*)

**209** 'Eve of Agincourt'
(*Henry V*)

**210** Hamlet contemplating
Yorick's skull (*Hamlet*)
and Queen Elizabeth II

## Shakespeare Festival

**1964** (23 Apr.) Perf 11 × 12 (2s6d) or 15 × 14 (others)

| | | | | | | | |
|---|---|---|---|---|---|---|---|
| 646 | **206** | 3d | bistre, black and violet-blue | 15 | 15 | ☐ | ☐ |
| | | p. | Phosphor | 25 | 30 | ☐ | ☐ |
| 647 | **207** | 6d | multicoloured | 30 | 30 | ☐ | ☐ |
| | | p. | Phosphor | 75 | 1·00 | ☐ | ☐ |
| 648 | **208** | 1s3d | multicoloured | 75 | 1·00 | ☐ | ☐ |
| | | p. | Phosphor | 4·00 | 6·50 | ☐ | ☐ |
| 649 | **209** | 1s6d | multicoloured | 1·00 | 85 | ☐ | ☐ |
| | | p. | Phosphor | 8·00 | 8·00 | ☐ | ☐ |
| 650 | **210** | 2s6d | deep slate-purple | 2·75 | 2·75 | ☐ | ☐ |
| *Set of* 5 (Ordinary) | | | | 4·50 | 4·50 | ☐ | ☐ |
| *Set of* 4 (Phosphor) | | | | 12·00 | 14·00 | ☐ | ☐ |
| First Day Cover (Ordinary) | | | | | 12·00 | ☐ | |
| First Day Cover (Phosphor) | | | | | 17·00 | ☐ | |
| Presentation Pack (Ordinary) | | | | 30·00 | | ☐ | |

**PRESENTATION PACKS** were first introduced by the G.P.O. for the Shakespeare Festival issue. The packs include one set of stamps and details of the designs, the designer and the stamp printer. They were issued for almost all later definitive and special issues.

**211** Flats near Richmond
Park ('Urban Development')

**212** Shipbuilding Yards,
Belfast. ('Industrial Activity')

**213** Beddgelert Forest. Park,
Snowdonia ('Forestry')

**214** Nuclear Reactor, Dounreay
('Technological Development')

## 20th International Geographical Congress, London

**1964** (1 July)

| | | | | | | | |
|---|---|---|---|---|---|---|---|
| 651 | **211** | 2½d | multicoloured | 10 | 10 | ☐ | ☐ |
| | | p. | Phosphor | 40 | 50 | ☐ | ☐ |
| 652 | **212** | 4d | multicoloured | 30 | 30 | ☐ | ☐ |
| | | p. | Phosphor | 1·20 | 1·20 | ☐ | ☐ |
| 653 | **213** | 8d | multicoloured | 75 | 85 | ☐ | ☐ |
| | | p. | Phosphor | 2·50 | 3·50 | ☐ | ☐ |
| 654 | **214** | 1s6d | multicoloured | 3·50 | 3·50 | ☐ | ☐ |
| | | p. | Phosphor | 28·00 | 22·00 | ☐ | ☐ |
| *Set of* 4 (Ordinary) | | | | 4·50 | 4·50 | ☐ | ☐ |
| *Set of* 4 (Phosphor) | | | | 30·00 | 25·00 | ☐ | ☐ |
| First Day Cover (Ordinary) | | | | | 22·00 | ☐ | |
| First Day Cover (Phosphor) | | | | | 40·00 | ☐ | |
| Presentation Pack (Ordinary) | | | | £160 | | ☐ | |

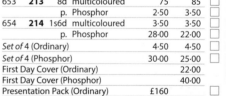

**215** Spring Gentian

**216** Dog Rose

**217** Honeysuckle

**218** Fringed Water Lily

## Tenth International Botanical Congress, Edinburgh

**1964** (5 Aug.)

| | | | | | | |
|---|---|---|---|---|---|---|
| 655 | **215** | 3d | violet, blue and green | 25 | 25 | ☐ ☐ |
| | | p. | Phosphor | 40 | 40 | ☐ ☐ |
| 656 | **216** | 6d | multicoloured | 50 | 50 | ☐ ☐ |
| | | p. | Phosphor | 2·50 | 2·75 | ☐ ☐ |
| 657 | **217** | 9d | multicoloured | 1·70 | 2·25 | ☐ ☐ |
| | | p. | Phosphor | 4·50 | 4·50 | ☐ ☐ |
| 658 | **218** | 1s3d | multicoloured | 2·50 | 2·50 | ☐ ☐ |
| | | p. | Phosphor | 25·00 | 20·00 | ☐ ☐ |
| *Set of* 4 (Ordinary) | | | | 4·50 | 4·50 | ☐ |
| *Set of* 4 (Phosphor) | | | | 30·00 | 25·00 | ☐ |
| First Day Cover (Ordinary) | | | | | 30·00 | ☐ |
| First Day Cover (Phosphor) | | | | | 40·00 | ☐ |
| Presentation Pack (Ordinary) | | | | £160 | | ☐ |

**219** Forth Road Bridge  **220** Forth Road and Railway Bridges

## Opening of Forth Road Bridge

**1964** (4 Sept.)

| | | | | | | |
|---|---|---|---|---|---|---|
| 659 | **219** | 3d | black, blue and violet | 10 | 10 | ☐ ☐ |
| | | p. | Phosphor | 1·00 | 1·50 | ☐ ☐ |
| 660 | **220** | 6d | blackish lilac, blue and red | 40 | 40 | ☐ ☐ |
| | | p. | Phosphor | 4·50 | 4·75 | ☐ ☐ |
| *Set of* 2 (Ordinary) | | | | 50 | 50 | ☐ ☐ |
| *Set of* 2 (Phosphor) | | | | 5·00 | 5·75 | ☐ ☐ |
| First Day Cover (Ordinary) | | | | | 7·00 | ☐ |
| First Day Cover (Phosphor) | | | | | 18·00 | ☐ |
| Presentation Pack (Ordinary) | | | | £450 | | ☐ |

**221** Sir Winston Churchill  **221a** Sir Winston Churchill

## Churchill Commemoration

**1965** (8 July)

| | | | | | | |
|---|---|---|---|---|---|---|
| 661 | **221** | 4d | black and drab | 15 | 10 | ☐ ☐ |
| | | p. | Phosphor | 25 | 25 | ☐ ☐ |
| 662 | **221a** | 1s3d | black and grey | 45 | 40 | ☐ ☐ |
| | | p. | Phosphor | 2·50 | 3·00 | ☐ ☐ |
| *Set of* 2 (Ordinary) | | | | 60 | 50 | ☐ ☐ |
| *Set of* 2 (Phosphor) | | | | 2·75 | 3·25 | ☐ ☐ |
| First Day Cover (Ordinary) | | | | | 7·00 | ☐ |
| First Day Cover (Phosphor) | | | | | 9·00 | ☐ |
| Presentation Pack (Ordinary) | | | | 70·00 | | ☐ |

**222** Simon de Montfort's Seal

**223** Parliament Buildings (after engraving by Hollar, 1647)

## 700th Anniversary of Simon de Montfort's Parliament

**1965** (19 July)

| | | | | | | |
|---|---|---|---|---|---|---|
| 663 | **222** | 6d | green | 20 | 20 | ☐ ☐ |
| | | p. | Phosphor | 60 | 1·00 | ☐ ☐ |
| 664 | **223** | 2s6d | black, grey and drab | 80 | 1·50 | ☐ ☐ |
| *Set of* 2 (Ordinary) | | | | 1·00 | 1·50 | ☐ ☐ |
| First Day Cover (Ordinary) | | | | | 15·00 | ☐ |
| First Day Cover (Phosphor) | | | | | 26·00 | ☐ |
| Presentation Pack (Ordinary) | | | | 85·00 | | ☐ |

**224** Bandsmen and Banner  **225** Three Salvationists

## Salvation Army Centenary

**1965** (9 Aug.)

| | | | | | | |
|---|---|---|---|---|---|---|
| 665 | **224** | 3d | multicoloured | 25 | 25 | ☐ ☐ |
| | | p. | Phosphor | 25 | 40 | ☐ ☐ |
| 666 | **225** | 1s6d | multicoloured | 1·00 | 1·50 | ☐ ☐ |
| | | p. | Phosphor | 2·50 | 2·75 | ☐ ☐ |
| *Set of* 2 (Ordinary) | | | | 1·10 | 1·60 | ☐ ☐ |
| *Set of* 2 (Phosphor) | | | | 2·50 | 3·00 | ☐ ☐ |
| First Day Cover (Ordinary) | | | | | 23·00 | ☐ |
| First Day Cover (Phosphor) | | | | | 33·00 | ☐ |

**226** Lister's Carbolic Spray  **227** Lister and Chemical Symbols

## Centenary of Joseph Lister's Discovery of Antiseptic Surgery

**1965** (1 Sept.)

| | | | | | | |
|---|---|---|---|---|---|---|
| 667 | **226** | 4d | indigo, chestnut and grey | 25 | 15 | ☐ ☐ |
| | | p. | Phosphor | 25 | 25 | ☐ ☐ |
| 668 | **227** | 1s | black, purple and blue | 1·00 | 1·10 | ☐ ☐ |
| | | p. | Phosphor | 2·00 | 2·50 | ☐ ☐ |
| *Set of* 2 (Ordinary) | | | | 1·00 | 1·20 | ☐ ☐ |
| *Set of* 2 (Phosphor) | | | | 2·00 | 2·50 | ☐ ☐ |
| First Day Cover (Ordinary) | | | | | 12·00 | ☐ |
| First Day Cover (Phosphor) | | | | | 15·00 | ☐ |

**228** Trinidad Carnival Dancers  **229** Canadian Folk Dancers

## Commonwealth Arts Festival

**1965** (1 Sept.)

| | | | | | | |
|---|---|---|---|---|---|---|
| 669 | **228** | 6d | black and orange | 20 | 20 | ☐ ☐ |
| | | p. | Phosphor | 30 | 50 | ☐ ☐ |
| 670 | **229** | 1s6d | black and violet | 80 | 1·10 | ☐ ☐ |
| | | p. | Phosphor | 2·50 | 3·50 | ☐ ☐ |
| *Set of* 2 (Ordinary) | | | | 1·00 | 1·25 | ☐ ☐ |
| *Set of* 2 (Phosphor) | | | | 2·50 | 3·50 | ☐ ☐ |
| First Day Cover (Ordinary) | | | | | 16·50 | ☐ |
| First Day Cover (Phosphor) | | | | | 22·00 | ☐ |

**230** Flight of Supermarine Spitfires    **231** Pilot in Hawker Hurricane Mk I

**232** Wing-tips of Supermarine Spitfire and Messerschmitt Bf 109    **233** Supermarine Spitfires attacking Heinkel HE 111H Bomber

**234** Supermarine Spitfire attacking Junkers Ju 87B 'Stuka' Dive Bomber    **235** Hawker Hurricanes Mk I over Wreck of Dornier Do-17Z Bomber

**236** Anti-aircraft Artillery in Action    **237** Air Battle over St. Paul's Cathedral

### 25th Anniversary of Battle of Britain

**1965** (13 Sept.)

| | | | | | | | |
|---|---|---|---|---|---|---|---|
| 671 | **230** | 4d | olive and black | 25 | 25 | ☐ | ☐ |
| | a. | | Block of 6. | | | | |
| | | | Nos. 671/6 | 8·00 | 8·00 | ☐ | ☐ |
| | p. | | Phosphor | 50 | 50 | ☐ | ☐ |
| | pa. | | Block of 6. | | | | |
| | | | Nos. 671p/6p | 10·00 | 12·00 | ☐ | ☐ |
| 672 | **231** | 4d | olive, blackish olive and black | 25 | 25 | ☐ | ☐ |
| | p. | | Phosphor | 50 | 50 | ☐ | ☐ |
| 673 | **232** | 4d | multicoloured | 25 | 25 | ☐ | ☐ |
| | p. | | Phosphor | 50 | 50 | ☐ | ☐ |
| 674 | **233** | 4d | olive and black | 25 | 25 | ☐ | ☐ |
| | p. | | Phosphor | 50 | 50 | ☐ | ☐ |
| 675 | **234** | 4d | olive and black | 25 | 25 | ☐ | ☐ |
| | p. | | Phosphor | 50 | 50 | ☐ | ☐ |
| 676 | **235** | 4d | multicoloured | 25 | 25 | ☐ | ☐ |
| | p. | | Phosphor | 50 | 50 | ☐ | ☐ |
| 677 | **236** | 9d | violet, orange and purple | 1·70 | 1·70 | ☐ | ☐ |
| | p. | | Phosphor | 1·70 | 2·50 | ☐ | ☐ |
| 678 | **237** | 1s3d | multicoloured | 1·70 | 1·70 | ☐ | ☐ |
| | p. | | Phosphor | 1·70 | 2·50 | ☐ | ☐ |
| *Set of* 8 (Ordinary) | | | | 10·00 | 10·00 | ☐ | ☐ |
| *Set of* 8 (Phosphor) | | | | 12·00 | 14·00 | ☐ | |
| First Day Cover (Ordinary) | | | | | 25·00 | ☐ | |
| First Day Cover (Phosphor) | | | | | 30·00 | ☐ | |
| Presentation Pack (Ordinary) | | | | 70·00 | | ☐ | |

Nos. 671/6 were issued together *se-tenant* in blocks of six (3 × 2) within the sheet.

**238** Tower and Georgian Buildings    **239** Tower and Nash Terrace, Regent's Park

### Opening of Post Office Tower

**1965** (8 Oct.)

| | | | | | | | |
|---|---|---|---|---|---|---|---|
| 679 | **238** | 3d | yellow, blue and green | 15 | 15 | ☐ | ☐ |
| | p. | | Phosphor | 15 | 15 | ☐ | ☐ |
| 680 | **239** | 1s3d | green and blue | 45 | 45 | ☐ | ☐ |
| | p. | | Phosphor | 50 | 50 | ☐ | ☐ |
| *Set of* 2 (Ordinary) | | | | 60 | 60 | ☐ | ☐ |
| *Set of* 2 (Phosphor) | | | | 65 | 65 | ☐ | ☐ |
| First Day Cover (Ordinary) | | | | | 6·50 | ☐ | |
| First Day Cover (Phosphor) | | | | | 7·00 | ☐ | |
| Presentation Pack (Ordinary) | | | | 10·00 | | ☐ | |
| Presentation Pack (Phosphor) | | | | 10·00 | | ☐ | |

**240** U.N. Emblem    **241** I.C.Y. Emblem

### 20th Anniversary of UNO and International Co-operation Year

**1965** (25 Oct.)

| | | | | | | | |
|---|---|---|---|---|---|---|---|
| 681 | **240** | 3d | black, orange and blue | 25 | 20 | ☐ | ☐ |
| | p. | | Phosphor | 25 | 30 | ☐ | ☐ |
| 682 | **241** | 1s6d | black, purple and blue | 1·00 | 80 | ☐ | ☐ |
| | p. | | Phosphor | 2·75 | 3·00 | ☐ | ☐ |
| *Set of* 2 (Ordinary) | | | | 1·00 | 90 | ☐ | ☐ |
| *Set of* 2 (Phosphor) | | | | 2·75 | 3·00 | ☐ | ☐ |
| First Day Cover (Ordinary) | | | | | 12·00 | ☐ | |
| First Day Cover (Phosphor) | | | | | 14·00 | ☐ | |

**242** Telecommunications Network    **243** Radio Waves and Switchboard

### I.T.U. Centenary

**1965** (15 Nov.)

| | | | | | | | |
|---|---|---|---|---|---|---|---|
| 683 | **242** | 9d | multicoloured | 50 | 40 | ☐ | ☐ |
| | p. | | Phosphor | 1·00 | 75 | ☐ | ☐ |
| 684 | **243** | 1s6d | multicoloured | 1·50 | 1·20 | ☐ | ☐ |
| | p. | | Phosphor | 4·25 | 5·25 | ☐ | ☐ |
| *Set of* 2 (Ordinary) | | | | 1·80 | 1·50 | ☐ | ☐ |
| *Set of* 2 (Phosphor) | | | | 4·75 | 5·50 | ☐ | ☐ |
| First Day Cover (Ordinary) | | | | | 17·00 | ☐ | |
| First Day Cover (Phosphor) | | | | | 20·00 | ☐ | |

**244** Robert Burns (after Skirving chalk drawing)
**245** Robert Burns (after Nasmyth portrait)

## Burns Commemoration

**1966** (25 Jan.)

| | | | | | | |
|---|---|---|---|---|---|---|
| 685 | **244** | 4d | black, indigo and blue | 20 | 15 | ☐ ☐ |
| | | p. | Phosphor | 50 | 50 | ☐ ☐ |
| 686 | **245** | 1s3d | black, blue and orange | 65 | 70 | ☐ ☐ |
| | | p. | Phosphor | 2·25 | 2·25 | ☐ ☐ |
| Set of 2 (Ordinary) | | | | 75 | 75 | ☐ ☐ |
| Set of 2 (Phosphor) | | | | 2·50 | 2·50 | ☐ ☐ |
| First Day Cover (Ordinary) | | | | | 4·00 | ☐ |
| First Day Cover (Phosphor) | | | | | 6·00 | ☐ |
| Presentation Pack (Ordinary) | | | | 60·00 | | ☐ |

**246** Westminster Abbey
**247** Fan Vaulting, Henry VII Chapel

## 900th Anniversary of Westminster Abbey

**1966** (28 Feb.) Perf 15 × 14 (3d) or 11 × 12 (2s6d)

| | | | | | | |
|---|---|---|---|---|---|---|
| 687 | **246** | 3d | black, brown and blue | 20 | 20 | ☐ ☐ |
| | | p. | Phosphor | 20 | 25 | ☐ ☐ |
| 688 | **247** | 2s6d | black | 80 | 80 | ☐ ☐ |
| Set of 2 | | | | 90 | 90 | ☐ ☐ |
| First Day Cover (Ordinary) | | | | | 6·00 | ☐ |
| First Day Cover (Phosphor) | | | | | 14·00 | ☐ |
| Presentation Pack (Ordinary) | | | | 55·00 | | ☐ |

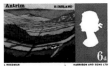

**248** View near Hassocks, Sussex
**249** Antrim, Northern Ireland

**250** Harlech Castle, Wales
**251** Cairngorm Mountains, Scotland

## Landscapes

**1966** (2 May)

| | | | | | | |
|---|---|---|---|---|---|---|
| 689 | **248** | 4d | black, yellow-green and blue | 10 | 15 | ☐ ☐ |
| | | p. | Phosphor | 10 | 15 | ☐ ☐ |
| 690 | **249** | 6d | black, green and blue | 15 | 20 | ☐ ☐ |
| | | p. | Phosphor | 15 | 20 | ☐ ☐ |
| 691 | **250** | 1s3d | black, yellow and blue | 25 | 35 | ☐ ☐ |
| | | p. | Phosphor | 25 | 35 | ☐ ☐ |
| 692 | **251** | 1s6d | black, orange and blue | 40 | 35 | ☐ ☐ |
| | | p. | Phosphor | 40 | 40 | ☐ ☐ |
| Set of 4 (Ordinary) | | | | 80 | 95 | ☐ ☐ |
| Set of 4 (Phosphor) | | | | 80 | 1·00 | ☐ ☐ |

| | | | |
|---|---|---|---|
| First Day Cover (Ordinary) | | 7·00 | ☐ |
| First Day Cover (Phosphor) | | 8·50 | ☐ |

**252** Players with Ball

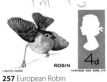

**253** Goalmouth Mêlée
**254** Goalkeeper saving Goal

## World Cup Football Championship

**1966** (1 June)

| | | | | | | |
|---|---|---|---|---|---|---|
| 693 | **252** | 4d | multicoloured | 10 | 25 | ☐ ☐ |
| | | p. | Phosphor | 10 | 25 | ☐ ☐ |
| 694 | **253** | 6d | multicoloured | 15 | 25 | ☐ ☐ |
| | | p. | Phosphor | 15 | 25 | ☐ ☐ |
| 695 | **254** | 1s3d | multicoloured | 50 | 1·00 | ☐ ☐ |
| | | p. | Phosphor | 50 | 1·00 | ☐ ☐ |
| Set of 3 (Ordinary) | | | | 70 | 1·25 | ☐ ☐ |
| Set of 3 (Phosphor) | | | | 70 | 1·25 | ☐ ☐ |
| First Day Cover (Ordinary) | | | | | 20·00 | ☐ |
| First Day Cover (Phosphor) | | | | | 22·00 | ☐ |
| Presentation Pack (Ordinary) | | | | 20·00 | | ☐ |

**255** Black-headed Gull
**256** Blue Tit

**257** European Robin
**258** Blackbird

## British Birds

**1966** (8 Aug.)

| | | | | | | |
|---|---|---|---|---|---|---|
| 696 | **255** | 4d | multicoloured | 20 | 20 | ☐ ☐ |
| | | a. | Block of 4. Nos. 696/9 | 1·00 | 2·00 | ☐ ☐ |
| | | p. | Phosphor | 20 | 20 | ☐ ☐ |
| | | pa. | Block of 4. Nos. 696p/9p | 1·00 | 2·00 | ☐ ☐ |
| 697 | **256** | 4d | multicoloured | 20 | 20 | ☐ ☐ |
| | | p. | Phosphor | 20 | 20 | ☐ ☐ |
| 698 | **257** | 4d | multicoloured | 20 | 20 | ☐ ☐ |
| | | p. | Phosphor | 20 | 20 | ☐ ☐ |
| 699 | **258** | 4d | multicoloured | 20 | 20 | ☐ ☐ |
| | | p. | Phosphor | 20 | 20 | ☐ ☐ |
| Set of 4 (Ordinary) | | | | 1·00 | 2·00 | ☐ ☐ |
| Set of 4 (Phosphor) | | | | 1·00 | 2·00 | ☐ ☐ |
| First Day Cover (Ordinary) | | | | | 8·00 | ☐ |
| First Day Cover (Phosphor) | | | | | 8·00 | ☐ |
| Presentation Pack (Ordinary) | | | | 13·00 | | ☐ |

Nos. 696/9 were issued *se-tenant* in blocks of four within the sheet.

**259** Cup Winners

**268**

**269**

**270** Norman Ship

## England's World Cup Football Victory

**1966** (18 Aug.)

| | | | | | | | |
|---|---|---|---|---|---|---|---|
| 700 | **259** | 4d | multicoloured | 30 | 30 | ☐ | ☐ |
| First Day Cover | | | | | 13·00 | | ☐ |

**260** Jodrell Bank Radio Telescope.

**261** British Motor-cars

**262** SR N6 Hovercraft

**263** Windscale Reactor

## British Technology

**1966** (19 Sept.)

| | | | | | | | |
|---|---|---|---|---|---|---|---|
| 701 | **260** | 4d | black and lemon | 15 | 10 | ☐ | ☐ |
| | | p. | Phosphor | 10 | 10 | ☐ | ☐ |
| 702 | **261** | 6d | red, blue and orange | 25 | 20 | ☐ | ☐ |
| | | p. | Phosphor | 15 | 25 | ☐ | ☐ |
| 703 | **262** | 1s3d | multicoloured | 50 | 40 | ☐ | ☐ |
| | | p. | Phosphor | 35 | 40 | ☐ | ☐ |
| 704 | **263** | 1s6d | multicoloured | 50 | 60 | ☐ | ☐ |
| | | p. | Phosphor | 50 | 60 | ☐ | ☐ |
| *Set of* 4 (Ordinary) | | | | 1·25 | 1·10 | ☐ | ☐ |
| *Set of* 4 (Phosphor) | | | | 1·00 | 1·10 | ☐ | ☐ |
| First Day Cover (Ordinary) | | | | | 5·00 | | ☐ |
| First Day Cover (Phosphor) | | | | | 5·00 | | ☐ |
| Presentation Pack (Ordinary) | | | | 20·00 | | | ☐ |

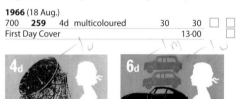

**264**

**265**

**266**

**267**

## 900th Anniversary of Battle of Hastings

**1966** (14 Oct.) Designs show scenes from Bayeux Tapestry Wmk **179** (sideways on 1s3d)

| | | | | | | | |
|---|---|---|---|---|---|---|---|
| 705 | **264** | 4d | multicoloured | 10 | 10 | ☐ | ☐ |
| | a. | Strip of 6. | | | | | |
| | | Nos. 705/10 | 1·90 | 2·25 | ☐ | ☐ |
| | p. | Phosphor | | 10 | 10 | ☐ | ☐ |
| | pa. | Strip of 6. Nos. | | | | | |
| | | 705p/10p | 1·90 | 2·25 | ☐ | ☐ |
| 706 | **265** | 4d | multicoloured | 10 | 10 | ☐ | ☐ |
| | | p. | Phosphor | 10 | 10 | ☐ | ☐ |
| 707 | **266** | 4d | multicoloured | 10 | 10 | ☐ | ☐ |
| | | p. | Phosphor | 10 | 10 | ☐ | ☐ |
| 708 | **267** | 4d | multicoloured | 10 | 10 | ☐ | ☐ |
| | | p. | Phosphor | 10 | 10 | ☐ | ☐ |
| 709 | **268** | 4d | multicoloured | 10 | 10 | ☐ | ☐ |
| | | p. | Phosphor | 10 | 10 | ☐ | ☐ |
| 710 | **269** | 4d | multicoloured | 10 | 10 | ☐ | ☐ |
| | | p. | Phosphor | 10 | 25 | ☐ | ☐ |
| 711 | **270** | 6d | multicoloured | 10 | 10 | ☐ | ☐ |
| | | p. | Phosphor | 10 | 10 | ☐ | ☐ |
| 712 | **271** | 1s3d | multicoloured | 20 | 75 | ☐ | ☐ |
| | | p. | Phosphor | 20 | 75 | ☐ | ☐ |
| *Set of* 8 (Ordinary) | | | | 2·00 | 2·25 | ☐ | ☐ |
| *Set of* 8 (Phosphor) | | | | 2·00 | 2·75 | ☐ | ☐ |
| First Day Cover (Ordinary) | | | | | 8·00 | | ☐ |
| First Day Cover (Phosphor) | | | | | 9·00 | | ☐ |
| Presentation Pack (Ordinary) | | | | 10·00 | | | ☐ |

Nos. 705/10 show battle scenes, they were issued together *se-tenant* in horizontal strips of six within the sheet.

**271** Norman Horsemen attacking Harold's Troops

**272** King of the Orient

**273** Snowman

## Christmas

**1966** (1 Dec.) Wmk 179 (upright on 1s6d)

| | | | | | | | |
|---|---|---|---|---|---|---|---|
| 713 | **272** | 3d | multicoloured | 10 | 25 | ☐ | ☐ |
| | | p. | Phosphor | 10 | 25 | ☐ | ☐ |
| 714 | **273** | 1s6d | multicoloured | 30 | 50 | ☐ | ☐ |
| | | p. | Phosphor | 30 | 50 | ☐ | ☐ |
| Set of 2 (Ordinary) | | | | 35 | 70 | ☐ | ☐ |
| Set of 2 (Phosphor) | | | | 35 | 70 | ☐ | ☐ |
| First Day Cover (Ordinary) | | | | | 2·50 | | ☐ |
| First Day Cover (Phosphor) | | | | | 2·00 | | ☐ |
| Presentation Pack (Ordinary) | | | | 12·00 | | | ☐ |

No. 713p exists with phosphor band at left or right.

**274** Sea Freight

**275** Air Freight

## European Free Trade Association (EFTA)

**1967** (20 Feb.)

| | | | | | | | |
|---|---|---|---|---|---|---|---|
| 715 | **274** | 9d | multicoloured | 25 | 20 | ☐ | ☐ |
| | | p. | Phosphor | 25 | 20 | ☐ | ☐ |
| 716 | **275** | 1s6d | multicoloured | 50 | 45 | ☐ | ☐ |
| | | p. | Phosphor | 25 | 40 | ☐ | ☐ |
| Set of 2 (Ordinary) | | | | 60 | 60 | ☐ | ☐ |
| Set of 2 (Phosphor) | | | | 60 | 55 | ☐ | ☐ |
| First Day Cover (Ordinary) | | | | | 3·00 | | ☐ |
| First Day Cover (Phosphor) | | | | | 3·00 | | ☐ |
| Presentation Pack (Ordinary) | | | | 25·00 | | | ☐ |

**276** Hawthorn and Bramble

**277** Larger Bindweed and Viper's Bugloss

**278** Ox-eye Daisy, Coltsfoot and Buttercup

**279** Bluebell, Red Campion and Wood Anemone

**280** Dog Violet

**281** Primroses

## British Wild Flowers

**1967** (24 Apr.)

| | | | | | | | |
|---|---|---|---|---|---|---|---|
| 717 | **276** | 4d | multicoloured | 20 | 20 | ☐ | ☐ |
| | | a. | Block of 4. Nos. 717/20 | 80 | 2·25 | ☐ | ☐ |
| | | p. | Phosphor | 10 | 15 | ☐ | ☐ |
| | | pa | Block of 4. Nos. 717p/20p | 80 | 2·00 | ☐ | ☐ |
| 718 | **277** | 4d | multicoloured | 20 | 20 | ☐ | ☐ |
| | | p. | Phosphor | 10 | 15 | ☐ | ☐ |

| | | | | | | | |
|---|---|---|---|---|---|---|---|
| 719 | **278** | 4d | multicoloured | 20 | 20 | ☐ | ☐ |
| | | p. | Phosphor | 10 | 15 | ☐ | ☐ |
| 720 | **279** | 4d | multicoloured | 20 | 20 | ☐ | ☐ |
| | | p. | Phosphor | 10 | 15 | ☐ | ☐ |
| 721 | **280** | 9d | multicoloured | 20 | 25 | ☐ | ☐ |
| | | p. | Phosphor | 15 | 25 | ☐ | ☐ |
| 722 | **281** | 1s9d | multicoloured | 25 | 35 | ☐ | ☐ |
| | | p. | Phosphor | 20 | 30 | ☐ | ☐ |
| Set of 6 (Ordinary) | | | | 1·00 | 2·25 | ☐ | ☐ |
| Set of 6 (Phosphor) | | | | 1·00 | 2·00 | ☐ | ☐ |
| First Day Cover (Ordinary) | | | | | 5·00 | | ☐ |
| First Day Cover (Phosphor) | | | | | 5·00 | | ☐ |
| Presentation Pack (Ordinary) | | | | 14·00 | | | ☐ |

Nos. 717/20 were issued together *se-tenant* in blocks of four within the sheet.

**282** (value at left)

**282a** (value at right)

I     II

Two types of the 2d.
I.   Value spaced away from left side of stamp.
II.   Value close to left side from new multi-positive. This results in the portrait appearing in the centre, thus conforming with the other values.

**1967** (5 June) **–69** Two phosphor bands, except where otherwise stated. No wmk

| | | | | | | | |
|---|---|---|---|---|---|---|---|
| 723 | **282** | ½d | orange-brown (5.2.68) | 30 | 75 | ☐ | ☐ |
| 724 | | 1d | light olive (2 bands) (5.2.68) | 20 | 10 | ☐ | ☐ |
| 725 | | 1d | yellowish olive (1 centre band) (16.9.68) | 30 | 35 | ☐ | ☐ |
| 726 | | 2d | lake-brown (Type I) (2 bands) (5.2.68) | 20 | 15 | ☐ | ☐ |
| 727 | | 2d | lake-brown (Type II) (2 bands) (1969) | 30 | 40 | ☐ | ☐ |
| 728 | | 2d | lake-brown (Type II) (1 centre band) (27.8.69) | 1·00 | 1·50 | ☐ | ☐ |
| 729 | | 3d | violet (1 centre band) (8.8.67) | 30 | 10 | ☐ | ☐ |
| 730 | | 3d | violet (2 bands)(6.4.68) | 30 | 45 | ☐ | ☐ |
| 731 | | 4d | deep sepia (2 bands) | 30 | 30 | ☐ | ☐ |
| 732 | | 4d | deep olive-brown (1 centre band) (16.9.68) | 20 | 10 | ☐ | ☐ |
| 733 | | 4d | bright vermilion (1 centre band) (6.1.69) | 20 | 10 | ☐ | ☐ |
| 734 | | 4d | vermilion (1 side band) (6.1.69) | 1·90 | 2·50 | ☐ | ☐ |
| 735 | | 5d | blue (1.7.68) | 20 | 20 | ☐ | ☐ |
| 736 | | 6d | purple (5.2.68) | 50 | 40 | ☐ | ☐ |
| 737 | **282a** | 7d | bright emerald (1.7.68) | 1·00 | 1·00 | ☐ | ☐ |
| 738 | | 8d | bright vermilion (1.7.68) | 50 | 1·25 | ☐ | ☐ |
| 739 | | 8d | turquoise-blue (6.1.69) | 1·00 | 1·50 | ☐ | ☐ |
| 740 | | 9d | green (8.8.67) | 1·00 | 1·50 | ☐ | ☐ |
| 741 | **282** | 10d | drab (1.7.68) | 1·00 | 1·00 | ☐ | ☐ |
| 742 | | 1s | light bluish violet | 45 | 45 | ☐ | ☐ |
| 743 | | 1s6d | blue and deep blue (8.8.67) | 50 | 50 | ☐ | ☐ |
| | | c. | Phosphorised paper (10.12.69) | 1·10 | 1·25 | ☐ | ☐ |
| 744 | | 1s9d | orange and black | 1·00 | 1·00 | ☐ | ☐ |
| Set of 16 (one of each value and colour) | | | | 7·00 | 8·00 | ☐ | ☐ |
| Presentation Pack (one of each value) | | | | 15·00 | | | ☐ |
| Presentation Pack (German) | | | | £150 | | | ☐ |
| First Day Covers | | | | | | | |
| 5 June 1967 | Nos. 731, 742, 744 | | | | 3·50 | | ☐ |

| 8 Aug. 1967 | Nos. 729, 740, 743 | 3·50 | |
| 5 Feb. 1968 | Nos. 723/4, 726, 736 | 3·75 | |
| 1 July 1968 | Nos. 735, 737/8, 741 | 4·50 | |

No. 734 exists with phosphor band at the left or right.

**283** 'Master Lambton'
(Sir Thomas Lawrence)

**284** 'Mares and Foals in a Landscape'    **285** 'Children Coming Out of
(George Stubbs)                            School' (L. S. Lowry)

### British Paintings

**1967** (10 July) Two phosphor bands. No wmk

| 748 | **283** | 4d | multicoloured | 10 | 10 | | |
| 749 | **284** | 9d | multicoloured | 15 | 15 | | |
| 750 | **285** | 1s6d | multicoloured | 35 | 35 | | |
| Set of 3 | | | | 50 | 50 | | |
| First Day Cover | | | | | 2·50 | | |
| Presentation Pack | | | | 35·00 | | | |

**286** Gipsy Moth IV

### Sir Francis Chichester's World Voyage

**1967** (24 July) Three phosphor bands. No wmk

| 751 | **286** | 1s9d | multicoloured | 20 | 20 | | |
| First Day Cover | | | | | 1·00 | | |

**287** Radar Screen    **288** *Penicillium notatum*

**289** Vickers VC-10 Jet Engines    **290** Television Equipment

### British Discovery and Invention

**1967** (19 Sept.) Two phosphor bands (except 4d. three bands).
Wmk **179** (sideways on 1s9d)

| 752 | **287** | 4d | yellow, black and vermilion | 10 | 10 | | |
| 753 | **288** | 1s | multicoloured | 20 | 20 | | |
| 754 | **289** | 1s6d | multicoloured | 25 | 25 | | |
| 755 | **290** | 1s9d | multicoloured | 30 | 30 | | |
| Set of 4 | | | | 75 | 75 | | |
| First Day Cover | | | | | 2·00 | | |
| Presentation Pack | | | | 6·00 | | | |

**NO WATERMARK.** All the following issues are on unwatermarked paper unless otherwise stated.

**291** 'The Adoration    **292** 'Madonna and
of the Shepherds'        Child' (Murillo)
(School of Seville)

**293** 'The Adoration of the
Shepherds' (Louis le Nain)

### Christmas

**1967** Two phosphor bands (except 3d, one phosphor band)

| 756 | **291** | 3d | multicoloured *(27 Nov.)* | 10 | 15 | | |
| 757 | **292** | 4d | multicoloured *(18 Oct.)* | 10 | 15 | | |
| 758 | **293** | 1s6d | multicoloured *(27 Nov.)* | 15 | 15 | | |
| Set of 3 | | | | 30 | 30 | | |
| First Day Covers (2) | | | | | 1·50 | | |

### Gift Pack 1967

**1967** (27 Nov.) Comprises Nos. 715p/22p and 748/58

| GP758c | Gift Pack | 3·00 | |

**1967–68** No wmk. Perf 11 × 12

| 759 | **166** | 2s6d | brown | 30 | 45 | | |
| 760 | **167** | 5s | red | 70 | 75 | | |
| 761 | **168** | 10s | blue | 7·75 | 4·00 | | |
| 762 | **169** | £1 | black | 7·50 | 4·50 | | |
| Set of 4 | | | | 15·00 | 8·00 | | |

**294** Tarr Steps, Exmoor    **295** Aberfeldy Bridge

**296** Menai Bridge    **297** M4 Viaduct

## British Bridges

**1968** (29 Apr.) Two phosphor bands

| | | | | | | | |
|---|---|---|---|---|---|---|---|
| 763 | **294** | 4d | multicoloured | 10 | 10 | ☐ | ☐ |
| 764 | **295** | 9d | multicoloured | 15 | 15 | ☐ | ☐ |
| 765 | **296** | 1s6d | multicoloured | 25 | 25 | ☐ | ☐ |
| 766 | **297** | 1s9d | multicoloured | 30 | 30 | ☐ | ☐ |
| Set of 4 | | | | 70 | 70 | ☐ | ☐ |
| First Day Cover | | | | | 1·50 | | ☐ |
| Presentation Pack | | | | 5·00 | | ☐ | |

**298** 'TUC' and Trades Unionists

**299** Mrs Emmeline Pankhurst. (statue)

**300** Sopwith Camel and English Electric Lightning Fighters

**301** Captain Cook's Endeavour and Signature

## British Anniversaries. Events described on stamps

**1968** (29 May) Two phosphor bands

| | | | | | | | |
|---|---|---|---|---|---|---|---|
| 767 | **298** | 4d | multicoloured | 10 | 10 | ☐ | ☐ |
| 768 | **299** | 9d | violet, grey and black | 15 | 15 | ☐ | ☐ |
| 769 | **300** | 1s | multicoloured | 15 | 15 | ☐ | ☐ |
| 770 | **301** | 1s9d | ochre and brown | 35 | 35 | ☐ | ☐ |
| Set of 4 | | | | 65 | 65 | ☐ | ☐ |
| First Day Cover | | | | | 5·00 | | ☐ |
| Presentation Pack | | | | 5·00 | | ☐ | |

**302** 'Queen Elizabeth I' (Unknown Artist)

**303** 'Pinkie' (Lawrence)

**304** 'Ruins of St. Mary Le Port' (John Piper)

**305** 'The Hay Wain' (John Constable)

## British Paintings

**1968** (12 Aug.) Two phosphor bands

| | | | | | | | |
|---|---|---|---|---|---|---|---|
| 771 | **302** | 4d | multicoloured | 10 | 10 | ☐ | ☐ |
| 772 | **303** | 1s | multicoloured | 10 | 20 | ☐ | ☐ |
| 773 | **304** | 1s6d | multicoloured | 20 | 25 | ☐ | ☐ |
| 774 | **305** | 1s9d | multicoloured | 25 | 40 | ☐ | ☐ |
| Set of 4 | | | | 60 | 85 | ☐ | ☐ |

| | | | |
|---|---|---|---|
| First Day Cover | | 2·00 | ☐ |
| Presentation Pack (P.O. Pack No.1) | 6·00 | | ☐ |
| Presentation Pack (German) | | | |
| (P.O. Pack No.1) | 19·00 | | ☐ |

## Gift Pack 1968

**1968** (16 Sept.) Comprises Nos. 763/74

| | | | |
|---|---|---|---|
| GP774c | Gift Pack | 6·00 | ☐ |
| GP774d | Gift Pack (German) | 80·00 | ☐ |

## Collectors Pack 1968

**1968** (16 Sept.) Comprises Nos. 752/8 and 763/74

| | | | |
|---|---|---|---|
| CP774e | Collectors Pack | 7·00 | ☐ |

**306** Girl and Boy with Rocking Horse

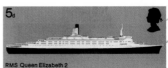

**307** Girl with Doll's House

**308** Boy with Train Set

## Christmas

**1968** (25 Nov.) Two phosphor bands (except 4d, one centre phosphor band)

| | | | | | | | |
|---|---|---|---|---|---|---|---|
| 775 | **306** | 4d | multicoloured | 10 | 15 | ☐ | ☐ |
| 776 | **307** | 9d | multicoloured | 15 | 25 | ☐ | ☐ |
| 777 | **308** | 1s6d | multicoloured | 15 | 50 | ☐ | ☐ |
| Set of 3 | | | | 1·35 | 80 | ☐ | ☐ |
| First Day Cover | | | | | 1·00 | | ☐ |
| Presentation Pack (P.O. Pack No.4) | | | 5·00 | | | ☐ | |
| Presentation Pack (German) | | | 19·00 | | | ☐ | |

**RMS Queen Elizabeth 2**

**309** *Queen Elizabeth 2*

**310** Elizabethan Galleon

**311** East. Indiaman

**312** *Cutty Sark*

**SS Great Britain**
**313** *Great Britain*

**RMS Mauretania**
**314** *Mauretania I*

### British Ships

**1969** (15 Jan.) One horiz phosphor band (5d), two phosphor bands (9d) or two vertical phosphor bands at right (1s)

| | | | | | | |
|---|---|---|---|---|---|---|
| 778 | **309** | 5d multicoloured | 10 | 15 | ☐ | ☐ |
| 779 | **310** | 9d multicoloured | 10 | 25 | ☐ | ☐ |
| | | a. Strip of 3. | | | | |
| | | Nos. 779/81 | 1·30 | 1·50 | ☐ | ☐ |
| 780 | **311** | 9d multicoloured | 10 | 25 | ☐ | ☐ |
| 781 | **312** | 9d multicoloured | 10 | 25 | ☐ | ☐ |
| 782 | **313** | 1s multicoloured | 40 | 45 | ☐ | ☐ |
| | | a. Pair. Nos. 782/3 | 1·30 | 1·50 | ☐ | ☐ |
| 783 | **314** | 1s multicoloured | 40 | 35 | ☐ | ☐ |
| Set of 6 | | | 2·40 | 2·80 | ☐ | ☐ |
| First Day Cover | | | | 6·00 | ☐ | |
| Presentation Pack (P.O. Pack No.5) | | | 6·00 | | ☐ | |
| Presentation Pack (German) | | | | | | |
| | | (P.O. Pack No.5) | 60·00 | | ☐ | |

The 9d and 1s values were arranged in horizontal strips of three and pairs respectively throughout the sheet.

**315** Concorde in Flight    **316** Plan and Elevation Views

**317** Concorde's Nose and Tail

### First Flight of Concorde

**1969** (3 Mar.) Two phosphor bands

| | | | | | | |
|---|---|---|---|---|---|---|
| 784 | **315** | 4d multicoloured | 25 | 25 | ☐ | ☐ |
| 785 | **316** | 9d multicoloured | 55 | 75 | ☐ | ☐ |
| 786 | **317** | 1s6d deep blue, grey and | | | | |
| | | light blue | 75 | 1·00 | ☐ | ☐ |
| Set of 3 | | | 1·00 | 1·50 | ☐ | ☐ |
| First Day Cover | | | | 3·00 | ☐ | |
| Presentation Pack (P.O. Pack No.6) | | | 12·00 | | ☐ | |
| Presentation Pack (German) | | | 95·00 | | ☐ | |

**318** (See also Type **357**)

**1969** (5 Mar.) Perf 12

| | | | | | | |
|---|---|---|---|---|---|---|
| 787 | **318** | 2s6d brown | 35 | 30 | ☐ | ☐ |
| 788 | | 5s lake | 1·80 | 60 | ☐ | ☐ |
| 789 | | 10s ultramarine | 6·00 | 7·00 | ☐ | ☐ |
| 790 | | £1 black | 3·25 | 1·50 | ☐ | ☐ |
| Set of 4 | | | 10·00 | 8·50 | ☐ | ☐ |
| First Day Cover | | | | 9·50 | ☐ | |
| Presentation Pack (P.O. Pack No.7) | | | 16·00 | | ☐ | |
| Presentation Pack (German) | | | 80·00 | | ☐ | |

**319** Page from the *Daily Mail*, and Vickers FB-27 Vimy Aircraft    **320** Europa and C.E.P.T. Emblems

**321** I.L.O. Emblem    **322** Flags of N.A.T.O. Countries

**323** Vickers FB-27 Vimy Aircraft and Globe showing Flight

### Anniversaries. Events described on stamps

**1969** (2 Apr.) Two phosphor bands

| | | | | | | |
|---|---|---|---|---|---|---|
| 791 | **319** | 5d multicoloured | 10 | 15 | ☐ | ☐ |
| 792 | **320** | 9d multicoloured | 15 | 25 | ☐ | ☐ |
| 793 | **321** | 1s claret, red and blue | 15 | 25 | ☐ | ☐ |
| 794 | **322** | 1s6d multicoloured | 15 | 30 | ☐ | ☐ |
| 795 | **323** | 1s9d olive, yellow and | | | | |
| | | turquoise-green | 40 | 40 | ☐ | ☐ |
| Set of 5 | | | 85 | 1·20 | ☐ | ☐ |
| First Day Cover | | | | 4·00 | ☐ | |
| Presentation Pack (P.O. Pack No.9) | | | 5·00 | | ☐ | |
| Presentation Pack (German) | | | 95·00 | | ☐ | |

**324** Durham Cathedral    **325** York Minster

**326** St. Giles' Cathedral, Edinburgh    **327** Canterbury Cathedral

**328** St. Paul's Cathedral    **329** Liverpool Metropolitan Cathedral

## British Architecture (Cathedrals)

**1969** (28 May) Two phosphor bands

| | | | | | | | |
|---|---|---|---|---|---|---|---|
| 796 | **324** | 5d | multicoloured | 10 | 10 | ☐ | ☐ |
| | | a. | Block of 4. | | | ☐ | ☐ |
| | | | Nos. 796/9 | 1·10 | 1·25 | ☐ | ☐ |
| 797 | **325** | 5d | multicoloured | 10 | 10 | ☐ | ☐ |
| 798 | **326** | 5d | multicoloured | 10 | 10 | ☐ | ☐ |
| 799 | **327** | 5d | multicoloured | 10 | 10 | ☐ | ☐ |
| 800 | **328** | 9d | multicoloured | 25 | 30 | ☐ | ☐ |
| 801 | **329** | 1s6d | multicoloured | 25 | 35 | ☐ | ☐ |
| *Set of 6* | | | | 1·40 | 1·70 | ☐ | ☐ |
| First Day Cover | | | | | 4·00 | ☐ | |
| Presentation Pack (P.O. Pack No.10) | | | | 6·00 | | ☐ | |
| Presentation Pack (German) | | | | 48·00 | | ☐ | |

Nos. 796/9 were issued together *se-tenant* in blocks of four within the sheet.

**330** The King's Gate, Caernarvon Castle  **331** The Eagle Tower, Caernarvon Castle  **332** Queen Eleanor's Gate, Caernarvon Castle

**333** Celtic Cross, Margam Abbey  **334** Prince Charles

## Investiture of H.R.H. The Prince of Wales

**1969** (1 July) Two phosphor bands

| | | | | | | | |
|---|---|---|---|---|---|---|---|
| 802 | **330** | 5d | multicoloured | 10 | 15 | ☐ | ☐ |
| | | a. | Strip of 3. Nos. 802/4 | 50 | 1·00 | ☐ | ☐ |
| 803 | **331** | 5d | multicoloured | 10 | 15 | ☐ | ☐ |
| 804 | **332** | 5d | multicoloured | 10 | 15 | ☐ | ☐ |
| 805 | **333** | 9d | multicoloured | 15 | 30 | ☐ | ☐ |
| 806 | **334** | 1s | black and gold | 15 | 30 | ☐ | ☐ |
| *Set of 5* | | | | 75 | 1·40 | ☐ | ☐ |
| First Day Cover | | | | | 1·70 | | ☐ |
| Presentation Pack (P.O. Pack No.11) | | | | 3·00 | | ☐ | |
| Presentation Pack (German) | | | | 48·00 | | ☐ | |
| Presentation Pack (Welsh) | | | | 40·00 | | ☐ | |

Nos. 802/4 were printed *se-tenant* in strips of three throughout the sheet.

**335** Mahatma Gandhi

## Gandhi Centenary Year

**1969** (13 Aug.) Two phosphor bands

| | | | | | | | |
|---|---|---|---|---|---|---|---|
| 807 | **335** | 1s6d | multicoloured | 40 | 30 | ☐ | ☐ |
| First Day Cover | | | | | 1·00 | | ☐ |

## Collectors Pack 1969

**1969** (15 Sept.) Comprises Nos. 775/86 and 791/807

| | | | |
|---|---|---|---|
| CP807b | Collectors Pack | 25·00 | ☐ |

**336** National Giro  **337** Telecommunications – International Subscriber Dialling

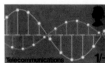

**338** Telecommunications – Pulse Code Modulation  **339** Postal Mechanisation – Automatic Sorting

## British Post Office Technology

**1969** (1 Oct.) Two phosphor bands. Perf 13½ × 14

| | | | | | | | |
|---|---|---|---|---|---|---|---|
| 808 | **336** | 5d | multicoloured | 10 | 10 | ☐ | ☐ |
| 809 | **337** | 9d | green, blue and black | 20 | 25 | ☐ | ☐ |
| 810 | **338** | 1s | green, lavender and black | 20 | 25 | ☐ | ☐ |
| 811 | **339** | 1s6d | multicoloured | 50 | 50 | ☐ | ☐ |
| *Set of 4* | | | | 90 | 1·00 | ☐ | ☐ |
| First Day Cover | | | | | 2·00 | | ☐ |
| Presentation Pack (P.O. Pack No.13) | | | | 5·00 | | ☐ | |

**340** Herald Angel  **341** The Three Shepherds

**342** The Three Kings

## Christmas

**1969** (26 Nov.) Two phosphor bands (5d, 1s6d) or one centre band (4d)

| | | | | | | | |
|---|---|---|---|---|---|---|---|
| 812 | **340** | 4d | multicoloured | 10 | 10 | ☐ | ☐ |
| 813 | **341** | 5d | multicoloured | 15 | 15 | ☐ | ☐ |
| 814 | **342** | 1s6d | multicoloured | 20 | 20 | ☐ | ☐ |
| *Set of 3* | | | | 40 | 40 | ☐ | ☐ |
| First Day Cover | | | | | 1·00 | | ☐ |
| Presentation Pack (P.O. Pack No.14) | | | | 5·00 | | ☐ | |

**343** Fife Harling  **344** Cotswold Limestone

**345** Welsh Stucco  **346** Ulster Thatch

## British Rural Architecture

**1970** (11 Feb.) Two phosphor bands

| | | | | | | | |
|---|---|---|---|---|---|---|---|
| 815 | **343** | 5d | multicoloured | 10 | 10 | ☐ | ☐ |
| 816 | **344** | 9d | multicoloured | 20 | 25 | ☐ | ☐ |
| 817 | **345** | 1s | multicoloured | 25 | 25 | ☐ | ☐ |
| 818 | **346** | 1s6d | multicoloured | 30 | 40 | ☐ | ☐ |
| *Set of 4* | | | | 75 | 90 | ☐ | ☐ |
| First Day Cover | | | | | 1·50 | | ☐ |
| Presentation Pack (P.O. Pack No.15) | | | 6·00 | | | ☐ | |

**347** Signing the Declaration of Arbroath

**348** Florence Nightingale attending Patients

**349** Signing of International Co-operative Alliance

**350** Pilgrims and *Mayflower*

**351** Sir William Herschel, Francis Baily, Sir John Herschel and Telescope

## Anniversaries. Events described on stamps

**1970** (1 Apr.) Two phosphor bands

| | | | | | | | |
|---|---|---|---|---|---|---|---|
| 819 | **347** | 5d | multicoloured | 10 | 10 | ☐ | ☐ |
| 820 | **348** | 9d | multicoloured | 15 | 15 | ☐ | ☐ |
| 821 | **349** | 1s | multicoloured | 20 | 25 | ☐ | ☐ |
| 822 | **350** | 1s6d | multicoloured | 20 | 30 | ☐ | ☐ |
| 823 | **351** | 1s9d | multicoloured | 25 | 30 | ☐ | ☐ |
| *Set of 5* | | | | 80 | 1·00 | ☐ | ☐ |
| First Day Cover | | | | | 2·00 | | ☐ |
| Presentation Pack (P.O. Pack No.16) | | | 5·00 | | | ☐ | |

**352** 'Mr Pickwick and Sam' (Pickwick Papers)

**353** 'Mr and Mrs Micawber' (David Copperfield)

**354** 'David Copperfield and Betsy Trotwood' (David Copperfield)

**355** 'Oliver asking for more'(Oliver Twist)

**356** 'Grasmere' (from engraving by J. Farrington, R.A.)

## Literary Anniversaries. Events described on stamps

**1970** (3 June) Two phosphor bands

| | | | | | | | |
|---|---|---|---|---|---|---|---|
| 824 | **352** | 5d | multicoloured | 10 | 25 | ☐ | ☐ |
| | | a. | Block of 4. Nos. 824/7 | 75 | 1·50 | ☐ | ☐ |
| 825 | **353** | 5d | multicoloured | 10 | 25 | ☐ | ☐ |
| 826 | **354** | 5d | multicoloured | 10 | 25 | ☐ | ☐ |
| 827 | **355** | 5d | multicoloured | 10 | 25 | ☐ | ☐ |
| 828 | **356** | 1s6d | multicoloured | 25 | 50 | ☐ | ☐ |
| *Set of 5* | | | | 95 | 1·80 | ☐ | ☐ |
| First Day Cover | | | | | 3·00 | | ☐ |
| Presentation Pack (P.O. Pack No.17) | | | 6·00 | | | ☐ | |

Nos. 824/7 were issued together *se-tenant* in blocks of four within the sheet.

**356a**

**357** (Value redrawn)

## Decimal Currency

**1970** (17 June)–**72** 10p and some printings of the 50p were issued on phosphor paper. Perf 12

| | | | | | | | |
|---|---|---|---|---|---|---|---|
| 829 | **356a** | 10p | cerise | 50 | 75 | ☐ | ☐ |
| 830 | | 20p | olive-green | 60 | 25 | ☐ | ☐ |
| 831 | | 50p | ultramarine | 1·50 | 40 | ☐ | ☐ |
| 831b | **357** | £1 | black *(6 Dec. 1972)* | 3·50 | 80 | ☐ | ☐ |
| *Set of 4* | | | | 5·50 | 2·00 | ☐ | ☐ |
| First Day Cover (Nos. 829/31) | | | | | 2·75 | | ☐ |
| First Day Cover (No. 831b) | | | | | 3·00 | | ☐ |
| Presentation Pack (P.O Pack No. 18) (Nos. 829/31) | | | | 10·00 | | ☐ | |
| Presentation Pack (P.O Pack No. 38) (Nos. 830/1, 790 or 831b) | | | | 17·00 | | ☐ | |

**358** Runners

**359** Swimmers

**360** Cyclists

## Ninth British Commonwealth Games, Edinburgh

**1970** (15 July) Two phosphor bands. Perf 13½ × 14

| | | | | | | | |
|---|---|---|---|---|---|---|---|
| 832 | **358** | 5d | pink, emerald, greenish yellow and yellow-green | 25 | 25 | ☐ | ☐ |
| 833 | **359** | 1s6d | greenish blue, lilac, brown and Prussian blue | 50 | 50 | ☐ | ☐ |
| 834 | **360** | 1s9d | yellow-orange, lilac, salmon and red-brown | 50 | 50 | ☐ | ☐ |
| *Set of 3* | | | | 1·10 | 1·10 | ☐ | ☐ |
| First Day Cover | | | | | 1·40 | | ☐ |
| Presentation Pack (P.O. Pack No.19) | | | 5·00 | | | ☐ | |

**Collectors Pack 1970**

**1970** (14 Sept.) Comprises Nos. 808/28 and 832/4

CP834a    Collectors Pack         35·00    ☐

| 5ᵈ | 9ᵈ | 1/6 |
|---|---|---|
| Philympia 1970 | Philympia 1970 | Philympia 1970 |

| 1840 first engraved issue | 1847 first embossed issue | 1855 first surface printed issue |
|---|---|---|
| **361** 1d Black (1840) | **362** 1s Green (1847) | **363** 4d Carmine (1855) |

**'Philympia 70' Stamp Exhibition**

**1970** (18 Sept.) Two phosphor bands. Perf 14 × 14½

| 835 | **361** | 5d | multicoloured | 25 | 10 | ☐ ☐ |
| 836 | **362** | 9d | multicoloured | 25 | 30 | ☐ ☐ |
| 837 | **363** | 1s6d | multicoloured | 25 | 45 | ☐ ☐ |
| *Set of 3* | | | | 70 | 75 | ☐ ☐ |
| First Day Cover | | | | | 1·50 | ☐ |
| Presentation Pack (P.O. Pack No.21) | | | 5·00 | | | ☐ |

**364** Shepherds and
Apparition of the Angel

**365** Mary, Joseph and
Christ. in Manger

**366** The Wise Men
bearing Gifts

**Christmas**

**1970** (25 Nov.) Two phosphor bands (5d, 1s6d) or one centre
phosphor band (4d)

| 838 | **364** | 4d | multicoloured | 15 | 10 | ☐ ☐ |
| 839 | **365** | 5d | multicoloured | 15 | 15 | ☐ ☐ |
| 840 | **366** | 1s6d | multicoloured | 25 | 30 | ☐ ☐ |
| *Set of 3* | | | | 50 | 50 | ☐ ☐ |
| First Day Cover | | | | | 1·00 | ☐ |
| Presentation Pack (P.O. Pack No.22) | | | 5·00 | | | ☐ |

# PRINTING PROCESSES

There is a basic distinction between stamps printed by
photogravure and those printed by lithography. Sorting the
two is not as difficult as it sounds and with a little experience
it should become easy to tell which method of production was
employed for a particular stamp.

The tiny dots of the printing screen give uneven edges to the values on
photogravure stamps (right). Litho values have clean, clear outlines (left).

All you need is a reasonably good glass giving a magnification
of ×4 or more (×10 is even better!).

The image on a photogravure stamp is created from a
pattern or 'screen', of minute dots which are not evident when
looking at the stamp without a glass but show up quite clearly
under magnification, especially in the Queen's face and around
the margin of the stamp design where it meets the white
background of the paper. Now look at the value; here also,
what looks to the naked eye like a straight line is in fact made
up of rows of tiny little dots.

'Screens' of dots are also used in the production of litho
printed stamps but they are only required where the printer
is attempting to produce shades and tints as is necessary in
the Queen's head portion of the stamp. Where solid colour is
used, as in the background of the majority of values, there is
no need to resort to a screen of dots and the background is
printed as a solid mass of colour. If you look at the margins
or the values of stamps produced in this way you will not
see any evidence of dots—just a clear clean break between
the inked portion of the stamp and the uninked white
of the paper.

**367**         **367a**

Two types of the 3p., 10p. and 26p. (Nos. X930/c, X886/b and
X971/b).

I         II

I         II

I         II

**Decimal Currency**

**1971 (15 Feb) –96.** Type **367**

(a) Printed in photogravure by Harrison and Sons (except for
some ptgs of Nos. X879 and X913 which were produced by
Enschedé) with phosphor bands. Perf 15×14

| X841 | ½p turquoise-blue (2 bands) | 10 | 10 | ☐ ☐ |
| X842 | ½p turquoise-blue (1 side band) | | | |
| | *(24.5.72)* | 55·00 | 30·00 | ☐ ☐ |

| | | | | |
|---|---|---|---|---|
| X843 | ½p turquoise-blue (1 centre band) *(14.12.77)* | 40 | 25 | ☐ ☐ |
| X844 | 1p crimson (2 bands) | 10 | 15 | ☐ ☐ |
| X845 | 1p crimson (1 centre band) *(14.12.77)* | 35 | 30 | ☐ ☐ |
| X846 | 1p crimson ('all-over' phosphor) *(10.10.79)* | 30 | 40 | ☐ ☐ |
| X847 | 1p crimson (1 side band at left) *(20.10.86)* | 1·00 | 1·25 | ☐ ☐ |
| X847Ea | Band at right *(3.3.87)* | 3·50 | 3·50 | ☐ ☐ |
| X848 | 1½p black (2 bands) | 20 | 30 | ☐ ☐ |
| X849 | 2p myrtle-green (face value as in T **367**) (2 bands) | 15 | 20 | ☐ ☐ |
| X850 | 2p myrtle-green (face value as in T **367**) ('all-over' phosphor) *(10.10.79)* | 25 | 30 | ☐ ☐ |
| X851 | 2½p magenta (1 centre band) | 20 | 15 | ☐ ☐ |
| X852 | 2½p magenta (1 side band) | 1·50 | 1·75 | ☐ ☐ |
| X853 | 2½p magenta (2 bands) *(21.5.75)* | 30 | 60 | ☐ ☐ |
| X854 | 2½p rose-red (2 bands) *(26.8.81)* | 55 | 750 | ☐ ☐ |
| X855 | 3p ultramarine (2 bands) | 20 | 25 | ☐ ☐ |
| X856 | 3p ultramarine (1 centre band) *(10.9.73)* | 15 | 20 | ☐ ☐ |
| X857 | 3p bright magenta (Type I) (2 bands) *(1.2.82)* | 35 | 35 | ☐ ☐ |
| X858 | 3½p olive-grey (2 bands) | 25 | 30 | ☐ ☐ |
| X859 | 3½p olive-grey (1 centre band) *(24.6.74)* | 30 | 35 | ☐ ☐ |
| X860 | 3½p purple-brown (1 centre band) *(5.4.83)* | 1·40 | 1·40 | ☐ ☐ |
| X861 | 4p ochre-brown (2 bands) | 40 | 50 | ☐ ☐ |
| X862 | 4p greenish blue (2 bands) *(26.8.81)* | 1·75 | 2·25 | ☐ ☐ |
| X863 | 4p greenish blue (1 centre band) *(3.9.84)* | 1·50 | 1·90 | ☐ ☐ |
| X864 | 4p greenish blue (1 side band) *(8.1.85)* | 2·00 | 2·25 | ☐ ☐ |
| X865 | 4½p grey-blue (2 bands) *(24.10.73)* | 40 | 50 | ☐ ☐ |
| X866 | 5p pale violet (2 bands) | 20 | 20 | ☐ ☐ |
| X867 | 5p claret (1 centre band) *(20.10.86)* | 2·25 | 2·25 | ☐ ☐ |
| X868 | 5½p violet (2 bands) *(24.10.73)* | 25 | 30 | ☐ ☐ |
| X869 | 5½p violet (1 centre band) *(17.3.75)* | 25 | 30 | ☐ ☐ |
| X870 | 6p light emerald (2 bands) | 25 | 40 | ☐ ☐ |
| X871 | 6½p greenish blue (2 bands) *(4.9.74)* | 50 | 60 | ☐ ☐ |
| X872 | 6½p greenish blue (1 centre band) *(24.9.75)* | 25 | 20 | ☐ ☐ |
| X873Ea | 6½p greenish blue (1 side band) *(26.1.77)* | 60 | 85 | ☐ ☐ |
| X874 | 7p purple-brown (2 bands) *(15.1.75)* | 30 | 35 | ☐ ☐ |
| X875 | 7p purple-brown (1 centre band) *(13.6.77)* | 25 | 30 | ☐ ☐ |
| X876Ea | 7p purple-brown (1 side band) *(13.6.77)* | 50 | 70 | ☐ ☐ |
| X877 | 7½p chestnut (2 bands) | 30 | 40 | ☐ ☐ |
| X878 | 8p rosine (2 bands) *(24.10.73)* | 30 | 30 | ☐ ☐ |
| X879 | 8p rosine (1 centre band) *(20.8.79)* | 30 | 30 | ☐ ☐ |
| X880 | 8p rosine (1 side band) *(28.8.79)* | 75 | 80 | ☐ ☐ |
| X881 | 8½p light yellowish green (2 bands) *(24.9.75)* | 30 | 30 | ☐ ☐ |
| X882 | 9p yellow-orange and black (2 bands) | 45 | 55 | ☐ ☐ |
| X883 | 9p deep violet (2 bands) *(25.2.76)* | 35 | 30 | ☐ ☐ |
| X884 | 9½p purple (2 bands) *(25.2.76)* | 75 | 1·00 | ☐ ☐ |
| X885 | 10p orange-brown and chestnut (2 bands) *(11.8.71)* | 35 | 35 | ☐ ☐ |
| X886 | 10p orange-brown (Type I) (2 bands) *(25.2.76)* | 35 | 30 | ☐ ☐ |
| | b. Type II *(4.9.84)* | 22·00 | 22·00 | ☐ ☐ |
| X887 | 10p orange-brown (Type I) ('all-over' phosphor) *(3.10.79)* | 35 | 45 | ☐ ☐ |
| X888 | 10p orange-brown (Type I) (1 centre band) *(4.2.80)* | 35 | 25 | ☐ ☐ |
| X889 | 10p orange-brown (Type I) (1 side band) *(4.2.80)* | 80 | 90 | ☐ ☐ |
| X890 | 10½p yellow (2 bands) *(25.2.76)* | 40 | 55 | ☐ ☐ |
| X891 | 10½p blue (2 bands) *(26.4.78)* | 45 | 75 | ☐ ☐ |
| X892 | 11p brown-red (2 bands) *(25.2.76)* | 40 | 40 | ☐ ☐ |
| X893 | 11½p drab (1 centre band) *(14.1.81)* | 40 | 35 | ☐ ☐ |
| X894 | 11½p drab (1 side band) *(26.1.81)* | 65 | 80 | ☐ ☐ |
| X895 | 12p yellowish green (2 bands) *(4.2.80)* | 45 | 45 | ☐ ☐ |
| X896 | 12p bright emerald (1 centre band) *(29.10.85)* | 45 | 45 | ☐ ☐ |
| X897 | 12p bright emerald (1 side band) *(14.1.86)* | 80 | 85 | ☐ ☐ |
| X898 | 12½p light emerald (1 centre band) *(27.1.82)* | 45 | 40 | ☐ ☐ |
| X899 | 12½p light emerald (1 side band) *(1.2.82)* | 70 | 75 | ☐ ☐ |
| X900 | 13p pale chestnut (1 centre band) *(28.8.84)* | 40 | 40 | ☐ ☐ |
| X901 | 13p pale chestnut (1 side band) *(3.9.84)* | 50 | 60 | ☐ ☐ |
| X902 | 14p grey-blue (2 bands) *(26.1.81)* | 75 | 80 | ☐ ☐ |
| X903 | 14p deep blue (1 centre band) *(23.8.88)* | 45 | 50 | ☐ ☐ |
| X904 | 14p deep blue (1 side band) *(5.9.88)* | 4·00 | 4·00 | ☐ ☐ |
| X905 | 15p bright blue (1 centre band) *(26.9.89)* | 65 | 65 | ☐ ☐ |
| X906a | 15p bright blue (1 side band) *(2.10.89)* | 4·00 | 4·00 | ☐ ☐ |
| X907 | 15½p pale violet (2 bands) *(1.2.82)* | 70 | 80 | ☐ ☐ |
| X908 | 16p olive-drab (2 bands) *(5.4.83)* | 1·40 | 1·60 | ☐ ☐ |
| X909 | 17p grey-blue (2 bands) *(3.9.84)* | 60 | 60 | ☐ ☐ |
| X910 | 17p deep blue (1 centre band) *(4.9.90)* | 80 | 85 | ☐ ☐ |
| X911Ea | 17p deep blue (1 side band) *(4.9.90)* | 1·25 | 1·25 | ☐ ☐ |
| X912 | 18p deep olive-grey (2 bands) *(20.10.86)* | 70 | 80 | ☐ ☐ |
| X913 | 18p bright green (1 centre band) *(10.9.91)* | 60 | 60 | ☐ ☐ |
| X914 | 19p bright orange-red (2 bands) *(5.9.88)* | 1·50 | 1·50 | ☐ ☐ |
| X915 | 20p dull purple (2 bands) *(25.2.76)* | 1·20 | 1·20 | ☐ ☐ |
| X916 | 20p brownish black (2 bands) *(2.10.89)* | 1·50 | 1·60 | ☐ ☐ |
| X917 | 22p bright orange-red (2 bands) *(4.9.90)* | 1·50 | 1·25 | ☐ ☐ |
| X917a | 25p rose-red (2 bands) *(6.2.96)* | 7·50 | 7·50 | ☐ ☐ |
| X918 | 26p rosine (Type I) (2 bands) *(3.3.87)* | 15·00 | 16·00 | ☐ ☐ |
| X919 | 31p purple (2 bands) *(18.3.86)* | 15·00 | 15·00 | ☐ ☐ |
| X920 | 34p ochre-brown (2 bands) *(8.1.85)* | 7·00 | 7·50 | ☐ ☐ |
| X921 | 50p ochre-brown (2 bands) *(2.2.77)* | 2·00 | 75 | ☐ ☐ |
| X922 | 50p ochre (2 bands) *(20.3.90)* | 4·50 | 4·50 | ☐ ☐ |

(b) Printed in photogravure by Harrison and Sons on phosphorised paper. Perf 15 × 14

| No. | Description | | |
|---|---|---|---|
| X924 | ½p turquoise-blue (10.12.80) | 10 | 20 |
| X925 | 1p crimson (12.12.79) | 10 | 15 |
| X926 | 2p myrtle-green (face value as in T **367**) (12.12.79) | 15 | 20 |
| X927 | 2p deep green (smaller value as in T **367a**) (26.7.88) | 20 | 20 |
| X928 | 2p myrtle-green (smaller value as in T **367a**) (5.9.88) | 4·25 | 4·25 |
| X929 | 2½p rose-red (14.1.81) | 25 | 40 |
| X930 | 3p bright magenta (Type I) (22.10.80) | 20 | 25 |
| | c. Type II (10.10.89) | 90 | 70 |
| X931 | 3½p purple-brown (30.3.83) | 60 | 70 |
| X932 | 4p greenish blue (30.12.81) | 35 | 50 |
| X933 | 4p new blue (26.7.88) | 20 | 25 |
| X934 | 5p pale violet (10.10.79) | 35 | 55 |
| X935 | 5p dull red-brown (26.7.88) | 25 | 30 |
| X936 | 6p yellow-olive (10.9.91) | 30 | 40 |
| X937 | 7p brownish red (29.10.85) | 1·40 | 1·50 |
| X938 | 8½p yellowish green (24.3.76) | 50 | 75 |
| X939 | 10p orange-brown (Type I) (11.79) | 35 | 35 |
| X940 | 10p dull orange (Type II) (4.9.90) | 40 | 35 |
| X941 | 11p brown-red (27.8.80) | 70 | 80 |
| X942 | 11½p ochre-brown (15.8.79) | 65 | 75 |
| X943 | 12p yellowish green (30.1.80) | 45 | 45 |
| X944 | 13p olive-grey (15.8.79) | 65 | 75 |
| X945 | 13½p purple-brown (30.1.80) | 70 | 80 |
| X946 | 14p grey-blue (14.1.81) | 50 | 50 |
| X947 | 15p ultramarine (15.8.79) | 60 | 60 |
| X948 | 15½p pale violet (14.1.81) | 60 | 50 |
| X949 | 16p olive-drab (30.8.83) | 55 | 55 |
| X950 | 16½p pale chestnut (27.1.82) | 90 | 1·00 |
| X951 | 17p light emerald (30.1.80) | 60 | 75 |
| X952 | 17p grey-blue (30.3.83) | 60 | 60 |
| X953 | 17½p pale chestnut (30.1.80) | 80 | 1·00 |
| X954 | 18p deep violet (14.1.81) | 70 | 80 |
| X955 | 18p deep olive-grey (28.8.84) | 75 | 60 |
| X956 | 19p bright orange-red (23.8.88) | 80 | 60 |
| X957 | 19½p olive-grey (27.1.82) | 2·00 | 2·00 |
| X958 | 20p dull purple (10.10.79) | 1·00 | 75 |
| X959 | 20p turquoise-green (23.8.88) | 75 | 70 |
| X960 | 20p brownish black (26.9.89) | 1·00 | 1·00 |
| X961 | 20½p ultramarine (30.3.83) | 1·25 | 1·25 |
| X962 | 22p blue (22.10.80) | 90 | 80 |
| X963 | 22p yellow-green (28.8.84) | 90 | 80 |
| X964 | 22p bright orange-red (4.9.90) | 90 | 80 |
| X965 | 23p brown-red (30.3.83) | 1·25 | 1·10 |
| X966 | 23p bright green (23.8.88) | 1·40 | 1·40 |
| X967 | 24p violet (28.8.84) | 1·40 | 1·50 |
| X968 | 24p Indian red (26.9.89) | 2·00 | 2·00 |
| X969 | 24p chestnut (10.9.91) | 80 | 80 |
| X970 | 25p purple (14.1.81) | 1·00 | 1·00 |
| X971 | 26p rosine (Type I) (27.1.82) | 1·10 | 80 |
| | b. Type II (4.8.87) | 6·00 | 7·00 |
| X972 | 26p drab (4.9.90) | 1·50 | 1·25 |
| X973 | 27p chestnut (23.8.88) | 1·25 | 1·25 |
| X974 | 27p violet (4.9.90) | 1·50 | 1·25 |
| X975 | 28p deep violet (20.3.83) | 1·25 | 1·25 |
| X976 | 28p ochre (23.8.88) | 1·40 | 1·25 |
| X977 | 28p deep bluish grey (10.9.91) | 1·40 | 1·25 |
| X978 | 29p ochre-brown (27.1.82) | 1·75 | 1·75 |
| X979 | 29p deep mauve (26.9.89) | 1·75 | 1·75 |
| X980 | 30p deep olive-grey (26.9.89) | 1·25 | 1·25 |
| X981 | 31p purple (30.8.83) | 1·25 | 1·25 |
| X982 | 31p ultramarine (4.9.90) | 1·60 | 1·75 |
| X983 | 32p greenish blue (23.8.88) | 1·90 | 1·75 |
| X984 | 33p light emerald (4.9.90) | 1·75 | 1·60 |
| X985 | 34p ochre-brown (28.8.84) | 1·75 | 1·75 |
| X986 | 34p deep bluish grey (26.9.89) | 2·00 | 2·00 |
| X987 | 34p deep mauve (10.9.91) | 1·75 | 1·75 |
| X988 | 35p sepia (23.8.88) | 1·60 | 1·60 |
| X989 | 35p yellow (10.9.91) | 1·75 | 1·60 |
| X990 | 37p rosine (26.9.89) | 2·00 | 1·75 |
| X991 | 39p bright mauve (10.9.91) | 1·75 | 1·75 |
| X991a | 50p ochre (21.1.92) | 5·00 | 2·00 |

(c) Printed in photogravure by Harrison and Sons on ordinary paper. Perf 15×14

| No. | Description | | |
|---|---|---|---|
| X992 | 50p ochre-brown (21.5.80) | 1·75 | 70 |
| X993 | 50p ochre (13.3.90) | 5·00 | 2·00 |
| X994 | 75p grey-black (smaller values as T **367a**) (26.7.88) | 3·25 | 1·50 |

(d) Printed in lithography by John Waddington. Perf 14

| No. | Description | | |
|---|---|---|---|
| X996 | 4p greenish blue (2 bands) (30.1.80) | 25 | 35 |
| X997 | 4p greenish blue (phosphorised paper) (11.81) | 45 | 40 |
| X998 | 20p dull purple (2 bands) (21.5.80) | 1·50 | 1·50 |
| X999 | 20p dull purple (phosphorised paper) (11.81) | 1·20 | 1·20 |

(e) Printed in lithography by Questa. Perf 14 (Nos. X1000, X1003/4 and X1023) or 15×14 (others)

| No. | Description | | |
|---|---|---|---|
| X1000 | 2p emerald-green (face value as in T **367**) (phosphorised paper) (21.5.80) | 20 | 25 |
| | a. Perf 15 × 14 (10.7.84) | 35 | 35 |
| X1001 | 2p bright green and deep green (smaller value as in T **367a**) (phosphorised paper) (23.2.88) | 75 | 80 |
| X1002 | 4p greenish blue (phosphorised paper) (13.5.86) | 1·80 | 90 |
| X1003 | 5p light violet (phosphorised paper) (21.5.80) | 1·60 | 75 |
| X1004 | 5p claret (phosphorised paper) (27.1.82) | 50 | 50 |
| | a. Perf 15 × 14 (21.2.84) | 65 | 60 |
| X1005 | 13p pale chestnut (1 centre band) (9.2.88) | 70 | 75 |
| X1006 | 13p pale chestnut (1 side band) (9.2.88) | 75 | 75 |
| X1007 | 14p deep blue (1 centre band) (11.10.88) | 2·00 | 2·00 |
| X1008 | 17p deep blue (1 centre band) (19.3.91) | 80 | 80 |
| X1009 | 18p deep olive-grey (phosphorised paper) (9.2.88) | 1·00 | 1·10 |
| X1010 | 18p deep olive-grey (2 bands) (9.2.88) | 7·50 | 7·50 |
| X1011 | 18p bright green (1 centre band) (27.10.92) | 75 | 75 |
| X1012 | 18p bright green (1 side band at right) (27.10.92) | 1·25 | 1·40 |
| X1013 | 19p bright orange-red (phosphorised paper) (11.10.88) | 2·20 | 2·00 |
| X1014 | 20p dull purple (phosphorised paper) (13.5.86) | 1·75 | 1·75 |
| X1015 | 22p yellow-green (2 bands) (9.2.88) | 9·00 | 9·00 |
| X1016 | 22p bright orange-red (phosphorised paper) (19.3.91) | 1·00 | 90 |

| | | | | |
|---|---|---|---|---|
| X1017 | 24p chestnut (phosphorised paper) *(27.10.92)* | 90 | 1·10 | ☐ ☐ |
| X1018 | 24p chestnut (2 bands) *(27.10.92)* | 1·40 | 1·40 | ☐ ☐ |
| X1019 | 33p light emerald (phosphorised paper) *(19.3.91)* | 2·50 | 2·50 | ☐ ☐ |
| X1020 | 33p light emerald (2 bands) *(25.2.92)* | 1·50 | 1·50 | ☐ ☐ |
| X1021 | 34p bistre-brown (2 bands) *(9.2.88)* | 7·50 | 7·50 | ☐ ☐ |
| X1022 | 39p bright mauve (2 bands) *(27.10.92)* | 1·75 | 1·75 | ☐ ☐ |
| X1023 | 75p black (face value as T **367**) (ordinary paper) *(30.1.80)* | 3·00 | 1·50 | ☐ ☐ |
| | a. Perf 15×14 *(21.2.84)* | 4·00 | 2·25 | ☐ ☐ |
| X1024 | 75p brownish grey and black (smaller value as T **367a**) (ordinary paper) *(23.2.88)* | 10·00 | 10·50 | ☐ ☐ |

### (f) Printed in lithography by Walsall. Perf 14

| | | | | |
|---|---|---|---|---|
| X1050 | 2p deep green (phosphorised paper) *(9.2.93)* | 1·50 | 1·40 | ☐ ☐ |
| X1051 | 14p deep blue (1 side band) *(25.4.89)* | 4·50 | 4·50 | ☐ ☐ |
| X1052 | 19p bright orange-red (2 bands) *(25.4.89)* | 3·00 | 3·00 | ☐ ☐ |
| X1053 | 24p chestnut (phosphorised paper) *(9.2.93)* | 1·10 | 1·25 | ☐ ☐ |
| X1054 | 29p deep mauve (2 bands) *(2.10.89)* | 3·00 | 3·00 | ☐ ☐ |
| X1055 | 29p deep mauve (phosphorised paper) *(17.4.90)* | 4·50 | 4·50 | ☐ ☐ |
| X1056 | 31p ultramarine (phosphorised paper) *(17.9.90)* | 1·75 | 1·75 | ☐ ☐ |
| X1057 | 33p light emerald (phosphorised paper) *(16.9.91)* | 1·50 | 1·50 | ☐ ☐ |
| X1058 | 39p bright mauve (phosphorised paper) *(16.9.91)* | 2·00 | 2·00 | ☐ ☐ |

*Presentation Pack* (P.O. Pack No. 26)
(contains ½p (X841), 1p (X844), 1½p (X848), 2p (X849), 2½p (X851), 3p (X855), 3½p (X858), 4p (X861), 5p (X866), 6p (X870), 7½p (X877), 9p (X882))     6·50     ☐

*Presentation Pack* ('Scandinavia 71')
(contents as above)     30·00     ☐

*Presentation Pack* (P.O. Pack No. 37)
(contains ½p (X841), 1p (X844), 1½p (X848), 2p (X849), 2½p (X851), 3p (X855 or X856), 3½p (X858 or X859), 4p (X861), 4½p (X865), 5p (X866), 5½p (X868 or X869), 6p (X870), 7½p (X877), 8p (X878), 9p (X882), 10p (X885))     30·00     ☐

Later issues of this pack included the 6½p (X871) or the 6½p (X872) and 7p (X874).

*Presentation Pack* (P.O. Pack No. 90)
(contains ½p (X841), 1p (X844), 1½p (X848), 2p (X849), 2½p (X851), 3p (X856), 5p (X866), 6½p (X872), 7p (X874 or X875), 7½p (X877), 8p (X878), 8½p (X881), 9p (X883), 9½p (X884), 10p (X886), 10½p (X890), 11p (X892), 20p (X915), 50p (X921))     6·00     ☐

*Presentation Pack* (P.O. Pack No. 129a)
(contains 2½p (X929), 3p (X930), 4p (X996), 10½p (X891), 11½p (X893), 11½p (X942), 12p (X943), 13p (X944), 13½p (X945), 14p (X946), 15p (X947), 15½p (X948), 17p (X951), 17½p (X953), 18p (X954), 22p (X962), 25p (X970), 75p (X1023)     20·00     ☐

*Presentation Pack* (P.O. Pack No. 1)
(contains ½p (X924), 1p (X925), 2p (X1000), 3p (X930), 3½p (X931), 4p (X997), 5p (X1004), 10p (X888), 12½p (X898), 16p (X949), 16½p (X950), 17p (X952), 20p (X999), 20½p (X961), 23p

---

(X965), 26p (X971), 28p (X975), 31p (X981), 50p (X992), 75p (X1023))     40·00     ☐

*Presentation Pack* (P.O. Pack No. 5)
(contains ½p (X924), 1p (X925), 2p (X1000a), 3p (X930), 4p (X997), 5p (X1004a), 10p (X939), 13p (X900), 16p (X949), 17p (X952), 18p (X955), 20p (X999), 22p (X963), 24p (X967), 26p (X971), 28p (X975), 31p (X981), 34p (X985), 50p (X992), 75p (X1023a))     36·00     ☐

*Presentation Pack* (P.O. Pack No. 9)
(contains 1p (X925), 2p (X1000a), 3p (X930), 4p (X997), 5p (X1004a), 7p (X937), 10p (X939), 12p (X896), 13p (X900), 17p (X952), 18p (X955), 20p (X999), 22p (X963), 24p (X967), 26p (X971), 28p (X975), 31p (X981), 34p (X985), 50p (X992), 75p (X1023a))     40·00     ☐

*Presentation Pack* (P.O. Pack No. 15)
(contains 14p (X903), 19p (X956), 20p (X959), 23p (X966), 27p (X973), 28p (X976), 32p (X983), 35p (X988))     12·00     ☐

*Presentation Pack* (P.O. Pack No. 19)
(contains 15p (X905), 20p (X960), 24p (X968), 29p (X979), 30p (X980), 34p (X986), 37p (X990))     10·00     ☐

*Presentation Pack* (P.O. Pack No. 22)
(contains 10p (X940), 17p (X910), 22p (X964), 26p (X972), 27p (X974), 31p (X982), 33p (X984))     9·00     ☐

*Presentation Pack* (P.O. Pack No. 24)
(contains 1p (X925), 2p (X927), 3p (X930), 4p (X933), 5p (X935), 10p (X940), 17p (X910), 20p (X959), 22p (X964), 26p (X972), 27p (X974), 30p (X980), 31p (X982), 32p (X983), 33p (X984), 37p (X990), 50p (X993), 75p (X994))     30·00     ☐

*Presentation Pack* (P.O. Pack No. 25)
(contains 6p (X936), 18p (X913), 24p (X969), 28p (X977), 34p (X987), 35p (X989), 39p (X991))     9·00     ☐

**First Day Covers**

| | | | |
|---|---|---|---|
| 15 Feb. 1971 | ½p, 1p, 1½p, 2p, 2½p, 3p, 3½p, 4p, 5p, 6p, 7½p, 9p (Nos. X841, X844, X848/9, X851, X855, X858, X861, X866, X870, X877, X882) (Covers carry 'POSTING DELAYED BY THE POST OFFICE STRIKE 1971' cachet) | 2·50 | ☐ |
| 11 Aug. 1971 | 10p (No. X885) | 1·50 | ☐ |
| 24 Oct. 1973 | 4½p, 5½p, 8p (Nos. X865, X868, X878) | 1·50 | ☐ |
| 4 Sept. 1974 | 6½p (No. X871) | 1·50 | ☐ |
| 15 Jan. 1975 | 7p (No. X874) | 1·00 | ☐ |
| 24 Sept. 1975 | 8½p (No. X881) | 1·50 | ☐ |
| 25 Feb. 1976 | 9p, 9½p, 10p, 10½p, 11p, 20p (Nos. X883/4, X886, X890, X892, X915) | 3·50 | ☐ |
| 2 Feb. 1977 | 50p (No. X921) | 1·75 | ☐ |
| 26 April 1978 | 10½p (No. X891) | 1·20 | ☐ |
| 15 Aug. 1979 | 11½p, 13p, 15p (Nos. X942, X944, X947) | 1·75 | ☐ |
| 30 Jan. 1980 | 4p, 12p, 13½p, 17p, 17½p, 75p (Nos. X996, X943, X945, X951, X953, X1023) | 3·25 | ☐ |
| 22 Oct. 1980 | 3p, 22p (Nos. X930, X962) | 1·50 | ☐ |
| 14 Jan. 1981 | 2½p, 11½p, 14p, 15½p, 18p, 25p (Nos. X929, X893, X946, X948, X954, X970) | 2·00 | ☐ |
| 27 Jan. 1982 | 5p, 12½p, 16½p, 19½p, 26p, 29p (Nos. X1004, X898, X950, X957, X971, X978) | 3·50 | ☐ |
| 30 Mar. 1983 | 3½p, 16p, 17p, 20½p, 23p, 28p, 31p (Nos. X931, X949, X952, X961, X965, X975, X981) | 5·00 | ☐ |

| 28 Aug. 1984 | 13p, 18p, 22p, 24p, 34p (Nos. X900, X955, X963, X967, X985) | 3·00 | ☐ |
| 29 Oct. 1985 | 7p, 12p (Nos. X937, X896) | 3·00 | ☐ |
| 23 Aug. 1988 | 14p, 19p, 20p, 23p, 27p, 28p, 32p, 35p (Nos. X903, X956, X959, X966, X973, X976, X983, X988) | 6·00 | ☐ |
| 26 Sept. 1989 | 15p, 20p, 24p, 29p, 30p, 34p, 37p (Nos. X905, X960, X968, X979/80, X986, X990) | 5·00 | ☐ |
| 4 Sept. 1990 | 10p, 17p, 22p, 26p, 27p, 31p, 33p (Nos. X940, X910, X964, X972, X974, X982, X984) | 5·50 | ☐ |
| 10 Sept. 1991 | 6p, 18p, 24p, 28p, 34p, 35p, 39p (Nos. X936, X913, X969, X977, X987, X989, X991) | 6·00 | ☐ |

For similar stamps, but with elliptical perforations see Nos. Y1667/1803 in 1993.

**PHOSPHOR BANDS**. See notes on page 15.

Phosphor bands are applied to the stamps, after the design has been printed, by a separate cylinder. On issues with 'all-over' phosphor the 'band' covers the entire stamp. Parts of the stamp covered by phosphor bands, or the entire surface for 'all-over' phosphor versions, appear matt.

Nos. X847, X852, X864, X873, X876, X880, X889, X894, X897, X899, X901, X906, X911, X1006 and X1012 exist with the phosphor band at the left or right of the stamp.

**PHOSPHORISED PAPER**. First introduced as an experiment for a limited printing of the 1s6d value (No. 743c) in 1969, this paper has the phosphor, to activate the automatic sorting machinery, added to the paper coating before the stamps were printed. Issues on this paper have a completely shiny surface. Although not adopted after this first trial further experiments on the 8½p in 1976 led to this paper being used for new printings of current values.

**368** 'A Mountain Road' (T.P. Flanagan)

**369** 'Deer's Meadow' (Tom Carr)

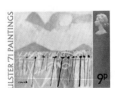

**370** 'Slieve na brock' (Colin Middleton)

### 'Ulster '71' Paintings

**1971** (16 June) Two phosphor bands

| 881 | **368** | 3p | multicoloured | 25 | 25 | ☐ | ☐ |
| 882 | **369** | 7½p | multicoloured | 50 | 50 | ☐ | ☐ |
| 883 | **370** | 9p | multicoloured | 50 | 50 | ☐ | ☐ |
| Set of 3 | | | | 1·00 | 1·00 | ☐ | |
| First Day Cover | | | | | 1·75 | | ☐ |
| Presentation Pack (P.O. Pack No. 26a) | | | 7·50 | | | ☐ | |

**371** John Keats (150th Death Anniv)

**372** Thomas Gray (Death Bicentenary)

**373** Sir Walter Scott (Birth Bicentenary)

### Literary Anniversaries. Events described above

**1971** (28 July) Two phosphor bands

| 884 | **371** | 3p | black, gold and blue | 25 | 10 | ☐ | ☐ |
| 885 | **372** | 5p | black, gold and olive | 45 | 50 | ☐ | ☐ |
| 886 | **373** | 7½p | black, gold and brown | 45 | 45 | ☐ | ☐ |
| Set of 3 | | | | 1·00 | 1·00 | ☐ | |
| First Day Cover | | | | | 2·00 | | ☐ |
| Presentation Pack (P.O. Pack No. 32) | | | 7·50 | | | ☐ | |

**374** Servicemen and Nurse of 1921   **375** Roman Centurion

**376** Rugby Football, 1871

### British Anniversaries. Events described on stamps

**1971** (25 Aug.) Two phosphor bands

| 887 | **374** | 3p | multicoloured | 25 | 25 | ☐ | ☐ |
| 888 | **375** | 7½p | multicoloured | 50 | 50 | ☑ | ☐ |
| 889 | **376** | 9p | multicoloured | 50 | 50 | ☐ | ☐ |
| Set of 3 | | | | 1·10 | 1·10 | ☐ | |
| First Day Cover | | | | | 2·50 | | ☐ |
| Presentation Pack (P.O. Pack No. 32A) | | | 7·50 | | | ☐ | |

**377** Physical Sciences Building, University College of Wales, Aberystwyth

**378** Faraday Building, Southampton University

**379** Engineering Department,
Leicester University

**380** Hexagon Restaurant,
Essex University

**386** Henry Hudson

**387** Capt. Robert F. Scott

## British Architecture (Modern University Buildings)

**1971** (22 Sept.) Two phosphor bands

| | | | | | | |
|---|---|---|---|---|---|---|
| 890 | **377** | 3p multicoloured | 10 | 10 | ☐ | ☐ |
| 891 | **378** | 5p multicoloured | 25 | 20 | ☐ | ☐ |
| 892 | **379** | 7½p ochre, black and purple-brown | 45 | 55 | ☐ | ☐ |
| 893 | **380** | 9p multicoloured | 75 | 80 | ☐ | ☐ |
| *Set of 4* | | | 1·40 | 1·50 | ☐ | |
| First Day Cover | | | | 2·00 | ☐ | |
| Presentation Pack (P.O. Pack No. 33) | | | 10·00 | | ☐ | |

## British Polar Explorers

**1972** (16 Feb.) Two phosphor bands

| | | | | | | |
|---|---|---|---|---|---|---|
| 897 | **384** | 3p multicoloured | 10 | 10 | ☑ | ☐ |
| 898 | **385** | 5p multicoloured | 15 | 15 | ☐ | ☐ |
| 899 | **386** | 7½p multicoloured | 45 | 50 | ☐ | ☐ |
| 900 | **387** | 9p multicoloured | 70 | 85 | ☐ | ☐ |
| *Set of 4* | | | 1·20 | 1·50 | ☐ | ☐ |
| First Day Cover | | | | 2·50 | ☐ | |
| Presentation Pack (P.O. Pack No. 39) | | | 7·00 | | ☐ | |

## Collectors Pack 1971

**1971** (29 Sept.) Comprises Nos. 835/40 and 881/93

| | | | |
|---|---|---|---|
| CP893a | Collectors Pack | 50·00 | ☐ |

**381** "Dream of the Wise Men"

**382** "Adoration of the Magi"

**388** Statuette of Tutankhamun

**389** 19th-century Coastguard

**383** "Ride of the Magi"

**390** Ralph Vaughan Williams
and Score

## Christmas

**1971** (13 Oct.) Two phosphor bands (3p, 7½p) or one centre phosphor band (2½p)

| | | | | | | |
|---|---|---|---|---|---|---|
| 894 | **381** | 2½p multicoloured | 10 | 10 | ☐ | ☐ |
| 895 | **382** | 3p multicoloured | 10 | 10 | ☐ | ☐ |
| 896 | **383** | 7½p multicoloured | 55 | 75 | ☐ | ☐ |
| *Set of 3* | | | 70 | 85 | ☐ | ☐ |
| First Day Cover | | | | 2·00 | ☐ | |
| Presentation Pack (P.O. Pack No. 35) | | | 6·00 | | ☐ | |

## Anniversaries. Events described on stamps

**1972** (26 Apr.) Two phosphor bands

| | | | | | | |
|---|---|---|---|---|---|---|
| 901 | **388** | 3p multicoloured | 25 | 25 | ☐ | ☐ |
| 902 | **389** | 7½p multicoloured | 50 | 50 | ☐ | ☐ |
| 903 | **390** | 9p multicoloured | 50 | 50 | ☐ | ☐ |
| *Set of 3* | | | 1·10 | 1·10 | ☐ | ☐ |
| First Day Cover | | | | 2·25 | ☐ | |
| Presentation Pack (P.O. Pack No. 40) | | | 7·00 | | ☐ | |

**384** Sir James Clark Ross

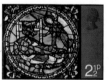

**385** Sir Martin Frobisher

**391** St. Andrew's,
Greensted - juxta-Ongar,
Essex

**392** All Saints, Earls
Barton, Northants

**393** St. Andrew's, Letheringsett, Norfolk

**394** St. Andrew's, Helpringham, Lincs

**395** St. Mary the Virgin, Huish Episcopi, Somerset

### British Architecture (Village Churches)

**1972** (21 June) Two phosphor bands

| | | | | | | |
|---|---|---|---|---|---|---|
| 904 | **391** | 3p multicoloured | 10 | 10 | ☐ | ☐ |
| 905 | **392** | 4p multicoloured | 10 | 20 | ☐ | ☐ |
| 906 | **393** | 5p multicoloured | 15 | 20 | ☐ | ☐ |
| 907 | **394** | 7½p multicoloured | 50 | 75 | ☐ | ☐ |
| 908 | **395** | 9p multicoloured | 50 | 80 | ☐ | ☐ |
| *Set of 5* | | | 1·20 | 1·90 | ☐ | ☐ |
| First Day Cover | | | | 2·75 | ☐ | |
| Presentation Pack (P.O. Pack No. 41) | | | 10·00 | | ☐ | |

### 'Belgica '72' Souvenir Pack

**1972** (24 June) Comprises Nos. 894/6 and 904/8

| | | | | |
|---|---|---|---|---|
| CP908b | Souvenir Pack | 10·00 | | ☐ |

**396** Microphones, 1924–69

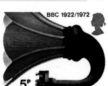

**397** Horn Loudspeaker

**398** TV Camera, 1972

**399** Oscillator and Spark Transmitter, 1897

### Broadcasting Anniversaries. Events described on stamps

**1972** (13 Sept.) Two phosphor bands

| | | | | | | |
|---|---|---|---|---|---|---|
| 909 | **396** | 3p multicoloured | 10 | 10 | ☐ | ☐ |
| 910 | **397** | 5p multicoloured | 10 | 20 | ☐ | ☐ |
| 911 | **398** | 7½p multicoloured | 45 | 50 | ☐ | ☐ |
| 912 | **399** | 9p multicoloured | 50 | 50 | ☐ | ☐ |
| *Set of 4* | | | 1·00 | 1·10 | ☐ | ☐ |
| First Day Cover | | | | 2·75 | ☐ | |
| Presentation Pack (P.O. Pack No. 43) | | | 4·25 | | ☐ | |

**400** Angel holding Trumpet  **401** Angel playing Lute  **402** Angel playing Harp

### Christmas

**1972** (18 Oct.) Two phosphor bands (3p, 7½p) or one centre phosphor band (2½p)

| | | | | | | |
|---|---|---|---|---|---|---|
| 913 | **400** | 2½p multicoloured | 10 | 10 | ☐ | ☐ |
| 914 | **401** | 3p multicoloured | 10 | 10 | ☐ | ☐ |
| 915 | **402** | 7½p multicoloured | 50 | 45 | ☐ | ☐ |
| *Set of 3* | | | 60 | 60 | ☐ | ☐ |
| First Day Cover | | | | 1·50 | ☐ | |
| Presentation Pack (P.O. Pack No. 44) | | | 4·00 | | ☐ | |

**403** Queen Elizabeth II and Prince Philip  **404** Europe

### Royal Silver Wedding

**1972** (20 Nov.) 3p 'all-over' phosphor, 20p without phosphor

| | | | | | | |
|---|---|---|---|---|---|---|
| 916 | **403** | 3p brownish black, deep blue and silver | 40 | 40 | ☐ | ☐ |
| 917 | | 20p brownish black, reddish purple and silver | 1·20 | 1·20 | ☐ | ☐ |
| *Set of 2* | | | 1·50 | 1·50 | ☐ | ☐ |
| First Day Cover | | | | 2·00 | ☐ | |
| Presentation Pack (P.O. Pack No. 45) | | | 4·00 | | ☐ | |
| Presentation Pack (Japanese) | | | 9·50 | | ☐ | |
| Souvenir Book (P.O. Pack No. 46) | | | 4·00 | 1·00 | ☐ | |
| Gutter Pair (3p) | | | 80 | | ☐ | |
| Traffic Light Gutter Pair (3p) | | | 20·00 | | ☐ | |

### Collectors Pack 1972

**1972** (20 Nov.) Comprises Nos. 897/917

| | | | |
|---|---|---|---|
| CP918a | Collectors Pack | 35·00 | ☐ |

### Britain's Entry into European Communities

**1973** (3 Jan.) Two phosphor bands

| | | | | | | |
|---|---|---|---|---|---|---|
| 919 | **404** | 3p multicoloured | 25 | 25 | ☐ | ☐ |
| 920 | | 5p multicoloured (blue jigsaw) | 25 | 50 | ☐ | ☐ |
| | | a. Pair. Nos. 920/1 | 1·00 | 1·25 | ☐ | ☐ |
| 921 | | 5p multicoloured (green jigsaw) | 25 | 50 | ☐ | ☐ |
| *Set of 3* | | | 1·10 | 1·40 | ☐ | ☐ |
| First Day Cover | | | | 2·00 | ☐ | |
| Presentation Pack (P.O. Pack No. 48) | | | 3·00 | | ☐ | |

Nos. 920/1 were issued horizontally *se-tenant* throughout the sheet.

Oak: Quercus robur
**405** Oak Tree

## British Trees (1st Issue)

**1973** (28 Feb.) Two phosphor bands

| | | | | | | |
|---|---|---|---|---|---|---|
| 922 | **405** | 9p | multicoloured | 35 | 40 | ☐ ☐ |
| First Day Cover | | | | | 1·70 | ☐ |
| Presentation Pack (P.O. Pack No. 49) | | | 2·75 | | | ☐ |

See also No. 949.

**406** David Livingstone

**407** H. M. Stanley

**408** Sir Francis Drake

**409** Sir Walter Raleigh

**410** Charles Sturt

## British Explorers

**1973** (18 Apr.) 'All-over' phosphor

| | | | | | | |
|---|---|---|---|---|---|---|
| 923 | **406** | 3p | multicoloured | 40 | 25 | ☐ ☐ |
| | | a. Pair. Nos. 923/4 | | 80 | 1·00 | ☐ ☐ |
| 924 | **407** | 3p | multicoloured | 40 | 25 | ☐ ☐ |
| 925 | **408** | 5p | multicoloured | 40 | 50 | ☐ ☐ |
| 926 | **409** | 7½p | multicoloured | 40 | 50 | ☐ ☐ |
| 927 | **410** | 9p | multicoloured | 40 | 75 | ☐ ☐ |
| Set of 5 | | | | 1·70 | 1·70 | ☐ |
| First Day Cover | | | | | 2·50 | ☐ |
| Presentation Pack (P.O. Pack No. 50) | | | 4·50 | | | ☐ |

Nos. 923/4 were issued horizontally *se-tenant* throughout the sheet.

**411**      **412**      **413**

County Cricket 1873-1973   County Cricket 1873-1973   County Cricket 1873-1973

## County Cricket 1873–1973

**1973** (16 May) Designs show sketches of W. G. Grace by Harry Furniss. Queen's head in gold. 'All-over' phosphor

| | | | | | | |
|---|---|---|---|---|---|---|
| 928 | **411** | 3p | black and brown | 25 | 25 | ☐ ☐ |
| 929 | **412** | 7½p | black and green | 75 | 75 | ☐ ☐ |
| 930 | **413** | 9p | black and blue | 1·25 | 1·00 | ☐ ☐ |
| Set of 3 | | | | 2·00 | 1·75 | ☐ ☐ |
| First Day Cover | | | | | 2·50 | ☐ |
| Presentation Pack (P.O. Pack No. 51) | | | 5·00 | | | ☐ |
| Souvenir Book | | | | 7·00 | | ☐ |
| PHQ Card (No. 928)(1) | | | | 70·00 | £275 | ☐ ☐ |

The PHQ Card did not become available until mid-July. The used price quoted is for an example used in July or August 1973.

**414** 'Self-portrait' (Sir Joshua Reynolds)

**415** 'Self-portrait' (Sir Henry Raeburn)

**416** 'Nelly O'Brien' (Sir Joshua Reynolds)

**417** 'Rev R. Walker (The Skater)' (Sir Henry Raeburn)

## British Paintings. 250th Birth Anniv of Sir Joshua Reynolds and 150th Death Anniv of Sir Henry Raeburn

**1973** (4 July) 'All-over' phosphor

| | | | | | | |
|---|---|---|---|---|---|---|
| 931 | **414** | 3p | multicoloured | 10 | 10 | ☐ ☐ |
| 932 | **415** | 5p | multicoloured | 30 | 30 | ☐ ☐ |
| 933 | **416** | 7½p | multicoloured | 30 | 30 | ☐ ☐ |
| 934 | **417** | 9p | multicoloured | 60 | 60 | ☐ ☐ |
| Set of 4 | | | | 1·20 | 1·20 | ☐ ☐ |
| First Day Cover | | | | | 2·00 | ☐ |
| Presentation Pack (P.O. Pack No. 52) | | | 3·25 | | | ☐ |

418 Court Masque Costumes

419 St. Paul's Church, Covent Garden

420 Prince's Lodging, Newmarket

421 Court Masque Stage Scene

### 400th Anniversary of the Birth of Inigo Jones (architect and designer)

**1973** (15 Aug.) 'All-over' phosphor

| | | | | | | |
|---|---|---|---|---|---|---|
| 935 | 418 | 3p | deep mauve, black and gold | 10 | 25 | |
| | | a. | Pair. Nos. 935/6 | 30 | 50 | |
| 936 | 419 | 3p | deep brown, black and gold | 10 | 25 | |
| 937 | 420 | 5p | blue, black and gold | 35 | 50 | |
| | | a. | Pair. Nos. 937/8 | 1·00 | 1·00 | |
| 938 | 421 | 5p | grey-olive, black and gold | 35 | 50 | |
| Set of 4 | | | | 1·20 | 1·40 | |
| First Day Cover | | | | | 2·00 | |
| Presentation Pack (P.O. Pack No.53) | | | | 3·50 | | |
| PHQ Card (No. 936) (2) | | | | £200 | £200 | |

The 3p and 5p values were printed horizontally *se-tenant* within the sheet.

422 Palace of Westminster seen from Whitehall

423 Palace of Westminster seen from Millbank

### 19th Commonwealth Parliamentary Conference

**1973** (12 Sept.) 'All-over' phosphor

| | | | | | | |
|---|---|---|---|---|---|---|
| 939 | 422 | 8p | black, grey and pale buff | 45 | 50 | |
| 940 | 423 | 10p | gold and black | 45 | 40 | |
| Set of 2 | | | | 80 | 80 | |
| First Day Cover | | | | | 1·50 | |
| Presentation Pack (P.O. Pack No. 54) | | | | 3·00 | | |
| Souvenir Book (P.O. Pack No. 55) | | | | 7·00 | | |
| PHQ Card (No. 939) (3) | | | | 40·00 | £150 | |

424 Princess Anne and Captain Mark Phillips

### Royal Wedding

**1973** (14 Nov.) 'All-over' phosphor

| | | | | | | |
|---|---|---|---|---|---|---|
| 941 | 424 | 3½p | violet and silver | 25 | 25 | |
| 942 | | 20p | brown and silver | 1·00 | 75 | |

| | | | |
|---|---|---|---|
| Set of 2 | | 1·10 | 90 |
| First Day Cover | | | 1·50 |
| Presentation Pack (P.O. Pack No. 56) | | 2·75 | |
| PHQ Card (No. 941) (4) | | 9·00 | 50·00 |
| Set of 2 Gutter Pairs | | 2·75 | |
| Set of 2 Traffic Light Gutter Pairs | | £110 | |

425

426

427

428

429

430 'Good King Wenceslas, the Page and Peasant'

### Christmas

**1973** (28 Nov.) One phosphor band (3p) or 'all-over' phosphor (3½p)

| | | | | | | |
|---|---|---|---|---|---|---|
| 943 | 425 | 3p | multicoloured | 20 | 25 | |
| | | a. | Strip of 5. Nos. 943/7 | 2·25 | 2·50 | |
| 944 | 426 | 3p | multicoloured | 20 | 25 | |
| 945 | 427 | 3p | multicoloured | 20 | 25 | |
| 946 | 428 | 3p | multicoloured | 20 | 25 | |
| 947 | 429 | 3p | multicoloured | 20 | 25 | |
| 948 | 430 | 3½p | multicoloured | 20 | 25 | |
| Set of 6 | | | | 2·25 | 2·50 | |
| First Day Cover | | | | | 3·00 | |
| Presentation Pack (P.O. Pack No. 57) | | | | 4·00 | | |

The 3p values depict the carol 'Good King Wenceslas' and were printed horizontally *se-tenant* within the sheet.

### Collectors Pack 1973

**1973** (28 Nov.) Comprises Nos. 919/48

| | | | |
|---|---|---|---|
| CP948k | Collectors Pack | 27·00 | |

431 Horse Chestnut

### British Trees (2nd issue)

**1974** (27 Feb.) 'All-over' phosphor

| | | | | | | |
|---|---|---|---|---|---|---|
| 949 | 431 | 10p | multicoloured | 40 | 35 | |
| First Day Cover | | | | | 1·20 | |
| Presentation Pack (P.O. Pack No. 59) | | | | 2·50 | | |
| PHQ Card (5) | | | | £150 | £150 | |

| | | | | |
|---|---|---|---|---|
| Gutter Pair | | 1·75 | | ☐ |
| Traffic Light Gutter Pair | | 65·00 | | ☐ |

The pack number is stated to be 58 on the reverse but the correct number is 59.

**432** First. Motor Fire-engine, 1904

**433** Prize-winning Fire-engine, 1863

**434** First. Steam Fire-engine, 1830

**435** Fire-engine, 1766

## Bicentenary of the Fire Prevention (Metropolis) Act

**1974** (24 Apr.) 'All-over' phosphor

| | | | | | | | |
|---|---|---|---|---|---|---|---|
| 950 | **432** | 3½p | multicoloured | 25 | 10 | ☐ | ☐ |
| 951 | **433** | 5½p | multicoloured | 25 | 30 | ☐ | |
| 952 | **434** | 8p | multicoloured | 50 | 50 | ☐ | |
| 953 | **435** | 10p | multicoloured | 50 | 50 | ☐ | |
| *Set of* 4 | | | | 1·40 | 1·30 | ☐ | |
| First Day Cover | | | | | 3·00 | ☐ | |
| Presentation Pack (P.O. Pack No. 60) | | | | 4·00 | | ☐ | |
| PHQ Card (No. 950) (6) | | | | £140 | £150 | ☐ | ☐ |
| *Set of* 4 Gutter Pairs | | | | 3·00 | | ☐ | |
| *Set of* 4 Traffic Light Gutter Pairs | | | | 60·00 | | ☐ | |

**436** P & O Packet *Peninsular*, 1888

**437** Farman H.F. III Biplane, 1911

**438** Airmail-blue Van and Postbox, 1930

**439** Imperial Airways Short S.21 Flying Boat *Maia*, 1937

## Centenary of Universal Postal Union

**1974** (12 June) 'All-over' phosphor

| | | | | | | | |
|---|---|---|---|---|---|---|---|
| 954 | **436** | 3½p | multicoloured | 25 | 10 | ☐ | ☐ |
| 955 | **437** | 5½p | multicoloured | 25 | 30 | ☐ | |
| 956 | **438** | 8p | multicoloured | 25 | 35 | ☐ | |
| 957 | **439** | 10p | multicoloured | 50 | 40 | ☐ | |
| *Set of* 4 | | | | 1·10 | 1·00 | ☐ | |
| First Day Cover | | | | | 2·00 | ☐ | |
| Presentation Pack (P.O. Pack No.64) | | | | 4·00 | | ☐ | |
| *Set of* 4 Gutter Pairs | | | | 2·50 | | ☐ | |
| *Set of* 4 Traffic Light Gutter Pairs | | | | 45·00 | | ☐ | |

**440** Robert the Bruce

**441** Owain Glyndŵr

**442** Henry V

**443** The Black Prince

## Medieval Warriors

**1974** (10 July) 'All-over' phosphor

| | | | | | | | |
|---|---|---|---|---|---|---|---|
| 958 | **440** | 4½p | multicoloured | 25 | 10 | ☐ | |
| 959 | **441** | 5½p | multicoloured | 25 | 35 | ☐ | |
| 960 | **442** | 8p | multicoloured | 50 | 50 | ☐ | |
| 961 | **443** | 10p | multicoloured | 50 | 50 | ☐ | |
| *Set of* 4 | | | | 1·40 | 1·30 | ☐ | |
| First Day Cover | | | | | 3·00 | ☐ | |
| Presentation Pack (P.O. Pack No. 65) | | | | 4·00 | | ☐ | |
| PHQ Cards (*set of* 4) (7) | | | | 28·00 | 65·00 | ☐ | ☐ |
| *Set of* 4 Gutter Pairs | | | | 3·00 | | ☐ | |
| *Set of* 4 Traffic Light Gutter Pairs | | | | 60·00 | | ☐ | |

**444** Churchill in Royal yacht Squadron Uniform

**445** Prime Minister, 1940

**446** Secretary for War and Air, 1919

**447** War Correspondent, South Africa, 1899

## Birth Centenary of Sir Winston Churchill

**1974** (9 Oct.) Queen's head and inscription in silver. 'All-over' phosphor

| | | | | | | | |
|---|---|---|---|---|---|---|---|
| 962 | **444** | 4½p | green and blue | 20 | 15 | ☐ | |
| 963 | **445** | 5½p | grey and black | 35 | 35 | ☐ | |
| 964 | **446** | 8p | rose and lake | 60 | 50 | ☐ | |
| 965 | **447** | 10p | stone and brown | 60 | 50 | ☐ | |
| *Set of* 4 | | | | 1·60 | 1·40 | ☐ | |
| First Day Cover | | | | | 2·00 | ☐ | |
| Presentation Pack (P.O. Pack No. 66) | | | | 4·00 | | ☐ | |
| Souvenir Book | | | | 3·00 | | ☐ | |
| PHQ Card (No. 963) (8) | | | | 6·00 | 32·00 | ☐ | ☐ |
| *Set of* 4 Gutter Pairs | | | | 4·00 | | ☐ | |
| *Set of* 4 Traffic Light Gutter Pairs | | | | 35·00 | | ☐ | |

3½p

4½p

**448** *"Adoration of the Magi"* (York Minister, c 1355)

**449** *"The Nativity"* (St. Helen's Church, Norwich, c 1480)

8p

10p

**450** *"Virgin and Child"* (Ottery St. Mary Church, c 1350)

**451** *"Virgin and Child"* (Worcester Cathedral, c 1224)

### Christmas

**1974** (27 Nov.) Designs show church roof bosses. One phosphor band (3½p) or 'all-over' phosphor (others)

| | | | | | | |
|---|---|---|---|---|---|---|
| 966 | **448** | 3½p multicoloured | 10 | 10 | | |
| 967 | **449** | 4½p multicoloured | 10 | 10 | | |
| 968 | **450** | 8p multicoloured | 25 | 50 | | |
| 969 | **451** | 10p multicoloured | 50 | 50 | | |
| Set of 4 | | | 80 | 1·10 | | |
| First Day Cover | | | | 2·00 | | |
| Presentation Pack (P.O. Pack No. 67) | | | 3·00 | | | |
| Set of 4 Gutter Pairs | | | 2·25 | | | |
| Set of 4 Traffic Light Gutter Pairs | | | 36·00 | | | |

### Collectors Pack 1974

**1974** (27 Nov.) Comprises Nos. 949/69

| | | | |
|---|---|---|---|
| CP969a | Collectors Pack | 16·00 | |

**452** Invalid in Wheelchair

### Health and Handicap Funds

**1975** (22 Jan.) 'All-over' phosphor

| | | | | | | |
|---|---|---|---|---|---|---|
| 970 | **452** | 4½p +1½p azure and blue | 25 | 25 | | |
| First Day Cover | | | | 1·00 | | |
| Gutter Pair | | | 60 | | | |
| Traffic Light Gutter Pair | | | 2·25 | | | |

4½p

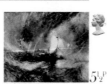

5½p

**453** 'Peace – Burial at Sea'

**454** 'Snowstorm – Steamer off a Harbour's Mouth'

8p

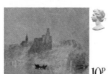

10p

**455** 'The Arsenal, Venice'

**456** 'St. Laurent'

### Birth Bicentenary of J. M. W. Turner (painter)

**1975** (19 Feb.) 'All-over' phosphor

| | | | | | | |
|---|---|---|---|---|---|---|
| 971 | **453** | 4½p multicoloured | 25 | 25 | | |
| 972 | **454** | 5½p multicoloured | 25 | 25 | | |
| 973 | **455** | 8p multicoloured | 25 | 50 | | |
| 974 | **456** | 10p multicoloured | 50 | 50 | | |
| Set of 4 | | | 1·10 | 1·10 | | |
| First Day Cover | | | | 1·50 | | |
| Presentation Pack (P.O. Pack No. 69) | | | 3·00 | | | |
| PHQ Card (No. 972) (9) | | | 30·00 | 34·00 | | |
| Set of 4 Gutter Pairs | | | 2·25 | | | |
| Set of 4 Traffic Light Gutter Pairs | | | 8·00 | | | |

7p

7p

**457** Charlotte Square, Edinburgh

**458** The Rows, Chester

8p

10p

**459** Royal Observatory, Greenwich

**460** St. George's Chapel, Windsor

12p

**461** National Theatre, London

### European Architectural Heritage Year

**1975** (23 Apr.) 'All-over' phosphor

| | | | | | | |
|---|---|---|---|---|---|---|
| 975 | **457** | 7p multicoloured | 15 | 15 | | |
| | | a. Pair. Nos. 975/6 | 90 | 1·00 | | |
| 976 | **458** | 7p multicoloured | 15 | 15 | | |
| 977 | **459** | 8p multicoloured | 40 | 30 | | |
| 978 | **460** | 10p multicoloured | 40 | 30 | | |
| 979 | **461** | 12p multicoloured | 40 | 35 | | |
| Set of 5 | | | 1·90 | 1·70 | | |
| First Day Cover | | | | 2·50 | | |
| Presentation Pack (P.O. Pack No.70) | | | 3·00 | | | |
| PHQ Cards (Nos. 975/7) (10) | | | 11·00 | 40·00 | | |
| Set of 5 Gutter Pairs | | | 4·00 | | | |
| Set of 5 Traffic Light Gutter Pairs | | | 22·00 | | | |

Nos. 975/6 were printed horizontally *se-tenant* throughout the sheet.

7p

8p

**462** Sailing Dinghies

**463** Racing Keel Boats

**464** Cruising Yachts

**465** Multihulls

### Sailing

**1975** (11 June) 'All-over' phosphor

| | | | | | | |
|---|---|---|---|---|---|---|
| 980 | **462** | 7p multicoloured | 25 | 20 | | |
| 981 | **463** | 8p multicoloured | 35 | 40 | | |
| 982 | **464** | 10p multicoloured | 35 | 45 | | |
| 983 | **465** | 12p multicoloured | 50 | 50 | | |
| *Set of 4* | | | 1·30 | 1·40 | | |
| First Day Cover | | | | 2·00 | | |
| Presentation Pack (P.O. Pack No. 71) | | | 2·50 | | | |
| PHQ Card (No. 981) (11) | | | 5·75 | 30·00 | | |
| *Set of 4 Gutter Pairs* | | | 2·75 | | | |
| *Set of 4 Traffic Light Gutter Pairs* | | | 25·00 | | | |

**466** Stephenson's *Locomotion*, 1825

Stephenson's Locomotion 7p
1825 Stockton and Darlington Railway

**467** *Abbotsford*, 1876

Waverley Class 8p
1876 North British Railway Drummond

**468** *Caerphilly Castle*, 1923

Caerphilly Castle 10p
1923 Great Western Railway Castle Class

**469** High Speed Train, 1975

High-Speed Train 12p
1975 British Rail Inter-City Service HST

### 150th Anniversary of Public Railways

**1975** (13 Aug.) 'All-over' phosphor

| | | | | | | |
|---|---|---|---|---|---|---|
| 984 | **466** | 7p multicoloured | 25 | 25 | | |
| 985 | **467** | 8p multicoloured | 50 | 50 | | |
| 986 | **468** | 10p multicoloured | 50 | 50 | | |
| 987 | **469** | 12p multicoloured | 40 | 50 | | |
| *Set of 4* | | | 1·50 | 1·50 | | |
| First Day Cover | | | | 2·50 | | |
| Presentation Pack (P.O. Pack No. 72) | | | 4·00 | | | |
| Souvenir Book (P.O. Pack No. 73) | | | | 4·00 | | |
| PHQ Cards (*set of 4*) (12) | | | 70·00 | 70·00 | | |
| *Set of 4 Gutter Pairs* | | | 3·25 | | | |
| *Set of 4 Traffic Light Gutter Pairs* | | | 12·00 | | | |

**470** Palace of Westminster

### 62nd Inter-Parliamentary Union Conference

**1975** (3 Sept.) 'All-over' phosphor

| | | | | | | |
|---|---|---|---|---|---|---|
| 988 | **470** | 12p multicoloured | 50 | 40 | | |
| First Day Cover | | | | 80 | | |
| Presentation Pack (P.O. Pack No. 74) | | | 1·80 | | | |
| Gutter Pair | | | 1·10 | | | |
| Traffic Light Gutter Pair | | | 3·00 | | | |

**471** Emma and Mr Woodhouse (*Emma*)

**472** Catherine Morland (*Northanger Abbey*)

**473** Mr Darcy (*Pride and Prejudice*)

**474** Mary and Henry Crawford (*Mansfield Park*)

### Birth Bicentenary of Jane Austen (novelist)

**1975** (22 Oct.) 'All-over' phosphor

| | | | | | | |
|---|---|---|---|---|---|---|
| 989 | **471** | 8½p multicoloured | 25 | 20 | | |
| 990 | **472** | 10p multicoloured | 45 | 45 | | |
| 991 | **473** | 11p multicoloured | 45 | 45 | | |
| 992 | **474** | 13p multicoloured | 50 | 50 | | |
| *Set of 4* | | | 1·50 | 1·40 | | |
| First Day Cover | | | | 2·50 | | |
| Presentation Pack (P.O. Pack No.75) | | | 5·00 | | | |
| PHQ Cards (*set of 4*) (13) | | | 24·00 | 42·00 | | |
| *Set of 4 Gutter Pairs* | | | 2·50 | | | |
| *Set of 4 Traffic Light Gutter Pairs* | | | 7·00 | | | |

**475** Angels with Harp and Lute

**476** Angel with Mandolin

**477** Angel with Horn

**478** Angel with Trumpet

### Christmas

**1975** (26 Nov.) One phosphor band (6½p). phosphor-inked (8½p) (background) or 'all-over' phosphor (others)

| | | | | | | |
|---|---|---|---|---|---|---|
| 993 | **475** | 6½p multicoloured | 25 | 25 | | |
| 994 | **476** | 8½p multicoloured | 25 | 40 | | |
| 995 | **477** | 11p multicoloured | 50 | 45 | | |
| 996 | **478** | 13p multicoloured | 50 | 45 | | |
| *Set of 4* | | | 1·40 | 1·40 | | |
| First Day Cover | | | | 1·80 | | |
| Presentation Pack (P.O. Pack No. 76) | | | 3·00 | | | |
| *Set of 4 Gutter Pairs* | | | 3·00 | | | |
| *Set of 4 Traffic Light Gutter Pairs* | | | 9·00 | | | |

## Collectors Pack 1975

**1975** (26 Nov.) Comprises Nos. 970/96
CP996a Collectors Pack     9·00 ☐

**479** Housewife

**480** Policeman

**481** District Nurse

**482** Industrialist

## Telephone Centenary

| | | | | | | |
|---|---|---|---|---|---|---|
| **1976** (10 Mar.) 'All-over' phosphor | | | | | | |
| 997 | **479** | 8½p | multicoloured | 25 | 20 | ☐ ☐ |
| 998 | **480** | 10p | multicoloured | 40 | 40 | ☐ ☐ |
| 999 | **481** | 11p | multicoloured | 50 | 50 | ☐ ☐ |
| 1000 | **482** | 13p | multicoloured | 60 | 60 | ☐ ☐ |
| Set of 4 | | | | 1·60 | 1·60 | ☐ ☐ |
| First Day Cover | | | | | 2·00 | ☐ |
| Presentation Pack (P.O. Pack No. 78) | | | | 3·00 | | ☐ |
| Set of 4 Gutter Pairs | | | | 3·25 | | ☐ |
| Set of 4 Traffic Light Gutter Pairs | | | | 9·00 | | ☐ |

**483** Hewing Coal
(Thomas Hepburn)

**484** Machinery
(Robert Owen)

**485** Chimney Cleaning
(Lord Shaftesbury)

**486** Hands clutching Prison Bars
(Elizabeth Fry)

## Social Reformers

| | | | | | | |
|---|---|---|---|---|---|---|
| **1976** (28 Apr.) 'All-over' phosphor | | | | | | |
| 1001 | **483** | 8½p | multicoloured | 25 | 20 | ☐ ☐ |
| 1002 | **484** | 10p | multicoloured | 40 | 40 | ☐ ☐ |
| 1003 | **485** | 11p | black, slate-grey and drab | 50 | 50 | ☐ ☐ |
| 1004 | **486** | 13p | slate-grey, black and green | 60 | 60 | ☐ ☐ |
| Set of 4 | | | | 1·60 | 1·60 | ☐ ☐ |
| First Day Cover | | | | | 2·00 | ☐ ☐ |
| Presentation Pack (P.O. Pack No. 79) | | | | 2·75 | | ☐ |
| PHQ Card (No. 1001) (14) | | | | 6·00 | 20·00 | ☐ ☐ |
| Set of 4 Gutter Pairs | | | | 3·25 | | ☐ |
| Set of 4 Traffic Light Gutter Pairs | | | | 9·00 | | ☐ |

**487** Benjamin Franklin
(bust. by Jean-Jacques Caffieri)

## Bicentenary of American Revolution

| | | | | | | |
|---|---|---|---|---|---|---|
| **1976** (2 June) 'All-over' phosphor | | | | | | |
| 1005 | **487** | 11p | multicoloured | 50 | 50 | ☐ ☐ |
| First Day Cover | | | | | 1·50 | ☐ |
| Presentation Pack (P.O. Pack No. 80) | | | | 1·50 | | ☐ |
| PHQ Card (15) | | | | 5·00 | 20·00 | ☐ ☐ |
| Gutter Pair | | | | 1·25 | | ☐ |
| Traffic Light Gutter Pair | | | | 2·50 | | ☐ |

**488** 'Elizabeth of Glamis'

**489** 'Grandpa Dickson'

**490** 'Rosa Mundi'

**491** 'Sweet Briar'

## Centenary of Royal National Rose Society

| | | | | | | |
|---|---|---|---|---|---|---|
| **1976** (30 June) 'All-over' phosphor | | | | | | |
| 1006 | **488** | 8½p | multicoloured | 15 | 10 | ☐ ☐ |
| 1007 | **489** | 10p | multicoloured | 40 | 40 | ☐ ☐ |
| 1008 | **490** | 11p | multicoloured | 50 | 50 | ☐ ☐ |
| 1009 | **491** | 13p | multicoloured | 65 | 65 | ☐ ☐ |
| Set of 4 | | | | 1·50 | 1·50 | ☐ ☐ |
| First Day Cover | | | | | 2·00 | ☐ |
| Presentation Pack (P.O. Pack No.81) | | | | 3·00 | | ☐ |
| PHQ Cards (set of 4) (16) | | | | 30·00 | 38·00 | ☐ ☐ |
| Set of 4 Gutter Pairs | | | | 3·25 | | ☐ |
| Set of 4 Traffic Light Gutter Pairs | | | | 10·00 | | ☐ |

**492** Archdruid

**493** Morris Dancing

| | |
|---|---|
| Highland Gathering Na Geamannan | Eisteddfod Genedlaethol Frenhinol Cymru Royal National Eisteddfod of Wales |
| **494** Scots Piper | **495** Welsh Harpist |

## British Cultural Traditions

**1976** (4 Aug.) 'All-over' phosphor

| | | | | |
|---|---|---|---|---|
| 1010 | **492** | 8½p multicoloured | 25 | 20 |
| 1011 | **493** | 10p multicoloured | 40 | 40 |
| 1012 | **494** | 11p multicoloured | 45 | 45 |
| 1013 | **495** | 13p multicoloured | 60 | 60 |
| Set of 4 | | | 1·50 | 1·50 |
| First Day Cover | | | | 2·00 |
| Presentation Pack (P.O. Pack No. 82) | | | 2·50 | |
| PHQ Cards (set of 4) (17) | | | 18·00 | 30·00 |
| Set of 4 Gutter Pairs | | | 3·25 | |
| Set of 4 Traffic Light Gutter Pairs | | | 12·00 | |

| | |
|---|---|
| William Caxton 1476 8½p | William Caxton 1476 10p |
| **496** The Canterbury Tales | **497** The Tretyse of Love |

| | |
|---|---|
| William Caxton 1476 11p | William Caxton 1476 13p |
| **498** Game and Playe of Chesse | **499** Early Printing Press |

## 500th Anniversary of British Printing

**1976** (29 Sept.) 'All-over' phosphor

| | | | | |
|---|---|---|---|---|
| 1014 | **496** | 8½p black, blue and gold | 25 | 20 |
| 1015 | **497** | 10p black, olive-green and gold | 40 | 40 |
| 1016 | **498** | 11p black, grey and gold | 45 | 45 |
| 1017 | **499** | 13p brown, ochre and gold | 60 | 60 |
| Set of 4 | | | 1·50 | 1·50 |
| First Day Cover | | | | 2·00 |
| Presentation Pack (P.O. Pack No. 83) | | | 2·75 | |
| PHQ Cards (set of 4) (18) | | | 10·00 | 28·00 |
| Set of 4 Gutter Pairs | | | 3·25 | |
| Set of 4 Traffic Light Gutter Pairs | | | 7·00 | |

| | |
|---|---|
| English Embroidery c.1272 6½p | English Embroidery c.1340 8½p |
| **500** Virgin and Child | **501** Angel with Crown |

| | |
|---|---|
| English Embroidery c.1320 11p | English Embroidery c.1320 13p |
| **502** Angel appearing to Shepherds | **503** The Three Kings |

## Christmas

**1976** (24 Nov.) Designs show English medieval embroidery. One phosphor band (6½p) or 'all-over' phosphor (others)

| | | | | |
|---|---|---|---|---|
| 1018 | **500** | 6½p multicoloured | 25 | 25 |
| 1019 | **501** | 8½p multicoloured | 35 | 25 |
| 1020 | **502** | 11p multicoloured | 40 | 45 |
| 1021 | **503** | 13p multicoloured | 45 | 50 |
| Set of 4 | | | 1·30 | 1·30 |
| First Day Cover | | | | 1·80 |
| Presentation Pack (P.O. Pack No. 87) | | | 2·75 | |
| PHQ Cards (set of 4) (19) | | | 4·50 | 26·00 |
| Set of 4 Gutter Pairs | | | 2·75 | |
| Set of 4 Traffic Light Gutter Pairs | | | 7·00 | |

## Collectors Pack 1976

**1976** (24 Nov.) Comprises Nos. 997/1021

| | | | |
|---|---|---|---|
| CP1021a | Collectors Pack | 14·00 | |

| | |
|---|---|
| 8½p | 10p |
| **504** Lawn Tennis | **505** Table Tennis |

| | |
|---|---|
| 11p | 13p |
| **506** Squash | **507** Badminton |

## Racket Sports

**1977** (12 Jan.) Phosphorised paper

| | | | | |
|---|---|---|---|---|
| 1022 | **504** | 8½p multicoloured | 25 | 20 |
| 1023 | **505** | 10p multicoloured | 40 | 40 |
| 1024 | **506** | 11p multicoloured | 45 | 40 |
| 1025 | **507** | 13p multicoloured | 45 | 50 |
| Set of 4 | | | 1·40 | 1·40 |
| First Day Cover | | | | 2·00 |
| Presentation Pack (P.O. Pack No. 89) | | | 3·00 | |
| PHQ Cards (set of 4) (20) | | | 8·00 | 24·00 |
| Set of 4 Gutter Pairs | | | 3·00 | |
| Set of 4 Traffic Light Gutter Pairs | | | 7·50 | |

**508**

**1977** (2 Feb.)–**87** Type **508** Ordinary paper

| | | | | | | |
|---|---|---|---|---|---|---|
| 1026 | £1 | bright yellow-green and blackish olive | 3·00 | 25 | ☐ | ☐ |
| 1026b | £1·30 | pale drab and deep greenish blue (3.8.83) | 5·50 | 6·00 | ☐ | ☐ |
| 1026c | £1·33 | pale mauve and grey-black (28.8.84) | 7·50 | 8·00 | ☐ | ☐ |
| 1026d | £1·41 | pale drab and deep greenish blue (17.9.85) | 8·50 | 8·50 | ☐ | ☐ |
| 1026e | £1·50 | pale mauve and grey-black (2.9.86) | 6·00 | 5·00 | ☐ | ☐ |
| 1026f | £1·60 | pale drab and deep greenish blue (15.9.87) | 6·50 | 7·00 | ☐ | ☐ |
| 1027 | £2 | light emerald and purple-brown | 9·00 | 50 | ☐ | ☐ |
| 1028 | £5 | salmon and chalky blue | 22·00 | 3·00 | ☐ | ☐ |
| *Set of 8* | | | 60·00 | 32·00 | ☐ | ☐ |

| | | | |
|---|---|---|---|
| Presentation pack (P.O. Pack No. 91 (small size)) (Nos. 1026, 1027/8) | 48·00 | | ☐ |
| Presentation Pack (P.O. Pack No 13 (large size)) (Nos. 1026, 1027/8) | £180 | | ☐ |
| Presentation Pack (P.O. Pack No. 14) (No. 1026f) | 22·00 | | ☐ |
| *Set of 8 Gutter Pairs* | £140 | | ☐ |
| *Set of 8 Traffic Light Gutter Pairs* | £170 | | ☐ |

First Day Covers

| | | | |
|---|---|---|---|
| 2 Feb. 1977 | Nos. 1026, 1027/8 | 14·00 | ☐ |
| 3 Aug. 1983 | No. 1026b | 6·50 | ☐ |
| 28th Aug. 1984 | No. 1026c | 8·00 | ☐ |
| 17 Sept. 1985 | No. 1026d | 9·00 | ☐ |
| 2 Sept. 1986 | No. 1026e | 6·50 | ☐ |
| 15 Sept. 1987 | No. 1026f | 8·50 | ☐ |

**509** Steroids — Conformational Analysis

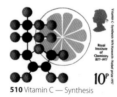

**510** Vitamin C — Synthesis

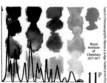

**511** Starch — Chromatography

**512** Salt — Crystallography

**Centenary of Royal Institute of Chemistry**

**1977** (2 Mar.) 'All-over' phosphor

| | | | | | | |
|---|---|---|---|---|---|---|
| 1029 | **509** | 8½p | multicoloured | 25 | 20 | ☐ ☐ |
| 1030 | **510** | 10p | multicoloured | 45 | 45 | ☐ ☐ |
| 1031 | **511** | 11p | multicoloured | 45 | 45 | ☐ ☐ |
| 1032 | **512** | 13p | multicoloured | 45 | 45 | ☐ ☐ |
| *Set of 4* | | | | 1·40 | 1·40 | ☐ ☐ |

| | | | | |
|---|---|---|---|---|
| First Day Cover | | 1·80 | | ☐ |
| Presentation Pack (P.O. Pack No. 92) | 3·00 | | | ☐ |
| PHQ Cards (*set of 4*) (21) | 8·00 | 18·00 | | ☐ ☐ |
| *Set of 4 Gutter Pairs* | 3·00 | | | ☐ |
| *Set of 4 Traffic Light Gutter Pairs* | 7·00 | | | ☐ |

**513**

**Silver Jubilee**

**1977** (11 May–15 June) 'All-over' phosphor

| | | | | | | |
|---|---|---|---|---|---|---|
| 1033 | **513** | 8½p | multicoloured | 25 | 25 | ☐ ☐ |
| 1034 | | 9p | multicoloured (15 June) | 25 | 25 | ☐ ☐ |
| 1035 | | 10p | multicoloured | 25 | 25 | ☐ ☐ |
| 1036 | | 11p | multicoloured | 50 | 50 | ☐ ☐ |
| 1037 | | 13p | multicoloured | 50 | 50 | ☐ ☐ |
| *Set of 5* | | | | 1·60 | 1·60 | ☐ ☐ |
| First Day Cover (2) | | | | | 2·50 | ☐ ☐ |

| | | | |
|---|---|---|---|
| Presentation Pack (ex 9p) (P.O. Pack No. 94) | 2·00 | | ☐ |
| Souvenir Book (ex 9p) (P.O. Pack No. 93) | 3·00 | | ☐ |
| PHQ Cards (*set of 5*) (22) | 14·00 | 20·00 | ☐ ☐ |
| *Set of 5 Gutter Pairs* | 3·50 | | ☐ |
| *Set of 5 Traffic Light Gutter Pairs* | 6·00 | | ☐ |

**517** 'Gathering of Nations'

**Commonwealth Heads of Government Meeting, London**

**1977** (8 June) 'All-over' phosphor

| | | | | | | |
|---|---|---|---|---|---|---|
| 1038 | **517** | 13p | black, deep green, rose and silver | 50 | 50 | ☐ ☐ |
| First Day Cover | | | | | 1·30 | ☐ ☐ |
| Presentation Pack (P.O. Pack No. 95) | | | 1·50 | | | ☐ |
| PHQ Card (23) | | | 5·00 | 6·00 | | ☐ ☐ |
| Gutter Pair | | | 1·10 | | | ☐ |
| Traffic Light Gutter Pair | | | 1·50 | | | ☐ |

**518** Hedgehog     **519** Brown Hare     **520** Red Squirrel

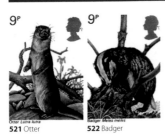

**521** Otter     **522** Badger

### British Wildlife

**1977** (5 Oct.) 'All-over' phosphor

| | | | | |
|---|---|---|---|---|
| 1039 | **518** | 9p multicoloured | 25 | 20 |
| | | a. Strip of 5. Nos.1039/43 | 1·50 | 1·80 |
| 1040 | **519** | 9p multicoloured | 25 | 20 |
| 1041 | **520** | 9p multicoloured | 25 | 20 |
| 1043 | **522** | 9p multicoloured | 25 | 20 |
| Set of 5 | | | 1·50 | 1·80 |
| First Day Cover | | | | 3·00 |
| Presentation Pack (P.O. Pack No. 96) | | | 2·50 | |
| PHQ Cards (set of 5) (25) | | | 3·00 | 7·00 |
| Set of 10 Gutter Strip | | | 3·25 | |
| Set of 10 Traffic Light Gutter Strip | | | 5·00 | |

Nos. 1039/43 were printed together, *se-tenant*, throughout the sheet.

**523** 'Three French Hens, Two Turtle Doves and a Partridge in a Pear Tree'
    **524** 'Six Geese a laying, Five Gold Rings, Four Colly Birds'

**525** 'Eight Maids a-milking, Seven Swans a-swimming'
    **526** 'Ten Pipers piping, Nine Drummers drumming'

**527** 'Twelve Lords a-leaping, Eleven Ladies Dancing'
    **528** 'A Partridge in a Pear Tree'

### Christmas

**1977** (23 Nov.) One centre phosphor band (7p) or 'all-over' phosphor (9p)

| | | | | |
|---|---|---|---|---|
| 1044 | **523** | 7p multicoloured | 20 | 15 |
| | | a. Strip of 5. Nos. 1044/8 | 1·50 | 1·50 |
| 1045 | **524** | 7p multicoloured | 20 | 15 |
| 1046 | **525** | 7p multicoloured | 20 | 15 |
| 1047 | **526** | 7p multicoloured | 20 | 15 |
| 1048 | **527** | 7p multicoloured | 20 | 15 |
| 1049 | **528** | 9p multicoloured | 35 | 30 |
| Set of 6 | | | 1·50 | 1·50 |

| | | | |
|---|---|---|---|
| First Day Cover | | | 2·25 |
| Presentation Pack (P.O. Pack No. 97) | | 2·25 | |
| PHQ Cards (set of 6) (26) | | 3·00 | 6·00 |
| Set of 6 Gutter Pairs | | 3·25 | |
| Set of 6 Traffic Light Gutter Pairs | | 5·50 | |

Nos. 1044/9 depict the carol 'The Twelve Days of Christmas'. Nos. 1044/8 were printed horizontally *se-tenant* throughout the sheet.

### Collectors Pack 1977

**1977** (23 Nov.) Comprises Nos. 1022/5, 1029/49

| | | |
|---|---|---|
| CP1049b | Collectors Pack | 9·00 |

**529** Oil — North Sea Production Platform
    **530** Coal — Modern Pithead

**531** Natural Gas — Flame Rising from Sea
    **532** Electricity — Nuclear Power Station and Uranium Atom

### Energy Resources

**1978** (25 Jan.) 'All-over' phosphor

| | | | | |
|---|---|---|---|---|
| 1050 | **529** | 9p multicoloured | 25 | 25 |
| 1051 | **530** | 10½p multicoloured | 25 | 25 |
| 1052 | **531** | 11p multicoloured | 50 | 50 |
| 1053 | **532** | 13p multicoloured | 50 | 50 |
| Set of 4 | | | 1·40 | 1·40 |
| First Day Cover | | | | 1·80 |
| Presentation Pack (P.O. Pack No. 99) | | | 2·00 | |
| PHQ Cards (set of 4) (27) | | | 3·00 | 6·00 |
| Set of 4 Gutter Pairs | | | 3·00 | |
| Set of 4 Traffic Light Gutter Pairs | | | 4·50 | |

**533** Tower of London
    **534** Holyroodhouse

**535** Caernarvon Castle
    **536** Hampton Court Palace

### British Architecture (Historic Buildings)

**1978** (1 Mar.) 'All-over' phosphor

| | | | | | | |
|---|---|---|---|---|---|---|
| 1054 | **533** | 9p | multicoloured | 25 | 20 | ☐ ☐ |
| 1055 | **534** | 10½p | multicoloured | 25 | 40 | ☐ ☐ |
| 1056 | **535** | 11p | multicoloured | 60 | 40 | ☐ ☐ |
| 1057 | **536** | 13p | multicoloured | 60 | 40 | ☐ ☐ |
| *Set of 4* | | | | 1·50 | 1·50 | ☐ ☐ |
| First Day Cover | | | | | 1·80 | ☐ |
| Presentation Pack (P.O. Pack No. 100) | | | | 2·00 | | ☐ |
| PHQ Cards (*set of 4*) (28) | | | | 3·00 | 6·00 | ☐ ☐ |
| *Set of 4 Gutter Pairs* | | | | 3·25 | | ☐ |
| *Set of 4 Traffic Light Gutter Pairs* | | | | 4·50 | | ☐ |
| **MS**1058 121 × 90 mm. Nos. 1054/7 | | | | 1·50 | 1·75 | ☐ ☐ |
| First Day Cover | | | | | 2·25 | ☐ |

No. **MS**1058 was sold at 53½p, the premium being used for the London 1980 Stamp Exhibition.

**537** State Coach

**538** St. Edward's Crown

**539** The Sovereign's Orb

**540** Imperial State Crown

### 25th Anniversary of Coronation

**1978** (31 May) 'All-over' phosphor

| | | | | | | |
|---|---|---|---|---|---|---|
| 1059 | **537** | 9p | gold and blue | 35 | 25 | ☐ ☐ |
| 1060 | **538** | 10½p | gold and red | 45 | 45 | ☐ ☐ |
| 1061 | **539** | 11p | gold and green | 45 | 45 | ☐ ☐ |
| 1062 | **540** | 13p | gold and violet | 50 | 50 | ☐ ☐ |
| *Set of 4* | | | | 1·60 | 1·50 | ☐ ☐ |
| First Day Cover | | | | | 2·00 | ☐ |
| Presentation Pack (P.O. Pack No. 101) | | | | 2·00 | | ☐ |
| Souvenir Book | | | | 3·00 | | ☐ |
| PHQ Cards (*set of 4*) (29) | | | | 3·00 | 6·00 | ☐ ☐ |
| *Set of 4 Gutter Pairs* | | | | 3·25 | | ☐ |
| *Set of 4 Traffic Light Gutter Pairs* | | | | 4·25 | | ☐ |

**541** Shire Horse

**542** Shetland Pony

**543** Welsh Pony

**544** Thoroughbred

### Horses

**1978** (5 July) 'All-over' phosphor

| | | | | | | |
|---|---|---|---|---|---|---|
| 1063 | **541** | 9p | multicoloured | 20 | 10 | ☐ ☐ |
| 1064 | **542** | 10½p | multicoloured | 35 | 40 | ☐ ☐ |
| 1065 | **543** | 11p | multicoloured | 35 | 45 | ☐ ☐ |
| 1066 | **544** | 13p | multicoloured | 45 | 50 | ☐ ☐ |
| *Set of 4* | | | | 1·20 | 1·30 | ☐ ☐ |
| First Day Cover | | | | | 1·80 | ☐ |
| Presentation Pack (P.O. Pack No. 102) | | | | 1·80 | | ☐ |
| PHQ Cards (*set of 4*) (30) | | | | 2·25 | 5·75 | ☐ ☐ |
| *Set of 4 Gutter Pairs* | | | | 3·00 | | ☐ |
| *Set of 4 Traffic Light Gutter Pairs* | | | | 4·50 | | ☐ |

**545** Penny-farthing and 1884 Safety Bicycle

**546** 1920 Touring Bicycles

**547** Modern Small-wheel Bicycles

**548** 1978 Road-racers

### Centenaries of Cyclists Touring Club and British Cycling Federation

**1978** (2 Aug.) 'All-over' phosphor

| | | | | | | |
|---|---|---|---|---|---|---|
| 1067 | **545** | 9p | multicoloured | 25 | 20 | ☐ ☐ |
| 1068 | **546** | 10½p | multicoloured | 35 | 40 | ☐ ☐ |
| 1069 | **547** | 11p | multicoloured | 40 | 40 | ☐ ☐ |
| 1070 | **548** | 13p | multicoloured | 50 | 50 | ☐ ☐ |
| *Set of 4* | | | | 1·30 | 1·40 | ☐ ☐ |
| First Day Cover | | | | | 1·80 | ☐ |
| Presentation Pack (P.O. Pack No. 103) | | | | 1·80 | | ☐ |
| PHQ Cards (*set of 4*) (31) | | | | 2·25 | 5·00 | ☐ ☐ |
| *Set of 4 Gutter Pairs* | | | | 2·75 | | ☐ |
| *Set of 4 Traffic Light Gutter Pairs* | | | | 4·50 | | ☐ |

**549** Singing Carols round the Christmas Tree

**550** The Waits

**551** 18th-Century Carol Singers

**552** 'The Boar's Head Carol'

### Christmas

**1978** (22 Nov.) One centre phosphor band (7p) or 'all-over' phosphor (others)

| | | | | | | |
|---|---|---|---|---|---|---|
| 1071 | **549** | 7p | multicoloured | 25 | 25 | ☐ ☐ |
| 1072 | **550** | 9p | multicoloured | 25 | 25 | ☐ ☐ |
| 1073 | **551** | 11p | multicoloured | 50 | 50 | ☐ ☐ |
| 1074 | **552** | 13p | multicoloured | 50 | 50 | ☐ ☐ |
| *Set of 4* | | | | 1·40 | 1·40 | ☐ ☐ |

| First Day Cover | | 1·80 | | ☑ |
|---|---|---|---|---|
| Presentation Pack (P.O. Pack No. 104) | 1·80 | | ☐ | |
| PHQ Cards (*set of* 4) (32) | 2·25 | 5·00 | ☐ | ☐ |
| *Set of* 4 Gutter Pairs | 3·00 | | ☐ | |
| *Set of* 4 Traffic Light Gutter Pairs | 4·25 | | ☐ | |

### Collectors Pack 1978

**1978** (22 Nov.) Comprises Nos. 1050/7, 1059/74
| CP1074a | Collectors Pack | 10·00 | ☐ |
|---|---|---|---|

9ᵖ

10½ᵖ

**553** Old English Sheepdog  **554** Welsh Springer Spaniel

11ᵖ

13ᵖ

**555** West. Highland Terrier  **556** Irish Setter

### Dogs

**1979** (7 Feb.) 'All-over' phosphor
| 1075 | **553** | 9p multicoloured | 25 | 20 | ☐ | ☐ |
|---|---|---|---|---|---|---|
| 1076 | **554** | 10½p multicoloured | 40 | 40 | ☐ | ☐ |
| 1077 | **555** | 11p multicoloured | 40 | 40 | ☐ | ☐ |
| 1078 | **556** | 13p multicoloured | 40 | 50 | ☐ | ☐ |
| *Set of* 4 | | | 1·30 | 1·30 | ☐ | ☐ |
| First Day Cover | | | | 1·80 | ☐ | |
| Presentation Pack (P.O. Pack No. 106) | | | 1·80 | | ☐ | |
| PHQ Cards (*set of* 4) (33) | | | 2·50 | 5·00 | ☐ | ☐ |
| *Set of* 4 Gutter Pairs | | | 2·75 | | ☐ | |
| *Set of* 4 Traffic Light Gutter Pairs | | | 4·25 | | ☐ | |

9ᵖ

10½ᵖ

**557** Primrose  **558** Daffodil

11ᵖ

13ᵖ

**559** Bluebell  **560** Snowdrop

### Spring Wild Flowers

**1979** (21 Mar.) 'All-over' phosphor
| 1079 | **557** | 9p multicoloured | 25 | 20 | ☐ | ☐ |
|---|---|---|---|---|---|---|
| 1080 | **558** | 10½p multicoloured | 25 | 45 | ☐ | ☐ |
| 1081 | **559** | 11p multicoloured | 50 | 45 | ☐ | ☐ |
| 1082 | **560** | 13p multicoloured | 50 | 40 | ☐ | ☐ |
| *Set of* 4 | | | 1·40 | 1·40 | ☐ | ☐ |

| First Day Cover | | 1·80 | | ☐ |
|---|---|---|---|---|
| Presentation Pack (P.O. Pack No. 107) | 1·80 | | ☐ | |
| PHQ Cards (*set of* 4) (34) | 2·50 | 4·50 | ☐ | ☐ |
| *Set of* 4 Gutter Pairs | 3·00 | | ☐ | |
| *Set of* 4 Traffic Light Gutter Pairs | 4·25 | | ☐ | |

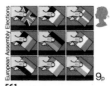
9ᵖ

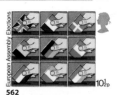
10½ᵖ

**561**  **562**

11ᵖ

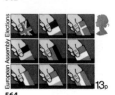
13ᵖ

**563**  **564**

### First Direct Elections to European Assembly

**1979** (9 May) Phosphorised paper
| 1083 | **561** | 9p multicoloured | 25 | 20 | ☐ | ☐ |
|---|---|---|---|---|---|---|
| 1084 | **562** | 10½p multicoloured | 35 | 35 | ☐ | ☐ |
| 1085 | **563** | 11p multicoloured | 40 | 40 | ☐ | ☐ |
| 1086 | **564** | 13p multicoloured | 45 | 40 | ☐ | ☐ |
| *Set of* 4 | | | 1·30 | 1·30 | ☐ | ☐ |
| First Day Cover | | | | 1·80 | ☐ | |
| Presentation Pack (P.O. Pack No. 108) | | | 1·80 | | ☐ | |
| PHQ Cards (*set of* 4) (35) | | | 2·25 | 4·50 | ☐ | ☐ |
| *Set of* 4 Gutter Pairs | | | 2·75 | | ☐ | |
| *Set of* 4 Traffic Light Gutter Pairs | | | 4·25 | | ☐ | |

Nos. 1083/6 show hands placing the flags of the member nations into ballot boxes.

9ᵖ

10½ᵖ

Saddling Mahmoud for The Derby 1936
**565** 'Saddling "Mahmoud" for the Derby, 1936' (Sir Alfred Munnings)

The Liverpool Great National Steeple Chase 1839
**566** 'The Liverpool Great National Steeple Chase, 1839' (aquatint by F. C.Turner)

11ᵖ

13ᵖ

The First Spring Meeting, Newmarket 1793
**567** 'The First. Spring Meeting, Newmarket, 1793' (J.N. Sartorius)

Racing at Dorsett Ferry, Windsor 1684
**568** 'Racing at Dorsett Ferry, Windsor, 1684' (Francis Barlow)

### Horseracing Paintings and Bicentenary of The Derby (9p)

**1979** (6 June) 'All-over' phosphor
| 1087 | **565** | 9p multicoloured | 25 | 25 | ☑ | ☐ |
|---|---|---|---|---|---|---|
| 1088 | **566** | 10½p multicoloured | 25 | 25 | ☐ | ☐ |
| 1089 | **567** | 11p multicoloured | 50 | 50 | ☐ | ☐ |
| 1090 | **568** | 13p multicoloured | 50 | 50 | ☐ | ☐ |
| *Set of* 4 | | | 1·40 | 1·40 | ☐ | ☐ |
| First Day Cover | | | | 1·80 | ☐ | |
| Presentation Pack (P.O. Pack No. 109) | | | 1·80 | | ☐ | |
| PHQ Cards (*set of* 4) (36) | | | 2·25 | 4·50 | ☐ | ☐ |
| *Set of* 4 Gutter Pairs | | | 3·00 | | ☐ | |

*Set of* 4 Traffic Light Gutter Pairs    4·25    ☐

**569** *The Tale of Peter Rabbit* (Beatrix Potter)

**570** *The Wind in the Willows* (Kenneth Grahame)

**571** *Winnie-the-Pooh* (A.A. Milne)

**572** *Alice's Adventures in Wonderland* (Lewis Carroll)

## International Year of the Child

**1979** (11 July) 'All-over' phosphor

| | | | | | | |
|---|---|---|---|---|---|---|
| 1091 | **569** | 9p | multicoloured | 30 | 25 | ☐ ☐ |
| 1092 | **570** | 10½p | multicoloured | 35 | 35 | ☐ ☐ |
| 1093 | **571** | 11p | multicoloured | 40 | 40 | ☐ ☐ |
| 1094 | **572** | 13p | multicoloured | 60 | 60 | ☐ ☐ |
| *Set of* 4 | | | | 1·50 | 1·50 | ☐ ☐ |
| First Day Cover | | | | | 2·00 | ☐ |
| Presentation Pack (P.O. Pack No. 110) | | | | 1·75 | | ☐ |
| PHQ Cards (*set of* 4) (37) | | | | 2·50 | 4·50 | ☐ ☐ |
| *Set of* 4 Gutter Pairs | | | | 3·50 | | ☐ |
| *Set of* 4 Traffic Light Gutter Pairs | | | | 4·25 | | ☐ |

Nos. 1091/4 depict original illustrations from the four books.

**573** Sir Rowland Hill, 1795-1879

**574** General Post, c 1839

**575** London Post, c 1839

**576** Uniform Postage, 1840

## Death Centenary of Sir Rowland Hill (postal reformer)

**1979** (22 Aug.–24 Oct.) 'All-over' phosphor

| | | | | | | |
|---|---|---|---|---|---|---|
| 1095 | **573** | 10p | multicoloured | 25 | 20 | ☐ ☐ |
| 1096 | **574** | 11½p | multicoloured | 25 | 35 | ☐ ☐ |
| 1097 | **575** | 13p | multicoloured | 50 | 45 | ☐ ☐ |
| 1098 | **576** | 15p | multicoloured | 75 | 50 | ☐ ☐ |
| *Set of* 4 | | | | 1·60 | 1·40 | ☐ ☐ |
| First Day Cover | | | | | 2·00 | ☐ |
| Presentation Pack (P.O. Pack No. 111) | | | | 1·50 | | ☐ |
| PHQ Cards (*set of* 4) (38) | | | | 2·25 | 4·25 | ☐ ☐ |
| *Set of* 4 Gutter Pairs | | | | 3·25 | | ☐ |
| *Set of* 4 Traffic Light Gutter Pairs | | | | 4·25 | | ☐ |
| **MS**1099 89 × 121 mm. Nos. 1095/8 | | | | 1·30 | 1·50 | ☐ ☐ |
| First Day Cover (24 Oct.) | | | | | 1·70 | ☐ |

No. **MS**1099 was sold at 59½p, the premium being used for the London 1980 Stamp Exhibition.

**577** Policeman on the Beat

**578** Policeman directing Traffic

**579** Mounted Policewoman

**580** River Patrol Boat

## 150th Anniversary of Metropolitan Police

**1979** (26 Sept.) Phosphorised paper

| | | | | | | |
|---|---|---|---|---|---|---|
| 1100 | **577** | 10p | multicoloured | 30 | 20 | ☐ ☐ |
| 1101 | **578** | 11½p | multicoloured | 35 | 35 | ☐ ☐ |
| 1102 | **579** | 13p | multicoloured | 40 | 55 | ☐ ☐ |
| 1103 | **580** | 15p | multicoloured | 60 | 55 | ☐ ☐ |
| *Set of* 4 | | | | 1·50 | 1·50 | ☐ ☐ |
| First Day Cover | | | | | 2·00 | ☐ |
| Presentation Pack (P.O. Pack No. 112) | | | | 1·80 | | ☐ |
| PHQ Cards (*set of* 4) (39) | | | | 2·25 | 4·25 | ☐ ☐ |
| *Set of* 4 Gutter Pairs | | | | 3·25 | | ☐ |
| *Set of* 4 Traffic Light Gutter Pairs | | | | 4·25 | | ☐ |

**581** The Three Kings

**582** Angel appearing to the Shepherds

**583** The Nativity

**584** Mary and Joseph travelling to Bethlehem

**585** The Annunciation

## Christmas

**1979** (21 Nov.) One centre phosphor band (8p) or phosphorised paper (others)

| | | | | | | | |
|---|---|---|---|---|---|---|---|
| 1104 | **581** | 8p | multicoloured | 25 | 20 | | |
| 1105 | **582** | 10p | multicoloured | 25 | 25 | | |
| 1106 | **583** | 11½p | multicoloured | 25 | 35 | | |
| 1107 | **584** | 13p | multicoloured | 50 | 50 | | |
| 1108 | **585** | 15p | multicoloured | 50 | 50 | | |
| Set of 5 | | | | 1·60 | 1·60 | | |
| First Day Cover | | | | | 2·00 | | |
| Presentation Pack (P.O. Pack No. 113) | | | | 2·00 | | | |
| PHQ Cards (set of 5) (40) | | | | 2·50 | 4·25 | | |
| Set of 5 Gutter Pairs | | | | 3·50 | | | |
| Set of 5 Traffic Light Gutter Pairs | | | | 4·50 | | | |

## Collectors Pack 1979

**1979** (21 Nov.) Comprises Nos. 1075/98, 1100/8

| | | | | |
|---|---|---|---|---|
| CP1108a | Collectors Pack | | 12·00 | |

**586** Common Kingfisher

**587** Dipper

**588** Moorhen

**589** Yellow Wagtails

## Centenary of Wild Bird Protection Act

**1980** (16 Jan.) Phosphorised paper

| | | | | | | | |
|---|---|---|---|---|---|---|---|
| 1109 | **586** | 10p | multicoloured | 20 | 10 | | |
| 1110 | **587** | 11½p | multicoloured | 40 | 35 | | |
| 1111 | **588** | 13p | multicoloured | 50 | 55 | | |
| 1112 | **589** | 15p | multicoloured | 50 | 55 | | |
| Set of 4 | | | | 1·50 | 1·40 | | |
| First Day Cover | | | | | 2·00 | | |
| Presentation Pack (P.O. Pack No. 115) | | | | 2·25 | | | |
| PHQ Cards (set of 4) (41) | | | | 2·25 | 4·50 | | |
| Set of 4 Gutter Pairs | | | | 3·50 | | | |

**590** *Rocket* approaching Moorish Arch, Liverpool

**591** First and Second Class Carriages passing through Olive Mount Cutting

**592** Third Class Carriage and Sheep Truck crossing Chat Moss

**593** Horsebox and Carriage Truck near Bridgewater Canal

**594** Goods Truck and Mail - coach at Manchester

## 150th Anniversary of Liverpool and Manchester Railway

**1980** (12 Mar.) Phosphorised paper

| | | | | | | | |
|---|---|---|---|---|---|---|---|
| 1113 | **590** | 12p | multicoloured | 20 | 15 | | |
| | | a. | Strip of 5. Nos. 1113/17 | 1·80 | 1·80 | | |
| 1114 | **591** | 12p | multicoloured | 20 | 15 | | |
| 1115 | **592** | 12p | multicoloured | 20 | 15 | | |
| 1116 | **593** | 12p | multicoloured | 20 | 15 | | |
| 1117 | **594** | 12p | multicoloured | 20 | 15 | | |
| Set of 5 | | | | 1·80 | 1·80 | | |
| First Day Cover | | | | | 2·25 | | |
| Presentation Pack (P.O. Pack No. 116) | | | | 2·00 | | | |
| PHQ Cards (set of 5) (42) | | | | 3·25 | 4·50 | | |
| Gutter block of 10 | | | | 3·75 | | | |

Nos. 1113/7 were printed together, *se-tenant*, in horizontal strips of 5 throughout the sheet.

**595** Montage of London Buildings

## 'London 1980' International Stamp Exhibition

**1980** (9 Apr.–7 May) Phosphorised paper. Perf 14½ × 14

| | | | | | | | |
|---|---|---|---|---|---|---|---|
| 1118 | **595** | 50p | agate | 1·50 | 1·50 | | |
| First Day Cover | | | | | 2·00 | | |
| Presentation Pack (P.O. Pack No. 117) | | | | 1·80 | | | |
| PHQ Card (43) | | | | 1·00 | 3·00 | | |
| Gutter Pair | | | | 3·25 | | | |

MS1119 90 × 123 mm. No. 1118          1·50     1·80  ☐ ☐
First Day Cover (7 May)                          2·00  ☐

No. **MS**1119 was sold at 75p, the premium being used for the exhibition.

10½P  Buckingham Palace     12P  The Albert Memorial     13½P  Royal Opera House
**596** Buckingham          **597** The Albert           **598** Royal Opera House
Palace                      Memorial

15P  Hampton Court          17½P  Kensington Palace
**599** Hampton Court       **600** Kensington Palace

## London Landmarks

**1980** (7 May) Phosphorised paper

| | | | | | | |
|---|---|---|---|---|---|---|
| 1120 | **596** | 10½p | multicoloured | 25 | 10 | ☐ ☐ |
| 1121 | **597** | 12p | multicoloured | 25 | 15 | ☐ ☐ |
| 1122 | **598** | 13½p | multicoloured | 40 | 50 | ☐ ☐ |
| 1123 | **599** | 15p | multicoloured | 50 | 75 | ☐ ☐ |
| 1124 | **600** | 17½p | multicoloured | 75 | 75 | ☐ ☐ |
| Set of 5 | | | | 2·00 | 2·00 | ☐ ☐ |
| First Day Cover | | | | | 2·50 | ☐ |
| Presentation Pack (P.O. Pack No. 118) | | | | 2·00 | | ☐ |
| PHQ Cards (set of 5) (43) | | | | 2·25 | 3·00 | ☐ ☐ |
| Set of 5 Gutter Pairs | | | | 4·25 | | ☐ |

**601** Charlotte Brontë         **602** George Eliot
(Jane Eyre)                      (The Mill on the Floss)

**603** Emily Brontë            **604** Mrs Gaskell
(Wuthering Heights)             (North and South)

## Famous Authoresses

**1980** (9 July) Phosphorised paper

| | | | | | | |
|---|---|---|---|---|---|---|
| 1125 | **601** | 12p | multicoloured | 35 | 20 | ☐ ☐ |
| 1126 | **602** | 13½p | multicoloured | 40 | 45 | ☐ ☐ |
| 1127 | **603** | 15p | multicoloured | 40 | 45 | ☐ ☐ |
| 1128 | **604** | 17½p | multicoloured | 50 | 50 | ☐ ☐ |
| Set of 4 | | | | 1·50 | 1·50 | ☐ ☐ |
| First Day Cover | | | | | 2·00 | ☐ |
| Presentation Pack (P.O. Pack No. 119) | | | | 1·75 | | ☐ |
| PHQ Cards (set of 4) (44) | | | | 2·50 | 3·00 | ☐ ☐ |

Set of 4 Gutter Pairs                  3·75          ☐

Nos. 1125/8 show authoresses and scenes from their novels.
Nos. 1125/6 also include the 'Europa' C.E.P.T. emblem.

**605** Queen Elizabeth
the Queen Mother

## 80th Birthday of Queen Elizabeth the Queen Mother

**1980** (4 Aug.) Phosphorised paper

| | | | | | | |
|---|---|---|---|---|---|---|
| 1129 | **605** | 12p | multicoloured | 30 | 50 | ☐ ☐ |
| First Day Cover | | | | | 1·50 | ☐ |
| PHQ Card (45) | | | | 1·00 | 2·00 | ☐ ☐ |
| Gutter Pair | | | | 1·10 | | ☐ |

**606** Sir Henry Wood          **607** Sir Thomas
                                Beecham

**608** Sir Malcolm            **609** Sir John Barbirolli
Sargent

## British Conductors

**1980** (10 Sept.) Phosphorised paper

| | | | | | | |
|---|---|---|---|---|---|---|
| 1130 | **606** | 12p | multicoloured | 30 | 10 | ☐ ☐ |
| 1131 | **607** | 13½p | multicoloured | 45 | 40 | ☐ ☐ |
| 1132 | **608** | 15p | multicoloured | 50 | 55 | ☐ ☐ |
| 1133 | **609** | 17½p | multicoloured | 50 | 55 | ☐ ☐ |
| Set of 4 | | | | 1·60 | 1·50 | ☐ ☐ |
| First Day Cover | | | | | 2·00 | ☐ |
| Presentation Pack (P.O. Pack No. 120) | | | | 1·80 | | ☐ |
| PHQ Cards (set of 4) (46) | | | | 2·25 | 3·75 | ☐ ☐ |
| Set of 4 Gutter Pairs | | | | 3·75 | | ☐ |

**610** Running

**611** Rugby

**612** Boxing

**613** Cricket

## Sports Centenaries

**1980** (10 Oct.) Phosphorised paper. Perf 14 × 14½

| | | | | | | |
|---|---|---|---|---|---|---|
| 1134 | **610** | 12p multicoloured | 25 | 20 | | |
| 1135 | **611** | 13½p multicoloured | 50 | 50 | | |
| 1136 | **612** | 15p multicoloured | 50 | 45 | | |
| 1137 | **613** | 17½p multicoloured | 50 | 50 | | |
| Set of 4 | | | 1·60 | 1·50 | | |
| First Day Cover | | | | 2·00 | | |
| Presentation Pack (P.O. Pack No. 121) | | | 1·75 | | | |
| PHQ Cards (set of 4) (47) | | | 2·25 | 3·75 | | |
| Set of 4 Gutter Pairs | | | 3·75 | | | |

Centenaries:—12p Amateur Athletics Association; 13½p Welsh Rugby Union; 15p Amateur Boxing Association; 17½p First England v Australia Test Match.

**614** Christmas Tree

**615** Candles

**616** Apples and Mistletoe

**617** Crown, Chains and Bell

**618** Holly

## Christmas

**1980** (19 Nov.) One centre phosphor band (10p) or phosphorised paper (others)

| | | | | | | |
|---|---|---|---|---|---|---|
| 1138 | **614** | 10p multicoloured | 20 | 10 | | |
| 1139 | **615** | 12p multicoloured | 20 | 20 | | |
| 1140 | **616** | 13½p multicoloured | 40 | 40 | | |
| 1141 | **617** | 15p multicoloured | 55 | 50 | | |
| 1142 | **618** | 17½p multicoloured | 55 | 50 | | |
| Set of 5 | | | 1·80 | 1·50 | | |
| First Day Cover | | | | 2·00 | | |
| Presentation Pack (P.O. Pack No. 122) | | | 2·00 | | | |
| PHQ Cards (set of 5) (48) | | | 2·25 | 4·00 | | |
| Set of 5 Gutter Pairs | | | 4·50 | | | |

## Collectors Pack 1980

**1980** (19 Nov.) Comprises Nos. 1109/18, 1120/42

| | | | | |
|---|---|---|---|---|
| CP1142a | Collectors Pack | 15·00 | | |

**619** St. Valentine's Day

**620** Morris Dancers

**621** Lammastide

**622** Medieval Mummers

## Folklore

**1981** (6 Feb.) Phosphorised paper

| | | | | | | |
|---|---|---|---|---|---|---|
| 1143 | **619** | 14p multicoloured | 25 | 25 | | |
| 1144 | **620** | 18p multicoloured | 50 | 50 | | |
| 1145 | **621** | 22p multicoloured | 75 | 80 | | |
| 1146 | **622** | 25p multicoloured | 1·00 | 1·10 | | |
| Set of 4 | | | 2·25 | 2·40 | | |
| First Day Cover | | | | 2·00 | | |
| Presentation Pack (P.O. Pack No. 124) | | | 2·25 | | | |
| PHQ Cards (set of 4) (49) | | | 2·25 | 3·25 | | |
| Set of 4 Gutter Pairs | | | 4·50 | | | |

Nos. 1143/4 also include the 'Europa' C.E.P.T. emblem.

**623** Blind Man with Guide Dog

**624** Hands spelling 'Deaf' in Sign Language

**625** Disabled Man in Wheelchair

**626** Disabled Artist. painting with Foot

## International Year of the Disabled

**1981** (25 Mar.) Phosphorised paper

| | | | | | | |
|---|---|---|---|---|---|---|
| 1147 | **623** | 14p multicoloured | 50 | 25 | | |
| 1148 | **624** | 18p multicoloured | 50 | 50 | | |
| 1149 | **625** | 22p multicoloured | 75 | 85 | | |
| 1150 | **626** | 25p multicoloured | 1·00 | 1·00 | | |
| Set of 4 | | | 2·50 | 2·40 | | |
| First Day Cover | | | | 3·00 | | |
| Presentation Pack (P.O. Pack No. 125) | | | 2·25 | | | |
| PHQ Cards (set of 4) (50) | | | 2·25 | 6·00 | | |
| Set of 4 Gutter Pairs | | | 5·25 | | | |

Small Tortoiseshell
**627** Aglais urticae

Large Blue
**628** Maculinea arion

Peacock
**629** Inachis io

Chequered Skipper
**630** Carterocephalus palaemon

## Butterflies

**1981** (13 May) Phosphorised paper

| | | | | | | |
|---|---|---|---|---|---|---|
| 1151 | **627** | 14p multicoloured | 25 | 20 | | |
| 1152 | **628** | 18p multicoloured | 75 | 70 | | |
| 1153 | **629** | 22p multicoloured | 70 | 85 | | |
| 1154 | **630** | 25p multicoloured | 75 | 85 | | |
| Set of 4 | | | 2·25 | 2·40 | | |
| First Day Cover | | | | 3·00 | | |
| Presentation Pack (P.O. Pack No. 126) | | | 2·25 | | | |
| PHQ Cards (set of 4) (51) | | | 2·25 | 6·00 | | |
| Set of 4 Gutter Pairs | | | 4·75 | | | |

Glenfinnan Scotland
**631** Glenfinnan, Scotland

Derwentwater England
**632** Derwentwater, England

Stackpole Head Wales
**633** Stackpole Head, Wales

Giant's Causeway N. Ireland
**634** Giant's Causeway, N. Ireland

St Kilda Scotland
**635** St. Kilda, Scotland

## 50th Anniversary of National Trust for Scotland (British landscapes)

**1981** (24 June) Phosphorised paper

| | | | | | | |
|---|---|---|---|---|---|---|
| 1155 | **631** | 14p multicoloured | 15 | 25 | | |
| 1156 | **632** | 18p multicoloured | 45 | 50 | | |
| 1157 | **633** | 20p multicoloured | 70 | 75 | | |
| 1158 | **634** | 22p multicoloured | 75 | 1·00 | | |
| 1159 | **635** | 25p multicoloured | 90 | 1·00 | | |
| Set of 5 | | | 2·60 | 3·00 | | |
| First Day Cover | | | | 3·50 | | |
| Presentation Pack (P.O. Pack No. 127) | | | 3·00 | | | |
| PHQ Cards (set of 5) (52) | | | 2·50 | 5·00 | | |
| Set of 5 Gutter Pairs | | | 5·50 | | | |

14ᵖ
**636** Prince Charles and Lady Diana Spencer

## Royal Wedding

**1981** (22 July) Phosphorised paper

| | | | | | | |
|---|---|---|---|---|---|---|
| 1160 | **636** | 14p multicoloured | 75 | 25 | | |
| 1161 | | 25p multicoloured | 1·50 | 1·50 | | |
| Set of 2 | | | 2·00 | 1·50 | | |
| First Day Cover | | | | 2·75 | | |
| Presentation Pack (P.O. Pack No. 127a) | | | 3·00 | | | |
| Souvenir Book | | | 3·00 | | | |
| PHQ Cards (set of 2) (53) | | | 1·50 | 5·00 | | |
| Set of 2 Gutter Pairs | | | 4·25 | | | |

The Duke of Edinburgh's Award
14ᵖ Expeditions
**637** 'Expeditions'

The Duke of Edinburgh's Award
18ᵖ Skills
**638** 'Skills'

The Duke of Edinburgh's Award
22ᵖ Service
**639** 'Service'

The Duke of Edinburgh's Award
25ᵖ Recreation
**640** 'Recreation'

## 25th Anniversary of Duke of Edinburgh's Award Scheme

**1981** (12 Aug.) Phosphorised paper. Perf 14

| | | | | | | |
|---|---|---|---|---|---|---|
| 1162 | **637** | 14p multicoloured | 25 | 20 | | |
| 1163 | **638** | 18p multicoloured | 45 | 50 | | |
| 1164 | **639** | 22p multicoloured | 80 | 80 | | |
| 1165 | **640** | 25p multicoloured | 90 | 1·00 | | |

| | | | |
|---|---|---|---|
| Set of 4 | | 2·25 | 2·40 |
| First Day Cover | | | 3·00 |
| Presentation Pack (P.O. Pack No. 128) | | 2·50 | |
| PHQ Cards (set of 4) (54) | | 2·50 | 4·50 |
| Set of 4 Gutter Pairs | | 5·00 | |

**641** Cockle-dredging from *Lindsey II*

**642** Hauling Trawl Net

**643** Lobster Potting

**644** Hoisting Seine Net

### Fishing Industry

**1981** (23 Sept.) Phosphorised paper

| | | | | | |
|---|---|---|---|---|---|
| 1166 | **641** | 14p | multicoloured | 25 | 25 |
| 1167 | **642** | 18p | multicoloured | 50 | 50 |
| 1168 | **643** | 22p | multicoloured | 85 | 85 |
| 1169 | **644** | 25p | multicoloured | 85 | 85 |
| Set of 4 | | | | 2·25 | 2·25 |
| First Day Cover | | | | | 2·40 |
| Presentation Pack (P.O. Pack No. 129) | | | | 2·50 | |
| PHQ Cards (set of 4) (55) | | | | 2·25 | 4·50 |
| Set of 4 Gutter Pairs | | | | 5·00 | |

Nos. 1166/9 were issued on the occasion of the centenary of Royal National Mission to Deep Sea Fishermen.

**645** Father Christmas

**646** Jesus Christ

**647** Flying Angel

**648** Joseph and Mary arriving at Bethlehem

**649** Three Kings approaching Bethlehem

### Christmas. Children's Pictures

**1981** (18 Nov.) One phosphor band (11½p) or phosphorised paper (others)

| | | | | | |
|---|---|---|---|---|---|
| 1170 | **645** | 11½p | multicoloured | 25 | 20 |
| 1171 | **646** | 14p | multicoloured | 35 | 20 |
| 1172 | **647** | 18p | multicoloured | 50 | 60 |
| 1173 | **648** | 22p | multicoloured | 75 | 75 |
| 1174 | **649** | 25p | multicoloured | 85 | 85 |
| Set of 5 | | | | 2·50 | 2·40 |
| First Day Cover | | | | | 3·00 |
| Presentation Pack (P.O. Pack No. 130) | | | | 3·00 | |
| PHQ Cards (set of 5) (56) | | | | 2·25 | 5·50 |
| Set of 5 Gutter Pairs | | | | 5·25 | |

### Collectors Pack 1981

**1981** (18 Nov.) Comprises Nos. 1143/74

| | | | |
|---|---|---|---|
| CP1174a | Collectors Pack | 19·00 | |

**650** Charles Darwin and Giant Tortoises

**651** Darwin and Marine Iguanas

**652** Darwin, Cactus Ground Finch and Large Ground Finch

**653** Darwin and Prehistoric Skulls

### Death Centenary of Charles Darwin

**1982** (10 Feb.) Phosphorised paper

| | | | | | |
|---|---|---|---|---|---|
| 1175 | **650** | 15½p | multicoloured | 50 | 20 |
| 1176 | **651** | 19½p | multicoloured | 50 | 60 |
| 1177 | **652** | 26p | multicoloured | 75 | 85 |
| 1178 | **653** | 29p | multicoloured | 95 | 90 |
| Set of 4 | | | | 2·50 | 2·40 |
| First Day Cover | | | | | 3·00 |
| Presentation Pack (P.O. Pack No. 132) | | | | 3·00 | |
| PHQ Cards (set of 4) (57) | | | | 2·50 | 6·00 |
| Set of 4 Gutter Pairs | | | | 5·25 | |

**654** Boys' Brigade

**655** Girls' Brigade

**656** Boy Scout Movement

**657** Girl Guide Movement

**662** Henry VIII and *Mary Rose*  **663** Admiral Blake and *Triumph*

**664** Lord Nelson and HMS *Victory*  **665** Lord Fisher and HMS *Dreadnought*

**666** Viscount Cunningham and HMS *Warspite*

## Youth Organizations

**1982** (24 Mar.) Phosphorised paper

| | | | | | | |
|---|---|---|---|---|---|---|
| 1179 | **654** | 15½p multicoloured | 25 | 15 | | |
| 1180 | **655** | 19½p multicoloured | 50 | 50 | | |
| 1181 | **656** | 26p multicoloured | 85 | 85 | | |
| 1182 | **657** | 29p multicoloured | 1·00 | 1·10 | | |
| Set of 4 | | | 2·40 | 2·40 | | |
| First Day Cover | | | | 3·00 | | |
| Presentation Pack (P.O. Pack No. 133) | | | 3·00 | | | |
| PHQ Cards (*set of* 4) (58) | | | 2·50 | 6·00 | | |
| Set of 4 Gutter Pairs | | | 5·25 | | | |

Nos. 1179/82 were issued on the occasion of the 75th anniversary of the Boy Scout Movement, the 125th birth anniversary of Lord Baden-Powell and the centenary of the Boys' Brigade (1983).

**658** Ballerina

**659** Harlequin

**660** Hamlet

**661** Opera Singer

## Europa. British Theatre

**1982** (28 Apr.) Phosphorised paper

| | | | | | | |
|---|---|---|---|---|---|---|
| 1183 | **658** | 15½p multicoloured | 25 | 15 | | |
| 1184 | **659** | 19½p multicoloured | 50 | 50 | | |
| 1185 | **660** | 26p multicoloured | 85 | 1·00 | | |
| 1186 | **661** | 29p multicoloured | 1·00 | 1·00 | | |
| Set of 4 | | | 2·40 | 2·40 | | |
| First Day Cover | | | | 3·00 | | |
| Presentation Pack (P.O. Pack No. 134) | | | 3·00 | | | |
| PHQ Cards (*set of* 4) (59) | | | 2·50 | 6·00 | | |
| Set of 4 Gutter Pairs | | | 5·25 | | | |

## Maritime Heritage

**1982** (16 June) Phosphorised paper

| | | | | | | |
|---|---|---|---|---|---|---|
| 1187 | **662** | 15½p multicoloured | 35 | 25 | | |
| 1188 | **663** | 19½p multicoloured | 50 | 50 | | |
| 1189 | **664** | 24p multicoloured | 75 | 85 | | |
| 1190 | **665** | 26p multicoloured | 75 | 85 | | |
| 1191 | **666** | 29p multicoloured | 1·00 | 1·00 | | |
| Set of 5 | | | 3·00 | 3·25 | | |
| First Day Cover | | | | 4·00 | | |
| Presentation Pack (P.O. Pack No. 136) | | | 3·50 | | | |
| PHQ Cards (*set of* 5) (60) | | | 2·50 | 6·00 | | |
| Set of 5 Gutter Pairs | | | 6·50 | | | |

**667** 'Strawberry Thief' (William Morris)

**668** Untitled (Steiner and Co)

**669** 'Cherry Orchard' (Paul Nash)

**670** 'Chevron' (Andrew Foster)

### British Textiles

**1982** (23 July) Phosphorised paper

| | | | | | | |
|---|---|---|---|---|---|---|
| 1192 | **667** | 15½p multicoloured | 25 | 25 | ☐ | ☐ |
| 1193 | **668** | 19½p multicoloured | 75 | 75 | ☐ | ☐ |
| 1194 | **669** | 26p multicoloured | 75 | 1·00 | ☐ | ☐ |
| 1195 | **670** | 29p multicoloured | 1·00 | 1·25 | ☐ | ☐ |
| *Set of 4* | | | 2·50 | 2·75 | ☐ | ☐ |
| First Day Cover | | | | 3·25 | ☐ | |
| Presentation Pack (P.O. Pack No. 137) | | | 3·00 | | ☐ | |
| PHQ Cards (*set of 4*) (61) | | | 2·50 | 6·00 | ☐ | ☐ |
| *Set of 4 Gutter Pairs* | | | 5·50 | | | |

Nos 1192/5 were issued on the occasion of the 250th birth anniversary of Sir Richard Arkwright (inventor of spinning machine).

671 Development of Communications

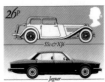

672 Modern Technological Aids

### Information Technology

**1982** (8 Sept.) Phosphorised paper. Perf 14 × 15

| | | | | | | |
|---|---|---|---|---|---|---|
| 1196 | **671** | 15½p multicoloured | 50 | 25 | ☐ | ☐ |
| 1197 | **672** | 26p multicoloured | 75 | 1·00 | ☐ | ☐ |
| *Set of 2* | | | 1·10 | 1·10 | ☐ | ☐ |
| First Day Cover | | | | 1·75 | | ☐ |
| Presentation Pack (P.O. Pack No. 138) | | | 2·00 | | ☐ | |
| PHQ Cards (*set of 2*) (62) | | | 2·00 | 5·25 | ☐ | ☐ |
| *Set of 2 Gutter Pairs* | | | 2·75 | | ☐ | |

673 Austin 'Seven' and 'Metro'    674 Ford 'Model T' and 'Escort'

675 Jaguar 'SS1' and 'XJ6'    676 Rolls-Royce 'Silver Ghost' and 'Silver Spirit'

### British Motor Industry

**1982** (13 Oct.) Phosphorised paper. Perf 14½ × 14

| | | | | | | |
|---|---|---|---|---|---|---|
| 1198 | **673** | 15½p multicoloured | 50 | 25 | ☐ | ☐ |
| 1199 | **674** | 19½p multicoloured | 75 | 75 | ☐ | ☐ |
| 1200 | **675** | 26p multicoloured | 75 | 75 | ☐ | ☐ |
| 1201 | **676** | 29p multicoloured | 1·00 | 1·00 | ☐ | ☐ |
| *Set of 4* | | | 2·75 | 2·75 | ☐ | ☐ |
| First Day Cover | | | | 3·00 | | ☐ |
| Presentation Pack (P.O. Pack No. 139) | | | 3·25 | | ☐ | |
| PHQ Cards (*set of 4*) (63) | | | 2·50 | 6·00 | ☐ | ☐ |
| *Set of 4 Gutter Pairs* | | | 5·50 | | ☐ | |

677 'While Shepherds Watched'    678 'The Holly and the Ivy'

679 'I Saw Three Ships'    680 'We Three Kings'

681 'Good King Wenceslas'

### Christmas. Carols

**1982** (17 Nov.) One phosphor band (12½p) or phosphorised paper (others)

| | | | | | | |
|---|---|---|---|---|---|---|
| 1202 | **677** | 12½p multicoloured | 30 | 30 | ☐ | ☐ |
| 1203 | **678** | 15½p multicoloured | 50 | 30 | ☐ | ☐ |
| 1204 | **679** | 19½p multicoloured | 65 | 75 | ☐ | ☐ |
| 1205 | **680** | 26p multicoloured | 75 | 90 | ☐ | ☐ |
| 1206 | **681** | 29p multicoloured | 1·00 | 1·00 | ☐ | ☐ |
| *Set of 5* | | | 3·00 | 3·00 | ☐ | ☐ |
| First Day Cover | | | | 3·25 | | ☐ |
| Presentation Pack (P.O. Pack No. 140) | | | 3·50 | | ☐ | |
| PHQ Cards (*set of 5*) (64) | | | 2·50 | 6·00 | ☐ | ☐ |
| *Set of 5 Gutter Pairs* | | | 6·50 | | ☐ | |

### Collectors Pack 1982

**1982** (17 Nov.) Comprises Nos. 1175/1206

| | | | | |
|---|---|---|---|---|
| CP1206a | Collectors Pack | | 22·00 | ☐ |

682 Atlantic Salmon    683 Northern Pike

684 Brown Trout    685 Eurasian Perch

### British River Fish

**1983** (26 Jan.) Phosphorised paper

| | | | | | | |
|---|---|---|---|---|---|---|
| 1207 | **682** | 15½p multicoloured | 30 | 35 | ☐ | ☐ |
| 1208 | **683** | 19½p multicoloured | 60 | 60 | ☐ | ☐ |
| 1209 | **684** | 26p multicoloured | 75 | 85 | ☐ | ☐ |
| 1210 | **685** | 29p multicoloured | 1·00 | 1·10 | ☐ | ☐ |
| *Set of 4* | | | 2·50 | 2·50 | ☐ | ☐ |

| First Day Cover | | 3·00 | ☐ |
| Presentation Pack (P.O. Pack No. 142) | 3·00 | | ☐ |
| PHQ Cards (*set of* 4) (65) | 3·00 | 7·00 | ☐ ☐ |
| *Set of* 4 Gutter Pairs | 5·50 | | ☐ |

**686** Tropical Island

**687** Desert

**688** Temperate Farmland

**689** Mountain Range

## Commonwealth Day. Geographical Regions

**1983** (9 Mar.) Phosphorised paper

| 1211 | **686** | 15½p | multicoloured | 40 | 30 | ☐ ☐ |
| 1212 | **687** | 19½p | multicoloured | 75 | 75 | ☐ ☐ |
| 1213 | **688** | 26p | multicoloured | 75 | 75 | ☐ ☐ |
| 1214 | **689** | 29p | multicoloured | 1·00 | 1·00 | ☐ ☐ |
| *Set of* 4 | | | | 2·50 | 2·50 | ☐ ☐ |
| First Day Cover | | | | | 3·00 | ☐ |
| Presentation Pack (P.O. Pack No. 143) | | | | 3·00 | | ☐ |
| PHQ Cards (*set of* 4) (66) | | | | 2·50 | 6·50 | ☐ ☐ |
| *Set of* 4 Gutter Pairs | | | | 5·50 | | ☐ |

**690** Humber Bridge

**691** Thames Flood Barrier

**692** *Iolair* (oilfield emergency support vessel)

## Europa. Engineering Achievements

**1983** (25 May) Phosphorised paper

| 1215 | **690** | 16p | multicoloured | 50 | 40 | ☐ ☐ |
| 1216 | **691** | 20½p | multicoloured | 1·00 | 1·00 | ☐ ☐ |
| 1217 | **692** | 28p | multicoloured | 1·00 | 1·00 | ☐ ☐ |
| *Set of* 3 | | | | 2·25 | 2·00 | ☐ ☐ |
| First Day Cover | | | | | 2·50 | ☐ |
| Presentation Pack (P.O. Pack No. 144) | | | | 3·00 | | ☐ |
| PHQ Cards (*set of* 3) (67) | | | | 2·50 | 5·75 | ☐ ☐ |
| *Set of* 3 Gutter Pairs | | | | 5·00 | | ☐ |

**693** Musketeer and Pikeman, The Royal Scots (1633)

**694** Fusilier and Ensign, The Royal Welch Fusiliers (mid-18th century)

**695** Riflemen, 95th Rifles (The Royal Green Jackets) (1805)

**696** Sergeant (khaki service uniform) and Guardsman full dress), The Irish Guards (1900).

**697** Paratroopers, The Parachute Regiment (1983)

## British Army Uniforms

**1983** (6 July) Phosphorised paper

| 1218 | **693** | 16p | multicoloured | 50 | 30 | ☐ ☐ |
| 1219 | **694** | 20½p | multicoloured | 50 | 60 | ☐ ☐ |
| 1220 | **695** | 26p | multicoloured | 75 | 90 | ☐ ☐ |
| 1221 | **696** | 28p | multicoloured | 75 | 90 | ☐ ☐ |
| 1222 | **697** | 31p | multicoloured | 75 | 85 | ☐ ☐ |
| *Set of* 5 | | | | 3·00 | 3·25 | ☐ ☐ |
| First Day Cover | | | | | 3·75 | ☐ |
| Presentation Pack (P.O. Pack No. 145) | | | | 3·50 | | ☐ |
| PHQ Cards (*set of* 5) (68) | | | | 3·50 | 6·50 | ☐ ☐ |
| *Set of* 5 Gutter Pairs | | | | 6·50 | | ☐ |

Nos. 1218/22 were issued on the occasion of the 350th anniversary of The Royal Scots, the senior line regiment of the British Army.

20TH CENTURY GARDEN
SISSINGHURST
**698** 20th-Century Garden, Sissinghurst

19TH CENTURY GARDEN
BIDDULPH GRANGE
**699** 19th-Century Garden, Biddulph Grange

18TH CENTURY GARDEN
**BLENHEIM**
**700** 18th-Century
Garden, Blenheim

17TH CENTURY GARDEN
**PITMEDDEN**
**701** 17th-Century
Garden, Pitmedden

## British Gardens

**1983** (24 Aug.) Phosphorised paper. Perf 14

| | | | | | | |
|---|---|---|---|---|---|---|
| 1223 | **698** | 16p | multicoloured | 50 | 30 | ☐ ☐ |
| 1224 | **699** | 20½p | multicoloured | 50 | 55 | ☐ ☐ |
| 1225 | **700** | 28p | multicoloured | 75 | 1·00 | ☐ ☐ |
| 1226 | **701** | 31p | multicoloured | 1·00 | 1·00 | ☐ ☐ |
| Set of 4 | | | | 2·50 | 2·50 | ☐ ☐ |
| First Day Cover | | | | | 3·00 | ☐ |
| Presentation Pack (P.O. Pack No. 146) | | | | 3·00 | | ☐ |
| PHQ Cards (set of 4) (69) | | | | 3·00 | 6·25 | ☐ ☐ |
| Set of 4 Gutter Pairs | | | | 5·50 | | ☐ |

**702** Merry-go-round

**703** Big Wheel, Helter-skelter and
Performing Animals

**704** Side-shows

**705** Early Produce Fair

## British Fairs

**1983** (5 Oct.) Phosphorised paper

| | | | | | | |
|---|---|---|---|---|---|---|
| 1227 | **702** | 16p | multicoloured | 35 | 35 | ☐ ☐ |
| 1228 | **703** | 20½p | multicoloured | 75 | 75 | ☐ ☐ |
| 1229 | **704** | 28p | multicoloured | 75 | 1·00 | ☐ ☐ |
| 1230 | **705** | 31p | multicoloured | 1·00 | 1·00 | ☐ ☐ |
| Set of 4 | | | | 2·50 | 2·75 | ☐ ☐ |
| First Day Cover | | | | | 3·25 | ☐ |
| Presentation Pack (P.O. Pack No. 147) | | | | 3·00 | | ☐ |
| PHQ Cards (set of 4) (70) | | | | 3·00 | 6·25 | ☐ ☐ |
| Set of 4 Gutter Pairs | | | | 5·50 | | ☐ |

Nos. 1227/30 were issued to mark the 850th anniversary of St Bartholomew's Fair, Smithfield, London.

**706** 'Christmas Post'
(Pillar box)

**707** 'The Three Kings'
(chimney-pots)

**708** 'World at Peace'
(Dove and Blackbird)

**709** 'Light of Christmas'
(street lamp)

**710** 'Christmas Dove'
(hedge sculpture)

## Christmas

**1983** (16 Nov.) One phosphor band (12½p) or phosphorised paper (others)

| | | | | | | |
|---|---|---|---|---|---|---|
| 1231 | **706** | 12½p | multicoloured | 30 | 30 | ☐ ☐ |
| 1232 | **707** | 16p | multicoloured | 50 | 35 | ☐ ☐ |
| 1233 | **708** | 20½p | multicoloured | 75 | 1·00 | ☐ ☐ |
| 1234 | **709** | 28p | multicoloured | 75 | 1·00 | ☐ ☐ |
| 1235 | **710** | 31p | multicoloured | 1·25 | 1·25 | ☐ ☐ |
| Set of 5 | | | | 3·25 | 3·50 | ☐ ☐ |
| First Day Cover | | | | | 4·00 | ☐ |
| Presentation Pack (P.O. Pack No. 148) | | | | 3·50 | | ☐ |
| PHQ Cards (set of 5) (71) | | | | 3·00 | 6·25 | ☐ ☐ |
| Set of 5 Gutter Pairs | | | | 7·00 | | ☐ |

## Collectors Pack 1983

**1983** (16 Nov.) Comprises Nos. 1207/35

| | | | |
|---|---|---|---|
| CP1235a | Collectors Pack | 25·00 | ☐ |

**711** Arms of the College
of Arms

**712** Arms of King Richard III (founder)

**713** Arms of the Earl
Marshal of England

**714** Arms of the City of
London

## 500th Anniversary of College of Arms

**1984** (17 Jan.) Phosphorised paper. Perf 14½

| | | | | | | |
|---|---|---|---|---|---|---|
| 1236 | **711** | 16p | multicoloured | 50 | 30 | ☐ ☐ |
| 1237 | **712** | 20½p | multicoloured | 50 | 65 | ☐ ☐ |
| 1238 | **713** | 28p | multicoloured | 1·00 | 1·10 | ☐ ☐ |
| 1239 | **714** | 31p | multicoloured | 1·25 | 1·25 | ☐ ☐ |
| Set of 4 | | | | 3·00 | 3·00 | ☐ ☐ |
| First Day Cover | | | | | 3·50 | ☐ |
| Presentation Pack (P.O. Pack No. 150) | | | | 3·25 | | ☐ |

| | | | | |
|---|---|---|---|---|
| PHQ Cards (*set of* 4) (72) | 3·00 | 6·50 | ☐ | ☐ |
| *Set of* 4 Gutter Pairs | 6·50 | | ☐ | |

**16ᴾ** Highland Cow
**715** Highland Cow

**20½ᴾ** Chillingham Wild Bull
**716** Chillingham Wild Bull

**26ᴾ** Hereford Bull
**717** Hereford Bull

**28ᴾ** Welsh Black Bull
**718** Welsh Black Bull

**31ᴾ** Irish Moiled Cow
**719** Irish Moiled Cow

## British Cattle

**1984** (6 Mar.) Phosphorised paper

| | | | | | | | |
|---|---|---|---|---|---|---|---|
| 1240 | **715** | 16p | multicoloured | 35 | 30 | ☐ | ☐ |
| 1241 | **716** | 20½p | multicoloured | 60 | 60 | ☐ | ☐ |
| 1242 | **717** | 26p | multicoloured | 80 | 80 | ☐ | ☐ |
| 1243 | **718** | 28p | multicoloured | 90 | 90 | ☐ | ☐ |
| 1244 | **719** | 31p | multicoloured | 1·00 | 1·20 | ☐ | ☐ |
| *Set of* 5 | | | | 3·50 | 3·50 | ☐ | ☐ |
| First Day Cover | | | | | 4·00 | ☐ | |
| Presentation Pack (P.O. Pack No.151) | | | | 4·00 | | ☐ | |
| PHQ Cards (*set of* 5) (73) | | | | 3·00 | 6·50 | ☐ | ☐ |
| *Set of* 5 Gutter Pairs | | | | 7·25 | | ☐ | |

Nos. 1240/4 marked the centenary of the Highland Cattle Society and the bicentenary of the Royal Highland and Agricultural Society of Scotland.

**720** Festival Hall, Liverpool

**721** Milburngate Shopping Centre, Durham

**722** Bush House, Bristol

**723** Commercial Street Housing Scheme, Perth

## Urban Renewal

**1984** (10 Apr.) Phosphorised paper

| | | | | | | | |
|---|---|---|---|---|---|---|---|
| 1245 | **720** | 16p | multicoloured | 35 | 35 | ☐ | ☐ |
| 1246 | **721** | 20½p | multicoloured | 50 | 60 | ☐ | ☐ |
| 1247 | **722** | 28p | multicoloured | 1·25 | 1·25 | ☐ | ☐ |
| 1248 | **723** | 31p | multicoloured | 1·25 | 1·25 | ☐ | ☐ |
| *Set of* 4 | | | | 3·00 | 3·00 | ☐ | ☐ |
| First Day Cover | | | | | 3·50 | ☐ | |
| Presentation Pack (P.O. Pack No.152) | | | | 3·50 | | ☐ | |
| PHQ Cards (*set of* 4) (74) | | | | 3·00 | 6·25 | ☐ | ☐ |
| *Set of* 4 Gutter Pairs | | | | 6·50 | | ☐ | |

Nos. 1245/8 marked the opening of the International Gardens Festival, Liverpool, and the 150th anniversaries of the Royal Institute of British Architects and the Chartered Institute of Building.

**724** C.E.P.T. 25th Anniversary Logo

**725** Abduction of Europa

## Europa. 25th Anniversary of C.E.P.T. and 2nd European Parliamentary Elections

**1984** (15 May) Phosphorised paper

| | | | | | | | |
|---|---|---|---|---|---|---|---|
| 1249 | **724** | 16p | greenish slate, deep blue and gold | 60 | 50 | ☐ | ☐ |
| | | a. | Horiz pair. Nos. 1249/50 | 1·50 | 1·50 | ☐ | ☐ |
| 1250 | **725** | 16p | greenish slate, deep blue, black and gold | 60 | 50 | ☐ | ☐ |
| 1251 | **724** | 20½p | Venetian red, deep magenta and gold | 70 | 40 | ☐ | ☐ |
| | | a. | Horiz pair. Nos. 1251/2 | 2·50 | 2·50 | ☐ | ☐ |
| 1252 | **725** | 20½p | Venetian red, deep magenta, black and gold | 70 | 40 | ☐ | ☐ |
| *Set of* 4 | | | | 3·50 | 3·50 | ☐ | ☐ |
| First Day Cover | | | | | 4·00 | ☐ | |
| Presentation Pack (P.O. Pack No. 153) | | | | 4·00 | | ☐ | |
| PHQ Cards (*set of* 4) (75) | | | | 3·00 | 6·25 | ☐ | ☐ |
| *Set of* 2 Gutter Blocks of 4 | | | | 7·50 | | ☐ | |

Nos. 1249/50 and 1251/2 were each printed together, *se-tenant*, in horizontal pairs throughout the sheets.

**726** Lancaster House

## London Economic Summit Conference

**1984** (5 June) Phosphorised paper

| | | | | | | | |
|---|---|---|---|---|---|---|---|
| 1253 | **726** | 31p | multicoloured | 1·25 | 1·25 | ☐ | ☐ |
| First Day Cover | | | | | 2·25 | ☐ | |
| PHQ Card (76) | | | | 1·00 | 3·50 | ☐ | ☐ |
| Gutter Pair | | | | 2·75 | | ☐ | |

**727** View of Earth from 'Apollo 11'

**728** Navigational Chart of English Channel

**729** Greenwich Observatory

**730** Sir George Airey's Transit Telescope

## Centenary of Greenwich Meridian

**1984** (26 June) Phosphorised paper. Perf 14 × 14½

| | | | | | | |
|---|---|---|---|---|---|---|
| 1254 | **727** | 16p multicoloured | 50 | 35 | ☑ | ☐ |
| 1255 | **728** | 20½p multicoloured | 75 | 80 | ☐ | ☐ |
| 1256 | **729** | 28p multicoloured | 1·00 | 1·00 | ☐ | ☐ |
| 1257 | **730** | 31p multicoloured | 1·00 | 1·10 | ☐ | ☐ |
| Set of 4 | | | 3·00 | 3·00 | ☐ | ☐ |
| First Day Cover | | | | 3·50 | | ☐ |
| Presentation Pack (P.O. Pack No. 154) | | | 3·50 | | ☐ | |
| PHQ Cards (set of 4) (77) | | | 3·00 | 6·25 | ☐ | ☐ |
| Set of 4 Gutter Pairs | | | 6·50 | | ☐ | |

**731** Bath Mail Coach, 1784

**732** Attack on Exeter Mail, 1816

**733** Norwich Mail in Thunderstorm, 1827

**734** Holyhead and Liverpool Mails leaving London, 1828

**735** Edinburgh Mail Snowbound, 1831

## Bicentenary of First Mail Coach Run, Bath and Bristol to London

**1984** (31 July) Phosphorised paper

| | | | | | | |
|---|---|---|---|---|---|---|
| 1258 | **731** | 16p multicoloured | 40 | 35 | ☐ | ☐ |
| | | a. Horiz strip of 5. Nos. 1258/62 | 2·50 | 2·75 | ☐ | ☐ |
| 1259 | **732** | 16p multicoloured | 40 | 35 | ☐ | ☐ |
| 1260 | **733** | 16p multicoloured | 40 | 35 | ☐ | ☐ |
| 1261 | **734** | 16p multicoloured | 40 | 35 | ☐ | ☐ |
| 1262 | **735** | 16p multicoloured | 40 | 35 | ☐ | ☐ |
| Set of 5 | | | 2·50 | 2·75 | ☐ | ☐ |
| First Day Cover | | | | 3·25 | | ☐ |
| Presentation Pack (P.O. Pack No. 155) | | | 3·00 | | ☐ | |
| Souvenir Book | | | 7·50 | | ☐ | |
| PHQ Cards (set of 5) (78) | | | 3·00 | 6·50 | ☐ | ☐ |
| Gutter Block of 10 | | | 6·00 | | ☐ | |

Nos. 1285/62 were printed together, se-tenant, in horizontal strips of five throughout the sheet.

**736** Nigerian Clinic

**737** Violinist and Acropolis, Athens

**738** Building Project, Sri Lanka

**739** British Council Library

## 50th Anniversary of The British Council

**1984** (25 Sept.) Phosphorised paper

| | | | | | | |
|---|---|---|---|---|---|---|
| 1263 | **736** | 17p multicoloured | 50 | 35 | ☐ | ☐ |
| 1264 | **737** | 22p multicoloured | 85 | 1·00 | ☐ | ☐ |
| 1265 | **738** | 31p multicoloured | 85 | 1·00 | ☐ | ☐ |
| 1266 | **739** | 34p multicoloured | 1·00 | 1·00 | ☐ | ☐ |
| Set of 4 | | | 3·00 | 3·00 | ☐ | ☐ |
| First Day Cover | | | | 3·50 | | ☐ |
| Presentation Pack (P.O. Pack No. 156) | | | 3·25 | | ☐ | |
| PHQ Cards (set of 4) (79) | | | 3·00 | 6·25 | ☐ | ☐ |
| Set of 4 Gutter Pairs | | | 6·50 | | | |

**740** The Holy Family

**741** Arrival in Bethlehem

**742** Shepherd and Lamb

**743** Virgin and Child

**744** Offering of Frankincense

## Christmas

**1984** (20 Nov.) One phosphor band (13p) or phosphorised paper (others)

| | | | | |
|---|---|---|---|---|
| 1267 | **740** | 13p multicoloured | 30 | 30 |
| 1268 | **741** | 17p multicoloured | 50 | 50 |
| 1269 | **742** | 22p multicoloured | 75 | 75 |
| 1270 | **743** | 31p multicoloured | 1·00 | 1·00 |
| 1271 | **744** | 34p multicoloured | 1·00 | 1·00 |
| Set of 5 | | | 3·25 | 3·25 |
| First Day Cover | | | | 3·75 |
| Presentation Pack (P.O. Pack No. 157) | | | 3·75 | |
| PHQ Cards (set of 5) (80) | | | 3·00 | 6·25 |
| Set of 5 Gutter Pairs | | | 7·00 | |

## Collectors Pack 1984

**1984** (20 Nov.) Comprises Nos. 1236/71

| | | | |
|---|---|---|---|
| CP1271a | Collectors Pack | 38·00 | |

## Post Office Yearbook

**1984** Comprises Nos. 1236/71 in hardbound book with slip case

| | | | |
|---|---|---|---|
| YB1271a | Yearbook | 85·00 | |

**745** 'Flying Scotsman'

**746** 'Golden Arrow'

**747** 'Cheltenham Flyer'

**748** 'Royal Scot'

**749** 'Cornish Riviera'

## Famous Trains

**1985** (22 Jan.) Phosphorised paper

| | | | | |
|---|---|---|---|---|
| 1272 | **745** | 17p multicoloured | 75 | 35 |
| 1273 | **746** | 22p multicoloured | 75 | 1·00 |
| 1274 | **747** | 29p multicoloured | 1·00 | 1·25 |
| 1275 | **748** | 31p multicoloured | 1·25 | 1·50 |
| 1276 | **749** | 34p multicoloured | 2·50 | 2·50 |
| Set of 5 | | | 5·75 | 6·00 |
| First Day Cover | | | | 6·50 |
| Presentation Pack (P.O. Pack No. 159) | | | 6·00 | |
| PHQ Cards (set of 5) (81) | | | 6·00 | 15·00 |

| | | |
|---|---|---|
| Set of 5 Gutter Pairs | 13·00 | |

Nos. 1272/6 were issued on the occasion of the 150th anniversary of the Great Western Railway Company.

Buff Tailed Bumble Bee
**750** Bombus terrestris (Bee)

Seven Spotted Ladybird
**751** Coccinella septempunctata (ladybird)

**752** Decticus verrucivorus (bush-cricket)

Wart-Biter Bush-Cricket

Stag Beetle
**753** Lucanus cervus (stag beetle)

**754** Anax imperator (dragonfly)

Emperor Dragonfly

## Insects

**1985** (12 Mar.) Phosphorised paper

| | | | | |
|---|---|---|---|---|
| 1277 | **750** | 17p multicoloured | 40 | 35 |
| 1278 | **751** | 22p multicoloured | 60 | 60 |
| 1279 | **752** | 29p multicoloured | 85 | 90 |
| 1280 | **753** | 31p multicoloured | 1·00 | 1·00 |
| 1281 | **754** | 34p multicoloured | 1·00 | 90 |
| Set of 5 | | | 3·25 | 3·50 |
| First Day Cover | | | | 4·00 |
| Presentation Pack (P.O. Pack No. 160) | | | 4·50 | |
| PHQ Cards (set of 5) (82) | | | 3·00 | 7·50 |
| Set of 5 Gutter Pairs | | | 7·00 | |

Nos. 1277/81 were issued on the occasion of the centenaries of the Royal Entomological Society of London's Royal Charter and of the Selborne Society.

SEVENTEEN·PENCE
WATER·MUSIC
George Frideric Handel
**755** 'Water Music', by Handel

TWENTY·TWO·PENCE
THE·PLANETS·SUITE
Gustav Holst
**756** 'The Planets', by Holst

THIRTY·ONE·PENCE
THE·FIRST·CUCKOO
Frederick Delius
**757** 'The First Cuckoo', by Delius

THIRTY·FOUR·PENCE
SEA·PICTURES
Edward Elgar
**758** 'Sea Pictures', by Elgar

## Europa. European Music Year

**1985** (14 May) Phosphorised paper. Perf 14½

| | | | | | | |
|---|---|---|---|---|---|---|
| 1282 | **755** | 17p multicoloured | 55 | 40 | | |
| 1283 | **756** | 22p multicoloured | 75 | 90 | | |
| 1284 | **757** | 31p multicoloured | 1·50 | 1·25 | | |
| 1285 | **758** | 34p multicoloured | 1·50 | 1·25 | | |
| *Set of 4* | | | 4·00 | 3·50 | | |
| First Day Cover | | | | 4·00 | | |
| Presentation Pack (P.O. Pack No. 161) | | | 4·75 | | | |
| PHQ Cards (*set of 4*) (83) | | | 3·00 | 6·50 | | |
| *Set of 4 Gutter Pairs* | | | 8·50 | | | |

Nos. 1282/5 were issued on the occasion of the 300th birth anniversary of Handel.

**759** R.N.L.I. Lifeboat and Signal Flags

**760** Beachy Head Lighthouse and Chart

**761** 'Marecs A' Communications Satellite and Dish Aerials

**762** Buoys

## Safety at Sea

**1985** (18 June) Phosphorised paper. Perf 14

| | | | | | | |
|---|---|---|---|---|---|---|
| 1286 | **759** | 17p multicoloured | 40 | 40 | | |
| 1287 | **760** | 22p multicoloured | 60 | 75 | | |
| 1288 | **761** | 31p multicoloured | 1·00 | 1·00 | | |
| 1289 | **762** | 34p multicoloured | 1·50 | 1·25 | | |
| *Set of 4* | | | 3·00 | 3·25 | | |
| First Day Cover | | | | 3·75 | | |
| Presentation Pack (P.O. Pack No. 162) | | | 3·75 | | | |
| PHQ Cards (*set of 4*) (84) | | | 3·00 | 6·50 | | |
| *Set of 4 Gutter Pairs* | | | 7·00 | | | |

Nos. 1286/9 were issued to mark the bicentenary of the unimmersible lifeboat and the 50th anniversary of Radar.

**763** Datapost Motorcyclist, City of London

**764** Rural Postbus

**765** Parcel Delivery in Winter

**766** Town Letter Delivery

## 350 Years of Royal Mail Public Postal Service

**1985** (30 July) Phosphorised paper

| | | | | | | |
|---|---|---|---|---|---|---|
| 1290 | **763** | 17p multicoloured | 50 | 40 | | |
| 1291 | **764** | 22p multicoloured | 75 | 70 | | |
| 1292 | **765** | 31p multicoloured | 1·00 | 1·00 | | |
| 1293 | **766** | 34p multicoloured | 1·50 | 1·50 | | |
| *Set of 4* | | | 3·00 | 3·25 | | |
| First Day Cover | | | | 3·75 | | |
| Presentation Pack (P.O. Pack No. 163) | | | 3·75 | | | |
| PHQ Cards (*set of 4*) (85) | | | 3·00 | 6·50 | | |
| *Set of 4 Gutter Pairs* | | | 6·50 | | | |

**767** King Arthur and Merlin

**768** The Lady of the Lake

**769** Queen Guinevere and Sir Lancelot

**770** Sir Galahad

## Arthurian Legends

**1985** (3 Sept.) Phosphorised paper

| | | | | | | |
|---|---|---|---|---|---|---|
| 1294 | **767** | 17p multicoloured | 50 | 40 | | |
| 1295 | **768** | 22p multicoloured | 75 | 75 | | |
| 1296 | **769** | 31p multicoloured | 1·25 | 1·25 | | |
| 1297 | **770** | 34p multicoloured | 1·25 | 1·25 | | |
| *Set of 4* | | | 3·50 | 3·25 | | |
| First Day Cover | | | | 3·75 | | |
| Presentation Pack (P.O. Pack No.164) | | | 4·00 | | | |
| PHQ Cards (*set of 4*) (86) | | | 3·00 | 6·50 | | |
| *Set of 4 Gutter Pairs* | | | 7·50 | | | |

Nos. 1294/7 were issued to mark the 500th anniversary of the printing of Sir Thomas Malory's *Morte d'Arthur*.

**771** Peter Sellers (from photo by Bill Brandt)

**772** David Niven (from photo by Cornell Lucas)

**773** Charlie Chaplin (from photo by Lord Snowdon)

**774** Vivien Leigh (from photo by Angus McBean)

**775** Alfred Hitchcock
(from photo by Howard Coster)

## British Film Year

**1985** (8 Oct.) Phosphorised paper. Perf 14½

| | | | | | | |
|---|---|---|---|---|---|---|
| 1298 | **771** | 17p | multicoloured | 45 | 40 | |
| 1299 | **772** | 22p | multicoloured | 60 | 75 | |
| 1300 | **773** | 29p | multicoloured | 1·00 | 1·25 | |
| 1301 | **774** | 31p | multicoloured | 1·10 | 1·50 | |
| 1302 | **775** | 34p | multicoloured | 1·40 | 1·50 | |
| Set of 5 | | | | 4·00 | 4·75 | |
| First Day Cover | | | | | 5·50 | |
| Presentation Pack (P.O. Pack No. 165) | | | | 5·50 | | |
| Souvenir Book | | | | 11·50 | | |
| PHQ Cards (set of 5) (87) | | | | 3·00 | 10·00 | |
| Set of 5 Gutter Pairs | | | | 9·00 | | |

**776** Principal Boy

**777** Genie

**778** Dame

**779** Good Fairy

**780** Pantomime Cat

## Christmas. Pantomime Characters

**1985** (19 Nov.) One phosphor band (12p) or phosphorised paper (others)

| | | | | | | |
|---|---|---|---|---|---|---|
| 1303 | **776** | 12p | multicoloured | 50 | 30 | |
| 1304 | **777** | 17p | multicoloured | 50 | 40 | |
| 1305 | **778** | 22p | multicoloured | 75 | 1·10 | |
| 1306 | **779** | 31p | multicoloured | 1·25 | 1·40 | |
| 1307 | **780** | 34p | multicoloured | 1·25 | 1·40 | |
| Set of 5 | | | | 4·00 | 4·25 | |
| First Day Cover | | | | | 4·75 | |
| Presentation Pack (P.O. Pack No. 166) | | | | 4·25 | | |
| PHQ Cards (set of 5) (88) | | | | 3·00 | 6·50 | |
| Set of 5 Gutter Pairs | | | | 8·50 | | |

## Collectors Pack 1985

**1985** (19 Nov.) Comprises Nos. 1272/1307
CP1307a   Collectors Pack   35·00

## Post Office Yearbook

**1985** Comprises Nos. 1272/1307 in hardbound book with slip case
YB1307a   Yearbook   75·00

17 PENCE · INDUSTRY YEAR 1986
**781** Light Bulb and North
Sea Oil Drilling Rig (Energy)

22 PENCE · INDUSTRY YEAR 1986
**782** Thermometer and
Pharmaceutical Laboratory (Health)

31 PENCE · INDUSTRY YEAR 1986
**783** Garden Hoe and Steel Works
(Steel)

34 PENCE · INDUSTRY YEAR 1986
**784** Loaf of Bread and Cornfield
(Agriculture)

## Industry Year

**1986** (14 Jan.) Phosphorised paper. Perf 14½ × 14

| | | | | | | |
|---|---|---|---|---|---|---|
| 1308 | **781** | 17p | multicoloured | 75 | 40 | |
| 1309 | **782** | 22p | multicoloured | 50 | 75 | |
| 1310 | **783** | 31p | multicoloured | 1·25 | 1·40 | |
| 1311 | **784** | 34p | multicoloured | 1·25 | 1·40 | |
| Set of 4 | | | | 3·50 | 3·50 | |
| First Day Cover | | | | | 4·00 | |
| Presentation Pack (P.O. Pack No. 168) | | | | 3·75 | | |
| PHQ Cards (set of 4) (89) | | | | 3·50 | 6·50 | |
| Set of 4 Gutter Pairs | | | | 7·50 | | |

**785** Dr Edmond Halley as Comet

**786** Giotto Spacecraft approaching
Comet

**787** 'Twice in a Lifetime'

**788** Comet orbiting Sun
and Planets

## Appearance of Halley's Comet

**1986** (18 Feb.) Phosphorised paper

| | | | | | | |
|---|---|---|---|---|---|---|
| 1312 | **785** | 17p | multicoloured | 50 | 40 | |
| 1313 | **786** | 22p | multicoloured | 75 | 75 | |
| 1314 | **787** | 31p | multicoloured | 1·25 | 1·25 | |
| 1315 | **788** | 34p | multicoloured | 1·25 | 1·40 | |
| Set of 4 | | | | 3·50 | 3·50 | |
| First Day Cover | | | | | 4·00 | |
| Presentation Pack (P.O. Pack No. 169) | | | | 3·75 | | |
| PHQ Cards (set of 4) (90) | | | | 3·50 | 6·50 | |
| Set of 4 Gutter Pairs | | | | 7·50 | | |

**789** Queen Elizabeth II in 1928, 1942 and 1952    **790** Queen Elizabeth II in 1958, 1973 and 1982

### 60th Birthday of Queen Elizabeth II

**1986** (21 Apr.) Phosphorised paper

| | | | | | | |
|---|---|---|---|---|---|---|
| 1316 | **789** | 17p multicoloured | 60 | 50 | | |
| | | a. Horiz pair. | | | | |
| | | Nos. 1316/17 | 1·50 | 1·50 | | |
| 1317 | **790** | 17p multicoloured | 60 | 50 | | |
| 1318 | **789** | 34p multicoloured | 1·25 | 1·25 | | |
| | | a. Horiz pair. | | | | |
| | | Nos. 1318/19 | 3·00 | 4·00 | | |
| 1319 | **790** | 34p multicoloured | 1·25 | 1·25 | | |
| *Set of* 4 | | | 4·50 | 5·00 | | |
| First Day Cover | | | | 5·50 | | |
| Presentation Pack (P.O. Pack No. 170) | | | 5·50 | | | |
| Souvenir Book | | | 8·50 | | | |
| PHQ Cards (*set of* 4) (91) | | | 5·00 | 6·50 | | |
| *Set of* 2 Gutter Blocks of 4 | | | 9·50 | | | |

Nos. 1316/17 and 1318/19 were each printed together, *se-tenant*, in horizontal pairs throughout the sheets.

**791** Barn Owl    **792** Pine Marten

**793** Wild Cat    **794** Natterjack Toad

### Europa. Nature Conservation. Endangered Species

**1986** (20 May) Phosphorised paper. Perf 14½ × 14

| | | | | | | |
|---|---|---|---|---|---|---|
| 1320 | **791** | 17p multicoloured | 40 | 45 | | |
| 1321 | **792** | 22p multicoloured | 80 | 1·00 | | |
| 1322 | **793** | 31p multicoloured | 1·50 | 1·25 | | |
| 1323 | **794** | 34p multicoloured | 1·65 | 1·40 | | |
| *Set of* 4 | | | 4·00 | 3·75 | | |
| First Day Cover | | | | 4·25 | | |
| Presentation Pack (P.O. Pack No. 171) | | | 4·50 | | | |
| PHQ Cards (*set of* 4) (92) | | | 3·50 | 6·50 | | |
| *Set of* 4 Gutter Pairs | | | 8·50 | | | |

**795** Peasants Working in Fields    **796** Freemen working at Town Trades

**797** Knight and Retainers    **798** Lord at Banquet

### 900th Anniversary of Domesday Book

**1986** (17 June) Phosphorised paper

| | | | | | | |
|---|---|---|---|---|---|---|
| 1324 | **795** | 17p multicoloured | 40 | 45 | | |
| 1325 | **796** | 22p multicoloured | 85 | 85 | | |
| 1326 | **797** | 31p multicoloured | 1·25 | 1·40 | | |
| 1327 | **798** | 34p multicoloured | 1·25 | 1·40 | | |
| *Set of* 4 | | | 3·50 | 3·75 | | |
| First Day Cover | | | | 4·25 | | |
| Presentation Pack (P.O. Pack No. 172) | | | 4·00 | | | |
| PHQ Cards (*set of* 4) (93) | | | 3·50 | 6·50 | | |
| *Set of* 4 Gutter Pairs | | | 7·50 | | | |

**799** Athletics    **800** Rowing

**801** Weightlifting    **802** Rifle-shooting

**803** Hockey

### Thirteenth Commonwealth Games, Edinburgh (Nos. 1328/31) and World Men's Hockey Cup, London (No. 1332)

**1986** (15 July) Phosphorised paper

| | | | | | | |
|---|---|---|---|---|---|---|
| 1328 | **799** | 17p multicoloured | 40 | 45 | | |
| 1329 | **800** | 22p multicoloured | 55 | 75 | | |
| 1330 | **801** | 29p multicoloured | 75 | 1·00 | | |
| 1331 | **802** | 31p multicoloured | 1·50 | 1·75 | | |
| 1332 | **803** | 34p multicoloured | 1·75 | 1·75 | | |
| *Set of* 5 | | | 4·00 | 4·50 | | |
| First Day Cover | | | | 5·00 | | |
| Presentation Pack (P.O. Pack No. 173) | | | 4·50 | | | |
| PHQ Cards (*set of* 5) (94) | | | 3·50 | 7·50 | | |
| *Set of* 5 Gutter Pairs | | | 8·75 | | | |

No. 1332 also marked the centenary of the Hockey Association.

**804** Prince Andrew and Miss Sarah Ferguson

**805** Prince Andrew and Miss Sarah Ferguson

### Royal Wedding

**1986** (22 July) One side band (12p) or phosphorised paper (17p)

| | | | | | | |
|---|---|---|---|---|---|---|
| 1333 | **804** | 12p multicoloured | 50 | 45 | ☐ | ☐ |
| 1334 | **805** | 17p multicoloured | 1·00 | 1·25 | ☐ | ☐ |
| *Set of 2* | | | 1·50 | 1·50 | ☐ | ☐ |
| First Day Cover | | | | 2·00 | | ☐ |
| Presentation Pack (P.O. Pack No. 174) | | | 1·75 | | ☐ | |
| PHQ Cards (*set of 2*) (95) | | | 2·25 | 5·00 | ☐ | ☐ |
| *Set of 2 Gutter Pairs* | | | 3·25 | | ☐ | |

**806** Stylised Cross on Ballot Paper

### 32nd Commonwealth Parliamentary Conference, London

**1986** (19 Aug.) Phosphorised paper. Perf 14 × 14½

| | | | | | | |
|---|---|---|---|---|---|---|
| 1335 | **806** | 34p multicoloured | 1·25 | 1·25 | ☐ | ☐ |
| First Day Cover | | | | 1·75 | | ☐ |
| PHQ Card (96) | | | 1·00 | 3·00 | ☐ | ☐ |
| Gutter Pair | | | 2·75 | | ☐ | |

**807** Lord Dowding and Hawker Hurricane Mk. I

**808** Lord Tedder and Hawker Typhoon 1B

**809** Lord Trenchard and de Havilland D.H.9A

**810** Sir Arthur Harris and Avro Type 683 Lancaster

**811** Lord Portal and de Havilland DH.98 Mosquito

### History of the Royal Air Force

**1986** (16th Sept.) Phosphorised paper. Perf 14½ × 14

| | | | | | | |
|---|---|---|---|---|---|---|
| 1336 | **807** | 17p multicoloured | 50 | 45 | ☐ | ☐ |
| 1337 | **808** | 22p multicoloured | 75 | 95 | ☐ | ☐ |
| 1338 | **809** | 29p multicoloured | 1·25 | 1·25 | ☐ | ☐ |
| 1339 | **810** | 31p multicoloured | 1·75 | 1·60 | ☐ | ☐ |
| 1340 | **811** | 34p multicoloured | 1·75 | 1·90 | ☐ | ☐ |
| *Set of 5* | | | 5·00 | 5·50 | ☐ | ☐ |
| First Day Cover | | | | 6·00 | | ☐ |
| Presentation Pack (P.O. Pack No. 175) | | | 5·50 | | ☐ | |
| PHQ Cards (*set of 5*) (97) | | | 4·50 | 10·00 | ☐ | ☐ |
| *Set of 5 Gutter Pairs* | | | 12·00 | | ☐ | |

Nos. 1336/40 were issued to celebrate the 50th anniversary of the first R.A.F. Commands.

**812** The Glastonbury Thorn

**813** The Tanad Valley Plygain

**814** The Hebrides Tribute

**815** The Dewsbury Church Knell

**816** The Hereford Boy Bishop

### Christmas. Folk Customs

**1986** (18 Nov.–2 Dec.) One phosphor band (12p, 13p) or phosphorised paper (others)

| | | | | | | |
|---|---|---|---|---|---|---|
| 1341 | **812** | 12p multicoloured *(2 Dec.)* | 50 | 50 | ☐ | ☐ |
| 1342 | | 13p multicoloured | 30 | 40 | ☐ | ☐ |
| 1343 | **813** | 18p multicoloured | 50 | 50 | ☐ | ☐ |
| 1344 | **814** | 22p multicoloured | 1·00 | 1·00 | ☐ | ☐ |
| 1345 | **815** | 31p multicoloured | 1·25 | 1·00 | ☐ | ☐ |
| 1346 | **816** | 34p multicoloured | 1·25 | 1·10 | ☐ | ☐ |
| *Set of 6* | | | 4·25 | 4·00 | ☐ | ☐ |
| First Day Covers (2) | | | | 4·50 | | ☐ |
| Presentation Pack (Nos. 1342/6) (P.O. Pack No. 176) | | | 5·00 | | ☐ | |
| PHQ Cards (*set of 5*) (Nos. 1342/6) (98) | | | 3·50 | 6·50 | ☐ | ☐ |
| *Set of 6 Gutter Pairs* | | | 9·00 | | ☐ | |

## Collectors Pack 1986

**1986** (18 Nov.) Comprises Nos. 1308/40, 1342/6

| | | | | |
|---|---|---|---|---|
| CP1346a | Collectors Pack | 37·00 | | ☐ |

## Post Office Yearbook

**1986** Comprises Nos. 1308/40, 1342/6 in hardbound book with slip case

| | | | | |
|---|---|---|---|---|
| YB1346a | Yearbook | 70·00 | | ☐ |

**817** North American Blanket Flower

**818** Globe Thistle

**819** Echeveria

**820** Autumn Crocus

### Flower Photographs by Alfred Lammer

**1987** (20 Jan.) Phosphorised paper. Perf 14½ × 14

| | | | | | | |
|---|---|---|---|---|---|---|
| 1347 | **817** | 18p multicoloured | 40 | 40 | ☐ | ☐ |
| 1348 | **818** | 22p multicoloured | 70 | 85 | ☐ | ☐ |
| 1349 | **819** | 31p multicoloured | 1·10 | 1·25 | ☐ | ☐ |
| 1350 | **820** | 34p multicoloured | 1·10 | 1·25 | ☐ | ☐ |
| Set of 4 | | | 3·25 | 3·50 | ☐ | ☐ |
| First Day Cover | | | | 4·00 | | ☐ |
| Presentation Pack (P.O. Pack No. 178) | | | 4·00 | | | ☐ |
| PHQ Cards (set of 4) (99) | | | 3·00 | 7·00 | ☐ | ☐ |
| Set of 4 Gutter Pairs | | | 7·50 | | | ☐ |

**821** The Principia Mathematica

**822** Motion of Bodies in Ellipses

**823** Optick Treatise

**824** The System of the World

### 300th Anniversary of The Principia Mathematica by Sir Isaac Newton

**1987** (24 Mar.) Phosphorised paper

| | | | | | | |
|---|---|---|---|---|---|---|
| 1351 | **821** | 18p multicoloured | 50 | 40 | ☐ | ☐ |
| 1352 | **822** | 22p multicoloured | 75 | 75 | ☐ | ☐ |
| 1353 | **823** | 31p multicoloured | 1·25 | 1·50 | ☐ | ☐ |
| 1354 | **824** | 34p multicoloured | 1·25 | 1·25 | ☐ | ☐ |
| Set of 4 | | | 3·50 | 3·50 | ☐ | ☐ |
| First Day Cover | | | | 4·00 | | ☐ |
| Presentation Pack (P.O. Pack No. 179) | | | 4·00 | | | ☐ |
| PHQ Cards (set of 4) (100) | | | 3·00 | 6·50 | ☐ | ☐ |
| Set of 4 Gutter Pairs | | | 8·00 | | | ☐ |

**825** Willis Faber and Dumas Building, Ipswich  **826** Pompidou Centre, Paris

**827** Staatsgalerie, Stuttgart

**828** European Investment Bank, Luxembourg

### Europa. British Architects in Europe

**1987** (12 May) Phosphorised paper

| | | | | | | |
|---|---|---|---|---|---|---|
| 1355 | **825** | 18p multicoloured | 50 | 40 | ☐ | ☐ |
| 1356 | **826** | 22p multicoloured | 75 | 75 | ☐ | ☐ |
| 1357 | **827** | 31p multicoloured | 1·25 | 1·25 | ☐ | ☐ |
| 1358 | **828** | 34p multicoloured | 1·25 | 1·25 | ☐ | ☐ |
| Set of 4 | | | 3·50 | 3·50 | ☐ | ☐ |
| First Day Cover | | | | 4·00 | | ☐ |
| Presentation Pack (P.O. Pack No. 180) | | | 4·00 | | | ☐ |
| PHQ Cards (set of 4) (101) | | | 3·00 | 6·50 | ☐ | ☐ |
| Set of 4 Gutter Pairs | | | 8·00 | | | ☐ |

**829** Brigade Members with Ashford Litter, 1887

**830** Bandaging Blitz Victim, 1940

**831** Volunteer with fainting Girl, 1965

**832** Transport of Transplant Organ by Air Wing, 1987

## Centenary of St John Ambulance Brigade

**1987** (16 June) Phosphorised paper. Perf 14 × 14½

| | | | | | |
|---|---|---|---|---|---|
| 1359 | **829** | 18p multicoloured | 40 | 45 | |
| 1360 | **830** | 22p multicoloured | 60 | 75 | |
| 1361 | **831** | 31p multicoloured | 1·25 | 1·25 | |
| 1362 | **832** | 34p multicoloured | 1·25 | 1·25 | |
| *Set of* 4 | | | 3·25 | 3·50 | |
| First Day Cover | | | | 4·00 | |
| Presentation Pack (P.O. Pack No. 181) | | | 4·00 | | |
| PHQ Cards (*set of* 4) (102) | | | 3·00 | 6·50 | |
| *Set of* 4 Gutter Pairs | | | 8·00 | | |

**833** Arms of the Lord Lyon King of Arms

**834** Scottish Heraldic Banner of Prince Charles

**835** Arms of Royal Scottish Academy of Painting, Sculpture and Architecture

**836** Arms of Royal Society of Edinburgh

## 300th Anniversary of Revival of Order of the Thistle

**1987** (21 July) Phosphorised paper. Perf 14½

| | | | | | |
|---|---|---|---|---|---|
| 1363 | **833** | 18p multicoloured | 50 | 40 | |
| 1364 | **834** | 22p multicoloured | 75 | 90 | |
| 1365 | **835** | 31p multicoloured | 1·40 | 1·40 | |
| 1366 | **836** | 34p multicoloured | 1·50 | 1·40 | |
| *Set of* 4 | | | 3·75 | 3·75 | |
| First Day Cover | | | | 4·25 | |
| Presentation Pack (P.O. Pack No.182) | | | 4·00 | | |
| PHQ Cards (*set of* 4) (103) | | | 3·00 | 6·50 | |
| *Set of* 4 Gutter Pairs | | | 8·00 | | |

**837** Crystal Palace, 'Monarch of the Glen' (Landseer) and Grace Darling

**838** Great Eastern, Beeton's Book of Household Management and Prince Albert

**839** Albert Memorial, Ballot Box and Disraeli

**840** Diamond Jubilee Emblem, Morse Key and Newspaper Placard for Relief of Mafeking

## 150th Anniversary of Queen Victoria's Accession

**1987** (8 Sept.) Phosphorised paper

| | | | | | |
|---|---|---|---|---|---|
| 1367 | **837** | 18p multicoloured | 50 | 45 | |
| 1368 | **838** | 22p multicoloured | 80 | 75 | |
| 1369 | **839** | 31p multicoloured | 1·25 | 1·50 | |
| 1370 | **840** | 34p multicoloured | 1·35 | 1·60 | |
| *Set of* 4 | | | 3·50 | 4·00 | |
| First Day Cover | | | | 4·50 | |
| Presentation Pack (P.O. Pack No. 183) | | | 4·25 | | |
| PHQ Cards (*set of* 4) (104) | | | 3·00 | 6·50 | |
| *Set of* 4 Gutter Pairs | | | 7·50 | | |

**841** Pot by Bernard Leach

**842** Pot by Elizabeth Fritsch

**843** Pot by Lucie Rie

**844** Pot by Hans Coper

## Studio Pottery

**1987** (13 Oct.) Phosphorised paper. Perf 14½ × 14

| | | | | | |
|---|---|---|---|---|---|
| 1371 | **841** | 18p multicoloured | 50 | 40 | |
| 1372 | **842** | 26p multicoloured | 70 | 75 | |
| 1373 | **843** | 31p multicoloured | 1·25 | 1·25 | |
| 1374 | **844** | 34p multicoloured | 1·40 | 1·50 | |
| *Set of* 4 | | | 3·50 | 3·50 | |
| First Day Cover | | | | 4·00 | |
| Presentation Pack (P.O. Pack No. 184) | | | 4·00 | | |
| PHQ Cards (*set of* 4) (105) | | | 3·00 | 6·50 | |
| *Set of* 4 Gutter Pairs | | | 7·50 | | |

Nos. 1371/4 also mark the birth centenary of Bernard Leach, the potter.

**845** Decorating the Christmas Tree

**846** Waiting for Father Christmas

**847** Sleeping Child and Father Christmas in Sleigh

**848** Child reading

**849** Child playing Flute and Snowman

## Christmas

**1987** (17 Nov.) One phosphor band (13p) or phosphorised paper (others)

| | | | | | |
|---|---|---|---|---|---|
| 1375 | **845** | 13p multicoloured | 30 | 30 | |
| 1376 | **846** | 18p multicoloured | 40 | 40 | |
| 1377 | **847** | 26p multicoloured | 80 | 1·00 | |
| 1378 | **848** | 31p multicoloured | 1·10 | 1·25 | |
| 1379 | **849** | 34p multicoloured | 1·25 | 1·50 | |
| Set of 5 | | | 3·50 | 4·00 | |
| First Day Cover | | | | 4·50 | |
| Presentation Pack (P.O. Pack No. 185) | | | 4·00 | | |
| PHQ Cards (set of 5) (106) | | | 3·00 | 6·50 | |
| Set of 5 Gutter Pairs | | | 7·50 | | |

## Collectors Pack 1987

**1987** (17 Nov.) Comprises Nos. 1347/79

| | | | |
|---|---|---|---|
| CP1379a | Collectors Pack | 38·00 | |

## Post Office Yearbook

**1987** Comprises Nos. 1347/79 in hardbound book with slip case

| | | | |
|---|---|---|---|
| YB1379a | Yearbook | 35·00 | |

**850** Short-spined Seascorpion ('Bull-rout') (Jonathan Couch)   **851** Yellow Waterlily (Major Joshua Swatkin)

**852** Whistling ('Bewick's') Swan (Edward Lear)   **853** Morchella esculenta (James Sowerby)

## Bicentenary of Linnean Society. Archive Illustrations

**1988** (19 Jan.) Phosphorised paper

| | | | | | |
|---|---|---|---|---|---|
| 1380 | **850** | 18p multicoloured | 55 | 35 | |
| 1381 | **851** | 26p multicoloured | 85 | 1·00 | |
| 1382 | **852** | 31p multicoloured | 1·10 | 1·25 | |
| 1383 | **853** | 34p multicoloured | 1·25 | 1·40 | |
| Set of 4 | | | 3·25 | 3·50 | |
| First Day Cover | | | | 4·00 | |
| Presentation Pack (P.O. Pack No.187) | | | 4·00 | | |
| PHQ Cards (set of 4) (107) | | | 3·00 | 6·50 | |
| Set of 4 Gutter Pairs | | | 8·00 | | |

**854** Revd William Morgan (Bible translator, 1588)   **855** William Salesbury (New Testament translator, 1567)

**856** Bishop Richard Davies (New Testament translator, 1567)   **857** Bishop Richard Parry (editor of Revised Welsh Bible, 1620)

## 400th Anniversary of Welsh Bible

**1988** (1 Mar.) Phosphorised paper. Perf 14½ × 14

| | | | | | |
|---|---|---|---|---|---|
| 1384 | **854** | 18p multicoloured | 40 | 40 | |
| 1385 | **855** | 26p multicoloured | 70 | 95 | |
| 1386 | **856** | 31p multicoloured | 1·25 | 1·25 | |
| 1387 | **857** | 34p multicoloured | 1·40 | 1·25 | |
| Set of 4 | | | 3·25 | 3·50 | |
| First Day Cover | | | | 4·00 | |
| Presentation Pack (P.O. Pack No. 188) | | | 4·00 | | |
| PHQ Cards (set of 4) (108) | | | 3·00 | 6·50 | |
| Set of 4 Gutter Pairs | | | 8·00 | | |

**858** Gymnastics (Centenary of British Amateur Gymnastics Association)   **859** Downhill Skiing (Ski Club of Great Britain)

**860** Tennis (Centenary of Lawn Tennis Association)   **861** Football (Centenary of Football League)

## Sports Organizations

**1988** (22 Mar.) Phosphorised paper. Perf 14½

| | | | | | |
|---|---|---|---|---|---|
| 1388 | **858** | 18p multicoloured | 40 | 40 | |
| 1389 | **859** | 26p multicoloured | 70 | 80 | |
| 1390 | **860** | 31p multicoloured | 1·10 | 1·25 | |
| 1391 | **861** | 34p multicoloured | 1·25 | 1·25 | |
| Set of 4 | | | 3·25 | 3·25 | |
| First Day Cover | | | | 3·75 | |
| Presentation Pack (P.O. Pack No. 189) | | | 4·00 | | |
| PHQ Cards (set of 4) (109) | | | 2·50 | 6·00 | |
| Set of 4 Gutter Pairs | | | 8·00 | | |

**862** *Mallard* and Mailbags on Pick-up Arms

**863** Loading Transatlantic Mail on Liner *Queen Elizabeth*

**864** Glasgow Tram No. 1173 and Pillar Box

**865** Imperial Airways Handley Page H.P.45 *Horatius* and Airmail Van

### Europa. Transport and Mail Services in 1930's

**1988** (10 May) Phosphorised paper

| | | | | | | |
|---|---|---|---|---|---|---|
| 1392 | **862** | 18p multicoloured | 50 | 35 | | |
| 1393 | **863** | 26p multicoloured | 1·00 | 1·00 | | |
| 1394 | **864** | 31p multicoloured | 1·25 | 1·25 | | |
| 1395 | **865** | 34p multicoloured | 1·60 | 1·50 | | |
| *Set of 4* | | | 4·00 | 3·75 | | |
| First Day Cover | | | | 4·25 | | |
| Presentation Pack (P.O. Pack No.190) | | | 4·25 | | | |
| PHQ Cards (*set of 4*) (110) | | | 2·25 | 6·00 | | |
| *Set of 4 Gutter Pairs* | | | 9·00 | | | |

**866** Early Settler and Sailing Clipper

**867** Queen Elizabeth II with British and Australian Parliament Buildings

**868** W. G. Grace (cricketer) and Tennis Racquet

**869** Shakespeare, John Lennon (entertainer) and Sydney Landmarks

### Bicentenary of Australian Settlement

**1988** (21 June) Phosphorised paper. Perf 14½

| | | | | | | |
|---|---|---|---|---|---|---|
| 1396 | **866** | 18p multicoloured | 40 | 50 | | |
| | | a. Horiz pair. Nos. 1396/7 | 1·25 | 1·50 | | |
| 1397 | **867** | 18p multicoloured | 40 | 50 | | |
| 1398 | **868** | 34p multicoloured | 1·00 | 1·25 | | |
| | | a. Horiz pair. Nos. 1398/9 | 2·50 | 3·00 | | |
| 1399 | **869** | 34p multicoloured | 1·00 | 1·25 | | |
| *Set of 4* | | | 3·50 | 4·00 | | |
| First Day Cover | | | | 4·50 | | |
| Presentation Pack (P.O. Pack No. 191) | | | 4·00 | | | |
| Souvenir Book | | | 15·00 | | | |
| PHQ Cards (*set of 4*) (111) | | | 2·25 | 6·00 | | |
| *Set of 2 Gutter Blocks of 4* | | | 8·25 | | | |

Nos. 1396/7 and 1398/9 were each printed together, *se-tenant*, in horizontal pairs throughout the sheets, each pair showing a background design of the Australian flag.

Stamps in similar designs were also issued by Australia. These are included in the Souvenir Book.

**870** Spanish Galeasse off The Lizard

**871** English Fleet leaving Plymouth

**872** Engagement off Isle of Wight

**873** Attack of English Fire-ships, Calais

**874** Armada in Storm, North Sea

### 400th Anniversary of Spanish Armada

**1988** (19 July) Phosphorised paper

| | | | | | | |
|---|---|---|---|---|---|---|
| 1400 | **870** | 18p multicoloured | 45 | 50 | | |
| | | a. Horiz strip of 5. Nos. 1400/4 | 3·00 | 3·00 | | |
| 1401 | **871** | 18p multicoloured | 45 | 50 | | |
| 1402 | **872** | 18p multicoloured | 45 | 50 | | |
| 1403 | **873** | 18p multicoloured | 45 | 50 | | |
| 1404 | **874** | 18p multicoloured | 45 | 50 | | |
| *Set of 5* | | | 3·00 | 3·00 | | |
| First Day Cover | | | | 3·75 | | |
| Presentation Pack (P.O. Pack No.192) | | | 3·75 | | | |
| PHQ Cards (*set of 5*) (112) | | | 2·75 | 7·00 | | |
| Gutter Block of 10 | | | 8·00 | | | |

Nos. 1400/4 were printed together, *se-tenant*, in horizontal strips of 5 throughout the sheet, forming a composite design.

**875** 'The Owl and the pussy-cat'

**876** 'Edward Lear as a Bird' (self-portrait)

**877** 'Cat' (from alphabet book)

**878** 'There was a Young Lady whose Bonnet . . .' (limerick)

### Death Centenary of Edward Lear (artist and author)

**1988** (6–27 Sept.) Phosphorised paper

| | | | | | |
|---|---|---|---|---|---|
| 1405 | **875** | 19p black, pale cream and carmine | 65 | 40 | ☐ ☐ |
| 1406 | **876** | 27p black, pale cream and yellow | 1·00 | 1·00 | ☐ ☐ |
| 1407 | **877** | 32p black, pale cream and emerald | 1·25 | 1·40 | ☐ ☐ |
| 1408 | **878** | 35p black, pale cream and blue | 1·40 | 1·40 | ☐ ☐ |
| *Set of 4* | | | 4·00 | 3·75 | |
| First Day Cover | | | | 4·25 | ☐ |
| Presentation Pack (P.O. Pack No. 193) | | | 4·25 | | ☐ |
| PHQ Cards (*set of 4*) (113) | | | 2·25 | 6·00 | ☐ ☐ |
| *Set of 4 Gutter Pairs* | | | 9·00 | | ☐ |
| **MS**1409 122 × 90 mm. Nos. 1405/8 | | | 7·00 | 8·50 | ☐ ☐ |
| First Day Cover (27 Sept.) | | | | 8·50 | ☐ |

No. **MS**1409 was sold at £1·35, the premium being used for the 'Stamp World London 90' International Stamp Exhibition.

**CARRICKFERGUS CASTLE**

**879** Carrickfergus Castle

**CAERNARFON CASTLE**

**880** Caernarfon Castle

**EDINBURGH CASTLE**

**881** Edinburgh Castle

**WINDSOR CASTLE**

**882** Windsor Castle

**1988** (18 Oct.) Ordinary paper

| | | | | | |
|---|---|---|---|---|---|
| 1410 | **879** | £1 deep green | 4·25 | 60 | ☐ ☐ |
| 1411 | **880** | £1·50 maroon | 4·50 | 1·25 | ☐ ☐ |
| 1412 | **881** | £2 indigo | 8·00 | 1·50 | ☐ ☐ |
| 1413 | **882** | £5 deep brown | 21·00 | 5·50 | ☐ ☐ |
| *Set of 4* | | | 35·00 | 8·00 | ☐ ☐ |
| First Day Cover | | | | 35·00 | ☐ |
| Presentation Pack (P.O. Pack No. 18) | | | 36·00 | | ☐ |
| *Set of 4 Gutter pairs* | | | 80·00 | | ☐ |

For similar designs, but with silhouette of Queen's head see Nos. 1611/14 and 1993/6.

**883** Journey to Bethlehem

**884** Shepherds and Star

**885** Three Wise Men

**886** Nativity

**887** The Annunciation

### Christmas

**1988** (15 Nov.) One phosphor band (14p) or phosphorised paper (others)

| | | | | | |
|---|---|---|---|---|---|
| 1414 | **883** | 14p multicoloured | 45 | 35 | ☐ ☐ |
| 1415 | **884** | 19p multicoloured | 50 | 50 | ☐ ☐ |
| 1416 | **885** | 27p multicoloured | 90 | 1·00 | ☐ ☐ |
| 1417 | **886** | 32p multicoloured | 1·10 | 1·25 | ☐ ☐ |
| 1418 | **887** | 35p multicoloured | 1·40 | 1·25 | ☐ ☐ |
| *Set of 5* | | | 4·00 | 3·75 | ☐ ☐ |
| First Day Cover | | | | 4·25 | ☐ |
| Presentation Pack (P.O. Pack No. 194) | | | 4·50 | | ☐ |
| PHQ Cards (*set of 5*) (114) | | | 3·00 | 6·00 | ☐ ☐ |
| *Set of 5 Gutter Pairs* | | | 9·50 | | ☐ |

### Collectors Pack 1988

**1988** (15 Nov.) Comprises Nos. 1380/1408, 1414/18

| | | | |
|---|---|---|---|
| CP1418a | Collectors Pack | 35·00 | ☐ |

### Post Office Yearbook

**1988** Comprises Nos. 1380/1404, **MS**1409, 1414/18 in hardbound book with slip case

| | | | |
|---|---|---|---|
| YB1418a | Yearbook | 38·00 | ☐ |

**19P**

PUFFIN *Fratercula arctica*

RSPB 1889-1989
**888** Atlantic Puffin

**27P**

AVOCET *Recurvirostra avosetta*

RSPB 1889-1989
**889** Avocet

**32P**

OYSTERCATCHER *Haematopus ostralegus*

RSPB 1889-1989
**890** Oystercatcher

**35P**

GANNET *Sula bassana*

RSPB 1889-1989
**891** Northern Gannet

### Centenary of Royal Society for the Protection of Birds

**1989** (17 Jan.) Phosphorised paper

| | | | | | |
|---|---|---|---|---|---|
| 1419 | **888** | 19p multicoloured | 35 | 40 | ☐ ☐ |
| 1420 | **889** | 27p multicoloured | 1·25 | 1·25 | ☐ ☐ |
| 1421 | **890** | 32p multicoloured | 1·25 | 1·25 | ☐ ☐ |
| 1422 | **891** | 35p multicoloured | 1·25 | 1·25 | ☐ ☐ |
| *Set of 4* | | | 3·50 | 3·50 | ☐ ☐ |
| First Day Cover | | | | 4·00 | ☐ |
| Presentation Pack (P.O. Pack No. 196) | | | 4·00 | | ☐ |
| PHQ Cards (*set of 4*) (115) | | | 3·00 | 7·00 | ☐ ☐ |
| *Set of 4 Gutter Pairs* | | | 8·50 | | ☐ |

**892** Rose

**893** Cupid

**894** Yachts

**895** Fruit

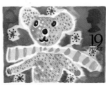
**896** Teddy Bear

## Greetings Booklet Stamps

**1989** (31 Jan.) Phosphorised paper

| | | | | | | | |
|---|---|---|---|---|---|---|---|
| 1423 | **892** | 19p multicoloured | 3·00 | 3·00 | ☐ | ☐ |
| | | a. Booklet pane. | | | | |
| | | Nos. 1423/7 × 2 | 50·00 | | ☐ | |
| | | b. Horiz strip of 5. | | | | |
| | | Nos. 1423/7 | 25·00 | 25·00 | ☐ | ☐ |
| 1424 | **893** | 19p multicoloured | 3·00 | 3·00 | ☐ | ☐ |
| 1425 | **894** | 19p multicoloured | 3·00 | 3·00 | ☐ | ☐ |
| 1426 | **895** | 19p multicoloured | 3·00 | 3·00 | ☐ | ☐ |
| 1427 | **896** | 19p multicoloured | 3·00 | 3·00 | ☐ | ☐ |
| Set of 5 | | | 25·00 | 25·00 | ☐ | ☐ |
| First Day Cover | | | | 20·00 | ☐ | |

Nos. 1423/7 were printed together, *se-tenant*, in horizontal strips of five, two such strips forming the booklet pane with twelve half stamp-size labels.

FOOD AND FARMING YEAR 1989
**897** Fruit and Vegetables

FOOD AND FARMING YEAR 1989
**898** Meat Products

FOOD AND FARMING YEAR 1989
**899** Dairy Produce

FOOD AND FARMING YEAR 1989
**900** Cereal Products

## Food and Farming Year

**1989** (7 Mar.) Phosphorised paper. Perf 14 × 14½

| | | | | | | |
|---|---|---|---|---|---|---|
| 1428 | **897** | 19p multicoloured | 45 | 50 | ☐ | ☐ |
| 1429 | **898** | 27p multicoloured | 90 | 85 | ☐ | ☐ |
| 1430 | **899** | 32p multicoloured | 1·25 | 1·40 | ☐ | ☐ |
| 1431 | **900** | 35p multicoloured | 1·40 | 1·50 | ☐ | ☐ |
| Set of 4 | | | 3·50 | 3·50 | ☐ | ☐ |

| | | | | |
|---|---|---|---|---|
| First Day Cover | | 4·00 | ☐ | |
| Presentation Pack (P.O. Pack No. 197) | 4·00 | | ☐ | |
| PHQ Cards (*set of* 4) (116) | 2·25 | 6·50 | ☐ | ☐ |
| Set of 4 Gutter Pairs | 8·50 | | ☐ | |

**901** Mortar Board (150th Anniv of Public Education in England)

**902** Cross on Ballot Paper (3rd Direct Elections to European Parliament)

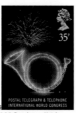
**903** Posthorn (26th Postal, Telegraph and Telephone International Congress, Brighton)

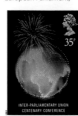
**904** Globe (Inter - Parliamentry Union Centenary Conference, London)

## Anniversaries

**1989** (11 Apr.) Phosphorised paper. Perf 14 × 14½

| | | | | | | |
|---|---|---|---|---|---|---|
| 1432 | **901** | 19p multicoloured | 60 | 60 | ☐ | ☐ |
| | | a. Horiz pair. | | | | |
| | | Nos. 1432/3 | 1·50 | 1·50 | ☐ | ☐ |
| 1433 | **902** | 19p multicoloured | 60 | 60 | ☐ | ☐ |
| 1434 | **903** | 35p multicoloured | 1·00 | 1·00 | ☐ | ☐ |
| | | a. Horiz pair. | | | | |
| | | Nos. 1434/5 | 2·50 | 2·50 | ☐ | ☐ |
| 1435 | **904** | 35p multicoloured | 1·00 | 1·00 | ☐ | ☐ |
| Set of 4 | | | 3·50 | 3·50 | ☐ | ☐ |
| First Day Cover | | | | 4·50 | ☐ | |
| Presentation Pack (P.O. Pack No. 198) | | 4·00 | | ☐ | |
| PHQ Cards (*set of* 4) (117) | | 2·25 | 6·50 | ☐ | ☐ |
| Set of 2 Gutter Strips of 4 | | 8·00 | | ☐ | |

Nos. 1432/3 and 1434/5 were each printed together, *se-tenant*, in horizontal pairs throughout the sheets.

**905** Toy Train and Aeroplanes

**906** Building Bricks

**907** Dice and Board Games

**908** Toy Robot, Boat and Doll's House

## Europa. Games and Toys

**1989** (16 May) Phosphorised paper

| | | | | | | | |
|---|---|---|---|---|---|---|---|
| 1436 | **905** | 19p | multicoloured | 65 | 50 | ☐ | ☐ |
| 1437 | **906** | 27p | multicoloured | 95 | 1·00 | ☐ | ☐ |
| 1438 | **907** | 32p | multicoloured | 1·40 | 1·25 | ☐ | ☐ |
| 1439 | **908** | 35p | multicoloured | 1·50 | 1·25 | ☐ | ☐ |
| *Set of 4* | | | | 4·00 | 3·75 | ☐ | ☐ |
| First Day Cover | | | | | 4·25 | ☐ | ☐ |
| Presentation Pack (P.O. Pack No. 199) | | | | 4·25 | | ☐ | |
| PHQ Cards (*set of 4*) (118) | | | | 2·25 | 6·50 | ☐ | ☐ |
| *Set of 4 Gutter Pairs* | | | | 9·00 | | ☐ | |

**909** Ironbridge,
Shropshire

**910** Tin Mine.
St Agnes Head,
Cornwall

**911** Cotton Mills,
New Lanark, Strathclyde

**912** Pontcysyllite
Aqueduct, Clwyd

**912a**

## Industrial Archaeology

**1989** (4–25 July) Phosphorised paper

| | | | | | | | |
|---|---|---|---|---|---|---|---|
| 1440 | **909** | 19p | multicoloured | 60 | 15 | ☐ | ☐ |
| 1441 | **910** | 27p | multicoloured | 1·00 | 1·10 | ☐ | ☐ |
| 1442 | **911** | 32p | multicoloured | 1·10 | 1·25 | ☐ | ☐ |
| 1443 | **912** | 35p | multicoloured | 1·25 | 1·50 | ☐ | ☐ |
| *Set of 4* | | | | 3·50 | 4·00 | ☐ | ☐ |
| First Day Cover | | | | | 4·50 | ☐ | ☐ |
| Presentation Pack (P.O. Pack No. 200) | | | | 4·00 | | ☐ | |
| PHQ Cards (*set of 4*) (119) | | | | 2·25 | 6·50 | ☐ | ☐ |
| *Set of 4 Gutter Pairs* | | | | 8·50 | | ☐ | |
| **MS**1444 122 × 90 mm. **912a** As Nos. 1440/3 but designs horizontal | | | | 6·00 | 6·50 | ☐ | ☐ |
| First Day Cover (25 July) | | | | | 7·00 | | ☐ |

No. **MS**1444 was sold at £1·40, the premium being used for the 'Stamp World London 90' International Stamp Exhibition.

**913**

**914**

## Booklet Stamps

**1989** (22 Aug.)–**92**

(a) Printed in photogravure by Harrison and Sons. Perf 15 × 14

| | | | | | | | |
|---|---|---|---|---|---|---|---|
| 1445 | **913** | (2nd) | bright blue (1 centre band) | 1·25 | 1·50 | ☐ | ☐ |
| 1446 | | (2nd) | bright blue (1 side band) *(20.3.90)* | 3·00 | 3·25 | ☐ | ☐ |
| 1447 | **914** | (1st) | brownish black (phosphorised paper) | 1·75 | 1·50 | ☐ | ☐ |
| 1448 | | (1st) | brownish black (2 bands) *(20.3.90)* | 3·25 | 3·00 | ☐ | ☐ |

(b) Printed in lithography by Walsall. Perf 14

| | | | | | | | |
|---|---|---|---|---|---|---|---|
| 1449 | **913** | (2nd) | bright blue (1 centre band) | 1·00 | 1·00 | ☐ | ☐ |
| 1450 | **914** | (1st) | blackish brown (2 bands) | 2·50 | 2·75 | ☐ | ☐ |

(c) Printed in lithography by Questa. Perf 15 × 14

| | | | | | | | |
|---|---|---|---|---|---|---|---|
| 1451 | **913** | (2nd) | bright blue (1 centre band) *(19.9.89)* | 1·00 | 1·00 | ☐ | ☐ |
| 1451a | | (2nd) | bright blue (1 side band) *(25.2.92)* | 3·00 | 3·00 | ☐ | ☐ |
| 1452 | **914** | (1st) | brownish black (phosphorised paper) *(19.9.89)* | 2·75 | 2·50 | ☐ | ☐ |
| First Day Cover (Nos. 1445, 1447) | | | | | 6·00 | | ☐ |

For similar stamps showing changed colours see Nos. 1511/16, for those with elliptical perforations Nos. 1664/71 and for self-adhesive versions Nos. 2039/40, 2295, U2941/2, U2945, U2948, U3001/2 and U3271.

No. 1451a exists with the phosphor band at the left or right of the stamp.

**915** Snowflake (×10)

**916** *Calliphora erythrocephala* (fly) (×5)

**917** Blood Cells (×500)

**918** Microchip (×600)

## 150th Anniversary of Royal Microscopical Society

**1989** (5 Sept.) Phosphorised paper. Perf 14½ × 14

| | | | | | | |
|---|---|---|---|---|---|---|
| 1453 | **915** | 19p multicoloured | 45 | 45 | | |
| 1454 | **916** | 27p multicoloured | 95 | 1·00 | | |
| 1455 | **917** | 32p multicoloured | 1·10 | 1·25 | | |
| 1456 | **918** | 35p multicoloured | 1·25 | 1·25 | | |
| *Set of* 4 | | | 3·50 | 3·75 | | |
| First Day Cover | | | | 4·25 | | |
| Presentation Pack (P.O. Pack No. 201) | | | 4·00 | | | |
| PHQ Cards (*set of* 4) (120) | | | 2·25 | 6·50 | | |
| *Set of* 4 Gutter Pairs | | | 8·50 | | | |

**919** Royal Mail Coach

**920** Escort of Blues and Royals

**921** Lord Mayor's Coach

**922** Coach Team passing St Paul's

**923** Blues and Royals Drum Horse

## Lord Mayor's Show, London

**1989** (17 Oct.) Phosphorised paper

| | | | | | | |
|---|---|---|---|---|---|---|
| 1457 | **919** | 20p multicoloured | 45 | 50 | | |
| | | a. Horiz strip of 5. Nos. 1457/61 | 3·00 | 3·00 | | |
| 1458 | **920** | 20p multicoloured | 45 | 50 | | |
| 1459 | **921** | 20p multicoloured | 45 | 50 | | |
| 1460 | **922** | 20p multicoloured | 45 | 50 | | |
| 1461 | **923** | 20p multicoloured | 45 | 50 | | |
| *Set of* 5 | | | 3·00 | 3·00 | | |
| First Day Cover | | | | 3·50 | | |
| Presentation Pack (P.O. Pack No. 202) | | | 3·50 | | | |
| PHQ Cards (*set of* 5) (121) | | | 3·00 | 6·50 | | |
| Gutter Strip of 10 | | | 8·00 | | | |

Nos. 1457/61 commemorate the 800th anniversary of the installation of the first Lord Mayor of London.

Nos. 1457/61 were printed together, *se-tenant*, in horizontal strips of five throughout the sheet, forming a composite design. See also No. 2957.

**924** 14th-century Peasants from Stained-glass Window

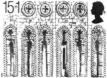

**925** Arches and Roundels, West Front

**926** Octagon Tower

**927** Arcade from West Transept

**928** Triple Arch from West Front

## Christmas. 800th Anniversary of Ely Cathedral

**1989** (14 Nov.) One phosphor band (Nos. 1462/3) or phosphorised paper (others)

| | | | | | | |
|---|---|---|---|---|---|---|
| 1462 | **924** | 15p gold, silver and blue | 40 | 40 | | |
| 1463 | **925** | 15p +1p gold, silver and blue | 50 | 40 | | |
| 1464 | **926** | 20p +1p gold, silver and rosine | 65 | 80 | | |
| 1465 | **927** | 34p +1p gold, silver and emerald | 1·25 | 1·75 | | |
| 1466 | **928** | 37p +1p gold, silver and yellow-olive | 1·40 | 1·90 | | |
| *Set of* 5 | | | 3·75 | 4·75 | | |
| First Day Cover | | | | 5·50 | | |
| Presentation Pack (P.O. Pack No. 203) | | | 4·50 | | | |
| PHQ Cards (*set of* 5) (122) | | | 3·00 | 6·00 | | |
| *Set of* 5 Gutter Pairs | | | 8·50 | | | |

## Collectors Pack 1989

**1989** (14 Nov.) Comprises Nos. 1419/22, 1428/43 and 1453/66

| | | | |
|---|---|---|---|
| CP1466a | Collectors Pack | 38·00 | |

## Post Office Yearbook

**1989** (14 Nov.) Comprises Nos. 1419/22, 1428/44 and 1453/66 in hardback book with slip case

| | | | |
|---|---|---|---|
| YB1466a | Yearbook | 42·00 | |

**929** Queen Victoria
and Queen Elizabeth II

1840·RSPCA·1990
**932** Duckling

1840·RSPCA·1990
**933** Puppy

**150th Anniversary of the Penny Black**

**1990** (10 Jan.–17 Apr.)

(a) Printed in photogravure by Harrison and Sons (Nos. 1468, 1470, 1472 from booklets only). Perf 15 × 14

| | | | | | | |
|---|---|---|---|---|---|---|
| 1467 | **929** | 15p | bright blue (1 centre band) | 80 | 80 | ☐ ☐ |
| 1468 | | 15p | bright blue (1 side band) (30 Jan.) | 3·75 | 3·75 | ☐ ☐ |
| 1469 | | 20p | brownish black and cream (phosphorised paper) | 1·00 | 1·00 | ☐ ☐ |
| 1470 | | 20p | brownish black and cream (2 bands) (30 Jan.) | 2·75 | 2·75 | ☐ ☐ |
| 1471 | | 29p | deep mauve (phosphorised paper) | 1·75 | 1·75 | ☐ ☐ |
| 1472 | | 29p | deep mauve (2 bands) (20 Mar.) | 9·00 | 9·00 | ☐ ☐ |
| 1473 | | 34p | deep bluish grey (phosphorised paper) | 2·00 | 2·00 | ☐ ☐ |
| 1474 | | 37p | rosine (phosphorised paper) | 2·25 | 2·25 | ☐ ☐ |

*Set of* 5 (Nos. 1467, 1469, 1471, 1473/4)  7·00  7·00  ☐ ☐
First Day Cover (Nos. 1467, 1469, 1471, 1473/4)  7·00  ☐
Presentation Pack (Nos. 1467, 1469, 1471, 1473/4) (P.O. Pack No. 21)  9·00  ☐

(b) Litho Walsall (booklets). Perf 14 (30 Jan.)

| | | | | | | |
|---|---|---|---|---|---|---|
| 1475 | **929** | 15p | bright blue (1 centre band) *(30 Jan)* | 1·50 | 1·75 | ☐ ☐ |
| 1476 | | 20p | brownish black and cream (phosphorised paper) *(30 Jan)* | 1·60 | 1·75 | ☐ ☐ |

(c) Litho Questa (booklets). Perf 15 × 14 (17 Apr.)

| | | | | | | |
|---|---|---|---|---|---|---|
| 1477 | **929** | 15p | bright blue (1 centre band) *(17 Apr)* | 2·25 | 2·25 | ☐ ☐ |
| 1478 | | 20p | brownish black (phosphorised paper) *(17 Apr)* | 2·00 | 2·25 | ☐ ☐ |

No. 1468 exists with the phosphor band at the left or right of the stamp.
For Type **929** redrawn with "1st" face value see Nos. 2133 and 2956.

1840·RSPCA·1990
**930** Kitten

1840·RSPCA·1990
**931** Rabbit

**150th Anniversary of Royal Society for Prevention of Cruelty to Animals**

**1990** (23 Jan.) Phosphorised paper. Perf 14 × 14½

| | | | | | |
|---|---|---|---|---|---|
| 1479 | **930** | 20p | multicoloured | 75 | 50 | ☐ ☐ |
| 1480 | **931** | 29p | multicoloured | 1·25 | 1·25 | ☐ ☐ |
| 1481 | **932** | 34p | multicoloured | 1·25 | 1·50 | ☐ ☐ |
| 1482 | **933** | 37p | multicoloured | 1·50 | 1·50 | ☐ ☐ |

*Set of* 4  4·50  4·25  ☐ ☐
First Day Cover  4·75  ☐
Presentation Pack (P.O. Pack No. 205)  4·75  ☐
PHQ Cards (*set of* 4) (123)  3·00  7·50  ☐ ☐
*Set of* 4 Gutter Pairs  9·50  ☐

**934** Teddy Bear

**935** Dennis the Menace

**936** Punch

**937** Cheshire Cat

**938** The Man in the Moon

**939** The Laughing Policeman

**940** Clown

**941** Mona Lisa

**942** Queen of Hearts

**943** Stan Laurel (comedian)

**Greetings Booklet Stamps. 'Smiles'**

**1990** (6 Feb.) Two phosphor bands

| | | | | | | | |
|---|---|---|---|---|---|---|---|
| 1483 | **934** | 20p multicoloured | | 2·25 | 2·40 | | |
| | | a. Booklet pane. | | | | | |
| | | Nos. 1483/92 | | 30·00 | 26·00 | | |
| 1484 | **935** | 20p multicoloured | | 2·25 | 2·40 | | |
| 1485 | **936** | 20p multicoloured | | 2·25 | 2·40 | | |
| 1486 | **937** | 20p multicoloured | | 2·25 | 2·40 | | |
| 1487 | **938** | 20p multicoloured | | 2·25 | 2·40 | | |
| 1488 | **939** | 20p multicoloured | | 2·25 | 2·40 | | |
| 1489 | **940** | 20p multicoloured | | 2·25 | 2·40 | | |
| 1490 | **941** | 20p multicoloured | | 2·25 | 2·40 | | |
| 1491 | **942** | 20p multicoloured | | 2·25 | 2·40 | | |
| 1492 | **943** | 20p gold and grey-black | 2·25 | 2·40 | | |
| Set of 10 | | | | 30·00 | 26·00 | | |
| First Day Cover | | | | | 28·00 | | |

Nos. 1483/92 were printed together, *se-tenant*, in booklet panes of 10.

For these designs with the face value expressed as '1st' see Nos. 1550/9.

> **SET PRICES.** Please note that set prices for booklet greetings stamps are for complete panes. Sets of single stamps are worth considerably less.

**944** Alexandra Palace ('Stamp World London 90' Exhibition)

**945** Glasgow School of Art

**946** British Philatelic Bureau, Edinburgh

**947** Templeton Carpet Factory, Glasgow

**Europa (Nos. 1493 and 1495) and 'Glasgow 1990 European City of Culture' (Nos. 1494 and 1496)**

**1990** (6 Mar.) Phosphorised paper

| | | | | | | |
|---|---|---|---|---|---|---|
| 1493 | **944** | 20p multicoloured | 50 | 40 | | |
| 1494 | **945** | 20p multicoloured | 50 | 40 | | |
| 1495 | **946** | 29p multicoloured | 1·25 | 1·75 | | |
| 1496 | **947** | 37p multicoloured | 1·50 | 1·75 | | |
| Set of 4 | | | 3·50 | 4·00 | | |
| First Day Cover | | | | 4·25 | | |
| Presentation Pack (P.O. Pack No. 206) | | 4·25 | | | |
| PHQ Cards (*set of* 4) (124) | | 3·00 | 6·00 | | |
| Set of 4 Gutter Pairs | | 8·00 | | | |

**948** Export Achievement Award

**949** Technological Achievement Award

**25th Anniversary of Queen's Awards for Export and Technology**

**1990** (10 Apr.) Phosphorised paper. Perf 14 × 14½

| | | | | | | |
|---|---|---|---|---|---|---|
| 1497 | **948** | 20p multicoloured | 50 | 60 | | |
| | | a. Horiz pair. | | | | |
| | | Nos. 1497/8 | 1·40 | 1·60 | | |
| 1498 | **949** | 20p multicoloured | 50 | 60 | | |
| 1499 | **948** | 37p multicoloured | 1·25 | 1·25 | | |
| | | a. Horiz pair. | | | | |
| | | Nos. 1499/1500 | 3·00 | 3·00 | | |
| 1500 | **949** | 37p multicoloured | 1·25 | 1·25 | | |
| Set of 4 | | | 4·00 | 4·25 | | |
| First Day Cover | | | | 4·75 | | |
| Presentation Pack (P.O. Pack No. 207) | | 4·50 | | | |
| PHQ Cards (*set of* 4) (125) | | 3·00 | 6·00 | | |
| Set of 2 Gutter Strips of 4 | | 8·50 | | | |

Nos. 1497/8 and 1499/500 were each printed together, *se-tenant*, in horizontal pairs throughout the sheets.

**949a**

**'Stamp World London 90' International Stamp Exhibition, London. Minature sheet**

**1990** (3 May) Sheet 122 × 90 mm. Phosphorised paper

| | | | | | | |
|---|---|---|---|---|---|---|
| **MS**1501 **949a** 20p brownish black | | | | | | |
| | and cream | | 5·50 | 5·50 | | |
| First Day Cover | | | | 5·75 | | |
| Souvenir Book (Nos. 1467, 1469, 1471, | | | | | | |
| 1473/4 and **MS**1501 | | 20·00 | | | |

No. **MS**1501 was sold at £1, the premium being used for the exhibition.

KEW GARDENS 1840-1990
**950** Cycad and Sir
Joseph Banks Building

KEW GARDENS 1840-1990
**951** Stone Pine and Princess
of Wales Conservatory

KEW GARDENS 1840-1990
**952** Willow Tree and
Palm House

KEW GARDENS 1840-1990
**953** Cedar Tree and
Pagoda

## 150th Anniversary of Kew Gardens

**1990** (5 June) Phosphorised paper

| | | | | | | | |
|---|---|---|---|---|---|---|---|
| 1502 | **950** | 20p | multicoloured | 55 | 40 | ☐ | ☐ |
| 1503 | **951** | 29p | multicoloured | 75 | 1·00 | ☐ | ☐ |
| 1504 | **952** | 34p | multicoloured | 1·25 | 1·60 | ☐ | ☐ |
| 1505 | **953** | 37p | multicoloured | 1·50 | 1·50 | ☐ | ☐ |
| *Set of* 4 | | | | 3·50 | 4·00 | ☐ | ☐ |
| First Day Cover | | | | | 4·50 | ☐ | |
| Presentation Pack (P.O. Pack No. 208) | | | | 4·00 | | ☐ | |
| PHQ Cards (*set of* 4) (126) | | | | 3·00 | 6·00 | ☐ | ☐ |
| *Set of* 4 Gutter Pairs | | | | 8·00 | | ☐ | |

**954** Thomas Hardy and Clyffe Clump, Dorset

## 150th Birth Anniversary of Thomas Hardy (author)

**1990** (10 July) Phosphorised paper

| | | | | | | | |
|---|---|---|---|---|---|---|---|
| 1506 | **954** | 20p | multicoloured | 80 | 75 | ☐ | ☐ |
| First Day Cover | | | | | 1·50 | ☐ | |
| Presentation Pack (P.O. Pack No. 209) | | | | 1·50 | | ☐ | |
| PHQ Card (127) | | | | 1·00 | 2·25 | ☐ | ☐ |
| Gutter Pair | | | | 1·75 | | ☐ | |

**955** Queen Elizabeth
the Queen Mother

**956** Queen Elizabeth

**957** Elizabeth,
Duchess of York

**958** Lady Elizabeth
Bowes-Lyon

## 90th Birthday of Queen Elizabeth the Queen Mother

**1990** (2 Aug.) Phosphorised paper

| | | | | | | | |
|---|---|---|---|---|---|---|---|
| 1507 | **955** | 20p | multicoloured | 95 | 60 | ☐ | ☐ |
| 1508 | **956** | 29p | silver, indigo and grey-blue | 1·40 | 1·50 | ☐ | ☐ |
| 1509 | **957** | 34p | multicoloured | 2·00 | 2·50 | ☐ | ☐ |
| 1510 | **958** | 37p | silver, sepia and stone | 2·25 | 2·50 | ☐ | ☐ |
| *Set of* 4 | | | | 6·00 | 6·50 | ☐ | ☐ |
| First Day Cover | | | | | 7·00 | | ☐ |
| Presentation Pack (P.O. Pack No. 210) | | | | 7·00 | | ☐ | |
| PHQ Cards (*set of* 4) (128) | | | | 5·50 | 8·00 | ☐ | ☐ |
| *Set of* 4 Gutter Pairs | | | | 15·00 | | ☐ | |

For these designs with Queen mother's head and frame in black see Nos. 2280/3.

## Booklet Stamps

**1990** (7 Aug.)–**92** As Types **913/14**, but colours changed

(a) Photo Harrison. Perf 15 × 14

| | | | | | | | |
|---|---|---|---|---|---|---|---|
| 1511 | **913** | (2nd) | deep blue (1 centre band) | 1·50 | 1·50 | ☐ | ☐ |
| 1512 | **914** | (1st) | bright orange-red (phosphorised paper) | 1·50 | 1·50 | ☐ | ☐ |

(b) Litho Questa. Perf 15 × 14

| | | | | | | | |
|---|---|---|---|---|---|---|---|
| 1513 | **913** | (2nd) | deep blue (1 centre band) | 2·50 | 2·75 | ☐ | ☐ |
| 1514 | **914** | (1st) | bright orange-red (phosphorised paper) | 1·50 | 1·00 | ☐ | ☐ |
| 1514a | | (1st) | bright orange-red (2 bands) (25.2.92) | 2·25 | 2·25 | ☐ | ☐ |

(c) Litho Walsall. Perf 14

| | | | | | | | |
|---|---|---|---|---|---|---|---|
| 1515 | **913** | (2nd) | deep blue (1 centre band) | 1·50 | 1·20 | ☐ | ☐ |
| 1516 | **914** | (1st) | bright orange-red (phosphorised paper) | 1·25 | 1·25 | ☐ | ☐ |
| | | c. | Perf 13 | 5·00 | 6·50 | ☐ | ☐ |
| First Day Cover (Nos. 1515/16) | | | | | 5·00 | | ☐ |

For similar stamps with elliptical perforations see Nos. 1664/71.

**959** Victoria Cross

**960** George Cross

**961** Distinguished Service Cross and Distinguished Service Medal

**962** Military Cross and Military Medal

**968** Building a Snowman

**969** Fetching the Christmas Tree

**963** Distinguished Flying Cross and Distinguished Flying Medal

**970** Carol Singing

**971** Tobogganing

### Gallantry Awards

**1990** (11 Sept.) Phosphorised paper

| | | | | | | |
|---|---|---|---|---|---|---|
| 1517 | **959** | 20p multicoloured | 80 | 75 | | |
| 1518 | **960** | 20p multicoloured | 80 | 75 | | |
| 1519 | **961** | 20p multicoloured | 80 | 75 | | |
| 1520 | **962** | 20p multicoloured | 80 | 75 | | |
| 1521 | **963** | 20p multicoloured | 80 | 75 | | |
| Set of 5 | | | 3·75 | 3·50 | | |
| First Day Cover | | | | 4·00 | | |
| Presentation Pack (P.O. Pack No. 211) | | | 4·00 | | | |
| PHQ Cards (set of 5) (129) | | | 3·00 | 8·00 | | |
| Set of 5 Gutter Pairs | | | 8·50 | | | |

For Type **959** with "all-over" phosphor and perf 14 see No. 2666.

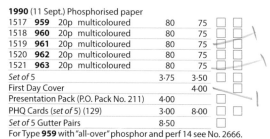

**964** Armagh Observatory, Jodrell Bank Radio Telescope and La Palma Telescope

**965** Newton's Moon and Tides Diagram with Early Telescopes

**966** Greenwich Old Observatory and Early Astronomical Equipment

**967** Stonehenge, Gyroscope and Navigating by Stars

### Astronomy

**1990** (16 Oct.) Phosphorised paper. Perf 14 × 14½

| | | | | | | |
|---|---|---|---|---|---|---|
| 1522 | **964** | 22p multicoloured | 65 | 50 | | |
| 1523 | **965** | 26p multicoloured | 1·00 | 1·10 | | |
| 1524 | **966** | 31p multicoloured | 1·25 | 1·40 | | |
| 1525 | **967** | 37p multicoloured | 1·50 | 1·40 | | |
| Set of 4 | | | 3·75 | 4·00 | | |
| First Day Cover | | | | 4·50 | | |
| Presentation Pack (P.O. Pack No. 212) | | | 4·50 | | | |
| PHQ Cards (set of 4) (130) | | | 3·00 | 7·00 | | |
| Set of 4 Gutter Pairs | | | 8·50 | | | |

Nos. 1522/5 commemorate the centenary of the British Astronomical Association and the bicentenary of the Armagh Observatory.

**972** Ice-skating

### Christmas

**1990** (13 Nov.) One phosphor band (17p) or phosphorised paper (others)

| | | | | | | |
|---|---|---|---|---|---|---|
| 1526 | **968** | 17p multicoloured | 50 | 40 | | |
| 1527 | **969** | 22p multicoloured | 70 | 50 | | |
| 1528 | **970** | 26p multicoloured | 70 | 1·10 | | |
| 1529 | **971** | 31p multicoloured | 1·25 | 1·50 | | |
| 1530 | **972** | 37p multicoloured | 1·25 | 1·50 | | |
| Set of 5 | | | 4·00 | 4·50 | | |
| First Day Cover | | | | 5·00 | | |
| Presentation Pack (P.O. Pack No. 213) | | | 4·50 | | | |
| PHQ Cards (set of 5) (131) | | | 3·00 | 7·00 | | |
| Set of 5 Gutter Pairs | | | 10·00 | | | |

### Collectors Pack 1990

**1990** (13 Nov.) Comprises Nos. 1479/82, 1493/1510 and 1517/30

| | | | |
|---|---|---|---|
| CP1530a | Collectors Pack | 30·00 | |

### Post Office Yearbook

**1990** Comprises Nos. 1479/82, 1493/1500, 1502/10 and 1517/30 in hardback book with slip case

| | | | |
|---|---|---|---|
| YB1530a | Yearbook | 45·00 | |

**973** 'King Charles Spaniel'

**974** 'A Pointer'

975 'Two Hounds in a Landscape'    976 'A Rough Dog'

977 'Fino and Tiny'

### Dogs. Paintings by George Stubbs

**1991** (8 Jan.) Phosphorised paper. Perf 14 × 14½

| | | | | |
|---|---|---|---|---|
| 1531 | **973** | 22p multicoloured | 50 | 50 |
| 1532 | **974** | 26p multicoloured | 75 | 1·25 |
| 1533 | **975** | 31p multicoloured | 1·00 | 1·25 |
| 1534 | **976** | 33p multicoloured | 1·25 | 1·25 |
| 1535 | **977** | 37p multicoloured | 1·25 | 1·25 |
| Set of 5 | | | 4·50 | 5·00 |
| First Day Cover | | | | 5·50 |
| Presentation Pack (P.O. Pack No. 215) | | | 5·00 | |
| PHQ Cards (set of 5) (132) | | | 3·50 | 8·00 |
| Set of 5 Gutter Pairs | | | 11·00 | |

978 Thrush's Nest    979 Shooting Star and Rainbow

980 Magpies and Charm Bracelet    981 Black Cat

982 Common Kingfisher with Key    983 Mallard and Frog

984 Four-leaf Clover in Boot and Match Box    985 Pot of Gold at End of Rainbow

986 Heart-shaped Butterflies    987 Wishing Well and Sixpence

### Greetings Booklet Stamps. 'Good Luck'

**1991** (5 Feb.) Two phosphor bands

| | | | | |
|---|---|---|---|---|
| 1536 | **978** | (1st) multicoloured | 1·25 | 1·00 |
| | | a. Booklet pane. Nos. 1536/45 | 15·00 | 17·00 |
| 1537 | **979** | (1st) multicoloured | 1·25 | 1·00 |
| 1538 | **980** | (1st) multicoloured | 1·25 | 1·00 |
| 1539 | **981** | (1st) multicoloured | 1·25 | 1·00 |
| 1540 | **982** | (1st) multicoloured | 1·25 | 1·00 |
| 1541 | **983** | (1st) multicoloured | 1·25 | 1·00 |
| 1542 | **984** | (1st) multicoloured | 1·25 | 1·00 |
| 1543 | **985** | (1st) multicoloured | 1·25 | 1·00 |
| 1544 | **986** | (1st) multicoloured | 1·25 | 1·00 |
| 1545 | **987** | (1st) multicoloured | 1·25 | 1·00 |
| Set of 10 | | | 15·00 | 17·00 |
| First Day Cover | | | | 19·00 |

Nos. 1536/45 were printed together, *se-tenant*, in booklet panes of 10 stamps and 12 half stamp-size labels, the backgrounds of the stamps forming a composite design.

> **SET PRICES.** Please note that set prices for booklet greetings stamps are for complete panes. Sets of single stamps are worth considerably less.

988 Michael Faraday (inventor of electric motor) (Birth Bicentenary)    989 Charles Babbage (computer science pioneer) (Birth Bicentenary)

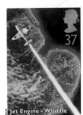

990 Radar Sweep of East Anglia (50th Anniv of Discovery by Sir Robert Watson-Watt)    991 Gloster Whittle E28/39 Aircraft over East Anglia (50th Anniv of First Flight of Sir Frank Whittle's Jet Engine)

### Scientific Achievements

**1991** (5 Mar.) Phosphorised paper

| | | | | |
|---|---|---|---|---|
| 1546 | **988** | 22p multicoloured | 60 | 60 |
| 1547 | **989** | 22p multicoloured | 60 | 60 |
| 1548 | **990** | 31p multicoloured | 1·20 | 1·50 |
| 1549 | **991** | 37p multicoloured | 1·40 | 1·75 |
| Set of 4 | | | 3·50 | 4·00 |
| First Day Cover | | | | 4·50 |

| | | | | | |
|---|---|---|---|---|---|
| Presentation Pack (P.O. Pack No. 216) | | 4·25 | | ☐ | |
| PHQ Cards (set of 4) (133) | | 3·50 | 7·00 | ☐ | ☐ |
| Set of 4 Gutter Pairs | | 8·50 | | ☐ | |

**992** Teddy Bear

### Greetings Booklet Stamps. 'Smiles'

**1991** (26 Mar.) As Nos. 1483/92, but inscribed '1st' as T **992**. Two phosphor bands. Perf 15 × 14

| | | | | | | | |
|---|---|---|---|---|---|---|---|
| 1550 | **992** | (1st) | multicoloured | 1·25 | 1·00 | ☐ | ☐ |
| | | a. | Booklet pane. | | | | |
| | | | Nos. 1550/9 | 12·00 | 13·00 | ☐ | ☐ |
| 1551 | **935** | (1st) | multicoloured | 1·25 | 1·00 | ☐ | ☐ |
| 1552 | **936** | (1st) | multicoloured | 1·25 | 1·00 | ☐ | ☐ |
| 1553 | **937** | (1st) | multicoloured | 1·25 | 1·00 | ☐ | ☐ |
| 1554 | **938** | (1st) | multicoloured | 1·25 | 1·00 | ☐ | ☐ |
| 1555 | **939** | (1st) | multicoloured | 1·25 | 1·00 | ☐ | ☐ |
| 1556 | **940** | (1st) | multicoloured | 1·25 | 1·00 | ☐ | ☐ |
| 1557 | **941** | (1st) | multicoloured | 1·25 | 1·00 | ☐ | ☐ |
| 1558 | **942** | (1st) | multicoloured | 1·25 | 1·00 | ☐ | ☐ |
| 1559 | **943** | (1st) | multicoloured | 1·25 | 1·00 | ☐ | ☐ |
| Set of 10 | | | | 12·00 | 13·00 | ☐ | ☐ |
| First Day Cover | | | | | 14·00 | | ☐ |

Nos. 1550/9 were originally printed together, se-tenant, in booklet panes of 10 stamps and 12 half stamp-size labels.

The stamps were re-issued in sheets of 10 each with se-tenant label on 22 May 2000 in connection with 'customised' stamps available at 'Stamp Show 2000'. The labels show either a pattern of ribbons or a personal photograph.

A similar sheet, but in lithography instead of photogravure, and perforated 14½ × 14, appeared on 3 July 2001 with the labels showing either greetings or a personal photograph.

Three further sheets, also in lithography, appeared on 1 October 2002. One contained Nos. 1550/1 each × 10 with greetings labels. Both designs were also available in sheets of 20 with personal photographs.

**993** Man looking at Space

**994**

**995** Space looking at Man

**996**

### Europa. Europe in Space

**1991** (23 Apr.) Phosphorised paper

| | | | | | | | |
|---|---|---|---|---|---|---|---|
| 1560 | **993** | 22p | multicoloured | 60 | 60 | ☐ | ☐ |
| | | a. | Horiz pair. | | | | |
| | | | Nos. 1560/1 | 1·50 | 1·50 | ☐ | ☐ |
| 1561 | **994** | 22p | multicoloured | 60 | 60 | ☐ | ☐ |
| 1562 | **995** | 37p | multicoloured | 1·25 | 1·25 | ☐ | ☐ |
| | | a. | Horiz pair. | | | | |
| | | | Nos. 1562/3 | 3·50 | 3·00 | ☐ | ☐ |
| 1563 | **996** | 37p | multicoloured | 1·25 | 1·25 | ☐ | ☐ |
| Set of 4 | | | | 4·50 | 4·50 | ☐ | ☐ |
| First Day Cover | | | | | 5·00 | | ☐ |
| Presentation Pack (P.O. Pack No. 217) | | | | 5·00 | | ☐ | |
| PHQ Cards (set of 4) (134) | | | | 3·00 | 7·00 | ☐ | ☐ |
| Set of 2 Gutter Strips of 4 | | | | 9·50 | | ☐ | |

Nos. 1560/1 and 1562/3 were each printed together, se-tenant, in horizontal pairs throughout the sheets, each pair forming a composite design.

**997** Fencing

**998** Hurdling

**999** Diving

**1000** Rugby

### World Student Games, Sheffield (Nos. 1564/6) and World Cup Rugby Championship, London (No. 1567)

**1991** (11 June) Phosphorised paper. Perf 14½ × 14

| | | | | | | | |
|---|---|---|---|---|---|---|---|
| 1564 | **997** | 22p | multicoloured | 60 | 50 | ☐ | ☐ |
| 1565 | **998** | 26p | multicoloured | 1·00 | 1·00 | ☐ | ☐ |
| 1566 | **999** | 31p | multicoloured | 1·25 | 1·25 | ☐ | ☐ |
| 1567 | **1000** | 37p | multicoloured | 1·50 | 1·50 | ☐ | ☐ |
| Set of 4 | | | | 3·50 | 3·75 | ☐ | ☐ |
| First Day Cover | | | | | 4·25 | | ☐ |
| Presentation Pack (P.O. Pack No. 218) | | | | 4·50 | | ☐ | |
| PHQ Cards (set of 4) (135) | | | | 3·00 | 7·00 | ☐ | ☐ |
| Set of 4 Gutter Pairs | | | | 8·00 | | ☐ | |

**1001** 'Silver Jubilee'

**1002** 'Mme Alfred Carrière'

*Rosa moyesii*
**1003** *Rosa moyesii*

*Rosa* Harvest Fayre
**1004** 'Harvest Fayre'

*Rosa* Mutabilis
**1005** 'Mutabilis'

## 9th World Congress of Roses, Belfast

**1991** (16 July) Phosphorised paper. Perf 14½ × 14

| | | | | | |
|---|---|---|---|---|---|
| 1568 | **1001** | 22p multicoloured | 50 | 50 | |
| 1569 | **1002** | 26p multicoloured | 75 | 1·25 | |
| 1570 | **1003** | 31p multicoloured | 1·00 | 1·25 | |
| 1571 | **1004** | 33p multicoloured | 1·25 | 1·50 | |
| 1572 | **1005** | 37p multicoloured | 1·50 | 1·50 | |
| *Set of 5* | | | 4·50 | 5·50 | |
| First Day Cover | | | | 6·00 | |
| Presentation Pack (P.O. Pack No. 219) | | | 5·00 | | |
| PHQ Cards (*set of 5*) (136) | | | 3·00 | 9·00 | |
| *Set of 5 Gutter Pairs* | | | 10·00 | | |

*Iguanodon.* Owen's Dinosauria 1841
**1006** Iguanodon

*Stegosaurus.* Owen's Dinosauria 1841
**1007** Stegosaurus

*Tyrannosaurus.* Owen's Dinosauria 1841
**1008** Tyrannosaurus

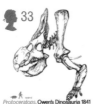

*Protoceratops.* Owen's Dinosauria 1841
**1009** Protoceratops

*Triceratops.* Owen's Dinosauria 1841
**1010** Triceratops

## 150th Anniversary of Dinosaurs' Identification by Owen

**1991** (20 Aug.) Phosphorised paper. Perf 14½ × 14

| | | | | | |
|---|---|---|---|---|---|
| 1573 | **1006** | 22p multicoloured | 60 | 50 | |
| 1574 | **1007** | 26p multicoloured | 1·10 | 1·25 | |
| 1575 | **1008** | 31p multicoloured | 1·25 | 1·25 | |
| 1576 | **1009** | 33p multicoloured | 1·50 | 1·50 | |
| 1577 | **1010** | 37p multicoloured | 1·60 | 1·50 | |
| *Set of 5* | | | 5·75 | 5·50 | |
| First Day Cover | | | | 6·00 | |
| Presentation Pack (P.O. Pack No. 220) | | | 6·00 | | |
| PHQ Cards (*set of 5*) (137) | | | 3·00 | 9·00 | |
| *Set of 5 Gutter Pairs* | | | 12·00 | | |

ORDNANCE SURVEY
1791 – 1991
**1011** Map of 1816

ORDNANCE SURVEY
1791 – 1991
**1012** Map of 1906

ORDNANCE SURVEY
1791 – 1991
**1013** Map of 1959

ORDNANCE SURVEY
1791 – 1991
**1014** Map of 1991

## Bicentenary of Ordnance Survey. Maps of Hamstreet, Kent

**1991** (17 Sept.) Phosphorised paper. Perf 14½ × 14

| | | | | | |
|---|---|---|---|---|---|
| 1578 | **1011** | 24p multicoloured | 60 | 50 | |
| 1579 | **1012** | 28p multicoloured | 1·00 | 95 | |
| 1580 | **1013** | 33p multicoloured | 1·25 | 1·40 | |
| 1581 | **1014** | 39p multicoloured | 1·50 | 1·40 | |
| *Set of 4* | | | 3·50 | 3·75 | |
| First Day Cover | | | | 4·25 | |
| Presentation Pack (P.O. Pack No. 221) | | | 4·50 | | |
| PHQ Cards (*set of 4*) (138) | | | 3·00 | 7·00 | |
| *Set of 4 Gutter Pairs* | | | 8·50 | | |

**1015** Adoration of the Magi

**1016** Mary and Baby Jesus in Stable

**1017** Holy Family and Angel

**1018** The Annunciation

**1019** The Flight into Egypt

### Christmas. Illuminated Manuscripts from the Bodleian Library, Oxford

**1991** (12 Nov.) One phosphor band (18p) or phosphorised paper (others)

| | | | | | |
|---|---|---|---|---|---|
| 1582 | **1015** | 18p multicoloured | 75 | 35 | |
| 1583 | **1016** | 24p multicoloured | 90 | 45 | |
| 1584 | **1017** | 28p multicoloured | 95 | 1·25 | |
| 1585 | **1018** | 33p multicoloured | 1·10 | 1·50 | |
| 1586 | **1019** | 39p multicoloured | 1·25 | 1·75 | |
| Set of 5 | | | 4·50 | 4·75 | |
| First Day Cover | | | | 5·50 | |
| Presentation Pack (P.O. Pack No. 222) | | | 5·00 | | |
| PHQ Cards (set of 5) (139) | | | 3·00 | 7·50 | |
| Set of 5 Gutter Pairs | | | 11·00 | | |

### Collectors Pack 1991

**1991** (12 Nov.) Comprises Nos. 1531/5, 1546/9 and 1560/86

| | | | |
|---|---|---|---|
| CP1586a | Collectors Pack | 32·00 | |

### Post Office Yearbook

**1991** Comprises Nos. 1531/5, 1546/9 and 1560/86 in hardback book with slip case

| | | | |
|---|---|---|---|
| YB1586a | Yearbook | 45·00 | |

**1020** Fallow Deer in Scottish Forest

**1021** Hare on North Yorkshire Moors

**1022** Fox in the Fens

**1023** Redwing and Home Counties Village

**1024** Welsh Mountain Sheep in Snowdonia

### The Four Seasons (1st series). Wintertime

**1992** (14 Jan.) One phosphor band (18p) or phosphorised paper (others)

| | | | | | |
|---|---|---|---|---|---|
| 1587 | **1020** | 18p multicoloured | 55 | 40 | |
| 1588 | **1021** | 24p multicoloured | 75 | 50 | |
| 1589 | **1022** | 28p multicoloured | 1·00 | 1·25 | |
| 1590 | **1023** | 33p multicoloured | 1·25 | 1·50 | |

| | | | | | |
|---|---|---|---|---|---|
| 1591 | **1024** | 39p multicoloured | 1·40 | 1·75 | |
| Set of 5 | | | 4·50 | 5·00 | |
| First Day Cover | | | | 5·50 | |
| Presentation Pack (P.O. Pack No. 224) | | | 5·00 | | |
| PHQ Cards (set of 5) (140) | | | 3·00 | 8·00 | |
| Set of 5 Gutter Pairs | | | 11·00 | | |

**1025** Flower Spray

**1026** Double Locket

**1027** Key

**1028** Model Car and Cigarette Cards

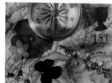

**1029** Compass and Map

**1030** Pocket Watch

**1031** 1854 1d. Red Stamp and Pen

**1032** Pearl Necklace

**1033** Marbles

**1034** Bucket, Spade and Starfish

### Greetings Booklet Stamps. 'Memories'

**1992** (28 Jan.) Two phosphor bands

| | | | | | |
|---|---|---|---|---|---|
| 1592 | **1025** | (1st) multicoloured | 1·25 | 1·00 | |
| | | a. Booklet pane. Nos. 1592/1601 | 13·00 | 13·00 | |
| 1593 | **1026** | (1st) multicoloured | 1·25 | 1·00 | |
| 1594 | **1027** | (1st) multicoloured | 1·25 | 1·00 | |
| 1595 | **1028** | (1st) multicoloured | 1·25 | 1·00 | |
| 1596 | **1029** | (1st) multicoloured | 1·25 | 1·00 | |
| 1597 | **1030** | (1st) multicoloured | 1·25 | 1·00 | |
| 1598 | **1031** | (1st) multicoloured | 1·25 | 1·00 | |
| 1599 | **1032** | (1st) multicoloured | 1·25 | 1·00 | |
| 1600 | **1033** | (1st) multicoloured | 1·25 | 1·00 | |
| 1601 | **1034** | (1st) multicoloured | 1·25 | 1·00 | |
| Set of 10 | | | 13·00 | 13·00 | |
| First Day Cover | | | | 15·00 | |
| Presentation Pack (P.O. Pack No. G1) | | | 17·00 | | |

Nos. 1592/1601 were printed together, se-tenant, in booklet panes of 10 stamps and 12 half stamp-size labels, the backgrounds of the stamps forming a composite design.

**SET PRICES.** Please note that set prices for booklet greetings stamps are for complete panes. Sets of single stamps are worth considerably less.

**1035** Queen Elizabeth in Coronation Robes and Parliamentary Emblem

**1036** Queen Elizabeth in Garter Robes and Archiepiscopal Arms

**1037** Queen Elizabeth with Baby Prince Andrew and Royal Arms

**1038** Queen Elizabeth at Trooping the Colour and Service Emblems

**1039** Queen Elizabeth and Commonwealth Emblem

## 40th Anniversary of Accession

**1992** (6 Feb.) Two phosphor bands. Perf 14½ × 14

| | | | | | |
|---|---|---|---|---|---|
| 1602 | **1035** | 24p | multicoloured | 90 | 90 |
| | | a. | Horiz strip of 5. | | |
| | | | Nos. 1602/6 | 6·00 | 6·50 |
| 1603 | **1036** | 24p | multicoloured | 90 | 90 |
| 1604 | **1037** | 24p | multicoloured | 90 | 90 |
| 1605 | **1038** | 24p | multicoloured | 90 | 90 |
| 1606 | **1039** | 24p | multicoloured | 90 | 90 |
| *Set of* 5 | | | | 6·00 | 6·50 |
| First Day Cover | | | | | 7·00 |
| Presentation Pack (P.O. Pack No. 225) | | | | 7·00 | |
| PHQ Cards (*set of* 5) (141) | | | | 3·00 | 7·50 |
| Gutter Block of 10 | | | | 15·00 | |

Nos. 1602/6 were printed together, *se-tenant*, in horizontal strips of five throughout the sheet.

**1040** Tennyson in 1888 and 'The Beguiling of Merlin' (Sir Edward Burne-Jones)

**1041** Tennyson in 1856 and 'April Love' (Arthur Hughes)

**1042** Tennyson in 1864 and 'I am Sick of the Shadows' (John Waterhouse)

**1043** Tennyson as a Young Man and 'Mariana' (Dante Gabriel Rossetti)

## Death Centenary of Alfred, Lord Tennyson (poet)

**1992** (10 Mar.) Phosphorised paper. Perf 14½ × 14

| | | | | | |
|---|---|---|---|---|---|
| 1607 | **1040** | 24p | multicoloured | 60 | 50 |
| 1608 | **1041** | 28p | multicoloured | 85 | 85 |
| 1609 | **1042** | 33p | multicoloured | 1·40 | 1·60 |
| 1610 | **1043** | 39p | multicoloured | 1·50 | 1·60 |
| *Set of* 4 | | | | 4·00 | 4·00 |
| First Day Cover | | | | | 4·50 |
| Presentation Pack (P.O. Pack No. 226) | | | | 4·50 | |
| PHQ Cards (*set of* 4) (142) | | | | 3·00 | 7·00 |
| *Set of* 4 Gutter Pairs | | | | 9·00 | |

£1·50

CAERNARFON CASTLE

**1044** Caernarfon Castle

**1992** (24 Mar.)–**95** Designs as Nos. 1410/13, but showing Queen's head in silhouette as T **1044**. Perf 15 × 14 (with one elliptical hole in each vertical side)

| | | | | | |
|---|---|---|---|---|---|
| 1611 | **879** | £1 | bottle green and gold† | 5·50 | 1·00 |
| 1612 | **1044** | £1·50 | maroon and gold† | 6·00 | 1·20 |
| 1613 | **881** | £2 | indigo and gold† | 8·00 | 1·20 |
| 1613a | **1044** | £3 | reddish violet and gold† (22.8.95) | 19·00 | 3·00 |
| 1614 | **882** | £5 | deep brown and gold† | 18·00 | 3·00 |
| *Set of* 5 | | | | 50·00 | 8·00 |
| First Day Cover (Nos. 1611/13, 1614) | | | | | 35·00 |
| First Day Cover (22 Aug. 1995) (No. 1613a) | | | | | 10·00 |
| Presentation Pack (P.O. Pack No. 27) | | | | | |
| (Nos. 1611/13, 1614) | | | | 38·00 | |
| Presentation Pack (P.O. Pack No 33) | | | | | |
| (No. 1613a) | | | | 30·00 | |
| PHQ Cards (Nos. 1611/13, 1614)(D2-5) | | | | 15·00 | 35·00 |
| PHQ Card (No. 1613a) (D8) | | | | 10·00 | 25·00 |
| *Set of* 5 Gutter Pairs | | | | £100 | |

†The Queen's head on these stamps is printed in optically variable ink which changes colour from gold to green when viewed from different angles.

PHQ cards for Nos. 1611/13 and 1614 were not issued until 16 February 1993.

Nos. 1611/14 were printed by Harrison. For stamps with different lettering by Enschedé see Nos. 1410/13 and 1993/6.

**1045** British Olympic Association Logo (Olympic Games, Barcelona)

**1046** British Paralympic Association Symbol (Paralympics '92, Barcelona)

**1047** *Santa Maria* (500th Anniv of Discovery of America by Columbus)

**1048** *Kaisei* (Japanese cadet brigantine) (Grand Regatta Columbus, 1992)

**1049** British Pavilion, 'EXPO 92', Seville

### Europa. International Events

**1992** (7 Apr.) Phosphorised paper. Perf 14 × 14½

| | | | | | | |
|---|---|---|---|---|---|---|
| 1615 | **1045** | 24p | multicoloured | 50 | 50 | |
| | | a. | Horiz. pair. | | | |
| | | | Nos. 1615/16 | 2·25 | 1·75 | |
| 1616 | **1046** | 24p | multicoloured | 50 | 50 | |
| 1617 | **1047** | 24p | multicoloured | 1·00 | 75 | |
| 1618 | **1048** | 39p | multicoloured | 1·40 | 1·50 | |
| 1619 | **1049** | 39p | multicoloured | 1·40 | 1·50 | |
| *Set of 5* | | | | 4·50 | 4·50 | |
| First Day Cover | | | | | 5·00 | |
| Presentation Pack (P.O. Pack No. 227) | | | | 5·25 | | |
| PHQ Cards (*set of 5*) (143) | | | | 3·00 | 7·00 | |
| *Set of 3 Gutter Pairs and a Gutter* | | | | | | |
| Strip of 4 | | | | 11·00 | | |

Nos. 1615/16 were printed together, *se-tenant*, in horizontal pairs throughout the sheet.

**1050** Pikeman

**1051** Drummer

**1052** Musketeer

**1053** Standard Bearer

### 350th Anniversary of the Civil War

**1992** (16 June) Phosphorised paper. Perf 14½ × 14

| | | | | | | |
|---|---|---|---|---|---|---|
| 1620 | **1050** | 24p | multicoloured | 60 | 50 | |
| 1621 | **1051** | 24p | multicoloured | 85 | 85 | |
| 1622 | **1052** | 33p | multicoloured | 1·40 | 1·50 | |
| 1623 | **1053** | 39p | multicoloured | 1·50 | 1·75 | |
| *Set of 4* | | | | 4·00 | 4·25 | |
| First Day Cover | | | | | 4·75 | |
| Presentation Pack (P.O. Pack No. 228) | | | | 4·50 | | |
| PHQ Cards (*set of 4*) (144) | | | | 3·00 | 7·00 | |
| *Set of 4 Gutter Pairs* | | | | 9·50 | | |

**1054** *The Yeomen of the Guard*

**1055** *The Gondoliers*

**1056** *The Mikado*

**1057** *The Pirates of Penzance*

**1058** *Iolanthe*

### 150th Birth Anniversary of Sir Arthur Sullivan (composer). Gilbert and Sullivan Operas

**1992** (21 July) One phosphor band (18p) or phosphorised paper (others). Perf 14½ × 14

| | | | | | | |
|---|---|---|---|---|---|---|
| 1624 | **1054** | 18p | multicoloured | 50 | 40 | |
| 1625 | **1055** | 24p | multicoloured | 80 | 60 | |
| 1626 | **1056** | 28p | multicoloured | 95 | 1·00 | |
| 1627 | **1057** | 33p | multicoloured | 1·50 | 1·60 | |
| 1628 | **1058** | 39p | multicoloured | 1·60 | 1·60 | |
| *Set of 5* | | | | 4·50 | 4·75 | |
| First Day Cover | | | | | 5·25 | |
| Presentation Pack (P.O. Pack No. 229) | | | | 5·00 | | |
| PHQ Cards (*set of 5*) (145) | | | | 3·00 | 6·25 | |
| *Set of 5 Gutter Pairs* | | | | 10·00 | | |

**1059** 'Acid Rain Kills'

**1060** 'Ozone Layer'

**1061** 'Greenhouse Effect'

**1062** 'Bird of Hope'

## Protection of the Environment. Children's Paintings

**1992** (15 Sept.) Phosphorised paper. Perf 14 × 14½

| | | | | | | |
|---|---|---|---|---|---|---|
| 1629 | **1059** | 24p | multicoloured | 70 | 60 | |
| 1630 | **1060** | 28p | multicoloured | 1·10 | 1·25 | |
| 1631 | **1061** | 33p | multicoloured | 1·25 | 1·50 | |
| 1632 | **1062** | 39p | multicoloured | 1·40 | 1·50 | |
| Set of 4 | | | | 4·00 | 4·25 | |
| First Day Cover | | | | | 4·75 | |
| Presentation Pack (P.O. Pack No. 230) | | | | 4·50 | | |
| PHQ Cards (set of 4) (146) | | | | 3·00 | 6·25 | |
| Set of 4 Gutter Pairs | | | | 9·00 | | |

**1063** European Star

## Single European Market

**1992** (13 Oct.) Phosphorised paper

| | | | | | | |
|---|---|---|---|---|---|---|
| 1633 | **1063** | 24p | multicoloured | 1·00 | 1·00 | |
| First Day Cover | | | | | 1·50 | |
| Presentation Pack (P.O. Pack No. 231) | | | 1·50 | | |
| PHQ Card (147) | | | | 1·50 | 4·00 | |
| Gutter Pair | | | | 2·25 | | |

**1064** 'Angel Gabriel', St. James's, Pangbourne

**1065** 'Madonna and Child', St. Mary's, Bibury

**1066** 'King with Gold', Our Lady and St. Peter, Leatherhead

**1067** 'Shepherds', All Saints, Porthcawl

**1068** 'Kings with Frankincense and Myrrh', Our Lady and St. Peter, Leatherhead

## Christmas. Stained Glass Windows

**1992** (10 Nov.) One phosphor band (18p) or phosphorised paper (others)

| | | | | | | | |
|---|---|---|---|---|---|---|---|
| 1634 | **1064** | 18p | multicoloured | 50 | 30 | | |
| 1635 | **1065** | 24p | multicoloured | 75 | 60 | | |
| 1636 | **1066** | 28p | multicoloured | 1·00 | 1·10 | | |
| 1637 | **1067** | 33p | multicoloured | 1·25 | 1·50 | | |
| 1638 | **1068** | 39p | multicoloured | 1·25 | 1·50 | | |
| Set of 5 | | | | 4·25 | 4·50 | | |
| First Day Cover | | | | | 5·00 | | |
| Presentation Pack (P.O. Pack No. 232) | | | 5·00 | | | |
| PHQ Cards (set of 5) (148) | | | | 3·00 | 7·50 | | |
| Set of 5 Gutter Pairs | | | | 9·50 | | | |

## Collectors Pack 1992

**1992** (10 Nov.) Comprises Nos. 1587/91, 1602/10 and 1615/38

| | | | |
|---|---|---|---|
| CP1638a | Collectors Pack | 32·00 | |

## Post Office Yearbook

**1992** (11 Nov.) Comprises Nos. 1587/91, 1602/10 and 1615/38 in hardback book with slip case

| | | | |
|---|---|---|---|
| YB1638a | Yearbook | 50·00 | |

**1069** Mute Swan Cob and St. Catherine's, Abbotsbury

**1070** Cygnet and Decoy

**1071** Swans and Cygnet

**1072** Eggs in Nest and Tithe Barn, Abbotsbury

**1073** Young Swan and the Fleet

**600th Anniversary of Abbotsbury Swannery**

**1993** (19 Jan.) One phosphor band (18p) or phosphorised paper (others)

| | | | | | | | |
|---|---|---|---|---|---|---|---|
| 1639 | **1069** | 18p | multicoloured | 1·25 | 70 | ☐ | ☐ |
| 1640 | **1070** | 24p | multicoloured | 1·10 | 70 | ☐ | ☐ |
| 1641 | **1071** | 28p | multicoloured | 1·40 | 2·25 | ☐ | ☐ |
| 1642 | **1072** | 33p | multicoloured | 1·75 | 2·50 | ☐ | ☐ |
| 1643 | **1073** | 39p | multicoloured | 1·90 | 2·50 | ☐ | ☐ |
| *Set of* 5 | | | | 6·50 | 8·00 | ☐ | ☐ |
| First Day Cover | | | | | 8·50 | ☐ | |
| Presentation Pack (P.O. Pack No. 234) | | | | 7·00 | | ☐ | |
| PHQ Cards (*set of* 5) (149) | | | | 4·25 | 8·50 | ☐ | ☐ |
| *Set of* 5 Gutter Pairs | | | | 15·00 | | ☐ | |

1074 Long John Silver and Parrot (Treasure Island)

1075 Tweedledum and Tweedledee (Alice Throughthe Looking-Glass)

1076 William (*William books*)

1077 Mole and Toad (*The Wind in the Willows*)

1078 Teacher and Wilfrid ('*The Bash Street Kids*')

1079 Peter Rabbit and Mrs Rabbit (*The Tale of PeterRabbit*)

1080 Snowman (*The Snowman*) and Father Christmas (Father Christmas)

1081 The Big Friendly Giant and Sophie (*The BFG*)

1082 Bill Badger and Rupert Bear

1083 Aladdin and the Genie

**Greetings Booklet Stamps. 'Gift Giving'**

**1993** (2 Feb.) Two phosphor bands. Perf 15 × 14 (with one elliptical hole in each vertical side)

| | | | | | | | |
|---|---|---|---|---|---|---|---|
| 1644 | **1074** | (1st) | multicoloured | 1·25 | 1·00 | ☐ | ☐ |
| | | a. | Booklet pane. Nos. 1644/53 | 14·00 | 12·00 | ☐ | ☐ |
| 1645 | **1075** | (1st) | gold, cream and black | 1·25 | 1·00 | ☐ | ☐ |
| 1646 | **1076** | (1st) | multicoloured | 1·25 | 1·00 | ☐ | ☐ |
| 1647 | **1077** | (1st) | multicoloured | 1·25 | 1·00 | ☐ | ☐ |
| 1648 | **1078** | (1st) | multicoloured | 1·25 | 1·00 | ☐ | ☐ |
| 1649 | **1079** | (1st) | multicoloured | 1·25 | 1·00 | ☐ | ☐ |
| 1650 | **1080** | (1st) | multicoloured | 1·25 | 1·00 | ☐ | ☐ |
| 1651 | **1081** | (1st) | multicoloured | 1·25 | 1·00 | ☐ | ☐ |
| 1652 | **1082** | (1st) | multicoloured | 1·25 | 1·00 | ☐ | ☐ |
| 1653 | **1083** | (1st) | multicoloured | 1·25 | 1·00 | ☐ | ☐ |
| *Set of* 10 | | | | 14·00 | 12·00 | ☐ | ☐ |
| First Day Cover | | | | | 13·00 | ☐ | |
| Presentation Pack (P.O. Pack No. G2) | | | | 16·00 | | ☐ | |
| PHQ Cards (*set of* 10) (GS1) | | | | 16·00 | 30·00 | ☐ | ☐ |

Nos. 1644/53 were printed together, *se-tenant*, in booklet panes of 10 stamps and 20 half stamp-size labels.

> **SET PRICES.** Please note that set prices for booklet greetings stamps are for complete panes. Sets of single stamps are worth considerably less.

1084 Decorated Enamel Dial

1085 Escapement, Remontoire and Fusee

1086 Balance, Spring and Temperature Compensator

1087 Back of Movement

**300th Birth Anniversary of John Harrison (inventor of the marine chronometer). Details of 'H4' Clock**

**1993** (16 Feb.) Phosphorised paper. Perf 14½ × 14

| | | | | | | | |
|---|---|---|---|---|---|---|---|
| 1654 | **1084** | 24p | multicoloured | 60 | 60 | ☐ | ☐ |
| 1655 | **1085** | 28p | multicoloured | 1·00 | 1·25 | ☐ | ☐ |
| 1656 | **1086** | 33p | multicoloured | 1·40 | 1·25 | ☐ | ☐ |
| 1657 | **1087** | 39p | multicoloured | 1·50 | 1·50 | ☐ | ☐ |
| *Set of* 4 | | | | 4·00 | 4·00 | ☐ | ☐ |
| First Day Cover | | | | | 4·50 | ☐ | |
| Presentation Pack (P.O. Pack No. 235) | | | | 4·50 | | ☐ | |
| PHQ Cards (*set of* 4) (150) | | | | 4·25 | 7·00 | ☐ | ☐ |
| *Set of* 4 Gutter Pairs | | | | 9·00 | | ☐ | |

1088 Britannia

**1993** (2 Mar.) Granite paper. Perf 14 × 14½ (with two elliptical holes in each horizontal side)

| | | | | | | | |
|---|---|---|---|---|---|---|---|
| 1658 | **1088** | £10 | multicoloured | 40·00 | 12·00 | ☐ | ☐ |
| First Day Cover | | | | | 25·00 | ☐ | |
| Presentation Pack (P.O. Pack No. 29) | | | | 45·00 | | ☐ | |
| PHQ Card (D1) | | | | 8·00 | 60·00 | ☐ | ☐ |

18

**1089** *Dendrobium hellwigianum*

24

**1090** *Paphiopedilum Maudiae 'Magnifcum'*

28

**1091** *Cymbidium lowianum*

33

**1092** *Vanda Rothschildiana*

39

**1093** *Dendrobium vexillarius var albiviride*

**1093a**

### 14th World Orchid Conference, Glasgow

**1993** (16 Mar.) One phosphor band (18p) or phosphorised paper (others)

| | | | | | | |
|---|---|---|---|---|---|---|
| 1659 | **1089** | 18p | multicoloured | 45 | 40 | ☐ ☐ |
| 1660 | **1090** | 24p | multicoloured | 75 | 60 | ☐ ☐ |
| 1661 | **1091** | 28p | multicoloured | 1·00 | 1·25 | ☐ ☐ |
| 1662 | **1092** | 33p | multicoloured | 1·25 | 1·50 | ☐ ☐ |
| 1663 | **1093** | 39p | multicoloured | 1·60 | 1·50 | ☐ ☐ |
| *Set of 5* | | | | 4·50 | 4·75 | ☐ ☐ |
| First Day Cover | | | | | 5·25 | ☐ |
| Presentation Pack (P.O. Pack No. 236) | | | | 5·00 | | ☐ |
| PHQ Cards (*set of 5*) (151) | | | | 4·50 | 7·00 | ☐ ☐ |
| *Set of 5 Gutter Pairs* | | | | 10·00 | | ☐ |

**1993** (6 Apr.)–**2008**. As T **913/14** and **1093a**, but Perf 14 (No. 1665) or 15 × 14 (others) (both with one elliptical hole in each vertical side)

(a) Photo

Harrison (No. 1666)
Questa (Nos. 1664a, 1667a)
Walsall (No. 1665)
Harrison (later De La Rue), Questa or Walsall (No. 1667)
Harrison (later De La Rue), Enschedé, Questa or Walsall (Nos. 1664, 1668, 1669)

| | | | | | | |
|---|---|---|---|---|---|---|
| 1664 | **913** | (2nd) | bright blue (1 centre band) *(7.9.93)* | 1·00 | 1·00 | ☐ ☐ |
| | a. | | Perf 14 *(1.12.98)* | 1·10 | 1·10 | ☐ ☐ |
| 1665 | | (2nd) | bright blue (1 side band) *(13.10.98)* | 1·50 | 1·50 | ☐ ☐ |
| 1666 | **914** | (1st) | bright orange-red (phosphorised paper) | 1·50 | 1·25 | ☐ ☐ |
| 1667 | | (1st) | bright orange-red (2 phosphor bands) *(4.4.95)* | 1·10 | 1·10 | ☐ ☐ |
| | a. | | Perf 14 *(1.12.98)* | 1·50 | 1·50 | ☐ ☐ |
| 1668 | | (1st) | gold (2 phosphor bands) *(21.4.97)* | 1·00 | 1·25 | ☐ ☐ |
| 1669 | **1093a** | (E) | deep blue (2 phosphor bands) *(19.1.99)* | 1·25 | 1·25 | ☐ ☐ |

(b) Litho Questa or Walsall (No. 1670), Questa, Enschedé or Walsall (No. 1671), De La Rue or Walsall (No. 1672)

| | | | | | | |
|---|---|---|---|---|---|---|
| 1670 | **913** | (2nd) | bright blue (1 centre band) | 90 | 90 | ☐ ☐ |
| 1671 | **914** | (1st) | bright orange-red (2 phosphor bands) | 1·00 | 1·00 | ☐ ☐ |

| | | | | | | |
|---|---|---|---|---|---|---|
| 1672 | | (1st) | gold (2 phosphor bands) *(8.1.08)* | 2·75 | 2·75 | ☐ ☐ |

First Day Covers
| | | | | |
|---|---|---|---|---|
| 21 Apr. 1997 | (1st), 26p (Nos 1668, Y1686) | | 3·50 | ☐ |
| 19 Jan. 1999 | (E) (No 1669) | | 3·50 | ☐ |

Nos. 1664, 1667, 1669 and 1670/1 also come from sheets.

No. 1665 exists with the phosphor band at the left or right of the stamp and was only issued in booklets.

No. 1668 was issued by Harrison in booklets and Walsall in sheets and booklets for the Queen's Golden Wedding on 21 April 1997. The gold colour was later adopted for the (1st) class rate, replacing bright orange-red.

For No. 1668 in presentation pack see Pack No. 38 listed below, No. Y1667 etc.

No. 1669 was valid for the basic European airmail rate, initially 30p.

No. 1672 was only issued in £7·40 or £7·15 stamp booklets.

> For self-adhesive versions in these colours see Nos. 2039/40 and 2295/8.

**II** Normal figures of face value    **III** Open '4' and open lower curve of '5'

**1993–2011** As Nos. X841 etc, but perf 14 (No. Y1678) or 15 × 14 (others) (both with one elliptical hole in each vertical side)

(a) Photo

Enschedé: 20p (Y1684), 29p, 35p (Y1698), 36p, 38p (Y1706), 41p (Y1712), 43p (Y1716)

Harrison: 20p (Y1686), 25p (Y1689), 26p (Y1692), 35p (Y1699), 41p (Y1713), 43p (Y1717)

Walsall: 10p (Y1676), 19p (Y1683), 38p (Y1707), 43p (Y1717)

Enschedé or Harrison (later De La Rue): 4p, 5p, 6p, 25p (Y1690), 31p, 39p (Y1708), £1 (Y1743)

Enschedé, Harrison (later De La Rue) or Questa: 1p

Enschedé, or Harrison (later De La Rue Questa or Walsall): 2p

Enschedé, Harrison (later De La Rue) or Walsall:— 10p. (Y1676), 30p, 37p (Y1703), 42p, 50p (Y1726), 63p

Harrison (later De La Rue) or Questa: 19p (Y1682), 20p (Y1685), 26p (Y1691)

De La Rue or Walsall: 38p (Y1707), 39p (Y1709), 40p (Y1710), 64p, 65p, 68p

De La Rue: 7p, 8p, 9p, 12p, 14p, 15p, 16p, 17p, 20p (Y1687), 22p, 33p, 34p, 35p (Y1700), 37p (Y1704/5), 41p (Y1714), 43p (Y1718), 44p, 45p, 48p, 49p, 50p (Y1727), 56p, 60p, 62p, 67p, 72p, 78p, 81p, 88p, 90p, 97p, £1 (Y1744), £1·46, £1·50, £2, £3, £5

Enschedé or De La Rue: 35p (Y1701), 40p (Y1711), 46p, 47p, 54p

| | | | | | | |
|---|---|---|---|---|---|---|
| Y1667 | **367** | 1p | crimson (2 bands) *(8.6.93)* | 25 | 25 | ☐ ☐ |
| Y1668 | | 2p | deep green (2 bands) | | | |
| | | | *(11.4.95)* | 25 | 30 | ☐ ☐ |
| Y1669 | | 4p | new blue (2 bands) | | | |
| | | | *(14.12.93)* | 25 | 60 | ☐ ☐ |
| Y1670 | | 5p | dull red-brown (2 bands) | | | |
| | | | (Type II) *(8.6.93)* | 25 | 35 | ☐ ☐ |
| Y1671 | | 6p | yellow-olive (2 bands) | | | |
| | | | *(27.4.93)* | 25 | 35 | ☐ ☐ |
| Y1672 | | 7p | grey (2 bands) *(20.4.99)* | 2·50 | 2·50 | ☐ ☐ |
| Y1673 | | 7p | bright magenta (2 bands) | | | |
| | | | *(1.4.04)* | 75 | 80 | ☐ ☐ |
| Y1674 | | 8p | yellow (2 bands) *(25.4.00)* | 35 | 35 | ☐ ☐ |
| Y1675 | | 9p | yellow-orange (2 bands) *(5.4.05)* | 15 | 20 | ☐ ☐ |
| Y1676 | | 10p | dull orange (2 bands) *(8.6.93)* | 35 | 35 | ☐ ☐ |

|  |  |  |  |  |  |
|---|---|---|---:|---:|---|
|  | a. Perf 14 *(13.10.98)* | 2·00 | 2·00 | ☐ ☐ |
| Y1677 | 12p greenish blue<br>(2 bands) *(1.8.06)* | 1·00 | 1·25 | ☐ ☐ |
| Y1678 | 14p rose-red (2 bands) *(1.8.06)* | 50 | 55 | ☐ ☐ |
| Y1679 | 15p bright magenta<br>(2 bands) *(1.4.08)* | 60 | 65 | ☐ ☐ |
| Y1680 | 16p pale cerise (2 bands)<br>*(27.3.07)* | 60 | 65 | ☐ ☐ |
| Y1681 | 17p brown-olive (2 bands)<br>*(31.3.09)* | 60 | 65 | ☐ ☐ |
| Y1682 | 19p bistre (1 centre band)<br>*(26.10.93)* | 40 | 45 | ☐ ☐ |
| Y1683 | 19p bistre (1 side band)<br>*(15.2.00)* | 2·25 | 2·25 | ☐ ☐ |
| Y1684 | 20p turquoise-green<br>(2 bands) *(14.12.93)* | 90 | 90 | ☐ ☐ |
| Y1685 | 20p bright green<br>(1 centre band) *(25.6.96)* | 50 | 50 | ☐ ☐ |
| Y1686 | 20p bright green<br>(1 side band) *(23.9.97)* | 1·50 | 1·50 | ☐ ☐ |
| Y1687 | 20p bright green<br>(2 bands) *(20.4.99)* | 75 | 75 | ☐ ☐ |
| Y1688 | 22p drab (2 bands) *(31.3.09)* | 70 | 70 | ☐ ☐ |
| Y1689 | 25p rose-red (phosphorised<br>paper) *(26.10.93)* | 1·10 | 1·10 | ☐ ☐ |
| Y1690 | 25p rose-red (2 bands)<br>*(20.12.94)* | 90 | 90 | ☐ ☐ |
| Y1691 | 26p red-brown (2 bands)<br>*(25.6.96)* | 1·10 | 1·10 | ☐ ☐ |
| Y1692 | 26p gold (2 bands) *(21.4.97)* | 1·10 | 1·10 | ☐ ☐ |
| Y1693 | 29p grey (2 bands) *(26.10.93)* | 1·25 | 1·25 | ☐ ☐ |
| Y1694 | 30p deep olive-grey<br>(2 bands) *(27.7.93)* | 1·10 | 1·10 | ☐ ☐ |
| Y1695 | 31p deep mauve<br>(2 bands) *(25.6.96)* | 1·20 | 1·20 | ☐ ☐ |
| Y1696 | 33p grey-green<br>(2 bands) *(25.4.00)* | 1·50 | 1·50 | ☐ ☐ |
| Y1697 | 34p yellow-olive<br>(2 bands) *(6.5.03)* | 4·00 | 3·00 | ☐ ☐ |
| Y1698 | 35p yellow (2 bands) *(17.8.93)* | 1·50 | 1·50 | ☐ ☐ |
| Y1699 | 35p yellow (phosphorised<br>paper) *(1.11.93)* | 12·00 | 12·00 | ☐ ☐ |
| Y1700 | 35p sepia (2 bands) *(1.4.04)* | 1·10 | 1·10 | ☐ ☐ |
| Y1701 | 35p yellow-olive<br>(1 centre band) *(5.4.05)* | 50 | 55 | ☐ ☐ |
| Y1702 | 36p bright ultramarine<br>(2 bands) *(26.10.93)* | 1·75 | 1·75 | ☐ ☐ |
| Y1703 | 37p bright mauve<br>(2 bands) *(25.6.96)* | 1·40 | 1·40 | ☐ ☐ |
| Y1704 | 37p grey-black (2 bands)<br>*(4.7.02)* | 1·50 | 1·50 | ☐ ☐ |
| Y1705 | 37p brown-olive (1 centre<br>band) *(28.3.06)* | 90 | 90 | ☐ ☐ |
| Y1706 | 38p rosine (2 bands) *(26.10.93)* | 1·50 | 1·50 | ☐ ☐ |
| Y1707 | 38p ultramarine (2 bands)<br>*(20.4.99)* | 2·00 | 2·00 | ☐ ☐ |
|  | a. Perf 14 *(15.2.00)* | 8·00 | 8·00 | ☐ ☐ |
| Y1708 | 39p bright magenta<br>(2 bands) *(25.6.96)* | 1·50 | 1·50 | ☐ ☐ |
| Y1709 | 39p grey (2 bands) *(1.4.04)* | 1·20 | 1·20 | ☐ ☐ |
| Y1710 | 40p deep azure<br>(2 bands) *(25.4.00)* | 1·40 | 1·40 | ☐ ☐ |
| Y1711 | 40p turquoise-blue<br>(2 bands) *(1.4.04)* | 1·40 | 1·40 | ☐ ☐ |
| Y1712 | 41p grey-brown<br>(2 bands) *(26.10.93)* | 1·75 | 1·75 | ☐ ☐ |
| Y1713 | 41p drab (phosphorised<br>paper) *(1.11.93)* | 12·00 | 12·00 | ☐ ☐ |
| Y1714 | 41p rosine (2 bands) *(25.4.00)* | 1·40 | 1·40 | ☐ ☐ |
| Y1715 | 42p deep olive-grey<br>(2 bands) *(4.7.02)* | 1·40 | 1·40 | ☐ ☐ |
| Y1716 | 43p deep olive-brown<br>(2 bands) *(25.6.96)* | 1·75 | 1·75 | ☐ ☐ |
| Y1717 | 43p sepia (2 bands) *(8.7.96)* | 2·50 | 2·50 | ☐ ☐ |

|  |  |  |  |  |  |
|---|---|---|---:|---:|---|
|  | a. Perf 14 *(13.10.98)* | 2·50 | 2·50 | ☐ ☐ |
| Y1718 | 43p emerald (2 bands) *(1.4.04)* | 1·40 | 1·40 | ☐ ☐ |
| Y1719 | 44p grey-brown<br>(2 bands) *(20.4.99)* | 5·00 | 5·00 | ☐ ☐ |
| Y1720 | 44p deep bright blue<br>(2 bands) *(28.3.06)* | 1·10 | 1·10 | ☐ ☐ |
| Y1721 | 45p bright mauve<br>(2 bands) *(25.4.00)* | 1·50 | 1·50 | ☐ ☐ |
| Y1722 | 46p yellow (2 bands) *(5.4.05)* | 1·00 | 1·00 | ☐ ☐ |
| Y1723 | 47p turquoise-green<br>(2 bands) *(4.7.02)* | 1·75 | 1·75 | ☐ ☐ |
| Y1724 | 48p bright mauve<br>(2 bands) *(27.3.07)* | 1·00 | 1·00 | ☐ ☐ |
| Y1725 | 49p red-brown (2 bands)<br>*(28.3.06)* | 1·50 | 1·50 | ☐ ☐ |
| Y1726 | 50p ochre (2 bands) *(14.12.93)* | 1·75 | 1·75 | ☐ ☐ |
| Y1727 | 50p grey (2 bands) *(27.3.07)* | 1·00 | 1·00 | ☐ ☐ |
| Y1728 | 54p red-brown (Type II)<br>(2 bands) *(27.3.07)* | 1·25 | 1·25 | ☐ ☐ |
| Y1729 | 56p yellow-olive<br>(2 bands) *(1.4.08)* | 1·10 | 1·10 | ☐ ☐ |
| Y1730 | 60p light emerald<br>(2 bands) *(30.3.10)* | 1·40 | 1·40 | ☐ ☐ |
| Y1731 | 62p rosine (2 bands) *(31.3.09)* | 1·40 | 1·40 | ☐ ☐ |
| Y1732 | 63p light emerald<br>(2 bands) *(25.6.96)* | 2·00 | 2·00 | ☐ ☐ |
| Y1733 | 64p turquoise-green<br>(2 bands) *(20.4.99)* | 2·25 | 2·25 | ☐ ☐ |
| Y1734 | 65p greenish blue<br>(2 bands) *(25.4.00)* | 2·10 | 2·10 | ☐ ☐ |
| Y1735 | 67p bright mauve<br>(2 bands) *(30.3.10)* | 1·50 | 1·50 | ☐ ☐ |
| Y1736 | 68p grey-brown<br>(2 bands) *(4.7.02)* | 2·10 | 2·10 | ☐ ☐ |
| Y1737 | 72p rosine (2 bands) *(28.3.06)* | 1·50 | 1·50 | ☐ ☐ |
| Y1738 | 78p emerald (2 bands) *(27.3.07)* | 1·50 | 1·50 | ☐ ☐ |
| Y1739 | 81p turquoise-green<br>(2 bands) *(1.4.08)* | 1·50 | 1·50 | ☐ ☐ |
| Y1740 | 88p bright magenta<br>(2 bands) *(30.3.10)* | 2·00 | 2·00 | ☐ ☐ |
| Y1741 | 90p ultramarine (2 bands)<br>*(31.3.09)* | 2·25 | 2·25 | ☐ ☐ |
| Y1742 | 97p violet (2 bands) *(30.3.10)* | 3·00 | 3·00 | ☐ ☐ |
| Y1743 | £1 bluish violet<br>(2 bands) *(22.8.95)* | 2·50 | 2·50 | ☐ ☐ |
| Y1744 | £1 magenta (2 bands) *(5.6.07)* | 2·00 | 2·00 | ☐ ☐ |
| Y1745 | £1·46 greenish-blue<br>(2 bands) *(30.3.10)* | 4·00 | 4·00 | ☐ ☐ |
| Y1746 | £1·50 brown-red (2 bands)<br>*(1.7.03)* | 4·00 | 4·00 | ☐ ☐ |
| Y1747 | £2 deep blue-green<br>(2 bands) *(1.7.03)* | 5·50 | 5·50 | ☐ ☐ |
| Y1748 | £3 deep mauve<br>(2 bands) *(1.7.03)* | 8·00 | 8·00 | ☐ ☐ |
| Y1749 | £5 azure (2 bands) *(1.7.03)* | 14·00 | 14·00 | ☐ ☐ |

(b) Litho Cartor (1p (Y1761), 5p (Y1765),10p (Y1767), 16p, 17p, 20p (Y1773), 22p, 50p, 54p, 60p (Y1785), 62p, 67p, 90p, 97p), De La Rue (48p), Cartor, Questa or De La Rue (10p)(Y1767), Questa or Walsall (25p, 35p, 41p), Walsall (37p, 60p (Y1784), 63p), Questa (others), Cartor or De La Rue (5p (Y1762)

|  |  |  |  |  |  |
|---|---|---|---:|---:|---|
| Y1760 | **367** 1p lake (2 bands) *(8.7.96)* | 80 | 80 | ☐ ☐ |
| Y1761 | 1p reddish purple<br>(2 bands) *(17.9.09)* | 2·50 | 2·50 | ☐ ☐ |
| Y1763 | 5p Red-brown (Type II)<br>*(12.2.09)* | 2·50 | 2·50 | ☐ ☐ |
| Y1765 | 5p red-brown (2 bands)<br>(Type III) *(7.1.10)* | 3·75 | 3·75 | ☐ ☐ |
| Y1766 | 6p yellow-olive<br>(2 bands) *(26.7.94)* | 12·00 | 13·00 | ☐ ☐ |
| Y1767 | 10p dull orange<br>(2 bands) *(25.4.95)* | 3·50 | 3·50 | ☐ ☐ |
| Y1769 | 16p pale cerise (2 bands)<br>*(13.1.09)* | 3·00 | 1·95 | ☐ ☐ |

| | | | |
|---|---|---|---|
| Y1770 | 17p bistre (2 bands) *(18.8.09)* | 1·50 | 1·50 |
| Y1771 | 19p bistre (1 side band at left) *(26.7.94)* | 1·90 | 1·75 |
| Y1772 | 20p bright yellow-green (1 centre band) *(8.7.96)* | 2·25 | 2·25 |
| Y1773 | 20p light green (2 bands) *(7.1.10)* | 3·00 | 3·00 |
| Y1774 | 22p olive-brown (2 bands)*(18.8.09)* | 2·50 | 2·50 |
| Y1775 | 25p red (2 bands)*(1.11.93)* | 1·10 | 1·10 |
| Y1776 | 26p chestnut (2 bands)*(8.7.96)* | 1·00 | 1·00 |
| Y1777 | 30p olive-grey (2 bands) *(25.4.95)* | 4·25 | 4·25 |
| Y1778 | 35p yellow (2 bands)*(1.11.93)* | 1·60 | 1·60 |
| Y1779 | 37p bright mauve (2 bands)*(8.7.96)* | 3·50 | 3·50 |
| Y1780 | 41p drab (2 bands)*(1.11.93)* | 1·75 | 1·75 |
| Y1781 | 48p bright mauve (2 bands) *(12.2.09)* | 2·75 | 2·75 |
| Y1782 | 50p grey (2 bands) *(13.1.09)* | 3·50 | 2·50 |
| Y1783 | 54p chestnut (2 bands) (Type III) *(7.1.10)* | 2·00 | 2·00 |
| Y1784 | 60p dull blue-grey (2 bands) *(9.8.94)* | 2·50 | 2·50 |
| Y1785 | 60p emerald (2 bands) *(13.5.10)* | 4·75 | 3·25 |
| Y1786 | 62p rosine (2 bands) *(18.8.09)* | 1·75 | 1·75 |
| Y1787 | 63p light emerald (2 bands) *(8.7.96)* | 3·50 | 3·50 |
| Y1788 | 67p bright mauve (2 bands) *(22.3.11)* | 6·00 | 5·00 |
| Y1789 | 90p bright blue (2 bands) *(17.9.09)* | 4·00 | 4·00 |
| Y1790 | 97p bluish violet (2 bands) *(22.3.11)* | 6·50 | 5·50 |

**(c) Recess Enschedé or De La Rue**

| | | | |
|---|---|---|---|
| Y1800 | **367** £1·50 red *(9.3.99)* | 4·50 | 2·00 |
| Y1801 | £2 dull blue *(9.3.99)* | 6·00 | 2·25 |
| Y1802 | £3 dull violet *(9.3.99)* | 9·00 | 3·00 |
| Y1803 | £5 brown *(9.3.99)* | 15·50 | 5·00 |
| PHQ Card (No. Y1725) (D7) | | 3·00 | 15·00 |

*PHQ Cards* (Nos. 1664, 1668, Y1667/8, Y1670, Y1675/6, Y1679/80, Y1687, Y1724, Y1727, Y1729, Y1739, Y1744, Y1746/9, 2357a, 2358, 2359, 2652/3)(D30)   15·00

*Presentation Pack* (P.O. Pack No. 30) (contains 19p (Y1682), 25p (Y1689), 29p (Y1693), 36p (Y1702), 38p (Y1706), 41p (Y1712))   7·00

*Presentation Pack* (P.O. Pack No. 34) (contains 1p (Y1667), 2p (Y1668), 4p (Y1669), 5p (Y1670), 6p (Y1671), 10p (Y1676), 19p (Y1682), 20p (Y1684), 25p (Y1690), 29p (Y1693), 30p (Y1694), 35p (Y1698), 36p (Y1702), 38p (Y1706), 41p (Y1712), 50p (Y1726), 60p (Y1730), £1 (Y1743))   30·00

*Presentation Pack* (P.O. Pack No. 35) (contains 20p (Y1685), 26p (Y1691), 31p (Y1695), 37p (Y1703), 39p (Y1708), 43p (Y1716), 63p (Y1732))   9·50

*Presentation Pack* (P.O. Pack No. 38) (contains 1st (Y1668), 26p (Y1692))   7·50

*Presentation Pack* (P.O. Pack No. 41) (contains 2nd (1664), 1st (Y1667), 1p (Y1667), 2p (Y1668), 4p (Y1669), 5p (Y1670), 6p (Y1671), 10p (Y1676), 20p (Y1685), 26p (Y1691), 30p (Y1694), 31p (Y1695), 37p (Y1703), 39p (Y1708), 43p (Y1717), 50p (Y1726), 63p (Y1732), £1 (Y1743))   16·00

*Presentation Pack* (P.O. Pack No. 43 or 43A) (contains £1·50 (Y1800), £2 (Y1801), £3 (Y1802), £5 (Y1803))   55·00

*Presentation Pack* (P.O. Pack No. 44) contains 7p (Y1672), 19p (Y1682), 38p (Y1707), 44p (Y1719), 64p (Y1733))   11·00

*Presentation Pack* (P.O. Pack No. 49) (contains 8p (Y1674), 33p (Y1696), 40p (Y1710), 41p (Y1714), 45p (Y1721), 65p (Y1734))   10·00

*Presentation Pack* (P.O. Pack No.57) (contains 2nd (1664), 1st (1667), E (1669), 1p (Y1667), 2p (Y1668), 4p (Y1669), 5p (Y1670), 8p (Y1674), 10p (Y1676), 20p (Y1687), 33p (Y1696), 40p (Y1710), 41p (Y1714), 45p (Y1721), 50p (Y1726), 65p (Y1734), £1 (Y1743))   16·00

*Presentation Pack* (P.O. Pack No. 58) (contains 37p (Y1704), 42p (Y1715), 47p (Y1723), 68p (Y1736))   7·50

*Presentation Pack* (P.O. Pack No. 62) (contains £1·50 (Y1746), £2 (Y1747), £3 (Y1748), £5 (Y1749))   23·00

*Presentation Pack* (P.O. Pack No. 67) (contains 7p (No. Y1673), 1st (1668), 35p (Y1700), 39p (Y1709), 40p (Y1711), 43p (Y1718), Worldwide postcard (2357a)   9·00

*Presentation Pack* (P.O. Pack No. 71) (contains 1p (Y1667), 2p (Y1668), 5p (Y1670), 9p (Y1675), 10p (Y1676), 20p (Y1687), 35p (Y1701), 40p (Y1711), 42p (Y1715), 46p (Y1722), 47p (Y1723), 50p (Y1726), 68p (Y1736), £1 (Y1743), 2nd (2039), 1st (2295), Worldwide postcard (2357a), Europe up to 40 grams (2358), Worldwide up to 40 grams (2359)   38·00

*Presentation Pack* (P.O. Pack No. 72) (contains 37p (Y1705), 44p (Y1720), 49p (Y1725), 72p (Y1737)   10·00

*Presentation Pack* (P.O. Pack No.75) (contains 16p (Y1680), 48p (Y1724), 50p (Y1727), 54p (Y1728), 78p (Y1738)   9·00

*Presentation Pack* (P.O. Pack No.77) (contains 1p (Y1667), 2p (Y1668), 5p (Y1670), 10p (Y1676), 14p (Y1678), 16p (Y1679), 20p (Y1687), 46p (Y1722), 48p (Y1724), 50p (Y1727), 54p (Y1728), 78p (Y1738), £1 (Y1744), 2nd (1664), 1st (1668), 2nd Large (2652), 1st Large (2653), Worldwide postcard (2357a), Europe up to 40 grams (2358), Worldwide up to 40 grams (2359)   28·00

*Presentation Pack* (P.O. Pack No.78) (contains 15p (Y1679), 56p (Y1729), 81p (Y1739)   6·00

*Presentation Pack* (P.O. Pack No. 84) (contains 17p (Y1681), 22p (Y1688), 62p (Y1731), 90p (Y1741)   8·00

*Presentation Pack* (P.O. Pack No. 86) (contains 60p (Y1730), 67p (Y1735), 88p (Y1740), 97p (Y1742), £1·46 (Y1745), Europe up to 20 grams (2357b), Worldwide up to 20 grams (2358a), Recorded Signed for 1st (U2981), Recorded Signed for 1st Large (U2982)   20·00

*Presentation Pack* (P.O. Pack No. 88) (contains 1p (Y1667), 2p (Y1668), 5p (Y1670), 9p (Y1675), 10p (Y1676), 20p (Y1687), 50p (Y1727), 60p (Y1730), 67p (Y1735), 88p (Y1740), 97p (Y1742), £1 (Y1744), £1·46 (Y1745), Worldwide postcard (2357a), Europe up to 20 grams (2357b), Europe up to 40 grams (2358), Worldwide up to 20 grams (2358a), Worldwide up to 40 grams (2359a), 2nd (1664), 1st (1668), 2nd Large (2652), 1st Large (2653), Recorded Signed for 1st

(U2981),  Recorded Signed for 1st Large
(U2982)  35·00 ☐

For P.O. Pack No. 37 see below No. 1977.

For P.O. Pack No. 74 containing Nos. Y1677/8 see below No. 2657.

First Day Covers

| | | | |
|---|---|---|---|
| 26 Oct. 1993 | 19p, 25p, 29p, 36p, 38p, 41p (Nos. Y1682, Y1689, Y1693, Y1702, Y1706, Y1712) | 6·00 | ☐ |
| 9 Aug. 1994 | 60p (No. Y1784) | 4·00 | ☐ |
| 22 Aug. 1995 | £1 (No. Y1743) | 3·50 | ☐ |
| 25 June 1996 | 20p, 26p, 31p, 37p, 39p, 43p, 63p (Nos. Y1685, Y1691, Y1695, Y1703, Y1708, Y1716, Y1732) | 8·00 | ☐ |
| 9 March 1999 | £1·50, £2, £3, £5 (Nos. Y1800/3) | 27·00 | ☐ |
| 20 April 1999 | 7p, 38p, 44p, 64p (Nos. Y1672, Y1707,  Y1719, Y1733) | 5·00 | ☐ |
| 25 April 2000 | 8p, 33p, 40p, 41p, 45p, 65p (Nos. Y1674, Y1696, Y1710, Y1714, Y1721, Y1734) | 5·00 | ☐ |
| 4 July 2002 | 37p, 42p, 47p, 68p, (Nos. Y1704, Y1715, Y1722, Y1736) | 4·00 | ☐ |
| 6 May 2003 | 34p (No. Y1697) | 1·20 | ☐ |
| 1 July 2003 | £1·50, £2, £3, £5 (Nos. Y1746/9) | 21·00 | ☐ |
| 1 April 2004 | 7p, 35p, 39p, 40p, 43p, Worldwide post- card (Nos. Y1673, Y1700, Y1709, Y1711, Y1718, 2357a) | 9·00 | ☐ |
| 5 April 2005 | 9p, 35p, 46p (Nos. Y1675, Y1701, Y1722) | 2·20 | ☐ |
| 28 March 2006 | 37p, 44p, 49p, 72p (Nos. Y1705, Y1720, Y1725, Y1737) | 4·25 | ☐ |
| 27 March 2007 | 16p, 48p, 50p, 54p, 78p (Nos. Y1680, Y1724, Y1727/8, Y1738) | 6·00 | ☐ |
| 1 April 2008 | 15p, 56p, 81p (Nos. Y1679, Y1729, Y1739) | 4·50 | ☐ |
| 31 March 2009 | 17p, 22p, 62p, 90p, (Nos. Y1681, Y1688, Y1731, Y1741) | 6·00 | ☐ |
| 30 March 2010 | 60p, 67p, 88p, 97p, £1·46, Europe up to 20 grams, Worldwide up to 20 grams  (Nos. Y1730, 1735, Y1740,  Y1742, Y1745, 2357b, 2358a) | 16·00 | ☐ |

For Nos. Y1677/8 on first day cover see under Nos. 2650/7.

Nos. Y1743/9 are printed in Iriodin ink which gives a shiny effect to the solid part of the background behind the Queen's head.

Nos. Y1699 and Y1713 were only issued in coils and Nos. Y1676, Y1683, Y1678, Y1686, Y1707, Y1717 and Y1660/89 only in booklets.

No. Y1771 exists with the phosphor band at the left or right of the stamp, but Nos. Y1683 and Y1686 exist with band at right only.

For self-adhesive versions of the 42p and 68p see Nos. 2297/8.

**1094** 'Family Group'
(bronze sculpture) (Henry Moore)

**1095** 'Kew Gardens'
(lithograph) (Edward Bawden)

**1096** 'St Francis and
the Birds' (Stanley Spencer)

**1097** 'Still Life: Odyssey I'
(Ben Nicholson)

**Europa. Contemporary Art**

**1993** (11 May) Phosphorised paper. Perf 14 × 14½

| | | | | | | |
|---|---|---|---|---|---|---|
| 1767 | **1094** | 24p | multicoloured | 60 | 60 | ☐ ☐ |
| 1768 | **1095** | 28p | multicoloured | 90 | 1·00 | ☐ ☐ |
| 1769 | **1096** | 33p | multicoloured | 1·25 | 1·40 | ☐ ☐ |
| 1770 | **1097** | 39p | multicoloured | 1·75 | 1·75 | ☐ ☐ |
| Set of 4 | | | | 4·00 | 4·25 | ☐ ☐ |
| First Day Cover | | | | | 4·75 | ☐ |
| Presentation Pack (P.O. Pack No. 237) | | | | 4·50 | | ☐ |
| PHQ Cards (set of 4) (152) | | | | 4·00 | 7·00 | ☐ ☐ |
| Set of 4 Gutter Pairs | | | | 9·00 | | ☐ |

**1098** Emperor Claudius
(from gold coin)

**1099** Emperor Hadrian
(bronze head)

**1100** Goddess Roma
(from gemstone)

**1101** Christ (Hinton
St. Mary mosaic)

**Roman Britain**

**1993** (15 June) Phosphorised paper with two phosphor bands. Perf 14 × 14½

| | | | | | | |
|---|---|---|---|---|---|---|
| 1771 | **1098** | 24p | multicoloured | 60 | 50 | ☐ ☐ |
| 1772 | **1099** | 28p | multicoloured | 90 | 1·00 | ☐ ☐ |
| 1773 | **1100** | 33p | multicoloured | 1·30 | 1·50 | ☐ ☐ |
| 1774 | **1101** | 39p | multicoloured | 1·50 | 1·60 | ☐ ☐ |
| Set of 4 | | | | 4·00 | 4·25 | ☐ ☐ |
| First Day Cover | | | | | 4·75 | ☐ |
| Presentation Pack (P.O. Pack No. 238) | | | | 4·50 | | ☐ |
| PHQ Cards (set of 4) (153) | | | | 4·25 | 7·00 | ☐ ☐ |
| Set of 4 Gutter Pairs | | | | 9·00 | | ☐ |

**1102** *Midland Maid* and other Narrow Boats, Grand Junction Canal

**1103** *Yorkshire Maid* and other Humber Keels, Stainforth and Keadby Canal

**1104** *Valley Princess* and other Horse-drawn Barges, Brecknock and Abergavenny Canal

**1105** Steam Barges including *Pride of Scotland* and Fishing Boats, Crinan Canal

**Inland Waterways**

**1993** (20 July) Two phosphor bands. Perf 14½ × 14

| | | | | |
|---|---|---|---|---|
| 1775 | **1102** | 24p multicoloured | 50 | 50 |
| 1776 | **1103** | 28p multicoloured | 1·00 | 1·00 |
| 1777 | **1104** | 33p multicoloured | 1·25 | 1·25 |
| 1778 | **1105** | 39p multicoloured | 1·50 | 1·40 |
| *Set of* 4 | | | 3·75 | 3·75 |
| First Day Cover | | | | 4·25 |
| Presentation Pack (P.O. Pack No. 239) | | | 4·50 | |
| PHQ Cards (*set of* 4) (154) | | | 4·25 | 7·00 |
| *Set of* 4 Gutter Pairs | | | 8·50 | |

Nos. 1775/8 commemorate the bicentenaries of the Acts of Parliament authorising the canals depicted.

**1106** Horse Chestnut

**1107** Blackberry

**1108** Hazel

**1109** Rowan

**1110** Pear

**The Four Seasons. (2nd series) Autumn. Fruits and Leaves**

**1993** (14 Sept.) One phosphor band (18p) or phosphorised paper (others) 1779 **1106** 18p multicoloured 50 30

| | | | | |
|---|---|---|---|---|
| 1780 | **1107** | 24p multicoloured | 75 | 50 |
| 1781 | **1108** | 28p multicoloured | 1·10 | 1·25 |
| 1782 | **1109** | 33p multicoloured | 1·40 | 1·50 |
| 1783 | **1110** | 39p multicoloured | 1·50 | 1·50 |
| *Set of* 5 | | | 4·75 | 4·50 |

| | | |
|---|---|---|
| First Day Cover | | 5·00 |
| Presentation Pack (P.O. Pack No. 240) | 5·00 | |
| PHQ Cards (*set of* 5) (155) | 4·50 | 7·00 |
| *Set of* 5 Gutter Pairs | 10·50 | |

**1111** *The Reigate Square*

**1112** *The Hound of the Baskervilles*

**1113** *The Six Napoleons*

**1114** *The Greek Interpreter*

**1115** *The Final Problem*

**Sherlock Holmes. Centenary of the Publication of The Final Problem**

**1993** (12 Oct.) Phosphorised paper. Perf 14 × 14½

| | | | | |
|---|---|---|---|---|
| 1784 | **1111** | 24p multicoloured | 50 | 60 |
| | | a. Horiz strip of 5. | | |
| | | Nos. 1784/8 | 5·00 | 5·25 |
| 1785 | **1112** | 24p multicoloured | 50 | 60 |
| 1786 | **1113** | 24p multicoloured | 50 | 60 |
| 1787 | **1114** | 24p multicoloured | 50 | 60 |
| 1788 | **1115** | 24p multicoloured | 50 | 60 |
| *Set of* 5 | | | 5·00 | 5·25 |
| First Day Cover | | | | 5·75 |
| Presentation Pack (P.O. Pack No. 241) | | | 5·50 | |
| PHQ Cards (*set of* 5) (156) | | | 4·50 | 10·00 |
| Gutter Strip of 10 | | | 11·00 | |

Nos. 1784/8 were printed together, *se-tenant*, in horizontal strips of five throughout the sheet.

**1116**

### Self-adhesive Booklet Stamp

**1993** (19 Oct.) Litho Walsall. Two phosphor bands. Die-cut perf 14 × 15 (with one elliptical hole in each vertical side)

| 1789 | **1116** | (1st) orange-red | 2·50 | 2·75 | ☐ ☐ |
|---|---|---|---|---|---|
| First Day Cover | | | | 5·50 | ☐ |
| Presentation Pack (booklet pane of 20) | | | | | |
| | (P.O. Pack No. 29) | | 25·00 | | ☐ |
| PHQ Card (D6) | | | 4·00 | 8·00 | ☐ ☐ |

For similar 2nd and 1st designs printed in photogravure by Enschedé see Nos. 1976/7.

**1117** Bob Cratchit and Tiny Tim

**1118** Mr and Mrs Fezziwig

**1119** Scrooge    **1120** The Prize Turkey

**1121** Mr Scrooge's Nephew

### Christmas. 150th Anniversary of Publication of A Christmas Carol

**1993** (9 Nov.) One phosphor band (19p) or phosphorised paper (others)

| 1790 | **1117** | 19p multicoloured | 60 | 40 | ☐ ☐ |
|---|---|---|---|---|---|
| 1791 | **1118** | 25p multicoloured | 90 | 60 | ☐ ☐ |
| 1792 | **1119** | 30p multicoloured | 1·25 | 1·50 | ☐ ☐ |
| 1793 | **1120** | 35p multicoloured | 1·40 | 1·60 | ☐ ☐ |
| 1794 | **1121** | 41p multicoloured | 1·40 | 1·60 | ☐ ☐ |
| *Set of* 5 | | | 4·50 | 5·25 | ☐ |
| First Day Cover | | | | 5·75 | ☐ |
| Presentation Pack (P.O. Pack No. 242) | | | 5·00 | | ☐ |
| PHQ Cards (*set of* 5) (157) | | | 4·50 | 8·00 | ☐ ☐ |
| *Set of* 5 Gutter Pairs | | | 10·00 | | ☐ |

### Collectors Pack 1993

**1993** (9 Nov.) Comprises Nos. 1639/43, 1654/7, 1659/63, 1767/88 and 1790/4

| CP1794a | Collectors Pack | 45·00 | ☐ |
|---|---|---|---|

### Post Office Yearbook

**1993** (9 Nov.) Comprises Nos. 1639/43, 1654/7, 1659/63, 1767/88 and 1790/4 in hardback book with slip case

| YB1794a | Yearbook | 50·00 | ☐ |
|---|---|---|---|

**1122** Class 5 No. 44957 and Class B1 No. 61342 on West Highland Line

**1123** Class A1 No. 60149 *Amadis* at Kings Cross

**1124** Class 4 No. 43000 on Turntable at Blythe North

**1125** Class 4 No. 42455 near Wigan Central

**1126** Castle Class No. 7002 *Devizes Castle* on Bridge crossing Worcester and Birmingham Canal

### The Age of Steam. Railway Photographs by Colin Gifford

**1994** (18 Jan.) One phosphor band (19p) or phosphorised paper with two bands (others). Perf 14½

| 1795 | **1122** | 19p deep blue-green, grey-black and black | 55 | 45 | ☐ ☐ |
|---|---|---|---|---|---|
| 1796 | **1123** | 25p slate-lilac, grey-black and black | 90 | 95 | ☐ ☐ |
| 1797 | **1124** | 30p lake-brown, grey-black and black | 1·40 | 1·50 | ☐ ☐ |
| 1798 | **1125** | 35p deep claret, grey-black and black | 1·75 | 1·80 | ☐ ☐ |
| 1799 | **1126** | 41p indigo, grey-black and black | 1·80 | 1·90 | ☐ ☐ |
| *Set of* 5 | | | 6·00 | 6·00 | ☐ ☐ |
| First Day Cover | | | | 6·50 | ☐ |
| Presentation Pack (P.O. Pack No. 244) | | | 6·50 | | ☐ |
| PHQ Cards (*set of* 5) (158) | | | 5·75 | 17·00 | ☐ ☐ |
| *Set of* 5 Gutter Pairs | | | 12·00 | | ☐ |

**1127** Dan Dare and the Mekon

**1128** The Three Bears

**1129** Rupert Bear

**1130** Alice (*Alice in Wonderland*)

**1131** Noggin and the Ice Dragon

**1132** Peter Rabbit posting Letter

**1133** Red Riding Hood and Wolf

**1134** Orlando the Marmalade Cat

**1135** Biggles

**1136** Paddington Bear on Station

## Greeting Stamps Booklet. 'Messages'

**1994** (1 Feb.) Two phosphor bands. Perf 15 × 14 (with one elliptical hole in each vertical side)

| | | | | | | |
|---|---|---|---|---|---|---|
| 1800 | **1127** | (1st) | multicoloured | 1·25 | 1·00 | ☐ ☐ |
| | | a. | Booklet pane. Nos. 1800/9 | 15·00 | 15·00 | ☐ ☐ |
| 1801 | **1128** | (1st) | multicoloured | 1·25 | 1·00 | ☐ ☐ |
| 1802 | **1129** | (1st) | multicoloured | 1·25 | 1·00 | ☐ ☐ |
| 1803 | **1130** | (1st) | gold, bistre-yellow and black | 1·25 | 1·00 | ☐ ☐ |
| 1804 | **1131** | (1st) | multicoloured | 1·25 | 1·00 | ☐ ☐ |
| 1805 | **1132** | (1st) | multicoloured | 1·25 | 1·00 | ☐ ☐ |
| 1806 | **1133** | (1st) | multicoloured | 1·25 | 1·00 | ☐ ☐ |
| 1807 | **1134** | (1st) | multicoloured | 1·25 | 1·00 | ☐ ☐ |
| 1808 | **1135** | (1st) | multicoloured | 1·25 | 1·00 | ☐ ☐ |
| 1809 | **1136** | (1st) | multicoloured | 1·25 | 1·00 | ☐ ☐ |
| *Set of* 10 | | | | 15·00 | 15·00 | ☐ ☐ |
| First Day Cover | | | | | 16·00 | ☐ |
| Presentation Pack (P.O. Pack No. G3) | | | | 18·00 | | ☐ |
| PHQ Cards (*set of* 10) (GS2) | | | | 16·00 | 30·00 | ☐ ☐ |

Nos. 1800/9 were printed together, *se-tenant*, in booklet panes of 10 stamps and 20 half stamp-size labels.

**SET PRICES.** Please note that set prices for booklet greetings stamps are for complete panes. Sets of single stamps are worth considerably less.

Castell Y Waun / Chirk Castle, Clwyd, Cymru / Wales
**1137** Castell Y Waun (Chirk Castle), Clwyd, Wales

Ben Arkle, Sutherland, Scotland
**1138** Ben Arkle, Sutherland, Scotland

Mourne Mountains, County Down, Northern Ireland
**1139** Mourne Mountains, County Down, Northern Ireland

Dersingham, Norfolk, England
**1140** Dersingham, Norfolk, England

Dolwyddelan, Gwynedd, Cymru / Wales
**1141** Dolwyddelan, Gwynedd, Wales

## 25th Anniversary of Investiture of the Prince of Wales. Paintings by Prince Charles

**1994** (1 Mar.) One phosphor band (19p) or phosphorised paper (others)

| | | | | | | |
|---|---|---|---|---|---|---|
| 1810 | **1137** | 19p | multicoloured | 55 | 40 | ☐ ☐ |
| 1811 | **1138** | 25p | multicoloured | 1·00 | 60 | ☐ ☐ |
| 1812 | **1139** | 30p | multicoloured | 1·10 | 1·50 | ☐ ☐ |
| 1813 | **1140** | 35p | multicoloured | 1·40 | 1·75 | ☐ ☐ |
| 1814 | **1141** | 41p | multicoloured | 1·50 | 1·75 | ☐ ☐ |
| *Set of* 5 | | | | 5·00 | 5·50 | ☐ ☐ |
| First Day Cover | | | | | 6·00 | ☐ |
| Presentation Pack (P.O. Pack No. 245) | | | | 5·50 | | ☐ |
| PHQ Cards (*set of* 5) (159) | | | | 5·75 | 11·50 | ☐ ☐ |
| *Set of* 5 Gutter Pairs | | | | 11·00 | | ☐ |

PICTORIAL POSTCARDS 1894-1994
**1142** Bather at Blackpool

PICTORIAL POSTCARDS 1894-1994
**1143** 'Where's my Little Lad?'

PICTORIAL POSTCARDS 1894-1994
**1144** 'Wish You were Here!'

PICTORIAL POSTCARDS 1894-1994
**1145** Punch and Judy Show

PICTORIAL POSTCARDS 1894-1994
**1146** 'The Tower Crane' Machine

## Centenary of Picture Postcards

**1994** (12 Apr.) One side band (19p) or two phosphor bands (others). Perf 14 × 14½

| | | | | | | |
|---|---|---|---|---|---|---|
| 1815 | **1142** | 19p | multicoloured | 60 | 40 | ☐ ☐ |
| 1816 | **1143** | 25p | multicoloured | 90 | 60 | ☐ ☐ |
| 1817 | **1144** | 30p | multicoloured | 1·10 | 1·50 | ☐ ☐ |
| 1818 | **1145** | 35p | multicoloured | 1·40 | 1·75 | ☐ ☐ |
| 1819 | **1146** | 41p | multicoloured | 1·50 | 1·75 | ☐ ☐ |
| *Set of* 5 | | | | 5·00 | 5·50 | ☐ ☐ |
| First Day Cover | | | | | 6·00 | ☐ |
| Presentation Pack (P.O. Pack No. 246) | | | | 5·50 | | ☐ |

| | | | | |
|---|---|---|---|---|
| PHQ Cards (*set of 5*) (160) | 5·75 | 11·50 | ☐ | ☐ |
| *Set of 5* Gutter Pairs | 11·00 | | ☐ | |

**1147** British Lion and French Cockerel over Tunnel

**1148** Symbolic Hands over Train

### Opening of Channel Tunnel

**1994** (3 May) Phosphorised paper. Perf 14 × 14½

| | | | | | | | |
|---|---|---|---|---|---|---|---|
| 1820 | **1147** | 25p | multicoloured | 75 | 60 | ☐ | ☐ |
| | | a. | Horiz pair. | | | | |
| | | | Nos. 1820/1 | 1·75 | 2·00 | ☐ | ☐ |
| 1821 | **1148** | 25p | multicoloured | 75 | 60 | ☐ | ☐ |
| 1822 | **1147** | 41p | multicoloured | 1·00 | 1·00 | ☐ | ☐ |
| | | a. | Horiz pair. | | | | |
| | | | Nos. 1822/3 | 3·25 | 2·50 | ☐ | ☐ |
| 1823 | **1148** | 41p | multicoloured | 1·00 | 1·00 | ☐ | ☐ |
| *Set of 4* | | | | 4·50 | 4·75 | ☐ | ☐ |
| First Day Cover | | | | | 5·25 | | ☐ |
| First Day Covers (2) (UK and | | | | | | | |
| French stamps) | | | | | 20·00 | | ☐ |
| Presentation Pack (P.O. Pack No. 247) | | | | 5·00 | | | ☐ |
| Presentation Pack (UK and | | | | | | | |
| French stamps) | | | | 25·00 | | | ☐ |
| Souvenir Book | | | | 50·00 | | | ☐ |
| PHQ Cards (*set of 4*) (161) | | | | 5·75 | 9·00 | ☐ | ☐ |

Stamps in similar designs were also issued by France and these are included in the joint Presentation Pack and Souvenir Book.

Nos. 1820/1 and 1822/3 were printed together, *se-tenant*, in horizontal pairs throughout the sheets.

**1149** Groundcrew replacing Smoke Canisters on Douglas Boston of 88 Sqn

**1150** H.M.S. Warspite (battleship) shelling Enemy Positions

**1151** Commandos Landing on Gold Beach

**1152** Infantry regrouping on Sword Beach

**1153** Tank and Infantry advancing, Ouistreham

### 50th Anniversary of D-Day

**1994** (6 June) Two phosphor bands. Perf 14½ × 14

| | | | | | | | |
|---|---|---|---|---|---|---|---|
| 1824 | **1149** | 25p | multicoloured | 60 | 60 | ☐ | ☐ |
| | | a. | Horiz strip of 5. | | | | |
| | | | Nos. 1824/8 | 4·25 | 5·00 | ☐ | ☐ |
| 1825 | **1150** | 25p | multicoloured | 60 | 60 | ☐ | ☐ |
| 1826 | **1151** | 25p | multicoloured | 60 | 60 | ☐ | ☐ |
| 1827 | **1152** | 25p | multicoloured | 60 | 60 | ☐ | ☐ |
| 1828 | **1153** | 25p | multicoloured | 60 | 60 | ☐ | ☐ |
| *Set of 5* | | | | 4·25 | 5·00 | ☐ | ☐ |
| First Day Cover | | | | | 5·50 | | ☐ |
| Presentation Pack (P.O. Pack No. 248) | | | | 5·50 | | | ☐ |
| PHQ Cards (*set of 5*) (162) | | | | 5·00 | 11·50 | ☐ | ☐ |
| Gutter Block of 10 | | | | 11·00 | | | ☐ |

Nos. 1824/8 were printed together, *se-tenant*, in horizontal strips of five throughout the sheet.

**1154** The Old Course, St Andrews

**1155** The 18th Hole, Muirfield

**1156** The 15th Hole ('Luckyslap'), Carnoustie

**1157** The 8th Hole ('The Postage Stamp'), Royal Troon

**1158** The 9th Hole, Turnberry

### Scottish Golf Courses

**1994** (5 July) One phosphor band (19p) or phosphorised paper (others). Perf 14½ × 14

| | | | | | | | |
|---|---|---|---|---|---|---|---|
| 1829 | **1154** | 19p | multicoloured | 50 | 40 | ☐ | ☐ |
| 1830 | **1155** | 25p | multicoloured | 75 | 60 | ☐ | ☐ |
| 1831 | **1156** | 30p | multicoloured | 1·10 | 1·40 | ☐ | ☐ |
| 1832 | **1157** | 35p | multicoloured | 1·25 | 1·40 | ☐ | ☐ |
| 1833 | **1158** | 41p | multicoloured | 1·40 | 1·40 | ☐ | ☐ |
| *Set of 5* | | | | 4·50 | 4·75 | ☐ | ☐ |

| | | | | |
|---|---|---|---|---|
| First Day Cover | | 5·25 | ☐ | |
| Presentation Pack (P.O. Pack No. 249) | 5·00 | | ☐ | |
| PHQ Cards (*set of* 5) (163) | 5·75 | 11·50 | ☐ | ☐ |
| *Set of* 5 Gutter Pairs | | 10·00 | ☐ | |

Nos. 1829/33 commemorate the 250th anniversary of golf's first set of rules produced by the Honourable Company of Edinburgh Golfers.

**1159** Royal Welsh Show, Llanelwedd

**1160** All England Tennis Championships, Wimbledon

**1161** Cowes Week

**1162** Test Match, Lord's

SUMMERTIME *Braemar*
**1163** Braemar Gathering

### The Four Seasons (3rd series). Summertime. Events

**1994** (2 Aug.) One phosphor band (19p) or phosphorised paper (others)

| | | | | | | |
|---|---|---|---|---|---|---|
| 1834 | **1159** | 19p | multicoloured | 50 | 40 | ☐ ☐ |
| 1835 | **1160** | 25p | multicoloured | 75 | 60 | ☐ ☐ |
| 1836 | **1161** | 30p | multicoloured | 1·10 | 1·25 | ☐ ☐ |
| 1837 | **1162** | 35p | multicoloured | 1·25 | 1·60 | ☐ ☐ |
| 1838 | **1163** | 41p | multicoloured | 1·40 | 1·60 | ☐ ☐ |
| *Set of* 5 | | | | 4·50 | 5·00 | ☐ ☐ |
| First Day Cover | | | | | 5·50 | ☐ |
| Presentation Pack (P.O. Pack No. 250) | | | | 5·00 | | ☐ |
| PHQ Cards (*set of* 5) (164) | | | | 5·75 | 11·50 | ☐ ☐ |
| *Set of* 5 Gutter Pairs | | | | 10·00 | | ☐ |

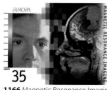
**1164** Ultrasonic Imaging

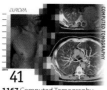
**1165** Scanning Electron Microscopy

**1166** Magnetic Resonance Imaging

**1167** Computed Tomography

### Europa. Medical Discoveries

**1994** (27 Sept.) Phosphorised paper. Perf 14 × 14½

| | | | | | | |
|---|---|---|---|---|---|---|
| 1839 | **1164** | 25p | multicoloured | 75 | 60 | ☐ ☐ |
| 1840 | **1165** | 30p | multicoloured | 1·00 | 1·25 | ☐ ☐ |
| 1841 | **1166** | 35p | multicoloured | 1·50 | 1·75 | ☐ ☐ |
| 1842 | **1167** | 41p | multicoloured | 1·75 | 1·75 | ☐ ☐ |
| *Set of* 4 | | | | 4·50 | 4·75 | ☐ ☐ |
| First Day Cover | | | | | 5·25 | ☐ |
| Presentation Pack (P.O. Pack No. 251) | | | | 5·00 | | ☐ |
| PHQ Cards (*set of* 4) (165) | | | | 5·75 | 10·00 | ☐ ☐ |
| *Set of* 4 Gutter Pairs | | | | 10·00 | | ☐ |

**1168** Virgin Mary and Joseph

**1169** Three Wise Men

**1170** Virgin and Child

**1171** Shepherds

**1172** Angels

### Christmas. Children's Nativity Plays

**1994** (1 Nov.) One phosphor band (19p) or phosphorised paper (others)

| | | | | | | |
|---|---|---|---|---|---|---|
| 1843 | **1168** | 19p | multicoloured | 50 | 40 | ☐ ☐ |
| 1844 | **1169** | 25p | multicoloured | 75 | 60 | ☐ ☐ |
| 1845 | **1170** | 30p | multicoloured | 1·00 | 1·50 | ☐ ☐ |
| 1846 | **1171** | 35p | multicoloured | 1·25 | 1·50 | ☐ ☐ |
| 1847 | **1172** | 41p | multicoloured | 1·50 | 1·75 | ☐ ☐ |
| *Set of* 5 | | | | 4·50 | 5·25 | ☐ ☐ |
| First Day Cover | | | | | 5·75 | ☐ |
| Presentation Pack (P.O. Pack No. 252) | | | | 5·00 | | ☐ |
| PHQ Cards (*set of* 5) (166) | | | | 5·75 | 11·50 | ☐ ☐ |
| *Set of* 5 Gutter Pairs | | | | 10·50 | | ☐ |

### Collectors Pack 1994

**1994** (14 Nov.) Comprises Nos. 1795/1847

| | | | |
|---|---|---|---|
| CP1847a | Collectors Pack | 48·00 | ☐ |

### Post Office Yearbook

**1994** (14 Nov.) Comprises Nos. 1795/9 and 1810/47 in hardback book with slip case

| | | | |
|---|---|---|---|
| YB1847a | Yearbook | 50·00 | ☐ |

**1173** Sophie (black cat)

**1174** Puskas (Siamese) and Tigger (tabby)

**1175** Chloe (ginger cat)

**1176** Kikko (tortoiseshell) and Rosie (Abyssinian)

**1177** Fred (black and white cat)

## Cats

**1995** (17 Jan.) One phosphor band (19p) or two phosphor bands (others). Perf 14½ × 14

| | | | | | | |
|---|---|---|---|---|---|---|
| 1848 | **1173** | 19p | multicoloured | 75 | 40 | |
| 1849 | **1174** | 25p | multicoloured | 75 | 60 | |
| 1850 | **1175** | 30p | multicoloured | 1·00 | 1·50 | |
| 1851 | **1176** | 35p | multicoloured | 1·25 | 1·50 | |
| 1852 | **1177** | 41p | multicoloured | 1·50 | 1·50 | |
| Set of 5 | | | | 4·75 | 5·00 | |
| First Day Cover | | | | | 5·00 | |
| Presentation Pack (P.O. Pack No. 254) | | | | 5·50 | | |
| PHQ Cards (set of 5) (167) | | | | 6·00 | 11·50 | |
| Set of 5 Gutter Pairs | | | | 11·00 | | |

**1178** Dandelions

**1179** Sweet Chestnut Leaves

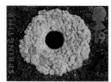

**1180** Garlic Leaves

**1181** Hazel Leaves

**1182** Spring Grass

## The Four Seasons (4th series). Springtime. Plant Sculptures by Andy Goldsworthy

**1995** (14 Mar.) One phosphor band (19p) or two phosphor bands (others)

| | | | | | | |
|---|---|---|---|---|---|---|
| 1853 | **1178** | 19p | multicoloured | 75 | 40 | |
| 1854 | **1179** | 25p | multicoloured | 75 | 60 | |
| 1855 | **1180** | 30p | multicoloured | 1·00 | 1·50 | |
| 1856 | **1181** | 35p | multicoloured | 1·25 | 1·50 | |
| 1857 | **1182** | 41p | multicoloured | 1·50 | 1·75 | |
| Set of 5 | | | | 4·75 | 5·25 | |
| First Day Cover | | | | | 5·75 | |
| Presentation Pack (P.O. Pack No. 255) | | | | 5·50 | | |
| PHQ Cards (set of 5) (168) | | | | 6·00 | 11·50 | |
| Set of 5 Gutter Pairs | | | | 11·00 | | |

**1183** 'La Danse à la Campagne' (Renoir)

**1184** 'Troilus and Criseyde' Peter Brookes)

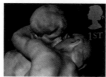

**1185** 'The Kiss' (Rodin)

**1186** 'Girls on the Town' (Beryl Cook)

**1187** 'Jazz' (Andrew Mockett)

**1188** 'Girls performing a Kathal Dance' (Aurangzeb period)

**1189** 'Alice Keppel with her Daughter' (Alice Hughes)

**1190** 'Children Playing' (L. S. Lowry)

**1191** 'Circus Clowns' (Emily Firmin and Justin Mitchell)

**1192** Decoration from 'All the Love Poems of Shakespeare' (Eric Gill)

## Greetings Booklet Stamp. 'Greetings in Art'

**1995** (21 Mar.) Two phosphor bands. Perf 14½ × 14 (with one elliptical hole in each vertical side)

| | | | | | | | |
|---|---|---|---|---|---|---|---|
| 1858 | **1183** | (1st) | multicoloured | 1·25 | 1·00 | | |
| | | a. | Booklet pane. Nos. 1858/67 | 14·00 | 11·00 | | |
| 1859 | **1184** | (1st) | multicoloured | 1·25 | 1·00 | | |
| 1860 | **1185** | (1st) | multicoloured | 1·25 | 1·00 | | |
| 1861 | **1186** | (1st) | multicoloured | 1·25 | 1·00 | | |

| | | | | | | | |
|---|---|---|---|---|---|---|---|
| 1862 | **1187** | (1st) | multicoloured | 1·25 | 1·00 | ☐ | ☐ |
| 1863 | **1188** | (1st) | multicoloured | 1·25 | 1·00 | ☐ | ☐ |
| 1864 | **1189** | (1st) | purple-brown and silver | 1·25 | 1·00 | ☐ | ☐ |
| 1865 | **1190** | (1st) | multicoloured | 1·25 | 1·00 | ☐ | ☐ |
| 1866 | **1191** | (1st) | multicoloured | 1·25 | 1·00 | ☐ | ☐ |
| 1867 | **1192** | (1st) | black, greenish yellow and silver | 1·25 | 1·00 | ☐ | ☐ |
| *Set of* 10 | | | | 14·00 | 11·00 | ☐ | ☐ |
| First Day Cover | | | | | 12·00 | | ☐ |
| Presentation Pack (P.O. Pack No. G4) | | | | 15·00 | | ☐ | |
| PHQ Cards (*set of* 10) (GS3) | | | | 16·00 | 30·00 | ☐ | ☐ |

Nos. 1858/67 were printed together, *se-tenant*, in booklet panes of 10 stamps and 20 half stamp-size labels.

*The National Trust
Celebrating 100 Years* **19**

**1193** Fireplace Decoration, Attingham Park, Shropshire

*The National Trust
Protecting Land* **25**

**1194** Oak Seedling

*The National Trust
Conserving Art* **30**

**1195** Carved Table Leg, Attingham Park

*The National Trust
Saving Coast* **35**

**1196** St. David's Head, Dyfed, Wales

*The National Trust
Repairing Buildings* **41**

**1197** Elizabethan Window, Little Moreton Hall, Cheshire

### Centenary of The National Trust

**1995** (11 Apr.) One phosphor band (19p), two phosphor bands (25p, 35p) or phosphorised paper (30p, 41p)

| | | | | | | |
|---|---|---|---|---|---|---|
| 1868 | **1193** | 19p | multicoloured | 60 | 40 | ☐ ☐ |
| 1869 | **1194** | 25p | multicoloured | 80 | 60 | ☐ ☐ |
| 1870 | **1195** | 30p | multicoloured | 1·00 | 1·50 | ☐ ☐ |
| 1871 | **1196** | 35p | multicoloured | 1·25 | 1·50 | ☐ ☐ |
| 1872 | **1197** | 41p | multicoloured | 1·40 | 1·75 | ☐ ☐ |
| *Set of* 5 | | | | 4·50 | 5·25 | ☐ ☐ |
| First Day Cover | | | | | 5·75 | ☐ |
| Presentation Pack (P.O. Pack No. 256) | | | | 5·00 | | ☐ |
| PHQ Cards (*set of* 5) (169) | | | | 6·00 | 11·50 | ☐ ☐ |
| *Set of* 5 Gutter Pairs | | | | 10·50 | | ☐ |

**1198** British Troops and French Civilians celebrating

**1199** Symbolic Hands and Red Cross

**1200** St. Paul's Cathedral and Searchlights

**1201** Symbolic Hand releasing Peace Dove

**1202** Symbolic Hands

### Europa. Peace and Freedom

**1995** (2 May) One phosphor band (Nos. 1873/4) or two phosphor bands (others). Perf 14½ × 14

| | | | | | | |
|---|---|---|---|---|---|---|
| 1873 | **1198** | 19p | silver, bistre-brown and grey-black | 70 | 50 | ☐ ☐ |
| 1874 | **1199** | 19p | multicoloured | 70 | 50 | ☐ ☐ |
| 1875 | **1200** | 25p | silver, blue and grey-black | 1·00 | 1·00 | ☐ ☐ |
| 1876 | **1201** | 25p | multicoloured | 1·00 | 1·00 | ☐ ☐ |
| 1877 | **1202** | 30p | multicoloured | 1·25 | 2·25 | ☐ ☐ |
| *Set of* 5 | | | | 4·25 | 4·75 | ☐ ☐ |
| First Day Cover | | | | | 5·25 | ☐ |
| Presentation Pack (P.O. Pack No. 257) | | | | 5·00 | | ☐ |
| PHQ Cards (*set of* 5) (170) | | | | 6·00 | 11·50 | ☐ ☐ |
| *Set of* 5 Gutter Pairs | | | | 10·50 | | ☐ |

Nos. 1873 and 1875 commemorate the 50th anniversary of the end of the Second World War, No. 1874 the 125th anniversary of the British Red Cross Society and Nos. 1876/7 the 50th anniversary of the United Nations.

Nos. 1876/7 include the 'EUROPA' emblem.

For Type **1200** with the face value expressed as '1st' see No. MS2547.

**1203** *The Time Machine*

**1204** *The First Men in the Moon*

**1205** *The War of the Worlds*

**1206** *The Shape of Things to Come*

### Science Fiction. Novels by H. G. Wells

**1995** (6 June) Two phosphor bands. Perf 14½ × 14

| | | | | | | |
|---|---|---|---|---|---|---|
| 1878 | **1203** | 25p | multicoloured | 75 | 60 | ☐ ☐ |
| 1879 | **1204** | 30p | multicoloured | 1·25 | 1·50 | ☐ ☐ |
| 1880 | **1205** | 35p | multicoloured | 1·25 | 1·60 | ☐ ☐ |
| 1881 | **1206** | 41p | multicoloured | 1·50 | 1·60 | ☐ ☐ |
| *Set of 4* | | | | 4·25 | 4·75 | ☐ ☐ |
| First Day Cover | | | | | 5·25 | ☐ |
| Presentation Pack (P.O. Pack No. 258) | | | | 5·00 | | ☐ |
| PHQ Cards (*set of 4*) (171) | | | | 6·00 | 11·50 | ☐ ☐ |
| *Set of 4 Gutter Pairs* | | | | 10·00 | | ☐ |

Nos. 1878/81 commemorate the centenary of publication of Wells's *The Time Machine*.

**1207** The Swan, 1595

**1208** The Rose, 1592

**1209** The Globe, 1599

**1210** The Hope, 1613

**1211** The Globe, 1614

### Reconstruction of Shakespeare's Globe Theatre

**1995** (8 Aug.) Two phosphor bands. Perf 14½

| | | | | | | |
|---|---|---|---|---|---|---|
| 1882 | **1207** | 25p | multicoloured | 60 | 60 | ☐ ☐ |
| | | a. | Horiz strip of 5. | | | |
| | | | Nos. 1882/6 | 4·50 | 4·75 | ☐ ☐ |
| 1883 | **1208** | 25p | multicoloured | 60 | 60 | ☐ ☐ |
| 1884 | **1209** | 25p | multicoloured | 60 | 60 | ☐ ☐ |
| 1885 | **1210** | 25p | multicoloured | 60 | 60 | ☐ ☐ |
| 1886 | **1211** | 25p | multicoloured | 60 | 60 | ☐ ☐ |
| *Set of 5* | | | | 4·50 | 4·75 | ☐ ☐ |
| First Day Cover | | | | | 5·50 | ☐ |
| Presentation Pack (P.O. Pack No. 259) | | | | 5·00 | | ☐ |

| | | | |
|---|---|---|---|
| PHQ Cards (*set of 5*) (172) | | 6·00 | 11·50 | ☐ ☐ |
| Gutter Strip of 10 | | 10·50 | | ☐ |

Nos. 1882/6 were printed together, *se-tenant*, in horizontal strips of 5 throughout the sheet, the backgrounds forming a composite design.

**1212** Sir Rowland Hill and Uniform Penny Postage Petition

**1213** Hill and Penny Black

**1214** Guglielmo Marconi and Early Wireless

**1215** Marconi and Sinking of *Titanic* (liner)

### Pioneers of Communications

**1995** (5 Sept.) One phosphor band (19p) or phosphorised paper (others). Perf 14½ × 14

| | | | | | | |
|---|---|---|---|---|---|---|
| 1887 | **1212** | 19p | silver, red and black | 75 | 40 | ☐ ☐ |
| 1888 | **1213** | 25p | silver, brown and black | 1·00 | 60 | ☐ ☐ |
| 1889 | **1214** | 41p | silver, grey-green and black | 1·50 | 1·75 | ☐ ☐ |
| 1890 | **1215** | 60p | silver, deep ultramarine and black | 1·75 | 2·25 | ☐ ☐ |
| *Set of 4* | | | | 4·50 | 4·50 | ☐ ☐ |
| First Day Cover | | | | | 5·00 | ☐ |
| Presentation Pack (P.O. Pack No. 260) | | | | 5·00 | | ☐ |
| PHQ Cards (*set of 4*) (173) | | | | 5·75 | 11·50 | ☐ ☐ |
| *Set of 4 Gutter Pairs* | | | | 10·00 | | ☐ |

Nos. 1887/8 mark the birth bicentenary of Sir Rowland Hill and Nos. 1889/90 the centenary of the first radio transmissions.

**1216** Harold Wagstaff

**1217** Gus Risman

**1218** Jim Sullivan

**1219** Billy Batten

**1220** Brian Bevan

### Centenary of Rugby League

**1995** (3 Oct.) One phosphor band (19p) or two phosphor bands (others). Perf 14 × 14½

| | | | | |
|---|---|---|---|---|
| 1891 | **1216** | 19p multicoloured | 75 | 40 |
| 1892 | **1217** | 25p multicoloured | 75 | 60 |
| 1893 | **1218** | 30p multicoloured | 1·00 | 1·50 |
| 1894 | **1219** | 35p multicoloured | 1·00 | 1·60 |
| 1895 | **1220** | 41p multicoloured | 1·50 | 1·60 |
| Set of 5 | | | 4·75 | 5·25 |
| First Day Cover | | | | 5·75 |
| Presentation Pack (P.O. Pack No. 261) | | | 5·50 | |
| PHQ Cards (set of 5) (174) | | | 6·00 | 11·50 |
| Set of 5 Gutter Pairs | | | 11·00 | |

**1221** European Robin in Mouth of Pillar Box

**1222** European Robin on Railings and Holly

**1223** European Robin on Snow-covered Milk Bottles

**1224** European Robin on Road Sign

**1225** European Robin on Door Knob and Christmas Wreath

### Christmas. Christmas Robins

**1995** (30 Oct.) One phosphor band (19p) or two phosphor bands (others)

| | | | | |
|---|---|---|---|---|
| 1896 | **1221** | 19p multicoloured | 60 | 40 |
| 1897 | **1222** | 25p multicoloured | 85 | 60 |
| 1898 | **1223** | 30p multicoloured | 1·25 | 1·50 |
| 1899 | **1224** | 41p multicoloured | 1·60 | 1·75 |
| 1900 | **1225** | 60p multicoloured | 1·75 | 1·90 |
| Set of 5 | | | 5·50 | 6·00 |
| First Day Cover | | | | 6·50 |
| Presentation Pack (P.O. Pack No. 262) | | | 6·00 | |
| PHQ Cards (set of 5) (175) | | | 6·00 | 11·50 |
| Set of 5 Gutter Pairs | | | 12·00 | |

The 19p value was re-issued on 3 October 2000 and 9 October 2001 in sheets of 20 each with se-tenant label, in connection with 'customised' stamps available from the Philatelic Bureau. The labels show either Christmas greetings or a personal photograph.

### Collectors Pack 1995

**1995** (30 Oct.) Comprises Nos. 1848/1900

| | | | |
|---|---|---|---|
| CP1900a | Collectors Pack | 48·00 | |

### Post Office Yearbook

**1995** (30 Oct.) Comprises Nos. 1848/57 and 1868/1900 in hardback book with slip case

| | | | |
|---|---|---|---|
| YB1900a | Yearbook | 50·00 | |

**1226** Opening Lines of 'To a Mouse' and Fieldmouse

**1227** 'O my Luve's like a red, red rose' and Wild Rose

**1228** 'Scots, wha hae wi Wallace bled' and Sir William Wallace

**1229** 'Auld Lang Syne' and Highland Dancers

### Death Bicentenary of Robert Burns (Scottish poet)

**1996** (25 Jan.) One phosphor band (19p) or two phosphor bands (others). Perf 14½

| | | | | |
|---|---|---|---|---|
| 1901 | **1226** | 19p cream, bistre-brown and black | 75 | 40 |
| 1902 | **1227** | 25p multicoloured | 1·00 | 60 |
| 1903 | **1228** | 41p multicoloured | 1·50 | 2·00 |
| 1904 | **1229** | 60p multicoloured | 1·75 | 2·50 |
| Set of 4 | | | 4·50 | 5·00 |
| First Day Cover | | | | 5·50 |
| Presentation Pack (P.O. Pack No. 264) | | | 5·00 | |
| PHQ Cards (set of 4) (176) | | | 6·00 | 11·50 |
| Set of 4 Gutter Pairs | | | 10·50 | |

**1230** 'MORE! LOVE' (Mel Calman)

**1231** 'Sincerely' (Charles Barsotti)

**1232** 'Do you have something for the HUMAN CONDITION?' (Mel Calman)

**1233** 'MENTAL FLOSS' (Leo Cullum)

**1234** '4.55 P.M.'
(Charles Barsotti)

**1235** 'Dear lottery prize winner' (Larry)

**1236** 'I'm writing to you because...'
(Mel Calman)

**1237** 'FETCH THIS, FETCH THAT'
(Charles Barsotti)

**1238** 'My day starts before I'm ready for it' (Mel Calman)

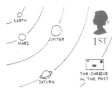

**1239** 'THE CHEQUE IN THE POST'
(Jack Ziegler)

### Greetings Booklet Stamps. Cartoons

**1996** (26 Feb.–11 Nov.) 'All-over' phosphor. Perf 14½ × 14 (with one elliptical hole in each vertical side)

| | | | | | | |
|---|---|---|---|---|---|---|
| 1905 | **1230** | (1st) | black and bright mauve | 1·25 | 75 | ☐ ☐ |
| | | a. | Booklet pane. Nos. 1905/14 | 14·00 | 11·00 | ☐ ☐ |
| | | p. | Two phosphor bands | 2·00 | 80 | ☐ ☐ |
| | | pa. | Booklet pane. Nos. 1905p/14p (11 Nov.) | 38·00 | 36·00 | ☐ ☐ |
| 1906 | **1231** | (1st) | black and blue-green | 1·25 | 75 | ☐ ☐ |
| | | p. | Two phosphor bands | 2·00 | 80 | ☐ ☐ |
| 1907 | **1232** | (1st) | black and new blue | 1·25 | 75 | ☐ ☐ |
| | | p. | Two phosphor bands | 2·00 | 80 | ☐ ☐ |
| 1908 | **1233** | (1st) | black and bright violet | 1·25 | 75 | ☐ ☐ |
| | | p. | Two phosphor bands | 2·00 | 80 | ☐ ☐ |
| 1909 | **1234** | (1st) | black and vermilion | 1·25 | 75 | ☐ ☐ |
| | | p. | Two phosphor bands | 2·00 | 80 | ☐ ☐ |
| 1910 | **1235** | (1st) | black and new blue | 1·25 | 75 | ☐ ☐ |
| | | p. | Two phosphor bands | 2·00 | 80 | ☐ ☐ |
| 1911 | **1236** | (1st) | black and vermilion | 1·25 | 75 | ☐ ☐ |
| | | p. | Two phosphor bands | 2·00 | 80 | ☐ ☐ |
| 1912 | **1237** | (1st) | black and bright violet | 1·25 | 75 | ☐ ☐ |
| | | p. | Two phosphor bands | 2·00 | 80 | ☐ ☐ |
| 1913 | **1238** | (1st) | black and blue-green | 1·25 | 75 | ☐ ☐ |
| | | p. | Two phosphor bands | 2·00 | 80 | ☐ ☐ |
| 1914 | **1239** | (1st) | black and bright mauve | 1·25 | 75 | ☐ ☐ |
| | | p. | Two phosphor bands | 2·00 | 80 | ☐ ☐ |
| Set of 10 (Nos. 1905/14) | | | | 14·00 | 11·00 | ☐ ☐ |
| Set of 10 (Nos. 1905p/14p) | | | | 38·00 | 36·00 | ☐ ☐ |
| First Day Cover (Nos. 1905/14) | | | | | 12·00 | ☐ |
| Presentation Pack (Nos. 1905/14) (P.O. Pack No. G5) | | | | 16·00 | | ☐ |
| PHQ Cards (set of 10) (GS4) | | | | 16·00 | 30·00 | ☐ ☐ |

Nos. 1905/14 were printed together, *se-tenant*, in booklet panes of 10 stamps and 20 half stamp-size labels.

Nos. 1905/14 were re-issued on 18 December 2001 in sheets of 10, each stamp with a *se-tenant* label showing cartoon titles. They were again issued on 29 July 2003 in sheets of 20 containing two of each design, each stamp accompanied by a half stamp size label showing a crossword grid or personal photograph. Such sheets are perforated without elliptical holes.

> **SET PRICES.** Please note that set prices for booklet greetings stamps are for complete panes. Sets of single stamps are worth considerably less.

**1240** 'Muscovy Duck'

**1241** 'Lapwing'

**1242** 'White-fronted Goose'

**1243** 'Bittern'

**1244** 'Whooper Swan'

### 50th Anniversary of the Wildfowl and Wetlands Trust. Bird Paintings by C. F. Tunnicliffe

**1996** (12 Mar.) One phosphor band (19p) or phosphorised paper (others). Perf 14 × 14½

| | | | | | |
|---|---|---|---|---|---|
| 1915 | **1240** | 19p multicoloured | 70 | 40 | ☐ ☐ |
| 1916 | **1241** | 25p multicoloured | 90 | 60 | ☐ ☐ |
| 1917 | **1242** | 30p multicoloured | 1·00 | 1·25 | ☐ ☐ |
| 1918 | **1243** | 35p multicoloured | 1·10 | 1·50 | ☐ ☐ |
| 1919 | **1244** | 41p multicoloured | 1·50 | 1·60 | ☐ ☐ |
| Set of 5 | | | 4·75 | 4·75 | ☐ ☐ |
| First Day Cover | | | | 5·50 | ☐ |
| Presentation Pack (P.O. Pack No. 265) | | | 5·50 | | ☐ |
| PHQ Cards (set of 5) (177) | | | 6·00 | 11·50 | ☐ ☐ |
| Set of 5 Gutter Pairs | | | 10·50 | | ☐ |

**1245** The Odeon, Harrogate

**1246** Laurence Olivier and Vivien Leigh in Lady Hamilton (film)

**1247** Old Cinema Ticket

**1248** Pathé News Still

**1249** Cinema Sign,
The Odeon, Manchester

## Centenary of Cinema

**1996** (16 Apr.) One phosphor band (19p) or two phosphor bands (others). Perf 14 × 14½

| | | | | | | |
|---|---|---|---|---|---|---|
| 1920 | **1245** | 19p | multicoloured | 50 | 40 | |
| 1921 | **1246** | 25p | multicoloured | 70 | 60 | |
| 1922 | **1247** | 30p | multicoloured | 1·00 | 1·75 | |
| 1923 | **1248** | 35p | black, red and silver | 1·25 | 2·00 | |
| 1924 | **1249** | 41p | multicoloured | 1·50 | 2·25 | |
| Set of 5 | | | | 4·75 | 6·25 | |
| First Day Cover | | | | | 7·00 | |
| Presentation Pack (P.O. Pack No. 266) | | | 5·50 | | | |
| PHQ Cards (set of 5) (178) | | | 6·00 | 11·50 | | |
| Set of 5 Gutter Pairs | | | 11·00 | | | |

**1250** Dixie Dean

**1251** Bobby Moore

**1252** Duncan Edwards

**1253** Billy Wright

**1254** Danny Blanchflower

## European Football Championship

**1996** (14 May) One phosphor band (19p) or two phosphor bands (others). Perf 14½ × 14

| | | | | | | |
|---|---|---|---|---|---|---|
| 1925 | **1250** | 19p | multicoloured | 50 | 40 | |
| 1926 | **1251** | 25p | multicoloured | 75 | 60 | |
| 1927 | **1252** | 35p | multicoloured | 1·25 | 1·75 | |
| 1928 | **1253** | 41p | multicoloured | 1·50 | 1·75 | |
| 1929 | **1254** | 60p | multicoloured | 1·75 | 2·00 | |
| Set of 5 | | | | 5·50 | 6·00 | |

| | | |
|---|---|---|
| First Day Cover | | 6·50 |
| Presentation Pack (P.O. Pack No. 267) | 6·00 | |
| PHQ Cards (set of 5) (179) | 6·00 | 11·50 |
| Set of 5 Gutter Pairs | 12·00 | |

**1255** Athlete on Starting Blocks

**1256** Throwing the Javelin

**1257** Basketball

**1258** Swimming

**1259** Athlete celebrating and Olympic Rings

## Olympic and Paralympic Games, Atlanta

**1996** (9 July) Two phosphor bands. Perf 14½ × 14

| | | | | | | | |
|---|---|---|---|---|---|---|---|
| 1930 | **1255** | 26p | multicoloured | 60 | 70 | | |
| | | a. | Horiz strip of 5. Nos. 1930/4 | 4·50 | 4·50 | | |
| 1931 | **1256** | 26p | multicoloured | 60 | 70 | | |
| 1932 | **1257** | 26p | multicoloured | 60 | 70 | | |
| 1933 | **1258** | 26p | multicoloured | 60 | 70 | | |
| 1934 | **1259** | 26p | multicoloured | 60 | 70 | | |
| Set of 5 | | | | 4·50 | 4·50 | | |
| First Day Cover | | | | | 5·00 | | |
| Presentation Pack (P.O. Pack No. 268) | | | 5·00 | | | | |
| PHQ Cards (set of 5) (180) | | | 6·00 | 11·50 | | | |
| Gutter Strip of 10 | | | 10·00 | | | | |

Nos. 1930/4 were printed together, *se-tenant*, in horizontal strips of 5 throughout the sheet.

For these designs with the face value expressed as '1st' see **MS**2554.

**1260** Prof. Dorothy Hodgkin (scientist)

**1261** Dame Margot Fonteyn (ballerina)

**1262** Dame Elisabeth Frink (sculptress)

**1263** Dame Daphne du Maurier (novelist)

**1264** Dame Marea Hartman (sports administrator)

## Europa. Famous Women

**1996** (6 Aug.) One phosphor band (20p) or two phosphor bands (others). Perf 14½

| | | | | |
|---|---|---|---|---|
| 1935 **1260** | 20p | dull blue-green, brownish grey and black | 60 | 50 |
| 1936 **1261** | 26p | dull mauve, brownish grey and black | 75 | 60 |
| 1937 **1262** | 31p | bronze, brownish grey and black | 1·10 | 1·10 |
| 1938 **1263** | 37p | silver, brownish grey and black | 1·25 | 1·40 |
| 1939 **1264** | 43p | gold, brownish grey and black | 1·50 | 1·50 |
| Set of 5 | | | 4·75 | 4·50 |
| First Day Cover | | | | 5·00 |
| Presentation Pack (P.O. Pack No. 269) | | | 8·50 | |
| PHQ Cards (set of 5) (181) | | | 6·00 | 11·50 |
| Set of 5 Gutter Pairs | | | 11·00 | |

Nos. 1936/7 include the 'EUROPA' emblem.

**1265** Muffin the Mule

**1266** Sooty

**1267** Stingray

**1268** The Clangers

**1269** Dangermouse

## 50th Anniversary of Children's Television

**1996** (3 Sept.)–**97** One phosphor band (20p) or two phosphor bands (others). Perf 14½ × 14

| | | | | |
|---|---|---|---|---|
| 1940 **1265** | 20p | multicoloured | 55 | 30 |
| | a. | Perf 15 × 14 (23.9.97) | 2·00 | 2·00 |
| 1941 **1266** | 26p | multicoloured | 80 | 40 |
| 1942 **1267** | 31p | multicoloured | 1·00 | 1·50 |
| 1943 **1268** | 37p | multicoloured | 1·40 | 1·75 |
| 1944 **1269** | 43p | multicoloured | 1·60 | 2·00 |
| Set of 5 | | | 4·75 | 5·50 |
| First Day Cover | | | | 6·00 |
| Presentation Pack (P.O. Pack No. 270) | | | 3·50 | |

| | | |
|---|---|---|
| PHQ Cards (set of 5) (182) | 6·00 | 11·50 |
| Set of 5 Gutter Pairs | 10·50 | |

No. 1940a was only issued in the £6.15 'Celebrating 75 years of the BBC' stamp booklet.

**1270** Triumph TR3

**1271** MG TD

**1272** Austin-Healey 100

**1273** Jaguar XK120

**1274** Morgan Plus 4

## Classic Sports Cars

**1996** (1 Oct.) One phosphor band (20p) or two phosphor bands (others). Perf 14½

| | | | | |
|---|---|---|---|---|
| 1945 **1270** | 20p | multicoloured | 55 | 40 |
| 1946 **1271** | 26p | multicoloured | 1·10 | 50 |
| 1947 **1272** | 37p | multicoloured | 1·40 | 1·90 |
| 1948 **1273** | 43p | multicoloured | 1·60 | 1·90 |
| 1949 **1274** | 63p | multicoloured | 1·75 | 2·00 |
| Set of 5 | | | 5·75 | 6·00 |
| First Day Cover | | | | 6·50 |
| Presentation Pack (P.O. Pack No. 271) | | | 6·50 | |
| PHQ Cards (set of 5) (183) | | | 6·00 | 11·50 |
| Set of 5 Gutter Pairs | | | 13·00 | |

**1275** The Three Kings

**1276** The Annunciation

**1277** The Journey to Bethlehem

**1278** The Nativity

**1279** The Shepherds

## Christmas. Biblical Scenes

**1996** (28 Oct.) One phosphor band (2nd) or two phosphor bands (others)

| | | | | |
|---|---|---|---|---|
| 1950 **1275** | (2nd) | multicoloured | 1·00 | 60 |
| 1951 **1276** | (1st) | multicoloured | 1·25 | 70 |
| 1952 **1277** | 31p | multicoloured | 1·25 | 1·75 |
| 1953 **1278** | 43p | multicoloured | 1·25 | 1·75 |
| 1954 **1279** | 63p | multicoloured | 1·50 | 2·00 |
| *Set of 5* | | | 5·50 | 6·00 |
| First Day Cover | | | | 6·50 |
| Presentation Pack (P.O. Pack No. 272) | | | 6·00 | |
| PHQ Cards (*set of 5*) (184) | | | 6·00 | 11·50 |
| *Set of 5 Gutter Pairs* | | | 12·50 | |

## Collectors Pack 1996

**1996** (28 Oct.) Comprises Nos. 1901/54

| | | |
|---|---|---|
| CP1954a | Collectors Pack | 55·00 |

## Post Office Yearbook

**1996** (28 Oct.) Comprises Nos. 1901/4 and 1915/54 in hardback book with slip case

| | | |
|---|---|---|
| YB1954a | Yearbook | 55·00 |

**1280** *Gentiana acaulis* (Georg Ehret)

**1281** *Magnolia grandiflora* (Ehret)

**1282** *Camellia japonica* (Alfred Chandler)

**1283** *Tulipa* (Ehret)

**1284** *Fuchsia* 'Princess of Wales' (Augusta Sowerby)

**1285** *Tulipa gesneriana* (Ehret)

**1286** *Gazania splendens* (Charlotte Sowerby)

**1287** *Iris latifolia* (Ehret)

**1288** Hippeastrum rutilum (Pierre-Joseph Redoute)

**1289** Passiflora coerulea (Ehret)

## Greetings Stamps Booklet. 19th-century Flower Paintings

**1997** (6 Jan.) Two phosphor bands. Perf 14½ × 14 (with one elliptical hole in each vertical side)

| | | | | |
|---|---|---|---|---|
| 1955 **1280** | (1st) | multicoloured | 1·25 | 1·00 |
| | a. | Booklet pane. Nos. 1955/64 | 14·00 | 14·00 |
| 1956 **1281** | (1st) | multicoloured | 1·25 | 1·00 |
| 1957 **1282** | (1st) | multicoloured | 1·25 | 1·00 |
| 1958 **1283** | (1st) | multicoloured | 1·25 | 1·00 |
| 1959 **1284** | (1st) | multicoloured | 1·25 | 1·00 |
| 1960 **1285** | (1st) | multicoloured | 1·25 | 1·00 |
| 1961 **1286** | (1st) | multicoloured | 1·25 | 1·00 |
| 1962 **1287** | (1st) | multicoloured | 1·25 | 1·00 |
| 1963 **1288** | (1st) | multicoloured | 1·25 | 1·00 |
| 1964 **1289** | (1st) | multicoloured | 1·25 | 1·00 |
| *Set of 10* | | | 14·00 | 14·00 |
| First Day Cover | | | | 15·00 |
| Presentation Pack (P.O. Pack No. G6) | | | 16·00 | |
| PHQ Cards (*set of 10*) (GS5) | | | 16·00 | 30·00 |

Nos. 1955/64 were printed together, *se-tenant*, in booklet panes of 10 stamps and 20 half stamp-size labels.

Nos. 1955/64 were re-issued on 21 January 2003 in *se-tenant* sheets of 20, each accompanied by a label showing flowers or personal photograph. Such sheets are perforated without elliptical holes.

For Types **1280, 1283** and **1287** perf 15 × 14 see Nos. 2463/5. For Types **1283** and **1287** printed in photogravure and perf 14, see Nos. 2942/3.

**1290** 'King Henry VIII'

**1291** 'Catherine of Aragon'

**1292** 'Anne Boleyn'

**1293** 'Jane Seymour'

**1294** 'Anne of Cleves'

**1295** 'Catherine Howard'

**1296** 'Catherine Parr'

## 450th Death Anniversary of King Henry VIII

**1997** (21 Jan.) Two phosphor bands. Perf 15 (No. 1965) or 14 × 15 (others)

| | | | | |
|---|---|---|---|---|
| 1965 **1290** | 26p multicoloured | 60 | 60 | |
| 1966 **1291** | 26p multicoloured | 60 | 60 | |
| | a. Horiz strip of 6. | | | |
| | Nos. 1966/71 | 8·00 | 8·50 | |
| 1967 **1292** | 26p multicoloured | 60 | 60 | |
| 1968 **1293** | 26p multicoloured | 60 | 60 | |
| 1969 **1294** | 26p multicoloured | 60 | 60 | |
| 1970 **1295** | 26p multicoloured | 60 | 60 | |
| 1971 **1296** | 26p multicoloured | 60 | 60 | |
| *Set of 7* | | 8·00 | 8·50 | |
| First Day Cover | | | 9·50 | |
| Presentation Pack (P.O. Pack No. 274) | | 10·00 | | |
| PHQ Cards (*set of 7*) (185) | | 10·00 | 18·00 | |
| Gutter Pair and Gutter Block of 12 | | 17·00 | | |

Nos. 1966/71 were printed together, *se-tenant*, in horizontal strips of 6 throughout the sheet.

**1297** St. Columba in Boat

**1298** St. Columba on Iona

**1299** St. Augustine with King Ethelbert

**1300** St. Augustine with Model of Cathedral

### Religious Anniversaries

**1997** (11 Mar.) Two phosphor bands. Perf 14½

| | | | | |
|---|---|---|---|---|
| 1972 **1297** | 26p multicoloured | 75 | 60 | |
| 1973 **1298** | 37p multicoloured | 1·10 | 1·50 | |
| 1974 **1299** | 43p multicoloured | 1·50 | 1·50 | |
| 1975 **1300** | 63p multicoloured | 2·00 | 2·10 | |
| *Set of 4* | | 4·75 | 5·25 | |
| First Day Cover | | | 5·75 | |
| Presentation Pack (P.O. Pack No. 275) | | 5·25 | | |
| PHQ Cards (*set of 4*) (186) | | 5·75 | 11·50 | |
| *Set of 4 Gutter Pairs* | | 11·50 | | |

Nos. 1972/3 commemorate the 1400th death anniversary of St Columba and Nos. 1974/5 the 1400th anniversary of the arrival of St Augustine of Canterbury in Kent.

**1301**

**1302**

### Self-adhesive Coil Stamps

**1997** (18 Mar.) Photo Enschedé. One centre phosphor band (2nd) or two phosphor bands (1st). Perf 14 × 15 die-cut (with one elliptical hole in each vertical side)

| | | | | | |
|---|---|---|---|---|---|
| 1976 **1301** | (2nd) bright blue | 2·50 | 2·50 | | |
| 1977 **1302** | (1st) bright orange-red | 2·75 | 2·75 | | |
| *Set of 2* | | 5·00 | 5·00 | | |
| First Day Cover | | | 5·50 | | |
| Presentation Pack (P.O. Pack No. 37) | | 7·00 | | | |

Nos. 1976/7, which were priced at 20p and 26p, were each sold in rolls of 100 with the stamps separate on the backing paper.

> Machin stamps printed in gold were issued on 21 April 1997 for the Royal Golden Wedding. These are listed as definitives under Nos. 1668 (1st) and Y1692 26p. Nos. 1978/9 are vacant

**1303** *Dracula*

**1304** *Frankenstein*

**1305** *Dr Jekyll and Mr Hyde*

**1306** *The Hound of the Baskervilles*

### Europa. Tales and Legends. Horror Stories

**1997** (13 May) Two phosphor bands. Perf 14 × 15

| | | | | | |
|---|---|---|---|---|---|
| 1980 **1303** | 26p multicoloured | 1·00 | 60 | | |
| 1981 **1304** | 31p multicoloured | 1·10 | 1·50 | | |
| 1982 **1305** | 37p multicoloured | 1·30 | 1·75 | | |
| 1983 **1306** | 43p multicoloured | 2·00 | 1·95 | | |
| *Set of 4* | | 5·00 | 5·50 | | |
| First Day Cover | | | 6·00 | | |
| Presentation Pack (P.O. Pack No. 276) | | 5·50 | | | |
| PHQ Cards (*set of 4*) (187) | | 5·75 | 11·50 | | |
| *Set of 4 Gutter Pairs* | | 11·50 | | | |

Nos. 1980/3 commemorate the birth bicentenary of Mary Shelley (creator of Frankenstein) with the 26p and 31p values incorporating the 'EUROPA' emblem.

**1307** Reginald Mitchell and Supermarine Spitfire MkIIA

**1308** Roy Chadwick and Avro Lancaster MkI

**1309** Ronald Bishop and de Havilland Mosquito B MkXVI

**1310** George Carter and Gloster Meteor T Mk7

**1311** Sir Sidney Camm and
Hawker Hunter FGA Mk9

## British Aircraft Designers

**1997** (10 June) One phosphor band (20p) or two phosphor bands (others)

| | | | | | | |
|---|---|---|---|---|---|---|
| 1984 | **1307** | 20p | multicoloured | 75 | 50 | |
| 1985 | **1308** | 26p | multicoloured | 1·10 | 1·25 | |
| 1986 | **1309** | 37p | multicoloured | 1·40 | 1·25 | |
| 1987 | **1310** | 43p | multicoloured | 1·50 | 1·60 | |
| 1988 | **1311** | 63p | multicoloured | 2·00 | 2·00 | |
| *Set of* 5 | | | | 6·00 | 6·00 | |
| First Day Cover | | | | | 6·50 | |
| Presentation Pack (P.O. Pack No. 277) | | | | 6·50 | | |
| PHQ Cards (188) | | | | 6·00 | 13·00 | |
| *Set of* 5 Gutter Pairs | | | | 14·00 | | |

For Type **1307** printed in lithography and perf 14, see No. 2868.

**1312** Carriage Horse and
Coachman

**1313** Lifeguards Horse
and Trooper

**1314** Household Cavalry
Drum Horse and Drummer

**1315** Duke of Edinburgh's
Horse and Groom

## 50th Anniv of the British Horse Society
**'All The Queen's Horses'.**

**1997** (8 July) One phosphor band (20p) or two phosphor bands (others). Perf 14½

| | | | | | | |
|---|---|---|---|---|---|---|
| 1989 | **1312** | 20p | multicoloured | 80 | 45 | |
| 1990 | **1313** | 26p | multicoloured | 1·10 | 1·50 | |
| 1991 | **1314** | 43p | multicoloured | 1·50 | 1·50 | |
| 1992 | **1315** | 63p | multicoloured | 2·00 | 2·00 | |
| *Set of* 4 | | | | 5·00 | 5·25 | |
| First Day Cover | | | | | 5·75 | |
| Presentation Pack (P.O. Pack No. 278) | | | | 5·50 | | |
| PHQ Cards (*set of* 4) (189) | | | | 5·75 | 11·50 | |
| *Set of* 4 Gutter Pairs | | | | 12·00 | | |

**CASTLE**

Harrison printing (Nos. 1611/14)

**CASTLE**

Enschedé printing (Nos. 1993/6)

**1315a** Caernarfon Castle

Differences between Harrison and Enschedé printings:

Harrison – 'C' has top serif and tail of letter points to right. 'A' has flat top. 'S' has top and bottom serifs.

Enschedé – 'C' has no top serif and tail of letter points upwards. 'A' has pointed top. 'S' has no serifs.

**1997** (29 July) Designs as Nos. 1611/14 with Queen's head in silhouette as T **1044**, but re-engraved as above. Perf 15 × 14 (with one elliptical hole in each vertical side)

| | | | | | |
|---|---|---|---|---|---|
| 1993 | **1315a** | £1·50 | deep claret and gold† | 12·00 | 6·00 |
| 1994 | **881** | £2 | indigo and gold† | 14·00 | 2·25 |
| 1995 | **1044** | £3 | violet and gold† | 30·00 | 3·50 |
| 1996 | **882** | £5 | deep brown and gold† | 36·00 | 10·00 |
| *Set of* 4 | | | | 80·00 | 18·00 |
| *Set of* 4 Gutter Pairs | | | | £175 | |
| Presentation Pack (P.O. Pack No. 40) | | | | £150 | |

† The Queen's head on these stamps is printed in optically variable ink which changes colour from gold to green when viewed from different angles. See also Nos. 1410/13.

**1316** Haroldswick,
Shetland

**1317** Painswick,
Gloucestershire

**1318** Beddgelert,
Gwynedd

**1319** Ballyroney, County
Down

## Sub-Post Offices

**1997** (12 Aug.) One phosphor band (20p) or two phosphor bands (others). Perf 14½

| | | | | | | |
|---|---|---|---|---|---|---|
| 1997 | **1316** | 20p | multicoloured | 75 | 50 | |
| 1998 | **1317** | 26p | multicoloured | 1·00 | 1·00 | |
| 1999 | **1318** | 43p | multicoloured | 1·50 | 1·50 | |
| 2000 | **1319** | 63p | multicoloured | 2·25 | 2·25 | |
| *Set of* 4 | | | | 5·50 | 5·00 | |
| First Day Cover | | | | | 5·75 | |
| Presentation Pack (P.O. Pack No. 279) | | | | 6·00 | | |
| PHQ Cards (*set of* 4) (190) | | | | 5·75 | 11·50 | |
| *Set of* 4 Gutter Pairs | | | | 12·00 | | |

Nos. 1997/2000 also mark the centenary of the National Federation of Sub-Postmasters.

Enid Blyton's *Noddy*
**1320** 'Noddy'

Enid Blyton's *Famous Five*
**1321** 'Famous Five'

Enid Blyton's *Secret Seven*
**1322** 'Secret Seven'

Enid Blyton's *Faraway Tree*
**1323** 'Faraway Tree'

Enid Blyton's *Malory Towers*
**1324** 'Malory Towers'

### Birth Centenary of Enid Blyton (children's author)

**1997** (9 Sept.) One phosphor band (20p) or two phosphor bands (others). Perf 14 × 14½

| | | | | | | |
|---|---|---|---|---|---|---|
| 2001 | **1320** | 20p | multicoloured | 50 | 45 | ☐ ☐ |
| 2002 | **1321** | 26p | multicoloured | 1·00 | 1·25 | ☐ |
| 2003 | **1322** | 37p | multicoloured | 1·25 | 1·25 | ☐ |
| 2004 | **1323** | 43p | multicoloured | 1·50 | 2·00 | ☐ |
| 2005 | **1324** | 63p | multicoloured | 1·75 | 2·00 | ☐ |
| *Set of* 5 | | | | 5·50 | 6·00 | ☐ |
| First Day Cover | | | | | 6·50 | ☐ |
| Presentation Pack (P.O. Pack No. 280) | | | | 6·00 | | ☐ |
| PHQ Cards (*set of* 5) (191) | | | | 6·00 | 13·00 | ☐ ☐ |
| *Set of* 5 Gutter Pairs | | | | 12·00 | | ☐ |

**1325** Children and Father Christmas pulling Cracker

**1326** Father Christmas with Traditional Cracker

**1327** Father Christmas riding Cracker

**1328** Father Christmas on Snowball

**1329** Father Christmas and Chimney

### Christmas. 150th Anniversary of the Christmas Cracker

**1997** (27 Oct.) One phosphor band (2nd) or two phosphor bands (others)

| | | | | | | |
|---|---|---|---|---|---|---|
| 2006 | **1325** | (2nd) | multicoloured | 75 | 40 | ☐ ☐ |
| 2007 | **1326** | (1st) | multicoloured | 1·25 | 60 | ☐ ☐ |

| | | | | | |
|---|---|---|---|---|---|
| 2008 | **1327** | 31p | multicoloured | 1·00 | 1·50 | ☐ ☐ |
| 2009 | **1328** | 43p | multicoloured | 1·25 | 1·75 | ☐ ☐ |
| 2010 | **1329** | 63p | multicoloured | 1·60 | 2·00 | ☐ ☐ |
| *Set of* 5 | | | | 5·50 | 5·75 | ☐ ☐ |
| First Day Cover | | | | | 6·50 | ☐ |
| Presentation Pack (P.O. Pack No. 282) | | | 6·00 | | ☐ |
| PHQ Cards (*set of* 5) (192) | | | 6·00 | 13·00 | ☐ ☐ |
| *Set of* 5 Gutter Pairs | | | 12·00 | | |

The 1st value was re-issued on 3 October 2000 and 9 October 2001, in sheets of 10 in photogravure, each stamp with a *se-tenant* label, in connection with 'customised' service available from the Philatelic Bureau. On 1 October 2002 in sheet size of 20 in lithography the 1st value was again issued but perforated 14½ × 14. The labels show either Christmas greetings or a personal photograph.

**1330** Wedding Photograph, 1947

**1331** Queen Elizabeth II and Prince Philip, 1997

### Royal Golden Wedding

**1997** (13 Nov.) One phosphor band (20p) or two phosphor bands (others). Perf 15

| | | | | | |
|---|---|---|---|---|---|
| 2011 | **1330** | 20p | gold, yellow-brown and grey-black | 85 | 45 | ☐ ☐ |
| 2012 | **1331** | 26p | multicoloured | 1·10 | 70 | ☐ ☐ |
| 2013 | **1330** | 43p | gold, bluish green and grey-black | 1·90 | 2·25 | ☐ ☐ |
| 2014 | **1331** | 63p | multicoloured | 2·50 | 3·00 | ☐ ☐ |
| *Set of* 4 | | | | 5·75 | 5·75 | ☐ ☐ |
| First Day Cover | | | | | 7·00 | ☐ |
| Presentation Pack (P.O. Pack No. 281) | | | 6·25 | | ☐ |
| Souvenir Book (contains Nos. 1668, 1989/92 and 2011/14) | | | 50·00 | | ☐ |
| PHQ Cards (*set of* 4) (192) | | | 5·75 | 11·50 | ☐ ☐ |
| *Set of* 4 Gutter Pairs | | | 12·00 | | ☐ |

### Collectors Pack 1997

**1997** (13 Nov.) Comprises Nos. 1965/75, 1980/92 and 1997/2014

| | | | |
|---|---|---|---|
| CP2014a | Collectors Pack | 55·00 | ☐ |

### Post Office Yearbook

**1997** (13 Nov.) Comprises Nos. 1965/75, 1980/92 and 1997/2014 in hardback book with slip case

| | | | |
|---|---|---|---|
| YB2014a | Yearbook | 50·00 | ☐ |

Decline in distribution

Decline in sites

**20** ENDANGERED SPECIES
Common dormouse
*Muscardinus avellanarius*
**1332** Common Doormouse

**26** ENDANGERED SPECIES
Lady's slipper orchid
*Cypripedium calceolus*
**1333** Lady's Slipper Orchid

Decline in population

Decline in distribution

31 **ENDANGERED SPECIES**
Song thrush
*Turdus philomelos*

**1334** Song Thrush

37 **ENDANGERED SPECIES**
Shining ram's-horn snail
*Segmentina nitida*

**1335** Shining
Ram's-horn Snail

Decline in sightings

Decline in sites

43 **ENDANGERED SPECIES**
Mole cricket
*Gryllotalpa gryllotalpa*

**1336** Mole Cricket

63 **ENDANGERED SPECIES**
Devil's bolete
*Boletus satanas*

**1337** Devil's Bolete

## Endangered Species

**1998** (20 Jan.) One side phosphor band (20p) or two phosphor bands (others). Perf 14 × 14½

| | | | | |
|---|---|---|---|---|
| 2015 **1332** | 20p | multicoloured | 60 | 40 |
| 2016 **1333** | 26p | multicoloured | 75 | 40 |
| 2017 **1334** | 31p | multicoloured | 1·00 | 2·00 |
| 2018 **1335** | 37p | multicoloured | 1·25 | 1·25 |
| 2019 **1336** | 43p | multicoloured | 1·40 | 1·75 |
| 2020 **1337** | 63p | multicoloured | 1·90 | 2·25 |
| *Set of 6* | | | 6·25 | 7·50 |
| First Day Cover | | | | 8·00 |
| Presentation Pack (P.O. Pack No. 284) | | | 6·75 | |
| PHQ Cards (*Set of 6*) (194) | | | 6·00 | 14·00 |
| *Set of 6 Gutter Pairs* | | | 14·00 | |

1961–1997

**1338** Diana, Princess of Wales (photo by Lord Snowdon)

1961–1997

**1339** At British Lung Foundation Function, April 1997 (photo by John Stillwell)

1961–1997

**1340** Wearing Tiara, 1991 (photo by Lord Snowdon)

1961–1997

**1341** On Visit to Birmingham, October 1995 (photo by Tim Graham)

1961–1997

**1342** In Evening Dress, 1987 (photo by Terence Donovan)

## Diana, Princess of Wales Commemoration

**1998** (3 Feb.) Two phosphor bands

| | | | | |
|---|---|---|---|---|
| 2021 **1338** | 26p | multicoloured | 50 | 50 |
| | | a. Horiz strip of 5. Nos. 2021/5 | 4·50 | 4·50 |
| 2022 **1339** | 26p | multicoloured | 50 | 50 |
| 2023 **1340** | 26p | multicoloured | 50 | 50 |
| 2024 **1341** | 26p | multicoloured | 50 | 50 |
| 2025 **1342** | 26p | multicoloured | 50 | 50 |
| *Set of 5* | | | 4·50 | 4·50 |
| First Day Cover | | | | 5·00 |
| Presentation Pack (Unnumbered) | | | 16·00 | |
| Presentation Pack (Welsh) | | | 70·00 | |
| Gutter Strip of 10 | | | 10·00 | |

Nos. 2021/5 were printed together, *se-tenant*, in horizontal strips of 5 throughout the sheet.

**1343** Lion of England and Griffin of Edward III

**1344** Falcon of Plantagenet and Bull of Clarence

**1345** Lion of Mortimer and Yale of Beaufort

**1346** Greyhound of Richmond and Dragon of Wales

**1347** Unicorn of Scotland and Horse of Hanover

## 650th Anniversary of the Order of the Garter. The Queen's Beasts

**1998** (24 Feb.) Two phosphor bands

| | | | | |
|---|---|---|---|---|
| 2026 **1343** | 26p | multicoloured | 90 | 90 |
| | | a. Horiz strip of 5. Nos. 2026/30 | 4·50 | 4·50 |
| 2027 **1344** | 26p | multicoloured | 90 | 90 |
| 2028 **1345** | 26p | multicoloured | 90 | 90 |
| 2029 **1346** | 26p | multicoloured | 90 | 90 |
| 2030 **1347** | 26p | multicoloured | 90 | 90 |
| *Set of 5* | | | 4·50 | 4·50 |
| First Day Cover | | | | 5·25 |
| Presentation Pack (P.O. Pack No. 285) | | | 5·00 | |
| PHQ Cards (*set of 5*) (195) | | | 6·00 | 13·00 |
| Gutter Block of 10 | | | 10·00 | |

Nos. 2026/30 were printed together, *se-tenant*, in horizontal strips of 5 throughout the sheet.

The phosphor bands on Nos. 2026/30 are only half the height of the stamps and do not cover the silver parts of the designs.

**1348**

## Wilding definitives. The Definitive Portrait.
## Booklet Stamps

**1998** (10 Mar.) Design as T **157** (issued 1952–54), but with face values in decimal currency as T **1348**. One side phosphor band (20p) or two phosphor bands (others). Perf 14 (with one elliptical hole in each vertical side)

| | | | | | | |
|---|---|---|---|---|---|---|
| 2031 | **1348** | 20p | light green | 70 | 75 | ☐ ☐ |
| 2032 | | 26p | red-brown | 90 | 95 | ☐ ☐ |
| 2033 | | 37p | light purple | 2·75 | 2·75 | ☐ ☐ |
| *Set of* 3 | | | | 4·00 | 4·00 | ☐ ☐ |

Nos. 2031/3 were only issued in the £7.49 'The Definitive Portrait' booklet

---

For further Wilding designs in decimal currency see Nos. 2258/9, **MS**2326, **MS**2367, 2378/80 and 3329.

---

**1349** St. John's Point Lighthouse, County Down

**1350** Smalls Lighthouse, Pembrokeshire

**1351** Needles Rock Lighthouse, Isle of Wight, *c* 1900

**1352** Bell Rock Lighthouse, Arbroath, mid-19th-century

**1353** Eddystone Lighthouse, Plymouth, 1698

## Lighthouses

**1998** (24 Mar.) One side phosphor band (20p) or two phosphor bands (others). Perf 14½ × 14

| | | | | | | |
|---|---|---|---|---|---|---|
| 2034 | **1349** | 20p | multicoloured | 50 | 40 | ☐ ☐ |
| 2035 | **1350** | 26p | multicoloured | 75 | 50 | ☐ ☐ |
| 2036 | **1351** | 37p | multicoloured | 1·10 | 1·50 | ☐ ☐ |
| 2037 | **1352** | 43p | multicoloured | 1·50 | 1·75 | ☐ ☐ |
| 2038 | **1353** | 63p | multicoloured | 2·10 | 2·50 | ☐ ☐ |
| *Set of* 5 | | | | 5·50 | 6·00 | ☐ ☐ |
| First Day Cover | | | | | 6·50 | ☐ |
| Presentation Pack (P.O. Pack No. 286) | | | | 6·00 | | ☐ |
| PHQ Cards (*set of* 5) (196) | | | | 6·00 | 13·00 | ☐ ☐ |
| *Set of* 5 Gutter Pairs | | | | 13·00 | | ☐ |

Nos. 2034/8 commemorate the 300th anniversary of the first Eddystone Lighthouse and the final year of manned lighthouses.

## Self-adhesive stamps

**1998** (6 Apr.–22 June) Photo Enschedé, Questa or Walsall. Designs as T **913/14**. One centre phosphor band (2nd) or two phosphor bands (1st). Perf 15 × 14 die-cut (with one elliptical hole in each vertical side)

| | | | | | |
|---|---|---|---|---|---|
| 2039 | (2nd) | bright blue | 1·20 | 80 | ☐ ☐ |
| | b. | Perf 14½ × 14 die-cut *(22.6.98)* | £250 | | ☐ |
| 2040 | (1st) | bright orange-red | 1·50 | 1·50 | ☐ ☐ |
| | b. | Perf 14½ × 14 die-cut *(22.6.98)* | £250 | | ☐ |
| *Set of* 2 | | | 2·50 | 2·50 | ☐ ☐ |

Nos. 2039/40 were initially priced at 20p and 26p, and were available in coils of 200 (Enschedé), sheets of 100 (Enschedé, Questa or Walsall) or self-adhesive booklets (Questa or Walsall). See also Nos. 2295/8.

**1354** Tommy Cooper          **1355** Eric Morecambe

**1356** Joyce Grenfell          **1357** Les Dawson

**1358** Peter Cook

## Comedians

**1998** (23 Apr.) One phosphor band (20p) or two phosphor bands (others). Perf 14½ × 14

| | | | | | | |
|---|---|---|---|---|---|---|
| 2041 | **1354** | 20p | multicoloured | 50 | 50 | ☐ ☐ |
| 2042 | **1355** | 26p | multicoloured | 75 | 85 | ☐ ☐ |
| 2043 | **1356** | 37p | multicoloured | 1·25 | 1·25 | ☐ ☐ |
| 2044 | **1357** | 43p | multicoloured | 1·50 | 1·50 | ☐ ☐ |
| 2045 | **1358** | 63p | multicoloured | 1·75 | 2·10 | ☐ ☐ |
| *Set of* 5 | | | | 5·25 | 5·50 | ☐ ☐ |

| | | | | | | | |
|---|---|---|---|---|---|---|---|
| First Day Cover | | | 6·00 | | ☐ | | |
| Presentation Pack (P.O. Pack No. 287) | | 6·00 | | | ☐ | | |
| PHQ Cards (*set of* 5) (197) | | | 6·00 | 13·00 | ☐ | ☐ | |
| *Set of* 5 Gutter Pairs | | | 13·50 | | ☐ | | |

**1359** Hands forming Heart

**1360** Adult and Child holding Hands

**1361** Hands forming Cradle

**1362** Hands taking Pulse

### 50th Anniversary of National Health Service

**1998** (23 June) One side phosphor band (20p) or two phosphor bands (others). Perf 14 × 14½

| | | | | | | |
|---|---|---|---|---|---|---|
| 2046 | **1359** | 20p | multicoloured | 50 | 50 | ☐ ☐ |
| 2047 | **1360** | 26p | multicoloured | 90 | 90 | ☐ ☐ |
| 2048 | **1361** | 43p | multicoloured | 1·50 | 1·50 | ☐ ☐ |
| 2049 | **1362** | 63p | multicoloured | 2·10 | 2·10 | ☐ ☐ |
| *Set of* 4 | | | | 4·50 | 4·50 | ☐ ☐ |
| First Day Cover | | | | | 5·00 | ☐ |
| Presentation Pack (P.O. Pack No. 288) | | | | 5·50 | | ☐ |
| PHQ Cards (*set of* 4) (198) | | | | 5·75 | 11·50 | ☐ ☐ |
| *Set of* 4 Gutter Pairs | | | | 11·00 | | ☐ |

**1363** 'The Hobbit' (J.R.R. Tolkien)

**1364** 'The Lion, The Witch and the Wardrobe' (C. S. Lewis)

**1365** 'The Phoenix and the Carpet' (E. Nesbit)

**1366** 'The Borrowers' (Mary Norton)

**1367** 'Through the Looking Glass' (Lewis Carroll)

### Famous Children's Fantasy Novels

**1998** (21 July) One phosphor band (20p) or two phosphor bands (others)

| | | | | | | | |
|---|---|---|---|---|---|---|---|
| 2050 | **1363** | 20p | multicoloured | 50 | 50 | ☐ ☐ | |
| 2051 | **1364** | 26p | multicoloured | 90 | 90 | ☐ ☐ | |
| 2052 | **1365** | 37p | multicoloured | 1·25 | 1·50 | ☐ ☐ | |
| 2053 | **1366** | 43p | multicoloured | 1·50 | 1·50 | ☐ ☐ | |
| 2054 | **1367** | 63p | multicoloured | 2·10 | 2·00 | ☐ ☐ | |
| *Set of* 5 | | | | 5·75 | 5·75 | ☐ ☐ | |
| First Day Cover | | | | | 6·50 | ☐ | |
| Presentation Pack (P.O. Pack No. 289) | | | | 6·50 | | ☐ | |
| PHQ Cards (*set of* 5) (199) | | | | 6·00 | 13·00 | ☐ ☐ | |
| *Set of* 5 Gutter Pairs | | | | 13·00 | | ☐ | |

Nos. 2050/4 commemorate the birth centenary of C. S. Lewis and the death centenary of Lewis Carroll.

**1368** Woman in Yellow Feathered Costume

**1369** Woman in Blue Costume and Headdress

**1370** Group of Children in White and Gold Robes

**1371** Child in 'Tree' Costume

### Europa. Festivals. Notting Hill Carnival

**1998** (25 Aug.) One centre phosphor band (20p) or two phosphor bands (others). Perf 14 × 14½

| | | | | | | | |
|---|---|---|---|---|---|---|---|
| 2055 | **1368** | 20p | multicoloured | 75 | 45 | ☐ ☐ | |
| 2056 | **1369** | 26p | multicoloured | 95 | 55 | ☐ ☐ | |
| 2057 | **1370** | 43p | multicoloured | 1·50 | 2·00 | ☐ ☐ | |
| 2058 | **1371** | 63p | multicoloured | 2·00 | 2·75 | ☐ ☐ | |
| *Set of* 4 | | | | 4·75 | 5·25 | ☐ ☐ | |
| First Day Cover | | | | | 5·75 | ☐ | |
| Presentation Pack (P.O. Pack No. 290) | | | | 5·25 | | ☐ | |
| PHQ Cards (*set of* 4) (200) | | | | 5·75 | 11·50 | ☐ ☐ | |
| *Set of* 4 Gutter Pairs | | | | 11·50 | | ☐ | |

Nos. 2055/6 include the 'EUROPA' emblem.

**1372** Sir Malcolm Campbell's 'Bluebird', 1925

**1373** Sir Henry Segrave's Sunbeam, 1926

**1374** John G. Parry Thomas's Babs, 1926

**1375** John R. Cobb's Railton Mobil Special, 1947

**1376** Donald Campbell's 'Bluebird' CN7, 1964

### British Land Speed Record Holders

**1998** (29 Sept.–13 Oct.) One phosphor band (20p) or two phosphor bands (others). Perf 15 × 14

| | | | | | | |
|---|---|---|---|---|---|---|
| 2059 **1372** | 20p | multicoloured (centre band) | 50 | 40 | ☐ | ☐ |
| | | a. Perf 14½ × 13½ (side band) (13 Oct.) | 1·40 | 1·20 | ☐ | ☐ |
| 2060 **1373** | 26p | multicoloured | 75 | 50 | ☐ | ☐ |
| 2061 **1374** | 30p | multicoloured | 1·25 | 1·50 | ☐ | ☐ |
| 2062 **1375** | 43p | multicoloured | 1·50 | 1·60 | ☐ | ☐ |
| 2063 **1376** | 63p | multicoloured | 2·00 | 2·40 | ☐ | ☐ |
| Set of 5 | | | 5·50 | 5·75 | ☐ | ☐ |
| First Day Cover | | | | 6·50 | | ☐ |
| Presentation Pack (P.O. Pack No. 291) | | | 6·25 | | ☐ | |
| PHQ Cards (set of 5) (201) | | | 6·00 | 13·00 | ☐ | ☐ |
| Set of 5 Gutter Pairs | | | 13·00 | | ☐ | |

No. 2059a, which occurs with the phosphor band at the left or right of the stamp, was only issued in the £6.16 "Breaking Barriers" booklet. There are minor differences of design between No. 2059 and No. 2059a, which also omits the copyright symbol and date.

Nos. 2059/63 commemorate the 50th death anniversary of Sir Malcolm Campbell.

**1377** Angel with Hands raised in Blessing

**1378** Angel praying

**1379** Angel playing Flute

**1380** Angel playing Lute

**1381** Angel praying

### Christmas. Angels

**1998** (2 Nov.) One phosphor band (20p) or two phosphor bands (others)

| | | | | | | |
|---|---|---|---|---|---|---|
| 2064 **1377** | 20p | multicoloured | 50 | 50 | ☐ | ☐ |
| 2065 **1378** | 26p | multicoloured | 75 | 60 | ☐ | ☐ |
| 2066 **1379** | 30p | multicoloured | 1·25 | 1·50 | ☐ | ☐ |
| 2067 **1380** | 43p | multicoloured | 1·50 | 1·60 | ☐ | ☐ |
| 2068 **1381** | 63p | multicoloured | 2·00 | 2·25 | ☐ | ☐ |
| Set of 5 | | | 5·75 | 5·75 | ☐ | ☐ |

| | | | |
|---|---|---|---|
| First Day Cover | | 6·50 | ☐ |
| Presentation Pack (P.O. Pack No. 292) | 6·50 | | ☐ |
| PHQ Cards (set of 5) (202) | 6·00 | 13·00 | ☐ ☐ |
| Set of 5 Gutter Pairs | 12·50 | | |

### Collectors Pack 1998

**1998** (2 Nov.) Comprises Nos. 2015/30, 2034/8 and 2041/68

| | | |
|---|---|---|
| CP2068a | Collectors Pack | 65·00 | ☐ |

### Post Office Yearbook

**1998** (2 Nov.) Comprises Nos. 2015/30, 2034/8 and 2041/68 in hardback book with slip case

| | | |
|---|---|---|
| YB2068a | Yearbook | 60·00 | ☐ |

**1382** Greenwich Meridian and Clock (John Harrison's Chronometer)

**1383** Industrial Worker and Blast Furnace (James Watt's discovery of steam power)

**1384** Early Photos of Leaves (Henry Fox-Talbot's photographic experiments)

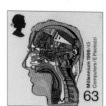

**1385** Computer inside Human Head (Alan Turing's work on computers)

### Millennium Series. The Inventors' Tale

**1999** (12 Jan.–21 Sept.) One centre phosphor band (20p) or two phosphor bands (others). Perf 14 × 14½

| | | | | | | |
|---|---|---|---|---|---|---|
| 2069 **1382** | 20p | multicoloured | 75 | 70 | ☐ | ☐ |
| 2070 **1383** | 26p | multicoloured | 95 | 1·00 | ☐ | ☐ |
| 2071 **1384** | 43p | multicoloured | 1·50 | 1·60 | ☐ | ☐ |
| 2072 **1385** | 63p | multicoloured | 2·25 | 2·40 | ☐ | ☐ |
| | | a. Perf 13½ × 14 (21 Sept.) | 3·50 | 3·50 | ☐ | ☐ |
| Set of 4 | | | 5·25 | 5·25 | ☐ | ☐ |
| First Day Cover | | | | 10·00 | | ☐ |
| Presentation Pack (P.O. Pack No. 294) | | | 7·50 | | ☐ | |
| PHQ Cards (set of 4) (203) | | | 6·00 | 13·00 | ☐ | ☐ |
| Set of 4 Gutter Pairs | | | 13·00 | | ☐ | |

No. 2072a was only issued in the £6.99 "World Changers" booklet.

**1386** Airliner hugging Globe (International air travel)

**1387** Woman on Bicycle (Development of the bicycle)

**1388** Victorian Railway
Station (Growth of public transport)

**1389** Captain Cook and
Maori (Captain James Cook's voyages)

**1393** Penicillin Mould
(Fleming's discovery of Penicillin)

**1394** Sculpture of Test-tube Baby
(development of in vitro fertilization)

## Millennium Series. The Patients' Tale

**1999** (2 Mar.) One centre phosphor band (20p) or two phosphor bands (others). Perf 13½ × 14

| | | | | | |
|---|---|---|---|---|---|
| 2080 | **1391** | 20p multicoloured | 75 | 70 | ☐ ☐ |
| 2081 | **1392** | 26p multicoloured | 95 | 1·00 | ☐ ☐ |
| 2082 | **1393** | 43p multicoloured | 1·50 | 1·60 | ☐ ☐ |
| 2083 | **1394** | 63p multicoloured | 2·25 | 2·40 | ☐ ☐ |
| *Set of* 4 | | | 5·25 | 5·25 | ☐ |
| First Day Cover | | | | 7·00 | ☐ |
| Presentation Pack (P.O. Pack No. 296) | | | 7·00 | | ☐ |
| PHQ Cards (*set of* 4) (205) | | | 6·00 | 13·00 | ☐ ☐ |
| *Set of* 4 Gutter Pairs | | | 12·00 | | ☐ |

**1395** Dove and Norman
Settler (medieval migration
to Scotland)

**1396** Pilgrim Fathers and
Red Indian (17th-century migration
to America)

## Millennium Series. The Travellers' Tale

**1999** (2 Feb.) One centre phosphor band (20p) or two phosphor bands (others). Perf 14 × 14½

| | | | | | |
|---|---|---|---|---|---|
| 2073 | **1386** | 20p multicoloured | 75 | 70 | ☐ ☐ |
| 2074 | **1387** | 26p multicoloured | 95 | 1·00 | ☐ ☐ |
| 2075 | **1388** | 43p grey-black, stone and bronze | 1·50 | 1·60 | ☐ ☐ |
| 2076 | **1389** | 63p multicoloured | 2·25 | 2·40 | ☐ ☐ |
| *Set of* 4 | | | 5·25 | 5·25 | ☐ ☐ |
| First Day Cover | | | | 7·00 | ☐ |
| Presentation Pack (P.O. Pack No. 295) | | | 7·50 | | ☐ |
| PHQ Cards (*set of* 4) (204) | | | 6·00 | 13·00 | ☐ ☐ |
| *Set of* 4 Gutter Pairs | | | 12·00 | | ☐ |

**1390**

### Booklet Stamps
**1999** (16 Feb.)

(a) Embossed and litho Walsall. Self-adhesive.
Die-cut perf 14 × 15

| | | | | | |
|---|---|---|---|---|---|
| 2077 | **1390** | (1st) grey (face value) (Queen's head in colourless relief) (phosphor background around head) | 3·00 | 2·50 | ☐ ☐ |

(b) Recess Enschedé. Perf 14 × 14½

| | | | | | |
|---|---|---|---|---|---|
| 2078 | **1390** | (1st) grey-black (2 phosphor bands) | 3·00 | 2·50 | ☐ ☐ |

(c) Typo Harrison. Perf 14 × 15

| | | | | | |
|---|---|---|---|---|---|
| 2079 | **1390** | (1st) black (2 phosphor bands) | 3·00 | 2·50 | ☐ ☐ |
| *Set of* 3 | | | 8·00 | 7·00 | ☐ ☐ |

Nos. 2077/9 were only issued in £7·54 'Profile on Print' stamp booklet.

**1391** Vaccinating Child
(pattern in cow markings) (Jenner's
development of smallpox vaccine)

**1392** Patient on Trolley
(nursing care)

**1397** Sailing Ship and
Aspects of Settlement
(19th-century migration
to Australia)

**1398** Hummingbird and
Superimposed Stylised
Face (20th-century
migration to Great Britain)

## Millennium Series. The Settlers' Tale

**1999** (6 Apr.) One centre phosphor band (20p) or two phosphor bands (others). Perf 14 × 14½

| | | | | | |
|---|---|---|---|---|---|
| 2084 | **1395** | 20p multicoloured | 75 | 70 | ☐ ☐ |
| 2085 | **1396** | 26p multicoloured | 95 | 1·00 | ☐ ☐ |
| 2086 | **1397** | 43p multicoloured | 2·00 | 1·75 | ☐ ☐ |
| 2087 | **1398** | 63p multicoloured | 3·00 | 3·00 | ☐ ☐ |
| *Set of* 4 | | | 5·75 | 5·75 | ☐ ☐ |
| First Day Cover | | | | 7·50 | ☐ |
| Presentation Pack (P.O. Pack No. 297) | | | 7·00 | | ☐ |
| PHQ Cards (*set of* 4) (206) | | | 8·50 | 13·00 | ☐ ☐ |
| *Set of* 4 Gutter Pairs | | | 12·00 | | ☐ |

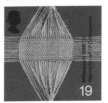

**1399** Woven Threads
(woollen industry)

**1400** Salts Mill, Saltaire
(worsted cloth industry)

**1401** Hull on Slipway (shipbuilding)

**1402** Lloyd's Building (City of London finance centre)

## Millennium Series. The Workers' Tale

**1999** (4 May) One centre phosphor band (19p) or two phosphor bands (others). Perf 14 × 14½

| | | | | | | |
|---|---|---|---|---|---|---|
| 2088 | **1399** | 19p multicoloured | 75 | 70 | ☐ | ☐ |
| 2089 | **1400** | 26p multicoloured | 95 | 1·00 | ☐ | ☐ |
| 2090 | **1401** | 44p multicoloured | 1·75 | 1·60 | ☐ | ☐ |
| 2091 | **1402** | 64p multicoloured | 2·25 | 2·40 | ☐ | ☐ |
| *Set of 4* | | | 5·25 | 5·25 | ☐ | |
| First Day Cover | | | | 7·00 | ☐ | |
| Presentation Pack (P.O. Pack No. 298) | | | 7·50 | | ☐ | |
| PHQ Cards (*set of 4*) (207) | | | 8·50 | 13·00 | ☐ | ☐ |
| *Set of 4 Gutter Pairs* | | | 12·00 | | ☐ | |

**1403** Freddie Mercury (lead singer of Queen) ('Popular Music')

**1404** Bobby Moore with World Cup, 1966 ('Sport')

**1405** Dalek from Dr Who (science-fiction series) ('Television')

**1406** Charlie Chaplin (film star) ('Cinema')

## Millennium Series. The Entertainers' Tale

**1999** (1 June) One centre phosphor band (19p) or two phosphor bands (others). Perf 14 × 14½

| | | | | | | |
|---|---|---|---|---|---|---|
| 2092 | **1403** | 19p multicoloured | 75 | 70 | ☐ | ☐ |
| 2093 | **1404** | 26p multicoloured | 95 | 1·00 | ☐ | ☐ |
| 2094 | **1405** | 44p multicoloured | 1·50 | 1·60 | ☐ | ☐ |
| 2095 | **1406** | 64p multicoloured | 2·25 | 2·40 | ☐ | ☐ |
| *Set of 4* | | | 5·25 | 5·25 | ☐ | |
| First Day Cover | | | | 7·00 | ☐ | |
| Presentation Pack (P.O. Pack No. 299) | | | 7·50 | | ☐ | |
| PHQ Cards (*set of 4*) (208) | | | 8·50 | 13·00 | ☐ | ☐ |
| *Set of 4 Gutter Pairs* | | | 12·00 | | ☐ | |

**1407** Prince Edward and Miss Sophie Rhys-Jones (from photos by John Swannell)

**1408** Prince Edward and Miss Sophie Rhys-Jones (from photos by John Swannell)

### Royal Wedding

**1999** (15 June) Two phosphor bands

| | | | | | | |
|---|---|---|---|---|---|---|
| 2096 | **1407** | 26p multicoloured | 85 | 85 | ☐ | |
| 2097 | **1408** | 64p multicoloured | 2·50 | 2·50 | ☐ | |
| *Set of 2* | | | 3·00 | 3·00 | ☐ | |
| First Day Cover | | | | 4·00 | ☐ | |
| Presentation Pack (P.O. Pack No. M01) | | | 4·00 | | ☐ | |
| PHQ Cards (*set of 2*) (PSM1) | | | 8·50 | 6·75 | ☐ | ☐ |
| *Set of 2 Gutter Pairs* | | | 7·00 | | ☐ | |

**1409** Suffragette behind Prison Window ('Equal Rights for Women')

**1410** Water Tap ('Right to Health')

**1411** Generations of School Children ('Right to Education')

**1412** 'MAGNA CARTA' ('Human Rights')

## Millennium Series. The Citizens' Tale

**1999** (6 July) One centre phosphor band (19p) or two phosphor bands (others). Perf 14 × 14½

| | | | | | | |
|---|---|---|---|---|---|---|
| 2098 | **1409** | 19p multicoloured | 75 | 70 | ☐ | ☐ |
| 2099 | **1410** | 26p multicoloured | 95 | 1·00 | ☐ | ☐ |
| 2100 | **1411** | 44p multicoloured | 1·75 | 1·60 | ☐ | ☐ |
| 2101 | **1412** | 64p multicoloured | 2·50 | 2·40 | ☐ | ☐ |
| *Set of 4* | | | 5·75 | 5·25 | ☐ | |
| First Day Cover | | | | 7·00 | ☐ | |
| Presentation Pack (P.O. Pack No. 300) | | | 7·50 | | ☐ | |
| PHQ Cards (*set of 4*) (209) | | | 8·50 | 13·00 | ☐ | ☐ |
| *Set of 4 Gutter Pairs* | | | 13·00 | | ☐ | |

**1413** Molecular Structures ('DNA decoding')

**1414** Galapagos Finch and Fossilized Skeleton ('Darwin's theory of evolution')

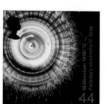

**1415** Rotation of Polarized Light by Magnetism (Faraday's work on electricity)

**1416** Saturn (development of astronomical telescopes)

## Millennium Series. The Scientists' Tale

**1999** (3 Aug.–21 Sept.) One centre phosphor band (19p) or two phosphor bands (others). Perf 13½ × 14 (19p, 64p) or 14 × 14½ (26p, 44p)

| | | | | | | |
|---|---|---|---|---|---|---|
| 2102 | **1413** | 19p multicoloured | 75 | 70 | ☐ | ☐ |
| 2103 | **1414** | 26p multicoloured | 1·50 | 1·00 | ☐ | ☐ |
| | | b. Perf 14½ × 14 | | | | |
| | | (21 Sept.) | 2·50 | 2·50 | ☐ | ☐ |
| 2104 | **1415** | 44p multicoloured | 1·50 | 1·60 | ☐ | ☐ |
| | | a. Perf 14½ × 14 | | | | |
| | | (21 Sept.) | 2·75 | 2·75 | ☐ | ☐ |
| 2105 | **1416** | 64p multicoloured | 2·25 | 2·40 | ☐ | ☐ |
| *Set of* 4 | | | 5·25 | 5·25 | ☐ | ☐ |
| First Day Cover | | | | 7·00 | | ☐ |
| Presentation Pack (P.O. Pack No. 301) | | | 7·50 | | ☐ | |
| PHQ Cards (*set of* 4) (210) | | | 8·50 | 13·00 | ☐ | ☐ |
| *Set of* 4 Gutter Pairs | | | 13·00 | | ☐ | |

Nos. 2103b and 2104a were only issued in the £6.99 'World Changers' booklet.

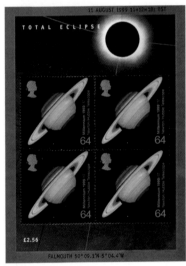

1416a

**Solar Eclipse miniature sheet**

**1999** (11 Aug.) Sheet 89 × 121 mm. Two phosphor bands. Perf 14 × 14½

| | | | | | |
|---|---|---|---|---|---|
| **MS**2106 | **1416a** | 64p × 4 multicoloured | 22·00 | 22·00 | ☐ ☐ |
| First Day Cover | | | | 24·00 | ☐ |

**1417** Upland Landscape (Strip farming)

**1418** Horse-drawn Rotary Seed Drill (Mechanical farming)

**1419** Man peeling Potato (Food imports)

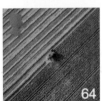

**1420** Aerial View of Combine Harvester (Satellite agriculture)

## Millennium Series. The Farmers' Tale

**1999** (7 Sept.) One centre phosphor band (19p) or two phosphor bands (others). Perf 14 × 14½

| | | | | | | |
|---|---|---|---|---|---|---|
| 2107 | **1417** | 19p multicoloured | 75 | 70 | ☐ | ☐ |
| 2108 | **1418** | 26p multicoloured | 95 | 1·00 | ☐ | |
| 2109 | **1419** | 44p multicoloured | 2·00 | 1·60 | ☐ | ☐ |
| 2110 | **1420** | 64p multicoloured | 2·50 | 2·40 | ☐ | ☐ |
| *Set of* 4 | | | 5·75 | 5·25 | ☐ | ☐ |
| First Day Cover | | | | 7·00 | | ☐ |
| Presentation Pack (P.O. Pack No. 302) | | | 7·50 | | ☐ | |
| PHQ Cards (*set of* 4) (211) | | | 8·50 | 13·00 | ☐ | ☐ |
| *Set of* 4 Gutter Pairs | | | 13·00 | | ☐ | |

No. 2107 includes the 'EUROPA' emblem.

**1421** Robert the Bruce (Battle of Bannockburn, 1314)

**1422** Cavalier and Horse (English Civil War)

**1423** War Graves Cemetery, The Somme (World Wars)

**1424** Soldiers with Boy (Peace-keeping)

## Millennium Series. The Soldiers' Tale

**1999** (5 Oct.) One centre phosphor band (19p) or two phosphor bands (others). Perf 14 × 14½

| | | | | | | |
|---|---|---|---|---|---|---|
| 2111 | **1421** | 19p black, stone and silver | 75 | 70 | ☐ | ☐ |
| 2112 | **1422** | 26p multicoloured | 95 | 1·00 | ☐ | ☐ |
| 2113 | **1423** | 44p grey-black, black | | | | |
| | | and silver | 2·00 | 1·60 | ☐ | ☐ |
| 2114 | **1424** | 64p multicoloured | 2·50 | 2·40 | ☐ | ☐ |
| *Set of* 4 | | | 5·75 | 5·25 | ☐ | ☐ |
| First Day Cover | | | | 7·00 | | ☐ |
| Presentation Pack (P.O. Pack No. 303) | | | 7·50 | | ☐ | |
| PHQ Cards (*set of* 4) (212) | | | 8·50 | 13·00 | ☐ | ☐ |
| *Set of* 4 Gutter Pairs | | | 13·00 | | ☐ | |

**1425** 'Hark the herald angels sing' and Hymn book (John Wesley)

**1426** King James I and Bible (Authorised Version of Bible)

**1427** St. Andrews Cathedral, Fife ('Pilgrimage')

**1428** Nativity ('First Christmas')

### Millennium Series. The Christians' Tale

**1999** (2 Nov.) One centre phosphor band (19p) or two phosphor bands (others). Perf 14 × 14½

| | | | | | | |
|---|---|---|---|---|---|---|
| 2115 | **1425** | 19p | multicoloured | 75 | 70 | ☐ ☐ |
| 2116 | **1426** | 26p | multicoloured | 95 | 1·00 | ☐ ☐ |
| 2117 | **1427** | 44p | multicoloured | 1·50 | 1·60 | ☐ ☐ |
| 2118 | **1428** | 64p | multicoloured | 2·25 | 2·40 | ☐ ☐ |
| *Set of 4* | | | | 5·25 | 5·25 | ☐ ☐ |
| First Day Cover | | | | | 7·00 | ☐ |
| Presentation Pack (P.O. Pack No. 304) | | | | 7·50 | | ☐ |
| PHQ Cards (*set of 4*) (213) | | | | 8·50 | 13·00 | ☐ ☐ |
| *Set of 4 Gutter Pairs* | | | | 13·00 | | ☐ |

**1429** 'World of the Stage' (Allen Jones)

**1430** 'World of Music' (Bridget Riley)

**1431** 'World of Literature' (Lisa Milroy)

**1432** 'New Worlds' (Sir Howard Hodgkin)

### Millennium Series. The Artists' Tale

**1999** (7 Dec.) One centre phosphor band (19p) or two phosphor bands (others). Perf 14 × 14½

| | | | | | | |
|---|---|---|---|---|---|---|
| 2119 | **1429** | 19p | multicoloured | 75 | 70 | ☐ ☐ |
| 2120 | **1430** | 26p | multicoloured | 95 | 1·00 | ☐ ☐ |
| 2121 | **1431** | 44p | multicoloured | 1·50 | 1·60 | ☐ ☐ |
| 2122 | **1432** | 64p | multicoloured | 2·25 | 2·40 | ☐ ☐ |
| *Set of 4* | | | | 5·25 | 5·25 | ☐ ☐ |
| First Day Cover | | | | | 7·00 | ☐ |
| Presentation Pack (P.O. Pack No. 305) | | | | 7·50 | | ☐ |
| PHQ Cards (*set of 4*) (214) | | | | 8·50 | 13·00 | ☐ ☐ |
| *Set of 4 Gutter Pairs* | | | | 13·00 | | ☐ |

### Collectors Pack 1999

**1999** (7 Dec.) Comprises Nos. 2069/76, 2080/105 and 2107/22

| | | | |
|---|---|---|---|
| CP2122a | Collectors Pack | 90.00 | ☐ |

### Post Office Yearbook

**1999** (7 Dec.) Comprises Nos. 2069/76, 2080/105 and 2107/22 in hardback book with slip case

| | | | |
|---|---|---|---|
| YB2122a | Yearbook | 90.00 | ☐ |

**1433a**

### Millennium Series. 'Millennium Timekeeper'

**1999** (14 Dec.) Sheet 120 × 89 mm. Multicoloured. Two phosphor bands. Perf 14 × 14½

**MS**2123 **1433a** 64p Clock face and map of North America; 64p Clock face and map of Asia; 64p Clock face and map of Middle East; 64p Clock face and map of Europe

| | | | |
|---|---|---|---|
| Clock face and map of Europe | 20·00 | 20·00 | ☐ ☐ |
| First Day Cover | | 21·00 | ☐ |
| Presentation Pack (P.O. Pack No. M02) | 22·00 | | ☐ |
| PHQ Cards (*set of 5*) (PSM02) | 11·00 | 24·00 | ☐ ☐ |

No. **MS**2123 also exists overprinted 'EARLS COURT, LONDON 22–28 MAY 2000 THE STAMP SHOW 2000' from Exhibition Premium Passes, costing £10, available from 1 March 2000.

The five PHQ cards show the four individual stamps and the complete miniature sheet.

**1437** Queen Elizabeth II

### New Millennium

**2000** (6 Jan.) Photo De La Rue, Questa or Walsall (No. 2124); Questa or Walsall (No. 2124d). Two phosphor bands. Perf 15 × 14 (with one elliptical hole in each vertical side)

| | | | | | | |
|---|---|---|---|---|---|---|
| 2124 | **1437** | (1st) | olive-brown | 1·50 | 1·00 | ☐ ☐ |
| | | d. | Perf 14 | 1·50 | 1·00 | ☐ ☐ |
| First Day Cover | | | | | 3·00 | ☐ |
| Presentation Pack (P.O. Pack No. 48) | | | | 9·00 | | ☐ |
| PHQ Card (*23 May*) (D16) | | | | 5·00 | 16·00 | ☐ ☐ |

No. 2124 comes from sheets or stamp booklets and No. 2124d from booklets only.

**1438** Barn Owl (World Owl Trust, Muncaster)

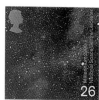

**1439** Night Sky (National Space Science Centre, Leicester)

**1440** River Goyt and Textile Mills (Torrs Walkaway, New Mills)

**1441** Cape Gannets (Seabird Centre, North Berwick)

**1446** Queen Victoria and Queen Elizabeth II

## Millennium Projects (1st series). 'Above and Beyond'

**2000** (18 Jan.–26 May) One centre phosphor band (19p) or two phosphor bands (others). Perf 14 × 14½ (1st, 44p) or 13½ × 14 (others)

| | | | | | |
|---|---|---|---|---|---|
| 2125 | **1438** | 19p multicoloured | 1·25 | 70 | ☐ ☐ |
| 2126 | **1439** | 26p multicoloured | 95 | 1·00 | ☐ ☐ |
| 2126a | | (1st) multicoloured | | | |
| | | (26 May) | 5·25 | 4·50 | ☐ ☐ |
| 2127 | **1440** | 44p multicoloured | 1·75 | 1·75 | ☐ ☐ |
| 2128 | **1441** | 64p multicoloured | 2·75 | 2·75 | ☐ ☐ |
| Set of 4 (ex No. 2126a) | | | 6·00 | 6·00 | ☐ ☐ |
| First Day Cover | | | | 7·00 | ☐ |
| Presentation Pack (P.O. Pack No. 307) | | | 7·00 | | ☐ |
| PHQ Cards (set of 4) (215) | | | 8·50 | 13·00 | ☐ ☐ |
| Set of 4 Gutter Pairs | | | 13·00 | | ☐ |

No. 2126a was only issued in the £2·70 Millennium booklet and, on 24 Sept 2002 in the £6·83 'Across the Universe' booklet.

**1442** Millennium Beacon (Beacons across the Land)

**1443** Garratt Steam Locomotive No. 143 pulling Train (Rheilffordd Eryri, Welsh Highland Railway)

**1444** Lightning (Dynamic Earth Centre, Edinburgh)

**1445** Multicoloured Lights (Lighting Croydon's Skyline)

## Millennium Projects (2nd series). 'Fire and Light'

**2000** (1 Feb.) One centre phosphor band (19p) or two phosphor bands (others). Perf 14 × 14½

| | | | | | |
|---|---|---|---|---|---|
| 2129 | **1442** | 19p multicoloured | 75 | 70 | ☐ ☐ |
| 2130 | **1443** | 26p multicoloured | 1·25 | 1·00 | ☐ ☐ |
| 2131 | **1444** | 44p multicoloured | 1·50 | 1·50 | ☐ ☐ |
| 2132 | **1445** | 64p multicoloured | 2·25 | 2·50 | ☐ ☐ |
| Set of 4 | | | 5·50 | 5·50 | ☐ |
| First Day Cover | | | | 7·00 | ☐ |
| Presentation Pack (P.O. Pack No. 308) | | | 7·00 | | ☐ |
| PHQ Cards (set of 4) (216) | | | 8·50 | 13·00 | ☐ ☐ |
| Set of 4 Gutter Pairs | | | 13·00 | | ☐ |

### Booklet Stamp

**2000** (15 Feb.) Design T **929**, but redrawn with '1st' face value as T **1446**. Two phosphor bands. Perf 14 (with one elliptical hole in each vertical side)

| | | | | | |
|---|---|---|---|---|---|
| 2133 | **1446** | (1st) brownish black and cream | 2·00 | 2·00 | ☐ ☐ |

No. 2133 was only issued in the £7·50 'Special by Design' booklet. See also No. 2956

**1447** Beach Pebbles (Turning the Tide, Durham Coast)

**1448** Frog's Legs and Water Lilies (National Pondlife Centre, Merseyside)

**1449** Cliff Boardwalk (Parc Ardfordirol, Llanelli Coast)

**1450** Reflections in Water (Portsmouth Harbour Development)

## Millennium Projects (3rd series). 'Water and Coast'

**2000** (7 Mar.) One centre phosphor band (19p) or two phosphor bands (others). Perf 14 × 14½

| | | | | | |
|---|---|---|---|---|---|
| 2134 | **1447** | 19p multicoloured | 75 | 70 | ☐ ☐ |
| 2135 | **1448** | 26p multicoloured | 1·25 | 1·00 | ☐ ☐ |
| 2136 | **1449** | 44p black, grey and silver | 1·50 | 1·50 | ☐ ☐ |
| 2137 | **1450** | 64p multicoloured | 2·25 | 2·50 | ☐ ☐ |
| Set of 4 | | | 5·50 | 5·50 | ☐ |
| First Day Cover | | | | 7·00 | ☐ |
| Presentation Pack (P.O. Pack No. 309) | | | 7·00 | | ☐ |
| PHQ Cards (set of 4) (217) | | | 8·50 | 13·00 | ☐ ☐ |
| Set of 4 Gutter Pairs | | | 13·00 | | ☐ |

**1451** Reed Beds, River Braid (ECOS, Ballymena)

**1452** South American Leaf-cutter Ants ('Web of Life' Exhibition, London Zoo)

**1453** Solar Sensors
(Earth Centre, Doncaster)

**1454** Hydroponic Leaves (Project SUZY, Teesside)

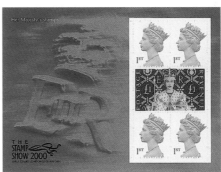

**1459**

### Millennium Projects (4th series). 'Life and Earth'

**2000** (4 Apr.) One centre phosphor band (2nd) or two phosphor bands (others). Perf 14 × 14½

| | | | | | |
|---|---|---|---|---|---|
| 2138 | **1451** | (2nd) multicoloured | 1·00 | 70 | ☐ ☐ |
| 2139 | **1452** | (1st) multicoloured | 1·25 | 1·00 | ☐ ☐ |
| 2140 | **1453** | 44p multicoloured | 1·50 | 1·50 | ☐ ☐ |
| 2141 | **1454** | 64p multicoloured | 2·25 | 1·50 | ☐ ☐ |
| *Set of* 4 | | | 5·75 | 5·50 | |
| First Day Cover | | | | 7·00 | ☐ |
| Presentation Pack (P.O. Pack No. 310) | | | 7·00 | | ☐ |
| PHQ Cards (*set of* 4) (218) | | | 8·50 | 13·00 | ☐ ☐ |
| *Set of* 4 Gutter Pairs | | | 13·00 | | ☐ |

**1455** Pottery Glaze (Ceramic Museum, Stoke-on-Trent)

**1456** Bankside Galleries (Tate Modern, London)

**1457** Road Marking (Cycle Network Artworks)

**1458** People of Salford (Lowry Centre, Salford)

### Millennium Projects (5th series). 'Art and Craft'

**2000** (2 May) One centre phosphor band (2nd) or two phosphor bands (others). Perf 14 × 14½

| | | | | | |
|---|---|---|---|---|---|
| 2142 | **1455** | (2nd) multicoloured | 1·00 | 70 | ☐ ☐ |
| 2143 | **1456** | (1st) multicoloured | 1·25 | 1·00 | ☐ ☐ |
| 2144 | **1457** | 45p multicoloured | 1·50 | 1·50 | ☐ ☐ |
| 2145 | **1458** | 65p multicoloured | 2·25 | 2·50 | ☐ ☐ |
| *Set of* 4 | | | 5·75 | 5·50 | |
| First Day Cover | | | | 7·00 | ☐ |
| Presentation Pack (P.O. Pack No. 311) | | | 7·50 | | ☐ |
| PHQ Cards (*set of* 4) (219) | | | 8·50 | 13·00 | ☐ ☐ |
| *Set of* 4 Gutter Pairs | | | 13·00 | | ☐ |

### 'Stamp Show 2000' International Stamp Exhibition, (1st issue) London. Jeffrey Matthews Colour Palette minature sheet

**2000** (22 May) Sheet, 124 × 70 mm, containing stamps as T **367** with two labels. Phosphorised paper. Perf 15 × 14 (with one elliptical hole in each vertical side)

| | | | |
|---|---|---|---|
| MS·2146 **1459** 4p new blue; 5p dull red-brown; 6p yellow-olive; 10p dull orange; 31p dp mauve; 39p brt magenta; 64p turq-green; £1 bluish violet | 30·00 | 30·00 | ☐ ☐ |
| First Day Cover | | 30·00 | ☐ |
| Exhibition Card (wallet, sold at £4·99, containing one mint sheet and one cancelled on postcard) | 75·00 | | ☐ |

The £1 value is printed in Iriodin ink which gives a shiny effect to the solid part of the background behind the Queen's head.

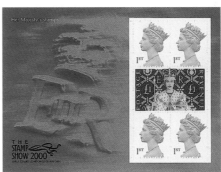

**1459a**

### 'Stamp Show 2000' International Stamp Exhibition, (2nd issue) London. 'Her Majesty's Stamps' miniature sheet

**2000** (23 May) Sheet 121 × 89 mm. Phosphorised paper. Perf 15 × 14 (with one elliptical hole in each vertical side of stamps as T **1437**)

| | | | |
|---|---|---|---|
| MS·2147 **1459a** (1st) olive-brown (Type **1437**) × 4; £1 slate-green (as Type **163**) 21·00 | 21·00 | | ☐ ☐ |
| First Day Cover | | 22·00 | ☐ |
| Presentation Pack (P.O. Pack No. M03) | 80 | | ☐ |
| PHQ Cards (*set of* 2) (PSM03) | 16·00 | 34·00 | ☐ ☐ |

The £1 value is an adaptation of the 1953 Coronation 1s3d stamp. It is shown on one of the PHQ cards with the other depicting the complete miniature sheet.

See also No. 2380 for T **163** from £7·46 stamp booklet.

**1460** Children playing (Millenium Greens Project)

**1461** Millennium Bridge, Gateshead

**1468** Tree Roots ('Yews for the Millennium' Project)

**1469** Sunflower ('Eden' Project, St. Austell)

**1462** Daisies (Mile End Park, London)

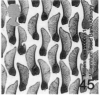

**1463** African Hut and Thatched Cottage ('On the Meridian Line' Project)

**1470** Sycamore Seeds (Millennium Seed Bank, Wakehurst Place, Surrey)

**1471** Forest, Doire Dach ('Forest for Scotland')

### Millennium Projects (6th series). 'People and Places'

**2000** (6 June) One centre phosphor band (2nd) or two phosphor bands (others). Perf 14 × 14½

| | | | | | | |
|---|---|---|---|---|---|---|
| 2148 | **1460** | (2nd) | multicoloured | 1·00 | 70 | |
| 2149 | **1461** | (1st) | multicoloured | 1·25 | 1·00 | |
| 2150 | **1462** | 45p | multicoloured | 1·50 | 1·50 | |
| 2151 | **1463** | 65p | multicoloured | 2·25 | 2·50 | |
| Set of 4 | | | | 5·75 | 5·50 | |
| First Day Cover | | | | | 7·00 | |
| Presentation Pack (P.O. Pack No. 312) | | | 7·50 | | |
| PHQ Cards (set of 4) (220) | | | 8·50 | 13·00 | |
| Set of 4 Gutter Pairs | | | 13·00 | | |

### Millennium Projects (8th series). 'Tree and Leaf'

**2000** (1 Aug.) One centre phosphor band (2nd) or two phosphor bands (others). Perf 14 × 14½

| | | | | | | |
|---|---|---|---|---|---|---|
| 2156 | **1468** | (2nd) | multicoloured | 1·00 | 70 | |
| 2157 | **1469** | (1st) | multicoloured | 1·25 | 1·00 | |
| 2158 | **1470** | 45p | multicoloured | 1·50 | 1·60 | |
| 2159 | **1471** | 65p | multicoloured | 2·50 | 2·50 | |
| Set of 4 | | | | 5·75 | 5·50 | |
| First Day Cover | | | | | 7·00 | |
| Presentation Pack (P.O. Pack No. 314) | | | 7·50 | | |
| PHQ Cards (set of 4) (222) | | | 8·50 | 13·00 | |
| Set of 4 Gutter Pairs | | | 13·00 | | |

**1464** Raising the Stone (Strangford Stone, Killyleagh)

**1465** Horse's Hooves (Trans Pennine Trail, Derbyshire)

**1466** Cyclist (Kingdom of Fife Cycle Ways, Scotland)

**1467** Bluebell Wood (Groundwork's 'Changing Places' Project)

### Millennium Projects (7th series). 'Stone and Soil'

**2000** (4 July) One centre phosphor band (2nd) or two phosphor bands (others). Perf 14 × 14½

| | | | | | | |
|---|---|---|---|---|---|---|
| 2152 | **1464** | (2nd) | brownish black, grey-black and silver | 1·00 | 70 | |
| 2153 | **1465** | (1st) | multicoloured | 1·25 | 1·00 | |
| 2154 | **1466** | 45p | multicoloured | 1·50 | 1·75 | |
| 2155 | **1467** | 65p | multicoloured | 2·50 | 2·50 | |
| Set of 4 | | | | 5·75 | 5·75 | |
| First Day Cover | | | | | 7·00 | |
| Presentation Pack (P.O. Pack No. 313) | | | 7·50 | | |
| PHQ Cards (set of 4) (221) | | | 8·50 | 13·00 | |
| Set of 4 Gutter Pairs | | | 13·00 | | |

**1472** Queen Elizabeth the Queen Mother

**1472a** Royal Family on Queen Mother's 100th Birthday (from photo by J. Swannell)

**Queen Elizabeth the Queen Mother's 100th Birthday**

**2000** (4 Aug.) Phosphorised paper plus two phosphor bands. Perf 14½

| 2160 | **1472** | 27p multicoloured | 2·50 | 2·75 | ☐ ☐ |

**MS**2161 121 × 89 mm. **1472a** 27p Queen Elizabeth II; 27p Prince William; 27p Queen Elizabeth the Queen Mother; 27p Prince Charles 11·00 11·00 ☐ ☐

| First Day Cover (**MS**2161) | | 12·00 | ☐ |
| Presentation Pack (**MS**2161) (P.O. Pack No. M04) | 38·00 | | ☐ |
| PHQ Cards (*set of 5*) (PSM04) | 11·00 | 24·00 | ☐ ☐ |

No. 2160 was only issued in the £7.03 "Life of the Century" booklet and in No. **MS**2161.

The complete miniature sheet is shown on one of the PHQ cards with the others depicting individual stamps.

**1473** Head of Gigantiops destructor (Ant) (Wildscreen at Bristol)

**1474** Gathering Water Lilies on Broads (Norfolk and Norwich Project)

**1475** X-ray of Hand holding Computer Mouse (Millennium Point, Birmingham

**1476** Tartan Wool Holder (Scottish Cultural Resources Access Network)

**Millennium Projects (9th series). 'Mind and Matter'**

**2000** (5 Sept.) One centre phosphor band (2nd) or two phosphor bands (others). Perf 14 × 14½

| 2162 | **1473** | (2nd) multicoloured | 1·00 | 70 | ☐ ☐ |
| 2163 | **1474** | (1st) multicoloured | 1·25 | 1·00 | ☐ ☐ |
| 2164 | **1475** | 45p multicoloured | 1·50 | 1·75 | ☐ ☐ |
| 2165 | **1476** | 65p multicoloured | 2·25 | 2·50 | ☐ ☐ |
| *Set of 4* | | | 5·75 | 5·75 | |
| First Day Cover | | | | 7·00 | ☐ |
| Presentation Pack (P.O. Pack No. 315) | | 7·50 | | ☐ |
| PHQ Cards (*set of 4*) (223) | | 8·50 | 13·00 | ☐ ☐ |
| *Set of 4 Gutter Pairs* | | | 13·00 | | |

**1477** Acrobatic Performers (Millennium Dome)

**1478** Football Players (Hampden Park, Glasgow)

**1479** Bather (Bath Spa Project)

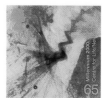

**1480** Hen's Egg under Magnification (Centre for Life, Newcastle)

**Millennium Projects (10th series). 'Body and Bone'**

**2000** (3 Oct.) One centre phosphor band (2nd) or two phosphor bands (others). Perf 14 × 14½ (2nd) or 13½ × 14 (others)

| 2166 | **1477** | (2nd) black, slate-blue and silver | 1·00 | 70 | ☐ ☐ |
| 2167 | **1478** | (1st) multicoloured | 1·25 | 1·00 | ☐ ☐ |
| 2168 | **1479** | 45p multicoloured | 1·50 | 1·50 | ☐ ☐ |
| 2169 | **1480** | 65p multicoloured | 2·25 | 2·50 | ☐ ☐ |
| *Set of 4* | | | 5·75 | 5·75 | ☐ ☐ |
| First Day Cover | | | | 7·00 | ☐ |
| Presentation Pack (P.O. Pack No. 316) | | 7·50 | | ☐ |
| PHQ Cards (*set of 4*) (224) | | 8·50 | 13·00 | ☐ ☐ |
| *Set of 4 Gutter Pairs* | | | 13·00 | | ☐ |

**1481** Virgin and Child Stained Glass Window, St. Edmundsbury Cathedral (Suffolk Cathedral Millennium Project)

**1482** Floodlit Church of St. Peter and St. Paul, Overstowey (Church Floodlighting Trust)

**1483** 12th-cent. Latin Gradual (St. Patrick Centre, Downpatrick)

**1484** Chapter House Ceiling, York Minster (York Millennium Mystery Plays)

**Millennium Projects (11th series). 'Spirit and Faith'**

**2000** (7 Nov.) One centre phosphor band (2nd) or two phosphor bands (others). Perf 14 × 14½

| 2170 | **1481** | (2nd) multicoloured | 1·00 | 70 | ☐ ☐ |
| 2171 | **1482** | (1st) multicoloured | 1·25 | 1·00 | ☐ ☐ |
| 2172 | **1483** | 45p multicoloured | 1·50 | 1·50 | ☐ ☐ |
| 2173 | **1484** | 65p multicoloured | 2·25 | 2·50 | ☐ ☐ |
| *Set of 4* | | | 5·75 | 5·50 | ☐ ☐ |
| First Day Cover | | | | 7·00 | ☐ |
| Presentation Pack (P.O. Pack No. 317) | | 7·50 | | ☐ |
| PHQ Cards (*set of 4*) (225) | | 8·50 | 13·00 | ☐ ☐ |
| *Set of 4 Gutter Pairs* | | | 13·00 | | ☐ |

**Post Office Yearbook**

**2000** (7 Nov.) Comprises Nos. 2125/6, 2127/32, 2134/45, 2148/59 and **MS**2161/77 in hardback book with slip case

| YB2177a | Yearbook | £100 | |

The last two issues in the Millennium Projects Series were supplied for insertion into the above at a later date.

**1485** Church Bells (Ringing in the Millennium)

**1486** Eye (Year of the Artist)

**1487** Top of Harp (Canolfan Mileniwn, Cardiff)

**1488** Figure within Latticework (TS2K Creative Enterprise Centres, London)

**Millennium Projects (12th series). 'Sound and Vision'**

**2000** (5 Dec.) One centre phosphor band (2nd) or two phosphor bands (others). Perf 14 × 14½

| | | | | | | |
|---|---|---|---|---|---|---|
| 2174 | **1485** | (2nd) | multicoloured | 1·00 | 70 | ☐ ☐ |
| 2175 | **1486** | (1st) | multicoloured | 1·25 | 1·00 | ☐ ☐ |
| 2176 | **1487** | 45p | multicoloured | 1·50 | 1·50 | ☐ ☐ |
| 2177 | **1488** | 65p | multicoloured | 2·25 | 2·50 | ☐ ☐ |
| Set of 4 | | | | 5·75 | 5·50 | ☐ |
| First Day Cover | | | | | 7·00 | ☐ |
| Presentation Pack (P.O. Pack No. 318) | | | | 7·50 | | ☐ |
| PHQ Cards (set of 4) (226) | | | | 8·50 | 13·00 | ☐ ☐ |
| Set of 4 Gutter Pairs | | | | 13·00 | | ☐ |

**Collectors Pack 2000**

**2000** (5 Dec.) Comprises Nos. 2125/6, 2127/32, 2134/45, 2148/59 and MS2161/77

| | | | |
|---|---|---|---|
| CP2177a | Collectors Pack | £100 | ☐ |

**1489** 'Flower' ('Nurture Children')

**1490** 'Tiger' ('Listen to Children')

**1491** 'Owl' ('Teach Children')

**1492** 'Butterfly' ('Ensure Children's Freedom')

**New Millennium. Rights of the Child.**
**Face Paintings**

**2001** (16 Jan.) One centre phosphor band (2nd) or two phosphor bands (others). Perf 14 × 14½

| | | | | | | |
|---|---|---|---|---|---|---|
| 2178 | **1489** | (2nd) | multicoloured | 1·00 | 75 | ☐ ☐ |
| 2179 | **1490** | (1st) | multicoloured | 1·25 | 1·10 | ☐ ☐ |
| 2180 | **1491** | 45p | multicoloured | 1·60 | 1·75 | ☐ ☐ |

| | | | | | | |
|---|---|---|---|---|---|---|
| 2181 | **1492** | 65p | multicoloured | 2·40 | 2·50 | ☐ ☐ |
| Set of 4 | | | | 5·75 | 5·75 | ☐ ☐ |
| First Day Cover | | | | | 7·00 | ☐ |
| Presentation Pack (P.O. Pack No. 319) | | | | 7·50 | | ☐ |
| PHQ Cards (set of 4) (227) | | | | 7·50 | 10·00 | ☐ ☐ |
| Set of 4 Gutter Pairs | | | | 14·00 | | ☐ |

**1493** 'Love'

**1494** 'THANKS'

**1495** 'abc' (New Baby)

**1496** 'WELCOME'

**1497** 'Cheers'

**'Occasions' Greetings Stamps (1st series)**

**2001** (6 Feb.) Two phosphor bands. Perf 14½ × 14

| | | | | | | |
|---|---|---|---|---|---|---|
| 2182 | **1493** | (1st) | multicoloured | 1·30 | 1·30 | ☐ ☐ |
| 2183 | **1494** | (1st) | multicoloured | 1·30 | 1·30 | ☐ ☐ |
| 2184 | **1495** | (1st) | multicoloured | 1·30 | 1·30 | ☐ ☐ |
| 2185 | **1496** | (1st) | multicoloured | 1·30 | 1·30 | ☐ ☐ |
| 2186 | **1497** | (1st) | multicoloured | 1·30 | 1·30 | ☐ ☐ |
| Set of 5 | | | | 5·75 | 5·75 | ☐ ☐ |
| First Day Cover | | | | | 7·50 | ☐ |
| Presentation Pack (13 Feb.) | | | | | | |
| (P.O. Pack No. M05) | | | | 10·00 | | ☐ |
| PHQ Cards (set of 5) (PSM05) | | | | 8·50 | 11·00 | ☐ ☐ |
| Set of 5 Gutter Pairs | | | | 13·00 | | ☐ |

The silver-grey backgrounds are printed in Iriodin ink which gives a shiny effect.

Further packs of Nos. 2182/6 were sold from 3 July 2001. These comprised the listed stamps in blocks of ten (from sheets) with an insert describing the occasion (Price £10 per pack).

Nos. 2182/6 were printed in photogravure. They were subsequently re-issued on 1 May, as sheets of 20, printed in lithography instead of photogravure with each stamp accompanied by a half stamp-size label showing either postal symbols or a personal photograph.

**1498** Dog and Owner on Bench

**1499** Dog in Bath

**1500** Boxer at Dog Show

**1501** Cat in Handbag

**1502** Cat on Gate

**1503** Dog in Car

**1504** Cat at Window

**1505** Dog behind Fence

**1506** Cat watching Bird

**1507** Cat in Washbasin

## Cats and Dogs

**2001** (13 Feb.) Self-adhesive. Two phosphor bands. Die-cut perf 15 × 14

| | | | | | | | |
|---|---|---|---|---|---|---|---|
| 2187 | **1498** | (1st) | black, grey and silver | 1·25 | 1·00 | ☐ | ☐ |
| | | a. | Sheetlet. | | | | |
| | | | Nos. 2187/96 | 15·00 | 15·00 | ☐ | ☐ |
| | | b. | Booklet pane. | | | | |
| | | | Nos.2187/96 plus | | | | |
| | | | Nos. 2040 × 2 | 30·00 | | ☐ | |
| 2188 | **1499** | (1st) | black, grey and silver | 1·25 | 1·00 | ☐ | ☐ |
| 2189 | **1500** | (1st) | black, grey and silver | 1·25 | 1·00 | ☐ | ☐ |
| 2190 | **1501** | (1st) | black, grey and silver | 1·25 | 1·00 | ☐ | ☐ |
| 2191 | **1502** | (1st) | black, grey and silver | 1·25 | 1·00 | ☐ | ☐ |
| 2192 | **1503** | (1st) | black, grey and silver | 1·25 | 1·00 | ☐ | ☐ |
| 2193 | **1504** | (1st) | black, grey and silver | 1·25 | 1·00 | ☐ | ☐ |
| 2194 | **1505** | (1st) | black, grey and silver | 1·25 | 1·00 | ☐ | ☐ |
| 2195 | **1506** | (1st) | black, grey and silver | 1·25 | 1·00 | ☐ | ☐ |
| 2196 | **1507** | (1st) | black, grey and silver | 1·25 | 1·00 | ☐ | ☐ |
| *Set of* 10 | | | | 15·00 | 15·00 | ☐ | ☐ |
| First Day Cover | | | | | 15·00 | | ☐ |
| Presentation Pack (P.O. Pack No. 320) | | | | 20·00 | | ☐ | |
| PHQ Cards (*set of* 10) (228) | | | | 14·00 | 30·00 | ☐ | ☐ |

Nos. 2187/96 were printed together in sheetlets of ten (5 × 2), with the surplus self-adhesive paper around each stamp retained. They were also issued in £3.24 booklets, the booklet pane has vertical roulettes between rows 2/3 and 4/5.

**1508** 'RAIN'

**1509** 'FAIR'

**1510** 'STORMY'

**1511** 'VERY DRY'

## The Weather

**2001** (13 Mar.) One side phosphor band (19p) or two phosphor bands (others). Perf 14½

| | | | | | | | |
|---|---|---|---|---|---|---|---|
| 2197 | **1508** | 19p | multicoloured | 70 | 75 | ☐ | ☐ |
| 2198 | **1509** | 27p | multicoloured | 85 | 1·00 | ☐ | ☐ |
| 2199 | **1510** | 45p | multicoloured | 1·50 | 1·50 | ☐ | ☐ |
| 2200 | **1511** | 65p | multicoloured | 2·40 | 2·50 | ☐ | ☐ |
| *Set of* 4 | | | | 5·00 | 5·50 | ☐ | ☐ |
| First Day Cover | | | | | 7·50 | | ☐ |
| Presentation Pack (P.O. Pack No. 321) | | | 14·00 | | ☐ | |
| *Set of* 4 Gutter Pairs | | | | 14·00 | | | |
| **MS**2201 105 × 105 mm. Nos. 2197/200 | | | 18·00 | 18·00 | ☐ | ☐ |
| First Day Cover | | | | | 19·00 | | ☐ |
| PHQ Cards (*set of* 5) (229) | | | | 8·50 | 20·00 | ☐ | ☐ |

Nos. 2197/200 show the four quadrants of a barometer dial which are combined on the miniature sheet.

The reddish violet on both the 27p and the miniature sheet is printed in thermochromic ink which changes from reddish violet to light blue when exposed to heat.

The PHQ cards depict the four values and the miniature sheet.

**1512** Vanguard Class Submarine, 1992

**1513** Swiftsure Class Submarine, 1973

**1514** Unity Class Submarine, 1939

**1515** 'Holland' Type Submarine, 1901

**1516** White Ensign

**1517** Union Jack

**1518** Jolly Roger flown by H.M.S. Proteus (submarine)

**1519** Flag of Chief of Defence Staff

### Centenary of the Royal Navy Submarine Service

**2001** (10 Apr.–22 Oct.) One centre phosphor band (2nd) or two phosphor bands (others).

(a) Submarines. Ordinary gum. Perf 15 × 14

| | | | | | | |
|---|---|---|---|---|---|---|
| 2202 | **1512** | (2nd) | multicoloured | 1·00 | 75 | ☐ ☐ |
| | a. | Perf 15½ × 15 | | | | |
| | | (22 Oct.) | | 3·75 | 3·00 | ☐ ☐ |
| 2203 | **1513** | (1st) | multicoloured | 1·25 | 90 | ☐ ☐ |
| | a. | Perf 15½ × 15 | | | | |
| | | (22 Oct.) | | 3·75 | 3·00 | ☐ ☐ |
| 2204 | **1514** | 45p | multicoloured | 1·75 | 1·60 | ☐ ☐ |
| | a. | Perf 15½ × 15 | | | | |
| | | (22 Oct.) | | 3·75 | 3·00 | ☐ ☐ |
| 2205 | **1515** | 65p | multicoloured | 2·40 | 2·50 | ☐ ☐ |
| | a. | Perf 15½ × 15 | | | | |
| | | (22 Oct.) | | 3·75 | 3·00 | ☐ ☐ |
| *Set of 4* | | | | 5·75 | 5·25 | ☐ |
| First Day Cover | | | | | 7·50 | ☐ |
| Presentation Pack (P.O. Pack No. 322) | | | | 20·00 | | ☐ |
| PHQ Cards (*set of 4*) (230) | | | | 7·50 | 12·00 | ☐ ☐ |
| *Set of 4 Gutter Pairs* | | | | 13·50 | | ☐ |

(b) Flags. Sheet 92 × 97 mm. Ordinary gum. Perf 14½

**MS**2206  **1516**  (1st)  multicoloured;
**1517**  (1st) multicoloured; **1518**
(1st) multicoloured; **1519** (1st)

| | | | |
|---|---|---|---|
| multicoloured *(22 Oct.)* | 9·00 | 9·00 | ☐ ☐ |
| First Day Cover | | 11·00 | ☐ |
| Presentation Pack (P.O. Pack No. M06) | 30·00 | | ☐ |
| PHQ Cards (*set of 5*) (PSM07) | 12·00 | 15·00 | ☐ ☐ |

(c) Self-adhesive. Die-cut perf 15½ × 14 (No. 2207)
or 14½ (others)

| | | | | | | |
|---|---|---|---|---|---|---|
| 2207 | **1513** | (1st) | multicoloured | | | |
| | | (17 Apr.) | | 50·00 | 40·00 | ☐ ☐ |
| 2208 | **1516** | (1st) | multicoloured | | | |
| | | (22 Oct.) | | 15·00 | 15·00 | ☐ ☐ |
| 2209 | **1518** | (1st) | multicoloured | | | |
| | | (22 Oct.) | | 15·00 | 15·00 | ☐ ☐ |

Nos. 2202a/5a were only issued in the £6.76 "Unseen and Unheard" booklet.

The five PHQ cards depict the four designs and the complete miniature sheet, **MS**2206.

Nos. 2207/9 only come from two different £1·62 booklets.

Type **1516** was re-issued on 21 June 2005 in sheets of 20, printed in lithography instead of photogravure, with half stamp-size *se-tenant* labels showing signal flags.

Designs as Type **1517** were issued on 27 July 2004 in sheets of 20 printed in lithography instead of photogravure with each vertical row of stamps alternated with half stamp-size labels. See also Nos. 2581, 2805 and 2970.

**1520** Leyland X2 Open-top, London
General B Type,
Leyland Titan TD1 and
AEC Regent 1

**1521** AEC Regent 1, Daimler COG5,
Utility Guy Arab Mk II
and AEC Regent III RT Type

**1522** AEC Regent III RT Type, Bristol
KSW5G Open-Top, AEC Routemaster
and Bristol Lodekka FSF6G

**1523** Bristol Lodekka FSF6G, Leyland
Titan PD3/4, Leyland Atlantean
PDR1/1 and Daimler Fleetline
CRG6LX-33

**1524** Daimler Fleetline CRG6LX-33, MCW Metrobus DR102/43,
Leyland Olympian ONLXB/1R and Dennis Trident

### 150th Anniversary of First Double-decker Bus

**2001** (15 May) 'All-over' phosphor. Perf 14½ × 14

| | | | | | | |
|---|---|---|---|---|---|---|
| 2210 | **1520** | (1st) | multicoloured | 1·25 | 1·00 | ☐ ☐ |
| | a. | Horiz strip of 5. | | | | |
| | | Nos. 2210/14 | 7·00 | 7·00 | ☐ ☐ |
| 2211 | **1521** | (1st) | multicoloured | 1·25 | 1·00 | ☐ ☐ |
| 2212 | **1522** | (1st) | multicoloured | 1·25 | 1·00 | ☐ ☐ |
| 2213 | **1523** | (1st) | multicoloured | 1·25 | 1·00 | ☐ ☐ |
| 2214 | **1524** | (1st) | multicoloured | 1·25 | 1·00 | ☐ ☐ |
| *Set of 5* | | | | 7·00 | 7·00 | ☐ ☐ |
| First Day Cover | | | | | 8·00 | ☐ |
| Presentation Pack (P.O. Pack No. 323) | | | 10·00 | | ☐ |
| PHQ Cards (*set of 6*) (231) | | | 14·00 | 16·00 | ☐ ☐ |
| Gutter Strip of 10 | | | | 15·00 | | ☐ |
| **MS**2215 120 × 105 mm. Nos. 2210/14 | | 10·50 | 12·50 | ☐ ☐ |
| First Day Cover | | | | | 15·00 | ☐ |

Nos. 2210/4 were printed together, *se-tenant*, in horizontal strips of five throughout the sheet. The illustrations of the first bus on No. 2210 and the last bus on No. 2214 continue onto the sheet margins.

In No. **MS**2215 the illustrations of the AEC Regent III RT Type and the Daimler Fleetline CRG6LX-33 appear twice.

The six PHQ cards show the stamps and the miniature sheet.

**1525** Toque Hat by Pip Hackett

**1526** Butterfly Hat by Dai Rees

**1527** Top Hat by
Stephen Jones

**1528** Spiral Hat by Philip
Treacy

### Fashion Hats

**2001** (19 June) 'All-over' phosphor. Perf 14½

| | | | | | | |
|---|---|---|---|---|---|---|
| 2216 | **1525** | (1st) | multicoloured | 1·25 | 90 | ☐ ☐ |
| 2217 | **1526** | (E) | multicoloured | 1·50 | 1·25 | ☐ ☐ |
| 2218 | **1527** | 45p | multicoloured | 1·60 | 1·60 | ☐ ☐ |
| 2219 | **1528** | 65p | multicoloured | 2·50 | 2·50 | ☐ ☐ |
| *Set of 4* | | | | 6·00 | 5·50 | ☐ ☐ |
| First Day Cover | | | | | 6·50 | ☐ |
| Presentation Pack (P.O. Pack No. 324) | | | 7·50 | | ☐ |
| PHQ Cards (*set of 4*) (232) | | | 8·50 | 14·00 | ☐ ☐ |
| *Set of 4 Gutter Pairs* | | | | 13·00 | | ☐ |

**1529** Common Frog

**1530** Great Diving Beetle

**1531** Three-spined Stickleback

**1532** Southern Hawker Dragonfly

## Europa. Pond Life

**2001** (10 July) Two phosphor bands

| | | | | | | |
|---|---|---|---|---|---|---|
| 2220 | **1529** | (1st) | multicoloured | 1·25 | 1·00 | ☐ ☐ |
| 2221 | **1530** | (E) | multicoloured | 1·50 | 1·25 | ☐ ☐ |
| 2222 | **1531** | 45p | multicoloured | 1·50 | 1·50 | ☐ ☐ |
| 2223 | **1532** | 65p | multicoloured | 2·00 | 2·25 | ☐ ☐ |
| *Set of 4* | | | | 6·00 | 5·75 | ☐ ☐ |
| First Day Cover | | | | | 9·00 | ☐ |
| Presentation Pack (P.O. Pack No. 325) | | | | 7·50 | | ☐ |
| PHQ Cards (*set of 4*) (233) | | | | 8·50 | 14·00 | ☐ ☐ |
| *Set of 4 Gutter Pairs* | | | | 13·00 | | ☐ |

The 1st and E values incorporate the 'EUROPA' emblem.
The bluish silver on all four values is in Iriodin ink and was used as a background for those parts of the design below the water line.

**1533** Policeman

**1534** Clown

**1535** Mr. Punch

**1536** Judy

**1537** Beadle

**1538** Crocodile

## Punch and Judy Show Puppets

**2001** (4 Sept.) Two phosphor bands

| | | | | | | |
|---|---|---|---|---|---|---|
| | | | (a) Ordinary gum. Perf 14 × 15 | | | |
| 2224 | **1533** | (1st) | multicoloured | 1·25 | 1·00 | ☐ ☐ |
| | | a. | Horiz strip of 6. | | | |
| | | | Nos. 2224/9 | 6·50 | 6·50 | ☐ ☐ |
| 2225 | **1534** | (1st) | multicoloured | 1·25 | 1·00 | ☐ ☐ |
| 2226 | **1535** | (1st) | multicoloured | 1·25 | 1·00 | ☐ ☐ |
| 2227 | **1536** | (1st) | multicoloured | 1·25 | 1·00 | ☐ ☐ |
| 2228 | **1537** | (1st) | multicoloured | 1·25 | 1·00 | ☐ ☐ |
| 2229 | **1538** | (1st) | multicoloured | 1·25 | 1·00 | ☐ ☐ |
| *Set of 6* | | | | 6·50 | 6·50 | ☐ ☐ |
| First Day Cover | | | | | 7·00 | ☐ |
| Presentation Pack (P.O. Pack No. 326) | | | | 7·00 | | ☐ |
| PHQ Cards (*set of 6*) (234) | | | | 8·50 | 18·00 | ☐ ☐ |
| Gutter Block of 12 | | | | 14·00 | | ☐ |
| | | | (b) Self-adhesive. Die-cut perf 14 × 15½ | | | |
| 2230 | **1535** | (1st) | multicoloured | 17·00 | 17·00 | ☐ ☐ |
| 2231 | **1536** | (1st) | multicoloured | 17·00 | 17·00 | ☐ ☐ |

Nos. 2230/1 were only issued in £1·62 stamp booklets.
Nos. 2224/9 were printed together, *se-tenant*, in horizontal strips of 6 throughout the sheet.

CHEMISTRY
**Nobel Prize** 100th Anniversary
**1539** Carbon 60
Molecule (Chemistry)

ECONOMIC SCIENCES
**Nobel Prize** 100th Anniversary
**1540** Globe
(Economic Sciences)

E

PEACE
**Nobel Prize** 100th Anniversary
**1541** Embossed Dove
(Peace)

40

PHYSIOLOGY OR MEDICINE
**Nobel Prize** 100th Anniversary
**1542** Crosses
(Physiology or Medicine)

45

LITERATURE
**Nobel Prize** 100th Anniversary
**1543** Poem 'The
Addressing of Cats' by
T.S. Eliot in Open Book (Literature)

65

PHYSICS
**Nobel Prize** 100th Anniversary
**1544** Hologram of
Boron Molecule (Physics)

## Centenary of Nobel Prizes

**2001** (2 Oct.) One side phosphor band (2nd) or phosphor frame (others). Perf 14½

| | | | | | | |
|---|---|---|---|---|---|---|
| 2232 | **1539** | (2nd) | black, silver and grey-black | 1·00 | 80 | ☑ ☐ |
| 2233 | **1540** | (1st) | multicoloured | 1·50 | 1·00 | ☐ ☐ |
| 2234 | **1541** | (E) | black, silver and bright green | 1·50 | 1·50 | ☐ ☐ |
| 2235 | **1542** | 40p | multicoloured | 2·00 | 1·50 | ☐ ☐ |
| 2236 | **1543** | 45p | multicoloured | 3·00 | 2·00 | ☐ ☐ |
| 2237 | **1544** | 65p | black and silver | 5·00 | 2·50 | ☐ ☐ |
| *Set of 6* | | | | 12·00 | 8·00 | ☐ ☐ |
| First Day Cover | | | | | 9·00 | ☐ |

| | | |
|---|---|---|
| Presentation Pack (P.O. Pack No. 327) | 40·00 | ☐ |
| PHQ Cards (*set of* 6) (235) | 10·00  14·00 | ☐ ☐ |
| *Set of* 6 Gutter Pairs | 25·00 | ☐ |

The grey-black on No. 2232 is printed in thermochromic ink which temporarily changes to pale grey when exposed to heat. The centre of No. 2235 is coated with a eucalyptus scent.

**1545** Robins with Snowman

**1546** Robins on Bird Table

**1547** Robins skating on Bird Bath

**1548** Robins with Christmas Pudding

**1549** Robins in Paper Chain Nest

### Christmas. Robins

**2001** (6 Nov.) Self-adhesive. One centre phosphor band (2nd) or two phosphor bands (others). Die-cut perf 14½

| | | | | | |
|---|---|---|---|---|---|
| 2238 | **1545** | (2nd) | multicoloured | 1·00  80 | ☐ ☐ |
| 2239 | **1546** | (1st) | multicoloured | 1·25  1·00 | ☐ ☐ |
| 2240 | **1547** | (E) | multicoloured | 1·50  1·50 | ☐ ☐ |
| 2241 | **1548** | 45p | multicoloured | 2·00  2·00 | ☐ ☐ |
| 2242 | **1549** | 65p | multicoloured | 3·00  3·00 | ☐ ☐ |
| *Set of* 5 | | | | 7·50  7·50 | ☐ ☐ |
| First Day Cover | | | | 8·50 | ☐ |
| Presentation Pack (P.O. Pack No. 328) | | | | 8·00 | ☐ |
| PHQ Cards (*set of* 5) (236) | | | | 11·00  16·00 | ☐ ☐ |

The 1st value was re-issued on 30 September 2003, in sheets of 20, in lithography instead of photogravure, each stamp *se-tenant* with a Christmas label or a personal photograph. The sheet contained die-cut perforated stamps and labels.

The 2nd and 1st class stamps were issued again on 1 November 2005 in sheets of 20 containing ten 1st class and ten 2nd class stamps, each stamp accompanied by a *se-tenant* label showing a snowman.

### Collectors Pack 2001

**2001** (6 Nov.) Comprises Nos. 2178/2200, 2202/**MS**2206, 2210/14, 2216/29 and 2232/42

| | | | |
|---|---|---|---|
| CP2242a | Collectors Pack | £110 | ☐ |

### Post Office Yearbook

**2001** (6 Nov.) Comprises Nos. 2178/96, **MS**2201/6, **MS**2215/29 and 2232/42 in hardback book with slip case

| | | | |
|---|---|---|---|
| YB2242a | Yearbook | £110 | ☐ |

**1550** 'How the Whale got his Throat'

**1551** 'How the Camel got his Hump'

**1552** 'How the Rhinoceros got his Skin'

**1553** 'How the Leopard got his Spots'

**1554** 'The Elephant's Child'

**1555** 'The Sing-Song of Old Man Kangaroo'

**1556** 'The Beginning of the Armadillos'

**1557** 'The Crab that played with the Sea'

**1558** 'The Cat that walked by Himself'

**1559** 'The Butterfly that stamped'

### Centenary of Publication of Rudyard Kipling's Just So Stories

**2002** (15 Jan.) Self-adhesive. Two phosphor bands. Die-cut perf 15 × 14

| | | | | | | |
|---|---|---|---|---|---|---|
| 2243 | **1550** | (1st) | multicoloured | 1·25 | 1·00 | ☐ ☐ |
| | | a. | Sheetlet. Nos. 2243/52 | 14·00 | 11·00 | ☐ ☐ |
| 2244 | **1551** | (1st) | multicoloured | 1·25 | 1·00 | ☐ ☐ |
| 2245 | **1552** | (1st) | multicoloured | 1·25 | 1·00 | ☐ ☐ |
| 2246 | **1553** | (1st) | multicoloured | 1·25 | 1·00 | ☐ ☐ |
| 2247 | **1554** | (1st) | multicoloured | 1·25 | 1·00 | ☐ ☐ |
| 2248 | **1555** | (1st) | multicoloured | 1·25 | 1·00 | ☐ ☐ |
| 2249 | **1556** | (1st) | multicoloured | 1·25 | 1·00 | ☐ ☐ |
| 2250 | **1557** | (1st) | multicoloured | 1·25 | 1·00 | ☐ ☐ |
| 2251 | **1558** | (1st) | multicoloured | 1·25 | 1·00 | ☐ ☐ |
| 2252 | **1559** | (1st) | multicoloured | 1·25 | 1·00 | ☐ ☐ |
| *Set of* 10 | | | | 14·00 | 11·00 | ☐ ☐ |
| First Day Cover | | | | | 12·00 | ☐ |
| Presentation Pack (P.O. Pack No. 330) | | | | 16·00 | | ☐ |
| PHQ Cards (*set of* 10) (237) | | | | 10·00 | 28·00 | ☐ ☐ |

Nos. 2243/52 were printed together in sheetlets of ten (5 × 2), with the surplus self-adhesive paper around each stamp retained.

**1560** Queen Elizabeth II,
1952 (Dorothy Wilding)

**1561** Queen Elizabeth II,
1968 (Cecil Beaton)

**1562** Queen Elizabeth II,
1978 (Lord Snowdon)

**1563** Queen Elizabeth II,
1984 (Yousef Karsh)

**1564** Queen Elizabeth II,
1996 (Tim Graham)

**1565**

**Golden Jubilee. Studio portraits of Queen Elizabeth II by photographers named**

**2002** (6 Feb.) One centre phosphor band (2nd) or two phosphor bands (others). W **1565** (sideways). Perf 14½ × 14

| | | | | | | |
|---|---|---|---|---|---|---|
| 2253 | **1560** | (2nd) | multicoloured | 1·00 | 80 | |
| 2254 | **1561** | (1st) | multicoloured | 1·25 | 90 | |
| 2255 | **1562** | (E) | multicoloured | 1·50 | 1·50 | |
| 2256 | **1563** | 45p | multicoloured | 1·75 | 2·00 | |
| 2257 | **1564** | 65p | multicoloured | 2·75 | 3·00 | |
| Set of 5 | | | | 7·50 | 7·50 | |
| First Day Cover | | | | | 8·50 | |
| Presentation Pack (P.O. Pack No. 331) | | | | 9·00 | | |
| PHQ Cards (set of 5) (238) | | | | 4·50 | 14·00 | |
| Set of 5 Gutter Pairs | | | | 16·00 | | |

Nos. 2253/7 were also issued with watermark upright, in the £7·29 'A Gracious Accession' booklet.

**1566**

**Booklet Stamps**

**2002** (6 Feb.) Designs as 1952-54 issue, but with service indicator as T **1566**. One centre phosphor band (2nd) or two phosphor bands (1st). W 1565. Uncoated paper. Perf 15 × 14 (with one elliptical hole in each vertical side)

| | | | | | | |
|---|---|---|---|---|---|---|
| 2258 | **1566** | (2nd) | carmine-red | 1·20 | 1·00 | |
| 2259 | **154** | (1st) | green | 1·25 | 1·25 | |
| Set of 2 | | | | 2·40 | 2·25 | |

Nos. 2258/9 were only issued in the £7·29 'The Gracious Accession' booklet.

For other Wilding designs with decimal face vace values, see

Nos. 2031/3, **MS**2326, **MS**2367, 2378/80 and 3329.

**1567** Rabbits ('a new baby')

**1568** 'LOVE'

**1569** Aircraft Sky-writing 'hello'

**1570** Bear pulling Potted Topiary Tree (Moving Home)

**1571** Flowers ('best wishes')

**'Occasions' Greetings Stamps**

**2002** (5 Mar.)-**03** Two phosphor bands

| | | | (a) Litho. Ordinary gum. Perf 15 × 14 | | | |
|---|---|---|---|---|---|---|
| 2260 | **1567** | (1st) | multicoloured | 1·50 | 1·10 | |
| 2261 | **1568** | (1st) | multicoloured | 1·50 | 1·10 | |
| 2262 | **1569** | (1st) | multicoloured | 1·50 | 1·10 | |
| 2263 | **1570** | (1st) | multicoloured | 1·50 | 1·10 | |
| 2264 | **1571** | (1st) | multicoloured | 1·50 | 1·10 | |
| Set of 5 | | | | 6·50 | 5·00 | |
| First Day Cover | | | | | 6·00 | |
| Presentation Pack (P.O. Pack No. M07) | | | | 7·50 | | |
| PHQ Cards (set of 5) (PSM08) | | | | 4·50 | 14·00 | |
| Set of 5 Gutter Pairs | | | | 13·00 | | |

| | | | (b) Photo. Self-adhesive. Die-cut perf 15 × 14 | | | |
|---|---|---|---|---|---|---|
| 2264a | **1569** | (1st) | multicoloured *(4.3.03)* 6·00 | | 6·00 | |

Nos. 2260/4 were re-issued on 23 April 2002 in sheets of 20 perforated 14, either of one design or *se-tenant*, with each stamp accompanied by a half stamp-size label showing either greetings or a personal photograph.

No. 2262 was also issued in sheets of 20 with *se-tenant* labels in connection with the Hong Kong Stamp Expo on 30 January 2004. It was issued in sheets of 20 perforated 14 with *se-tenant* labels on 21 April 2005 for Pacific Explorer 2005 World Stamp Expo, on 25 May 2006 for Washington 2006 International Stamp Exhibition, on 14 November 2006 for Belgica 2006 International Stamp Exhibition, on 5 August 2008 for Beijing 2008 Olympic Expo, on 3 August 2009 for Thaipex 09 Stamp Exhibition, on 21 October 2009 for Italia 2009 International Stamp Exhibition and on 4 December 2009 for MonacoPhil International Stamp Exhibition.

No. 2264a was only issued in £1·62 stamp booklets in which the surplus self-adhesive paper around each stamp was removed.

**1572** Studland Bay, Dorset

**1573** Luskentyre, South Harris

**1582** Slack Wire Act

**1583** Lion Tamer

**1574** Cliffs, Dover, Kent

**1575** Padstow Harbour, Cornwall

**1584** Trick Tri-cyclists

**1585** Krazy Kar

**1576** Broadstairs, Kent

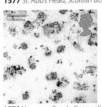
**1577** St. Abb's Head, Scottish Borders

**1586** Equestrienne

### Europa. Circus

**2002** (10 Apr.) One centre phosphor band (2nd) or two phosphor bands (others). Perf 14½

| | | | | | |
|---|---|---|---|---|---|
| 2275 | **1582** | (2nd) | multicoloured | 1·00 | 80 |
| 2276 | **1583** | (1st) | multicoloured | 1·25 | 1·00 |
| 2277 | **1584** | (E) | multicoloured | 1·50 | 1·25 |
| 2278 | **1585** | 45p | multicoloured | 1·75 | 1·50 |
| 2279 | **1586** | 65p | multicoloured | 2·75 | 2·25 |
| Set of 5 | | | | 6·50 | 6·25 |
| First Day Cover | | | | | 7·00 |
| Presentation Pack (P.O. Pack No. 333) | | | | 7·50 | |
| PHQ Cards (set of 5) (240) | | | | 4·50 | 14·00 |
| Set of 5 Gutter Pairs | | | | 14·00 | |

The 1st and E values incorporate the "EUROPA" emblem.

Due to the funeral of the Queen Mother, the actual issue of Nos. 2275/9 was delayed from 9 April which is the date that appears on first day covers.

**1578** Dunster Beach, Somerset

**1579** Newquay Beach, Cornwall

**1587** Queen Elizabeth the Queen Mother

**1580** Portrush, County Antrim

**1581** Sand-spit, Conwy

### British Coastlines

**2002** (19 Mar.) Two phosphor bands. Perf 14½

| | | | | | |
|---|---|---|---|---|---|
| 2265 | **1572** | 27p | multicoloured | 80 | 70 |
| | a. | Block of 10. | | | |
| | | Nos. 2265/74 | | 8·75 | 8·75 |
| 2266 | **1573** | 27p | multicoloured | 80 | 70 |
| 2267 | **1574** | 27p | multicoloured | 80 | 70 |
| 2268 | **1575** | 27p | multicoloured | 80 | 70 |
| 2269 | **1576** | 27p | multicoloured | 80 | 70 |
| 2270 | **1577** | 27p | multicoloured | 80 | 70 |
| 2271 | **1578** | 27p | multicoloured | 80 | 70 |
| 2272 | **1579** | 27p | multicoloured | 80 | 70 |
| 2273 | **1580** | 27p | multicoloured | 80 | 70 |
| 2274 | **1581** | 27p | multicoloured | 80 | 70 |
| Set of 10 | | | | 8·75 | 8·75 |
| First Day Cover | | | | | 10·00 |
| Presentation Pack (P.O. Pack No. 332) | | | | 10·50 | |
| PHQ Cards (set of 10) (239) | | | | 9·25 | 28·00 |
| Gutter Block of 20 | | | | 19·00 | |

Nos. 2265/74 were printed together, se-tenant, in blocks of ten (5 × 2) throughout the sheet.

### Queen Elizabeth the Queen Mother Commemoration

**2002** (25 Apr.) Vert designs as T **955/8** with changed face values and showing both the Queen's head and frame in black as in T **1587**. Two phosphor bands. Perf 14 × 15

| | | | | | |
|---|---|---|---|---|---|
| 2280 | **1587** | (1st) | multicoloured | 1·25 | 85 |
| 2281 | **956** | (E) | black and indigo | 1·50 | 1·10 |
| 2282 | **957** | 45p | multicoloured | 1·50 | 1·50 |
| 2283 | **958** | 65p | black, stone & sepia | 2·00 | 2·25 |
| Set of 4 | | | | 5·50 | 5·50 |
| First Day Cover | | | | | 7·00 |
| Presentation Pack (P.O. Pack No. M08) | | | | 7·00 | |
| Set of 4 Gutter Pairs | | | | 14·00 | |

**1588** Airbus A340-600 (2002)

**1589** Concorde (1976)

**1590** Trident (1964)

**1591** VC 10 (1964)

**1592** Comet (1952)

**50th Anniversary of Passenger Jet Aviation. Airliners**

**2002** (2 May) One centre phosphor band (2nd) or two phosphor bands (others). Perf 14½

(a) Photo De La Rue. Ordinary gum

| | | | | |
|---|---|---|---|---|
| 2284 | **1588** | (2nd) multicoloured | 1·00 | 70 |
| 2285 | **1589** | (1st) multicoloured | 1·25 | 1·00 |
| 2286 | **1590** | (E) multicoloured | 1·50 | 1·50 |
| 2287 | **1591** | 45p multicoloured | 2·00 | 2·00 |
| 2288 | **1592** | 65p multicoloured | 3·00 | 3·00 |
| *Set of 5* | | | 8·00 | 7·50 |
| First Day Cover | | | | 8·00 |
| Presentation Pack (P.O. Pack No. 334) | | | 10·00 | |
| *Set of 5 Gutter Pairs* | | | 17·00 | |
| **MS**2289 120 × 105 mm. Nos. 2284/8 | | | 12·00 | 11·00 |
| First Day Cover | | | | 12·00 |
| PHQ Cards (*set of* 6) (241) | | | 5·25 | 18·00 |

(b) Photo Questa. Self-adhesive

| | | | | |
|---|---|---|---|---|
| 2290 | **1589** | (1st) multicoloured | 7·00 | 7·00 |

The complete miniature sheet is shown on one of the PHQ cards with the others depicting individual stamps.

No. 2290 was only issued in £1·62 stamp booklets. For Type **1589** printed by lithography see No. 2897.

**1593** Crowned Lion with Shield of St. George

**1594** Top Left Quarter of English Flag, and Football

**1595** Top Right Quarter of English Flag, and Football

**1596** Bottom Left Quarter of English Flag, and Football

**1597** Bottom Right Quarter of English Flag, and Football

**World Cup Football Championship, Japan and Korea**

**2002** (21 May) Two phosphor bands. Perf 14½ × 14

(a) Ordinary gum

| | | | | |
|---|---|---|---|---|
| 2291 | **1593** | (1st) deep turquoise-blue, scarlet-vermilion and silver | 2·50 | 2·50 |
| **MS**2292 145 × 74 mm. No. 2291; **1594** (1st) multicoloured; **1595** (1st) multicoloured; **1596** (1st) multicoloured; **1597** (1st) multicoloured | | | 7·50 | 7·50 |
| First Day Cover (**MS**2292) | | | | 8·50 |
| Presentation Pack (**MS**2292) (P.O. Pack No. 335) | | | 8·50 | |
| PHQ Cards (*set of* 6) (242) | | | 5·25 | 15·00 |
| Gutter Pair (No. 2291) | | | 6·00 | |

(b) Self-adhesive. Die-cut perf 15 × 14

| | | | | |
|---|---|---|---|---|
| 2293 | **1594** | (1st) multicoloured | 6·00 | 6·00 |
| 2294 | **1595** | (1st) multicoloured | 6·00 | 6·00 |

The complete miniature sheet is shown on one of the PHQ cards with the others depicting individual stamps from **MS**2292 and No. 2291.

Nos. 2293/4 were only issued in £1·62 stamp booklets.

Stamps as Type **1597** were also issued in sheets of 20, *se-tenant* with half stamp-sized labels, printed in lithography instead of photogravure. The labels show either match scenes or personal photographs.

Stamps as Type **1593** but with 'WORLD CUP 2002' inscription omitted were issued on 17 May 2007 in sheets of 20 with *se-tenant* labels showing scenes from Wembley Stadium the same date as **MS**2740.

**Self-adhesive Stamps**

**2002** (5 June–4 July) Self-adhesive. Photo Questa, Walsall, De La Rue or Enschedé (No. 2295) or Walsall (others). Two phosphor bands. Perf 15 × 14 die-cut (with one elliptical hole in each vertical side)

| | | | | |
|---|---|---|---|---|
| 2295 | **914** | (1st) gold | 1·50 | 1·00 |
| 2296 | **1093a** | (E) deep blue (*4 July*) | 2·50 | 2·50 |
| 2297 | **367a** | 42p deep olive-grey (*4 July*) | 3·75 | 3·75 |
| 2298 | | 68p grey-brown (*4 July*) | 4·25 | 4·25 |
| *Set of 4* | | | 11·00 | 10·50 |
| PHQ Card (No. 2295) Walsall (*27.3.03*)(D22) | | | 60 | 3·50 |

Further printings of No. 2295 in sheets of 100 appeared on 4 July 2002 produced by Enschedé and on 18 March 2003 printed by Walsall.

**1598** Swimming

**1599** Running

**1600** Cycling

**1601** Long Jumping

### 17th Commonwealth Games, Manchester

**2002** (16 July) One side phosphor band (2nd) or two phosphor bands (others). Perf 14½

| | | | | | | |
|---|---|---|---|---|---|---|
| 2299 | **1598** | (2nd) | multicoloured | 1·00 | 80 | |
| 2300 | **1599** | (1st) | multicoloured | 1·25 | 1·00 | |
| 2301 | **1600** | (E) | multicoloured | 1·50 | 1·25 | |
| 2302 | **1601** | 47p | multicoloured | 1·50 | 1·50 | |
| 2303 | **1602** | 68p | multicoloured | 2·00 | 2·25 | |
| *Set of 5* | | | | 6·50 | 6·00 | |
| First Day Cover | | | | | 7·00 | |
| Presentation Pack (P.O. Pack No. 336) | | | | 7·50 | | |
| PHQ Cards (*set of 5*) (243) | | | | 4·75 | 16·00 | |
| *Set of 5 Gutter Pairs* | | | | 14·00 | | |

**1603** Tinkerbell

**1604** Wendy, John and Michael Darling in front of Big Ben

**1605** Crocodile and Alarm Clock

**1606** Captain Hook

**1607** Peter Pan

---

### 150th Anniversary of Great Ormond Street Children's Hospital. Peter Pan by Sir James Barrie

**2002** (20 Aug.) One centre phosphor band (2nd) or two phosphor bands (others). Perf 15 × 14

| | | | | | | |
|---|---|---|---|---|---|---|
| 2304 | **1603** | (2nd) | multicoloured | 1·00 | 80 | |
| 2305 | **1604** | (1st) | multicoloured | 1·25 | 1·00 | |
| 2306 | **1605** | (E) | multicoloured | 1·50 | 1·25 | |
| 2307 | **1606** | 47p | multicoloured | 1·50 | 1·50 | |
| 2308 | **1607** | 68p | multicoloured | 2·00 | 2·25 | |
| *Set of 5* | | | | 6·50 | 6·00 | |
| First Day Cover | | | | | 7·00 | |
| Presentation Pack (P.O. Pack No. 337) | | | | 7·50 | | |
| PHQ Cards (*set of 5*) (244) | | | | 4·75 | 15·00 | |
| *Set of 5 Gutter Pairs* | | | | 14·00 | | |

**1608** Millennium Bridge, 2001

**1609** Tower Bridge, 1894

**1610** Westminster Bridge, 1864

**1611** 'Blackfriars Bridge, *c* 1800' (William Marlow)

**1612** 'London Bridge, *c* 1670' (Wenceslaus Hollar)

### Bridges of London

**2002** (10 Sept.) One centre phosphor band (2nd) or two phosphor bands (others)

(a) Litho. Ordinary gum. Perf 15 × 14

| | | | | | | |
|---|---|---|---|---|---|---|
| 2309 | **1608** | (2nd) | multicoloured | 1·00 | 80 | |
| 2310 | **1609** | (1st) | multicoloured | 1·25 | 80 | |
| 2311 | **1610** | (E) | multicoloured | 2·00 | 1·50 | |
| 2312 | **1611** | 47p | multicoloured | 2·50 | 2·00 | |
| 2313 | **1612** | 68p | multicoloured | 3·50 | 3·00 | |
| *Set of 5* | | | | 9·00 | 8·50 | |
| First Day Cover | | | | | 9·00 | |
| Presentation Pack (P.O. Pack No. 338) | | | | 45·00 | | |
| PHQ Cards (*set of 5*) (245) | | | | 4·00 | 12·00 | |
| *Set of 5 Gutter Pairs* | | | | 20·00 | | |

(b) Photo. Self-adhesive. Die-cut perf 15 × 14

| | | | | | | |
|---|---|---|---|---|---|---|
| 2314 | **1609** | (1st) | multicoloured | 6·00 | 6·00 | |

No. 2314 was only issued in £1·62 stamp booklets.

**1613** Galaxies and Nebula

## Astronomy

**2002** (24 Sept.) Sheet 120 × 89 mm. Multicoloured. Two phosphor bands. Perf 14½ × 14

MS2315 **1613** (1st) Planetary nebula in Aquila; (1st) Seyfert 2 galaxy in Pegasus; (1st) Planetary nebula in Norma; (1st) Seyfert 2 galaxy in

| | | | | |
|---|---|---|---|---|
| Circinus | 6·00 | 6·00 | ☐ | ☐ |
| First Day Cover | | 7·00 | | ☐ |
| Presentation Pack (P.O. Pack No. 339) | 20·00 | | ☐ | |
| PHQ Cards (*set of* 5) (246) | 4·75 | 18·00 | ☐ | ☐ |

The five PHQ cards depict the four designs and the complete miniature sheet.

No. **MS**2315 was also issued as a booklet paine in the £6.83 'Across the Universe' booklet.

**1614** Green Pillar Box, 1857

**1615** Horizontal Aperture Box, 1874

**1616** Air Mail Box, 1934

**1617** Double Aperture Box, 1939

**1618** Modern Style Box, 1980

## 150th Anniversary of the First Pillar Box

**2002** (8 Oct.) One centre phosphor band (2nd) or two phosphor bands (others). Perf 14 × 14½

| | | | | | |
|---|---|---|---|---|---|
| 2316 | **1614** (2nd) | multicoloured | 1·00 | 80 | ☐ ☐ |
| 2317 | **1615** (1st) | multicoloured | 1·25 | 1·00 | ☐ ☐ |
| 2318 | **1616** (E) | multicoloured | 1·75 | 1·75 | ☐ ☐ |
| 2319 | **1617** | 47p multicoloured | 2·00 | 2·50 | ☐ ☐ |
| 2320 | **1618** | 68p multicoloured | 2·50 | 3·00 | ☐ ☐ |
| *Set of* 5 | | | 7·50 | 8·00 | ☐ ☐ |
| First Day Cover | | | | 9·00 | ☐ |
| Presentation Pack (P.O. Pack No. 340) | | | 8·00 | | ☐ |
| PHQ Cards (*set of* 5) (247) | | | 4·75 | 16·00 | ☐ ☐ |
| *Set of* 5 Gutter Pairs | | | 16·00 | | ☐ |

**1619** Blue Spruce Star

**1620** Holly

**1621** Ivy

**1622** Mistletoe

**1623** Pine Cone

## Christmas. Plants

**2002** (5 Nov.) Self-adhesive. One centre phosphor band (2nd) or two phosphor bands (others). Die-cut perf 14½ × 14

| | | | | | |
|---|---|---|---|---|---|
| 2321 | **1619** (2nd) | multicoloured | 1·00 | 80 | ☐ ☐ |
| 2322 | **1620** (1st) | multicoloured | 1·25 | 80 | ☐ ☐ |
| 2323 | **1621** (E) | multicoloured | 1·50 | 1·50 | ☐ |
| 2324 | **1622** | 47p multicoloured | 2·00 | 1·75 | ☐ |
| 2325 | **1623** | 68p multicoloured | 3·00 | 2·75 | ☐ |
| *Set of* 5 | | | 8·00 | 7·00 | ☐ ☐ |
| First Day Cover | | | | 8·00 | ☐ |
| Presentation Pack (P.O. Pack No. 341) | | | 8·50 | | ☐ |
| PHQ Cards (*set of* 5) (248) | | | 4·75 | 16·00 | ☐ ☐ |

## Collectors Pack 2002

**2002** (5 Nov.) Comprises Nos. 2243/57, 2260/4, 2265/88, **MS**2292, 2299/313 and **MS**2315/25

| | | |
|---|---|---|
| CP2325a | Collectors Pack | £110 | ☐ |

## Post Office Yearbook

**2002** (5 Nov.) Comprises Nos. 2243/57, 2260/4, 2265/88, 2291/2, 2299/313 and **MS**2315/25 in hardback book with slip case

| | | |
|---|---|---|
| YB2325a | Yearbook | £100 | ☐ |

The Wilding definitives collection 1 ~ 1952 ~ 1953

**1623a**

## 50th Anniversary of Wilding Definitives (1st issue)

**2002** (5 Dec.) Sheet, 124 × 70 mm,

MS2326 1p orange-red; 2p ultramarine;
5p red-brown; (2nd) carmine-
red; (1st) green; 33p brown; 37p
magenta; 47p bistre-brown; 50p
green and label showing national

| | | |
|---|---|---|
| emblems | 10·00 | 10·00 ☐ ☐ |
| First Day Cover | | 11·00 ☐ |
| Presentation Pack (P.O. Pack No. 59) | 65·00 | ☐ ☐ |
| PHQ Cards (set of 5) (D21) | 3·00 | 12·00 ☐ ☐ |

The PHQ cards depict the (2nd), (1st), 33p, 37p and 47p stamps.

For othe Wilding designs with decimal face values, see Nos. 2031/3, 2258/9, **MS**2367, 2378/80 and 3829.

**1624** Barn Owl landing

**1625** Barn Owl with folded Wings and Legs down

**1626** Barn Owl with extended Wings and Legs down

**1627** Barn Owl in Flight with Wings lowered

**1628** Barn Owl in Flight with Wings raised

**1629** Kestrel with Wings folded

**1630** Kestrel with Wings fully extended upwards

**1631** Kestrel with Wings horizontal

**1632** Kestrel with Wings partly extended downwards

**1633** Kestrel with Wings fully extended downwards

## Birds of Prey

**2003** (14 Jan.) Phosphor background. Perf 14½

| | | | | | | | |
|---|---|---|---|---|---|---|---|
| 2327 | **1624** | (1st) | multicoloured | 1·25 | 1·00 | ☐ | ☐ |
| | a. | Block of 10. | | | | | |
| | | Nos. 2327/36 | | 14·00 | 14·00 | ☐ | ☐ |
| 2328 | **1625** | (1st) | multicoloured | 1·25 | 1·00 | ☐ | ☐ |
| 2329 | **1626** | (1st) | multicoloured | 1·25 | 1·00 | ☐ | ☐ |
| 2330 | **1627** | (1st) | multicoloured | 1·25 | 1·00 | ☐ | ☐ |
| 2331 | **1628** | (1st) | multicoloured | 1·25 | 1·00 | ☐ | ☐ |
| 2332 | **1629** | (1st) | multicoloured | 1·25 | 1·00 | ☐ | ☐ |
| 2333 | **1630** | (1st) | multicoloured | 1·25 | 1·00 | ☐ | ☐ |
| 2334 | **1631** | (1st) | multicoloured | 1·25 | 1·00 | ☐ | ☐ |
| 2335 | **1632** | (1st) | multicoloured | 1·25 | 1·00 | ☐ | ☐ |
| 2336 | **1633** | (1st) | multicoloured | 1·25 | 1·00 | ☐ | ☐ |
| Set of 10 | | | | 14·00 | 11·00 | ☐ | ☐ |
| First Day Cover | | | | | 12·00 | ☐ | |
| Presentation Pack (P.O. Pack No. 343) | | | | 15·00 | | ☐ | |
| PHQ Cards (set of 10) (249) | | | | 9·25 | 28·00 | ☐ | ☐ |
| Gutter Block of 20 | | | | 28·00 | | ☐ | |

Nos. 2327/36 were printed together, se-tenant, in blocks of ten (5 × 2) throughout the sheet.

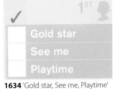

**1634** 'Gold star, See me, Playtime'

**1635** '1♥U, XXXX, S.W.A.L.K.'

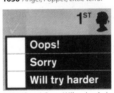

**1636** 'Angel, Poppet, Little terror'

**1637** 'Yes, No, Maybe'

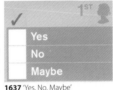

**1638** 'Oops!, Sorry, Will try harder'

**1639** 'I did it!, You did it!, We did it!'

### 'Occasions' Greetings Stamps (3rd series)

**2003** (4 Feb.) Two phosphor bands. Perf 14½ × 14

| | | | | | | | |
|---|---|---|---|---|---|---|---|
| 2337 | **1634** | (1st) | lemon and new blue | 1·25 | 1·00 | ☐ | ☐ |
| | a. | Block of 6. | | | | | |
| | | Nos. 2337/42 | | 8·00 | 6·50 | ☐ | ☐ |
| 2338 | **1635** | (1st) | red and deep ultramarine | 1·25 | 1·00 | ☐ | ☐ |
| 2339 | **1636** | (1st) | purple and bright yellow-green | 1·25 | 1·00 | ☐ | ☐ |
| 2340 | **1637** | (1st) | bright yellow-green and red | 1·25 | 1·00 | ☐ | ☐ |
| 2341 | **1638** | (1st) | deep ultramarine and lemon | 1·25 | 1·00 | ☐ | ☐ |
| 2342 | **1639** | (1st) | new blue and purple | 1·25 | 1·00 | ☐ | ☐ |
| Set of 6 | | | | 8·00 | 6·50 | ☐ | ☐ |
| First Day Cover | | | | | 7·50 | ☐ | ☐ |
| Presentation Pack (P.O. Pack No. M09) | | | | 10·00 | | ☐ | |
| PHQ Cards (set of 6) (PSM09) | | | | 5·25 | 18·00 | ☐ | ☐ |
| Gutter Block of 12 | | | | 17·00 | | ☐ | |

Nos. 2337/42 were printed together, se-tenant, in blocks of six (3 × 2) throughout the sheet.

Nos. 2337/42 were also available in se-tenant sheets of 20 containing four examples of Nos. 2338 and 2340 and three of each of the others. The stamps are accompanied by half stamp-size printed labels or a personal photograph.

**1640** Completing the Genome Jigsaw

**1641** Ape with Moustache and Scientist

**1642** DNA Snakes and Ladders

**1643** 'Animal Scientists'

**1644** Genome Crystal Ball

### 50th Anniversary of Discovery of DNA

**2003** (25 Feb.) One centre phosphor band (2nd) or two phosphor bands (others). Perf 14½

| | | | | | | |
|---|---|---|---|---|---|---|
| 2343 | **1640** | (2nd) | multicoloured | 1·00 | 80 | |
| 2344 | **1641** | (1st) | multicoloured | 1·25 | 1·00 | |
| 2345 | **1642** | (E) | multicoloured | 1·50 | 1·25 | |
| 2346 | **1643** | 47p | multicoloured | 1·50 | 1·50 | |
| 2347 | **1644** | 68p | multicoloured | 2·00 | 2·25 | |
| Set of 5 | | | | 6·50 | 6·00 | |
| First Day Cover | | | | | 8·00 | |
| Presentation Pack (P.O. Pack No. 344) | | | | 9·00 | | |
| PHQ Cards (set of 5) (250) | | | | 4·75 | 18·00 | |
| Set of 5 Gutter Pairs | | | | 15·00 | | |

Nos. 2343/7 were also issued in a £6.99 'Microcosmos' booklet

**1645** Strawberry
**1646** Potato
**1647** Apple
**1648** Red Pepper

**1649** Pear
**1650** Orange

**1651** Tomato
**1652** Lemon

**1653** Brussels Sprout
**1654** Aubergine

### Fruit and Vegetables

**2003** (25 Mar.) Self-adhesive. Two phosphor bands. Perf 14½ × 14 die-cut (without teeth around protruding tops or bottoms of the designs).

| | | | | | | |
|---|---|---|---|---|---|---|
| 2348 | **1645** | (1st) | multicoloured | 1·25 | 1·00 | |
| | | a. | Sheetlet. Nos. 2348/57 and pane of decorative labels | 14·00 | 14·00 | |
| 2349 | **1646** | (1st) | multicoloured | 1·25 | 1·00 | |
| 2350 | **1647** | (1st) | multicoloured | 1·25 | 1·00 | |
| 2351 | **1648** | (1st) | multicoloured | 1·25 | 1·00 | |
| 2352 | **1649** | (1st) | multicoloured | 1·25 | 1·00 | |
| 2353 | **1650** | (1st) | multicoloured | 1·25 | 1·00 | |
| 2354 | **1651** | (1st) | multicoloured | 1·25 | 1·00 | |
| 2355 | **1652** | (1st) | multicoloured | 1·25 | 1·00 | |
| 2356 | **1653** | (1st) | multicoloured | 1·25 | 1·00 | |
| 2357 | **1654** | (1st) | multicoloured | 1·25 | 1·00 | |
| Set of 10 | | | | 14·00 | 10·00 | |
| First Day Cover | | | | | 12·00 | |
| Presentation Pack (P.O. Pack No. 345) | | | | 35·00 | | |
| PHQ Cards (set of 10) (251) | | | | 9·25 | 25·00 | |

Nos. 2348/57 were printed together in sheets of ten with the surplus self-adhesive paper around each stamp retained. The stamp pane is accompanied by a similar-sized pane of self-adhesive labels showing ears, eyes, mouths, hats, etc which are intended for the adornment of fruit and vegetables depicted. This pane is separated from the stamps by a line of roulettes.

Nos. 2348/57 were re-issued on 7th March 2006 in sheets of 20 containing two of each of the ten designs, each stamp accompanied by a se-tenant speech bubble label. These sheets were printed in lithography instead of photogravure, and have stickers showing eyes, hats, etc in the sheet margin.

**1655**

## Overseas Booklet Stamps

**2003** (27 Mar.)–2010 Self-adhesive. Two phosphor bands. Perf 15 × 14 die-cut with one elliptical hole in each vertical side

| | | | |
|---|---|---|---|
| 2357a | (Worldwide postcard) grey-black, rosine and ultramarine *(1.4.04)* | 1·75 | 1·75 ☐ ☐ |
| 2357b | (Europe up to 20 grams) deep blue-green, new blue and rosine *(30.3.10)* | 1·75 | 1·75 ☐ ☐ |
| 2358 **1655** | (Europe up to 40 grams)new blue and rosine | 2·50 | 2·50 ☐ ☐ |
| 2358a | (Worldwide up to 20grams) deep mauve, new blue and rosine *(30.3.10)* | 2·60 | 2·60 ☐ ☐ |
| 2359 | (Worldwide up to 40 grams) rosine and new blue | 4·00 | 4·05 ☐ ☐ |
| First Day Cover (Nos. 2358, 2359) | | | 6·50 ☐ |
| Presentation Pack (Nos. 2358, 2359) (P.O. Pack No. 60) | | 6·50 | ☐ |
| PHQ Card (No. 2358) (D23) | | 45 | 3·50 ☐ ☐ |

Nos. 2358 and 2359 were intended to pay postage on mail up to 40 grams to either Europe (52p) or to foreign destinations outside Europe (£1·12). No. 2357a was intended to pay postcard rate to foreign destinations (43p).

Operationally they were only available in separate booklets of 4, initially sold at £2·08, £4·48 and £1·72, with the surplus self-adhesive paper around each stamp removed. Single examples of the stamps were available from philatelic outlets as sets of two or in presentation packs.

Nos. 2357b and 2358a were intended to pay postage on mail up to 20 grams to either Europe (initially 56p, or to foreign destinations outside Europe (90p).

They were only available in separate booklets of four (Nos. MI3 and MJ3) initially sold at £2·24 and £3·60, increasing to £2·40 and £3·88 from 6 April 2010, with the surplus self-adhesive paper around each stamp removed.

For first day covers and presentation packs for Nos. 2357a/b and 2358a and PHQ cards for Nos. 2357a, 2358 and 2359 see below Nos. Y1667/1803.

**1656** Amy Johnson (pilot) and Biplane

**1657** Members of 1953 Everest Team

**1658** Freya Stark (traveller and writer) and Desert

**1659** Ernest Shackleton (Antarctic explorer) and Wreck of *Endurance*

**1660** Francis Chichester (yachtsman) and *Gipsy Moth IV*

**1661** Robert Falcon Scott (Antarctic explorer) and Norwegian Expedition at the Pole

### Extreme Endeavours (British Explorers)

**2003** (29 Apr.) One centre phosphor band (2nd) or two phosphor bands (others)

| | | | | | |
|---|---|---|---|---|---|
| (a) Ordinary gum. Perf 15 × 14½ | | | | | |
| 2360 **1656** | 2nd) | multicoloured | 1·00 | 1·00 ☐ ☐ |
| 2361 **1657** | (1st) | multicoloured | 1·25 | 1·00 ☐ ☐ |
| 2362 **1658** | (E) | multicoloured | 1·50 | 1·50 ☐ ☐ |
| 2363 **1659** | 42p | multicoloured | 1·75 | 1·75 ☐ ☐ |
| 2364 **1660** | 47p | multicoloured | 2·00 | 2·00 ☐ ☐ |
| 2365 **1661** | 68p | multicoloured | 2·50 | 2·50 ☐ ☐ |
| *Set of* 6 | | | 8·00 | 8·50 |
| First Day Cover | | | | 10·00 ☐ |
| Presentation Pack (P.O. Pack No. 346) | | | 10·00 | ☐ |
| PHQ Cards (*set of* 6) (252) | | | 3·25 | 14·00 ☐ ☐ |
| *Set of* 6 Gutter Pairs | | | 17·00 | ☐ |

| | | | | | |
|---|---|---|---|---|---|
| (b) Self-adhesive. Die-cut perf 14½ | | | | | |
| 2366 **1657** | (1st) | multicoloured | 5·00 | 5·00 ☐ ☐ |

The phosphor bands on Nos. 2361/5 are at the centre and right of each stamp.

No. 2366 was only issued in £1·62 stamp booklets in which the surplus self-adhesive paper around each stamp was removed.

### 50th Anniversary of Wilding Definitives (2nd issue)

**2003** (20 May) Sheet, 124 × 70 mm, containing designs as T 155/8 and 160 (1952–54 issue), but with values in decimal currency as T **1348** or with service indicator as T **1566**, printed on pale cream. One centre phosphor band (20p) or two phosphor bands (others). W 1565. P 15 × 14 (with one elliptical hole in each vertical side).

| | | | |
|---|---|---|---|
| **MS**2367 | 4p deep lilac; 8p ultramarine; 10p reddish purple; 20p bright green; 28p bronze-green; 34p brown-purple; (E) chestnut; 42p Prussian blue; 68p grey-blue and label showing national emblems | 10·50 | 11·25 ☐ ☐ |
| First Day Cover | | | 13·00 ☐ ☐ |
| Presentation Pack (P.O. Pack No. 61) | | 15·00 | ☐ ☐ |

**1662** Guardsmen in Coronation Procession

**1663** East End Children reading Coronation Party Poster

**1664** Queen Elizabeth II in Coronation Chair with Bishops of Durham and Bath & Wells

**1665** Children in Plymouth working on Royal Montage

**1666** Queen Elizabeth II in Coronation Robes (photograph by Cecil Beaton)

**1667** Children's Race at East End Street Party

**1668** Coronation Coach passing through Marble Arch

**1669** Children in Fancy Dress

**1670** Coronation Coach outside Buckingham Palace

**1671** Children eating at London Street Party

## 50th Anniversary of Coronation

**2003** (2 June) W **1565**. Two phosphor bands. Perf 14½ × 14

| | | | | | | | |
|---|---|---|---|---|---|---|---|
| 2368 | **1662** | (1st) | multicoloured | 1·25 | 1·00 | ☐ | ☐ |
| | a. | Block of 10. | | | | | |
| | | Nos. 2368/77 | 14·00 | 11·00 | ☐ | ☐ |
| 2369 | **1663** | (1st) | black and gold | 1·25 | 1·00 | ☐ | ☐ |
| 2370 | **1664** | (1st) | multicoloured | 1·25 | 1·00 | ☐ | ☐ |
| 2371 | **1665** | (1st) | black and gold | 1·25 | 1·00 | ☐ | ☐ |
| 2372 | **1666** | (1st) | multicoloured | 1·25 | 1·00 | ☐ | ☐ |
| 2373 | **1667** | (1st) | black and gold | 1·25 | 1·00 | ☐ | ☐ |
| 2374 | **1668** | (1st) | multicoloured | 1·25 | 1·00 | ☐ | ☐ |
| 2375 | **1669** | (1st) | black and gold | 1·25 | 1·00 | ☐ | ☐ |
| 2376 | **1670** | (1st) | multicoloured | 1·25 | 1·00 | ☐ | ☐ |
| 2377 | **1671** | (1st) | black and gold | 1·25 | 1·00 | ☐ | ☐ |
| Set of 10 | | | | 14·00 | 11·00 | ☐ | ☐ |
| First Day Cover | | | | | 12·00 | ☐ | |
| Presentation Pack (P.O. Pack No. 347) | | | 20·00 | | | ☐ | |
| PHQ Cards (set of 10) (253) | | | 9·25 | 20·00 | ☐ | ☐ |
| Gutter Block of 20 | | | 30·00 | | | ☐ | |

Nos. 2368/77 were printed together, *se-tenant*, as blocks of ten (5 × 2) in sheets of 60 (2 panes of 30).

No. 2372 does not show the Queen's head in gold as do the other nine designs.

### 50th Anniversary of Coronation. Booklet Stamps

**2003** (2 June) Designs as T **160** (Wilding definitive of 1952) and 163 (Coronation commemorative of 1953), but with values in decimal currency as T **134**8. W **1565**. Two phosphor bands. P 15 × 14 (with one elliptical hole in each vertical side for Nos. 2378/9)

| | | | | | | | |
|---|---|---|---|---|---|---|---|
| 2378 | **160** | 47p bistre-brown | 5·00 | 2·50 | ☐ | ☐ |
| 2379 | | 68p grey-blue | 5·00 | 4·00 | ☐ | ☐ |
| 2380 | **163** | £1 deep yellow-green | 50·00 | 45·00 | ☐ | ☐ |
| Set of 3 | | | 55·00 | 47·00 | ☐ | ☐ |

Nos. 2378/80 were only available in £7·46 'A Perfect Coronation' stamp booklets. Stamps as Nos. 2378/9, but on pale cream, were also included in the Wilding miniature sheets, Nos. **MS**2326 or **MS**2367. A £1 design as No. 2380, but on phosphorised paper, was previously included in the "Stamp Show 2000" miniature sheet, No. **MS**2147.

**1672** Prince William in September 2001 (Brendan Beirne)

**1673** Prince William in September 2000 (Tim Graham)

**1674** Prince William in September 2001 (Camera Press)

**1675** Prince William in September 2001 (Tim Graham)

### 21st Birthday of Prince William of Wales

**2003** (17 June) Phosphor backgrounds. Perf 14½

| | | | | | | |
|---|---|---|---|---|---|---|
| 2381 | **1672** | 28p multicoloured | 1·00 | 80 | ☐ | ☐ |
| 2382 | **1673** | (E) dull mauve, grey-black and light green | 2·25 | 1·50 | ☐ | ☐ |
| 2383 | **1674** | 47p multicoloured | 2·75 | 2·00 | ☐ | ☐ |
| 2384 | **1675** | 68p sage-green, black and bright green | 4·00 | 2·50 | ☐ | ☐ |
| Set of 4 | | | 9·00 | 6·00 | ☐ | |
| First Day Cover | | | | 8·00 | | |
| Presentation Pack (P.O. Pack No. 348) | | 20·00 | | | ☐ | |
| PHQ Cards (set of 4) (254) | | 7·50 | 20·00 | ☐ | ☐ |
| Set of 4 Gutter Pairs | | 19·00 | | | ☐ | |

**1676** Loch Assynt, Sutherland

**1677** Ben More, Isle of Mull

**1680** Glenfinnan Viaduct, Lochaber **1681** Papa Little, Shetland Islands

## A British Journey (1st series): Scotland

**2003** (15 July) One centre phosphor band (2nd) or two phosphor bands (others). Perf 14½

| | | | (a) Ordinary gum | | |
|---|---|---|---|---|---|
| 2385 | **1676** | (2nd) | multicoloured | 1·00 | 90 |
| 2386 | **1677** | (1st) | multicoloured | 1·25 | 1·00 |
| 2387 | **1678** | (E) | multicoloured | 1·50 | 1·25 |
| 2388 | **1679** | 42p | multicoloured | 1·25 | 1·50 |
| 2389 | **1680** | 47p | multicoloured | 1·50 | 2·00 |
| 2390 | **1681** | 68p | multicoloured | 2·00 | 2·50 |
| *Set of 6* | | | | 7·00 | 8·50 |
| First Day Cover | | | | | 10·00 |
| Presentation Pack (P.O. Pack No. 349) | | | | 9·50 | |
| PHQ Cards (*set of 6*) (255) | | | | 3·00 | 14·00 |
| *Set of 6 Gutter Pairs* | | | | 15·00 | |

| | | | (b) Self-adhesive. Die-cut perf 14½ | | |
|---|---|---|---|---|---|
| 2391 | **1677** | (1st) | multicoloured | 6·00 | 6·00 |

No. 2391 was only issued in £1·68 stamp booklets in which the surplus self-adhesive paper around each stamp was removed.

**1682** 'The Station' (Andrew Davidson)  **1683** 'Black Swan' (Stanley Chew)  **1684** 'The Cross Keys' (George Mackenney)

**1685** 'The Mayflower' (Ralph Ellis)  **1686** 'The Barley Sheaf' (Joy Cooper)

## Europa. British Pub Signs

**2003** (12 Aug.) Two phosphor bands. Perf 14 × 14½

| | | | | | |
|---|---|---|---|---|---|
| 2392 | **1682** | (1st) | multicoloured | 1·25 | 70 |
| 2393 | **1683** | (E) | multicoloured | 2·00 | 2·00 |
| 2394 | **1684** | 42p | multicoloured | 1·50 | 1·50 |
| 2395 | **1685** | 47p | multicoloured | 1·75 | 2·00 |
| 2396 | **1686** | 68p | multicoloured | 2·00 | 2·25 |
| *Set of 5* | | | | 7·50 | 8·00 |
| First Day Cover | | | | | 9·00 |
| Presentation Pack (P.O. Pack No. 350) | | | | 11·00 | |
| PHQ Cards (*set of 5*) (256) | | | | 3·00 | 12·00 |
| *Set of 5 Gutter Pairs* | | | | 16·00 | |

The 1st and E values incorporate the "EUROPA" emblem.

No. 2392 was also issued in the £7.44 @Letters by Night' booklet.

**1687** Meccano Constructor Biplane, c. 1931  **1688** Wells-Brimtoy Clockwork Double-decker Omnibus, c. 1938

**1689** Hornby M1 Clockwork Locomotive and Tender, c. 1948  **1690** Dinky Toys Ford Zephyr, c. 1956

**1691** Mettoy Friction Drive Space Ship Eagle, c. 1960

## Classic Transport Toys

**2003** (18 Sept.) Two phosphor bands

| | | | (a) Ordinary gum. Perf 14½ × 14 | | |
|---|---|---|---|---|---|
| 2397 | **1687** | (1st) | multicoloured | 1·25 | 70 |
| 2398 | **1688** | (E) | multicoloured | 1·50 | 1·25 |
| 2399 | **1689** | 42p | multicoloured | 1·50 | 1·50 |
| 2400 | **1690** | 47p | multicoloured | 1·75 | 1·75 |
| 2401 | **1691** | 68p | multicoloured | 2·50 | 2·50 |
| *Set of 5* | | | | 7·50 | 7·00 |
| First Day Cover | | | | | 8·50 |
| Presentation Pack (P.O. Pack No. 351) | | | | 12·00 | |
| PHQ Cards (*set of 6*) (257) | | | | 3·00 | 14·00 |
| *Set of 5 Gutter Pairs* | | | | 16·00 | |
| **MS**2402 115 × 105 mm. Nos. 2397/401 | | | | 8·00 | 8·50 |
| First Day Cover | | | | | 11·00 |

| | | | (b) Self-adhesive. Die-cut perf 14½ × 14 | | |
|---|---|---|---|---|---|
| 2403 | **1687** | (1st) | multicoloured | 6·00 | 6·00 |

The complete miniature sheet is shown on one of the PHQ cards with the others depicting individual stamps.

No. 2403 was only issued in £1·68 stamp booklets in which the surplus self-adhesive paper around each stamp was removed.

**1692** Coffin of Denytenamun, Egyptian, c. 900BC  **1693** Alexander the Great, Greek, c. 200BC

**1694** Sutton Hoo
Helmet, Anglo-Saxon,
c. AD600

**1695** Sculpture of
Parvati, South Indian,
c. AD1550

**1696** Mask of Xiutecuhtli,
Mixtec-Aztec, c. AD1500

**1697** Hoa Hakananai'a,
Easter Island, c. AD1000

### 250th Anniversary of the British Museum

**2003** (7 Oct.) One side phosphor band (2nd), two phosphor
bands ((1st), (E), 47p) or phosphor background at left and band
at right (42p, 68p). Perf 14 × 14½

| | | | | |
|---|---|---|---|---|
| 2404 | **1692** | (2nd) | multicoloured | 1·00 | 70 |
| 2405 | **1693** | (1st) | multicoloured | 1·25 | 90 |
| 2406 | **1694** | (E) | multicoloured | 1·50 | 1·25 |
| 2407 | **1695** | 42p | multicoloured | 1·50 | 1·50 |
| 2408 | **1696** | 47p | multicoloured | 2·00 | 2·00 |
| 2409 | **1697** | 68p | multicoloured | 2·75 | 2·75 |
| *Set of* 6 | | | | 9·00 | 8·00 |
| First Day Cover | | | | | 10·00 |
| Presentation Pack (P.O. Pack No. 352) | | | 11·00 | |
| PHQ Cards (*set of* 6) (258) | | | 3·00 | 14·00 |
| *Set of* 6 Gutter Pairs | | | | 19·00 | |

**1698** Ice Spiral      **1699** Icicle Star

**1700** Wall of Ice Blocks      **1701** Ice Ball

**1702** Ice Hole      **1703** Snow Pyramids

### Christmas. Ice Sculptures by Andy Goldsworthy

**2003** (4 Nov.) Self-adhesive. One side phosphor band (2nd),
'all-over' phosphor (1st) or two bands (others). Die-cut perf
14½ × 14

| | | | | | |
|---|---|---|---|---|---|
| 2410 | **1698** | (2nd) | multicoloured | 1·00 | 70 |
| 2411 | **1699** | (1st) | multicoloured | 1·25 | 90 |
| 2412 | **1700** | (E) | multicoloured | 1·50 | 1·50 |
| 2413 | **1701** | 53p | multicoloured | 2·00 | 2·00 |
| 2414 | **1702** | 68p | multicoloured | 2·50 | 2·50 |
| 2415 | **1703** | £1·12 | multicoloured | 3·00 | 3·00 |
| *Set of* 6 | | | | 10·00 | 9·50 |
| First Day Cover | | | | | 11·00 |
| Presentation Pack (P.O. Pack No. 353) | | 12·00 | |
| PHQ Cards (*set of* 6) (259) | | | 4·00 | 14·00 |

The 2nd and 1st class were also issued in separate sheets of
20, each stamp printed in lithography instead of photogravure
and accompanied by a half stamp-size *se-tenant* label showing
either animals, ice sculptures or a personal photograph.

### Collectors Pack 2003

**2003** (4 Nov.) Comprises Nos. 2327/57, 2360/5, 2368/77,
2381/90, 2392/401 and 2404/15

| | | | |
|---|---|---|---|
| CP2415a | Collectors Pack | £120 | |

### Post Office Yearbook

**2003** (4 Nov.) Comprises Nos. 2327/57, 2360/5, 2368/77,
2381/90, 2392/401 and 2404/15

| | | | |
|---|---|---|---|
| YB2415a | Yearbook | £100 | |

**1704** Rugby Scenes

### England's Victory in Rugby World Cup Championship, Australia, Miniature sheet

**2003** (19 Dec.) Sheet 115 × 85 mm. Multicoloured. Two
phosphor bands. Perf 14

| | | |
|---|---|---|
| MS2416 1704 (1st) England flags and fans; (1st) England team standing in circle before match; 68p World Cup trophy; 68p Victorious England players after match | 14·00 | 14·00 |
| First Day Cover | | 15·00 |
| Presentation Pack (P.O. Pack No. M9B) | 20·00 | |

**1705** *Dolgoch*, Rheilffordd Talyllyn Railway, Gwynedd

**1706** CR Class 439, Bo'ness and Kinneil Railway, West Lothian

**1707** GCR Class 8K, Leicestershire

**1708** GWR Manor Class *Bradley Manor*, Severn Valley Railway, Worcestershire

**1709** SR West Country class *Blackmoor Vale*, Bluebell Railway, East Sussex

**1710** BR Standard class, Keighley & Worth Valley Railway, Yorkshire

## Classic Locomotives

**2004** (13 Jan.) One side phosphor band (20p) or two phosphor bands (others). Perf 14½

| | | | | | | |
|---|---|---|---|---|---|---|
| 2417 | **1705** | 20p | multicoloured | 65 | 65 | |
| 2418 | **1706** | 28p | multicoloured | 90 | 90 | |
| 2419 | **1707** | (E) | multicoloured | 1·50 | 1·20 | |
| 2420 | **1708** | 42p | multicoloured | 1·50 | 1·50 | |
| 2421 | **1709** | 47p | multicoloured | 2·00 | 2·00 | |
| 2422 | **1710** | 68p | multicoloured | 3·00 | 3·50 | |
| *Set of* 6 | | | | 8·00 | 8·50 | |
| First Day Cover | | | | | 10·00 | |
| Presentation Pack (P.O. Pack No. 355) | | | | 25·00 | | |
| PHQ Cards (*set of* 7) (260) | | | | 8·50 | 15·00 | |
| *Set of* 6 Gutter Pairs | | | | 17·00 | | |
| **MS**2423 190 × 67 mm. Nos. 2417/22 | | | | 25·00 | 25·00 | |
| First Day Cover | | | | | 26·00 | |

The seven PHQ cards depict the six stamps and the miniature sheet.

No.s 2418/20 were also issued in the £7.44 'Letters by Night' booklet

**1711** Postman

**1712** Face

**1713** Duck

**1714** Baby

**1715** Aircraft

## 'Occasions' Greetings Stamps (4th series)

**2004** (3 Feb.) Two phosphor bands. Perf 14½ × 14

| | | | | | | |
|---|---|---|---|---|---|---|
| 2424 | **1711** | (1st) | bright mauve and black | 1·25 | 1·00 | |
| | | a. | Horiz strip of 5. Nos. 2424/8 | 7·00 | 6·00 | |
| 2425 | **1712** | (1st) | magenta and black | 1·25 | 1·00 | |
| 2426 | **1713** | (1st) | lemon and black | 1·25 | 1·00 | |
| 2427 | **1714** | (1st) | pale turquoise-green and black | 1·25 | 1·00 | |
| 2428 | **1715** | (1st) | bright new blue and black | 1·25 | 1·00 | |
| *Set of* 5 | | | | 7·00 | 6·00 | |
| First Day Cover | | | | | 8·00 | |
| Presentation Pack (P.O. Pack No. M10) | | | | 8·00 | | |
| PHQ Cards (*set of* 5) (PSM10) | | | | 4·75 | 12·00 | |
| Gutter Block of 10 | | | | 15·00 | | |

Nos. 2424/8 were printed together, *se-tenant*, as horizontal strips of five in sheets of 25 (5 × 5).

Nos. 2424/8 were also issued in sheets of 20 containing the five designs *se-tenant* with half stamp-size printed message labels. Similar sheets containing either Nos. 2424 and 2428 or Nos. 2425/7 came with personal photographs on the labels.

**1716** Map showing Middle Earth

**1717** Forest of Lothlórien in Spring

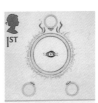
**1718** Dust-jacket for The Fellowship of the Ring

**1719** Rivendell

**1720** The Hall at Bag End

**1721** Orthanc

JRR TOLKIEN · THE LORD OF THE RINGS
**1722** Doors of Durin

JRR TOLKIEN · THE LORD OF THE RINGS
**1723** Barad-dûr

JRR TOLKIEN · THE LORD OF THE RINGS
**1724** Minas Tirith

JRR TOLKIEN · THE LORD OF THE RINGS
**1725** Fangorn Forest

### 50th Anniversary of Publication of The Fellowship of the Ring and The Two Towers by J. R. R. Tolkien

**2004** (26 Feb.) Two phosphor bands. Perf 14½

| | | | | | | |
|---|---|---|---|---|---|---|
| 2429 | **1716** | (1st) | multicoloured | 1·25 | 1·00 | ☐ ☐ |
| | | a. | Block of 10. | | | |
| | | | Nos. 2429/38 | 14·00 | 12·00 | ☐ ☐ |
| 2430 | **1717** | (1st) | multicoloured | 1·25 | 1·00 | ☐ ☐ |
| 2431 | **1718** | (1st) | multicoloured | 1·25 | 1·00 | ☐ ☐ |
| 2432 | **1719** | (1st) | multicoloured | 1·25 | 1·00 | ☐ ☐ |
| 2433 | **1720** | (1st) | multicoloured | 1·25 | 1·00 | ☐ ☐ |
| 2434 | **1721** | (1st) | multicoloured | 1·25 | 1·00 | ☐ ☐ |
| 2435 | **1722** | (1st) | multicoloured | 1·25 | 1·00 | ☐ ☐ |
| 2436 | **1723** | (1st) | multicoloured | 1·25 | 1·00 | ☐ ☐ |
| 2437 | **1724** | (1st) | multicoloured | 1·25 | 1·00 | ☐ ☐ |
| 2438 | **1725** | (1st) | multicoloured | 1·25 | 1·00 | ☐ ☐ |
| Set of 10 | | | | 14·00 | 11·00 | ☐ ☐ |
| First Day Cover | | | | | 12·00 | ☐ |
| Presentation Pack (P.O. Pack No. 356) | | | 20·00 | | ☐ |
| PHQ Cards (set of 10) (261) | | | 9·75 | 18·00 | ☐ ☐ |
| Gutter Block of 20 | | | 30·00 | | ☐ |

Nos. 2429/38 were printed together, *se-tenant*, in blocks of ten (5 × 2) throughout the sheet.

**1726** Ely Island, Lower Lough Erne

**1727** Giant's Causeway, Antrim Coast

**1728** Slemish, Antrim Mountains

**1729** Banns Road, Mourne Mountains

**1730** Glenelly Valley, Sperrins

**1731** Islandmore, Strangford Lough

### A British Journey (2nd series): Northern Ireland

**2004** (16 Mar.) One side phosphor band (2nd) or two phosphor bands (others). Perf 14½

#### (a) Ordinary gum

| | | | | | | |
|---|---|---|---|---|---|---|
| 2439 | **1726** | (2nd) | multicoloured | 1·00 | 75 | ☐ ☐ |
| 2440 | **1727** | (1st) | multicoloured | 1·25 | 90 | ☐ ☐ |
| 2441 | **1728** | (E) | multicoloured | 1·50 | 1·20 | ☐ ☐ |
| 2442 | **1729** | 42p | multicoloured | 1·30 | 1·30 | ☐ ☐ |
| 2443 | **1730** | 47p | multicoloured | 1·50 | 1·50 | ☐ ☐ |
| 2444 | **1731** | 68p | multicoloured | 2·20 | 2·20 | ☐ ☐ |
| Set of 6 | | | | 8·00 | 7·00 | ☐ ☐ |
| First Day Cover | | | | | 10·00 | ☐ |
| Presentation Pack (P.O. Pack No. 357) | | 12·00 | | ☐ |
| PHQ Cards (set of 6) (262) | | | 5·75 | 14·00 | ☐ ☐ |
| Set of 6 Gutter Pairs | | | 17·00 | | ☐ |

#### (b) Self-adhesive. Die-cut perf 14½

| | | | | | | |
|---|---|---|---|---|---|---|
| 2445 | **1727** | (1st) | multicoloured | 6·00 | 6·00 | ☐ ☐ |

No. 2445 was only issued in £1·68 stamp booklets in which the surplus self-adhesive paper around each stamp was removed.

**28**
**1732** 'Lace 1 (trial proof) 1968' (Sir Terry Frost)

**57**
**1733** 'Coccinelle' (Sonia Delaunay)

### Centenary of the Entente Cordiale. Contemporary Paintings

**2004** (6 Apr.) Two phosphor bands. Perf 14 × 14½

| | | | | | | |
|---|---|---|---|---|---|---|
| 2446 | **1732** | 28p | grey, black and rosine | 1·00 | 85 | ☐ ☐ |
| 2447 | **1733** | 57p | multicoloured | 2·25 | 2·00 | ☐ ☐ |
| Set of 2 | | | | 3·00 | 2·75 | ☐ ☐ |
| First Day Cover | | | | | 3·75 | ☐ ☐ |
| Presentation Pack (P.O. Pack No. 358) | | 35·00 | | ☐ |
| Presentation Pack (UK and French stamps) | | | 25·00 | | ☐ |
| PHQ Cards (set of 2) (263) | | | 3·50 | 6·00 | ☐ ☐ |
| Set of 2 Gutter Pairs | | | 7·00 | | ☐ |
| Set of 2 Traffic Light Gutter Blocks of 4 | 15·00 | | ☐ |

Stamps in similar designs were issued by France and these are included in the joint Presentation Pack.

**1734** 'RMS Queen Mary 2, 2004' (Edward D. Walker)

**1735** 'SS Canberra 1961' (David Cobb)

**1736** 'RMS *Queen Mary* 1936' (Charles Pears)

**1737** 'RMS *Mauretania*, 1907' (Thomas Henry)

**1744** Lilium 'Lemon Pixie'

**1745** Delphinium 'Clifford Sky'

**1738** 'SS *City of New York*, 1888' (Raphael Monleaon y Torres)

**1739** 'PS *Great Western*, 1838' (Joseph Walter)

## Ocean Liners

**2004** (13 Apr.) Two phosphor bands.

(a) Photo. Ordinary gum. Perf 14½ × 14

| | | | | | | |
|---|---|---|---|---|---|---|
| 2448 | **1734** | (1st) | multicoloured | 1·25 | 90 | ☐ ☐ |
| 2449 | **1735** | (E) | multicoloured | 1·50 | 1·30 | ☐ ☐ |
| 2450 | **1736** | 42p | multicoloured | 1·30 | 1·30 | ☐ ☐ |
| 2451 | **1737** | 47p | multicoloured | 1·50 | 1·50 | ☐ ☐ |
| 2452 | **1738** | 57p | multicoloured | 1·80 | 1·80 | ☐ ☐ |
| 2453 | **1739** | 68p | multicoloured | 2·20 | 2·20 | ☐ ☐ |
| *Set of* 6 | | | | 9·00 | 9·00 | ☐ ☐ |
| First Day Cover | | | | | 11·00 | ☐ |
| Presentation Pack (P.O. Pack No. 359) | | | | 11·00 | | ☐ |
| PHQ Cards (*set of* 7) (264) | | | | 6·75 | 20·00 | ☐ ☐ |
| *Set of* 6 Gutter Pairs | | | | 20·00 | | |
| **MS**2454 114 × 104 mm. Nos. 2448/53 | | | | 20·00 | 18·00 | ☐ ☐ |
| First Day Cover | | | | | 19·00 | ☐ |

(b) Self-adhesive. Die-cut perf 14½ × 14

| | | | | | | |
|---|---|---|---|---|---|---|
| 2455 | **1734** | (1st) | multicoloured | 6·00 | 6·00 | ☐ ☐ |

Nos. 2448/55 commemorate the introduction to service of the Queen Mary 2.

No. 2455 was only issued in £1·68 stamp booklets in which the surplus self-adhesive paper around each stamp was removed.

The complete miniature sheet is shown on one of the PHQ cards with the others depicting individual stamps. See also No. 2614

For Type **1739** printed in lithography, see No. 2514.

**1740** Dianthus Allwoodii Group

**1741** Dahlia 'Garden Princess'

**1742** Clematis 'Arabella'

**1743** Miltonia 'French Lake'

## Bicentenary of the Royal Horticultural Society (1st issue)

**2004** (25 May) One side phosphor band (2nd) or 'all-over' phosphor (others). Perf 14½

| | | | | | | |
|---|---|---|---|---|---|---|
| 2456 | **1740** | (2nd) | multicoloured | 1·00 | 80 | ☐ ☐ |
| 2457 | **1741** | (1st) | multicoloured | 1·25 | 1·00 | ☐ ☐ |
| 2458 | **1742** | (E) | multicoloured | 1·50 | 1·30 | ☐ ☐ |
| 2459 | **1743** | 42p | multicoloured | 2·00 | 2·00 | ☐ ☐ |
| 2460 | **1744** | 47p | multicoloured | 2·50 | 2·50 | ☐ ☐ |
| 2461 | **1745** | 68p | multicoloured | 3·50 | 3·50 | ☐ ☐ |
| *Set of* 6 | | | | 11·00 | 10·00 | ☐ ☐ |
| First Day Cover | | | | | 12·00 | ☐ |
| Presentation Pack (P.O. Pack No. 360) | | | | 12·00 | | ☐ |
| PHQ Cards (*set of* 7) (265) | | | | 6·75 | 20·00 | ☐ ☐ |
| *Set of* 6 Gutter Pairs | | | | 23·00 | | |
| **MS**2462 115 × 105 mm. Nos. 2456/61 | | | | 14·00 | 14·00 | ☐ ☐ |
| First Day Cover | | | | | 16·00 | ☐ |

The complete miniature sheet is shown on one of the PHQ cards with the others depicting individual stamps.

The 1st class stamp was also issued in sheets of 20, printed in lithography instead of photogravure, each stamp accompanied by a *se-tenant* stamp-size label.

Nos. 2456/61 were also, issued in the £7·23 'The Glory of the Garden' booklet.

## Bicentenary of the Royal Horticultural Society (2nd issue). Booklet stamps

**2004** (25 May) Designs as Nos. 1955, 1958 and 1962 (1997 Greeting Stamps 19th-century Flower Paintings). Two phosphor bands. Perf 15 × 14 (with one elliptical hole in each vertical side)

| | | | | | | |
|---|---|---|---|---|---|---|
| 2463 | **1280** | (1st) | multicoloured | 8·00 | 8·00 | ☐ ☐ |
| 2464 | **1283** | (1st) | multicoloured | 4·00 | 4·00 | ☐ ☐ |
| 2465 | **1287** | (1st) | multicoloured | 8·00 | 8·00 | ☐ ☐ |
| *Set of* 3 | | | | 18·00 | 18·00 | ☐ ☐ |

On Nos. 2463/5 the phosphor bands appear at the left and the centre of each stamp.

Nos. 2463/5 were only issued in the in £7·23 'The Glory of the Garden' booklet.

**1746** Barmouth Bridge

**1747** Hyddgen, Plynlimon

**1748** Brecon Beacons

**1749** Pen-pych, Rhondda Valley

**1750** Rhewl, Dee Valley

**1751** Marloes Sands

## A British Journey (3rd series): Wales

**2004** (15 June) One centre phosphor band (2nd), 'all-over' phosphor (1st) or two phosphor bands (others)

(a) Ordinary gum. Perf 14½

| | | | | |
|---|---|---|---|---|
| 2466 **1746** | (2nd) | multicoloured | 1·00 | 80 |
| 2467 **1747** | (1st) | multicoloured | 1·25 | 1·00 |
| 2468 **1748** | 40p | multicoloured | 1·75 | 1·50 |
| 2469 **1749** | 43p | multicoloured | 2·00 | 2·00 |
| 2470 **1750** | 47p | multicoloured | 2·50 | 3·00 |
| 2471 **1751** | 68p | multicoloured | 3·50 | 4·00 |
| Set of 6 | | | 10·00 | 11·00 |
| First Day Cover | | | | 12·00 |
| Presentation Pack (P.O. Pack No. 361) | | | 11·00 | |
| PHQ Cards (set of 6) (266) | | | 5·75 | 12·00 |
| Set of 6 Gutter Pairs | | | 22·00 | |

(b) Self-adhesive. Die-cut perf 14½

| | | | | |
|---|---|---|---|---|
| 2472 **1747** | (1st) | multicoloured | 8·00 | 8·00 |

The 1st and 40p values include the 'EUROPA' emblem.

No. 2472 was only issued in £1·68 stamp booklets in which the surplus self-adhesive paper around each stamp was removed.

**1752** Sir Rowland Hill Award

**1753** William Shipley (Founder of Royal Society of Arts)

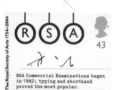

**1754** 'RSA' as Typewriter Keys and Shorthand

**1755** Chimney Sweep

**1756** 'Gill Typeface'

**1757** 'Zero Waste'

## 250th Anniversary of the Royal Society of Arts

**2004** (10 Aug.) Two phosphor bands. Perf 14

| | | | | |
|---|---|---|---|---|
| 2473 **1752** | (1st) | multicoloured | 1·25 | 95 |
| 2474 **1753** | 40p | multicoloured | 1·30 | 1·30 |
| 2475 **1754** | 43p | multicoloured | 1·40 | 1·40 |
| 2476 **1755** | 47p | multicoloured | 1·50 | 1·50 |
| 2477 **1756** | 57p | silver, vermilion and black | 2·20 | 2·20 |

| | | | | |
|---|---|---|---|---|
| 2478 **1757** | 68p | silver, vermilion and black | 3·00 | 3·00 |
| Set of 6 | | | 10·00 | 10·00 |
| First Day Cover | | | | 12·00 |
| Presentation Pack (P.O. Pack No. 362) | | | 11·00 | |
| PHQ Cards (set of 6) (267) | | | 5·75 | 14·00 |
| Set of 6 Gutter Pairs | | | 22·00 | |

**1758** Pine Marten

**1759** Roe Deer

**1760** Badger

**1761** Yellow-necked Mouse

**1762** Wild Cat

**1763** Red Squirrel

**1764** Stoat

**1765** Natterer's Bat

**1766** Mole

**1767** Fox

## Woodland Animals

**2004** (16 Sept.) Two phosphor bands. Perf 14½

| | | | | |
|---|---|---|---|---|
| 2479 **1758** | (1st) | multicoloured | 1·25 | 1·00 |
| | a. | Block of 10. Nos. 2479/88 | 14·00 | 12·00 |
| 2480 **1759** | (1st) | multicoloured | 1·25 | 1·00 |
| 2481 **1760** | (1st) | multicoloured | 1·25 | 1·00 |
| 2482 **1761** | (1st) | multicoloured | 1·25 | 1·00 |
| 2483 **1762** | (1st) | multicoloured | 1·25 | 1·00 |

| | | | | | | | |
|---|---|---|---|---|---|---|---|
| 2484 | **1763** | (1st) multicoloured | 1·25 | 1·00 | ☐ | ☐ |
| 2485 | **1764** | (1st) multicoloured | 1·25 | 1·00 | ☐ | ☐ |
| 2486 | **1765** | (1st) multicoloured | 1·25 | 1·00 | ☐ | ☐ |
| 2487 | **1766** | (1st) multicoloured | 1·25 | 1·00 | ☐ | ☐ |
| 2488 | **1767** | (1st) multicoloured | 1·25 | 1·00 | ☐ | ☐ |
| Set of 10 | | | 14·00 | 12·00 | ☐ | ☐ |
| First Day Cover | | | | 13·00 | | ☐ |
| Presentation Pack (P.O. Pack No. 363) | | | 16·00 | | ☐ | |
| PHQ Cards (set of 10) (268) | | | 9·75 | 18·00 | ☐ | ☐ |
| Gutter Block of 20 | | | 30·00 | | ☐ | |

Nos. 2479/88 were printed together, *se-tenant*, in blocks of ten (5 × 2) throughout the sheet.

For the miniature sheet celebrating the opening of the new Scottish Parliament Building, Ediburgh, issued 5 October 2004, see the Regionals section.

**1768** Pte. McNamara,
5th Dragoon Guards,
Heavy Brigade Charge,
Battle of Balaklava

**1769** Piper Muir,
42nd Regt of Foot,
Amphibious Assault
on Kerch

**1770** Sgt. Maj. Edwards,
Scots Fusilier Guards,
Gallant Action,
Battle of Inkerman

**1771** Sgt. Powell,
1st Regt of Foot
Guards, Battles of
Alma and Inkerman

**1772** Sgt. Maj. Poole,
Royal Sappers and
Miners, Defensive Line,
Battle of Inkerman

**1773** Sgt. Glasgow,
Royal Artillery, Gun
Battery besieged
Sevastopol

**150th Anniversary of the Crimean War**

**2004** (12 Oct.) One centre phosphor band (2nd) or two phosphor bands (others). Perf 14

| | | | | | | |
|---|---|---|---|---|---|---|
| 2489 | **1768** (2nd) multicoloured | 1·00 | 80 | ☐ | ☐ |
| 2490 | **1769** (1st) multicoloured | 1·25 | 1·00 | ☐ | ☐ |
| 2491 | **1770** 40p multicoloured | 2·00 | 2·00 | ☐ | ☐ |
| 2492 | **1771** 57p multicoloured | 2·50 | 2·50 | ☐ | ☐ |
| 2493 | **1772** 68p multicoloured | 2·75 | 3·00 | ☐ | ☐ |
| 2494 | **1773** £1·12 multicoloured | 4·50 | 5·00 | ☐ | ☐ |
| Set of 6 | | 12·00 | 13·00 | ☐ | ☐ |
| First Day Cover | | | 14·00 | | ☐ |
| Presentation Pack (P.O. Pack No. 364) | | 14·00 | | ☐ | |
| PHQ Cards (set of 6) (269) | | 5·75 | 16·00 | ☐ | ☐ |
| Set of 6 Gutter Pairs | | 25·00 | | ☐ | |

| | | | |
|---|---|---|---|
| Set of 6 Traffic Light Pairs | | 30·00 | ☐ |

Nos. 2489/94 show 'Crimean Heroes' photographs taken in 1856.

**1774** Father Christmas
on Snowy Roof

**1775** Celebrating the
Sunrise

**1776** On Roof in Gale

**1777** With Umbrella
in Rain

**1778** In Fog on Edge
of Roof with Torch

**1779** Sheltering from
Hailstorm behind Chimney

**Christmas. Father Christmas**

**2004** (2 Nov.) One centre phosphor band (2nd) or two phosphor bands (others). Perf 14½ ×14

(a) Self-adhesive

| | | | | | | |
|---|---|---|---|---|---|---|
| 2495 | **1774** (2nd) multicoloured | 1·00 | 80 | ☐ | ☐ |
| 2496 | **1775** (1st) multicoloured | 1·25 | 1·00 | ☐ | ☐ |
| 2497 | **1776** 40p multicoloured | 1·30 | 1·30 | ☐ | ☐ |
| 2498 | **1777** 57p multicoloured | 1·80 | 1·80 | ☐ | ☐ |
| 2499 | **1778** 68p multicoloured | 2·20 | 2·20 | ☐ | ☐ |
| 2500 | **1779** £1·12 multicoloured | 3·75 | 3·75 | ☐ | ☐ |
| Set of 6 | | 11·00 | 12·00 | ☐ | ☐ |
| First Day Cover | | | 13·50 | | ☐ |
| Presentation Pack (P.O. Pack No. 365) | 12·50 | | ☐ | |
| PHQ Cards (set of 7) (270) | | 6·75 | 18·00 | ☐ | ☐ |

(b) Ordinary gum

| | | | | | |
|---|---|---|---|---|---|
| **MS**2501 115 × 105 mm. | | | | | |
| As Nos. 2495/500 | 12·00 | 13·00 | ☐ | ☐ |
| First Day Cover | | 14·00 | | ☐ |

The seven PHQ cards depict the six individual stamps and the miniature sheet.

The 2nd and 1st class stamps were also issued in sheets of 20 printed in lithography instead of photogravure containing ten 1st class and ten 2nd class stamps, each stamp accompanied by a *se-tenant* stamp-size label showing Father Christmas.

Separate sheets of either 20 1st or 20 2nd class were available with personal photographs.

**Collectors Pack 2004**

**2004** (2 Nov.) Comprises Nos. 2417/22, 2424/44, 2446/53, 2456/61, 2466/71 and 2473/2500

| | | | |
|---|---|---|---|
| CP2500a | Collectors Pack | £120 | ☐ |

**Post Office Yearbook**

**2004** (2 Nov.) Comprises Nos. 2417/22, 2424/44, 2446/53, 2456/61, 2466/71 and 2473/2500

| | | | |
|---|---|---|---|
| YB2500a | Yearbook | £110 | ☐ |

**1780** British Saddleback
Pigs

**1781** Khaki Campbell
Ducks

**1782** Clydesdale Mare
and Foal

**1783** Dairy Shorthorn
Cattle

**1784** Border Collie Dog

**1785** Light Sussex Chicks

**1786** Suffolk Sheep

**1787** Bagot Goat

**1788** Norfolk Black Turkeys

**1789** Embden Geese

**Farm Animals**

**2005** (11 Jan.) Two phosphor bands. Perf 14½

| | | | | | | |
|---|---|---|---|---|---|---|
| 2502 | **1780** | (1st) | multicoloured | 1·25 | 1·00 | |
| | a. | Block of 10. | | | | |
| | | Nos. 2502/11 | | 14·00 | 12·00 | |
| 2503 | **1781** | (1st) | multicoloured | 1·25 | 1·00 | |
| 2504 | **1782** | (1st) | multicoloured | 1·25 | 1·00 | |
| 2505 | **1783** | (1st) | multicoloured | 1·25 | 1·00 | |
| 2506 | **1784** | (1st) | multicoloured | 1·25 | 1·00 | |
| 2507 | **1785** | (1st) | multicoloured | 1·25 | 1·00 | |
| 2508 | **1786** | (1st) | multicoloured | 1·25 | 1·00 | |
| 2509 | **1787** | (1st) | multicoloured | 1·25 | 1·00 | |
| 2510 | **1788** | (1st) | multicoloured | 1·25 | 1·00 | |
| 2511 | **1789** | (1st) | multicoloured | 1·25 | 1·00 | |
| Set of 10 | | | | 14·00 | 12·00 | |
| First Day Cover | | | | | 13·00 | |
| Presentation Pack (P.O. Pack No. 367) | | | | 15·00 | | |
| PHQ Cards (set of 10) (271) | | | | 9·75 | 18·00 | |
| Gutter Block of 20 | | | | 30·00 | | |
| Traffic Light Gutter Block of 20 | | | | 30·00 | | |

Nos. 2502/11 were printed together, *se-tenant*, in blocks of ten (5 × 2) throughout the sheet.

Nos. 2502/11 were also issued in sheets of 20, printed in lithography instead of photogravure, containing two of each of the ten designs, arranged in vertical strips of five alternated with printed labels.

**1790** Old Harry Rocks,
Studland Bay

**1791** Wheal Coates,
St. Agnes

**1792** Start Point, Start Bay

**1793** Horton Down, Wiltshire

**1794** Chiselcombe,
Exmoor

**1795** St. James's Stone,
Lundy

**A British Journey (4th series). South West England**

**2005** (8 Feb.) One centre phosphor band (2nd) or two phosphor bands (others). Perf 14½

| | | | | | |
|---|---|---|---|---|---|
| 2512 | **1790** | (2nd) | multicoloured | 1·00 | 80 |
| 2513 | **1791** | (1st) | multicoloured | 1·25 | 90 |
| 2514 | **1792** | 40p | multicoloured | 1·50 | 1·75 |
| 2515 | **1793** | 43p | multicoloured | 1·75 | 2·00 |
| 2516 | **1794** | 57p | multicoloured | 2·50 | 2·50 |
| 2517 | **1795** | 68p | multicoloured | 3·50 | 3·00 |
| Set of 6 | | | | 10·00 | 10·00 |
| First Day Cover | | | | | 12·00 |
| Presentation Pack (P.O. Pack No. 368) | | | | 11·00 | |
| PHQ Cards (set of 6) (262) | | | | 6·00 | 14·00 |
| Set of 6 Gutter Pairs | | | | 21·00 | |

**1796** 'Mr Rochester'

**1797** 'Come to Me'

**1798** 'In the Comfort
of her Bonnet'

**1799** 'La Ligne des Rats'  **1800** 'Refectory'  **1801** 'Inspection'

**150th Death Anniversary of Charlotte Brontë.**
**Illustrations of Scenes from Jane Eyre by Paula Rego**

**2005** (24 Feb.) One centre phosphor band (2nd) or two phosphor bands (others). Perf 14 × 14½

| | | | | | | |
|---|---|---|---|---|---|---|
| 2518 | **1796** | (2nd) | multicoloured | 1·00 | 80 | |
| 2519 | **1797** | (1st) | multicoloured | 1·25 | 1·00 | |
| 2520 | **1798** | 40p | multicoloured | 1·50 | 1·50 | |
| 2521 | **1799** | 57p | silver, brownish grey and black | 3·00 | 2·50 | |
| 2522 | **1800** | 68p | multicoloured | 3·75 | 3·00 | |
| 2523 | **1801** | £1·12 | silver, brownish grey and black | 4·50 | 3·50 | |
| Set of 6 | | | | 12·00 | 11·00 | |
| First Day Cover | | | | | 12·00 | |
| Presentation Pack (P.O. Pack No. 369) | | | | 13·00 | | |
| PHQ Cards (set of 6) (273) | | | | 6·00 | 18·00 | |
| Set of 6 Gutter Pairs | | | | 25·00 | | |
| Set of 6 Traffic Light gutter blocks of four | | | | 48·00 | | |
| **MS**2524 114 × 105 mm. Nos. 2518/23 | | | | 12·00 | 11·00 | |
| First Day Cover | | | | | 12·00 | |

The complete miniature sheet is shown on one of the PHQ cards with the others depicting individual stamps.

Nos. 2518/23 were also issued in the £7.43 'The Brontë Sisters' booklet.

**1802** Spinning Coin  **1803** Rabbit out of Hat Trick

**1804** Knotted Scarf Trick  **1805** Card Trick

**1806** Pyramid under Fez Trick

**Centenary of the Magic Circle**

**2005** (15 Mar.) Two phosphor bands. Perf 14½ × 14

| | | | | | | |
|---|---|---|---|---|---|---|
| 2525 | **1802** | (1st) | multicoloured | 1·25 | 80 | |
| 2526 | **1803** | 40p | multicoloured | 1·00 | 90 | |
| 2527 | **1804** | 47p | multicoloured | 2·50 | 2·75 | |
| 2528 | **1805** | 68p | multicoloured | 3·00 | 3·00 | |
| 2529 | **1806** | £1·12 | multicoloured | 3·50 | 3·50 | |

| | | | |
|---|---|---|---|
| Set of 5 | | 10·00 | 11·00 |
| First Day Cover | | | 12·00 |
| Presentation Pack (P.O. Pack No. 370) | | 15·00 | |
| PHQ Cards (set of 5) (274) | | 5·00 | 12·00 |
| Set of 5 Gutter Pairs | | 21·00 | |

Nos. 2525/9 are each printed with instructions for the illusion or trick on the stamp.

No. 2525 can be rubbed with a coin to reveal the 'head' or 'tail' of a coin. The two versions, which appear identical before rubbing, are printed in alternate rows of the sheet, indicated by the letters H and T in the side margins of the sheet.

No. 2525 was also issued in sheets of 20 with se-tenant labels showing magic tricks, printed in lithography instead of photogravure.

Nos. 2526 and 2528 each show optical illusions.

The spotted scarf on No. 2527 and the fezzes on No. 2529 are printed in thermochromic inks which fade temporarily when exposed to heat, making the pyramid under the centre fez visible.

**1806a** (Illustration reduced. Actual size 127×73 mm)

**50th Anniversary of First Castles Definitives miniature sheet**

**2005** (22 Mar.) Sheet 127 × 73 mm, printed on pale cream. 'All-over' phosphor. Perf 11 × 11½

| | | |
|---|---|---|
| **MS**2530 1806a 50p brownish-black; 50p black; £1 dull vermilion; £1 royal blue | 10·00 | 10·00 |
| First Day Cover | | 12·00 |
| Presentation Pack (P.O. Pack No. 69) | 15·00 | |
| PHQ Cards (set of 5) (D28) | 5·00 | 12·00 |

See also No. 3221

**1807** Prince Charles and Mrs Camilla Parker Bowles

## Royal Wedding miniature sheet

**2005** (9 Apr.) Sheet 85 × 115 mm. Multicoloured. 'All-over' phosphor. Perf 13½ × 14

**MS**2531 1807 30p × 2 Prince Charles and Mrs Camilla Parker Bowles laughing; 68p × 2 Prince Charles and Mrs Camilla Parker Bowles smiling into camera ....... 8·00 ... 9·00

First Day Cover ....... 10·00

Presentation Pack (P.O. Pack No. M10) ... 18·00

**1808** Hadrian's Wall, England

**1809** Uluru-Kata Tjuta National Park, Australia

**1810** Stonehenge, England

**1811** Wet Tropics of Queensland, Australia

**1812** Blenheim Palace, England

**1813** Greater Blue Mountains Area, Australia

**1814** Heart of Neolithic Orkney, Scotland

**1815** Purnululu National Park, Australia

## World Heritage Sites

**2005** (21 Apr.) One side phosphor band (2nd) or two phosphor bands (others). Perf 14½

| | | | | | | |
|---|---|---|---|---|---|---|
| 2532 | **1808** | (2nd) | multicoloured | 90 | 80 | |
| | | a. | Horiz pair. | | | |
| | | | Nos. 2532/3 | 1·75 | 1·60 | |
| 2533 | **1809** | (2nd) | multicoloured | 90 | 80 | |
| 2534 | **1810** | (1st) | multicoloured | 1·25 | 90 | |
| | | a. | Horiz pair. | | | |
| | | | Nos. 2534/5 | 2·50 | 2·00 | |
| 2535 | **1811** | (1st) | multicoloured | 1·25 | 90 | |
| 2536 | **1812** | 47p | multicoloured | 1·00 | 1·00 | |
| | | a. | Horiz pair. | | | |
| | | | Nos. 2536/7 | 3·00 | 3·50 | |
| 2537 | **1813** | 47p | multicoloured | 1·00 | 1·00 | |
| 2538 | **1814** | 68p | multicoloured | 1·50 | 1·40 | |

| | | | | | | |
|---|---|---|---|---|---|---|
| | | a. | Horiz pair. | | | |
| | | | Nos. 2538/9 | 5·00 | 5·00 | |
| 2539 | **1815** | 68p | multicoloured | 1·50 | 1·40 | |
| Set of 8 | | | | 11·00 | 11·50 | |
| First Day Cover | | | | | 13·00 | |
| Presentation Pack (P.O. Pack No. 371) | | | | 12·00 | | |
| Presentation Pack | | | | | | |
| | (UK and Australian stamps) | | | | 18·00 | |
| PHQ Cards (set of 8) (275) | | | | 7·00 | 16·00 | |
| Set of 4 Gutter Strips of 4 | | | | 23·00 | | |
| Set of 4 Traffic Light Gutter Blocks of 8 | | 45·00 | | | | |

Nos. 2532/3, 2534/5, 2536/7 and 2538/9 were each printed together, *se-tenant*, in horizontal pairs.

Stamps in these designs were also issued by Australia and these are included in the joint Presentation Pack.

**1816** Ensign of the Scots Guards, 2002

**1817** Queen taking the salute as Colonel-in-Chief of the Grenadier Guards, 1983

**1818** Trumpeter of the Household Calvalry, 2004

**1819** Welsh Guardsman, 1990s

**1820** Queen riding side-saddle, 1972

**1821** Queen and Duke of Edinburgh in Carriage, 2004

## Trooping the Colour

**2005** (7 June) One phosphor band (2nd), two phosphor bands (others). Perf 14½

| | | | | | | |
|---|---|---|---|---|---|---|
| 2540 | **1816** | (2nd) | multicoloured | 1·00 | 80 | |
| 2541 | **1817** | (1st) | multicoloured | 1·25 | 1·00 | |
| 2542 | **1818** | 42p | multicoloured | 1·00 | 1·20 | |
| 2543 | **1819** | 60p | multicoloured | 2·00 | 2·00 | |
| 2544 | **1820** | 68p | multicoloured | 2·50 | 2·50 | |
| 2545 | **1821** | £1·12 | multicoloured | 3·50 | 3·50 | |
| Set of 6 | | | | 10·00 | 10·00 | |
| First Day Cover | | | | | 12·00 | |
| Presentation Pack (P.O. Pack No. 372) | | | 14·00 | | | |
| PHQ Cards (set of 6) (276) | | | | 5·00 | 20·00 | |
| Set of 6 Gutter Pairs | | | | 21·00 | | |
| **MS**2546 115 × 105 mm. Nos. 2540/5 | | | 11·00 | 11·00 | | |
| First Day Cover | | | | | 12·00 | |

The six PHQ cards show the six stamps and the miniature sheet.

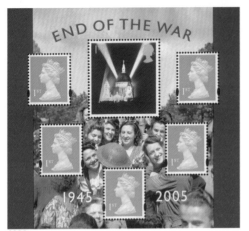

1822

**60th Anniversary of End of the Second World War miniature sheet**

**2005** (5 July) Sheet 115 × 105 mm containing design as T **1200** (1995 Peace and Freedom) but with service indicator and No. 1664b × 5. Two phosphor bands. Perf 15 × 14 (with one elliptical hole in each vertical side) (1664b) or 14½ × 14 (T **1200**)

**MS**2547 1822 (1st) gold × 5; (1st) silver,
blue and grey-black                    7.50    7.00 ☐ ☐
First Day Cover                                 8.00         ☐

**1823** Norton F.1, Road Version of Race Winner (1991)

**1824** BSA Rocket 3, Early Three Cylinder 'Superbike' (1969)

**1825** Vincent Black Shadow, Fastest Standard Motorcycle (1949)

**1826** Triumph Speed Twin, Two Cylinder Innovation (1938)

**1827** Brough Superior, Bespoke Luxury Motorcycle (1930)

**1828** Royal Enfield, Small Engined Motor Bicycle (1914)

**Motorcycles**

**2005** (19 July) Two phosphor bands. Perf 14 × 14½

| | | | | | | |
|---|---|---|---|---|---|---|
| 2548 | **1823** | (1st) | multicoloured | 1·25 | 1·00 | ☐ ☐ |
| 2549 | **1824** | 40p | multicoloured | 90 | 1·00 | ☐ ☐ |
| 2550 | **1825** | 42p | multicoloured | 1·25 | 1·00 | ☐ ☐ |
| 2551 | **1826** | 47p | multicoloured | 1·75 | 2·00 | ☐ ☐ |
| 2552 | **1827** | 60p | multicoloured | 2·50 | 2·50 | ☐ ☐ |
| 2553 | **1828** | 68p | multicoloured | 3·00 | 3·00 | ☐ ☐ |

| | | | | |
|---|---|---|---|---|
| Set of 6 | | 9·00 | 9·0 | ☐ ☐ |
| First Day Cover | | | 11·00 | ☐ |
| Presentation Pack (P.O. Pack No. 373) | | 13·00 | | ☐ |
| PHQ Cards (*set of* 6) (277) | | 5·00 | 14·00 | ☐ ☐ |
| Set of 6 Gutter Pairs | | 19·00 | | ☐ |

1829

**London's Successful Bid for Olympic Games, 2012 miniature sheet**

**2005** (5 Aug.) Sheet 115 × 105 mm containing designs as T 1255/9, but with service indicator. Multicoloured. Two phosphor bands. Perf 14½

**MS**2554 1829 (1st) Athlete celebrating
× 2; (1st) Throwing the javelin;
(1st) Swimming; (1st) Athlete on
starting blocks; (1st) Basketball    6·50    6·50 ☐ ☐
First Day Cover                                 8·00         ☐
Presentation Pack (P.O. Pack No. M11)  12·00        ☐ ☐

Stamps from **MS**2554 are all inscribed 'London 2012—Host City' and have imprint date '2005'. The design as Type **1259** omits the Olympic rings.

**1830** African Woman eating Rice

**1831** Indian Womandrinking Tea

**1832** Boy eating Sushi

**1833** Woman eating Pasta

**1834** Woman eating Chips

**1835** Teenage Boy eating Apple

**Europa. Gastronomy. Changing Tastes in Britain**

**2005** (23 Aug.) One side phosphor band (2nd) or two phosphor bands (others). Perf 14½

| | | | | | |
|---|---|---|---|---|---|
| 2555 | **1830** | (2nd) | multicoloured | 1·00 | 80 |
| 2556 | **1831** | (1st) | multicoloured | 1·25 | 1·00 |
| 2557 | **1832** | 42p | multicoloured | 1·30 | 1·40 |
| 2558 | **1833** | 47p | multicoloured | 1·50 | 1·60 |
| 2559 | **1834** | 60p | multicoloured | 2·00 | 1·90 |
| 2560 | **1835** | 68p | multicoloured | 2·50 | 2·20 |
| *Set of* 6 | | | | 8·00 | 8·00 |
| First Day Cover | | | | | 10·00 |
| Presentation Pack (P.O. Pack No. 374) | | | 9·00 | | |
| PHQ Cards (*set of* 6) (278) | | | 5·00 | 12·00 | |
| *Set of* 6 Gutter Pairs | | | 17·00 | | |

The 1st and 42p values include the 'EUROPA' emblem.

**1836** 'Inspector Morse'

**1837** 'Emmerdale'

**1838** 'Rising Damp'

**1839** 'The Avengers'

**1840** 'The South Bank Show'

**1841** 'Who Wants to be a Millionaire'

**50th Anniversary of Independent Television. Classic ITV Programmes**

**2005** (15 Sept.) One side phosphor band (2nd) or two phosphor bands (others). Perf 14½ × 14

| | | | | | |
|---|---|---|---|---|---|
| 2561 | **1836** | (2nd) | multicoloured | 1·00 | 1·00 |
| 2562 | **1837** | (1st) | multicoloured | 1·25 | 1·00 |
| 2563 | **1838** | 42p | multicoloured | 1·30 | 1·40 |
| 2564 | **1839** | 47p | multicoloured | 1·40 | 1·50 |
| 2565 | **1840** | 60p | multicoloured | 2·00 | 1·90 |
| 2566 | **1841** | 68p | multicoloured | 2·20 | 2·20 |
| *Set of* 6 | | | | 8·00 | 8·00 |
| First Day Cover | | | | | 10·00 |
| Presentation Pack (P.O. Pack No. 375) | | | 9·00 | | |
| PHQ Cards (*set of* 6) (279) | | | 5·00 | 12·00 | |
| *Set of* 6 Gutter Pairs | | | 17·00 | | |

The 1st class stamps were also issued in sheets of 20 with each stamp accompanied by a half stamp-size *se-tenant* label.

**1842** *Gazania Splendens* (Charlotte Sowerby)

**1842a** "LOVE"

**'Smilers' (1st series) Booklet stamps**

**2005** (4 Oct.) Designs as Types 992, 1221, 1286, 1517 and 1568/9 but smaller, 20 × 23 mm, and inscribed 1st as T 1842. Self-adhesive. Two phosphor bands. Die-cut perf 15 × 14.

| | | | | | |
|---|---|---|---|---|---|
| 2567 | **1842** | (1st) | multicoloured | 2·00 | 2·00 |
| | | a. | Booklet pane. | | |
| | | | Nos· 2567/72 | 12·00 | |
| 2568 | **1569** | (1st) | multicoloured | 2·00 | 2·00 |
| 2569 | **1842**a | (1st) | multicoloured | 2·00 | 2·00 |
| 2570 | **1517** | (1st) | multicoloured | 2·00 | 2·00 |
| 2571 | **992** | (1st) | multicoloured | 2·00 | 2·00 |
| 2572 | **1221** | (1st) | multicoloured | 2·00 | 2·00 |
| *Set of* 6 | | | | 12·00 | 12·00 |
| First Day Cover | | | | | 13·00 |

Nos. 2567/72 were printed together, *se-tenant*, in booklet panes of six in which the surplus self-adhesive paper around each stamp was removed.

Nos. 2567/72 were re-issued on 4 July 2006 in sheets of 20 with *se-tenant* labels, printed in lithography instead of photogravure.

Nos. 2568/70 were re-issued on 18 January 2008 in sheets of 20 with circular *se-tenant* labels, printed in lithography.

No. 2567 was re-issued on 28 October 2008 in sheets of 10 with circular *se-tenant* 'Flower Fairy' labels, printed in lithography.

Stamps as Nos. 2569 and 2572 but perforated with one elliptical hole on each vertical side were issued, together with Nos. 2674 and 2821/3 and four designs from **MS**3024, on 8 May 2010 in sheets of 20 stamps with *se-tenant* greetings labels.

See also No. 2693 and Nos. 2819/24.

THE ASHES ENGLAND WINNERS 2005

**1843** Cricket Scenes

**England's Ashes Victory miniature sheet**

**2005** (6 Oct.) Sheet 115 × 90 mm. Multicoloured. Two phosphor bands. Perf 14½ ×14.

| | | | | | |
|---|---|---|---|---|---|
| **MS**2573 | 1843 | (1st) England team with Ashes trophy; (1st) Kevin Pieterson, Michael Vaughan and Andrew Flintoff on opening day of First Test, Lords; 68p Michael Vaughan, Third Test, Old Trafford; 68p Second Test Edgbaston | | 7·50 | 7·50 |
| First Day Cover | | | | | 9·00 |
| Presentation Pack (P.O. Pack No. M12) | | | 10·00 | | |

**1844** 'Entrepreante' with dismasted British 'Belle Isle'

1845 Nelson wounded on Deck of HMS 'Victory'

1846 British Cutter 'Entrepreante' attempting to rescue Crew of burning French 'Achille'

1847 Cutter and HMS 'Pickle' (schooner)

1848 British Fleet attacking in Two Columns

1849 Franco/Spanish Fleet putting to Sea from Cadiz

## Bicentenary of the Battle of Trafalgar (1st issue).
### Scenes from 'Panorama of the Battle of Trafalgar' by William Heath

**2005** (18 Oct.) Two phosphor bands. Perf 15 × 14½

| | | | | | | |
|---|---|---|---|---|---|---|
| 2574 | **1844** | (1st) multicoloured | 1·25 | 1·00 | ☐ | ☐ |
| | | a. Horiz pair. | | | | |
| | | Nos. 2574/5 | 2·50 | 2·25 | ☐ | ☐ |
| 2575 | **1845** | (1st) multicoloured | 1·25 | 1·00 | ☐ | ☐ |
| 2576 | **1846** | 42p multicoloured | 1·00 | 1·10 | ☐ | ☐ |
| | | a. Horiz pair. | | | | |
| | | Nos. 2576/7 | 2·50 | 2·75 | ☐ | ☐ |
| 2577 | **1847** | 42p multicoloured | 1·00 | 1·10 | ☐ | ☐ |
| 2578 | **1848** | 68p multicoloured | 1·25 | 1·50 | ☐ | ☐ |
| | | a. Horiz pair. | | | | |
| | | Nos. 2578/9 | 4·00 | 4·40 | ☐ | ☐ |
| 2579 | **1849** | 68p multicoloured | 1·25 | 1·50 | ☐ | ☐ |
| *Set of 6* | | | 8·00 | 8·50 | ☐ | |
| First Day Cover | | | | 10·00 | | ☐ |
| Presentation Pack (P.O. Pack No. 376) | | | 10·00 | | ☐ | |
| PHQ Cards (*set of 7*) (280) | | | 7·00 | 20·00 | ☐ | ☐ |
| *Set of 3 Gutter Strips of 4* | | | 18·00 | | ☐ | |
| **MS**2580 190 × 68 mm. Nos. 2574/9 | | | 10·00 | 11·00 | ☐ | ☐ |
| First Day Cover | | | | 12·00 | | ☐ |

Nos. 2574/5, 2576/7 and 2578/9 were each printed together, *se-tenant*, in horizontal pairs throughout the sheets, each pair forming a composite design and were also issued in the £7.26 'Bicentenary of the Battle of Trafalgar' booklet.

The phosphor bands are at just left of centre and at right of each stamp

The seven PHQ cards depict the six individual stamps and the miniature sheet.

## Bicentenary of the Battle of Trafalgar (2nd issue).
### Booklet stamp.

**2005** (18 Oct.) Design as Type **1516** (White Ensign from 2001 Submarine Centenary). Litho. Two phosphor bands. Perf 14½

| | | | | | |
|---|---|---|---|---|---|
| 2581 | **1516** | (1st) multicoloured | 5·00 | 5·00 | ☐ ☐ |

No. 2581 was only issued in the £7·26 'Bicentenary of the Battle of Trafalgar', the £7·40 'Ian Fleming's James Bond' booklet and £7·93 'Royal Navy Uniform booklet.

1850 Black Madonna and Child from Haiti

1851 'Madonna and Child' (Marianne Stokes)

1852 'The Virgin Mary with the Infant Christ'

1853 Choctaw Virgin Mother and Child (Fr. John Giuliani)

1854 'Madonna and the Infant Jesus' (from India)

1855 'Come let us adore Him' (Dianne Tchumut)

## Christmas. Madonna and Child Paintings

**2005** (1 Nov.) One side phosphor band (2nd) or two phosphor bands (others). Perf 14½ × 14

**(a) Self-adhesive**

| | | | | | | |
|---|---|---|---|---|---|---|
| 2582 | **1850** | (2nd) multicoloured | 1·00 | 80 | ☐ | ☐ |
| 2583 | **1851** | (1st) multicoloured | 1·25 | 1·00 | ☐ | ☐ |
| 2584 | **1852** | 42p multicoloured | 1·30 | 1·40 | ☐ | ☐ |
| 2585 | **1853** | 60p multicoloured | 1·80 | 1·90 | ☐ | ☐ |
| 2586 | **1854** | 68p multicoloured | 2·00 | 2·20 | ☐ | ☐ |
| 2587 | **1855** | £1·12 multicoloured | 3·40 | 3·60 | ☐ | ☐ |
| *Set of 6* | | | 9·50 | 10·00 | ☐ | |
| First Day Cover | | | | 12·00 | | ☐ |
| Presentation Pack (P.O. Pack No. 377) | | | 11·00 | | ☐ | |
| PHQ Cards (*set of 7*) (281) | | | 4·00 | 16·00 | ☐ | ☐ |

**(b) Ordinary gum**

| | | | | | |
|---|---|---|---|---|---|
| **MS**2588 115 × 102 mm. As Nos. | | | | | |
| 2582/7 | | | 10·50 | 11·00 | ☐ ☐ |
| First Day Cover | | | | 12·00 | ☐ |

The seven PHQ cards depict the six individual stamps and the miniature sheet.

## Collectors Pack

**2005** (1 Nov.) Comprises Nos. 2502/23, 2525/9, **MS**2531/45, 2548/53, 2555/66, 2574/9 and 2582/7

| | | | |
|---|---|---|---|
| CP2587a | Collectors Pack | £110 | ☐ |

## Post Office Yearbook

**2005** (1 Nov.) Comprises Nos. 2502/23, 2525/9, **MS**2531/45, 2548/53, 2555/66, 2574/9 and 2582/7

| | | | |
|---|---|---|---|
| YB2587a | Yearbook | 95·00 | ☐ |

## Miniature Sheet Collection

**2005** (21 Nov.) Comprises Nos. **MS**2524, **MS**2530/1, **MS**2546/7, **MS**2554, **MS**2573, **MS**2580, **MS**2588 and **MS**2588a

| | |
|---|---|
| Miniature Sheet Collection | 75·00 ☐ |

**1856** *The Tale of Mr. Jeremy Fisher* (Beatrix Potter)

**1857** *Kipper* (Mick Inkpen)

**1858** *The Enormous Crocodile* (Roald Dahl)

**1859** *More About Paddington* (Michael Bond)

**1860** *Comic Adventures of Boots* (Satoshi Kitamura)

**1861** *Alice's Adventures in Wonderland* (Lewis Carroll)

**1862** *The Very Hungry Caterpillar* (Eric Carle)

**1863** *Maisy's ABC* (Lucy Cousins)

## Animal Tales

**2006** (10 Jan.) One side phosphor band (2nd) or two phosphor bands (others). Perf 14½

| | | | | | | | |
|---|---|---|---|---|---|---|---|
| 2589 | **1856** | (2nd) | multicoloured | 90 | 75 | ☐ | ☐ |
| | | a. | Horiz pair. | | | | |
| | | | Nos. 2589/90 | 1·75 | 1·60 | ☐ | ☐ |
| 2590 | **1857** | (2nd) | multicoloured | 90 | 75 | ☐ | ☐ |
| 2591 | **1858** | (1st) | multicoloured | 1·25 | 1·00 | ☐ | ☐ |
| | | a. | Horiz pair. | | | | |
| | | | Nos. 2591/2 | 2·50 | 2·25 | ☐ | ☐ |
| 2592 | **1859** | (1st) | multicoloured | 1·25 | 1·00 | ☐ | ☐ |
| 2593 | **1860** | 42p | multicoloured | 90 | 1·10 | ☐ | ☐ |
| | | a. | Horiz pair. | | | | |
| | | | Nos. 2593/4 | 4·00 | 4·00 | ☐ | ☐ |
| 2594 | **1861** | 42p | multicoloured | 90 | 1·10 | ☐ | ☐ |
| 2595 | **1862** | 68p | multicoloured | 1·25 | 1·60 | ☐ | ☐ |
| | | a. | Horiz pair. | | | | |
| | | | Nos. 2595/6 | 5·00 | 5·00 | ☐ | ☐ |
| 2596 | **1863** | 68p | multicoloured | 1·25 | 1·60 | ☐ | ☐ |
| Set of 8 | | | | 12·00 | 11·50 | | ☐ |
| First Day Cover | | | | | 13·00 | | ☐ |
| Presentation Pack (P.O. Pack No. 379) | | | 13·00 | | | ☐ | |
| PHQ Cards (*set of 8*) (282) | | | 7·00 | 16·00 | | ☐ | ☐ |

| | | |
|---|---|---|
| *Set of* 4 Gutter Blocks of 4 | 25·00 | ☐ |
| *Set of* 4 Traffic Light Gutter Blocks of 8 | 50·00 | ☐ |

Nos. 2589/90, 2591/2, 2593/4 and 2595/6 were printed together, *se-tenant*, as horizontal pairs in sheets of 60 (2 panes 6 × 5).

No. 2595 contains two die-cut holes.

A design as No. 2592 but self-adhesive was also issued in sheets of 20 with each stamp accompanied by a *se-tenant* label.

**1864** Carding Mill Valley, Shropshire

**1865** Beachy Head, Sussex

**1866** St. Paul's Cathedral, London

**1867** Brancaster, Norfolk

**1868** Derwent Edge, Peak District

**1869** Robin Hood's Bay, Yorkshire

**1870** Buttermere, Lake District

**1871** Chipping Campden, Cotswolds

**1872** St. Boniface Down, Isle of Wight

**1873** Chamberlain Square, Birmingham

## A British Journey (5th series): England

**2006** (7 Feb.) Two phosphor bands. Perf 14½

| | | | | | | | |
|---|---|---|---|---|---|---|---|
| 2597 | **1864** | (1st) | multicoloured | 1·25 | 1·00 | ☐ | ☐ |
| | | a. | Block of 10. | | | | |
| | | | Nos. 2597/606 | 14·00 | 12·00 | ☐ | ☐ |
| 2598 | **1865** | (1st) | multicoloured | 1·25 | 1·00 | ☐ | ☐ |
| 2599 | **1866** | (1st) | multicoloured | 1·25 | 1·00 | ☐ | ☐ |
| 2600 | **1867** | (1st) | multicoloured | 1·25 | 1·00 | ☐ | ☐ |
| 2601 | **1868** | (1st) | multicoloured | 1·25 | 1·00 | ☐ | ☐ |
| 2602 | **1869** | (1st) | multicoloured | 1·25 | 1·00 | ☐ | ☐ |
| 2603 | **1870** | (1st) | multicoloured | 1·25 | 1·00 | ☐ | ☐ |
| 2604 | **1871** | (1st) | multicoloured | 1·25 | 1·00 | ☐ | ☐ |

| 2605 | **1872** | (1st) multicoloured | 1·25 | 1·00 | | |
|---|---|---|---|---|---|---|
| 2606 | **1873** | (1st) multicoloured | 1·25 | 1·00 | | |
| *Set of* 10 | | | 14·00 | 12·00 | | |
| First Day Cover | | | | 13·00 | | |
| Presentation Pack (P.O. Pack No. 380) | | | 15·00 | | | |
| PHQ Cards (*set of* 10) (283) | | | 9·00 | 18·00 | | |
| Gutter Block of 20 | | | 30·00 | | | |

Nos. 2597/606 were printed together, *se-tenant*, as blocks of ten (5 × 2) in sheets of 60 (2 panes of 30).

**1874** Royal Albert Bridge

**1875** Box Tunnel

**1876** Paddington Station

**1877** PSS *Great Eastern* (paddle steamer)

**1878** Clifton Suspension Bridge Design

**1879** Maidenhead Bridge

**Birth Bicentenary of Isambard Kingdom Brunel (engineer) (1st issue)**

**2006** (23 Feb.) Phosphor-coated paper (42p) or two phosphor bands (others). Perf 14 × 13½

| 2607 | **1874** | (1st) multicoloured | 1·25 | 80 | | |
|---|---|---|---|---|---|---|
| 2608 | **1875** | 40p multicoloured | 1·10 | 1·10 | | |
| 2609 | **1876** | 42p multicoloured | 1·10 | 1·10 | | |
| 2610 | **1877** | 47p multicoloured | 1·50 | 1·50 | | |
| 2611 | **1878** | 60p multicoloured | 2·00 | 1·75 | | |
| 2612 | **1879** | 68p multicoloured | 2·50 | 2·25 | | |
| *Set of* 6 | | | 7·50 | 7·50 | | |
| First Day Cover | | | | 9·00 | | |
| Presentation Pack (P.O. Pack No. 381) | | | 10·00 | | | |
| PHQ Cards (*set of* 7) (284) | | | 6·00 | 14·00 | | |
| *Set of* 6 Gutter Pairs | | | 16·00 | | | |
| **MS**2613 190 × 65 mm. Nos. 2607/12 | | | 8·50 | 8·50 | | |
| First Day Cover | | | | 9·00 | | |

The phosphor bands on Nos. 2607/8 and 2610/12 are at just left of centre and at right of each stamp.

The complete miniature sheet is shown on one of the PHQ cards with the others depicting individual stamps.

Nos. 2607/12 were also issued in the £7·40 'Isambard Kingdom Brunel' booklet.

**Birth Bicentenary of Isambard Kingdom Brunel (engineer) (2nd issue). Booklet stamp**

**2006** (23 Feb.) Design as Type **1739** (PS *Great Western* from 2004 Ocean Liners). Litho. Two phosphor bands. Perf 14½ × 14

| 2614 | **1739** | 68p multicoloured | 12·00 | 12·50 | | |
|---|---|---|---|---|---|---|

No. 2614 was only issued in the £7·40 'Isambard Kingdom Brunel' booklet.

For the miniature sheet celebrating the opening of the New Welsh Assembly building, Cardiff, issued 1 March 2006, see the Regionals section.

**1880** Sabre-tooth Cat

**1881** Giant Deer

**1882** Woolly Rhino

**1883** Woolly Mammoth

**1884** Cave Bear

**Ice Age Animals**

**2006** (21 Mar.) Two phosphor bands. Perf 14½

| 2615 | **1880** | (1st) black and silver | 1·25 | 1·00 | | |
|---|---|---|---|---|---|---|
| 2616 | **1881** | 42p black and silver | 1·00 | 1·00 | | |
| 2617 | **1882** | 47p black and silver | 2·00 | 2·00 | | |
| 2618 | **1883** | 68p black and silver | 2·25 | 2·25 | | |
| 2619 | **1884** | £1·12 black and silver | 3·25 | 3·25 | | |
| *Set of* 5 | | | 8·50 | 8·50 | | |
| First Day Cover | | | | 10·00 | | |
| Presentation Pack (P.O. Pack No. 382) | | | 12·00 | | | |
| PHQ Cards (*set of* 5) (285) | | | 4·00 | 12·00 | | |
| *Set of* 5 Gutter Pairs | | | 18·00 | | | |

**1885** On Britannia, 1972

**1886** At Royal Windsor Horse Show, 1985

**1887** At Heathrow Airport, 2001

**1888** As Young Princess Elizabeth with Duchess of York, 1931

**1889** At State Banquet, Ottawa, 1951

**1890** Queen Elizabeth II in 1960

**1891** As Princess Elizabeth, 1940

**1892** With Duke of Edinburgh, 1951

### 80th Birthday of Queen Elizabeth II

**2006** (18 Apr.) One side phosphor band (No. 2620), one centre phosphor band (No. 2621) or two phosphor bands (others). Perf 14½

| | | | | | | | |
|---|---|---|---|---|---|---|---|
| 2620 | **1885** | (2nd) | black, turquoise green and grey | 1·00 | 1·00 | ☐ | ☐ |
| | | a. | Horiz pair. Nos. 2620/1 | 2·25 | 2·25 | ☐ | ☐ |
| 2621 | **1886** | (2nd) | black, turquoise-green and grey | 1·00 | 1·00 | ☐ | |
| 2622 | **1887** | (1st) | black, turquoise-green and grey | 1·25 | 1·10 | ☐ | ☐ |
| | | a. | Horiz pair. Nos. 2622/3 | 2·50 | 2·40 | ☐ | ☐ |
| 2623 | **1888** | (1st) | black, turquoise-green and grey | 1·25 | 1·10 | ☐ | ☐ |
| 2624 | **1889** | 44p | black, turquoise-green and grey | 1·00 | 1·25 | ☐ | ☐ |
| | | a. | Horiz pair. Nos. 2624/5 | 2·75 | 2·75 | ☐ | ☐ |
| 2625 | **1890** | 44p | black, turquoise-green and grey | 1·00 | 1·25 | ☐ | ☐ |
| 2626 | **1891** | 72p | black, turquoise-green and grey | 1·50 | 2·00 | ☐ | ☐ |
| | | a. | Horiz pair. Nos. 2626/7 | 4·50 | 4·50 | ☐ | ☐ |
| 2627 | **1892** | 72p | black, turquoise-green and grey | 1·50 | 2·00 | ☐ | ☐ |
| Set of 8 | | | | 11·00 | 11·00 | ☐ | ☐ |
| First Day Cover | | | | | 12·00 | | ☐ |
| Presentation Pack (P.O. Pack No. 383) | | | | 12·00 | | ☐ | |
| PHQ Cards (set of 8) (286) | | | | 7·00 | 16·00 | ☐ | ☐ |
| Set of 4 Gutter Strips of 4 | | | | 23·00 | | ☐ | |

Nos. 2620/1, 2622/3, 2624/5 and 2626/7 were each printed together, *se-tenant*, as horizontal pairs in sheets of 60 (2 panes 6 × 5).

**1893** England (1966)

**1894** Italy (1934, 1938, 1982)

**44**
**1895** Argentina (1978, 1986)

**50**
**1896** Germany (1954, 1974, 1990)

**64**
**1897** France (1998)

**72**
**1898** Brazil (1958, 1962, 1970, 1994, 2002)

### World Cup Football Championship, Germany. World Cup Winners

**2006** (6 June) Two phosphor bands. Perf 14½

| | | | | | | |
|---|---|---|---|---|---|---|
| 2628 | **1893** | (1st) | multicoloured | 1·25 | 1·00 | ☐ ☐ |
| 2629 | **1894** | 42p | multicoloured | 1·25 | 1·10 | ☐ ☐ |
| 2630 | **1895** | 44p | multicoloured | 1·25 | 1·25 | ☐ ☐ |
| 2631 | **1896** | 50p | multicoloured | 2·00 | 2·00 | ☐ ☐ |
| 2632 | **1897** | 64p | multicoloured | 3·00 | 3·00 | ☐ ☐ |
| 2633 | **1898** | 72p | multicoloured | 3·50 | 3·50 | ☐ ☐ |
| Set of 6 | | | | 11·00 | 10·50 | ☐ ☐ |
| First Day Cover | | | | | 12·00 | ☐ |
| Presentation Pack (P.O. Pack No. 384) | | | | 12·00 | | ☐ |
| PHQ Cards (set of 6) (287) | | | | 5·00 | 12·00 | ☐ ☐ |
| Set of 6 Gutter Pairs | | | | 23·00 | | ☐ |

The 1st class stamp was also issued in sheets of 20 with each stamp accompanied by a *se-tenant* label showing scenes from the 1966 World Cup final.

**1899** 30 St. Mary Axe, London

**1900** Maggie's Centre, Dundee

**1901** Selfridges, Birmingham

**1902** Downland Gridshell, Chichester

**1903** An Turas, Isle of Tiree

**1904** The Deep, Hull

## Modern Architecture

**2006** (20 June). Two phosphor bands. Perf 14½

| | | | | |
|---|---|---|---|---|
| 2634 **1899** | (1st) multicoloured | 1·25 | 1·00 | |
| 2635 **1900** | 42p multicoloured | 1·10 | 1·10 | |
| 2636 **1901** | 44p multicoloured | 1·25 | 1·25 | |
| 2637 **1902** | 50p multicoloured | 2·00 | 2·00 | |
| 2638 **1903** | 64p multicoloured | 3·00 | 3·00 | |
| 2639 **1904** | 72p multicoloured | 3·50 | 3·50 | |
| *Set of 6* | | 11·00 | 10·50 | |
| First Day Cover | | | 12·00 | |
| Presentation Pack (P.O. Pack No. 385) | | 13·00 | | |
| PHQ Cards (*set of 6*) (288) | | 5·00 | 12·00 | |
| *Set of 6 Gutter Pairs* | | 23·00 | | |

**1905** 'Sir Winston Churchill' (Walter Sickert)

**1906** 'Sir Joshua Reynolds' (self-portrait)

**1907** 'T. S. Eliot' (Patrick Heron)

**1908** 'Emmeline Pankhurst' (Georgina Agnes Brackenbury)

**1909** Virginia Woolf (photo by George Charles Beresford)

**1910** Bust of Sir Walter Scott (Sir Francis Leggatt Chantry)

**1911** 'Mary Seacole' (Albert Charles Challen)

**1912** 'William Shakespeare' (attrib to John Taylor)

**1913** 'Dame Cicely Saunders' (Catherine Goodman)

**1914** 'Charles Darwin' (John Collier)

## 150th Anniversary of National Portrait Gallery, London

**2006** (18 July) Two phosphor bands. Perf 14½

| | | | | |
|---|---|---|---|---|
| 2640 **1905** | (1st) multicoloured | 1·25 | 1·00 | |
| | a. Block of 10. | | | |
| | Nos. 2640/9 | 14·00 | 12·00 | |
| 2641 **1906** | (1st) multicoloured | 1·25 | 1·00 | |

| | | | | |
|---|---|---|---|---|
| 2642 **1907** | (1st) multicoloured | 1·25 | 1·00 | |
| 2643 **1908** | (1st) multicoloured | 1·25 | 1·00 | |
| 2644 **1909** | (1st) multicoloured | 1·25 | 1·00 | |
| 2645 **1910** | (1st) multicoloured | 1·25 | 1·00 | |
| 2646 **1911** | (1st) multicoloured | 1·25 | 1·00 | |
| 2647 **1912** | (1st) multicoloured | 1·25 | 1·00 | |
| 2648 **1913** | (1st) multicoloured | 1·25 | 1·00 | |
| 2649 **1914** | (1st) multicoloured | 1·25 | 1·00 | |
| *Set of 10* | | 14·00 | 12·00 | |
| First Day Cover | | | 13·00 | |
| Presentation Pack (P.O. Pack No. 386) | | 15·00 | | |
| PHQ Cards (*set of 10*) (289) | | 9·00 | 18·00 | |
| Gutter Block of 20 | | 28·00 | | |
| Traffic Light Gutter Block of 20 | | 30·00 | | |

Nos. 2640/9 were printed together, *se-tenant*, as blocks of ten (5 × 2) in sheets of 60 (2 panes of 30).

**1915**          **1916**

### 'Pricing in Proportion'

**2006** (1 Aug.–12 Sept.) Perf 15 × 14 (with one elliptical hole in each vertical side).

(a) Ordinary gum. Photo De La Rue (No. 2651 also from Enschedé prestige booklet)

(i) As T **1915**

| | | | | |
|---|---|---|---|---|
| 2650 | (2nd) bright blue | | | |
| | (1 centre band) | 1·00 | 40 | |
| 2651 | (1st) gold (2 bands) | 1·25 | 50 | |

(ii) As T **1916**

| | | | | |
|---|---|---|---|---|
| 2652 (2nd Large) | bright blue | | | |
| | (2 bands) | 1·50 | 60 | |
| 2653 (1st Large) gold (2 bands) | | 2·00 | 70 | |

(b) Self-adhesive. Photo Walsall

(i) As T **1915**

| | | | | |
|---|---|---|---|---|
| 2654 | (2nd) bright blue (1 centre | | | |
| | band) *(12 Sept)* | 1·00 | 40 | |
| 2655 | (1st) gold (2 bands) | | | |
| | *(12 Sept)* | 1·25 | 50 | |

(ii) As T **1916**

| | | | | |
|---|---|---|---|---|
| 2656 (2nd Large) bright blue (2 bands) | | | | |
| | *(15 Aug)* | 1·50 | 60 | |
| 2657 (1st Large) gold (2 bands) *(15 Aug)* | | 2·00 | 70 | |
| First Day Cover (Nos. Y1676b/c, 2650/3) | | | 5·00 | |
| Presentation Pack (Nos. Y1676b/c, | | | | |
| 2650/3) (P.O. Pack No. 74) | | 7·00 | | |

No. 2650/3 were also issued in the £7.66 'The Machin. The Making of a masterpiece' booklet.

No. 2654 was issued in booklets of twelve sold at £2·76.

No. 2655 was available in booklets of six or twelve, sold at £1·92 or £3·84.

Nos. 2656/7 were issued in separate booklets of four, sold at £1·48 or £1·76.

All these booklets had the surplus self-adhesive paper around each stamp removed.

For PHQ cards for Nos. 2652/3 see below No. Y1803.

**1917**

## 70th Anniversary of the Year of Three Kings miniature sheet

**2006** (31 Aug.) Sheet 127 × 72 mm containing No. Y1748. Multicoloured. Two phosphor bands. Perf 15 × 14 (with one elliptical hole in each vertical side)

| | | | |
|---|---|---|---|
| **MS**2658 **1917** £3 deep mauve | 10·00 | 10·00 | ☐ ☐ |
| First Day Cover | | 11·00 | ☐ |

**1918** Corporal Agansing Rai    **1919** Boy Seaman Jack Cornwell

**1920** Midshipman Charles Lucas    **1921** Captain Noel Chavasse

**1922** Captain Albert Ball    **1923** Captain Charles Upham

## 150th Anniversary of the Victoria Cross (1st issue)

**2006** (21 Sept.) One side phosphor band. Perf 14½ × 14

| | | | | | |
|---|---|---|---|---|---|
| 2659 **1918** | (1st) | multicoloured | 1·25 | 1·10 | ☐ ☐ |
| | a. | Horiz pair. | | | |
| | | Nos. 2659/60 | 2·50 | 2·25 | ☐ ☐ |
| 2660 **1919** | (1st) | multicoloured | 1·25 | 1·10 | ☐ ☐ |
| 2661 **1920** | 64p | multicoloured | 1·25 | 1·50 | ☐ ☐ |
| | a. | Horiz pair. | | | |
| | | Nos. 2661/2 | 5·00 | 5·00 | ☐ ☐ |
| 2662 **1921** | 64p | multicoloured | 1·25 | 1·50 | ☐ ☐ |
| 2663 **1922** | 72p | multicoloured | 2·00 | 2·25 | ☐ ☐ |
| | a. | Horiz pair. | | | |
| | | Nos. 2663/4 | 7·00 | 7·00 | ☐ ☐ |
| 2664 **1923** | 72p | multicoloured | 2·00 | 2·25 | ☐ ☐ |
| Set of 6 | | | 13·00 | 13·00 | ☐ |
| First Day Cover | | | | 14·00 | ☐ |
| Presentation Pack (P.O. Pack No. 387) | | | 14·00 | | ☐ |
| Set of 3 Gutter Strips of 4 | | | 27·00 | | ☐ |
| **MS**2665 190 × 67 mm. No. 2666 and | | | | | |
| as Nos. 2659/64 but 'all-over' | | | | | |
| phosphor | | | 16·00 | 16·00 | ☐ ☐ |
| First Day Cover | | | | 17·00 | ☐ ☐ |

| | | | |
|---|---|---|---|
| PHQ Cards (set of 7) (290) | | 7·00 | 18·00 | ☐ ☐ |

Nos. 2659/60, 2661/2 and 2663/4 were each printed together, *se-tenant*, as horizontal pairs in sheets of 60 (2 panes 6 × 5) and were also issued in the £7.44 'Victoria Cross' booklet.

The seven PHQ cards depict the six individual stamps and the miniature sheet.

## 150th Anniversary of the Victoria Cross (2nd issue). Booklet stamp

**2006** (21 Sept.) Design as No. 1517 (1990 Gallantry Awards). 'All-over' phosphor. Perf 14 ×14½

| | | | | |
|---|---|---|---|---|
| 2666 **959** | 20p multicoloured | 10·00 | 10·00 | ☐ ☐ |

No. 2666 was only issued in the £7.44 'Victoria Cross' booklet and in **MS**2665.

**1924** Sitar Player and Dancer    **1925** Reggae Bass Guitarist and African Drummer

**1926** Fiddler and Harpist    **1927** Sax Player and Blues Guitarist

**1928** Maraca Player and Salsa Dancers

## Europa. Integration. Sounds of Britain

**2006** (3 Oct.) 'All-over' phosphor. Perf 14½

| | | | | | |
|---|---|---|---|---|---|
| 2667 **1924** | (1st) | multicoloured | 1·25 | 1·00 | ☐ ☐ |
| 2668 **1925** | 42p | multicoloured | 1·25 | 1·25 | ☐ ☐ |
| 2669 **1926** | 50p | multicoloured | 1·25 | 1·50 | ☐ ☐ |
| 2670 **1927** | 72p | multicoloured | 1·75 | 1·75 | ☐ ☐ |
| 2671 **1928** | £1·19 | multicoloured | 2·50 | 3·00 | ☐ ☐ |
| Set of 5 | | | 7·50 | 7·50 | ☐ ☐ |
| First Day Cover | | | | 9·00 | ☐ |
| Presentation Pack (P.O. Pack No. 388) | | | 9·00 | | ☐ |
| PHQ Cards (set of 5) (291) | | | 4·50 | 10·00 | ☐ ☐ |
| Set of 5 Gutter Pairs | | | 16·00 | | ☐ |
| Set of 5 Traffic Light Gutter Blocks of 4 | | | 38·00 | | ☐ |

The 1st class and 50p values include the 'EUROPA' emblem.

**1929** 'New Baby' (Alison Carmichael)

**1930** 'Best Wishes' (Alan Kitching)

**1931** 'THANK YOU' (Alan Kitching)

**1932** Balloons (Ivan Chermayeff)

**1933** Firework (Kam Tang)

**1934** Champagne, Flowers and Butterflies (Olaf Hajek)

## 'Smilers' Booklet stamps (2nd series). Occasions

**2006** (17 Oct.) Self-adhesive. Two phosphor bands. Die-cut perf 15 × 14

| | | | | | | |
|---|---|---|---|---|---|---|
| 2672 | **1929** | (1st) | chrome-yellow | 1·40 | 1·20 | ☐ ☐ |
| | | a. | Booklet pane. | | | |
| | | | Nos. 2672/7 | 9·00 | 7·00 | ☐ ☐ |
| 2673 | **1930** | (1st) | turquoise-blue | 1·40 | 1·20 | ☐ ☐ |
| 2674 | **1931** | (1st) | scarlet-vermilion, | | | |
| | | | rosine and yellow | 1·40 | 1·20 | ☐ ☐ |
| 2675 | **1932** | (1st) | multicoloured | 1·40 | 1·20 | ☐ ☐ |
| 2676 | **1933** | (1st) | multicoloured | 1·40 | 1·20 | ☐ ☐ |
| 2677 | **1934** | (1st) | multicoloured | 1·40 | 1·20 | ☐ ☐ |
| Set of 6 | | | | 9·00 | 7·00 | ☐ ☐ |
| First Day Cover | | | | | 8·00 | ☐ |
| Presentation Pack (P.O. Pack No. M13) | | | | 18·00 | | ☐ |
| PHQ Cards (D29) | | | | 5·00 | 12·00 | ☐ ☐ |

Nos. 2672/7 were printed together, *se-tenant*, in booklet panes of six in which the surplus self-adhesive paper around each stamp was removed.

They were also issued in sheets of 20, containing four of Nos. 2672 and 2677 and three of the other designs, and *se-tenant* labels. Separate sheets of each design were available with personal photographs on the labels.

Stamps as No. 2672 but perforated with one eliptical hole on each vertical side were issued on 28 October 2008 in sheets of 10 or 20 with circular *se-tenant* Peter Rabbit labels.

Stamps as Nos. 2674 but perforated with one elliptical hole in each vertical side were issued, together with Nos. 2569, 2572, 2821/3 and four designs from **MS**3024, on 8 May 2010 in sheets of 20 stamps with *se-tenant* greetings labels.

These generic sheets were all printed in lithography instead of photogravure.

**1935** Snowman

**1936** Father Christmas

**1937** Snowman

**1938** Father Christmas

**1939** Reindeer

**1940** Christmas Tree

## Christmas. Christmans scenes

**2006** (7 Nov.) One centre phosphor band (2nd) or two phosphor bands (others). Perf 15 × 14

(a) Self-adhesive

| | | | | | | |
|---|---|---|---|---|---|---|
| 2678 | **1935** | (2nd) | multicoloured | 1·00 | 90 | ☐ ☐ |
| 2679 | **1936** | (1st) | multicoloured | 1·25 | 1·00 | ☐ ☐ |
| 2680 | **1937** | (2nd Large) | multicoloured | 1·50 | 1·25 | ☐ ☐ |
| 2681 | **1938** | (1st Large) | multicoloured | 2·00 | 1·40 | ☐ ☐ |
| 2682 | **1939** | 72p | multicoloured | 3·25 | 3·25 | ☐ ☐ |
| 2683 | **1940** | £1·19 | multicoloured | 6·00 | 4·50 | ☐ ☐ |
| Set of 6 | | | | 12·00 | 12·00 | ☐ ☐ |
| First Day Cover | | | | | 13·00 | ☐ |
| Presentation Pack (P.O. Pack No. 389) | | | | 13·00 | | ☐ |
| PHQ Cards (set of 7) (292) | | | | 3·00 | 18·00 | ☐ ☐ |

(b) Ordinary gum

| | | | | |
|---|---|---|---|---|
| **MS**2684 115 × 102 mm. | | | | |
| As Nos. 2678/83 | 12·00 | 12·00 | ☐ ☐ |
| First Day Cover | | 13·00 | ☐ |

The seven PHQ cards depict the six individual stamps and the miniature sheet.

The 2nd and 1st class stamps were also issued in sheets of 20 printed in lithography instead of photogravure containing ten 1st class and ten 2nd class stamps, each stamp accompanied by a *se-tenant* label. Separate sheets of 20 1st or 20 2nd class were available with personal photographs.

**1941**

## 'Lest We Forget' (1st issue). 90th Anniversary of the Battle of the Somme, miniature sheet

**2006** (9 Nov.) Sheet 124 × 71 mm containing new stamp as No. 2883 and designs as Nos. EN15, W107, S118 and NI101. Multicoloured. Two phosphor bands. Perf 14½ (1st) or 15 × 14 (with one elliptical hole in each vertical side) (72p).

| | | | | |
|---|---|---|---|---|
| **MS**2685 1941 (1st) Poppies on barbed | | | | |
| wire stems; 72p ×4 As Nos. EN17, | | | | |
| W109, S120 and NI102 | 9·00 | 9·00 | ☐ ☐ |
| First Day Cover | | 10·00 | ☐ |
| Presentation Pack (P.O. Pack No. 390) | 12·00 | | ☐ |

No. **MS**2685 (including the Northern Ireland stamp) is printed in gravure.

The 1st class stamp was also issued in sheets of 20 with se-tenant labels showing war memorials, and on 6 Nov 2008, in a *se-tenant* strip of three, both issues printed in lithography instead of photogravure. See No. 2883.

For the miniature sheet entitled 'Celebrating Scotland', issued 30 November 2006, see the Regionals section.

## Collectors Pack

**2006** (9 Nov.) Comprises Nos. 2589/612, 2615/49, 2659/64, 2667/71, 2678/83 and **MS**2685

CP2685a Collectors Pack £120 ☐

## Post Office Yearbook

**2006** (9 Nov.) Comprises Nos. 2589/612, 2615/49, 2659/64, 2667/71, 2678/83 and **MS**2685

YB2685a Yearbook £100 ☐

## Miniature Sheet Collection

**2006** (30 Nov.) Comprises Nos. **MS**2613, **MS**2658, **MS**2665, **MS**2684/5, **MS**S153 and **MS**W143

**MS**2685a Miniature Sheet Collection 75·00 ☐

**1942** 'with the beatles'

**1943** 'Sgt Pepper's Lonely Hearts Club Band'

**1944** 'Help!'

**1945** 'Abbey Road'

**1946** 'Revolver'

**1947** 'Let It Be'

**1948** Beatles Memorabilia

## The Beatles. Album Covers

**2007** (9 Jan.) Two phosphor bands

(a) Photo Walsall. Self-adhesive. Die-cut irregular perf 13½ × 14½

| | | | | | | |
|---|---|---|---|---|---|---|
| 2686 | **1942** | (1st) | multicoloured | 1·25 | 1·00 | ☐ ☐ |
| | | a. Horiz pair. Nos. 2686/7 | | 2·50 | | ☐ |
| 2687 | **1943** | (1st) | multicoloured | 1·25 | 1·00 | ☐ ☐ |
| 2688 | **1944** | 64p | multicoloured | 1·50 | 1·50 | ☐ ☐ |
| | | a. Horiz pair. Nos. 2688/9 | | 4·00 | | ☐ |
| 2689 | **1945** | 64p | multicoloured | 1·50 | 1·50 | ☐ ☐ |
| 2690 | **1946** | 72p | multicoloured | 1·80 | 1·80 | ☐ ☐ |
| | | a. Horiz pair. Nos. 2690/1 | | 5·00 | | ☐ |
| 2691 | **1947** | 72p | multicoloured | 1·80 | 1·80 | ☐ ☐ |
| Set of 6 | | | | 10·00 | 8·00 | ☐ ☐ |
| First Day Cover | | | | | 11·00 | ☐ |
| Presentation Pack (Nos. 2686/92) | | | | | | |
| | | (P.O. Pack No. 392) | | 16·00 | | ☐ |
| PHQ Cards (set of 11) (293) | | | | 9·00 | 20·00 | ☐ ☐ |

(b) Litho Walsall. Ordinary gum. Two phosphor bands. Perf 14
**MS**2692 115 × 89 mm. 1948 (1st)
Guitar; (1st) Yellow Submarine
lunch-box and key-rings; (1st)
Record 'Love Me Do'; (1st) Beatles

| | | | | |
|---|---|---|---|---|
| badges | | 5·00 | 5·00 | ☐ ☐ |
| First Day Cover | | | 7·00 | ☐ |

Nos. 2686/91 are all die-cut in the shape of a pile of records.

Nos. 2686/7, 2688/9 and 2690/1 were each printed together in sheets of 60 (2 panes of 30), with the two designs alternating horizontally and the surplus backing paper around each stamp removed.

Nos. 2686/92 commemorate the 50th anniversary of the first meeting of Paul McCartney and John Lennon.

The complete miniature sheet is shown on one of the eleven PHQ cards, with the others depicting individual stamps, including those from **MS**2692.

### 'Smilers' Booklet stamp (3rd series)

**2007** (16 Jan.)–08 As No. 2569. Self-adhesive. Two phosphor bands. Die-cut Perf 15 × 14 (with one elliptical hole in each vertical side)

| | | | | | |
|---|---|---|---|---|---|
| 2693 | (1st) | multicoloured | 10·00 | 10·00 | ☐ ☐ |
| | a. Booklet pane. No. 2655 × 5 and No. 2693 | | 15·00 | | ☐ ☐ |
| | b. Booklet pane. No. 2693 × 2 with two attached labels and No. 2295 × 4 (15.1.08) | | 24·00 | | ☐ ☐ |

No. 2693 was issued in stamp booklets in which the surplus backing paper around each stamp was removed.
Nos. 2694/8 are left vacant.

**1949** Moon Jellyfish

**1950** Common Starfish

**1951** Beadlet Anemone

**1952** Bass

**1953** Thornback Ray

**1954** Lesser Octopus

**1955** Common Mussels

**1956** Grey Seal

**1957** Shore Crab

**1958** Common Sun Star

## Sea Life

2007 (1 Feb.) Two phosphor bands. Perf 14½

| | | | | | | | |
|---|---|---|---|---|---|---|---|
| 2699 | **1949** | (1st) | multicoloured | 1·25 | 90 | ☐ | ☐ |
| | a. Block of 10. | | | | | | |
| | | Nos. 2699/708 | 14·00 | 12·00 | | ☐ | ☐ |
| 2700 | **1950** | (1st) | multicoloured | 1·25 | 90 | ☐ | ☐ |
| 2701 | **1951** | (1st) | multicoloured | 1·25 | 90 | ☐ | ☐ |
| 2702 | **1952** | (1st) | multicoloured | 1·25 | 90 | ☐ | ☐ |
| 2703 | **1953** | (1st) | multicoloured | 1·25 | 90 | ☐ | ☐ |
| 2704 | **1954** | (1st) | multicoloured | 1·25 | 90 | ☐ | ☐ |
| 2705 | **1955** | (1st) | multicoloured | 1·25 | 90 | ☐ | ☐ |
| 2706 | **1956** | (1st) | multicoloured | 1·25 | 90 | ☐ | ☐ |
| 2707 | **1957** | (1st) | multicoloured | 1·25 | 90 | ☐ | ☐ |
| 2708 | **1958** | (1st) | multicoloured | 1·25 | 90 | ☐ | ☐ |
| *Set* of 10 | | | | 14·00 | 12·00 | ☐ | ☐ |
| First Day Cover | | | | | 13·00 | | ☐ |
| Presentation Pack (P.O. Pack No. 393) | | | | 16·00 | | ☐ | |
| PHQ Cards (*set of* 10) (294) | | | | 8·00 | 18·00 | ☐ | ☐ |
| Gutter Block of 20 | | | | 29·00 | | ☐ | |

Nos. 2699/708 were printed together, *se-tenant*, as blocks of ten (5 × 2) in sheets of 60 (2 panes of 30).

**1959** Saturn Nebula C55

**1960** Eskimo Nebula C39

**1961** Cat's Eye Nebula C6

**1962** Helix Nebula C63

**1963** Flaming Star Nebula C31

**1964** The Spindle C53

## 50th Anniversary of 'The Sky at Night' (TV programme). Nebulae

2007 (13 Feb.) Self-adhesive. Two phosphor bands. Die-cut perf 14½ × 14

| | | | | | | | |
|---|---|---|---|---|---|---|---|
| 2709 | **1959** | (1st) | multicoloured | 1·25 | 90 | ☐ | ☐ |
| | a. Horiz pair. Nos. 2709/10 | | | 2·50 | | ☐ | |
| 2710 | **1960** | (1st) | multicoloured | 1·25 | 90 | ☐ | ☐ |
| 2711 | **1961** | 50p | multicoloured | 1·20 | 1·20 | ☐ | ☐ |
| | a. Horiz pair. Nos. 2711/12 | | | 4·00 | | ☐ | |
| 2712 | **1962** | 50p | multicoloured | 1·20 | 1·20 | ☐ | ☐ |
| 2713 | **1963** | 72p | multicoloured | 1·70 | 1·70 | ☐ | ☐ |
| | a. Horiz pair. Nos. 2713/4 | | | 5·00 | | ☐ | |
| 2714 | **1964** | 72p | multicoloured | 1·70 | 1·70 | ☐ | ☐ |
| *Set of* 6 | | | | 10·00 | 7·00 | ☐ | ☐ |
| First Day Cover | | | | | 9·00 | | ☐ |
| Presentation Pack (P.O. Pack No. 394) | | | 12·00 | | ☐ | |
| PHQ Cards (*set of* 6) (295) | | | 4·50 | 14·00 | ☐ | ☐ |

Nos. 2709/10, 2711/12 and 2713/14 were each printed together in sheets of 60 (2 panes of 30), with the two designs alternating horizontally and the surplus backing paper around each stamp removed.

**1965** Iron Bridge (Thomas Telford)

**1966** Steam Locomotive and Railway Tracks

**1967** Map of British Isles and Australia (telephone)

**1968** Camera and Television (John Logie Baird)

**1969** Globe as Web (email and internet)

**1970** Couple with Suitcases on Moon (space travel)

## World of Invention (1st series)

2007 (1 Mar.) Self-adhesive. Two phosphor bands. Die-cut perf 14½ × 14

| | | | | | | | |
|---|---|---|---|---|---|---|---|
| 2715 | **1965** | (1st) | multicoloured | 1·25 | 90 | ☐ | ☐ |
| | a. Horiz pair. Nos. 2715/16 | | | 3·00 | | ☐ | |
| 2716 | **1966** | (1st) | multicoloured | 1·25 | 90 | ☐ | ☐ |
| 2717 | **1967** | 64p | multicoloured | 1·25 | 1·25 | ☐ | ☐ |
| | a. Horiz pair. Nos. 2717/18 | | | 3·00 | | ☐ | |
| 2718 | **1968** | 64p | multicoloured | 1·25 | 1·25 | ☐ | ☐ |
| 2719 | **1969** | 72p | multicoloured | 2·00 | 2·25 | ☐ | ☐ |

| | | | | | |
|---|---|---|---|---|---|
| | a. Horiz pair. Nos. 2719/20 | 5·00 | | ☐ | |
| 2720 **1970** | 72p multicoloured | 2·00 | 2·25 | ☐ | ☐ |
| *Set of 6* | | 10·00 | 8·00 | ☐ | ☐ |
| First Day Cover | | | 10·00 | | ☐ |
| Presentation Pack (P.O. Pack No. 395) | | 12·00 | | ☐ | |
| PHQ Cards (*set of 7*) (296) | | 6·00 | 14·00 | ☐ | ☐ |

The seven PHQ Cards depict the six individual stamps and **MS**2727.

Nos. 2715/16, 2717/18 and 2719/20 were each printed together in sheets of 60 (2 panes of 30), with the two designs alternating horizontally and the surplus backing paper around each stamp removed.

## World of Invention (2nd series)

**2007** (1 Mar.)Ordinary gum. Two phosphor bands. Perf 14½ × 14

| | | | | | | |
|---|---|---|---|---|---|---|
| 2721 | **1965** | (1st) multicoloured | 1·25 | 90 | ☐ | ☐ |
| 2722 | **1966** | (1st) multicoloured | 1·25 | 90 | ☐ | ☐ |
| 2723 | **1967** | 64p multicoloured | 2·50 | 2·50 | ☐ | ☐ |
| 2724 | **1968** | 64p multicoloured | 2·50 | 2·50 | ☐ | ☐ |
| 2725 | **1969** | 72p multicoloured | 4·50 | 4·50 | ☐ | ☐ |
| 2726 | **1970** | 72p multicoloured | 4·50 | 4·50 | ☐ | ☐ |
| *Set of 6* | | | 15·00 | 15·00 | | |
| **MS**2727 115 × 104 mm. Nos. 2721/6 | | | 15·00 | 15·00 | ☐ | |
| First Day Cover | | | | 16·00 | | ☐ |

Nos. 2721/6 were only issued in the £7·49 'World of Invention' booklet and in **MS**2727.

**1971** William Wilberforce and Anti-Slavery Poster

**1972** Olaudah Equiano and Map of Slave Trade Routes

**1973** Granville Sharp and Slave Ship

**1974** Thomas Clarkson and Diagram of Slave Ship

**1975** Hannah More and Title Page of 'The Sorrows of Yamba'

**1976** Ignatius Sancho and Trade/Business Card

## Bicentenary of the Abolition of the Slave Trade

**2007** (22 Mar.) Two phosphor bands. Perf 14½

| | | | | | | |
|---|---|---|---|---|---|---|
| 2728 | **1971** | (1st) multicoloured | 1·25 | 90 | ☐ | ☐ |
| | | a. Horiz pair. Nos. 2728/9 | 2·50 | 2·50 | ☐ | |
| 2729 | **1972** | (1st) multicoloured | 1·25 | 90 | ☐ | ☐ |
| 2730 | **1973** | 50p multicoloured | 1·20 | 1·20 | ☐ | ☐ |
| | | a. Horiz pair. Nos. 2730/1 | 3·00 | 3·00 | ☐ | |
| 2731 | **1974** | 50p multicoloured | 1·20 | 1·20 | ☐ | ☐ |
| 2732 | **1975** | 72p multicoloured | 1·80 | 1·80 | ☐ | ☐ |

| | | | | | |
|---|---|---|---|---|---|
| | a. Horiz pair. Nos. 2732/3 | 4·50 | 4·50 | ☐ | ☐ |
| 2733 **1976** | 72p multicoloured | 1·80 | 1·80 | ☐ | ☐ |
| *Set of 6* | | 9·00 | 9·00 | ☐ | ☐ |
| First Day Cover | | | 11·00 | | ☐ |
| Presentation Pack (P.O. Pack No. 396) | | 12·00 | | ☐ | |
| PHQ Cards (*set of 6*) (297) | | 4·50 | 14·00 | ☐ | ☐ |
| *Set of 3 Gutter Strips of 4* | | 20·00 | | ☐ | ☐ |
| *Set of 3 Traffic Light Gutter Strips of 4* | | 22·00 | | ☐ | ☐ |

Nos. 2728/9, 2730/1 and 2732/3 were each printed together, *se-tenant*, in horizontal pairs throughout the sheets.

For the miniature sheet entitled 'Celebrating England', issued 23 April 2007, see Regionals section.

**1977** Ice Cream Cone

**1978** Sandcastle

**1979** Carousel Horse

**1980** Beach Huts

**1981** Deckchairs

**1982** Beach Donkeys

## 'Beside the Seaside'

**2007** (15 May) Two phosphor bands. Perf 14½

| | | | | | | |
|---|---|---|---|---|---|---|
| 2734 | **1977** | (1st) multicoloured | 1·25 | 90 | ☐ | ☐ |
| 2735 | **1978** | 46p multicoloured | 1·20 | 1·10 | ☐ | ☐ |
| 2736 | **1979** | 48p multicoloured | 1·30 | 1·30 | ☐ | ☐ |
| 2737 | **1980** | 54p multicoloured | 1·40 | 1·40 | ☐ | ☐ |
| 2738 | **1981** | 69p multicoloured | 1·80 | 1·80 | ☐ | ☐ |
| 2739 | **1982** | 78p multicoloured | 2·00 | 2·00 | ☐ | ☐ |
| *Set of 6* | | | 8·00 | 8·00 | ☐ | ☐ |
| First Day Cover | | | | 10·00 | | ☐ |
| Presentation Pack (P.O. Pack No. 397) | | | 12·00 | | ☐ | |
| PHQ Cards (*set of 6*) (298) | | | 4·50 | 14·00 | ☐ | ☐ |
| *Set of 6 Gutter Pairs* | | | 18·00 | | ☐ | ☐ |

For Type **1977**, but self-adhesive , see No. 2848.

PHQ Cards (*Set of 3*) (Nos. 2741/
          **MS**2743) (299)    3·00   14·00 ☐ ☐
Nos. 2741/2 were only issued in the £7·66 'The Machin, the Making of a Masterpiece' booklet and in **MS**2743.
    Stamps as Type **1984** but with phosphor frames were issued in sheets of 20 with *se-tenant* labels showing the 1967–9 Machin definitives.

**1987** Stirling Moss in Vanwall 2.5L, 1957    **1988** Graham Hill in BRM P57, 1962

**1989** Jim Clark in Lotus 25 Climax, 1963    **1990** Jackie Stewart in Tyrrell 006/2, 1973

**1991** James Hunt in McLaren M23, 1976    **1992** Nigel Mansell in Williams FW11, 1986

### 50th Anniversary of the British Grand Prix, Silverstone. Racing Cars

**2007** (3 July) Two phosphor bands. Perf 14½

| | | | | | | |
|---|---|---|---|---|---|---|
| 2744 | **1987** | (1st) | multicoloured | 1·25 | 90 | ☐ ☐ |
| 2745 | **1988** | (1st) | multicoloured | 1·25 | 90 | ☐ ☐ |
| 2746 | **1989** | 54p | multicoloured | 1·50 | 1·50 | ☐ ☐ |
| 2747 | **1990** | 54p | multicoloured | 1·50 | 1·50 | ☐ ☐ |
| 2748 | **1991** | 78p | multicoloured | 2·00 | 2·00 | ☐ ☐ |
| 2749 | **1992** | 78p | multicoloured | 2·00 | 2·00 | ☐ ☐ |
| *Set of 6* | | | | 8·50 | 9·50 | ☐ ☐ |
| First Day Cover | | | | | 10·00 | ☐ |
| Presentation Pack (P.O. Pack No. 399) | | | | 11·00 | | ☐ |
| PHQ Cards (*set of 6*) (300) | | | | 4·50 | 14·00 | ☐ ☐ |
| *Set of 6 Gutter Pairs* | | | | 19·00 | | ☐ |

**1993** Harry Potter and the Philosopher's Stone    **1994** Harry Potter and the Chamber of Secrets    **1995** Harry Potter and the prisoner of Azkaban

---

**1983**

### New Wembley Stadium, London, miniature sheet

**2007** (17 May) Sheet 113 × 103 mm containing design as Type **1593** but with 'WORLD CUP 2002' inscription omitted, and Nos. EN6 and EN18, each × 2. One centre band (2nd) or two phosphor bands (others). Perf 14½ × 14 (1st) or 15 × 14 (with one elliptical hole in each vertical side) (2nd, 78p)

**MS**2740 **1983** (1st) As Type **1593**;
    (2nd) No. EN6 × 2; 78p No. EN18 ×
    2 and one central stamp-size label  8·00  8·00 ☐ ☐
First Day Cover             9·00 ☐

The design as Type **1593** was also issued in sheets of 20 with *se-tenant* labels showing scenes from Wembley Stadium.

**1984** Arnold Machin    **1985** 1967 4d. Machin

**1986**

### 40th Anniversary of the First Machin Definitives
### Booklet stamps and miniature sheet

**2007** (5 June) . Perf 14½ (1st) or 15 × 14 (with one elliptical hole in each vertical side) (£1)

| | | | | | |
|---|---|---|---|---|---|
| 2741 | **1984** | (1st) | multicoloured | 4·50 | 4·50 ☐ ☐ |
| 2742 | **1985** | (1st) | multicoloured | 4·50 | 4·50 ☐ ☐ |
| **MS**2743 127 × 73 mm. 1986 Nos. | | | | | |
|   2741/2, Y1725 and Y1725b | | | 12·00 | 12·00 ☐ ☐ |
| First Day Cover (**MS**2743) | | | | 13·00 | ☐ |
| Presentation Pack (**MS**2743) | | | | | |
|   (P.O. Pack No. 398) | | 14·00 | | | ☐ |

**1996** Harry Potter and the Goblet of Fire

**1997** Harry Potter and the Order of the Phoenix

**1998** Harry Potter and the Half-Blood Prince

**1999** Harry Potter and the Deathly Hallows

**2000** Crests of Hogwarts School and its Four Houses

## Publication of Final Book in the Harry Potter Series

**2007** (17 July)

(a) Book Covers. 'All-over' phosphor. Perf 14½

| | | | | | | | |
|---|---|---|---|---|---|---|---|
| 2750 | **1993** | (1st) | multicoloured | 1·25 | 90 | ☐ | ☐ |
| | | a. | Horiz strip of 7. | | | | |
| | | | Nos. 2750/6 | 9·00 | 8·00 | ☐ | ☐ |
| 2751 | **1994** | (1st) | multicoloured | 1·25 | 90 | ☐ | ☐ |
| 2752 | **1995** | (1st) | multicoloured | 1·25 | 90 | ☐ | ☐ |
| 2753 | **1996** | (1st) | multicoloured | 1·25 | 90 | ☐ | ☐ |
| 2754 | **1997** | (1st) | multicoloured | 1·25 | 90 | ☐ | ☐ |
| 2755 | **1998** | (1st) | multicoloured | 1·25 | 90 | ☐ | ☐ |
| 2756 | **1999** | (1st) | multicoloured | 1·25 | 90 | ☐ | ☐ |
| Set of 7 | | | | 9·00 | 8·00 | ☐ | |
| First Day Cover | | | | | 9·00 | | ☐ |
| Presentation Pack (Nos. 2750) | | | | | | | |
| | | (P.O. Pack No. M16) | | 17·00 | | ☐ | |
| PHQ Cards (set of 13) (HP) | | | | 11·00 | 27·00 | ☐ | ☐ |
| Gutter Block of 14 | | | | 20·00 | | ☐ | |
| Traffic Light Gutter Block of 14 | | | | 22·00 | | ☐ | |

(b) Crests of Hogwarts School and its Four Houses. Multicoloured. Two phosphor bands. Perf 15 × 14

**MS**2757  123 × 70 mm. 2000 (1st) Gryffindor; (1st) Hufflepuff; (1st) Hogwarts; (1st) Ravenclaw; (1st)

| | | | |
|---|---|---|---|
| Slytherin | 6·00 | 6·00 | ☐ ☐ |
| First Day Cover | | 7·50 | ☐ |

Nos. 2750/6 were printed together, *se-tenant*, as horizontal strips of seven stamps in sheets of 56 (2 panes 7 × 4).

The complete miniature sheet is shown on one of the thirteen PHQ cards with the others depicting the individual stamps including those from **MS**2757.

Stamps as those within **MS**2757 but self-adhesive were issued in sheets of 20 containing the five designs *se-tenant* with labels depicting either magic spells or personal photographs.

The magic spells labels are printed in thermochromic ink which fades temporarily when exposed to heat, revealing the meaning of the spells.

**2001** Scout and Camp Fire

**2002** Scouts Rock climbing

**2003** Scout planting Tree

**2004** Adult Volunteer teaching Scout Archery

**2005** Scouts learning gliding

**2006** Scouts from Many Nations

### Centenary of Scouting and 21st World Scout Jamboree, Chelmsford, Essex

**2007** (26 July) Two phosphor bands. Perf 14½ ×14

| | | | | | | | |
|---|---|---|---|---|---|---|---|
| 2758 | **2001** | (1st) | multicoloured | 1·25 | 90 | ☐ | ☐ |
| 2759 | **2002** | 46p | multicoloured | 1·20 | 1·20 | ☐ | ☐ |
| 2760 | **2003** | 48p | multicoloured | 1·20 | 1·20 | ☐ | ☐ |
| 2761 | **2004** | 54p | multicoloured | 1·40 | 1·40 | ☐ | ☐ |
| 2762 | **2005** | 69p | multicoloured | 1·80 | 1·80 | ☐ | ☐ |
| 2763 | **2006** | 78p | multicoloured | 2·00 | 2·00 | ☐ | ☐ |
| Set of 6 | | | | 8·00 | 8·00 | ☐ | ☐ |
| First Day Cover | | | | | 10·00 | | ☐ |
| Presentation Pack (P.O. Pack No. 400) | | | | 10·00 | | ☐ | |
| PHQ Cards (set of 6) (301) | | | | 4·50 | 14·00 | ☐ | ☐ |
| Set of 6 Gutter Pairs | | | | 18·00 | | ☐ | |

The 1st class and 48p values include the 'EUROPA' emblem.

**2007** White-tailed Eagle

**2008** Bearded Tit

**2009** Red Kite

**2010** Cirl Bunting

**2011** Marsh Harrier

**2012** Avocet

**2020** Rifleman,
95th Rifles, 1813

**2021** Grenadier,
Royal Regiment of
Foot of Ireland, 1704

**2022** Trooper, Earl
of Oxford's Horse,
1661

**2013** Bittern

**2014** Dartford Warbler

### Military Uniforms (1st series). British Army Uniforms

**2007** (20 Sept.) Two phosphor bands. Perf 14½

| | | | | | | |
|---|---|---|---|---|---|---|
| 2774 | **2017** | (1st) | multicoloured | 1·25 | 90 | ☐ ☐ |
| | a. | Horiz strip of 3. | | | | |
| | | Nos. 2774/6 | | 4·00 | 4·00 | ☐ ☐ |
| 2775 | **2018** | (1st) | multicoloured | 1·25 | 90 | ☐ ☐ |
| 2776 | **2019** | (1st) | multicoloured | 1·25 | 90 | ☐ ☐ |
| 2777 | **2020** | 78p | multicoloured | 2·00 | 2·00 | ☐ ☐ |
| | a. | Horiz strip of 3. | | | | |
| | | Nos. 2777/9 | | 7·00 | 7·00 | ☐ ☐ |
| 2778 | **2021** | 78p | multicoloured | 2·00 | 2·00 | ☐ ☐ |
| 2779 | **2022** | 78p | multicoloured | 1·70 | 1·70 | ☐ ☐ |
| *Set of* 6 | | | | | 10·00 | 10·00 | ☐ |
| First Day Cover | | | | | 11·00 | ☐ |
| Presentation Pack (P.O. Pack No. 402) | | | | 12·00 | | ☐ |
| PHQ Cards (*set of* 6) (303) | | | | 4·50 | 14·00 | ☐ ☐ |
| *Set of* 2 Gutter Strips of 6 | | | | 22·00 | | ☐ |
| *Set of* 2 Traffic Light Gutter Strips of 6 | | | 24·00 | | ☐ |

Nos. 2774/6 and 2777/9 were each printed together, *se-tenant*, in horizontal strips of three stamps in sheets of 60 (2 panes 6 × 5) and were also issued in the £7.66 'British Army Uniforms' booklet.

**2023** Leaving St. Paul's Cathedral after Thanksgiving Service, 2006

**2024** Inspecting King's Troop Royal Horse Artillery, Regents Park, 1997

### 'Action for Species' (1st series). Birds

**2007** (4 Sept.) Two phosphor bands. Perf 14½

| | | | | | | |
|---|---|---|---|---|---|---|
| 2764 | **2007** | (1st) | multicoloured | 1·25 | 90 | ☐ ☐ |
| | a. | Block of 10. | | | | |
| | | Nos. 2764/73 | | 14·00 | 10·00 | ☐ ☐ |
| 2765 | **2008** | (1st) | multicoloured | 1·25 | 90 | ☐ ☐ |
| 2766 | **2009** | (1st) | multicoloured | 1·25 | 90 | ☐ ☐ |
| 2767 | **2010** | (1st) | multicoloured | 1·25 | 90 | ☐ ☐ |
| 2768 | **2011** | (1st) | multicoloured | 1·25 | 90 | ☐ ☐ |
| 2769 | **2012** | (1st) | multicoloured | 1·25 | 90 | ☐ ☐ |
| 2770 | **2013** | (1st) | multicoloured | 1·25 | 90 | ☐ ☐ |
| 2771 | **2014** | (1st) | multicoloured | 1·25 | 90 | ☐ ☐ |
| 2772 | **2015** | (1st) | multicoloured | 1·25 | 90 | ☐ ☐ |
| 2773 | **2016** | (1st) | multicoloured | 1·25 | 90 | ☐ ☐ |
| *Set of* 10 | | | | 14·00 | 10·00 | ☐ ☐ |
| First Day Cover | | | | | 11·00 | ☐ |
| Presentation Pack (P.O. Pack No. 401) | | | 15·00 | | ☐ |
| PHQ Cards (*set of* 10) (302) | | | 9·00 | 18·00 | ☐ ☐ |
| Gutter Block of 20 | | | | 30·00 | | ☐ |

Nos. 2764/73 were printed together, *se-tenant*, in blocks of ten (5 × 2) in sheets of 60 (2 panes of 30).

**2015** Corncrake

**2016** Peregrine Falcon

**2017** NCO, Royal Military Police, 1999

**2018** Tank Commander, 5th Royal Tank Regiment, 1944

**2019** Observer, Royal Field Artillery, 1917

**2025** At Garter Ceremony, Windsor, 1980

**2026** At Royal Ascot, 1969

**2027** At Premiere of 'The Guns of Navarone', 1961

**2028** At Clydebank, 1947

**2029** Photographs of the Royal Family

### Royal Diamond Wedding Anniversary of Queen Elizabeth II and Duke of Edinburgh

**2007** (16 Oct.)

(a) Ordinary gum. Litho Cartor. 'All-over' phosphor.
Perf 14½ × 14

| | | | | | | |
|---|---|---|---|---|---|---|
| 2780 | **2023** | (1st) | blackish-brown and black | 1·25 | 90 | ☐ ☐ |
| | | a. | Horiz pair. Nos. 2780/1 | 2·50 | 2·00 | ☐ ☐ |
| 2781 | **2024** | (1st) | blackish-brown and black | 1·25 | 90 | ☐ ☐ |
| 2782 | **2025** | 54p | blackish-brown and black | 1·40 | 1·40 | ☐ ☐ |
| | | a. | Horiz pair. Nos. 2782/3 | 3·75 | 3·75 | ☐ ☐ |
| 2783 | **2026** | 54p | blackish-brown and black | 1·40 | 1·40 | ☐ ☐ |
| 2784 | **2027** | 78p | blackish-brown and black | 2·00 | 2·00 | ☐ ☐ |
| | | a. | Horiz pair. Nos. 2784/5 | 5·50 | 5·50 | ☐ ☐ |
| 2785 | **2028** | 78p | blackish-brown and black | 2·00 | 2·00 | ☐ ☐ |
| Set of 6 | | | | 11·00 | 11·00 | ☐ ☐ |
| First Day Cover | | | | | 12·00 | ☐ |
| Presentation Pack (Nos. 2780/**MS**2786) | | | | | | ☐ |
| | | (P.O. Pack No. 403) | | 19·00 | | |
| PHQ Cards (set of 11) (304) | | | | 9·00 | 27·00 | ☐ ☐ |
| Set of 3 Gutter Strips of 4 | | | | 23·00 | | ☐ |

Nos. 2780/1, 2782/3 and 2784/5 were each printed together, *se-tenant*, in horizontal pairs throughout the sheets.

(b) Self-adhesive. Photo Walsall. Two phosphor bands.
Perf 14½

**MS**2786 **2029** 115 × 89 mm. (1st)
Royal family, Balmoral, 1972; (1st) Queen and Prince Philip, Buckingham Palace, 2007; 69p. Royal family, Windsor Castle, 1965; 78p. Princess Elizabeth, Prince Philip, Prince Charles and Princess Anne, Clarence House, 1951 6·00 ☐ ☐

First Day Cover 7·00 ☐

The complete miniature sheet is shown on one of the eleven PHQ cards with the others depicting individual stamps including those from **MS**2786.

**2030** 'Madonna and Child' (William Dyce), c 1827

**2031** 'The Madonna of Humility' (Lippo di Dalmasio), c 1390–1400

### Christmas (1st issue). Paintings of the Madonna and Child

**2007** (6 Nov.) One centre band (2nd) or two phosphor bands (1st). Self-adhesive. Die-cut perf 15 × 14 (with one elliptical hole in each vertical side)

| | | | | | | |
|---|---|---|---|---|---|---|
| 2787 | **2030** | (2nd) | multicoloured | 1·00 | 80 | ☐ ☐ |
| 2788 | **2031** | (1st) | multicoloured | 1·25 | 90 | ☐ ☐ |
| First Day Cover | | | | | 4·00 | ☐ |

**2032** Angel playing Trumpet ('PEACE')

**2033** Angel playing Lute ('GOODWILL')

**2034** Angel playing Trumpet ('PEACE')

**2035** Angel playing Lute ('GOODWILL')

**2036** Angel playing Flute ('JOY')

**2037** Angel playing Tambourine ('GLORY')

### Christmas (2nd issue). Angels

**2007** (6 Nov.) One centre band (2nd) or two phosphor bands (others). Perf 15 × 14

(a) Self-adhesive

| | | | | | | |
|---|---|---|---|---|---|---|
| 2789 | **2032** | (2nd) | multicoloured | 1·00 | 80 | ☐ ☐ |
| 2790 | **2033** | (1st) | multicoloured | 1·25 | 90 | ☐ ☐ |
| 2791 | **2034** | (2nd Large) | multicoloured | 1·50 | 1·00 | ☐ ☐ |
| 2792 | **2035** | (1st Large) | multicoloured | 2·00 | 2·00 | ☐ ☐ |
| 2793 | **2036** | 78p | multicoloured | 2·00 | 2·00 | ☐ ☐ |
| 2794 | **2037** | £1·24 | multicoloured | 3·50 | 3·50 | ☐ ☐ |
| Set of 6 | | | | 10·00 | 10·00 | ☐ ☐ |
| First Day Cover | | | | | 10·00 | ☐ |
| Presentation Pack (Nos. 2787/94) | | | | | | ☐ |
| | | (P.O. Pack No. 404) | | 14·00 | | |
| PHQ Cards (set of 9) (305) | | | | 8·00 | 18·00 | ☐ ☐ |

(b) Ordinary gum

**MS**2795 115 × 102 mm.
As Nos. 2789/94 10·00 10·00 ☐ ☐
First Day Cover 11·00 ☐

The phosphor bands on Nos. 2791/2 are at the centre and right of each stamp.

The PHQ cards depict Nos. 2787/94 and **MS**2795.

The 2nd class, 1st class and 78p stamps were also issued in sheets of 20 printed in lithography instead of photogravure containing eight 1st class, eight 2nd class and four 78p stamps, each stamp accompanied by a *se-tenant* label. Separate sheets of 20 1st, 20 2nd or 10 78p were available with personal photographs.

**2038**

### 'Lest We Forget' (2nd issue). 90th Anniv of the Battle of Passchendaele, miniature sheet

**2007** (8 Nov.) Litho. Sheet 124 × 70 mm containing new stamp and designs as Nos. EN18, W110, S121 and NI128. Two phosphor bands. Perf 14½ (1st) or 15 × 14 (with one elliptical hole in each vertical side) (78p)

| | | | | |
|---|---|---|---|---|
| **MS**2796 | 2038 | (1st) Soldiers in poppy flower; 78p. × 4 As Nos. EN15, NI103, S118 and W107 | 10·00 | 10·00 |
| First Day Cover | | | | 11·00 |
| Presentation Pack (P.O. Pack No. 405) | | | 12·00 | |

The 1st class stamp was also issued in sheets of 20 with *se-tenant* labels showing soldiers and their letters home and, on 6 Nov. 2008 in a *se-tenant* strip of three, see No. 2884.

### Collectors Pack

**2007** (8 Nov.) Comprises Nos. 2686/92, 2699/720, 2728/39, **MS**2743/94 and **MS**2796

| CP2796a | Collectors Pack | £190 |
|---|---|---|

### Post Office Yearbook

**2007** (8 Nov.) Comprises Nos. 2686/92, 2699/720, 2728/39, **MS**2743/94 and **MS**2796

| YB2796a | Yearbook | £130 |
|---|---|---|

### Miniature Sheet Collection

**2007** (8 Nov.) Comprises Nos. **MS**2692, **MS**2727, **MS**2740, **MS**2743, **MS**2757, **MS**2786 and **MS**2795/6

| **MS**2796a Miniature Sheet Collection | 75·00 |
|---|---|

**2039** Casino Royale

**2040** Dr. No

**2041** Goldfinger

**2042** Diamonds are Forever

**2043** For Your Eyes Only

**2044** From Russia with Love

### Birth Centenary of Ian Fleming (author of James Bond books) (1st issue). Book Covers

**2008** (8 Jan.) Two phosphor bands. Perf 14½ × 14

| 2797 | **2039** | (1st) multicoloured | 1·25 | 90 | |
| --- | --- | --- | --- | --- | --- |
| 2798 | **2040** | (1st) multicoloured | 1·25 | 90 | |
| 2799 | **2041** | 54p multicoloured | 1·40 | 1·40 | |
| 2800 | **2042** | 54p multicoloured | 1·40 | 1·40 | |
| 2801 | **2043** | 78p multicoloured | 2·00 | 2·00 | |
| 2802 | **2044** | 78p multicoloured | 2·00 | 2·00 | |
| Set of 6 | | | 8·50 | 8·00 | |
| First Day Cover | | | | 10·00 | |
| Presentation Pack (P.O. Pack No. 407) | | | 11·00 | | |
| PHQ Cards (set of 7) (306) | | | 6·00 | 20·00 | |
| Set of 6 Gutter Pairs | | | 19·00 | | |
| **MS**2803 189 × 68 mm. Nos. 2797/802 | | | 9·00 | 9·00 | |
| First Day Cover | | | | 11·00 | |

No. 2797/802 were also issued in the £7·40 'Ian Fleming's James Bond' booklet.

The seven PHQ cards depict the individual stamps and **MS**2803.

### Birth Centenary of Ian Fleming (author of James Bond books) (2nd issue). Booklet stamps

**2008** (8 Jan.) Design as Type 1517 but printed in lithography. Two phosphor bands. Perf 14½

| 2805 | **1517** | (1st) multicoloured | 4·25 | 4·25 | |
|---|---|---|---|---|---|

No. 2805 was only issued in the £7·40 'Ian Fleming's James Bond' booklet. For White Ensign stamp from this booklet see No. 2581.

No. 2804 is vacant.

**2045** Assistance Dog carrying Letter (Labrador 'Rowan')

**2046** Mountain Rescue Dog (Cross-bred 'Merrick')

**2047** Police Dog (German Shepherd 'Max')

**2048** Customs Dog (Springer Spaniel 'Max')

**2049** Sheepdog
(Border Collie 'Bob')

**2050** Guide Dog
(Labrador 'Warwick')

## Working Dogs

**2008** (5 Feb.) Two phosphor bands. Perf 14½

| | | | | | | |
|---|---|---|---|---|---|---|
| 2806 | **2045** | (1st) | multicoloured | 1·25 | 90 | ☐ ☐ |
| 2807 | **2046** | 46p | multicoloured | 1·20 | 1·20 | ☐ ☐ |
| 2808 | **2047** | 48p | multicoloured | 1·20 | 1·20 | ☐ ☐ |
| 2809 | **2048** | 54p | multicoloured | 1·40 | 1·40 | ☐ ☐ |
| 2810 | **2049** | 69p | multicoloured | 1·80 | 1·80 | ☐ ☐ |
| 2811 | **2050** | 78p | multicoloured | 2·00 | 2·00 | ☐ ☐ |
| Set of 6 | | | | 8·00 | 8·00 | ☐ |
| First Day Cover | | | | | 10·00 | ☐ |
| Presentation Pack (P.O. Pack No. 408) | | | 10·00 | | ☐ |
| PHQ Cards (set of 6) (307) | | | 4·50 | 14·00 | ☐ ☐ |
| Set of 6 Gutter Pairs | | | 18·00 | | ☐ |

The 1st value includes the 'EUROPA' emblem.

**2051** Henry IV
(1399-1413)

**2052** Henry V
(1413–1422)

**2053** Henry VI (1422-
1461 & 1470-1471)

**2054** Edward IV
(1461–1470 &
1471–1473)

**2055** Edward V
(1483)

**2056** Richard III
(1483–1485)

**2057** The Age of Lancaster and York

## Kings and Queens (1st issue). The Houses of Lancaster and York

**2008** (28 Feb.) Two phosphor bands. Perf 14½

| | | | | | | |
|---|---|---|---|---|---|---|
| 2812 | **2051** | (1st) | multicoloured | 1·25 | 90 | ☐ ☐ |
| 2813 | **2052** | (1st) | multicoloured | 1·25 | 90 | ☐ ☐ |
| 2814 | **2053** | 54p | multicoloured | 1·40 | 1·40 | ☐ ☐ |
| 2815 | **2054** | 54p | multicoloured | 1·40 | 1·40 | ☐ ☐ |

| | | | | | | |
|---|---|---|---|---|---|---|
| 2816 | **2055** | 69p | multicoloured | 1·80 | 1·80 | ☐ ☐ |
| 2817 | **2056** | 69p | multicoloured | 1·80 | 1·80 | ☐ ☐ |
| Set of 6 | | | | 8·00 | 8·00 | ☐ ☐ |
| First Day Cover | | | | | 10·00 | ☐ |
| Presentation Pack (P.O. Pack No. 409) | | | 17·00 | | ☐ |
| PHQ Cards (set of 11) (308) | | | 9·00 | 27·00 | ☐ ☐ |
| Set of 6 Gutter Pairs | | | 18·00 | | ☐ |
| Set of 6 Traffic Light Gutter Blocks of 4 | | 38·00 | | ☐ |

**MS**2818 123 × 70 mm. **2057** (1st)
Owain Glyn Dwr ('Parliament'),
1404; (1st) Henry V's triumph
at Battle of Agincourt, 1415;
78p. Yorkish victory at Battle of
Tewkesbury, 1471; 78p. William
Caxton, first English printer, 1477    7·00    7·00  ☐ ☐

First Day Cover    8·00  ☐

The complete miniature sheet is shown on one of the eleven PHQ cards with the others depicting individual stamps including those from **MS**2818.

## 'Smilers' Booklet stamps (4th series)

**2008** (28 Feb.) Designs as Nos. 2567/8, 2570 and 2675/7. Self-adhesive. Two phosphor bands. Die-cut perf 15 × 14 (with one elliptical hole in each vertical side)

| | | | | | | |
|---|---|---|---|---|---|---|
| 2819 | **1569** | (1st) | multicoloured | 2·50 | 2·50 | ☐ ☐ |
| | | a. | Booklet pane. Nos. | | | |
| | | | 2819/24 | 15·00 | 15·00 | ☐ ☐ |
| 2820 | **1842** | (1st) | multicoloured | 2·50 | 2·50 | ☐ ☐ |
| 2821 | **1517** | (1st) | multicoloured | 2·50 | 2·50 | ☐ ☐ |
| 2822 | **1932** | (1st) | multicoloured | 2·50 | 2·50 | ☐ ☐ |
| 2823 | **1933** | (1st) | multicoloured | 2·50 | 2·50 | ☐ ☐ |
| 2824 | **1934** | (1st) | multicoloured | 2·50 | 2·50 | ☐ ☐ |
| Set of 6 | | | | 15·00 | 15·00 | ☐ ☐ |

Nos. 2819/24 were issued in £2·04 booklets in which the surplus backing paper around each stamp was removed.

Nos. 2820 and 2822 were reissued on 28 October 2008 in separate sheets of 10 or 20 with circular se-tenant labels showing the Almond Blossom fairy (2820), Mr. Men or Noddy (2822).

Nos. 2819, 2820 and 2822 were issued again on 30 April 2009 in separate sheets of 10 or 20 with circular se-tenant labels showing Jeremy Fisher (2820), Wild Cherry fairy (2820), Little Miss Sunshine or Big Ears (2822).

No. 2819 was issued in sheets of 20 with se-tenant labels on 8 May 2010, for London 2010 Festival of Stamps. on 28 July 2011 for Philanippon '11 International Stamp Exhibition, Yokohama, on 18 June 2012 for Indonesia 2012 International Stamp Exhibition, Jakarta, on 10 May 2013 for Australia 2013 World Stamp Exhibition, on 2 August 2013 for Bangkok 2013 World Stamp Exhibition and on 1 December 2014 for Kuala Lumpur 2014 FIP Exhibition.

Nos. 2821 (and Nos. 2822/3) were issued, together with Nos. 2569, 2572, 2674 and four designs from **MS**3024, on 8 May 2010 in sheets of 20 with se-tenant greetings labels.

No. 2821 was issued on 12 February 2011 in sheets of 20 with se-tenant labels for Indipex International Stamp Exhibition.

No. 2821 was issued on 30 March 2011 in sheets of ten with se-tenant labels for the 50th Anniversary of the Jaguar E-type car.

No. 2823 was issued in sheets of 20 with se-tenant labels on 20 January 2012 (Lunar New Year – Year of the Dragon), 7 February 2013 (Lunar New Year – Year of the Snake) and 10 December 2013 (Lunar New Year – Year of the Horse), and 19 November 2014 (Lunar New year – Year of the Sheep)..

All these sheets were printed in lithography instead of photogravure.

For the miniature sheet entitled 'Celebrating Northern Ireland', issued 11 March 2008, see the Regionals section.

**2058** Lifeboat, Barra

**2059** Lifeboat approaching Dinghy, Appledore

**2060** Helicopter Winchman, Portland

**2061** Inshore lifeboat, St. Ives

**2062** Rescue Helicopter, Lee-on-Solent

**2063** Launch of Lifeboat, Dinbych-y-Pysgod, Tenby

### Rescue at Sea

**2008** (13 Mar.) 'All-over' phosphor. Perf 14½ × 14

| | | | | | | | |
|---|---|---|---|---|---|---|---|
| 2825 | **2058** | (1st) | multicoloured | 1·25 | 90 | | |
| 2826 | **2059** | 46p | multicoloured | 1·20 | 1·20 | | |
| 2827 | **2060** | 48p | multicoloured | 1·20 | 1·20 | | |
| 2828 | **2061** | 54p | multicoloured | 1·40 | 1·40 | | |
| 2829 | **2062** | 69p | multicoloured | 1·80 | 1·80 | | |
| 2830 | **2063** | 78p | multicoloured | 2·00 | 2·00 | | |
| Set of 6 | | | | 8·00 | 8·00 | | |
| First Day Cover | | | | | 10·00 | | |
| Presentation Pack (P.O. Pack No. 411) | | | 10·00 | | | | |
| PHQ Cards (set of 6) (309) | | | 4·50 | 14·00 | | | |
| Set of 6 Gutter Pairs | | | 18·00 | | | | |

*Nos. 2825/30 have interrupted perforations along the top and bottom edges of the stamps, the gaps in the perforations forming the three dots and three dashes that spell out 'SOS' in morse code.

**2064** Lysandra bellargus (Adonis Blue)

**2065** Coenagrion mercuriale (southern damselfly)

**2066** Formica rufibarbis (red-barbed ant)

**2067** Pareulype berberata (barberry carpet moth)

**2068** Lucanus cervus (stag beetle)

**2069** Cryptocephalus coryli (hazel pot beetle)

**2070** Gryllus campestris (field cricket)

**2071** Hesperia comma (silver-spotted skipper)

**2072** Pseudepipona herrichii (Purbeck mason wasp)

**2073** Gnorimus nobilis (noble chafer)

### 'Action for Species' (2nd series). Insects

**2008** (15 Apr.) Phosphor background. Perf 14½

| | | | | | | | |
|---|---|---|---|---|---|---|---|
| 2831 | **2064** | (1st) | multicoloured | 1·25 | 90 | | |
| | | a. | Block of 10. | | | | |
| | | | Nos. 2831/40. | 14·00 | 10·00 | | |
| 2832 | **2065** | (1st) | multicoloured | 1·25 | 90 | | |
| 2833 | **2066** | (1st) | multicoloured | 1·25 | 90 | | |
| 2834 | **2067** | (1st) | multicoloured | 1·25 | 90 | | |
| 2835 | **2068** | (1st) | multicoloured | 1·25 | 90 | | |
| 2836 | **2069** | (1st) | multicoloured | 1·25 | 90 | | |
| 2837 | **2070** | (1st) | multicoloured | 1·25 | 90 | | |
| 2838 | **2071** | (1st) | multicoloured | 1·25 | 90 | | |
| 2839 | **2072** | (1st) | multicoloured | 1·25 | 90 | | |
| 2840 | **2073** | (1st) | multicoloured | 1·25 | 90 | | |
| Set of 10 | | | | 14·00 | 10·00 | | |
| First Day Cover | | | | | 11·00 | | |
| Presentation Pack (P.O. Pack No. 412) | | | 16·00 | | | | |
| PHQ Cards (set of 10) (310) | | | 9·00 | 16·00 | | | |
| Gutter Block of 20 | | | 30·00 | | | | |

Nos. 2831/40 were printed together, se-tenant, in blocks of ten (5 × 2) in sheets of 60 (2 panes of 30).

**2074** Lichfield Cathedral

**2075** Belfast Cathedral

**2076** Gloucester Cathedral

**2077** St. David's Cathedral

**2078** Westminster Cathedral

**2079** St. Magnus Cathedral, Kirkwall, Orkney

ST PAUL'S CATHEDRAL
BENEATH LIES BURIED THE FOUNDER OF THIS CHURCH AND CITY,
CHRISTOPHER WREN, WHO LIVED MORE THAN 90 YEARS,
NOT FOR HIMSELF BUT FOR THE PUBLIC GOOD.
READER, IF YOU SEEK HIS MONUMENT, LOOK AROUND YOU.

**2080** St. Paul's Cathedral

## Cathedrals

**2008** (13 May). 'All-over' phosphor. Perf 14½

| | | | | | | |
|---|---|---|---|---|---|---|
| 2841 | **2074** | (1st) | multicoloured | 1·25 | 90 | ☐ |
| 2842 | **2075** | 48p | multicoloured | 1·20 | 1·20 | ☐ |
| 2843 | **2076** | 50p | multicoloured | 1·30 | 1·30 | ☐ |
| 2844 | **2077** | 56p | multicoloured | 1·40 | 1·40 | ☐ |
| 2845 | **2078** | 72p | multicoloured | 1·80 | 1·80 | ☐ |
| 2846 | **2079** | 81p | multicoloured | 2·00 | 2·00 | ☐ |
| Set of 6 | | | | 8·00 | 8·00 | |
| First Day Cover | | | | | 10·00 | |
| Presentation Pack (P.O. Pack No. 413) | | | | 20·00 | | ☐ |
| PHQ Cards (set of 11) (311) | | | | 9·00 | 27·00 | ☐ ☐ |
| Set of 6 Gutter Pairs | | | | 17·00 | | |
| Set of 6 Traffic Light Gutter Pairs | | | | 20·00 | | |

**MS**2847 115 × 89 mm. (1st) multicoloured; (1st) multicoloured; 81p. multicoloured; 81p. multicoloured. Perf 14½ × 14 ... 7·00  7·00  ☐ ☐
First Day Cover ... 8·00  ☐

No. **MS**2847 commemorates the 300th anniversary of St. Paul's Cathedral.

The complete miniature sheet is shown on one of the eleven PHQ cards with the others depicting individual stamps including those from **MS**2847

## 'Beside the Seaside' (2nd series)

**2008** (13 May). As Type 1977 but self-adhesive. Two phosphor bands. Die-cut perf 14½

2848 1977 (1st) multicoloured ... 3·00  3·00  ☐ ☐

No. 2848 was only issued in £2·16 booklets.

**2081** 'Carry on Sergeant'

**2082** 'Dracula'

**2083** 'Carry on Cleo'

**2084** 'The Curse of Frankenstein'

**2085** 'Carry on Screaming'

**2086** 'The Mummy'

## Posters for Carry On and Hammer Horror Films

**2008** (10 June). Two phosphor bands. Perf 14

| | | | | | | |
|---|---|---|---|---|---|---|
| 2849 | **2081** | (1st) | multicoloured | 1·25 | 90 | ☐ |
| 2850 | **2082** | 48p | multicoloured | 1·20 | 1·20 | ☐ ☐ |
| 2851 | **2083** | 50p | multicoloured | 1·30 | 1·30 | ☐ ☐ |
| 2852 | **2084** | 56p | multicoloured | 1·40 | 1·40 | ☐ ☐ |
| 2853 | **2085** | 72p | multicoloured | 1·80 | 1·80 | ☐ ☐ |
| 2854 | **2086** | 81p | multicoloured | 2·00 | 2·00 | ☐ ☐ |
| Set of 6 | | | | 8·00 | 8·00 | ☐ |
| First Day Cover | | | | | 10·00 | ☐ |
| Presentation Pack (P.O. Pack No. 414) | | | | 10·00 | | ☐ |
| PHQ Cards (set of 6) (312) | | | | 4·50 | 14·00 | ☐ ☐ |
| PHQ Cards ("brick wall" background) and Stamps Set | | | | 9·00 | | ☐ |
| Set of 6 Gutter Pairs | | | | 18·00 | | ☐ |

Nos. 2849/54 commemorate the 50th anniversary of 'Dracula' and the first Carry On film ('Carry on Sergeant').

**2087** Red Arrows, Dartmouth Regatta Airshow, 2006

**2088** RAF Falcons Parachute Team, Biggin Hill, 2006

**2089** Spectator watching Red Arrows, Farnborough

**2090** Prototype Avro Vulcan Bombers and Avro 707s, Farnborough, 1953

**2091** Parachutist Robert Wyndham on Wing of Avro 504, 1933

**2092** Air Race rounding the Beacon, Hendon, c. 1912

## Air Displays

**2008** (17 July). Photo. Two phosphor bands. Perf 14½ × 14

| | | | | | | |
|---|---|---|---|---|---|---|
| 2855 | **2087** | (1st) | multicoloured | 1·25 | 90 | ☐ ☐ |
| 2856 | **2088** | 48p | multicoloured | 1·20 | 1·20 | ☐ ☐ |
| 2857 | **2089** | 50p | multicoloured | 1·30 | 1·30 | ☐ ☐ |

| | | | | | | | |
|---|---|---|---|---|---|---|---|
| 2858 **2090** | 56p multicoloured | 1·40 | 1·40 | ☐ | ☐ |
| 2859 **2091** | 72p multicoloured | 1·80 | 1·80 | ☐ | ☐ |
| 2860 **2092** | 81p multicoloured | 2·00 | 2·00 | ☐ | ☐ |
| *Set of 6* | | 8·00 | 8·00 | ☐ | ☐ |
| First Day Cover | | | 10·00 | | ☐ |
| Presentation Pack (P.O. Pack No. 415) | | 11·00 | | ☐ |
| PHQ Cards (*set of 6*) (313) | | 4·50 | 13·00 | ☐ | ☐ |
| *Set of 6 Gutter Pairs* | | 18·00 | | ☐ |

The 1st class stamp was also issued in sheets of 20 with *se-tenant* labels and, on 18 Sept., in booklets, both issues printed in lithography instead of photogravure. For the booklet stamps, see also No. 2869.

2093 Landmarks of Beijing and London

**Handover of Olympic Flag from Beijing to London miniature sheet**

**2008** (22 Aug.) Sheet 115 × 76 mm. Multicoloured. Phosphorised paper. Perf 14½
**MS**2861 2093 (1st) National Stadium, Beijing; (1st) London Eye; (1st) Tower of London; (1st) Corner Tower of the Forbidden City, Beijing

| | | | | | |
|---|---|---|---|---|---|
| Beijing | 7·00 | 7·00 | ☐ | ☐ |
| First Day Cover | | 8·00 | | ☐ |
| Presentation Pack (P.O. Pack No. M17) | 9·00 | | ☐ |
| PHQ Cards (*set of 5*) (OGH) | 4·00 | 15·00 | ☐ | ☐ |

The Olympic rings overprinted on **MS**2861 are in silk-screen varnish.

The five PHQ cards show the four individual stamps and the complete miniature sheet.

2094 Drum Major, RAF Central Band, 2007

2095 Helicopter Rescue Winchman, 1984

2096 Hawker Hunter Pilot, 1951

2097 Lancaster Air Gunner, 1944

2098 WAAF Plotter, 1940

2099 Pilot, 1918

**Military Uniforms (2nd series). RAF Uniforms**

**2008** (18 Sept.) Two phosphor bands. Perf 14

| | | | | | | |
|---|---|---|---|---|---|---|
| 2862 **2094** | (1st) multicoloured | 1·25 | 90 | ☐ | ☐ |
| | a. Horiz strip of 3. | | | | |
| | Nos. 2862/4 | 4·00 | 4·00 | ☐ | ☐ |
| 2863 **2095** | (1st) multicoloured | 1·25 | 90 | ☐ | ☐ |
| 2864 **2096** | (1st) multicoloured | 1·25 | 90 | ☐ | ☐ |
| 2865 **2097** | 81p multicoloured | 2·00 | 2·00 | ☐ | ☐ |
| | a. Horiz strip of 3. | | | | |
| | Nos. 2865/7 | 7·00 | 7·00 | ☐ | ☐ |
| 2866 **2098** | 81p multicoloured | 2·00 | 2·00 | ☐ | ☐ |
| 2867 **2099** | 81p multicoloured | 2·00 | 2·00 | ☐ | ☐ |
| *Set of 6* | | 10·00 | 10·00 | ☐ | ☐ |
| First Day Cover | | | 11·00 | | ☐ |
| Presentation Pack (P.O. Pack No. 416) | | 12·00 | | ☐ |
| PHQ Cards (*set of 6*) (314) | | 5·00 | 14·00 | ☐ | ☐ |
| *Set of 2 Gutter Strips of 6* | | 21·00 | | ☐ |
| *Set of 2 Traffic Light Gutter Blocks of 12* | 42·00 | | ☐ |

Nos. 2862/4 and 2865/7 were each printed together, *se-tenant*, in horizontal strips of three stamps in sheets of 60 (2 panes 6 × 5) and were also issued in the £7.15 'RAF Uniforms, 'Pilot to Plane' booklet.

**'Pilot to Plane'. RAF Uniforms. Booklet stamps**

**2008** (18 Sept.) Designs as Types 1307 (Spitfire from 1997 British Aircraft Designers) and 2087 (Red Arrows from 2008 Air Displays) but printed in lithography. Two phosphor bands. Perf 14

| | | | | | | |
|---|---|---|---|---|---|---|
| 2868 **1307** | 20p multicoloured | 4·00 | 4·00 | ☐ | ☐ |
| 2869 **2087** | (1st) multicoloured | 4·00 | 4·00 | ☐ | ☐ |

Nos. 2868/9 were only available from the £7·15 'RAF Uniforms, Pilot to Plane' booklet.

For the miniature sheet and booklet stamps issued 29 Sept. 2008 to celebrate the 50th Anniversary of the Country Definitives, see the Regional section.

2100 Millicent Garrett Fawcett (suffragist)

2101 Elizabeth Garrett Anderson (physician–women's health)

2102 Marie Stopes (family planning pioneer)

2103 Eleanor Rathbone (family allowance campaigner)

2104 Claudia Jones (civil rights activist)

2105 Barbara Castle (politician–Equal Pay Act)

## Women of Distinction

**2008** (14 Oct.) 'All-over' phosphor. Perf 14 × 14½

| | | | | | | | |
|---|---|---|---|---|---|---|---|
| 2870 | **2100** | (1st) | multicoloured | 1·25 | 90 | ☐ | ☐ |
| 2871 | **2101** | 48p | multicoloured | 1·20 | 1·20 | ☐ | ☐ |
| 2872 | **2102** | 50p | multicoloured | 1·30 | 1·30 | ☐ | ☐ |
| 2873 | **2103** | 56p | multicoloured | 1·40 | 1·40 | ☐ | ☐ |
| 2874 | **2104** | 72p | multicoloured | 1·80 | 1·80 | ☐ | ☐ |
| 2875 | **2105** | 81p | multicoloured | 2·00 | 2·00 | ☐ | ☐ |
| *Set of* 6 | | | | 8·00 | 8·00 | ☐ | ☐ |
| First Day Cover | | | | | 9·00 | | ☐ |
| Presentation Pack (P.O. Pack No. 417) | | | | 10·00 | | ☐ | |
| PHQ Cards (*set of* 6) (315) | | | | 4·50 | 13·00 | ☐ | ☐ |
| *Set of* 6 Gutter Pairs | | | | 17·00 | | ☐ | |

**2106** Ugly Sisters from Cinderella

**2107** Genie from Aladdin

**2108** Ugly Sisters from Cinderella

**2109** Captain Hook from Peter Pan

**2110** Genie from Aladdin

**2111** Wicked Queen from Snow White

## Christmas. Pantomimes

**2008** (4 Nov.) One centre band (2nd) or two phosphor bands (others). Perf 15 × 14

(a) Self-adhesive

| | | | | | | | |
|---|---|---|---|---|---|---|---|
| 2876 | 2106 | (2nd) | multicoloured | 1·00 | 60 | ☐ | ☐ |
| 2877 | 2107 | (1st) | multicoloured | 1·25 | 90 | ☐ | ☐ |
| 2878 | 2108 | (2nd Large) | multicoloured | 1·50 | 1·10 | ☐ | ☐ |
| 2879 | **2109** | 50p | multicoloured | 1·30 | 1·30 | ☐ | ☐ |
| 2880 | **2110** | (1st Large) | multicoloured | 2·00 | 1·50 | ☐ | ☐ |
| 2881 | **2111** | 81p | multicoloured | 2·00 | 2·00 | ☐ | ☐ |
| *Set of* 6 | | | | 8·00 | 7·00 | ☐ | ☐ |
| First Day Cover | | | | | 8·00 | | ☐ |
| Presentation Pack (P.O. Pack No. 418) | | | | 10·00 | | ☐ | |
| PHQ Cards (*set of* 7) (316) | | | | 6·00 | 24·00 | ☐ | ☐ |

(b) Ordinary gum

**MS**2882 114 × 102 mm.

| | | | | |
|---|---|---|---|---|
| As Nos. 2876/81 | 8·00 | 8·00 | @@ | |
| First Day Cover | | 9·00 | | ☐ |

The phosphor bands on Nos. 2878/9 are at the centre and right of each stamp.

The seven PHQ cards depict the six stamps and **MS**2882.

The 2nd class, 1st class and 81p stamps were also issued in sheets of 20 printed in lithography instead of photogravure containing eight 1st class, eight 2nd class and four 81p stamps, each stamp accompanied by a *se-tenant* label. Separate sheets of 20 1st, 20 2nd, 10 1st or 10 81p were available with personal photographs.

**2112** Poppies on Barbed Wire Stems

**2113** Soldiers in Poppy Flower

**2114** Soldier's Face in Poppy Flower

**2115**

## 'Lest We Forget' (3rd issue). 90th Anniversary of the Armistice

**2008** (6 Nov.) Phosphor background (No. 2885) or two phosphor bands (others). Perf 14½ (1st) or 15 × 14 (with one elliptical hole in each vertical side) (81p)

| | | | | | | | |
|---|---|---|---|---|---|---|---|
| 2883 | 2112 | (1st) | multicoloured | 1·25 | 90 | ☐ | ☐ |
| | | a. | Horiz strip of 3. | | | | |
| | | | Nos. 2883/5 | 4·00 | 4·00 | ☐ | ☐ |
| 2884 | 2113 | (1st) | multicoloured | 1·25 | 90 | ☐ | ☐ |
| 2885 | 2114 | (1st) | multicoloured | 1·25 | 90 | ☐ | ☐ |
| *Set of* 3 | | | | 4·00 | 4·00 | ☐ | ☐ |
| Presentation Pack (P.O. Pack No. 419) | | | | 16·00 | | ☐ | |
| PHQ Cards (*set of* 6) (317) | | | | 4·75 | 14·00 | ☐ | ☐ |
| Gutter Strip of 6 | | | | 9·00 | | ☐ | |
| Traffic Light Gutter Block of 12 | | | | 19·00 | | ☐ | |
| **MS**2886 124 × 70 mm. **2115** No. 2885 | | | | | | | |
| and as Nos. EN19, W111, S122 and | | | | | | | |
| NI129 | | | | 10·00 | 10·00 | ☐ | ☐ |
| First Day Cover | | | | | 11·00 | | ☐ |

Nos. 2883/5 were printed together, *se-tenant*, in horizontal strips of three stamps in sheets of 30.

No. **MS**2886 (including the Northern Ireland, Scotland and Wales stamps) is printed in lithography.

The six PHQ cards depict Nos. **MS**2685, **MS**2796 and 2883/ **MS**2886.

The 1st class stamp was also issued in sheets of 20 with se-tenant labels.

## Collectors Pack

**2008** (6 Nov.) Comprises Nos. 2797/802, 2806/**MS**2818, 2825/ **MS**2847, 2849/67, 2870/81, **MS**2886 and **MS**NI152

| | | | |
|---|---|---|---|
| CP2886a | Collectors Pack | £140 | ☐ |

## Post Office Yearbook

**2008** (6 Nov.) Comprises Nos. 2797/802, 2806/**MS**2818, 2825/**MS**2847, 2849/67, 2870/81, **MS**2886 and **MS**N152/3

| | | |
|---|---|---|
| YB2886a | Yearbook | £125 |

## Miniature Sheet Collection

**2008** (6 Nov.) Comprises Nos. **MS**2803, **MS**2818, **MS**2847, **MS**2861, **MS**2882, **MS**2886 and **MS**NI152/3

**MS**2886a Miniature Sheet Collection   75·00

|ST
**2116** Supermarine Spitfire
(R. J. Mitchell)

Supermarine Spitfire
Designed by R J Mitchell

|ST
**2117** Mini Skirt
(Mary Quant)

Mini Skirt
Designed by Mary Quant

|ST
**2118** Mini
(Sir Alec Issigonis)

Mini
Designed by Sir Alec Issigonis

|ST
**2119** Anglepoise Lamp
(George Carwardine)

Anglepoise Lamp
Designed by George Carwardine

|ST
**2120** Concorde
(Aérospatiale-BAC)

Concorde
Designed by Aérospatiale-BAC

|ST
**2121** K2 Telephone Kiosk
(Sir Giles Gilbert Scott)

K2 Telephone Kiosk
Designed by Sir Giles Gilbert Scott

|ST
**2122** Polypropylene Chair
(Robin Day)

Polypropylene Chair
Designed by Robin Day

|ST
**2123** Penguin Books
(Edward Young)

Penguin Books
Designed by Edward Young

|ST
**2124** London
Underground Map

London Underground Map
Designed by Harry Beck

|ST
**2125** Routemaster Bus
(design team led by AAM Durrant)

Routemaster Bus
Design team led by AAM Durrant

## British Design Classics (1st issue)

**2009** (13 Jan.) Printed in lithography. Phosphor background. Perf 14½

| | | | | | | |
|---|---|---|---|---|---|---|
| 2887 | **2116** | (1st) | multicoloured | 1·25 | 90 | ☐ ☐ |
| | | a. | Block of 10. Nos. | | | |
| | | | 2887/96 | 14·00 | 12·00 | ☐ ☐ |
| 2888 | **2117** | (1st) | multicoloured | 1·25 | 90 | ☐ ☐ |

| | | | | | | |
|---|---|---|---|---|---|---|
| 2889 | **2118** | (1st) | multicoloured | 1·25 | 90 | ☐ ☐ |
| 2890 | **2119** | (1st) | multicoloured | 1·25 | 90 | ☐ ☐ |
| 2891 | **2120** | (1st) | multicoloured | 1·25 | 90 | ☐ ☐ |
| 2892 | **2121** | (1st) | multicoloured | 1·25 | 90 | ☐ ☐ |
| 2893 | **2122** | (1st) | multicoloured | 1·25 | 90 | ☐ ☐ |
| 2894 | **2123** | (1st) | multicoloured | 1·25 | 90 | ☐ ☐ |
| 2895 | **2124** | (1st) | multicoloured | 1·25 | 90 | ☐ ☐ |
| 2896 | **2125** | (1st) | multicoloured | 1·25 | 90 | ☐ ☐ |
| *Set of* 10 | | | | 14·00 | 12·00 | ☐ |
| First Day Cover | | | | | 13·00 | ☐ |
| Presentation Pack (P.O. Pack No. 421) | | | | 16·00 | | ☐ |
| PHQ Cards (*set of* 10) (318) | | | | 9·00 | 20·00 | ☐ ☐ |
| Gutter Block of 20 | | | | 28·00 | | ☐ |

Nos. 2887/96 were printed together, *se-tenant*, in blocks of ten (2×5) throughout the sheet and also in the £7·68 'British Design Classics' booklet.

No. 2889 was also issued in sheets of 20 with *se-tenant* labels, perforated 14×14½, on 13 January 2009.

No. 2891 was also issued in sheets of 20 with *se-tenant* labels, perforated 14×14½, issued on 2 March 2009.

No. 2887 was also issued on 15 September 2010 in sheets of 20 with *se-tenant* labels, perforated 14×14½.

### British Design Classics (2nd issue). Booklet stamp

**2009** (13 Jan.) Design as Type 1589 (Concorde from 2002 Passenger Jet Aviation) but printed in lithography. Two phosphor bands. Perf 14½

| | | | | | | |
|---|---|---|---|---|---|---|
| 2897 | **1589** | (1st) | multicoloured | 10·00 | 9·50 | ☐ ☐ |

No. 2897 was only issued in the £7·68 'British Design Classics' booklet. For the miniature sheet celebrating the 250th anniversary of the Birth of Robert Burns, issued 22 Jan. 2009, see the Regionals section.

See also Nos. 2911/15b.

**2126** Charles Darwin

**2127** Marine Iguana

**2128** Finches

**2129** Atoll

**2130** Bee Orchid

**2131** Orang-utan

**2132** Fauna and Map of the Galapagos Islands

### Birth Bicentenary of Charles Darwin (naturalist and evolutionary theorist) (1st issue)

**2009** (12 Feb.)

(a) Self-adhesive. Printed in photogravure. 'All-over' phosphor. Perf 14

| | | | | | | |
|---|---|---|---|---|---|---|
| 2898 | **2126** | (1st) | multicoloured | 1·25 | 90 | |
| 2899 | **2127** | 48p | multicoloured | 1·20 | 1·20 | |
| 2900 | **2128** | 50p | multicoloured | 1·30 | 1·30 | |
| 2901 | **2129** | 56p | multicoloured | 1·40 | 1·40 | |
| 2902 | **2130** | 72p | multicoloured | 1·80 | 1·80 | |
| 2903 | **2131** | 81p | multicoloured | 2·00 | 2·00 | |

| | | |
|---|---|---|
| Set of 6 | 8·00 | 8·00 |
| First Day Cover | | 10·00 |
| Presentation Pack (P.O. Pack No. 423) | 18·00 | |
| PHQ Cards (set of 11) (320) | 9·00 | 20·00 |

(b) Ordinary gum. Printed in lithography. Two phosphor bands. Perf 14

**MS**2904   115×89 mm.   **2132**   (1st) Flightless Cormorant; Giant Tortoise and Cactus Finch; 81p Marine Iguana; 81p Floreana Mockingbird 8·00 8·00

| | |
|---|---|
| First Day Cover | 9·00 |

Nos. 2898/903 have 'jigsaw' perforations on the two vertical sides.

The complete miniature sheet is shown on one of the eleven PHQ cards with the others depicting individual stamps including those from **MS**2904.

### Birth Bicentenary of Charles Darwin (naturalist) (2nd issue). Booklet stamps

**2009** (12 Feb.) Printed in photogravure. 'All-over' phosphor. Perf 14

| | | | | | |
|---|---|---|---|---|---|
| 2905 | **2126** | (1st) | multicoloured | 4·50 | 4·50 |
| 2906 | **2127** | 48p | multicoloured | 5·00 | 5·00 |
| 2907 | **2128** | 50p | multicoloured | 5·50 | 5·50 |
| 2908 | **2129** | 56p | multicoloured | 6·00 | 6·00 |
| 2909 | **2130** | 72p | multicoloured | 6·50 | 6·50 |
| 2910 | **2131** | 81p | multicoloured | 7·00 | 7·00 |

| | | |
|---|---|---|
| Set of 6 | 30·00 | 30·00 |

Nos. 2905/10 were only issued in the £7·75 'Charles Darwin' booklet. They have 'jigsaw' perforations on both vertical sides.

**2132a**

**2132b**

**2132c**

**2132d**

**2009** (17 Feb.)–14. Self-adhesive. Designs as T **367**, T **913/14** or T **2132a/d**. One centre band (U2957, U3001) or two bands (others). U-shaped slits. Die-cut perf 14½×14 (with one elliptical hole in each vertical side).

(a) Self-adhesive. As T **367**. Iridescent overprint. Printed in gravure

| | | | | | | |
|---|---|---|---|---|---|---|
| U2920 | 1p | crimson (3.1.13) | | 10 | 10 | |
| U2921 | 2p | deep green (3.1.13) | | 10 | 10 | |
| U2922 | 5p | dull red-brown (3.1.13) | | 10 | 10 | |
| U2923 | 10p | dull orange (3.1.13) | | 20 | 20 | |
| U2924 | 20p | bright green (3.1.13) | | 40 | 40 | |
| U2911 | 50p | grey | | 1·50 | 1·50 | |
| U2925 | 50p | slate (3.1.13) | | 1·00 | 1·00 | |
| U2926 | 68p | deep turquoise-green (29.3.11) | | 2·00 | 2·00 | |
| U2927 | 76p | bright rose (29.3.11) | | 2·00 | 2·00 | |
| U2928 | 78p | deep mauve (27.3.13) | | 2·00 | 2·00 | |
| U2928a | 81p | emerald (26.3.13) | | 2·00 | 2·00 | |
| U2929 | 87p | yellow-orange (25.4.12) | | 2·00 | 2·00 | |
| U2930 | 88p | orange-yellow (27.3.13) | | 2·25 | 2·25 | |
| U2930a | 97p | bluish-violet (26.3.14) | | 2·50 | 2·50 | |
| U2912 | £1 | magenta | | 3·50 | 2·25 | |
| U2932 | £1 | bistre-brown (3.1.13) | | 2·25 | 2·25 | |
| U2933 | £1·10 | yellow-olive (29.3.11) | | 3·25 | 3·25 | |
| U2934 | £1·28 | emerald (25.4.12) | | 2·75 | 2·75 | |
| U2934a | £1·47 | lavender-grey (26.3.14) | | 3·50 | 3·50 | |
| U2913 | £1·50 | brown-red | | 3·25 | 3·25 | |
| U2935 | £1·65 | grey-olive (29.3.11) | | 3·50 | 3·50 | |
| U2936 | £1·88 | dull ultramarine (27.3.13) | | 3·75 | 3·75 | |
| U2937 | £1·90 | bright mauve (25.4.12) | | 3·75 | 3·75 | |
| U2914 | £2 | deep blue-green | | 5·00 | 4·25 | |
| U2939 | £2·15 | greenish-blue (26.3.14) | | 5·00 | 5·00 | |
| U2915 | £3 | deep mauve | | 6·25 | 6·25 | |
| U2916 | £5 | azure | | 10·50 | 10·50 | |

| | | |
|---|---|---|
| Set of 23 | 46·00 | 46·00 |
| First Day Cover (Nos. U2941/4 and U2911/12) | | 14·00 |
| First Day Cover (Nos. U2913/16) | | 30·00 |
| First Day Cover (Nos. U2926/7, U2933, U2935) | | 10·50 |
| First Day Cover (Nos. U2929, U2934, U2937 and U3276) | | 14·00 |
| First Day Cover (Nos. U2928, U2930, U2936, U2983a and U2984a) | | 16·00 |
| First Day Cover (Nos. U2928a, U2930a, U2934a, and U2939 | | 17·00 |
| Presentation Pack (Nos. U2941/4 and U2911/12) (P.O. Pack No· 82) | | 14·00 |
| Presentation Pack (Nos. U2913/16) (P.O. Pack No. 83) | | 30·00 |
| Presentation Pack (Nos. U2926/7, U2933, U2935 and U2991/5) (P.O. Pack No. 90) | | 30·00 |
| Presentation Pack (Nos. U2929, U2934, U2937, U3271 and U3276) (P·O· Pack No. 94) | | 14·00 |
| Presentation Pack (Nos· U2920/5, U2932, U2958a and U2960a (P.O. Pack No. 96) | | 10·00 |
| Presentation Pack (Nos. U2928, U2930, U2936, U2983a and U2984a)(P.O. Pack No. 97) | | 16·00 |
| Presentation Pack (Nos. U2928a, U2930a, U2934a, and U2939)( P.O. Pack No. 99) | | 16·00 |

(b) Self-adhesive. As T **913/14**, T **1916** or T **2132a/d**. Iridescent overprint. Printed in gravure

| | | | | | | |
|---|---|---|---|---|---|---|
| U2957 | (2nd) | bright blue (1.7.10) | | 1·50 | 1·25 | |

| | | | | | | |
|---|---|---|---|---|---|---|
| U2958 | (1st) | gold *(20.5.10)* | 2·75 | 80 | ☐ | ☐ |
| U3271 | (1st) | slate-blue *(6.2.12)* | 1·25 | 1·25 | ☐ | ☐ |
| U2958a | (1st) | vermilion *(3.1.13)* | 1·25 | 1·10 | ☐ | ☐ |
| U2959 | (2nd Large) bright blue *(26.1.11)* | | 2·00 | 90 | ☐ | ☐ |
| U2960 | (1st Large) | gold *(3.11.10)* | 3·00 | 1·10 | ☐ | ☐ |
| U3276 | (1st Large) | slate-blue *(25.4.12)* | 2·00 | 2·00 | ☐ | ☐ |
| U2960a | (1st Large) vermilion *(3.1.13)* | | 1·75 | 1·75 | ☐ | ☐ |

|  |  |  |  |  |
|---|---|---|---|---|
| U2981 (Recorded Signed for 1st) bright orange-red and lemon *(17.11.09)* | | 4·00 | 2·25 | ☐ ☐ |
| U2983a (Royal Mail Signed for 1st)bright orange-red and lemon *(27.3.13)* | | 3·75 | 3·50 | ☐ ☐ |
| U2982 (Recorded Signed for 1st Large) bright orange-red and lemon *(17.11.09)* | | 4·50 | 2·75 | ☐ ☐ |
| U2984a (Royal Mail Signed for 1st Large) bright orange-red and lemon *(27.3.13)* | | 4·25 | 4·00 | ☐ ☐ |
| U2985 (Special Delivery up to 100g) blue and silver *(26.10.10)* | | 10·00 | 10·00 | ☐ ☐ |
| U2986 (Special Delivery up to 500g) blue and silver *(26.10.10)* | | 11·00 | 11·00 | ☐ ☐ |
| First Day Cover (Nos. U2981/2) | | | 6·75 | ☐ ☐ |
| First Day Cover (Nos. U2985/6) | | | 25·00 | ☐ ☐ |
| Presentation Pack (Nos. U2985/6) (P.O. Pack No. 89) | | 25·00 | | ☐ ☐ |

**(c) Self-adhesive. Designs as T 367. No iridescent overprint. Printed in gravure**

| | | | | | | |
|---|---|---|---|---|---|---|
| U2991 | 1p | crimson *(8.3.11)* | 40 | 10 | ☐ | ☐ |
| U2992 | 2p | deep green *(8.3.11)* | 30 | 10 | ☐ | ☐ |
| U2993 | 5p | dull red-brown *(8.3.11)* | 30 | 10 | ☐ | ☐ |
| U2994 | 10p | dull orange *(8.3.11)* | 40 | 25 | ☐ | ☐ |
| U2995 | 20p | bright green *(8.3.11)* | 50 | 50 | ☐ | ☐ |
| *Set of 5* | | | 1·50 | 1·00 | ☐ | ☐ |
| First Day Cover (Nos. U2991/5) | | | 13·00 | | ☐ | ☐ |

**(d) Ordinary gum. Designs as T 367 and T 913/14. Iridescent overprint. Printed in gravure**

| | | | | | | |
|---|---|---|---|---|---|---|
| U3001 | (2nd) | bright blue *(13.5.10)* | 3·00 | 3·00 | ☐ | ☐ |
| U3002 | (1st) | gold *(13.5.10)* | 3·25 | 3·25 | ☐ | ☐ |
| U3005 | 68p | turquoise-green *(10.1.12)* | 3·75 | 3·75 | ☐ | ☐ |

**(e) Ordinary gum. As T 367 and T 913/14. Iridescent overprint. Printed in litho**

| | | | | | | |
|---|---|---|---|---|---|---|
| U3010 | 1p | crimson *(9.5.13)* | 1.00 | 1.00 | ☐ | ☐ |
| U3011 | 2p | deep green *(9.5.13)* | 1.00 | 1.00 | ☐ | ☐ |
| U3012 | 5p | red-brown *(26.3.13)* | 1.40 | 1.40 | ☐ | ☐ |
| U3013 | 10p | dull orange *(26.3.13)* | 1.75 | 1.75 | ☐ | ☐ |
| U3014 | 20p | bright green *(26.3.13)* | 1.25 | 1.25 | ☐ | ☐ |
| U3015 | (1st) | gold *(9.9.11)* | 3·75 | 3·50 | ☐ | ☐ |
| U3016 | (1st) | vermilion *(9.5.13)* | 1·50 | 1·50 | ☐ | ☐ |
| U3017 | 50p | slate-blue *(19.9.13)* | 2·00 | 2·00 | ☐ | ☐ |
| U3019 | 76p | bright rose *(9.9.11)* | 3·75 | 3·50 | ☐ | ☐ |
| U3020 | 87p | yellow-orange *(26.3.13)* | 2·25 | 2·25 | ☐ | ☐ |
| U3021 | £1 | sepia *(15.4.14)* | 4·50 | 4·50 | ☐ | ☐ |

No. U2981 originally sold for £1.14, U2982 for £1.36, U2983 for £5.05 and U2984 for £5.50.

No. U2983a was originally sold for £1.55 (£1.70 from 2 April 2013) and U2984a was originally sold for £1.85 (£2 from 2 April 2013).

On Nos. U3271 and U3276 the iridescent overprint reads 'DIAMOND JUBILEE'. The others have an iridescent overprint with the words 'ROYAL MAIL' repeated throughout.

Nos. U3001/2 were issued in coils of 500 or 1000.

Nos. U3005/21 all come from premium booklets as follows:

U3005 £11.47 Roald Dahl
U3010 £11.11 Football Heroes
U3011 £11.11 Football Heroes, £13.97 Classic Locomotives
· U3012 £13.77 Dr Who, £11.11 Football Heroes, £11.19 Merchant Navy, £13.97 Classic Locomotives
U3013 £13.77 Dr Who, £11.11 Football Heroes, £11.39 Buckingham Palace, £11.30 First World War Centenary
U3014 £13.77 Dr Who, £11.39 Buckingham Palace, £11.30 First World War Centenary
U3015 £9.97 Aerial Post Centenary
U3016 £11.11 Football Heroes
U3017 £11.19 Merchant Navy
U3019 £9.97 Aerial Post Centenary
U3020 £13.77 Dr Who
U3021 £11.39 Buckingham Palace, £11.30 First World War Centenary

For presentation pack containing Nos. U2981/2 see after No. Y1803.

Catalogue numbers U2941/4 from P.O. Pack No. 82 and first day cover are for 2nd bright blue, 1st gold, 2nd Large bright blue and 1st Large gold. They differ from the listed Nos. U2957/8 and U2959/60 by having no source or date codes in the iridescent overprint.

Catalogue numbers U2983/4 from P.O. Pack No. 89 and first day cover are for Recorded Signed for 1st and Recorded Signed for 1st Large. They differ from the listed Nos. U2983/4 by having source and date codes in the iridescent overprint.

Variations in the source and date codes incorporated into the iridescent overprint are outside the scope of this catalogue. Please refer to the Great Britain Concise Catalogue for further information. For the miniature sheet entitled 'Celebrating Wales', issued 26 Feb 2009, see the regionals section.

**British Design Classics (3rd series). Booklet stamps**

**2009** (10 Mar.)–10 Designs as Nos. 2887/9, 2891/2 and 2896. Printed in photogravure. Self-adhesive. Phosphor background. Die-cut perf 14½

| | | | | | | | |
|---|---|---|---|---|---|---|---|
| 2911 | **2121** | (1st) | multicoloured | 4·25 | 4·25 | ☐ | ☐ |
| 2912 | **2125** | (1st) | multicoloured | 4·25 | 4·25 | ☐ | ☐ |
| 2913 | **2118** | (1st) | multicoloured *(21.4.09)* | 3·25 | 2·50 | ☐ | ☐ |
| 2914 | **2120** | (1st) | multicoloured *(18.8.09)* | 3·25 | 2·50 | ☐ | ☐ |
| 2915 | **2117** | (1st) | multicoloured *(17.9.09)* | 3·25 | 2·50 | ☐ | ☐ |
| 2915b | **2116** | (1st) | multicoloured *(15.9.10)* | 3·25 | 2·50 | ☐ | ☐ |
| *Set of 6* | | | | 13·50 | 13·50 | ☐ | ☐ |

Nos. 2911/15b were only issued in booklets.

**2133** Matthew Boulton and Factory (manufacturing)

**2134** James Watt and Boulton & Watt Condensing Engine (steam engineering)

**2135** Richard Arkwright and Spinning Machine (textiles)

**2136** Josiah Wedgwood and Black Basalt Teapot and Vase (ceramics)

**2137** George Stephenson and Locomotion (railways)

**2138** Henry Maudslay and Table Engine (machine making)

**2139** James Brindley and Bridgewater Canal Aqueduct (canal engineering)

**2140** John McAdam (road building)

## Pioneers of the Industrial Revolution

**2009** (10 Mar.) 'All-over' phosphor. Perf 14×14½

| | | | | | | | |
|---|---|---|---|---|---|---|---|
| 2916 | 2133 | (1st) | multicoloured | 1·25 | 90 | | |
| | | a. | Horiz pair. | | | | |
| | | | Nos. 2916/17 | 2·75 | 2·75 | | |
| 2917 | 2134 | (1st) | multicoloured | 1·25 | 90 | | |
| 2918 | 2135 | 50p | multicoloured | 1·30 | 1·30 | | |
| | | a. | Horiz pair. | | | | |
| | | | Nos. 2918/19 | 3·00 | 3·00 | | |
| 2919 | 2136 | 50p | multicoloured | 1·30 | 1·30 | | |
| 2920 | 2137 | 56p | multicoloured | 1·40 | 1·40 | | |
| | | a. | Horiz pair. | | | | |
| | | | Nos. 2920/1 | 3·00 | 3·00 | | |
| 2921 | 2138 | 56p | multicoloured | 1·40 | 1·40 | | |
| 2922 | 2139 | 72p | multicoloured | 1·80 | 1·80 | | |
| | | a. | Horiz pair. | | | | |
| | | | Nos· 2922/3 | 4·00 | 4·00 | | |
| 2923 | 2140 | 72p | multicoloured | 1·80 | 1·80 | | |
| *Set of 8* | | | | 11·50 | 11·50 | | |
| First Day Cover | | | | | 13·00 | | |
| Presentation Pack (P.O. Pack No. 425) | | | | 14·00 | | | |
| PHQ Cards (*set of* 8) (321) | | | | 6·00 | 16·00 | | |
| *Set of 4 Gutter Strips of 4* | | | | 24·00 | | | |

Nos. 2916/17, 2918/19, 2920/1 and 2922/3 were each printed together, *se-tenant*, in horizontal pairs throughout the sheets.

**2141** Henry VII (1485–1509)

**2142** Henry VIII (1509–47)

**2143** Edward VI (1547–53)

**2144** Lady Jane Grey (1553)

**2145** Mary I (1553–8)

**2146** Elizabeth I (1558–1603)

**2147** The Age of the Tudors

## Kings and Queens (2nd issue). The House of Tudor

**2009** (21 Apr.) Two phosphor bands. Perf 14

| | | | | | | | |
|---|---|---|---|---|---|---|---|
| 2924 | **2141** | (1st) | multicoloured | 1·25 | 90 | | |
| 2925 | **2142** | (1st) | multicoloured | 1·25 | 90 | | |
| 2926 | **2143** | 62p | multicoloured | 1·60 | 1·60 | | |
| 2927 | **2144** | 62p | multicoloured | 1·60 | 1·60 | | |
| 2928 | **2145** | 81p | multicoloured | 2·10 | 2·10 | | |
| 2929 | **2146** | 81p | multicoloured | 2·10 | 2·10 | | |
| *Set of 6* | | | | 9·00 | 9·00 | | |
| First Day Cover | | | | | 10·00 | | |
| Presentation Pack (P.O. Pack No. 426) | | | | 18·00 | | | |
| PHQ Cards (*set of* 11) (322) | | | | 9·00 | 22·00 | | |
| *Set of 6 Gutter Pairs* | | | | 19·00 | | | |
| *Set of 6 Traffic Light Gutter Blocks of 4* | | | | 40·00 | | | |

**MS**2930 123×70 mm. 2147 (1st) *Mary Rose* (galleon), 1510; (1st) Field of Cloth of Gold Royal Conference, 1520; 90p Royal Exchange (centre of commerce), 1565; 90p Francis Drake (circumnavigation), 1580 — 7·00 — 7·00

First Day Cover — 8·00

The complete miniature sheet is shown on one of the eleven PHQ cards with the others depicting individual stamps including those from **MS**2930.

**2148** *Allium sphaerocephalon* (round-headed leek)

**2149** *Luronium natans* (floating water-plantain)

**2150** *Cypripedium calceolus* (lady's slipper orchid)

**2151** *Polygala amarella* (dwarf milkwort)

**2152** *Saxifraga hirculus* (marsh saxifrage)

**2153** *Stachys germanica* (downy woundwort)

**2154** *Euphorbia serrulata*
(upright spurge)

**2155** *Pyrus cordata*
(Plymouth pear)

**2156** *Polygonum maritimum*
(Sea knotgrass)

**2157** *Dianthus armeria*
(Deptford pink)

**2158** Royal Botanic Gardens, Kew

**'Action for Species' (3rd series). Plants and 250th Anniversary of Creation of Royal Botanic Gardens, Kew (MS2941)**

**2009** (19 May)

(a) Phosphor background. Perf 14½

| | | | | | | |
|---|---|---|---|---|---|---|
| 2931 | **2148** | (1st) | multicoloured | 1·25 | 90 | |
| | a. | Block of 10. | | | | |
| | | Nos. 2931/40 | 14·00 | 10·00 | | |
| 2932 | **2149** | (1st) | multicoloured | 1·25 | 90 | |
| 2933 | **2150** | (1st) | multicoloured | 1·25 | 90 | |
| 2934 | **2151** | (1st) | multicoloured | 1·25 | 90 | |
| 2935 | **2152** | (1st) | multicoloured | 1·25 | 90 | |
| 2936 | **2153** | (1st) | multicoloured | 1·25 | 90 | |
| 2937 | **2154** | (1st) | multicoloured | 1·25 | 90 | |
| 2938 | **2155** | (1st) | multicoloured | 1·25 | 90 | |
| 2939 | **2156** | (1st) | multicoloured | 1·25 | 90 | |
| 2940 | **2157** | (1st) | multicoloured | 1·25 | 90 | |
| *Set of* 10 | | | | 14·00 | 10·00 | |
| First Day Cover | | | | | 12·00 | |
| Presentation Pack (P.O. Pack No. 427) | | | 22·00 | | | |
| PHQ Cards (*set of* 15) (323) | | | 12·00 | 30·00 | | |
| Gutter Block of 10 | | | | 16·00 | | |

Nos. 2931/40 were printed together, *se-tenant*, in blocks of ten (5×2) throughout the sheet.

(b) Two phosphor bands. Perf 14×14½

**MS**2941  115×89 mm.  2158  (1st)
    Palm   House,  Kew  Gardens;
    (1st)  Millennium   Seed  Bank,
    Wakehurst Place; 90p  Pagoda,
    Kew   Gardens;  90p   Sackler
    Crossing, Kew Gardens    7·00   7·00
    First Day Cover                    8·00

The complete miniature sheet is shown on one of the 15 PHQ cards with the others depicting individual stamps including those from **MS**2941.

**50th Anniversary of NAFAS (National Association of Flower Arrangement Societies). Booklet stamps**

**2009** (21 May) Designs as Nos. 1958 and 1962 (1997 Greeting Stamps 19th-century FlowerPaintings) but printed in photogravure. Self-adhesive. Two phosphor bands. Die-cut perf 14 (with one elliptical hole in each vert side)

| | | | | | |
|---|---|---|---|---|---|
| 2942 | **1287** | (1st) | multicoloured | 4·00 | 4·00 |
| 2943 | **1283** | (1st) | multicoloured | 4·00 | 4·00 |

Nos. 2942/3 were only issued in £2.34 stamp booklets.

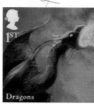

**2159** Dragon

**2160** Unicorn

**2161** Giant

**2162** Pixie

**2163** Mermaid

**2164** Fairy

**Mythical Creatures**

**2009** (16 June) 'All-over' phosphor. Perf 14½

| | | | | | |
|---|---|---|---|---|---|
| 2944 | **2159** | (1st) | multicoloured | 1·25 | 90 |
| 2945 | **2160** | (1st) | multicoloured | 1·25 | 90 |
| 2946 | **2161** | 62p | multicoloured | 1·60 | 1·60 |
| 2947 | **2162** | 62p | multicoloured | 1·60 | 1·60 |
| 2948 | **2163** | 90p | multicoloured | 2·25 | 2·25 |
| 2949 | **2164** | 90p | multicoloured | 2·25 | 2·25 |
| *Set of* 6 | | | | 9·00 | 9·00 |
| First Day Cover | | | | | 10·00 |
| Presentation Pack (P.O. Pack No. 428) | | | 11·00 | | |
| PHQ Cards (*set of* 6) (324) | | | 5·00 | 12·00 | |
| *Set of* 6 Gutter Pairs | | | 19·00 | | |

**2165** George V
Type B Wall Letter
Box, 1933–6

**2166** Edward VII
Ludlow Letter Box,
1901–10

**2167** Victorian Lamp Letter Box, 1896

**2168** Elizabeth II Type A Wall Letter Box, 1962–3

**2169** Post Boxes

**2170** Firefighting

**2171** Chemical Fire

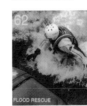

**2172** Emergency Rescue

**2173** Flood Rescue

**2174** Search and Rescue

**2175** Fire Safety

### Post Boxes

**2009** (18 Aug.) 'All-over' phosphor. Perf 14

| | | | | | | | |
|---|---|---|---|---|---|---|---|
| 2950 | **2165** | (1st) | multicoloured | 1·50 | 1·50 | ☐ | ☐ |
| 2951 | **2166** | 56p | multicoloured | 2·00 | 2·00 | ☐ | ☐ |
| 2952 | **2167** | 81p | multicoloured | 2·50 | 2·50 | ☐ | ☐ |
| 2953 | **2168** | 90p | multicoloured | 2·75 | 2·75 | ☐ | ☐ |
| *Set of 4* | | | | 8·50 | 8·50 | ☐ | ☐ |

**MS**2954 2169 145×74 mm.

| | | | | |
|---|---|---|---|---|
| Nos. 2950/3 | 7·00 | 7·00 | | @@ |
| First Day Cover | | 8·00 | | ☐ |
| Presentation Pack (P.O. Pack No. 430) | 8·00 | | ☐ | |
| PHQ Cards (*set of 5*) (325) | 4·00 | 10·00 | ☐ | ☐ |

Nos. 2950/3 were only issued in the £8·18 'Treasures of the Archive' booklet and in **MS**2954.

The five PHQ cards show the four individual stamps and the miniature sheet.

Type 2165 was also issued in sheets of 20 with *se-tenant* labels showing post boxes.

### 'Treasures of the Archive' (1st series). Booklet stamps

**2009** (18 Aug.) Designs as Type 929 (1990 150th anniv of the Penny Black) and 1446 (with with redrawn 1st face value). Printed in lithography. Two phosphor bands. Perf 14½ × 14 (with one elliptical hole in each vertical side)

| | | | | | | | |
|---|---|---|---|---|---|---|---|
| 2955 | **929** | 20p | brownish-black and grey-brown | 1·50 | 1·50 | ☐ | ☐ |
| 2956 | | (1st) | brownish-black and grey-brown | 1·50 | 1·50 | ☐ | ☐ |

Nos. 2955/6 were only issued in the £8·18 'Treasures of the Archive' stamp booklet.

### 'Treasures of the Archive' (2nd series). Booklet stamps

**2009** (18 Aug.) Design as Type 919 (1989 Lord Mayor's Show) but printed in lithography. 'All-over' phosphor. Perf 14

| | | | | | | |
|---|---|---|---|---|---|---|
| 2957 | **919** | 20p | multicoloured | 1·00 | 1·00 | ☐ ☐ |

No. 2957 was only available from £8·18 'Treasures of the Archive' stamp booklets.

### Fire and Rescue Service

**2009** (1 Sept.) 'All-over' phosphor. Perf 14×14½

| | | | | | | | |
|---|---|---|---|---|---|---|---|
| 2958 | **2170** | (1st) | multicoloured | 1·25 | 90 | ☐ | ☐ |
| 2959 | **2171** | 54p | multicoloured | 1·40 | 1·40 | ☐ | ☐ |
| 2960 | **2172** | 56p | multicoloured | 1·40 | 1·40 | ☐ | ☐ |
| 2961 | **2173** | 62p | multicoloured | 1·60 | 1·60 | ☐ | ☐ |
| 2962 | **2174** | 81p | multicoloured | 2·00 | 2·00 | ☐ | ☐ |
| 2963 | **2175** | 90p | multicoloured | 2·25 | 2·25 | ☐ | ☐ |
| *Set of 6* | | | | 10·00 | 10·00 | ☐ | ☐ |
| First Day Cover | | | | | 11·00 | | ☐ |
| Presentation Pack (P.O. Pack No. 429) | | | 12·00 | | | ☐ | |
| PHQ Cards (*set of 6*) (326) | | | 5·00 | 12·00 | | ☐ | ☐ |
| *Set of 6 Gutter Pairs* | | | | 21·00 | | ☐ | ☐ |

**2176** Flight Deck Officer, 2009

**2177** Captain, 1941

**2178** Second Officer WRNS, 1918

**2179** Able Seaman, 1880

**2180** Royal Marine, 1805

**2181** Admiral, 1795

**Military Uniforms (3rd series). Royal Navy Uniforms**

**2009** (17 Sept.) Phosphor background. Perf 14

| | | | | | | | |
|---|---|---|---|---|---|---|---|
| 2964 | **2176** | (1st) | multicoloured | 1·25 | 90 | ☐ | ☐ |
| | | a. | Horiz strip of 3. | | | | |
| | | | Nos. 2964/6 | 4·00 | 4·00 | ☐ | ☐ |
| 2965 | **2177** | (1st) | multicoloured | 1·25 | 90 | ☐ | ☐ |
| 2966 | **2178** | (1st) | multicoloured | 1·25 | 90 | ☐ | ☐ |
| 2967 | **2179** | 90p | multicoloured | 2·25 | 2·25 | ☐ | ☐ |
| | | a. | Horiz strip of 3. | | | | |
| | | | Nos. 2967/9 | 7·00 | 7·00 | ☐ | ☐ |
| 2968 | **2180** | 90p | multicoloured | 2·25 | 2·25 | ☐ | ☐ |
| 2969 | **2181** | 90p | multicoloured | 2·25 | 2·25 | ☐ | ☐ |
| *Set of* 6 | | | | 10·00 | 10·00 | ☐ | |
| First Day Cover | | | | | 11·00 | | ☐ |
| Presentation Pack (P.O. Pack No. 431) | | | | 12·00 | | ☐ | |
| PHQ Cards (*set of* 6) (327) | | | | 5·00 | 12·00 | ☐ | ☐ |
| *Set of* 2 Gutter Strips of 6 | | | | 21·00 | | ☐ | |
| *Set of* 2 Traffic Light Gutter Blocks of 12 | | | | 42·00 | | ☐ | ☐ |

Nos. 2964/6 and 2967/9 were each printed together, *se-tenant*, in horizontal strips of three stamps in sheets of 60 (2 panes 6×5) and in the £7.93 'Royal Navy' Uniforms booklet.

**Royal Navy Uniforms. Booklet stamp**

**2009** (17 Sept.) Design as Type 1518 (Jolly Roger flag from 2001 Submarine Centenary) but printed in lithography. Two phosphor bands. Perf 14½

| | | | | | | | |
|---|---|---|---|---|---|---|---|
| 2970 | **1518** | (1st) | multicoloured | 5·00 | 5·00 | ☐ | ☐ |

No. 2970 was only issued in the £7.93 'Royal Navy Uniforms' stamp booklet.

**2182** Fred Perry 1909–95 (lawn tennis champion)

**2183** Henry Purcell 1659–95 (composer and musician)

**2184** Sir Matt Busby 1909–94 (footballer and football manager)

**2185** William Gladstone 1809–98 (statesman and Prime Minister)

**2186** Mary Wollstonecraft 1759–97 (pioneering feminist)

**2187** Sir Arthur Conan Doyle 1859–1930 (writer and creator of Sherlock Holmes)

**2188** Donald Campbell 1921–67 (water speed record broken 1959)

**2189** Judy Fryd 1909–2000 (campaigner and founder of MENCAP)

**2190** Samuel Johnson 1709–84 (lexicographer, critic and poet)

**2191** Sir Martin Ryle 1918–84 (radio survey of the Universe 1959)

**Eminent Britons (1st series)**

**2009** (8 Oct.) Phosphor background. Perf 14½

| | | | | | | | |
|---|---|---|---|---|---|---|---|
| 2971 | **2182** | (1st) | multicoloured | 1·25 | 90 | ☐ | ☐ |
| | | a. | Horiz strip of 5. | | | | |
| | | | Nos. 2971/5 | 7·00 | 7·00 | ☐ | ☐ |
| 2972 | **2183** | (1st) | multicoloured | 1·25 | 90 | ☐ | ☐ |
| 2973 | **2184** | (1st) | multicoloured | 1·25 | 90 | ☐ | ☐ |
| 2974 | **2185** | (1st) | multicoloured | 1·25 | 90 | ☐ | ☐ |
| 2975 | **2186** | (1st) | multicoloured | 1·25 | 90 | ☐ | ☐ |
| 2976 | **2187** | (1st) | multicoloured | 1·25 | 90 | ☐ | ☐ |
| | | a. | Horiz strip of 5. | | | | |
| | | | Nos. 2976/80 | 7·00 | 7·00 | ☐ | ☐ |
| 2977 | **2188** | (1st) | multicoloured | 1·25 | 90 | ☐ | ☐ |
| 2978 | **2189** | (1st) | multicoloured | 1·25 | 90 | ☐ | ☐ |
| 2979 | **2190** | (1st) | multicoloured | 1·25 | 90 | ☐ | ☐ |
| 2980 | **2191** | (1st) | multicoloured | 1·25 | 90 | ☐ | ☐ |
| *Set of* 10 | | | | 13·00 | 13·00 | ☐ | |
| First Day Cover | | | | | 14·00 | | ☐ |
| Presentation Pack (P.O. Pack No. 432) | | | | 15·00 | 13·00 | ☐ | ☐ |
| PHQ Cards (*set of* 10) (328) | | | | 9·00 | 20·00 | ☐ | ☐ |
| *Set of* 2 Gutter Strips of 10 | | | | 28·00 | | ☐ | ☐ |

Nos. 2971/5 and 2976/80 were each printed together, se-tenant, in horizontal strips of five stamps throughout the sheets. No. 2980 includes the 'EUROPA' emblem.

**2192** Canoe Slalom

**2193** Paralympic Games Archery

**2194** Athletics: Track

**2195** Diving

**2196** Paralympic Games Boccia

**2197** Judo

**2205** Joseph (Henry Holiday), Parish Church of St. Michael, Minehead, Somerset

**2206** Madonna and Child (Henry Holiday), Church of Ormesby St. Michael, Great Yarmouth, Norfolk

**2207** Wise Man (Sir Edward Burne-Jones), Church of St. Mary the Virgin, Rye, East Sussex

**2198** Paralympic Games Dressage

**2199** Badminton

**2208** Shepherd (Henry Holiday), St. Mary's Church, Upavon, Wiltshire

### Christmas. Staned Glass windows

**2009** (3 Nov.) Photo. One centre band (2nd) or two phosphor bands (others). Perf 14½×14 (with one elliptical hole in- each vert side)

**2200** Weightlifting

**2201** Basketball

| (a) Self-adhesive | | | | |
|---|---|---|---|---|
| 2991 **2202** | (2nd) multicoloured | 1·00 | 60 | ☐ ☐ |
| 2992 **2203** | (1st) multicoloured | 1·25 | 85 | ☐ ☐ |
| 2993 **2204** | (2nd Large) multicoloured | 1·50 | 1·10 | ☐ ☐ |
| 2994 **2205** | 56p multicoloured | 1·40 | 1·40 | ☐ ☐ |
| 2995 **2206** | (1st Large) multicoloured | 2·00 | 1·25 | ☐ ☐ |
| 2996 **2207** | 90p multicoloured | 2·25 | 2·25 | ☐ ☐ |
| 2997 **2208** | £1·35 multicoloured | 3·50 | 3·00 | ☐ ☐ |
| Set of 7 | | 12·00 | 11·00 | ☐ ☐ |
| First Day Cover | | | 12·00 | ☐ |
| Presentation Pack (P.O. Pack No. 433) | | 14·00 | | ☐ ☐ |
| PHQ Cards (set of 8) (328) | | 6·00 | 16·00 | ☐ ☐ |

| (b) Ordinary gum | | | | |
|---|---|---|---|---|
| **MS**2998 115×102 mm. As Nos. 2991/7 | 12·00 | 11·00 | @@ |
| First Day Cover | | 12·00 | ☐ |

The eight PHQ cards show the seven individual stamps and the miniature sheet.

### Olympic and Paralympic Games, London (2012) (1st issue)

The 2nd class, 1st class, 56p and 90p stamps were also issued in sheets of 20 containing eight 2nd class, eight 1st class, two 56p and two 90p stamps, each stamp accompanied by a se-tenant label. Separate sheets of 20 2nd, 20 1st, ten 1st, ten 56p and ten 90p were available with personal photographs.

**2009** (22 Oct.) 'All-over' phosphor. Perf 14½

All these sheets wer printed in lithography instead of photgravure.

| 2981 **2192** | (1st) multicoloured | 1·25 | 90 | ☐ ☐ |
|---|---|---|---|---|
| | a. Horiz strip of 5. | | | |
| | Nos. 2981/5 | 7·00 | 7·00 | ☐ ☐ |
| 2982 **2193** | (1st) multicoloured | 1·25 | 90 | ☐ ☐ |
| 2983 **2194** | (1st) multicoloured | 1·25 | 90 | ☐ ☐ |
| 2984 **2195** | (1st) multicoloured | 1·25 | 90 | ☐ ☐ |
| 2985 **2196** | (1st) multicoloured | 1·25 | 90 | ☐ ☐ |
| 2986 **2197** | (1st) multicoloured | 1·25 | 90 | ☐ ☐ |
| | a. Horiz strip of 5. | | | |
| | Nos. 2986/90 | 7·00 | 7·00 | ☐ ☐ |
| 2987 **2198** | (1st) multicoloured | 1·25 | 90 | ☐ ☐ |
| 2988 **2199** | (1st) multicoloured | 1·25 | 90 | ☐ ☐ |
| 2989 **2200** | (1st) multicoloured | 1·25 | 90 | ☐ ☐ |
| 2990 **2201** | (1st) multicoloured | 1·25 | 90 | ☐ ☐ |
| Set of 10 | | 13·00 | 13·00 | ☐ ☐ |
| First Day Cover | | | 14·00 | ☐ |
| Presentation Pack (P.O. Pack No. M18) | | 15·00 | | ☐ ☐ |
| PHQ Cards (set of 10) (OXPG1) | | 9·00 | 20·00 | ☐ ☐ |
| Set of 2 Gutter Strips of 10 | | 27·00 | | ☐ ☐ |

For the 2nd class stampprinted in lithography with ordinary gum see No. 3186a.

### Collectors Pack

**2009** (3 Nov.) Comprises Nos. 2887/96, 2898/**MS**2904, 2916/**MS**2941, 2944/9, **MS**2954, 2958/69, 2971/97, **MS**S157 and **MS**W147

| CP2998a | Collectors Pack | £120 | ☐ ☐ |
|---|---|---|---|

Nos. 2981/5 and 2986/90 were each printed together, *se-tenant*, in horizontal strips of five stamps throughout the sheets and were also issued on 27 July 2011, in a sheetlet containing all 30 stamps in the series. See **MS**3204a.

See also Nos. 3020/3.

### Post Office Yearbook

**2009** (3 Nov.) Comprises Nos. 2887/96, 2898/**MS**2904, 2916/**MS**2941, 2944/9, **MS**2954, 2958/69, 2971/97, **MS**S157 and **MS**W147

| YB2998a | Yearbook | £130 | ☐ ☐ |
|---|---|---|---|

**2202** Angel playing Lute (William Morris), Church of St. James, Staveley, Kendal, Cumbria

**2203** Madonna and Child (Henry Holiday), Church of Ormesby St. Michael, Great Yarmouth, Norfolk

**2204** Angel playing Lute (William Morris), Church of St. James, Staveley, Kendal, Cumbria

### Miniature Sheet Collection

**2009** (3 Nov.) Comprises Nos. **MS**2904, **MS**2930, **MS**2941, **MS**2954, **MS**2998, **MS**S157 and **MS**W147

**MS**2998a Miniature Sheet Collection  70·00  ☐ ☐

**2209** *The Division Bell* (Pink Floyd)

**2210** *A Rush of Blood to the Head* (Coldplay)

**2211** *Parklife* (Blur)

**2212** *Power Corruption and Lies* (New Order)

**2213** *Let It Bleed* (Rolling Stones)

**2214** *London Calling* (The Clash)

**2215** *Tubular Bells* (Mike Oldfield)

**2216** *IV* (Led Zeppelin)

**2217** *Screamadelica* (Primal Scream)

**2218** The Rise and Fall of Ziggy Stardust and the Spiders from Mars (David Bowie)

### Classic Album Covers (1st issue)

**2010** (7 Jan.) "All-over" phosphor. Self-adhesive. Photo De La Rue. Die-cut perf 14½ (interrupted)

| | | | | | | |
|---|---|---|---|---|---|---|
| 2999 | **2209** | (1st) | multicoloured | 1·25 | 90 | ☐ ☐ |
| | a. | Horiz strip of 5. | | | | |
| | | Nos. 2999/3003 | | 7·00 | — | ☐ ☐ |
| 3000 | **2210** | (1st) | multicoloured | 1·25 | 90 | ☐ ☐ |
| 3001 | **2211** | (1st) | multicoloured | 1·25 | 90 | ☐ ☐ |
| 3002 | **2212** | (1st) | multicoloured | 1·25 | 90 | ☐ ☐ |
| 3003 | **2213** | (1st) | multicoloured | 1·25 | 90 | ☐ ☐ |
| 3004 | **2214** | (1st) | multicoloured | 1·25 | | ☐ ☐ |
| | a. | Horiz strip of 5. | | | | |
| | | Nos. 3004/8 | | 7·00 | — | ☐ ☐ |
| 3005 | **2215** | (1st) | multicoloured | 1·25 | 90 | ☐ ☐ |
| 3006 | **2216** | (1st) | multicoloured | 1·25 | 90 | ☐ ☐ |
| 3007 | **2217** | (1st) | multicoloured | 1·25 | 90 | ☐ ☐ |
| 3008 | **2218** | (1st) | multicoloured | 1·25 | 90 | ☐ ☐ |
| *Set of 10* | | | | 13·00 | 13·00 | ☐ ☐ |
| First Day Cover | | | | | 14·00 | ☐ |
| Presentation Pack (P.O. Pack No. 435) | | | 15·00 | | | ☐ ☐ |
| PHQ Cards (*set of 10*) (330) | | | 9·00 | 22·00 | | ☐ ☐ |

Nos. 2999/3003 and 3004/8 were each printed together as horizontal strips of five stamps in sheets of 50 (2 panes of 25).

### Classic Album Covers (2nd issue)

**2010** (7 Jan.) "All-over" phosphor. Litho Cartor. Perf 14½ (interrupted)

| | | | | | | |
|---|---|---|---|---|---|---|
| 3009 | **2213** | (1st) | multicoloured | 2·40 | 2·40 | ☐ ☐ |
| 3010 | **2216** | (1st) | multicoloured | 2·40 | 2·40 | ☐ ☐ |
| 3011 | **2218** | (1st) | multicoloured | 2·40 | 2·40 | ☐ ☐ |
| 3012 | **2212** | (1st) | multicoloured | 2·40 | 2·40 | ☐ ☐ |
| 3013 | **2217** | (1st) | multicoloured | 2·40 | 2·40 | ☐ ☐ |
| 3014 | **2209** | (1st) | multicoloured | 2·40 | 2·40 | ☐ ☐ |
| 3015 | **2215** | (1st) | multicoloured | 2·40 | 2·40 | ☐ ☐ |
| 3016 | **2214** | (1st) | multicoloured | 2·40 | 2·40 | ☐ ☐ |
| 3017 | **2211** | (1st) | multicoloured | 2·40 | 2·40 | ☐ ☐ |
| 3018 | **2210** | (1st) | multicoloured | 2·40 | 2·40 | ☐ ☐ |
| 3009/18 *Set of 10* | | | | 22·00 | 22·00 | ☐ ☐ |
| **MS**3019 223×189 mm. | | | | | | |
| | As Nos. 3009/18 | | | 30·00 | 30·00 | ☐ ☐ |
| First Day Cover | | | | | 32·00 | ☐ ☐ |

Nos. 3009/18 were only issued in the £8·06 'Classic Album Covers' and **MS**3019.

The right-hand edges of Nos. 2999/3018 and the miniature sheet **MS**3019 are all cut around in an imperforate section to show the vinyl disc protruding from the open edge of the album cover. Stamps from the miniature sheet have a white background, while those from the booklet have a brown background containing descriptive texts.

A miniature sheet containing No. 3014×10 The Division Bell (Pink Floyd) was issued on 6 March 2010 and sold for £4·75 per sheet.

### Olympic and Paralympic Games, London (2012) (2nd issue). Booklet stamps

**2010** (7 Jan.–25 Feb.) Designs as Nos. 2982/3, 2986 and 2990 but printed in photogravure. Self-adhesive. "All-over" phosphor. Die-cut perf 14½

| | | | | | | |
|---|---|---|---|---|---|---|
| 3020 | **2197** | (1st) | multicoloured | 2·75 | 2·75 | ☐ ☐ |
| 3021 | **2193** | (1st) | multicoloured | 2·75 | 2·75 | ☐ ☐ |
| 3022 | **2194** | (1st) | multicoloured | | | |
| | | | (25 Feb) | 2·75 | 2·75 | ☐ ☐ |
| 3023 | **2201** | (1st) | multicoloured | | | |
| | | | (25 Feb) | 2·75 | 2·75 | ☐ ☐ |
| *Set of 4* | | | | 10·00 | 10·00 | ☐ ☐ |

Nos. 3020/1 and 3022/3 were only issued in separate booklets, each originally sold for £2·34.

2219

### Business and Consumer Smilers

**2010** (26 Jan.) Sheet 124×71 mm. Multicoloured. Two phosphor bands. Perf 14½×14 (with one elliptical hole in each vertical side)

**MS**3024 2219 (1st) Propeller driven airplane; (1st) Vintage sports roadster; (1st) Recreation of crown seal; (1st) Birthday cake; (1st) Steam locomotive; (1st) Ocean liner; (1st) Poppies; (1st) Birthday present; (Europe up to 20 grams) Bird carrying envelope; (Worldwide up to 20 grams)

| | | | |
|---|---|---|---|
| "Hello" in plane vapour trail | 15·00 | 15·00 | ☐ ☐ |
| First Day Cover | | 16·00 | ☐ ☐ |
| Presentation Pack (P.O. Pack No. M19) | 18·00 | | ☐ ☐ |
| PHQ Cards (*set of* 11) (D31) | 9·00 | 22·00 | ☐ ☐ |

**MS**3024 was sold for £4·58.

The eleven PHQ cards show the ten individual stamps and the complete miniature sheet.

Stamps in designs as within **MS**3024 but self-adhesive were available printed together, *se-tenant*, in sheets of 20 containing two of each design with greetings labels.

The (1st) birthday cake, (1st) birthday present, Europe and Worldwide designs were also available in separate sheets with personal photographs.

A stamp as the crown seal design in **MS**3024 but self-adhesive was issued on 15 September 2011 in sheets of 20 with postmark labels for the 350th Anniversary of the Postmark.

The other 1st class designs were for the business customised service.

Stamps as the 1st Birthday cake (×4), 1st Birthday present (×4), Europe Bird carrying envelope (×2) and Worldwide "Hello" in plane vapour trail (×2) designs but self-adhesive were issued, together with Nos. 2569, 2572, 2674 and 2821/3 on 8 May 2010 in sheets of 20 stamps with *se-tenant* greetings labels.

**2220** Girlguiding UK

**Centenary of Girlguiding miniature sheet**

**2010** (2 Feb.) Sheet 190×67 mm. Multicoloured. Phosphor background. Perf 14×14½

| | | | |
|---|---|---|---|
| **MS**3025 2220 (1st) Rainbows; 56p Brownies; 81p Guides; 90p Senior Section members | 8·00 | 7·00 | ☐ ☐ |
| First Day Cover | | 8·00 | ☐ ☐ |
| Presentation Pack (P.O. Pack No. 436) | 12·00 | | ☐ ☐ |
| PHQ Cards (*set of* 5) (331) | 4·00 | 10·00 | ☐ ☐ |

The five PHQ cards show the four individual stamps and the complete miniature sheet.

**2221** Sir Robert Boyle (chemistry)

**2222** Sir Isaac Newton (optics)

**2223** Benjamin Franklin (electricity)

**2224** Edward Jenner (pioneer of smallpox vaccination)

**2225** Charles Babbage (computing)

**2226** Alfred Russel Wallace (theory of evolution)

**2227** Joseph Lister (antiseptic surgery)

**2228** Ernest Rutherford (atomic structure)

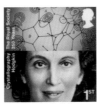

**2229** Dorothy Hodgkin (crystallography)

**2230** Sir Nicholas Shackleton (earth sciences)

**350th Anniversary of the Royal Society**

**2010** (25 Feb.) "All-over" phosphor. Perf 14½

| | | | | | |
|---|---|---|---|---|---|
| 3026 | **2221** | (1st) | multicoloured | 1·25 | 90 | ☐ ☐ |
| | | a. | Block of 10. Nos. 3026/35 | 15·00 | 13·00 | ☐ ☐ |
| 3027 | **2222** | (1st) | multicoloured | 1·25 | 90 | ☐ ☐ |
| 3028 | **2223** | (1st) | multicoloured | 1·25 | 90 | ☐ ☐ |
| 3029 | **2224** | (1st) | multicoloured | 1·25 | 90 | ☐ ☐ |
| 3030 | **2225** | (1st) | multicoloured | 1·25 | 90 | ☐ ☐ |
| 3031 | **2226** | (1st) | multicoloured | 1·25 | 90 | ☐ ☐ |
| 3032 | **2227** | (1st) | multicoloured | 1·25 | 90 | ☐ ☐ |
| 3033 | **2228** | (1st) | multicoloured | 1·25 | 90 | ☐ ☐ |
| 3034 | **2229** | (1st) | multicoloured | 1·25 | 90 | ☐ ☐ |
| 3035 | **2230** | (1st) | multicoloured | 1·25 | 90 | ☐ ☐ |
| Set of 10 | | | | 15·00 | 13·00 | ☐ ☐ |
| First Day Cover | | | | | 14·00 | ☐ ☐ |
| Presentation Pack (P.O. Pack No. 437) | | | | 17·00 | | ☐ ☐ |
| PHQ Cards (*set of* 10) (332) | | | | 9·00 | 20·00 | ☐ ☐ |
| Gutter Block of 20 | | | | 32·00 | | ☐ ☐ |

Nos. 3026/35 were printed together, *se-tenant*, as blocks of ten (5×2) in sheets of 60 (2 panes of 30) and were also issued in the £7.72 '350th Anniversary of the Royal Society' booklet.

**2231** "Pixie" (mastiff cross)

**2232** "Button"

**2233** "Herbie" (mongrel)

**2234** "Mr. Tumnus"

**2241** James I (1406–37)

**2242** James II (1437–60)

**2243** James III (1460–88)

**2235** "Tafka" (border collie)

**2236** "Boris" (bulldog cross)

**2244** James IV (1488–1513)

**2245** James V (1513–42)

**2246** Mary (1542–67)

**2237** "Casey" (lurcher)

**2238** "Tigger"

**2247** James VI (1567–1625)

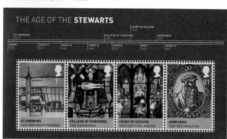

**2248** The Age of the Stewarts

**2239** "Leonard" (Jack Russell cross)

**2240** "Tia" (terrier cross)

## 150th Anniversary of Battersea Dogs and Cats Home.

**2010** (11 Mar.) Phosphor background. Perf 14½

| | | | | | | |
|---|---|---|---|---|---|---|
| 3036 | **2231** | (1st) | multicoloured | 1·25 | 90 | ☐ ☐ |
| | | a. Block of 10. | | | | |
| | | Nos. 3036/45 | | 15·00 | 13·00 | ☐ ☐ |
| 3037 | **2232** | (1st) | multicoloured | 1·25 | 90 | ☐ ☐ |
| 3038 | **2233** | (1st) | multicoloured | 1·25 | 90 | ☐ ☐ |
| 3039 | **2234** | (1st) | multicoloured | 1·25 | 90 | ☐ ☐ |
| 3040 | **2235** | (1st) | multicoloured | 1·25 | 90 | ☐ ☐ |
| 3041 | **2236** | (1st) | multicoloured | 1·25 | 90 | ☐ ☐ |
| 3042 | **2237** | (1st) | multicoloured | 1·25 | 90 | ☐ ☐ |
| 3043 | **2238** | (1st) | multicoloured | 1·25 | 90 | ☐ ☐ |
| 3044 | **2239** | (1st) | multicoloured | 1·25 | 90 | ☐ ☐ |
| 3045 | **2240** | (1st) | multicoloured | 1·25 | 90 | ☐ ☐ |
| *Set of 10* | | | | 15·00 | 13·00 | ☐ ☐ |
| First Day Cover | | | | | 14·00 | ☐ ☐ |
| Presentation Pack (P.O. Pack No. 438) | | | | 17·00 | | ☐ ☐ |
| PHQ Cards (*set of 10*) (333) | | | | 9·00 | 20·00 | ☐ ☐ |
| Gutter Block of 20 | | | | 32·00 | | ☐ ☐ |

Nos. 3036/45 were printed together, *se-tenant*, as blocks of ten (5×2) in sheets of 60 (2 panes of 30) .

## Kings and Queens (3rd issue). The House of Stewart

**2010** (23 Mar.) Two phosphor bands. Perf 14

| | | | | | | |
|---|---|---|---|---|---|---|
| 3046 | **2241** | (1st) | multicoloured | 1·25 | 90 | ☐ ☐ |
| 3047 | **2242** | (1st) | multicoloured | 1·25 | 90 | ☐ ☐ |
| 3048 | **2243** | (1st) | multicoloured | 1·25 | 90 | ☐ ☐ |
| 3049 | **2244** | 62p | multicoloured | 1·60 | 1·60 | ☐ ☐ |
| 3050 | **2245** | 62p | multicoloured | 1·60 | 1·60 | ☐ ☐ |
| 3051 | **2246** | 81p | multicoloured | 2·00 | 2·00 | ☐ ☐ |
| 3052 | **2247** | 81p | multicoloured | 2·00 | 2·00 | ☐ ☐ |
| *Set of 7* | | | | 10·00 | 10·00 | ☐ ☐ |
| First Day Cover | | | | | 11·00 | ☐ ☐ |
| Presentation Pack (P.O. Pack No. 439) | | | | 18·00 | | ☐ ☐ |
| PHQ Cards (*set of 12*) (334) | | | | 10·00 | 24·00 | ☐ ☐ |
| *Set of 7 Gutter Pairs* | | | | 21·00 | | ☐ ☐ |
| *Set of 7 Traffic Light Gutter Blocks of 4* | | | | 42·00 | | ☐ ☐ |

**MS**3053  123×70 mm. 2248 (1st) Foundation of the University of St. Andrews, 1413; (1st) Foundation of the College of Surgeons, Edinburgh, 1505; 81p Foundation of Court of Session, 1532; 81p John Knox (Reformation, 1559)  6·50  6·50  ☐ ☐

First Day Cover  7·50  ☐ ☐

The complete miniature sheet is shown on one of the twelve PHQ cards with the others depicting individual stamps including those from **MS**3053.

**2249** Humpback Whale (Megaptera novaeangliae)

**2250** Wildcat (Felis silvestris)

**2251** Brown Long-eared Bat (Plecotus auritus)

**2252** Polecat (Mustela putorius)

**2253** Sperm Whale (Physeter macrocephalus)

**2254** Water Vole (Arvicola terrestris)

**2255** Greater Horseshoe Bat (Rhinolophus ferrumequinum)

**2256** Otter (Lutra lutra)

**2257** Dormouse (Muscardinus avellanarius)

**2258** Hedgehog (Erinaceus europaeus)

## 'Action for Species' (4th series). Mammals.

**2010** (13 Apr.) 'All-over' phosphor. Perf 14½

| | | | | | | |
|---|---|---|---|---|---|---|
| 3054 | 2249 | (1st) multicoloured | 1·25 | 1·00 | ☐ | ☐ |
| | | a. Block of 10. | | | | |
| | | Nos. 3054/63 | 14·00 | 12·00 | ☐ | ☐ |
| 3055 | **2250** | (1st) multicoloured | 1·25 | 1·00 | ☐ | ☐ |
| 3056 | **2251** | (1st) multicoloured | 1·25 | 1·00 | ☐ | ☐ |
| 3057 | **2252** | (1st) multicoloured | 1·25 | 1·00 | ☐ | ☐ |
| 3058 | **2253** | (1st) multicoloured | 1·25 | 1·00 | ☐ | ☐ |
| 3059 | **2254** | (1st) multicoloured | 1·25 | 1·00 | ☐ | ☐ |
| 3060 | **2255** | (1st) multicoloured | 1·25 | 1·00 | ☐ | ☐ |
| 3061 | **2256** | (1st) multicoloured | 1·25 | 1·00 | ☐ | ☐ |
| 3062 | **2257** | (1st) multicoloured | 1·25 | 1·00 | ☐ | ☐ |
| 3063 | **2258** | (1st) multicoloured | 1·25 | 1·00 | ☐ | ☐ |
| *Set of* 10 | | | 14·00 | 12·00 | ☐ | ☐ |
| First Day Cover | | | | 13·00 | ☐ | ☐ |
| Presentation Pack (P.O. Pack No. 440) | | | 16·00 | | ☐ | ☐ |

| | | | | |
|---|---|---|---|---|
| PHQ Cards (*set of* 10) (335) | | 9·00 | 20·00 | ☐ ☐ |
| Gutter Block of 20 | | | 30·00 | ☐ ☐ |

Nos. 3054/63 were printed together, *se-tenant*, as blocks of ten (5×2) in sheets of 60 (2 panes of 30).

See also Nos. 3095/6.

No. 3064, and T 2259 are vacant.

**2260** King George V and Queen Elizabeth II (1st); Two portraits of King George V (£1)

### London 2010 Festival of Stamps and Centenary of Accession of King George V (1st issue)

**2010** (6 May) 'All-over' phosphor. Perf 14½×14. Sheet 141×74 mm

| | | | | |
|---|---|---|---|---|
| **MS**3065 2260 (1st) rosine; £1 blackish brown, grey-brown and silver | | 4·50 | 4·50 | ☐ ☐ |
| First Day Cover | | | 5·50 | ☐ ☐ |

A miniature sheet as No. **MS**3065 but inscr 'BUSINESS DESIGN CENTRE, LONDON 8–15 MAY 2010' along the top right margin was only available at London 2010 Festival of Stamps.

The eight PHQ cards depict the individual stamps from **MS**3065 and **MS**3072 and the complete miniature sheets.

**2261** King George V and Queen Elizabeth II

**2262** 1924 British Empire Exhibition 1½d. Brown Stamp

**2263** 1924 British Empire Exhibition 1d. Scarlet Stamp

**2264** Two Portraits of King George V

**2265** 1913 £1 Green 'Sea Horses' Design Stamp

**2266** 1913 10s. Blue 'Sea Horses' Design Stamp

**2267**

EXHIBITION SOUVENIR

**2268**

### London 2010 Festival of Stamps (3rd issue).
### Jeffery Matthews Colour Palette miniature sheet

**2010** (8 May) Sheet, 104×95 mm, containing stamps as T 367 with a label. Two phosphor bands. Perf 15×14 (with one elliptical hole in each vertical side).

| | | | |
|---|---|---|---|
| MS3073 **2268** 1p reddish purple; 2p deep grey-green; 5p reddish-brown; 9p bright orange; 10p orange; 20p light green; 60p emerald; 67p bright mauve; 88p bright magenta; 97p bluish violet; £1·46 turquoise-blue | 23·00 | 23·00 | ☐ ☐ |

### London 2010 Festival of Stamps (2nd issue) and
### Centenary of Accession of King George V

**2010** (6-8 May) Litho (Nos. 3066 and 3069) or recess and litho. 'All-over' phosphor. Perf 14½×14

| | | | | | | |
|---|---|---|---|---|---|---|
| 3066 | **2261** | (1st) | rosine (6 May) | 1·25 | 1·00 | ☐ ☐ |
| 3067 | **2262** | (1st) | multicoloured (8 May) | 1·25 | 1·00 | ☐ ☐ |
| 3068 | **2263** | (1st) | multicoloured (8 May) | 1·25 | 1·00 | ☐ ☐ |
| 3069 | **2264** | £1 | blackish brown, grey-brown and silver (8 May) | 2·50 | 2·50 | ☐ ☐ |
| 3070 | **2265** | £1 | multicoloured (8 May) | 2·50 | 2·50 | ☐ ☐ |
| 3071 | **2266** | £1 | multicoloured (8 May) | 2·50 | 2·50 | ☐ ☐ |
| 3066/71 | Set of 6 | | | 10·00 | 10·00 | ☐ ☐ |
| Gutter Pair (No. 3066) | | | | 3·00 | | ☐ ☐ |
| **MS**3072 115×90 mm. 2267 | | | | | | |
| Nos. 3067/8 and 3070/1 (8 May) | | | | 7·50 | 7·50 | ☐ ☐ |
| First Day Cover (**MS**3072) | | | | | 8·50 | ☐ |
| Presentation Pack (**MS**3065 and **MS**3072) | | | | | | |
| (P.O. Pack No. 441) | | | | 12·00 | | ☐ |
| PHQ Cards (set of 8) (336) | | | | 7·00 | 16·00 | ☐ ☐ |

No. 3066 was issued as a sheet stamp on 6 May 2010.

Nos. 3066/71 all come from the £11·15 '1910-1936, King George V' stamp booklet issued on 8 May 2010.

Nos. 3066 and 3069 also come from miniature sheet **MS**3065, issued on 6 May 2010.

Nos. 3067/8 and 3070/1 also come from **MS**3072, issued on 6 May 2010.

For presentation pack and PHQ cards for No. **MS**3072 see under **MS**3065.

**2269** Winston Churchill

**2270** Land Girl

**2271** Home Guard

**2272** Evacuees

**2273** Air Raid Wardens

**2274** Woman working in Factory

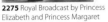

**2275** Royal Broadcast by Princess Elizabeth and Princess Margaret

**2276** Fire Service

### 'Britain Alone' (1st issue)

**2010** (13 May) 'All-over' phosphor. Perf 14½

| | | | | | | | |
|---|---|---|---|---|---|---|---|
| 3074 | **2269** | (1st) | pale stone, pale bistre and black | 1·25 | 1·00 | ☐ | ☐ |
| 3075 | **2270** | (1st) | pale stone, pale bistre and black | 1·25 | 1·00 | ☐ | ☐ |
| 3076 | **2271** | 60p | pale stone, pale bistre and black | 1·50 | 1·50 | ☐ | ☐ |
| 3077 | **2272** | 60p | pale stone, pale bistre and black | 1·50 | 1·50 | ☐ | ☐ |
| 3078 | **2273** | 67p | pale stone, pale bistre and black | 1·70 | 1·70 | ☐ | ☐ |
| 3079 | **2274** | 67p | pale stone, pale bistre and black | 1·70 | 1·70 | ☐ | ☐ |
| 3080 | **2275** | 97p | pale stone, pale bistre and black | 2·40 | 2·40 | ☐ | ☐ |
| 3081 | **2276** | 97p | pale stone, pale bistre and black | 2·40 | 2·40 | ☐ | ☐ |
| *Set of* 8 | | | | 12·00 | 12·00 | ☐ | ☐ |
| First Day Cover | | | | | 13·00 | | ☐ |
| Presentation Pack (P.O. Pack No. 442) | | | | 25·00 | | ☐ | |
| PHQ Cards (*set of* 13) (337) | | | | 11·00 | 29·00 | ☐ | ☐ |
| *Set of* 8 Gutter Pairs | | | | 25·00 | | ☐ | |

Nos. 3074/81 were also issued in the £9.76 'Britain Alone' booklet.

The thirteen PHQ cards depict Nos. 3074/85 and the complete miniature sheet **MS**3086.

**2277** Evacuation of British Soldiers from Dunkirk

**2278** Vessels from Upper Thames Patrol in 'Operation Little Ships'

**2279** Rescued Soldiers on Board Royal Navy Destroyer, Dover

**2280** Steamship and Other Boat loaded with Troops

**2281** Evacuation of British Troops from Dunkirk, 1940

### 'Britain Alone' (2nd issue)

**2010** (13 May) 'All-over' phosphor. Perf 14½

| | | | | | | | |
|---|---|---|---|---|---|---|---|
| 3082 | 2277 | (1st) | pale stone, pale bistre and black | 2·00 | 2·00 | ☐ | ☐ |
| 3083 | 2278 | 60p | pale stone, pale bistre and black | 3·00 | 3·00 | ☐ | ☐ |
| 3084 | 2279 | 88p | pale stone, pale bistre and black | 4·00 | 4·00 | ☐ | ☐ |
| 3085 | 2280 | 97p | pale stone, pale bistre and black | 4·00 | 4·00 | ☐ | ☐ |
| 3082/85 *Set of* 4 | | | | 12·00 | 12·00 | ☐ | ☐ |
| **MS**3086 115×89 mm. 2281 | | | | | | | |
| Nos. 3082/5 | | | | 7·50 | 7·50 | ☐ | |
| First Day Cover (**MS**3086) | | | | | 8·50 | | ☐ |

Nos. 3082/5 were only issued in the £9.76 'Britain Alone' booklets and in **MS**3086.

**2282** James I (1603–25)

**2283** Charles I (1625–49)

**2284** Charles II (1660–85)

**2285** James II (1685–8)

**2286** William III (1689–1702)

**2287** Mary II (1689–94)

**2288** Anne (1702–14)

THE AGE OF THE **STUARTS**

**2289** The Age of the Stuarts

### Kings and Queens (4th series). The House of Stuart

**2010** (15 June) Two phosphor bands. Perf 14

| | | | | | | | |
|---|---|---|---|---|---|---|---|
| 3087 | **2282** | (1st) | multicoloured | 1·25 | 1·00 | | |
| 3088 | **2283** | (1st) | multicoloured | 1·25 | 1·00 | | |
| 3089 | **2284** | 60p | multicoloured | 1·50 | 1·50 | | |
| 3090 | **2285** | 60p | multicoloured | 1·50 | 1·50 | | |
| 3091 | **2286** | 67p | multicoloured | 1·70 | 1·70 | | |
| 3092 | **2287** | 67p | multicoloured | 1·70 | 1·70 | | |
| 3093 | **2288** | 88p | multicoloured | 2·25 | 2·25 | | |
| *Set of* 7 | | | | 10·00 | 10·00 | | |
| First Day Cover | | | | | 11·00 | | |
| Presentation Pack (P.O. Pack No. 443) | | | | 19·00 | | | |
| PHQ Cards (*set of* 12) (338) | | | | 10·00 | 24·00 | | |
| *Set of* 7 Gutter Pairs | | | | 21·00 | | | |
| *Set of* 7 Traffic Light Gutter Blocks of 4 | | | 42·00 | | | | |

**MS**3094   123×70 mm. 2289 (1st) William Harvey (discovery of blood circulation, 1628); 60p Civil War Battle of Naseby, 1645; 88p John Milton (Paradise Lost, 1667); 97p Castle Howard (John Vanbrugh, 1712)   7·50   7·50

First Day Cover   8·50

The complete miniature sheet is shown on one of the twelve PHQ cards with the others depicting individual stamps including those from **MS**3094.

### Mammals. Booklet stamps.

**2010** (15 June) Designs as Nos. 3061 and 3063 but printed in photogravure. Self-adhesive. Die-cut perf 14½

| | | | | | | | |
|---|---|---|---|---|---|---|---|
| 3095 | **2256** | (1st) | multicoloured | 3·25 | 3·25 | | |
| 3096 | **2258** | (1st) | multicoloured | 3·25 | 3·25 | | |

Nos. 3095/6 were only issued in stamp booklets, originally sold for £2·46.

**2290** Paralympic Games: Rowing

**2291** Shooting

**2292** Modern Pentathlon

**2293** Taekwondo

**2294** Cycling

**2295** Paralympic Games: Table Tennis

**2296** Hockey

**2297** Football

**2298** Paralympic Games: Goalball

**2299** Boxing

### Olympic and Paralympic Games, London (2012) (3rd issue)

**2010** (27 July) 'All-over' phosphor. Perf 14½

| | | | | | | | |
|---|---|---|---|---|---|---|---|
| 3097 | **2290** | (1st) | multicoloured | 1·25 | 1·00 | | |
| | | a. Horiz strip of 5. Nos. 3097/101 | | 6·25 | 5·50 | | |
| 3098 | **2291** | (1st) | multicoloured | 1·25 | 1·00 | | |
| 3099 | **2292** | (1st) | multicoloured | 1·25 | 1·00 | | |
| 3100 | **2293** | (1st) | multicoloured | 1·25 | 1·00 | | |
| 3101 | **2294** | (1st) | multicoloured | 1·25 | 1·00 | | |
| 3102 | **2295** | (1st) | multicoloured | 1·25 | 1·00 | | |
| | | a. Horiz strip of 5. Nos. 3102/6 | | 6·25 | 5·50 | | |
| 3103 | **2296** | (1st) | multicoloured | 1·25 | 1·00 | | |
| 3104 | **2297** | (1st) | multicoloured | 1·25 | 1·00 | | |
| 3105 | **2298** | (1st) | multicoloured | 1·25 | 1·00 | | |
| 3106 | **2299** | (1st) | multicoloured | 1·25 | 1·00 | | |
| *Set of* 10 | | | | 12·00 | 10·00 | | |
| First Day Cover | | | | | 11·00 | | |
| Presentation Pack (P.O. Pack No. 444) | | | 13·00 | | | | |
| PHQ Cards (*set of* 10) (339) | | | | 9·00 | 20·00 | | |
| *Set of* 2 Gutter Strips of 10 | | | | 25·00 | | | |

Nos. 3097/101 and 3102/6 were each printed together, *se-tenant*, in horizontal strips of five stamps in sheets of 50 (2 panes 5×5) and were also issued on 27 July 2011 in a miniature sheet containing all 30 stamps in the series. See **MS**3204a.

### Olympic and Paralympic Games, London (2012) (4th issue). Booklet stamps

**2010** (27 July–12 Oct.) Designs as Nos. 3097, 3101/2 and 3104 but printed in photogravure. Self-adhesive. 'All-over' phosphor. Die-cut perf 14½

| | | | | | | | |
|---|---|---|---|---|---|---|---|
| 3107 | **2290** | (1st) | multicoloured | 3·25 | 3·25 | | |
| 3108 | **2295** | (1st) | multicoloured | 3·25 | 3·25 | | |
| 3108a | **2297** | (1st) | multicoloured (*12 Oct*) | 3·25 | 3·25 | | |
| 3108b | **2294** | (1st) | multicoloured (*12 Oct*) | 3·25 | 3·25 | | |
| *Set of* 4 | | | | 7·50 | 7·50 | | |

Nos. 3107/8 and 3108a/b were only issued in two separate stamp booklets each originally sold for £2·46.

**2300** LMS Coronation Class Locomotive, Euston Station, 1938

**2301** BR Class 9F Locomotive *Evening Star*, Midsomer Norton, 1962

**2302** GWR King Class Locomotive *King William IV*, near Teignmouth, 1935

**2303** LNER Class A1 Locomotive *Royal Lancer*, 1929

**2304** SR King Arthur Class Locomotive *Sir Mador de la Porte*, Bournemouth Central Station, 1935–9

**2305** LMS NCC Class WT No. 2, Larne Harbour, c. 1947

### Great British Railways

**2010** (19 Aug.) 'All-over' phosphor. Perf 14

| | | | | | | | |
|---|---|---|---|---|---|---|---|
| 3109 | **2300** | (1st) | gold, bluish grey and black | 1·25 | 1·00 | ☐ | ☐ |
| 3110 | **2301** | (1st) | gold, bluish grey and black | 1·25 | 1·00 | ☐ | ☐ |
| 3111 | **2302** | 67p | gold, bluish grey and black | 1·70 | 1·70 | ☐ | ☐ |
| 3112 | **2303** | 67p | gold, bluish grey and black | 1·70 | 1·70 | ☐ | ☐ |
| 3113 | **2304** | 97p | gold, bluish grey and black | 2·50 | 2·50 | ☐ | ☐ |
| 3114 | **2305** | 97p | gold, bluish grey and black | 2·50 | 2·50 | ☐ | ☐ |
| *Set of* 6 | | | | 10·00 | 10·00 | ☐ | ☐ |
| First Day Cover | | | | | 11·00 | | ☐ |
| Presentation Pack (P.O. Pack No. 445) | | | | 12·00 | | ☐ | |
| PHQ Cards (*set of* 6) (340) | | | | 5·00 | 12·00 | ☐ | ☐ |
| *Set of* 6 Gutter Pairs | | | | 21·00 | | ☐ | |

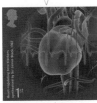

**2306** Heart-regulating Beta Blockers (Sir James Black, 1962)

**2307** Antibiotic Properties of Penicillin (Sir Alexander Fleming, 1928)

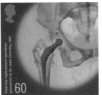

**2308** Total Hip Replacement Operation (Sir John Charnley, 1962)

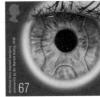

**2309** Artificial Lens Implant Surgery (Sir Harold Ridley, 1949)

**2310** Malaria Parasite transmitted by Mosquitoes (proved by Sir Ronald Ross, 1897)

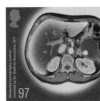

**2311** Computed Tomography Scanner (Sir Godfrey Hounsfield, 1971)

### Medical Breakthroughs

**2010** (16 Sept.) 'All-over' phosphor. Perf 14×14½

| | | | | | | | |
|---|---|---|---|---|---|---|---|
| 3115 | **2306** | (1st) | multicoloured | 1·25 | 1·00 | ☐ | ☐ |
| 3116 | **2307** | 58p | multicoloured | 1·50 | 1·50 | ☐ | ☐ |
| 3117 | **2308** | 60p | multicoloured | 1·50 | 1·50 | ☐ | ☐ |
| 3118 | **2309** | 67p | multicoloured | 1·70 | 1·70 | ☐ | ☐ |
| 3119 | **2310** | 88p | multicoloured | 2·25 | 2·25 | ☐ | ☐ |
| 3120 | **2311** | 97p | multicoloured | 2·50 | 2·50 | ☐ | ☐ |
| *Set of* 6 | | | | 9·50 | 9·50 | ☐ | ☐ |
| First Day Cover | | | | | 11·00 | | ☐ |
| Presentation Pack (P.O. Pack No. 446) | | | | 11·00 | | ☐ | |
| PHQ Cards (*set of* 6) (341) | | | | 5·00 | 12·50 | ☐ | ☐ |
| *Set of* 6 Gutter Pairs | | | | 20·00 | | ☐ | ☐ |

See also No. 3153.

**2312** Winnie the Pooh and Christopher Robin (*Now we are Six*)

**2313** Winnie the Pooh and Piglet (*The House at Pooh Corner*)

**2314** Winnie the Pooh and Rabbit (*Winnie the Pooh*)

**2315** Winnie the Pooh and Eeyore (*Winnie the Pooh*)

**2316** Winnie the Pooh and Friends (*Winnie the Pooh*)

**2317** Winnie the Pooh and Tigger (*The House at Pooh Corner*)

2318 *Winnie the Pooh* (Illustration reduced.
Actual size 115×89 mm)

**Europa. Children's Books. Winnie the Pooh by A. A.
Milne. Book Illustrations by E. H. Shepard**

**2010** (12 Oct.) 'All-over' phosphor. Perf 14×14½

| | | | | | | |
|---|---|---|---|---|---|---|
| 3121 | **2312** | (1st) | yellow-brown, pale stone and black | 1·25 | 1·00 | ☐ ☐ |
| 3122 | **2313** | 58p | yellow-brown, pale stone and black | 1·40 | 1·40 | ☐ ☐ |
| 3123 | **2314** | 60p | yellow-brown, pale stone and black | 1·50 | 1·50 | ☐ ☐ |
| 3124 | **2315** | 67p | yellow-brown, pale stone and black | 1·70 | 1·70 | ☐ ☐ |
| 3125 | **2316** | 88p | yellow-brown, pale stone and black | 2·25 | 2·25 | ☐ ☐ |
| 3126 | **2317** | 97p | yellow-brown, pale stone and black | 2·40 | 2·40 | ☐ ☐ |

| | | | |
|---|---|---|---|
| Set of 6 | | 9·50 | 9·50 | ☐ ☐ |
| First Day Cover | | | 11·00 | ☐ |
| Presentation Pack (P.O. Pack No. 447) | 19·00 | | ☐ |
| PHQ Cards (set of 11) (342) | 9·00 | 22·00 | ☐ ☐ |
| Set of 6 Gutter Pairs | 20·00 | | ☐ |

**MS**3127  115×89 mm. 2318 (1st)
Winnie the Pooh and Christopher
Robin (from *Now we are Six*);
60p Christopher Robin reads to
Winnie the Pooh (from *Winnie
the Pooh*); 88p Winnie the Pooh
and Christopher Robin sailing
in umbrella (from *Winnie the
Pooh*); 97p Christopher Robin
(putting on wellingtons) and Pooh
(from *Winnie the Pooh*). Perf 14½   7·50   7·50  ☐ ☐
First Day Cover                                       8·50  ☐

The 1st class value includes the 'EUROPA' emblem. Stamps
from **MS**3127 show lines from poem 'We Too' by A. A. Milne:
'Wherever I am, there's always Pooh' (1st); 'There's always Pooh
and Me. Whatever I do, he wants to do' (60p); "Where are you
going to-day?" says Pooh: "Well that's very odd 'cos I was too"
(88p); "Let's go together," says Pooh, says he. "Let's go together,"
says Pooh (97p).

The eleven PHQ cards show the six stamps, the four
individual stamps within **MS**3127 and the complete miniature
sheet.

2319 Wallace
and Gromit
carol singing

2320 Gromit
posting
Christmas Cards

2321 Wallace and
Gromit carol singing

2322 Wallace
and Gromit decorating
Christmas Tree

2323 Gromit
posting Christmas Cards

2324 Gromit carrying
Christmas
Pudding

2325 Gromit putting on Bone-themed Pullover

**Christmas with Wallace and Gromit**

**2010** (2 Nov.) One centre band (3128) or two phosphor bands
(others). Perf 14½×14 (with one elliptical hole in each vert side)

| | | | | | | |
|---|---|---|---|---|---|---|
| | | *(a) Self-adhesive* | | | | |
| 3128 | **2319** | (2nd) | multicoloured | 1·00 | 75 | ☐ ☐ |
| 3129 | **2320** | (1st) | multicoloured | 1·25 | 1·00 | ☐ ☐ |
| 3130 | **2321** | (2nd Large) | multicoloured | 1·50 | 1·50 | ☐ ☐ |
| 3131 | **2322** | 60p | multicoloured | 1·50 | 1·50 | ☐ ☐ |
| 3132 | **2323** | (1st Large) | multicoloured | 2·00 | 2·00 | ☐ ☐ |
| 3133 | **2324** | 97p | multicoloured | 2·40 | 2·40 | ☐ ☐ |
| 3134 | **2325** | £1·46 | multicoloured | 3·50 | 3·50 | ☐ ☐ |
| Set of 7 | | | | 12·00 | 11·00 | ☐ ☐ |
| First Day Cover | | | | | 12·00 | ☐ |
| Presentation Pack (P.O. Pack No. 448) | | 14·00 | | ☐ |
| PHQ Cards (set of 8) (343) | | | 6·00 | 17·00 | ☐ ☐ |

| | | | |
|---|---|---|---|
| | *(b) Ordinary gum* | | |
| **MS**3135 115×102 mm. As Nos. 3128/34 | 12·00 | 12·00 | ☐ ☐ |
| First Day Cover | | 13·00 | ☐ |

The eight PHQ cards show the seven individual stamps and the
miniature sheet.

The 2nd class, 1st class, 60p and 97p stamps were also issued
together in sheets of 20 containing eight 2nd class, eight 1st
class, two 60p and two 97p stamps, each stamps accompanied
by a *se-tenant* label. Separate sheets of 20 2nd, 20 1st, ten 1st,
ten 60p and ten 97p were available with personal photographs
on the labels. All these sheets were printed in lithography
instead of photogravure.

**Collectors Pack**

**2010** (2 Nov.) Comprises Nos. 2999/3008, **MS**3025/63, **MS**3065,
**MS**3072, 3074/81, **MS**3086/94, 3097/106 and 3109/34
CP3135a   Collectors Pack                £130   ☐

**Post Office Yearbook**

**2010** (2 Nov.) Comprises Nos. 2999/3008, **MS**3025/63, **MS**3065,
**MS**3072, 3074/81, **MS**3086/94, 3097/106 and 3109/34
YB3135a   Yearbook                       £130   ☐

**Miniature Sheet Collection**

**2010** (2 Nov.) Comprises Nos. **MS**3024, **MS**3025, **MS**3053,
**MS**3065, **MS**3072, **MS**3086, **MS**3094, **MS**3127 and **MS**3135
**MS**3135a Miniature Sheet Collection   60·00   ☐

2326 Joe 90

2327 Captain Scarlet

**2328** Thunderbird 2 (*Thunderbirds*)    **2329** Stingray

**2330** Fireball XL5    **2331** Supercar

**2332** Thunderbird 4; Thunderbird 3;
Thunderbird 2; Thunderbird 1

### 'F.A.B. The Genius of Gerry Anderson' (producer of TV programmes)

**2011** (11 Jan.) 'All-over' phosphor

| | | (a) Ordinary gum. Perf 14 | | | | |
|---|---|---|---|---|---|---|
| 3136 | **2326** | (1st) multicoloured | 1·25 | 1·00 | ☐ | ☐ |
| | a. | Horiz strip of 3. | | | | |
| | | Nos. 3136/8 | 4·00 | 4·00 | ☐ | ☐ |
| 3137 | **2327** | (1st) multicoloured | 1·25 | 1·00 | ☐ | ☐ |
| 3138 | **2328** | (1st) multicoloured | 1·25 | 1·00 | ☐ | ☐ |
| 3139 | **2329** | 97p multicoloured | 2·40 | 2·40 | ☐ | ☐ |
| | a. | Horiz strip of 3. | | | | |
| | | Nos. 3139/41 | 8·00 | 8·00 | ☐ | ☐ |
| 3140 | **2330** | 97p multicoloured | 2·40 | 2·40 | ☐ | ☐ |
| 3141 | **2331** | 97p multicoloured | 2·40 | 2·40 | ☐ | ☐ |
| Set of 6 | | | 11·00 | 11·00 | ☐ | |
| First Day Cover | | | | 12·00 | ☐ | |
| Presentation Pack (P.O. Pack No. 450) | | | 19·00 | | ☐ | |
| PHQ Cards (set of 11) (344) | | | 9·00 | 22·00 | ☐ | ☐ |
| Set of 2 Gutter Strips of 6 | | | 23·00 | | ☐ | |

(b) Microlenticular. Perf 14

MS3142   116×89 mm.   **2332** 41p
*Thunderbird 4*, 60p *Thunderbird
3*, 88p *Thunderbird 2*, 97p
*Thunderbird 1* multicoloured

| | | 8·00 | 8·00 | ☐ | ☐ |
|---|---|---|---|---|---|
| First Day Cover | | | 9·00 | ☐ | |

(c) Self-adhesive. As No. 3138 but printed
in photogravure. Die-cut perf 14

| 3143 | **2328** | (1st) multicoloured | 3·00 | 3·00 | ☐ | ☐ |
|---|---|---|---|---|---|---|

Nos. 3136/8 and 3139/41 were each printed together, se-tenant, as horizontal strips of three stamps in sheets of 60 (2 panes 6×5).

The stamps within **MS**3142 use microlenticular technology to show each vehicle's launch sequences when the miniature sheet is tilted. No. 3143 was only issued in booklets originally sold for £1·46.

**2333**

### Classic Locomotives (1st series). England miniature sheet

**2011** (1 Feb.) Sheet 180×74 mm. Multicoloured. 'All-over' phosphor. Perf 14

MS3144   **2333**  (1st) BR Dean Goods
No. 2532; 60p Peckett R2 *Thor*;
88p Lancashire and Yorkshire
Railway 1093 No. 1100; 97p
BR WD No. 90662

| | | | 7·50 | 7·50 | ☐ | ☐ |
|---|---|---|---|---|---|---|
| First Day Cover | | | | 8·50 | ☐ | |
| Presentation Pack (P.O. Pack No. 451) | | | 8·00 | | ☐ | |
| PHQ Cards (set of 5) (345) | | | 4·00 | 10·00 | ☐ | ☐ |

The five PHQ cards show the four individual stamps and the complete miniature sheet. See also No. 3215.

**2334** *Oliver*    **2335** *Blood Brothers*    **2336** *We Will Rock You*

**2337** *Spamalot*    **2338** *Rocky Horror Show*    **2339** *Me and My Girl*

**2340** *Return to the Forbidden Planet*    **2341** *Billy Elliot*

### Musicals

**2011** (24 Feb.) 'All-over' phosphor. Perf 14

| 3145 | **2334** | (1st) multicoloured | 1·25 | 1·00 | ☐ | ☐ |
|---|---|---|---|---|---|---|
| 3146 | **2335** | (1st) multicoloured | 1·25 | 1·00 | ☐ | ☐ |
| 3147 | **2336** | (1st) multicoloured | 1·25 | 1·00 | ☐ | ☐ |
| 3148 | **2337** | (1st) multicoloured | 1·25 | 1·00 | ☐ | ☐ |
| 3149 | **2338** | 97p multicoloured | 2·40 | 2·40 | ☐ | ☐ |
| 3150 | **2339** | 97p multicoloured | 2·40 | 2·40 | ☐ | ☐ |
| 3151 | **2340** | 97p multicoloured | 2·40 | 2·40 | ☐ | ☐ |
| 3152 | **2341** | 97p multicoloured | 2·40 | 2·40 | ☐ | ☐ |
| Set of 8 | | | 13·00 | 13·00 | ☐ | ☐ |
| First Day Cover | | | | 14·00 | ☐ | |
| Presentation Pack (P.O. Pack No. 452) | | | 15·00 | | ☐ | |

| PHQ Cards (*set of* 8) (346) | 6·00 | 17·00 | ☐ ☐ |
|---|---|---|---|
| *Set of* 8 Gutter Pairs | 27·00 | | ☐ |
| *Set of* 8 Traffic Light Gutter Pairs | 29·00 | | ☐ |

**50th Anniversary of the British Heart Foundation.**

**Booklet stamp**

**2011** (24 Feb.) Design as No. 3115 but printed in photogravure. Self-adhesive. 'All-over' phosphor. Die-cut perf 14×14½

| 3153 **2306** | (1st) multicoloured | 2·00 | 2·00 | ☐ ☐ |
|---|---|---|---|---|

No. 3153 was only issued in booklets originally sold for £2·46.

**2342** Rincewind (Terry Pratchett's *Discworld*)

**2343** Nanny Ogg (Terry Pratchett's *Discworld*)

**2344** Michael Gambon as Dumbledore (J. K. Rowling's *Harry Potter*)

**2345** Ralph Fiennes as Lord Voldemort (J. K. Rowling's *Harry Potter*)

**2346** Merlin (Arthurian Legend)

**2347** Morgan Le Fay (Arthurian Legend)

**2348** Aslan (C. S. Lewis's *Narnia*)

**2349** Tilda Swinton as The White Witch (C. S. Lewis's *Narnia*)

**Magical Realms**

**2011** (8 Mar.) 'All-over' phosphor. Perf 14½

| 3154 **2342** | (1st) multicoloured | 1·25 | 1·00 | ☐ ☐ |
|---|---|---|---|---|
| | a. Vert pair. | | | |
| | Nos. 3154/5 | 2·60 | 2·60 | ☐ ☐ |
| 3155 **2343** | (1st) multicoloured | 1·25 | 1·00 | ☐ ☐ |
| 3156 **2344** | (1st) multicoloured | 1·25 | 1·00 | ☐ ☐ |
| | a. Vert pair. | | | |
| | Nos. 3156/7 | 2·60 | 2·60 | ☐ ☐ |
| 3157 **2345** | (1st) multicoloured | 1·25 | 1·00 | ☐ ☐ |
| 3158 **2346** | 60p multicoloured | 1·50 | 1·50 | ☐ ☐ |

| | a. Vert pair. | | | |
|---|---|---|---|---|
| | Nos. 3158/9 | 3·25 | 3·25 | ☐ ☐ |
| 3159 **2347** | 60p multicoloured | 1·50 | 1·50 | ☐ ☐ |
| 3160 **2348** | 97p multicoloured | 2·40 | 2·40 | ☐ ☐ |
| | a. Vert pair. | | | |
| | Nos. 3160/1 | 5·00 | 5·00 | ☐ ☐ |
| 3161 **2349** | 97p multicoloured | 2·40 | 2·40 | ☐ ☐ |
| *Set of* 8 | | 12·00 | 12·00 | ☐ ☐ |
| First Day Cover | | | 13·00 | ☐ |
| Presentation Pack (P.O. Pack No. 453) | | 14·00 | | ☐ |
| Presentation Pack ('Heroes and Villains' containing Nos. 3156/7, each ×5) (2 Dec) | | 15·00 | | ☐ |
| PHQ Cards (*set of* 8) (347) | | 6·00 | 18·00 | ☐ ☐ |
| *Set of* 4 Gutter Strips of 4 | | 25·00 | | ☐ |

Nos. 3154/5, 3156/7, 3158/9 and 3160/1 were each printed together, *se-tenant*, as vertical pairs in sheets of 60 (2 panes 5×6).

**2350** African Elephant

**2351** Mountain Gorilla

**2352** Siberian Tiger

**2353** Polar Bear

**2354** Amur Leopard

**2355** Iberian Lynx

**2356** Red Panda

**2357** Black Rhinoceros

**2358** African Wild Dog

**2359** Golden Lion Tamarin

**2360** Wildlife of the Amazon Rainforest

### 50th Anniversary of the WWF

**2011** (22 Mar.) 'All-over' phosphor. Perf 14 (**MS**3172) or 14½ (others)

| | | | | | | |
|---|---|---|---|---|---|---|
| 3162 | **2350** | (1st) | multicoloured | 1·25 | 1·00 | ☐ ☐ |
| | | a. | Horiz strip of 5. | | | |
| | | | Nos. 3162/6 | 7·00 | 7·00 | ☐ ☐ |
| 3163 | **2351** | (1st) | multicoloured | 1·25 | 1·00 | ☐ ☐ |
| 3164 | **2352** | (1st) | multicoloured | 1·25 | 1·00 | ☐ ☐ |
| 3165 | **2353** | (1st) | multicoloured | 1·25 | 1·00 | ☐ ☐ |
| 3166 | **2354** | (1st) | multicoloured | 1·25 | 1·00 | ☐ ☐ |
| 3167 | **2355** | (1st) | multicoloured | 1·25 | 1·00 | ☐ ☐ |
| | | a. | Horiz strip of 5. | | | |
| | | | Nos. 3167/71 | 7·00 | 7·00 | ☐ ☐ |
| 3168 | **2356** | (1st) | multicoloured | 1·25 | 1·00 | ☐ ☐ |
| 3169 | **2357** | (1st) | multicoloured | 1·25 | 1·00 | ☐ ☐ |
| 3170 | **2358** | (1st) | multicoloured | 1·25 | 1·00 | ☐ ☐ |
| 3171 | **2359** | (1st) | multicoloured | 1·25 | 1·00 | ☐ ☐ |
| Set of 10 | | | | 12·50 | 12·50 | ☐ ☐ |
| First Day Cover | | | | | 13·00 | ☐ |
| Presentation Pack (P.O. Pack No. 454) | | | | 22·00 | | ☐ |
| PHQ Cards (set of 15) (348) | | | | 12·00 | 30·00 | ☐ ☐ |
| Set of 2 Gutter Strips of 10 | | | | 26·00 | | ☐ |

**MS**3172 115×89 mm. 2360 (1st) Spider monkey; 60p Hyacinth macaw; 88p Poison dart frog; 97p Jaguar  7·50  7·50 ☐ ☐
First Day Cover  8·50 ☐

Nos. 3162/6 and 3167/71 were each printed together, se-tenant, as horizontal strips of five stamps in sheets of 50 (2 panes 5 × 5) and were also issued in the £9.05 '50th Anniversary of the WWF' booklet.

The 1st class value from **MS**3172 includes the 'EUROPA' emblem.

**2361** David Tennant as *Hamlet*, 2008

**2362** Antony Sher as Prospero, *The Tempest*, 2009

**2363** Chuk Iwuji as *Henry VI*, 2006

**2364** Paul Schofield as *King Lear*, 1962

**2365** Sara Kestelman as Titania, A Midsummer Night's Dream, 1970

**2366** Ian McKellen and Francesca Annis as Romeo and Juliet, 1976

**2367** The Four Theatres of the Royal Shakespeare Company, Stratford-upon-Avon

### 50th Anniversary of the Royal Shakespeare Company

**2011** (12 Apr.) 'All-over' phosphor

(a) Photo Walsall. Perf 14½

| | | | | | | |
|---|---|---|---|---|---|---|
| 3173 | **2361** | (1st) | black, brownish black and bright scarlet | 1·25 | 1·00 | ☐ ☐ |
| 3174 | **2362** | 66p | black, brownish black and bright scarlet | 1·70 | 1·70 | ☐ ☐ |
| 3175 | **2363** | 68p | black, brownish black and bright scarlet | 1·70 | 1·70 | ☐ ☐ |
| 3176 | **2364** | 76p | black, brownish black and bright scarlet | 1·90 | 1·90 | ☐ ☐ |
| 3177 | **2365** | £1 | black, brownish black and bright scarlet | 2·50 | 2·50 | ☐ ☐ |
| 3178 | **2366** | £1·10 | black, brownish black and bright scarlet | 2·75 | 2·75 | ☐ ☐ |
| Set of 6 | | | | 10·50 | 10·50 | ☐ ☐ |
| First Day Cover | | | | | 12·00 | ☐ |
| Presentation Pack (P.O. Pack No. 455) | | | | 20·00 | | ☐ |
| PHQ Cards (set of 11) (349) | | | | 9·00 | 20·00 | ☐ ☐ |
| Set of 6 Gutter Pairs | | | | 22·00 | | ☐ |

(b) Litho Cartor. Multicoloured. Perf 14

**MS**3179 115×89 mm. 2367 (1st) Janet Suzman as Ophelia, *Hamlet*, 1965, Royal Shakespeare Theatre; 68p Patrick Stewart in *Antony and Cleopatra*, 2006, Swan Theatre; 76p Geoffrey Streatfeild in *Henry V*, 2007, The Courtyard Theatre; £1 Judy Dench as Lady Macbeth, 1976, The Other Place  7·50  7·50 ☐ ☐
First Day Cover  8·50 ☐

The eleven PHQ cards show the six stamps, the four individual stamps within **MS**3179 and the complete miniature sheet.

**2368** Prince William and Miss Catherine Middleton

### Royal Wedding. Official Engagement Portraits by Mario Testino miniature sheet

**2011** (21 Apr.) Sheet 115×89 mm. Multicoloured. 'All-over' phosphor. Perf 14½×14

**MS**3180 2368 (1st)×2 Prince William and Miss Catherine Middleton embracing; £1·10 × 2 Formal portrait of Prince William and Miss Catherine Middleton in Council Chamber, St. James's

| | | |
|---|---|---|
| Palace | 8·50 | 8·50 |
| First Day Cover | | 9·50 |
| Presentation Pack (P.O. Pack No. M20) | 13·00 | |
| Commemorative Document | 15·00 | |

**2369** Cray (fabric print by William Morris), 1884

**2370** Cherries (detail from panel by Philip Webb), 1867

**2371** Seaweed (wallpaper pattern by John Henry Dearle), 1901

**2372** Peony (ceramic tile design by Kate Faulkner), 1877

**2373** Acanthus (tile by William Morris and William De Morgan), 1876

**2374** The Merchant's Daughter (detail of stained glass window by Edward Burne-Jones), 1864

### 150th Anniversary of Morris and Company (designers and manufacturers of textiles, wallpaper and furniture) (1st issue)

**2011** (5 May) 'All-over' phosphor. Perf 14×14½

| | | | | |
|---|---|---|---|---|
| 3181 **2369** | (1st) multicoloured | 1·25 | 1·00 | |
| 3182 **2370** | (1st) multicoloured | 1·25 | 1·00 | |
| 3183 **2371** | 76p. multicoloured | 1·90 | 1·90 | |
| 3184 **2372** | 76p. multicoloured | 1·90 | 1·90 | |
| 3185 **2373** | £1·10 multicoloured | 2·75 | 2·75 | |
| 3186 **2374** | £1·10 multicoloured | 2·75 | 2·75 | |
| Set of 6 | | 10·50 | 10·50 | |
| First Day Cover | | | 12·50 | |
| Presentation Pack (P.O. Pack No. 456) | | 12·00 | | |
| PHQ Cards (set of 6) (350) | | 5·00 | 16·00 | |
| Set of 6 Gutter Pairs | | 22·00 | | |

Nos. 3181/6 were also issued in the £9.99 'Morris & Co' booklet

### 150th Anniversary of Morris and Company (2nd issue)

**2011** (5 May) Design as Type 2202 (2009 Christmas stained-glass windows). One centre band. Perf 14½×14 (with one elliptical hole in each vert side)

| | | | |
|---|---|---|---|
| 3186a **2202** | (2nd) multicoloured | 3·00 | 3·00 |

No. 3186a was only issued in the £9.99 'Morris & Co' stamp booklet.

**2375** Thomas the Tank Engine

**2376** James the Red Engine

**2377** Percy the Small Engine

**2378** Daisy (diesel railcar)

**2379** Toby the Tram Engine

**2380** Gordon the Big Engine

2381 Book Illustrations by John T. Kenny (76p.) or C. Reginald Dalby (others)

"Goodbye, Bertie," called Thomas

2382 "Goodbye, Bertie," called
Thomas (from Tank Engine Thomas Again)

## Thomas the Tank Engine

**2011** (14 June) 'All-over' phosphor

(a) Ordinary gum. Perf 14 (MS3193) or 14½×14 (others)

| | | | | | |
|---|---|---|---|---|---|
| 3187 | **2375** | (1st) multicoloured | 1·25 | 1·00 | ☐ ☐ |
| 3188 | **2376** | 66p multicoloured | 1·70 | 1·70 | ☐ ☐ |
| 3189 | **2377** | 68p multicoloured | 1·70 | 1·70 | ☐ ☐ |
| 3190 | **2378** | 76p multicoloured | 1·90 | 1·90 | ☐ ☐ |
| 3191 | **2379** | £1 multicoloured | 2·50 | 2·50 | ☐ ☐ |
| 3192 | **2380** | £1·10 multicoloured | 2·75 | 2·75 | ☐ ☐ |
| | *Set of* 6 | | 10·50 | 10·50 | ☐ ☐ |
| | First Day Cover | | | 12·00 | ☐ |
| | Presentation Pack (P.O. Pack No. 457) | | 20·00 | | ☐ |
| | PHQ Cards (*set of* 11) (351) | | 9·00 | 22·00 | ☐ ☐ |
| | *Set of* 6 Gutter Pairs | | 22·00 | | ☐ |

**MS**3193 115 × 89 mm. **2381**
"Goodbye, Bertie," called Thomas
(from *Tank Engine Thomas Again*)
(1st); James was more dirty than
hurt (from *Toby the Tram Engine*)
(68p.) "Yes Sir," Percy shivered
miserably (from *The Eight Famous
Engines*)(76p); They told Henry,
"We shall leave you there for
always" (from *The Three Railway
Engines*) (£1)        7·50   7·50  ☐ ☐
First Day Cover                      8·50  ☐

(b) Self-adhesive. Die-cut perf 14
3194 **2382** (1st) multicoloured   3·00   3·00  ☐ ☐

The eleven PHQ Cards show the six stamps, the four individual
stamps within **MS**3193 and the complete miniature sheet.

Nos. 3187/92 show scenes from TV series *Thomas and
Friends*, and Nos. **MS**3193/3194 book illustrations from *The
Railway Series*.

No. 3194 was only issued in stamp booklets originally sold
for £2·76.

2383 Paralympic Games:    2384 Athletics: Field
Sailing

2385 Volleyball           2386 Wheelchair Rugby

2387 Wrestling           2388 Wheelchair Tennis

2389 Fencing            2390 Gymnastics

2391 Triathlon          2392 Handball

## Olympic and Paralympic Games, London (2012)
(5th issue)

**2011** (27 July) 'All-over' phosphor Perf 14½

| | | | | | |
|---|---|---|---|---|---|
| 3195 | **2383** | (1st) multicoloured | 1·25 | 1·00 | ☐ ☐ |
| | | a. Horiz strip of 5. | | | |
| | | Nos. 3195/9 | 6·50 | 5·50 | ☐ ☐ |
| 3196 | **2384** | (1st) multicoloured | 1·25 | 1·00 | ☐ ☐ |
| 3197 | **2385** | (1st) multicoloured | 1·25 | 1·00 | ☐ ☐ |
| 3198 | **2386** | (1st) multicoloured | 1·25 | 1·00 | ☐ ☐ |
| 3199 | **2387** | (1st) multicoloured | 1·25 | 1·00 | ☐ ☐ |
| 3200 | **2388** | (1st) multicoloured | 1·25 | 1·00 | ☐ ☐ |
| | | b. Horiz strip of 5. | | | |
| | | Nos. 3200/4 | 6·50 | 5·50 | ☐ ☐ |
| 3201 | **2389** | (1st) multicoloured | 1·25 | 1·00 | ☐ ☐ |
| 3202 | **2390** | (1st) multicoloured | 1·25 | 1·00 | ☐ ☐ |
| 3203 | **2391** | (1st) multicoloured | 1·25 | 1·00 | ☐ ☐ |
| 3204 | **2392** | (1st) multicoloured | 1·25 | 1·00 | ☐ ☐ |
| | *Set of* 10 | | 12·00 | 10·00 | ☐ ☐ |

| | | | | |
|---|---|---|---|---|
| First Day Cover | | 11·00 | | ☐ |
| Presentation Pack (P.O. Pack No. 458) | 14·00 | | | ☐ |
| PHQ Cards (set of 10) (352) | | 9·00 | 20·00 | ☐ ☐ |
| Set of 2 Gutter Strips of 10 | | 25·00 | | ☐ |

**MS**3204a 210x300 mm. Nos. 2981/90,
3097/106 and 3195/204     38·00     38·00 ☐ ☐

Nos. 3195/9 and 3200/4 were each printed together, *se-tenant*, in horizontal strips of five stamps in sheets of 50 (2 panes 5×5) and in **MS**3204a.

### Olympic and Paralympic Games (2012) (6th issue)

**2011** (27 July) Booklet stamps. Designs as Nos. 3195, 3198 and 3201/2. Self-adhesive. 'All-over' phosphor. Die-cut perf 14½×14

| | | | | | |
|---|---|---|---|---|---|
| 3205 | **2386** | (1st) | multicoloured | 3·25 | 3·25 ☐ ☐ |
| 3206 | **2383** | (1st) | multicoloured | 3·25 | 3·25 ☐ ☐ |
| 3206a | **2390** | (1st) | multicoloured | 3·25 | 3·25 ☐ ☐ |
| 3206b | **2389** | (1st) | multicoloured | 3·25 | 3·25 ☐ ☐ |

Nos. 3205/6 and 3206a/b were only issued in two separate stamp booklets originally sold for £2·76.

**2393** The Sovereign's Sceptre with Cross

**2394** St. Edward's Crown

**2395** Rod and Sceptre with Doves

**2396** Queen Mary's Crown

**2397** The Sovereign's Orb

**2398** Jewelled Sword of Offering

**2399** Imperial State Crown

**2400** Coronation Spoon

### Crown Jewels

**2011** (23 Aug.) Phosphor background. Perf 14×14½

| | | | | | |
|---|---|---|---|---|---|
| 3207 | **2393** | (1st) | multicoloured | 1·25 | 1·00 ☐ ☐ |
| 3208 | **2394** | (1st) | multicoloured | 1·25 | 1·00 ☐ ☐ |
| 3209 | **2395** | 68p | multicoloured | 1·70 | 1·70 ☐ ☐ |
| 3210 | **2396** | 68p | multicoloured | 1·70 | 1·70 ☐ ☐ |
| 3211 | **2397** | 76p | multicoloured | 1·90 | 1·90 ☐ ☐ |
| 3212 | **2398** | 76p | multicoloured | 1·90 | 1·90 ☐ ☐ |
| 3213 | **2399** | £1·10 | multicoloured | 2·75 | 2·75 ☐ ☐ |
| 3214 | **2400** | £1·10 | multicoloured | 2·75 | 2·75 ☐ ☐ |

| | | | | |
|---|---|---|---|---|
| Set of 8 | | 14·00 | 14·00 | ☐ ☐ |
| First Day Cover | | | 15·00 | ☐ |
| Presentation Pack (P.O. Pack No. 459) | 16·00 | | | ☐ |
| PHQ Cards (set of 8) (353) | | 7·00 | 21·00 | ☐ ☐ |
| Set of 8 Gutter Pairs | | 29·00 | | ☐ |

**2401** BR Dean Goods Locomotive No. 2532, 1951

### Classic Locomotives. Booklet stamps

**2011** (23 Aug.) Design as 1st class stamp within **MS**3144 but printed in photogravure. Self-adhesive. 'All-over' phosphor. Die-cut perf 14

3215 **2401**   (1st)   black and gold       3·00     3·00 ☐ ☐

No. 3215 was only issued in stamp booklets originally sold for £2·76.

**2402** Pilot Gustav Hamel receiving mailbag

**2403** Gustav Hamel in cockpit

**2404** Pilot Clement Greswell and Blériot monoplane

**2405** Delivery of first airmail to Postmaster General at Windsor

**2406** First United Kingdom Aerial Post, 9 September 1911

### Centenary of First United Kingdom Aerial Post (1st issue)

**2011** (9 Sept.) 'All-over' phosphor. Perf 14

| | | | | | |
|---|---|---|---|---|---|
| 3216 | **2402** | (1st) | purple-black and pale grey-lilac | 1·25 | 1·00 ☐ ☐ |
| 3217 | **2403** | 68p | brownish black and stone | 1·70 | 1·70 ☐ ☐ |
| 3218 | **2404** | £1 | deep sepia and pale grey-brown | 2·50 | 2·50 ☐ ☐ |
| 3219 | **2405** | £1·10 | black and pale grey | 2·75 | 2·75 ☐ ☐ |
| Set of 4 | | | | 9·00 | 7·50 |
| **MS**3220 | **2406** | 146×74 mm. Nos. 3216/19 | | 9·00 | 7·50 |
| First Day Cover | | | | | 9·00 |
| Presentation Pack (P.O. Pack No. 460) | | | | 9·00 | ☐ |
| PHQ Cards (set of 5) (354) | | | | 4·50 | 12·00 ☐ ☐ |

Nos. 3216/19 were only issued in the £9·97 'First United Kingdom Aerial Post' booklet.

The five PHQ cards show the four individual stamps and the complete miniature sheet.

**2407** Windsor Castle

### Centenary of First United Kingdom Aerial Post (2nd issue)

**2011** (9 Sept.) Recess and Litho. Perf 11×11½

| | | | | | | |
|---|---|---|---|---|---|---|
| 3221 | **2407** | 50p black on cream | 4·00 | 4·00 | ☐ | ☐ |

No. 3221 was only issued in the £9·97 'First United Kingdom Aerial Post' booklet.

**2408**

### Birth Centenary of Arnold Machin (sculptor) miniature sheet

**2011** (14 Sept.) Sheet 124×71 mm containing stamps as No. U3002. Two phosphor bands. Perf 14½×14 (with one elliptical hole in each vertical side)

| | | | | | | |
|---|---|---|---|---|---|---|
| MS3222 | **2408** | (1st) gold×10 | 12·00 | 12·00 | ☐ | ☐ |
| | First Day Cover | | | 17·00 | | ☐ |

**2409** George I (1714–27)  **2410** George II (1727–60)  **2411** George III (1760–1820)

**2412** George IV (1820–30)  **2413** William IV (1830–7)  **2414** Victoria (1837–1901)

**2415** The Age of the Hanoverians

### Kings and Queens (5th issue). The House of Hanover

**2011** (15 Sept.) Two phosphor bands. Perf 14

| | | | | | | |
|---|---|---|---|---|---|---|
| 3223 | **2409** | (1st) multicoloured | 1·25 | 1·10 | ☐ | ☐ |
| 3224 | **2410** | (1st) multicoloured | 1·25 | 1·10 | ☐ | ☐ |
| 3225 | **2411** | 76p multicoloured | 1·90 | 1·90 | ☐ | ☐ |
| 3226 | **2412** | 76p multicoloured | 1·90 | 1·90 | ☐ | ☐ |
| 3227 | **2413** | £1·10 multicoloured | 2·75 | 2·75 | ☐ | ☐ |
| 3228 | **2414** | £1·10 multicoloured | 2·75 | 2·75 | ☐ | ☐ |
| Set of 6 | | | 10·50 | 10·50 | ☐ | ☐ |
| First Day Cover | | | | 13·00 | | ☐ |
| Presentation Pack (P.O. Pack No. 461) | | | 20·00 | | ☐ | |
| PHQ Cards (set of 11) (355) | | | 9·00 | 20·00 | ☐ | ☐ |
| Set of 6 Gutter Pairs | | | 22·00 | | ☐ | |
| Set of 6 Traffic Light Gutter Blocks of 4 | | | 42·00 | | ☐ | |

**MS**3229 123 × 70 mm. **2415** (1st) Robert Walpole (first Prime Minister), 1721; 68p Ceiling by Robert Adam, Kedleston Hall, 1763; 76p Penny Black (uniform postage), 1840; £1 Queen Victoria (Diamond Jubilee), 1897  7·50  7·50 ☐ ☐

| | | | | |
|---|---|---|---|---|
| First Day Cover | | 8·50 | | ☐ |

The complete miniature sheet is shown on one of the eleven PHQ cards with the others depicting individual stams including those from **MS**3229.

**2416** Angel of the North  **2417** Blackpool Tower

**2418** Carrick-a-Rede, Co. Antrim  **2419** Downing Street

 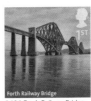

**2420** Edinburgh Castle  **2421** Forth Railway Bridge

**2422** Glastonbury Tor

**2423** Harlech Castle

**2424** Ironbridge

**2425** Jodrell Bank

**2426** Kursaal, Southend, Essex

**2427** Lindisfarne Priory

### UK A-Z (1st series). Famous Landmarks A-L

**2011** (13 Oct.) 'All-over' phosphor. Perf 14½

| | | | | | | |
|---|---|---|---|---|---|---|
| 3230 | **2416** | (1st) | multicoloured | 1·25 | 1·00 | ☐ ☐ |
| | | a. | Horiz strip of 6. Nos. 3230/35 | 7·50 | 6·00 | ☐ ☐ |
| 3231 | **2417** | (1st) | multicoloured | 1·25 | 1·00 | ☐ ☐ |
| 3232 | **2418** | (1st) | multicoloured | 1·25 | 1·00 | ☐ ☐ |
| 3233 | **2419** | (1st) | multicoloured | 1·25 | 1·00 | ☐ ☐ |
| 3234 | **2420** | (1st) | multicoloured | 1·25 | 1·00 | ☐ ☐ |
| 3235 | **2421** | (1st) | multicoloured | 1·25 | 1·00 | ☐ ☐ |
| 3236 | **2422** | (1st) | multicoloured | 1·25 | 1·00 | ☐ ☐ |
| | | a. | Horiz strip of 6. Nos. 3236/41 | 7·50 | 6·00 | ☐ ☐ |
| 3237 | **2423** | (1st) | multicoloured | 1·25 | 1·00 | ☐ ☐ |
| 3238 | **2424** | (1st) | multicoloured | 1·25 | 1·00 | ☐ ☐ |
| 3239 | **2425** | (1st) | multicoloured | 1·25 | 1·00 | ☐ ☐ |
| 3240 | **2426** | (1st) | multicoloured | 1·25 | 1·00 | ☐ ☐ |
| 3241 | **2427** | (1st) | multicoloured | 1·25 | 1·00 | ☐ ☐ |
| Set of 12 | | | | 14·00 | 11·00 | ☐ ☐ |
| First Day Covers (2) | | | | | 12·00 | ☐ |
| Presentation Pack (P.O. Pack No. 462) | | | | 16·00 | | ☐ |
| PHQ Cards (set of 12) (356) | | | | 10·00 | 20·00 | ☐ ☐ |
| Set of 2 Gutter Strips of 12 | | | | 29·00 | | ☐ |
| Set of 2 Traffic Light Gutter Strips of 24 | | | 50·00 | | | ☐ |

Nos. 3230/35 and 3236/41 were each printed together, se-tenant, as horizontal strips of six stamps in sheets of 60 (2 panes of 30) and were also issued on 10 April 2012 in a sheet containing all 26 stamps. See **MS**3308.

**2428** Joseph visited by the Angel (Matthew 1:21)

**2429** Madonna and Child (Matthew 1:23)

**2430** Joseph visited by the Angel (Matthew 1:21)

**2431** Madonna and Child (Matthew 1:23)

**2432** Baby Jesus in the Manger (Luke 2:7)

**2433** Shepherds visited by the Angel (Luke 2:10)

**2434** Wise Men and Star (Matthew 2:10)

### Christmas. 400th Anniversary of the King James Bible

**2011** (8 Nov.) One centre band (3242) or two phosphor bands (others). P 14½×14 (with one elliptical hole in each vert side)

| | | | | | | |
|---|---|---|---|---|---|---|
| (a) Self-adhesive | | | | | | |
| 3242 | **2428** | (2nd) multicoloured | 1·00 | 75 | ☐ ☐ |
| 3243 | **2429** | (1st) multicoloured | 1·25 | 1·00 | ☐ ☐ |
| 3244 | **2430** | (2nd Large) multicoloured | 1·50 | 1·25 | ☐ ☐ |
| 3245 | **2431** | (1st Large) multicoloured | 2·00 | 1·50 | ☐ ☐ |
| 3246 | **2432** | 68p multicoloured | 1·70 | 1·70 | ☐ ☐ |
| 3247 | **2433** | £1·10 multicoloured | 2·75 | 2·75 | ☐ ☐ |
| 3248 | **2434** | £1·65 multicoloured | 4·00 | 4·00 | ☐ ☐ |
| Set of 7 | | | 13·00 | 13·00 | ☐ ☐ |
| First Day Cover | | | | 14·00 | ☐ |
| Presentation Pack (P.O. Pack No. 463) | | 15·00 | | ☐ |
| PHQ Cards (set of 8) (357) | | 5·50 | 20·00 | ☐ ☐ |

| | | | | |
|---|---|---|---|---|
| (b) Ordinary gum | | | | |
| **MS**3249 116×102 mm. | | | | |
| As Nos. 3242/48 | | 13·00 | 13·00 | ☐ ☐ |
| First Day Cover | | | 14·00 | ☐ |

The eight PHQ cards show the seven individual stamps and the miniature sheet.

The 2nd class, 1st class, 68p, £1·10 and £1·65 stamps were also issued in sheets of 20 containing eight 2nd class, eight 1st class, two 68p and two £1·10 stamps, each stamp accompanied by a se-tenant label with a verse from the King James Bible.

Separate sheets of 20 2nd, ten 1st, ten 68p and ten £1·10 were available with personal photographs.

### Collectors Pack

**2011** (8 Nov.) Comprises Nos. 3136/42, **MS**3144/52, 3154/93, 3195/204, 3207/14, **MS**3220 and 3223/48

| | | | |
|---|---|---|---|
| CP3244a | Collectors Pack | £140 | ☐ |

### Post Office Yearbook

**2011** (8 Nov.) Comprises Nos. 3136/42, **MS**3144/52, 3154/93, 3195/204, 3207/14, **MS**3220 and 3223/48

| | | | |
|---|---|---|---|
| YB3244a | Yearbook | £140 | ☐ |

### Miniature Sheet Collection

**2011** (8 Nov.) Comprises Nos. **MS**3142, **MS**3144, **MS**3172, **MS**3179/80, **MS**3193, **MS**3220, **MS**3229 and **MS**3249

| | | |
|---|---|---|
| **MS**3244a   Miniature Sheet Collection   £130 | | ☐ |

**2435** Paralympic Games Emblem

**2436** Olympic Games Emblem

**Olympic and Paralympic Games (7th issue)**

2012 (5 Jan). Self-adhesive. Two phosphor bands. Die-cut perf 14½×14 (with one elliptical hole in each vert side)

| | | | | | | |
|---|---|---|---|---|---|---|
| 3250 | **2435** | (1st) | black and orange-red | 1·75 | 1·25 | ☐ ☐ |
| 3251 | **2436** | (1st) | black and orange-red | 1·75 | 1·25 | ☐ ☐ |
| 3252 | **2435** | (Worldwide up to 20g) black, bright scarlet and greenish blue | | 3·00 | 3·00 | ☐ ☐ |
| 3253 | **2436** | (Worldwide up to 20g) black, bright scarlet and greenish blue | | 3·00 | 3·00 | ☐ ☐ |
| Set of 4 | | | | 17·50 | 17·50 | ☐ ☐ |
| First Day Cover | | | | | 18.50 | ☐ |
| Presentation Pack (P.O. Pack No. 93) | | | | 18·00 | | ☐ |
| PHQ Cards (set of 4) (D32) | | | | 2·75 | 9·00 | ☐ ☐ |

Nos. 3250/1 were printed together in sheets of 50 (2 panes 5×5), with the two designs alternating horizontally and vertically. The upper pane had No. 3250 at top left and contained 13 of No. 3250 and 12 of No. 3251. The lower pane had No. 3251 at top left and contained 13 of No. 3251 and 12 of No. 3250.

Nos. 3250/1 were also issued in booklets of six originally sold for £2.76. The panes from this booklet exist in two versions which differ in the order of the stamps within the block of six.

Nos. 3252/3 were printed together in sheets of 25 (5×5) with the two designs alternating horizontally and vertically. There were two versions of the sheets of 25, one having No. 3252 at top left and containing 13 of No. 3252 and 12 of No. 3253, and the other having No. 3253 at top left and containing 13 of No. 3253 and 12 of No. 3252.

Nos. 3250/3 were also issued on 27 June 2012 in sheets of 20 with se-tenant labels showing Games venues, printed in lithography instead of photogravure, each sheet containing eight each of Nos. 3250/1 and two each of Nos. 3252/3.

**2437** Charlie and the Chocolate Factory

**2438** Fantastic Mr. Fox

**2439** James and the Giant Peach

**2440** Matilda

**2441** The Twits

**2442** The Witches

**Roald Dahl's Children's Stories (1st issue).**
**Book Illustrations by Quentin Blake**

2012 (10 Jan). 'All-over' phosphor. Perf 14

| | | | | | | |
|---|---|---|---|---|---|---|
| 3254 | **2437** | (1st) | multicoloured | 1·25 | 1·00 | ☐ ☐ |
| 3255 | **2438** | 66p | multicoloured | 1·70 | 1·70 | ☐ ☐ |
| 3256 | **2439** | 68p | multicoloured | 1·70 | 1·70 | ☐ ☐ |
| 3257 | **2440** | 76p | multicoloured | 1·90 | 1·90 | ☐ ☐ |
| 3258 | **2441** | £1 | multicoloured | 2·50 | 2·50 | ☐ ☐ |
| 3259 | **2442** | £1.10 | multicoloured | 2·75 | 2·75 | ☐ ☐ |
| Set of 6 | | | | 10·50 | 10·50 | ☐ ☐ |
| First Day Cover | | | | | 12·00 | ☐ |
| Presentation Pack (P.O. Pack No. 465) | | | | 20·00 | | ☐ |
| PHQ Cards (set of 11) (358) | | | | 7·50 | 17·00 | ☐ ☐ |
| Set of 6 Gutter Pairs | | | | 22·00 | | |

The complete miniature sheet is shown on one of the eleven PHQ cards with the others showing individual stamps including those from **MS**3264.

**2443** The BFG carrying Sophie in his Hand

**2444** The BFG wakes up the Giants

**2445** Sophie sat on Buckingham Palace Window-sill

**2446** The BFG and Sophie at Writing Desk

**2447** Roald Dahl's The BFG

**Roald Dahl's Children's Stories (2nd issue).**
**Book Illustrations by Quentin Blake**

2012 (10 Jan). 'All-over' phosphor. Perf 14×14½

| | | | | | | |
|---|---|---|---|---|---|---|
| 3260 | **2443** | (1st) | multicoloured | 1·25 | 1·25 | ☐ ☐ |
| 3261 | **2444** | 68p | multicoloured | 1·70 | 1·70 | ☐ ☐ |
| 3262 | **2445** | 76p | multicoloured | 1·90 | 1·90 | ☐ ☐ |
| 3263 | **2446** | £1 | multicoloured | 2·50 | 2·50 | ☐ ☐ |
| Set of 4 | | | | 6·75 | 6·75 | ☐ ☐ |
| **MS**3264 115×89 mm. 2447 Nos. 3260/3 | | | | 6·75 | 6·75 | ☐ ☐ |
| First Day Cover | | | | | 7.75 | ☐ |

Nos. 3260/3 were only issued in £11.47 'Roald Dahl, Master Storyteller' premium booklets, and in **MS**3264.

No. **MS**3264 commemorates the 30th anniversary of the publication of *The BFG*.

**2448** Edward VII (1901-10)

**2449** George V (1910-36)

**2450** Edward VIII (1936)

**2451** George VI (1936-52)

**2452** Elizabeth II (1952-)

**2453** The Age of the Windsors

### Kings and Queens (6th issue). The House of Windsor

2012 (2 Feb). Two phosphor bands. Perf 14

| | | | | | | |
|---|---|---|---|---|---|---|
| 3265 | **2448** | (1st) multicoloured | 1·25 | 1·00 | ☐ | ☐ |
| 3266 | **2449** | 68p multicoloured | 1·70 | 1·70 | ☐ | ☐ |
| 3267 | **2450** | 76p multicoloured | 1·90 | 1·90 | ☐ | ☐ |
| 3268 | **2451** | £1 multicoloured | 2·50 | 2·50 | ☐ | ☐ |
| 3269 | 2452 | £1.10 multicoloured | 2·75 | 2·75 | ☐ | ☐ |
| Set of 5 | | | 9·00 | 9·00 | ☐ | ☐ |
| First Day Cover | | | | 10·00 | | ☐ |
| Presentation Pack (P.O. Pack No. 466) | | | 17·00 | | ☐ | |
| PHQ Cards (*set of* 10) (359) | | | 6·75 | 14·00 | ☐ | ☐ |
| Commemorative Document (No. 3268 and £1·10 stamp from **MS**3229) *(6 Feb)* | | | 11·00 | | ☐ | ☐ |
| Set of 5 Gutter Pairs | | | 14·00 | | ☐ | ☐ |
| Set of 5 Traffic Light Gutter Blocks of 4 | | | 40·00 | | ☐ | ☐ |

**MS**3270 123×70 mm. **2453** (1st) Scott Expedition to South Pole, 1912; 68p Queen Elizabeth the Queen Mother and King George VI in bomb damaged street, c. 1940; 76p England's winning World Cup football team, 1966; £1 Channel Tunnel, 1999 .... 7·50   7·50   ☐ ☐

| | | | |
|---|---|---|---|
| First Day Cover | | 8·50 | ☐ |

The complete miniature sheet is shown on one of the ten PHQ cards with the others depicting individual stamps including those from **MS**3270.

**2454** Diamond Jubilee

### Diamond Jubilee

**2012** (6 Feb).Two phosphor bands. Perf 14½×14 (with one elliptical hole in each vertical side)

**MS**3272 146×74 mm. **2454** (1st)×6 Portrait from photograph by Dorothy Wilding; 1960 £1 Banknote portrait by Robert Austin; 1971 £5 Banknote portrait by Harry Eccleston; 1953 Coinage portrait by Mary Gillick; 1971 decimal coin portrait by Arnold Machin; As No. U3271 .... 9·00   9·00   ☐ ☐

| | | | |
|---|---|---|---|
| First Day Cover | | 10·00 | ☐ ☐ |
| Presentation Pack (P.O. Pack No. 93) | 11·00 | | ☐ ☐ |
| PHQ Cards (*set of* 7) (D33) | 4·75 | 13·00 | ☐ ☐ |

The 1st class slate-blue machin stamp from **MS**3272 has an iridescent overprint reading "DIAMOND JUBILEE".

The seven PHQ cards show the six individual stamps and the complete miniature sheet.

**2455** Coventry Cathedral, 1962 (Sir Basil Spence, architect)

**2456** Frederick Delius (1862-1934, composer)

**2457** Orange Tree Embroidery (Mary 'May' Morris 1862-1938, designer and textile artist)

**2458** Odette Hallowes (1912-95, SOE agent in occupied France)

**2459** Steam Engine, 1712 (Thomas Newcomen, inventor of atmospheric steam engine)

**2460** Kathleen Ferrier (1912-53, contralto)

**2461** Interior of Palace of Westminster (Augustus Pugin, 1812-52, Gothic revival architect and designer)

**2462** Montagu Rhodes James (1862-1936 scholar and author)

**2463** Bombe Code Breaking Machine (Alan Turing 1912-54, mathematician and World War II code breaker)

**2464** Joan Mary Fry (1862-1955 relief worker and social reformer)

### Britons of Distinction

**2012** (23 Feb). 'All-over' phosphor. Perf 14½

| | | | | | | |
|---|---|---|---|---|---|---|
| 3273 | **2455** | (1st) | multicoloured | 1·25 | 1·10 | ☐ ☐ |
| | | a. | Horiz strip of 5. | | | |
| | | | Nos. 3273/7 | 6·25 | 5·50 | ☐ ☐ |
| 3274 | **2456** | (1st) | multicoloured | 1·25 | 1·10 | ☐ ☐ |
| 3275 | **2457** | (1st) | multicoloured | 1·25 | 1·10 | ☐ ☐ |
| 3276 | **2458** | (1st) | multicoloured | 1·25 | 1·10 | ☐ ☐ |
| 3277 | **2459** | (1st) | multicoloured | 1·25 | 1·10 | ☐ ☐ |
| 3278 | **2460** | (1st) | multicoloured | 1·25 | 1·10 | ☐ ☐ |
| | | a. | Horiz strip of 5. | | | |
| | | | Nos. 3278/82 | 6·25 | 5·50 | ☐ ☐ |
| 3279 | **2461** | (1st) | multicoloured | 1·25 | 1·10 | ☐ ☐ |
| 3280 | **2462** | (1st) | multicoloured | 1·25 | 1·10 | ☐ ☐ |
| 3281 | **2463** | (1st) | multicoloured | 1·25 | 1·10 | ☐ ☐ |
| 3282 | **2464** | (1st) | multicoloured | 1·25 | 1·10 | ☐ ☐ |
| Set of 10 | | | | 12·00 | 12·00 | ☐ ☐ |
| First Day Cover | | | | | 12·00 | ☐ |
| Presentation Pack (P.O. Pack No. 467) | | | | 14·00 | | ☐ |
| PHQ Cards (set of 10) (360) | | | | 6·75 | 18·00 | ☐ ☐ |
| Set of 2 Gutter Strips of 10 | | | | 25·00 | | ☐ |

Nos. 3273/7 and 3278/82 were each printed together, se-tenant, as horizontal strips of five stamps in sheets of 50 (2 panes 5×5).

**2465**

### Classic Locomotives (2nd series). Scotland

**2012** (8 Mar). Sheet 180×74 mm. 'All-over' phosphor. Perf 14
**MS**3283 2465 (1st) BR Class D34 Nos. 62471 *Glen Falloch* and 62496 *Glen Loy* at Ardlui, 9 May 1959; 68p BR Class D40 No. 62276 *Andrew Bain* at Macduff, July 1950; £1 Andrew Barclay No. 807 *Bon Accord* propelling wagons

along Miller Street, Aberdeen, June 1962; £1.10 BR Class 4P No. 54767 *Clan Mackinnon* pulling fish train, Kyle of Lochalsh, October 1948

| | | | |
|---|---|---|---|
| | 8·00 | 8·00 | ☐ ☐ |
| First Day Cover | | 9·00 | ☐ |
| Presentation Pack (P.O. Pack No. 468) | 9·00 | | ☐ |
| PHQ Cards (set of 5) (361) | 3·25 | 10·00 | ☐ ☐ |

The five PHQ cards show the four individual stamps and the complete miniature sheet

**2466** The Dandy and Desperate Dan

**2467** The Beano and Dennis the Menace

**2468** Eagle and Dan Dare

**2469** The Topper and Beryl the Peril

**2470** Tiger and Roy of the Rovers

**2471** Bunty and the Four Marys

**2472** Buster and Cartoon Character Buster

**2473** Valiant and the Steel Claw

**2474** Twinkle and Nurse Nancy

**2475** 2000 AD and Judge Dredd

### Comics

**2012** (20 Mar). 'All-over' phosphor. Perf 14½

| | | | | | | |
|---|---|---|---|---|---|---|
| 3284 | **2466** | (1st) | multicoloured | 1·25 | 1·10 | ☐ ☐ |
| | | a. | Horiz strip of 5. | | | |
| | | | Nos. 3284/8 | 6·25 | 5·50 | ☐ ☐ |
| 3285 | **2467** | (1st) | multicoloured | 1·25 | 1·10 | ☐ ☐ |
| 3286 | **2468** | (1st) | multicoloured | 1·25 | 1·10 | ☐ ☐ |

| | | | | | | | |
|---|---|---|---|---|---|---|---|
| 3287 | **2469** | (1st) | multicoloured | 1·25 | 1·10 | ☐ | ☐ |
| 3288 | **2470** | (1st) | multicoloured | 1·25 | 1·10 | ☐ | ☐ |
| 3289 | **2471** | (1st) | multicoloured | 1·25 | 1·10 | ☐ | ☐ |
| | | a. | Horiz strip of 5. | | | | |
| | | | Nos. 3289/93 | 6·25 | 5·50 | ☐ | ☐ |
| 3290 | **2472** | (1st) | multicoloured | 1·25 | 1·10 | ☐ | ☐ |
| 3291 | **2473** | (1st) | multicoloured | 1·25 | 1·10 | ☐ | ☐ |
| 3292 | **2474** | (1st) | multicoloured | 1·25 | 1·10 | ☐ | ☐ |
| 3293 | **2475** | (1st) | multicoloured | 1·25 | 1·10 | ☐ | ☐ |
| *Set of* 10 | | | | 12·00 | 11·00 | ☐ | ☐ |
| First Day Cover | | | | | 12·00 | ☐ | |
| Presentation Pack (P.O. Pack No. 469) | | | | 14·00 | | ☐ | |
| PHQ Cards (*set of* 10) | | | | 6·75 | 17·00 | ☐ | ☐ |
| *Set of* 2 Gutter Strips of 5 | | | | 25·00 | | ☐ | |

**2476** Manchester Town Hall

**2477** Narrow Water Castle, Co. Down

**2478** Old Bailey, London

**2479** Portmeirion, Wales

**2480** The Queen's College, Oxford

**2481** Roman Baths, Bath

**2482** Stirling Castle, Scotland

**2483** Tyne Bridge, Newcastle

**2484** Urquhart Castle, Scotland

**2485** Victoria and Albert Museum, London

**2486** White Cliffs of Dover

**2487** Station X, Bletchley Park, Buckinghamshire

**2488** York Minster

**2489** London Zoo

## UK A-Z (2nd series)

**2012** (10 Apr). 'All-over' phosphor. Perf 14½

| | | | | | | | |
|---|---|---|---|---|---|---|---|
| 3294 | **2476** | (1st) | multicoloured | 1·25 | 1·10 | ☐ | ☐ |
| | | a. | Horiz strip of 5. | | | | |
| | | | Nos. 3294/9 | 7·50 | 6·50 | ☐ | ☐ |
| 3295 | **2477** | (1st) | multicoloured | 1·25 | 1·10 | ☐ | ☐ |
| 3296 | **2478** | (1st) | multicoloured | 1·25 | 1·10 | ☐ | ☐ |
| 3297 | **2479** | (1st) | multicoloured | 1·25 | 1·10 | ☐ | ☐ |
| 3298 | **2480** | (1st) | multicoloured | 1·25 | 1·10 | ☐ | ☐ |
| 3299 | **2481** | (1st) | multicoloured | 1·25 | 1·10 | ☐ | ☐ |
| 3300 | **2482** | (1st) | multicoloured | 1·25 | 1·10 | ☐ | ☐ |
| | | a. | Horiz strip of 5. | | | | |
| | | | Nos. 3300/5 | 7·50 | 6·50 | ☐ | ☐ |
| 3301 | **2483** | (1st) | multicoloured | 1·25 | 1·10 | ☐ | ☐ |
| 3302 | **2484** | (1st) | multicoloured | 1·25 | 1·10 | ☐ | ☐ |
| 3303 | **2485** | (1st) | multicoloured | 1·25 | 1·10 | ☐ | ☐ |
| 3304 | **2486** | (1st) | multicoloured | 1·25 | 1·10 | ☐ | ☐ |
| 3305 | **2487** | (1st) | multicoloured | 1·25 | 1·10 | ☐ | ☐ |
| 3306 | **2488** | (1st) | multicoloured | 1·25 | 1·10 | ☐ | ☐ |
| | | a. | Horiz pair. | | | | |
| | | | Nos. 3306/7 | 2·50 | 2·20 | ☐ | ☐ |
| 3307 | **2489** | (1st) | multicoloured | 1·25 | 1·10 | ☐ | ☐ |
| *Set of* 14 | | | | 14·00 | 12·00 | ☐ | ☐ |
| First Day Covers (2) | | | | | 14·00 | ☐ | |
| Presentation Pack (P.O. Pack No. 470) | | | | 16·00 | | ☐ | |
| PHQ Cards (*set of* 14) | | | | 9·50 | 20·00 | ☐ | ☐ |
| *Set of* 2 Gutter Strips of 12 and | | | | | | | |
| | | | 1 Gutter Strip of 4 | 30·00 | | ☐ | |
| *Set of* 2 Traffic Light Gutter Strips of 24 | | | | | | | |
| | | | and 1 Gutter Block of 8 | 60·00 | | ☐ | |
| **MS**3308 | 297×210 mm. Nos. 3230/41 | | | | | | |
| | and 3294/307 | | | 40·00 | 40·00 | ☐ | ☐ |

Nos. 3294/9 and 3300/5 were each printed together, 3 se-tenant, as horizontal strips of six stamps in sheets of 60 (2 panes 6×5).

Nos. 3306/7 were printed together, *se-tenant*, as horizontal pairs in sheets of 60 (2 panes 6×5).

No. 3303 includes the 'EUROPA' emblem.

**2490** Skirt Suit by Hardy Amies, late 1940s

**2491** Outfit by Norman Hartnell, 1950s

**2492** Jacket designed by John Pearce for Granny Takes a Trip Boutique, 1960s

**2493** Print by Celia Birtwell for Outfit by Ossie Clark, late 1960s

**2494** Suit designed for Ringo Starr by Tommy Nutter

**2495** Outfit by Jean Muir, late 1970s/early 1980s

**2496** 'Royal' Dress by Zandra Rhodes, 1981

**2497** Harlequin dress by Vivienne Westwood, 1993

**2498** Suit by Paul Smith, 2003

**2499** 'Black Raven' by Alexander McQueen, 2009

### Great British Fashion

2012 (15 May). Phosphor background. Perf 14½×14

| | | | | | | |
|---|---|---|---|---|---|---|
| 3309 | **2490** | (1st) | multicoloured | 1·25 | 1·25 | ☐ ☐ |
| | | a. | Horiz strip of 5. | | | |
| | | | Nos. 3309/13 | 6·50 | 6·50 | ☐ ☐ |
| 3310 | **2491** | (1st) | multicoloured | 1·25 | 1·25 | ☐ ☐ |
| 3311 | **2492** | (1st) | multicoloured | 1·25 | 1·25 | ☐ ☐ |
| 3312 | **2493** | (1st) | multicoloured | 1·25 | 1·25 | ☐ ☐ |
| 3313 | **2494** | (1st) | multicoloured | 1·25 | 1·25 | ☐ ☐ |
| 3314 | **2495** | (1st) | multicoloured | 1·25 | 1·25 | ☐ ☐ |
| | | a. | Horiz strip of 5. | | | |
| | | | Nos. 3314/18 | 6·50 | 6·50 | ☐ ☐ |
| 3315 | **2496** | (1st) | multicoloured | 1·25 | 1·25 | ☐ ☐ |
| 3316 | **2497** | (1st) | multicoloured | 1·25 | 1·25 | ☐ ☐ |
| 3317 | **2498** | (1st) | multicoloured | 1·25 | 1·25 | ☐ ☐ |
| 3318 | **2499** | (1st) | multicoloured | 1·25 | 1·25 | ☐ ☐ |
| Set of 10 | | | | 12·00 | 12·00 | ☐ |
| First Day Cover | | | | | 14·00 | ☐ |
| Presentation Pack (P.O. Pack No. 471) | | | 15·00 | | | ☐ |
| PHQ Cards (set of 10) | | | | 6·75 | 20·00 | ☐ ☐ |
| Set of 2 Gutter Strips of 10 | | | | 25·00 | | ☐ |
| Set of 2 Traffic Light Gutter Strips of 20 | | 50·00 | | | | ☐ |

Nos. 3309/13 and 3314/18 were each printed together, *se-tenant*, as horizontal strips of five stamps in sheets of 50 (2 panes 5×5).

**2500** Queen Elizabeth II at Golden Jubilee Thanksgiving Service, St. Paul's Cathedral, London, 2002

**2501** Queen Elizabeth II Trooping the Colour, 1967

**2502** Queen Elizabeth II inspecting 2nd Battalion Royal Welsh, Tidworth, 1 March 2007

**2503** First Christmas Television Broadcast, 1957

**2504** Silver Jubilee Walkabout, 1977

**2505** Queen Elizabeth II in Garter Ceremony Procession, 1997

**2506** Queen Elizabeth II addressing the UN General Assembly, 1957

**2507** Queen Elizabeth II at Commonwealth Games, Brisbane, Australia, 1982

### Diamond Jubilee (3rd issue)

2012 (31 May). 'All-over' phosphor.

(a) Sheet stamps. Ordinary gum. Photo. Perf 14×14½.

| | | | | | | |
|---|---|---|---|---|---|---|
| A3319 | **2500** | (1st) | multicoloured | 1·25 | 1·10 | ☐ ☐ |
| | | a) | Horiz pair. | | | |
| | | | Nos. 3319/20 | 2·50 | 2·50 | ☐ ☐ |
| A3320 | **2501** | (1st) | black and brownish grey | 1·25 | 1·10 | ☐ ☐ |
| A3321 | **2502** | 77p | multicoloured | 1·90 | 1·90 | ☐ ☐ |
| | | a. | Horiz pair. | | | |
| | | | Nos. 3321/2 | 3·75 | 3·75 | ☐ ☐ |
| A3322 | **2503** | 77p | black and brownish grey | 1·90 | 1·90 | ☐ ☐ |
| A3323 | **2504** | 87p | black and brownish grey | 2·25 | 2·25 | ☐ ☐ |
| | | a. | Horiz pair. | | | |
| | | | Nos. 3323/4 | 4·50 | 4·50 | ☐ ☐ |
| A3324 | **2505** | 87p. | multicoloured | 2·25 | 2·25 | ☐ ☐ |
| A3325 | **2506** | £1.28 | black and brownish grey | 3·25 | 3·25 | ☐ ☐ |
| | | a. | Horiz pair. | | | |
| | | | Nos. 3325/6 | 6·50 | 6·50 | ☐ ☐ |

| | | | | | | |
|---|---|---|---|---|---|---|
| A3326 | **2507** | £1.28 | multicoloured | 3·25 | 3·25 | ☐ ☐ |
| *Set of 8* | | | | 16·00 | 16·00 | ☐ ☐ |
| First Day Cover | | | | | 18·00 | ☐ |
| Presentation Pack (P.O. Pack No. 472) | | | | 21·00 | | ☐ |
| PHQ Cards (*set of 8*) | | | | | 5·50 | 21·00 | ☐ |
| *Set of 4 Gutter Strips of 4* | | | | 32·00 | | ☐ |

(b) Booklet stamps. Ordinary gum. Litho. Perf 14×14½.

| | | | | | | |
|---|---|---|---|---|---|---|
| B3319 | **2500** | (1st) | multicoloured | 1·50 | 1·50 | ☐ ☐ |
| B3320 | **2501** | (1st) | black and brownish grey | 1·50 | 1·50 | ☐ ☐ |
| B3321 | **2502** | 77p | multicoloured | 1·90 | 1·90 | ☐ ☐ |
| B3322 | **2503** | 77p | black and brownish grey | 1·90 | 1·90 | ☐ ☐ |
| B3323 | **2504** | 87p | black and brownish grey | 2·25 | 2·25 | ☐ ☐ |
| B3324 | **2505** | 87p | multicoloured | 2·25 | 2·25 | ☐ ☐ |
| B3325 | **2506** | £1.28 | black and brownish grey | 3·25 | 3·25 | ☐ ☐ |
| B3326 | **2507** | £1.28 | multicoloured | 3·25 | 3·25 | ☐ ☐ |

(c) Self-adhesive booklet stamp. Die-cut perf 14.

| | | | | | | |
|---|---|---|---|---|---|---|
| 3327 | **2500** | (1st) | multicoloured | 2·00 | 2·00 | ☐ ☐ |

Nos. A3319/20, A3321/2, A3323/4 and A3325/6 were printed together, *se-tenant*, as horizontal pairs in sheets of 60 (2 panes 6×5).

Nos. B3319/26 come from £12.77 Diamond Jubilee Prestige booklets.

No. 3327 was only issued in Diamond Jubilee stamp booklets, containing Nos. 3327×2 and U3271×4, originally sold for £3.60.

**Diamond Jubilee (4th issue)**

**2012** (31 May). As Type 159 but redrawn with 1st value indicator (3329). Two phosphor bands. Perf 14½×14 (with one elliptical hole in each vert side)

| | | | | | | |
|---|---|---|---|---|---|---|
| 3329 | | (1st) | light brown | 1·50 | 1·50 | ☐ ☐ |

No. 3329 was issued in £12.27 Diamond Jubilee booklets.
A similar stamp was issued in **MS**3272.

**2508** Mr. Bumble
(Oliver Twist)

**2509** Mr. Pickwick
(The Pickwick Papers)

**2510** The Marchioness
(The Old Curiosity Shop)

**2511** Mrs. Gamp
(Martin Chuzzlewit)

**2512** Captain Cuttle
(Dombey and Son)

**2513** Mr. Micawber
(David Copperfield)

**2514** Scenes from Nicholas Nickleby, Bleak House, Little Dorrit and A Tale of Two Cities

**Birth Bicentenary of Charles Dickens**

**2012** (19 June). Illustrations from Character Sketches from Charles Dickens, c. 1890 by Joseph Clayton Clarke ('Kyd') (3330/5) or Book Illustrations by Hablot Knight Browne ('Phiz') (**MS**3336). One centre band (2nd) or 'all-over' phosphor (others). Perf 14 (3330/5) or 14×14½ (**MS**3336)

| | | | | | | |
|---|---|---|---|---|---|---|
| 3330 | 2508 | (2nd) | multicoloured | 1·00 | 1·00 | ☐ ☐ |
| 3331 | 2509 | (1st) | multicoloured | 1·25 | 1·10 | ☐ ☐ |
| 3332 | 2510 | 77p | multicoloured | 1·90 | 1·90 | ☐ ☐ |
| 3333 | 2511 | 87p | multicoloured | 2·25 | 2·25 | ☐ ☐ |
| 3334 | 2512 | £1.28 | multicoloured | 3·25 | 3·25 | ☐ ☐ |
| 3335 | 2513 | £1.90 | multicoloured | 4·75 | 4·75 | ☐ ☐ |
| *Set of 6* | | | | 13·00 | 13·00 | ☐ ☐ |
| First Day Cover | | | | | 15·00 | ☐ |
| Presentation Pack (P.O. Pack No. 473) | | | 22·00 | | ☐ |
| PHQ Cards (*set of 11*) | | | | 7·50 | 20·00 | ☐ ☐ |
| *Set of 6 Gutter Pairs* | | | | 27·00 | | ☐ |
| *Set of 6 Traffic Light Gutter Blocks of 4* | | | 55·00 | | ☐ |

**MS**3336 190×67 mm. **2514** (1st)×4 Nicholas Nickleby caning headmaster Wackford Squeers (*Nicholas Nickleby*); Mrs. Bagnet is charmed with Mr. Bucket (*Bleak House*); Amy Dorrit introduces Maggy to Arthur Clennam (*Little Dorrit*); Charles Darnay arrested by French revolutionaries (*A Tale of Two Cities*) 6·00 6·00 ☐ ☐

| | | |
|---|---|---|
| First Day Cover | 8·00 | ☐ |

The complete miniature sheet is shown on one of the eleven PHQ cards with the others depicting individual stamps including those from **MS**3336.

**Olympic and Paralympic Games (8th issue)**

**2012** (27 July). Designs as Nos. 3250/3. Two phosphor bands. Perf 14½×14 (with one elliptical hole in each vert side)

| | | | | | | |
|---|---|---|---|---|---|---|
| 3337 | **2436** | (1st) | black and orange-red | 3·00 | 3·00 | ☐ ☐ |
| 3338 | **2435** | (1st) | black and orange-red | 3·00 | 3·00 | ☐ ☐ |
| 3339 | **2436** | (Worldwide up to 20g) | black, bright scarlet and greenish blue | 5·00 | 5·00 | ☐ ☐ |
| 3340 | **2435** | (Worldwide up to 20g) | black, bright scarlet and greenish blue | 5·00 | 5·00 | ☐ ☐ |
| *Set of 4* | | | | 14.00 | 14.00 | ☐ ☐ |
| First Day Cover | | | | | 16·00 | ☐ |

Nos. 3339/40 were for use on Worldwide Mail up to 20g.

Nos. 3337/40 were only issued in £10.71 Olympic and Paralympic Games stamp booklets.

**2515** Sports and London Landmarks

**Welcome to London, Olympic Games**

**2012** (27 July). Sheet 192×75 mm. 'All-over' phosphor. Perf 14½

**MS**3341 2515 (1st) Fencer and Tower Bridge; (1st) Athletes in race and Olympic Stadium; £1.28 Diver and Tate Modern;

| | | |
|---|---|---|
| £1.28 Cyclist and London Eye | 9·50 | 9·50 ☐ ☐ |
| First Day Cover | | 11·50 ☐ |
| Presentation Pack (P.O. Pack No. 474) | 12·00 | ☐ ☐ |
| PHQ Cards (*set of* 5) | 3·50 | 14·00 ☐ ☐ |

The five PHQ cards show the four individual stamps and the complete miniature sheet.

**2516** Helen Glover and Heather Stanning (rowing, women's pairs)

**2517** Bradley Wiggins (cycling: road, men's time trial)

**2518** Tim Baillie and Etienne Stott (canoe slalom: men's canoe double (C2))

**2519** Peter Wilson (shooting: shotgun men's double trap)

**2520** Philip Hindes, Chris Hoy and Jason Kenny (cycling: track men's team sprint)

**2521** Katherine Grainger and Anna Watkins (rowing: women's double sculls)

**2522** Steven Burke, Ed Clancy, Peter Kennaugh and Geraint Thomas (cycling: track men's team pursuit)

**2523** Victoria Pendleton (cycling: track women's keirin)

**2524** Alex Gregory, Tom James, Pete Reed and Andrew Triggs Hodge (rowing men's fours)

**2525** Katherine Copeland and Sophie Hosking (rowing: lightweight women's double sculls)

**2526** Dani King, Joanna Rowsell and Laura Trott (cycling: track women's team pursuit)

**2527** Jessica Ennis (athletics: combined women's heptathlon)

**2528** Greg Rutherford (athletics: field men's long jump)

**2529** Mo Farah (athletics: track men's 10,000m)

**2530** Ben Ainslie (sailing: Finn men's heavyweight dinghy)

**2531** Andy Murray (tennis: men's singles)

**2532** Scott Brash, Peter Charles, Ben Maher and Nick Skelton (equestrian: jumping team)

**2533** Jason Kenny (cycling: track men's sprint)

**2534** Alistair Brownlee (men's triathlon)

**2535** Laura Bechtolsheimer, Charlotte Dujardin and Carl Hester (equestrian: dressage team)

**2536** Laura Trott (cycling: track women's omnium)

**2537** Chris Hoy (cycling: track men's keirin)

**2538** Charlotte Dujardin (equestrian: dressage individual)

**2539** Nicola Adams (boxing: women's fly weight)

**2540** Jade Jones (taekwondo women's under 57kg)

**2541** Ed McKeever (canoe sprint: men's kayak single (K1) 200m)

**2542** Mo Farah (athletics: track men's 5000m)

**2543** Luke Campbell (boxing: men's bantam weight)

**2544** Anthony Joshua (boxing: men's super heavy weight)

**British Gold Medal Winners at London Olympic Games**

**2012** (2-13 Aug). Self-adhesive. Two phosphor panels. Die-cut perf 15×14½

| | | | | | | |
|---|---|---|---|---|---|---|
| 3342 | **2516** | (1st) | multicoloured | 1·50 | 1·50 | ☐ ☐ |
| | | a | Sheetlet. | | | |
| | | | No. 3342×6 | 8.50 | 8·50 | ☐ ☐ |
| 3343 | **2517** | (1st) | multicoloured | 1·50 | 1·50 | ☐ ☐ |
| | | a | Sheetlet. | | | |
| | | | No. 3343×6 | 8.50 | 8·50 | ☐ ☐ |
| 3344 | **2518** | (1st) | multicoloured (3 Aug) | 1·50 | 1·50 | ☐ ☐ |
| | | a | Sheetlet. | | | |
| | | | No. 3344×6 | 8.50 | 8·50 | ☐ ☐ |
| 3345 | **2519** | (1st) | multicoloured (3 Aug) | 1·50 | 1·50 | ☐ ☐ |
| | | a | Sheetlet. | | | |
| | | | No. 3345×6 | 8.50 | 8·50 | ☐ ☐ |
| 3346 | **2520** | (1st) | multicoloured (3 Aug) | 1·50 | 1·50 | ☐ ☐ |
| | | a | Sheetlet. | | | |
| | | | No. 3346×6 | 8.50 | 8·50 | ☐ ☐ |
| 3347 | **2521** | (1st) | multicoloured (4 Aug) | 1·50 | 1·50 | ☐ ☐ |
| | | a | Sheetlet. | | | |
| | | | No. 3347×6 | 8.50 | 8·50 | ☐ ☐ |
| 3348 | **2522** | (1st) | multicoloured (4 Aug) | 1·50 | 1·50 | ☐ ☐ |
| | | a | Sheetlet. | | | |
| | | | No. 3348×6 | 8.50 | 8·50 | ☐ ☐ |
| 3349 | **2523** | (1st) | multicoloured (4 Aug) | 1·50 | 1·50 | ☐ ☐ |
| | | a | Sheetlet. | | | |
| | | | No. 3349×6 | 8.50 | 8·50 | ☐ ☐ |
| 3350 | **2524** | (1st) | multicoloured (5 Aug) | 1·50 | 1·50 | ☐ ☐ |
| | | a | Sheetlet. | | | |
| | | | No. 3350×6 | 8.50 | 8·50 | ☐ ☐ |
| 3351 | **2525** | (1st) | multicoloured (5 Aug) | 1·50 | 1·50 | ☐ ☐ |
| | | a | Sheetlet. | | | |
| | | | No. 3351×6 | 8.50 | 8·50 | ☐ ☐ |
| 3352 | **2526** | (1st) | multicoloured (5 Aug) | 1·50 | 1·50 | ☐ ☐ |
| | | a | Sheetlet. | | | |
| | | | No. 3352×6 | 8.50 | 8·50 | ☐ ☐ |
| 3353 | **2527** | (1st) | multicoloured (5 Aug) | 1·50 | 1·50 | ☐ ☐ |
| | | a | Sheetlet. | | | |
| | | | No. 3353×6 | 8.50 | 8·50 | ☐ ☐ |
| 3354 | **2528** | (1st) | multicoloured (5 Aug) | 1·50 | 1·50 | ☐ ☐ |
| | | a | Sheetlet. | | | |
| | | | No. 3354×6 | 8.50 | 8·50 | ☐ ☐ |
| 3355 | **2529** | (1st) | multicoloured (5 Aug) | 1·50 | 1·50 | ☐ ☐ |
| | | a | Sheetlet. | | | |
| | | | No. 3355×6 | 8.50 | 8·50 | ☐ ☐ |
| 3356 | **2530** | (1st) | multicoloured (6 Aug) | 1·50 | 1·50 | ☐ ☐ |
| | | a | Sheetlet. | | | |
| | | | No. 3356×6 | 8.50 | 8·50 | ☐ ☐ |
| 3357 | **2531** | (1st) | multicoloured (6 Aug) | 1·50 | 1·50 | ☐ ☐ |
| | | a | Sheetlet. | | | |
| | | | No. 3357×6 | 8.50 | 8·50 | ☐ ☐ |
| 3358 | **2532** | (1st) | multicoloured (7 Aug) | 1·50 | 1·50 | ☐ ☐ |
| | | a | Sheetlet. | | | |
| | | | No. 3358×6 | 8.50 | 8·50 | ☐ ☐ |
| 3359 | **2533** | (1st) | multicoloured (7 Aug) | 1·50 | 1·50 | ☐ ☐ |
| | | a | Sheetlet. | | | |
| | | | No. 3359×6 | 8.50 | 8·50 | ☐ ☐ |
| 3360 | **2534** | (1st) | multicoloured (8 Aug) | 1·50 | 1·50 | ☐ ☐ |
| | | a | Sheetlet. | | | |
| | | | No. 3360×6 | 8.50 | 8·50 | ☐ ☐ |
| 3361 | **2535** | (1st) | multicoloured (8 Aug) | 1·50 | 1·50 | ☐ ☐ |
| | | a | Sheetlet. | | | |
| | | | No. 3361×6 | 8.50 | 8·50 | ☐ ☐ |
| 3362 | **2536** | (1st) | multicoloured (8 Aug) | 1·50 | 1·50 | ☐ ☐ |
| | | a | Sheetlet. | | | |
| | | | No. 3362×6 | 8.50 | 8·50 | ☐ ☐ |

| 3363 | 2537 | (1st) | multicoloured (8 Aug) | 1·50 | 1·50 | ☐ ☐ |
| | | a | Sheetlet. | | | |
| | | | No. 3363×6 | 8·50 | 8·50 | ☐ ☐ |
| 3364 | 2538 | (1st) | multicoloured (10 Aug) | 1·50 | 1·50 | ☐ ☐ |
| | | a | Sheetlet. | | | |
| | | | No. 3364×6 | 8·50 | 8·50 | ☐ ☐ |
| 3365 | 2539 | (1st) | multicoloured (10 Aug) | 1·50 | 1·50 | ☐ ☐ |
| | | a | Sheetlet. | | | |
| | | | No. 3365×6 | 8.50 | 8·50 | ☐ ☐ |
| 3366 | 2540 | (1st) | multicoloured (10 Aug) | 1·50 | 1·50 | ☐ ☐ |
| | | a | Sheetlet. | | | |
| | | | No. 3366×6 | 8·50 | 8·50 | ☐ ☐ |
| 3367 | 2541 | (1st) | multicoloured (12 Aug) | 1·50 | 1·50 | ☐ ☐ |
| | | a | Sheetlet. | | | |
| | | | No. 3367×6 | 8.50 | 8·50 | ☐ ☐ |
| 3368 | 2542 | (1st) | multicoloured (12 Aug) | 1·50 | 1·50 | ☐ ☐ |
| | | a | Sheetlet. | | | |
| | | | No. 3368×6 | 8.50 | 8·50 | ☐ ☐ |
| 3369 | 2543 | (1st) | multicoloured (12 Aug) | 1·50 | 1·50 | ☐ ☐ |
| | | a | Sheetlet. | | | |
| | | | No. 3369×6 | 8.50 | 8·50 | ☐ ☐ |
| 3370 | 2544 | (1st) | multicoloured (13 Aug) | 1·50 | 1·50 | ☐ ☐ |
| | | a | Sheetlet. | | | |
| | | | No. 3370×6 | 8.50 | 8·50 | ☐ ☐ |
| Set of 29 | | | | 40·00 | 40·00 | ☐ ☐ |
| First Day Covers (Nos. 3342a/70a) (29) | | | | | £325 | ☐ |
| First Day Cover (any gold medal stamp | | | | | 10·00 | ☐ |

The self-adhesive base sheetlets for Nos. 3342/70 were produced by Walsall with the image, name and event of the winning athletes digitally printed by regional printers in six different locations: Attleborough, Edinburgh, London, Preston, Solihull and Swindon. Nos. 3368/70 were not produced by the Preston printer due to machinery breakdown. These sheetlets of 24 stamps were divided by roulettes into four portions of six stamps (3×2) each with either of the following inscriptions on the left margin: emblem 'TEAM GB' and Olympic rings; 'The XXX Olympiad'; barcode; Sheet number, Issue date and Printer location.

**2545** Paralympic Sports and London Landmarks

**Welcome to London, Paralympic Games**

**2012** (29 Aug). Sheet 193 ×75 mm. 'All-over' phosphor. Perf 14½

| MS3371 | 2545 | (1st) | Athlete wearing running blades and Olympic Stadium; (1st) Wheelchair basketball player and Palace of Westminster; £1.28 Powerlifter, Millennium Bridge and St. Paul's Cathedral; £1.28 Cyclist and London Eye | 9·50 | 9·50 | ☐ ☐ |
| First Day Cover | | | | | 11·50 | ☐ |
| Presentation Pack (P.O. Pack No. 475) | | | | 12·00 | | ☐ |
| PHQ Cards | | | | 3·50 | 14·00 | ☐ ☐ |

The five PHQ cards show the four individual stamps and the complete miniature sheet.

**2546** Sarah Storey (cycling: track women's C5 pursuit)

**2547** Jonathan Fox (swimming: men's 100m backstroke, S7)

**2548** Mark Colbourne (cycling: track men's C1 pursuit)

**2549** Hannah Cockroft (athletics: track women's 100m, T34)

**2550** Neil Fachie and Barney Storey (cycling: men's B 1km time trial)

**2551** Richard Whitehead (athletics: track men's 200m, T42)

**2552** Natasha Baker (equestrian: individual championship test, grade II)

**2553** Sarah Storey (cycling: track – women's C4-5 500m time trial)

**2554** Ellie Simmonds (swimming: women's 400m freestyle, S6)

**2555** Pamela Relph, Naomi Riches, James Roe, David Smith and Lily van den Broecke (rowing: mixed coxed four, LTAmix4+)

**2556** Aled Davies (athletics: field men's discus, F42)

**2557** Anthony Kappes and Craig MacLean (cycling: track men's B sprint)

**2558** Jessica-Jane Applegate (swimming: women's 200m freestyle, S14)

**2559** Sophie Christiansen (equestrian: individual championship test, grade 1a)

**2560** David Weir (athletics: track men's 5000m, T54)

**2561** Natasha Baker (equestrian: individual freestyle test, grade II)

**2562** Ellie Simmonds (swimming: women's 200m individual medley, SM6)

**2563** Mickey Bushell (athletics: track men's 100m, T53)

**2564** Danielle Brown (archery: women's individual compound, open)

**2565** Heather Frederiksen (swimming: women's 100m backstroke, S8)

**2566** Sophie Christiansen (equestrian: individual freestyle test, grade 1a)

**2567** David Weir (athletics: track men's 1500m, T54)

**2568** Sarah Storey (cycling: road women's C5 time trial)

**2569** Ollie Hynd (swimming: men's 200m individual medley, SM8)

**2570** Sophie Christiansen, Deb Criddle, Lee Pearson and Sophie Wells (equestrian team, open)

**2571** Helena Lucas (sailing: single-person keelboat, 2.4mR)

**2572** Sarah Storey (cycling: road women's C4-5 road race)

**2573** Josef Craig (swimming: men's 400m freestyle, S7)

**2574** Hannah Cockroft (athletics: track women's 200m, T34)

**2575** David Weir (athletics: track men's 800m, T54)

**2576** Jonnie Peacock (athletics: track men's 100m, T44)

**2577** Josie Pearson (athletics: field women's discus, F51/52/53)

**2578** David Stone (cycling: road mixed T1-2 road race)

**2579** David Weir (athletics: road men's marathon, T54)

### British Gold Medal Winners at London Paralympic Games

**2012** (31 Aug-10 Sept). Self-adhesive. Two phosphor panels. Die-cut perf 15×14½

| | | | | | | | |
|---|---|---|---|---|---|---|---|
| 3372 | **2546** | (1st) | multicoloured | | 2·00 | 2·00 | ☐ ☐ |
| | a. | Sheetlet. No. 3372×2 | 4·00 | | | 4·00 | ☐ ☐ |
| 3373 | **2547** | (1st) | multicoloured (1 Sept) | | 2·00 | 2·00 | ☐ ☐ |
| | a. | Sheetlet. No. 3373×2 | 4·00 | | | 4·00 | ☐ ☐ |
| 3374 | **2548** | (1st) | multicoloured (3 Sept) | | 2·00 | 2·00 | ☐ ☐ |
| | a. | Sheetlet. No. 3374×2 | 4·00 | | | 4·00 | ☐ ☐ |
| 3375 | **2549** | (1st) | multicoloured (3 Sept) | | 2·00 | 2·00 | ☐ ☐ |
| | a. | Sheetlet. No. 3375×2 | 4·00 | | | 4·00 | ☐ ☐ |
| 3376 | **2550** | (1st) | multicoloured (3 Sept) | | 2·00 | 2·00 | ☐ ☐ |
| | a. | Sheetlet. No. 3376×2 | 4·00 | | | 4·00 | ☐ ☐ |
| 3377 | **2551** | (1st) | multicoloured (3 Sept) | | 2·00 | 2·00 | ☐ ☐ |
| | a. | Sheetlet. No. 3377×2 | 4·00 | | | 4·00 | ☐ ☐ |
| 3378 | **2552** | (1st) | multicoloured (3 Sept) | | 2·00 | 2·00 | ☐ ☐ |
| | a. | Sheetlet. No. 3378×2 | 4·00 | | | 4·00 | ☐ ☐ |
| 3379 | **2553** | (1st) | multicoloured (3 Sept) | | 2·00 | 2·00 | ☐ ☐ |
| | a. | Sheetlet. No. 3379×2 | 4·00 | | | 4·00 | ☐ ☐ |
| 3380 | **2554** | (1st) | multicoloured (3 Sept) | | 2·00 | 2·00 | ☐ ☐ |
| | a. | Sheetlet. No. 3380×2 | 4·00 | | | 4·00 | ☐ ☐ |
| 3381 | **2555** | (1st) | multicoloured (4 Sept) | | 2·00 | 2·00 | ☐ ☐ |
| | a. | Sheetlet. No. 3381×2 | 4·00 | | | 4·00 | ☐ ☐ |
| 3382 | **2556** | (1st) | multicoloured (4 Sept) | | 2·00 | 2·00 | ☐ ☐ |
| | a. | Sheetlet. No. 3382×2 | 4·00 | | | 4·00 | ☐ ☐ |
| 3383 | **2557** | (1st) | multicoloured (4 Sept) | | 2·00 | 2·00 | ☐ ☐ |
| | a. | Sheetlet. No. 3383×2 | 4·00 | | | 4·00 | ☐ ☐ |
| 3384 | **2558** | (1st) | multicoloured (4 Sept) | | 2·00 | 2·00 | ☐ ☐ |
| | a. | Sheetlet. No. 3384×2 | 4·00 | | | 4·00 | ☐ ☐ |
| 3385 | **2559** | (1st) | multicoloured (4 Sept) | | 2·00 | 2·00 | ☐ ☐ |
| | a. | Sheetlet. No. 3385×2 | 4·00 | | | 4·00 | ☐ ☐ |
| 3386 | **2560** | (1st) | multicoloured (4 Sept) | | 2·00 | 2·00 | ☐ ☐ |
| | a. | Sheetlet. No. 3386×2 | 4·00 | | | 4·00 | ☐ ☐ |
| 3387 | **2561** | (1st) | multicoloured (4 Sept) | | 2·00 | 2·00 | ☐ ☐ |
| | a. | Sheetlet. No. 3387×2 | 4·00 | | | 4·00 | ☐ ☐ |
| 3388 | **2562** | (1st) | multicoloured (4 Sept) | | 2·00 | 2·00 | ☐ ☐ |
| | a. | Sheetlet. No. 3388×2 | 4·00 | | | 4·00 | ☐ ☐ |
| 3389 | **2563** | (1st) | multicoloured (5 Sept) | | 2·00 | 2·00 | ☐ ☐ |
| | a. | Sheetlet. No. 3389×2 | 4·00 | | | 4·00 | ☐ ☐ |
| 3390 | **2564** | (1st) | multicoloured (5 Sept) | | 2·00 | 2·00 | ☐ ☐ |
| | a. | Sheetlet. No. 3390×2 | 4·00 | | | 4·00 | ☐ ☐ |
| 3391 | **2565** | (1st) | multicoloured (5 Sept) | | 2·00 | 2·00 | ☐ ☐ |
| | a. | Sheetlet. No. 3391×2 | 4·00 | | | 4·00 | ☐ ☐ |
| 3392 | **2566** | (1st) | multicoloured (5 Sept) | | 2·00 | 2·00 | ☐ ☐ |
| | a. | Sheetlet. No. 3392×2 | 4·00 | | | 4·00 | ☐ ☐ |
| 3393 | **2567** | (1st) | multicoloured (7 Sept) | | 4·00 | 4·00 | ☐ ☐ |
| | a. | Sheetlet. No. 3393×2 | 8·00 | | | 8·00 | ☐ ☐ |
| 3394 | **2568** | (1st) | multicoloured (7 Sept) | | 4·00 | 4·00 | ☐ ☐ |
| | a. | Sheetlet. No. 3394×2 | 8·00 | | | 8·00 | ☐ ☐ |
| 3395 | **2569** | (1st) | multicoloured (7 Sept) | | 4·00 | 4·00 | ☐ ☐ |
| | a. | Sheetlet. No. 3395×2 | 8·00 | | | 8·00 | ☐ ☐ |
| 3396 | **2570** | (1st) | multicoloured (7 Sept) | | 4·00 | 4·00 | ☐ ☐ |
| | a. | Sheetlet. No. 3396×2 | 8·00 | | | 8·00 | ☐ ☐ |
| 3397 | **2571** | (1st) | multicoloured (8 Sept) | | 2·00 | 2·00 | ☐ ☐ |
| | a. | Sheetlet No. 3397×2 | 4·00 | | | 4·00 | ☐ ☐ |
| 3398 | **2572** | (1st) | multicoloured (8 Sept) | | 2·00 | 2·00 | ☐ ☐ |
| | a. | Sheetlet. No. 3398×2 | 4·00 | | | 4·00 | ☐ ☐ |
| 3399 | **2573** | (1st) | multicoloured (8 Sept) | | 2·00 | 2·00 | ☐ ☐ |
| | a. | Sheetlet. No. 3399×2 | 4·00 | | | 4·00 | ☐ ☐ |
| 3400 | **2574** | (1st) | multicoloured (8 Sept) | | 2·00 | 2·00 | ☐ ☐ |
| | a. | Sheetlet. No. 3400×2 | 4·00 | | | 4·00 | ☐ ☐ |
| 3401 | **2575** | (1st) | multicoloured (10 Sept) | | 2·00 | 2·00 | ☐ ☐ |
| | a. | Sheetlet. No. 3401×2 | 4·00 | | | 4·00 | ☐ ☐ |
| 3402 | **2576** | (1st) | multicoloured (10 Sept) | | 2·00 | 2·00 | ☐ ☐ |
| | a. | Sheetlet. No. 3402×2 | 4·00 | | | 4·00 | ☐ ☐ |
| 3403 | **2577** | (1st) | multicoloured (10 Sept) | | 2·00 | 2·00 | ☐ ☐ |
| | a. | Sheetlet. No. 3403×2 | 4·00 | | | 4·00 | ☐ ☐ |
| 3404 | **2578** | (1st) | multicoloured (10 Sept) | | 2·00 | 2·00 | ☐ ☐ |
| | a. | Sheetlet. No. 3404×2 | 4·00 | | | 4·00 | ☐ ☐ |
| 3405 | **2579** | (1st) | multicoloured (10 Sept) | | 2·00 | 2·00 | ☐ ☐ |
| | a. | Sheetlet. No. 3405×2 | 4·00 | | | 4·00 | ☐ ☐ |

| | | | |
|---|---|---|---|
| Set of 34 | | 70·00 | 70·00 ☐ ☐ |
| First Day Covers (Nos. 3372a/405a) (34) | | | £200 ☐ ☐ |
| First Day Cover (any gold medal stamp) | | | 10·00 ☐ ☐ |

The self-adhesive base sheetlets for Nos. 3372/405 were produced by Walsall with the image, name and event of the winning athletes digitally printed by regional printers in six different locations: Attleborough, Edinburgh, London, Preston, Solihull and Swindon. These sheetlets of 16 stamps were divided by roulettes into eight panes of two stamps (1×2). The left margins were inscribed as follows (reading downwards): emblem and 'ParalympicsGB'; 'London 2012 Paralymic Games'; barcode; Sheet number, Issue date and Printer location.

Nos. 3372, 3373 and 3405 were each printed in separate sheetlets of 16 stamps. Nos. 3374/7, 3381/4, 3385/8, 3389/92, 3393/6, 3397/400 and 3401/4 were printed in sheetlets of 16 containing four stamps of each design. The sheetlets of 16 containing Nos. 3378/80 contained four each of Nos. 3378/9 and eight of No. 3380.

**2580** Scenes from Olympic and Paralympic Games

### Memories of London 2012 Olympic and Paralympic Games

**2012** (27 Sept). Sheet 192×75 mm. 'All-over' phosphor. Perf 14½

| | | | |
|---|---|---|---|
| MS3406 | **2580** | (1st) Procession of athletes, Paralympic Games; (1st) Games makers and Olympic Stadium; £1.28 Opening ceremony of Paralympic Games; £1.28 Olympic Games closing ceremony and handover to Rio | 9·50  9·50 ☐ ☐ |
| First Day Cover | | | 11·50 |
| Presentation Pack (P.O. Pack No. 476) | | 14·00 | ☐ ☐ |
| PHQ Cards (set of 5) | | 3·50 | 14·00 ☐ |

The five PHQ cards show the four individual stamps and the complete miniature sheet.

**2581** BR Class D34 Nos. 62471 Glen Falloch and 62496 Glen Loy at Ardlui, 9 May 1959

## Classic Locomotives of Scotland

**2012** (27 Sept). Booklet stamp. Design as 1st class stamp within **MS**3283 but printed in photogravure. Self-adhesive. 'All-over' phosphor. Die-cut perf 14

| 3407 | **2581** | (1st) multicoloured | 2·00 | 2·00 | ☐ ☐ |

No. 3407 was only issued in booklets containing No. 3407×2 and U3271×4, originally sold for £3.60.

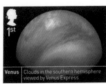

**2582** Sun and Particles ejected from Solar Surface seen from SOHO Observatory

**2583** Venus with Clouds in Southern Hemisphere seen from Venus Express

**2584** Ice in Martian Impact Crater seen from Mars Express

**2585** Surface of Asteroid Lutetia seen from Rosetta Probe

**2586** Saturn and its Rings seen from Cassini Satellite

**2587** Titan (Saturn's largest moon) seen from Huygens Probe

## Space Science

**2012** (16 Oct). 'All-over' phosphor. Perf 14

| 3408 | **2582** | (1st) multicoloured | 1·25 | 1·10 | ☐ ☐ |
| 3409 | **2583** | (1st) multicoloured | 1·25 | 1·10 | ☐ ☐ |
| 3410 | **2584** | 77p multicoloured | 1·90 | 1·90 | ☐ ☐ |
| 3411 | **2585** | 77p black | 1·90 | 1·90 | ☐ ☐ |
| 3412 | **2586** | £1.28 multicoloured | 3·25 | 3·25 | ☐ ☐ |
| 3413 | **2587** | £1.28 multicoloured | 3·25 | 3·25 | ☐ ☐ |
| Set of 6 | | | 11·50 | 11·50 | ☐ ☐ |
| First Day Cover | | | | 13·00 | ☐ |
| Presentation Pack (P.O. Pack No. 477) | | | 13.00 | | ☐ |
| PHQ Cards (set of 6) | | | 5·00 | 14·00 | ☐ ☐ |
| Set of 6 Gutter Pairs | | | 24·00 | | ☐ |

**2588** Poppies on Barbed Wire Stems

### "Lest We Forget" (4th issue)

**2012** (23 Oct). Self-adhesive. Two phosphor bands. Perf 14½×14 (with one eliptical hole in each vert side).

| 3414 | **2588** | (1st) multicoloured | 1·25 | 1·25 | ☐ ☐ |

**2589** Reindeer with Decorated Antlers

**2590** Santa with Robin

**2591** Reindeer with Decorated Antlers

**2592** Snowman and Penguin

**2593** Santa with Robin

**2594** Robin with Star Decoration in Beak

**2595** Cat and Mouse decorating Christmas Tree

## Christmas. Illustrations by Axel Scheffler

**2012** (6 Nov). One centre band (3415) or two phosphor bands (others). Perf 14½×14 (with one elliptical hole in each vert side)

| | | | (a) Self-adhesive | | | |
| 3415 | **2589** | (2nd) multicoloured | 1·00 | 90 | ☐ ☐ |
| 3416 | **2590** | (1st) multicoloured | 1·25 | 1·10 | ☐ ☐ |
| 3417 | **2591** | (2nd Large) multicoloured | 1·50 | 1·50 | ☐ ☐ |
| 3418 | **2592** | 87p. multicoloured | 2·25 | 2·25 | ☐ ☐ |
| 3419 | **2593** | (1st Large) multicoloured | 2·00 | 2·00 | ☐ ☐ |
| 3420 | **2594** | £1.28 multicoloured | 3·25 | 3·25 | ☐ ☐ |
| 3421 | **2595** | £1.90 multicoloured | 4·75 | 4·75 | ☐ ☐ |
| Set of 7 | | | 14·00 | 14·00 | ☐ ☐ |
| First Day Cover | | | | 16·00 | ☐ |
| Presentation Pack (P.O. Pack No. 478) | | | 29·00 | | ☐ ☐ |
| PHQ Cards (set of 8) | | | 5·50 | 18·00 | ☐ ☐ |

| | | | (b) Ordinary gum. | | | |
| MS3422 | 115×102 mm. As Nos. 3415/21 | | 14·00 | 14·00 | ☐ ☐ |
| First Day Cover | | | | 17·00 | ☐ |

### Collectors Pack

**2012** (6 Nov). Comprises Nos. 3254/9, **MS**3264/70, **MS**3272/307, 3309/18, A3319/26, 3330/6, **MS**3341, **MS**3371, **MS**3406, 3408/13 and 3415/21

| CP3422a Collectors Pack | £130 | ☐ ☐ |

### Post Office Yearbook

**2012** (6 Nov). Comprises Nos. 3254/9, **MS**3264/70, **MS**3272/307, 3309/18, A3319/26, 3330/6, **MS**3341, **MS**3371, **MS**3406, 3408/13 and 3415/21

| YB3422a Yearbook | £210 | ☐ ☐ |

### Miniature Sheet Collection

**2012** (6 Nov). Comprises Nos. **MS**3264, **MS**3270, **MS**3272, **MS**3283, **MS**3336, **MS**3341, **MS**3371, **MS**3406 and **MS**3422

| MS3422a Miniature Sheet Collection | 60·00 | ☐ ☐ |

**2596** Steam Locomotive on Metropolitan Railway, 1863

**2597** Navvies excavating 'Deep Cut' Tube Tunnel, 1898

**2598** Commuters in Carriage, 1911

**2599** Boston Manor Art Deco Station, 1934

**2600** Train on Deep Cut Line, 1938

**2601** Canary Wharf Station, 1999

**2602** Classic London Underground Posters

### 150th Anniversary of the London Underground

**2013** (9 Jan). One centre band (2nd) or 'all-over' phosphor (others)

(a) Ordinary gum. Perf 14½

| | | | | |
|---|---|---|---|---|
| 3423 | **2596**(2nd) multicoloured | 1·00 | 90 | |
| 3424 | **2597**(2nd) multicoloured | 1·00 | 90 | |
| 3425 | **2598** (1st) multicoloured | 1·25 | 1·10 | |
| 3426 | **2599** (1st) multicoloured | 1·25 | 1·10 | |
| 3427 | **2600**£1·28 multicoloured | 2·75 | 2·50 | |
| 3428 | **2601**£1·28 multicoloured | 2·75 | 2·50 | |
| Set of 6 | | 10·00 | 9·00 | |
| First Day Cover | | | 12·00 | |
| Presentation Pack (P.O. Pack No. 480) | | 18·00 | | |
| PHQ Cards (set of 11) (372) | | 7·50 | 17·00 | |
| Set of 6 Gutter Pairs | | 20·00 | | |

**MS**3429 184×74 mm. **2602** (1st) Golders Green, 1908, By Underground to fresh air (Maxwell Armfield), 1915 and Summer Sales (Mary Koop), 1925; 77p For the Zoo (Charles Paine), 1921, Power (Edward McKnight-Kauffer), 1931 and The Seen (James Fitton), 1948; 87p A train every 90 seconds (Abram Games), 1937, Thanks to the Underground (Zero (Hans Schleger), 1935 and Cut travelling time, Victoria Line (Tom Eckersley), 1969; £1·28 The London Transport Collection (Tom Eckersley), 1975, London Zoo (Abram Games), 1976 and The Tate Gallery by Tube (David Booth), 1987

| | | | | |
|---|---|---|---|---|
| | | 7·00 | 7·00 | |
| First Day Cover | | | 9·50 | |

(b) Self-adhesive. Die-cut perf 14½

| | | | | |
|---|---|---|---|---|
| 3430 | **2599** (1st) multicoloured | 1·25 | 1·10 | |

No. 3430 was issued in stamp booklets containing No. 3430×2 and 4× 1st vermilion, each booklet originally sold for £3.60.

The complete miniature sheet is shown on one of the eleven PHQ cards with the others depicting individual stamps, including those from **MS**3429.

**2603** Elinor and Marianne Dashwood (*Sense and Sensibility*)

**2604** Elizabeth Bennet and Portrait of Mr. Darcy (*Pride and Prejudice*)

**2605** Fanny Price (*Mansfield Park*)

**2606** Emma Woodhouse and Mr. Knightley (*Emma*)

**2607** Catherine Morland (*Northanger Abbey*)

**2608** Anne Elliot and Captain Wentworth (*Persuasion*)

### Bicentenary of the Publication of Jane Austen's Pride and Prejudice

**2013** (21 Feb). 'All-over' phosphor. Perf 14

| | | | | |
|---|---|---|---|---|
| 3431 | **2603** (1st) multicoloured | 1·25 | 1·10 | |
| 3432 | **2604** (1st) multicoloured | 1·25 | 1·10 | |
| 3433 | **2605** 77p multicoloured | 1·75 | 1·75 | |
| 3434 | **2606** 77p multicoloured | 1·75 | 1·75 | |
| 3435 | **2607**£1·28 multicoloured | 2·75 | 2·50 | |
| 3436 | **2608**£1·28 multicoloured | 2·75 | 2·50 | |
| Set of 6 | | 11·50 | 10·50 | |
| First Day Cover | | | 13·50 | |
| Presentation Pack (P.O. Pack No. 481) | | 13·00 | | |
| PHQ Cards (set of 6) (373) | | 4·00 | 16·00 | |
| Set of 6 Gutter Pairs | | 23·00 | | |
| Set of 6 Traffic Light Gutter Pairs | | 26·00 | | |

**2609** The Eleventh Doctor (Matt Smith, 2010-14)

**2610** The Tenth Doctor (David Tennant, 2005-10)

**2611** The Ninth Doctor (Christopher Eccleston, 2005)

**2612** The Eighth Doctor (Paul McGann, 1996)

2613 The Seventh Doctor (Sylvester McCoy, 1987-9) 2614 The Sixth Doctor (Colin Baker, 1984-6)

2615 The Fifth Doctor (Peter Davison, 1982-4) 2616 The Fourth Doctor (Tom Baker, 1974-81)

2617 The Third Doctor (Jon Pertwee, 1970-4) 2618 The Second Doctor (Patrick Troughton, 1966-9)

2619 The First Doctor (William Hartnell, 1963-6) 2620 TARDIS

2621 Dr. Who 1963-2013

**50th Anniversary of Doctor Who**
**(TV programme) (1st issue)**

**2013** (26 Mar). 'All-over' phosphor

(a) Ordinary gum. 'All-over' phosphor. Perf 14

| | | | | | | |
|---|---|---|---|---|---|---|
| 3437 | **2609** | (1st) | multicoloured | 1·25 | 1·10 | ☐ ☐ |
| | | a· | **Horiz** strip of 3· Nos. 3437/9 | 3·75 | 3·25 | ☐ ☐ |
| 3438 | **2610** | (1st) | multicoloured | 1·25 | 1·10 | ☐ ☐ |
| 3439 | **2611** | (1st) | multicoloured | 1·25 | 1·10 | ☐ ☐ |
| 3440 | **2612** | (1st) | multicoloured | 1·25 | 1·10 | ☐ ☐ |
| | | a. | Horiz strip of 4. Nos. 3440/3 | 5·00 | 4·25 | ☐ ☐ |
| 3441 | **2613** | (1st) | multicoloured | 1·25 | 1·10 | ☐ ☐ |
| 3442 | **2614** | (1st) | multicoloured | 1·25 | 1·10 | ☐ ☐ |

| | | | | | | |
|---|---|---|---|---|---|---|
| 3443 | **2615** | (1st) | multicoloured | 1·25 | 1·10 | ☐ ☐ |
| 3444 | **2616** | (1st) | multicoloured | 1·25 | 1·10 | ☐ ☐ |
| | | a. | Horiz strip of 4. Nos. 3444/7 | 5·00 | 4·25 | ☐ ☐ |
| 3445 | **2617** | (1st) | multicoloured | 1·25 | 1·10 | ☐ ☐ |
| 3446 | **2618** | (1st) | multicoloured | 1·25 | 1·10 | ☐ ☐ |
| 3447 | **2619** | (1st) | multicoloured | 1·25 | 1·10 | ☐ ☐ |
| Set of 11 | | | | 13·50 | 12·00 | ☐ |
| First Day Covers (2) | | | | | 18·00 | ☐ |
| Presentation Pack (P.O. Pack No. 482) | | | | 19·00 | | ☐ |
| PHQ Cards (set of 17) (374) | | | | 11·50 | 25·00 | ☐ ☐ |
| Set of 1 Gutter Strip of 3 and | | | | | | |
| | | | 2 Gutter Strips of 8 | 27·00 | | ☐ |

(b) Self-adhesive. One centre band (3449) or two bands (others). Die-cut perf 14½×14 (with one elliptical hole in each vert side) (3449) or 14½ (others)

| | | | | | | |
|---|---|---|---|---|---|---|
| 3448 | **2609** | (1st) | multicoloured | 1·25 | 1·10 | ☐ ☐ |
| 3449 | **2620** | (1st) | multicoloured | 1·25 | 1·10 | ☐ ☐ |
| 3450 | **2619** | (1st) | multicoloured | 1·25 | 1·10 | ☐ ☐ |
| MS3451 | 115×89 mm· | **2621** | (2nd) | | | |

Dalek; (2nd) The Ood; (2nd) Weeping Angel; (2nd) Cyberman;

| | | | | |
|---|---|---|---|---|
| (1st) TARDIS | | 5·25 | 5·25 | ☐ ☐ |
| First Day Cover | | | 7·25 | ☐ |

Nos. 3437/9 were printed together, se-tenant, as horizontal strips of three stamps in sheets of 48 (2 panes 6×4).

Nos. 3440/3 and 3444/7 were each printed together, se-tenant, as horizontal strips of four stamps in sheets of 60 (2 panes 4×6).

Nos. 3448/50 were issued in stamp booklets, each booklet containing Nos. 3448, 3449×4 and 3450 and originally sold for £3.60.

A 1st class TARDIS stamp perforated 15 all round comes from the £13.37 Dr. Who premium booklet.

The design area of No. 3449 measures 17½×21 mm, slightly smaller than the same TARDIS design (Type 2620) from the miniature sheet and premium booklet pane which measures 18×22 mm (all are 20×24 mm measured perf to perf edge).

The complete miniature sheet is shown on one of the seventeen PHQ cards with the others depicting individual stamps including those from the miniature sheet.

No. 3449 was also issued in sheets of 20 with se-tenant labels, printed in lithography instead of photogravure.

**50th Anniversary of Doctor Who**
**(TV programme) (2nd issue).**

**2013** (26 Mar). As No. 3449 but ordinary gum
| | | | | | | |
|---|---|---|---|---|---|---|
| 3452 | **2620** | (1st) | multicoloured | 1·40 | 1·40 | ☐ ☐ |

No. 3452 only comes from the £13.37 Dr. Who premium booklet.

2622 Norman Parkinson (1913-90, portrait and fashion photographer) 2623 Vivien Leigh (1913-67, actress)

2624 Peter Cushing (1913-94, actor) 2625 David Lloyd George (1863-1945, Prime Minister 1916-22)

**2626** Elizabeth David
(1913-92, cookery writer)

**2627** John Archer (1863-1932,
politician and civil rights campaigner)

**2628** Benjamin Britten
(1913-76, composer and
pianist)

**2629** Mary Leakey (1913-96,
archaeologist and
anthropologist)

**2630** Bill Shankly (1913-81, football
player and manager)

**2631** Richard Dimbleby (1913-65,
journalist and broadcaster)

### Great Britons

**2013** (16 Apr). 'All-over' phosphor. Perf 14½

| | | | | | | | |
|---|---|---|---|---|---|---|---|
| 3453 | **2622** | (1st) | multicoloured | 1·25 | 1·10 | ☐ | ☐ |
| | | a. | Horiz strip of 5. | | | | |
| | | | Nos. 3453/7 | 6·25 | 5·50 | ☐ | ☐ |
| 3454 | **2623** | (1st) | multicoloured | 1·25 | 1·10 | ☐ | ☐ |
| 3455 | **2624** | (1st) | multicoloured | 1·25 | 1·10 | ☐ | ☐ |
| 3456 | **2625** | (1st) | multicoloured | 1·25 | 1·10 | ☐ | ☐ |
| 3457 | **2626** | (1st) | multicoloured | 1·25 | 1·10 | ☐ | ☐ |
| 3458 | **2627** | (1st) | multicoloured | 1·25 | 1·10 | ☐ | ☐ |
| | | a. | Horiz strip of 5. | | | | |
| | | | Nos. 3458/62 | 6·25 | 5·50 | ☐ | ☐ |
| 3459 | **2628** | (1st) | multicoloured | 1·25 | 1·10 | ☐ | ☐ |
| 3460 | **2629** | (1st) | multicoloured | 1·25 | 1·10 | ☐ | ☐ |
| 3461 | **2630** | (1st) | multicoloured | 1·25 | 1·10 | ☐ | ☐ |
| 3462 | **2631** | (1st) | multicoloured | 1·25 | 1·10 | ☐ | ☐ |
| *Set of* 10 | | | | 12·50 | 11·00 | ☐ | ☐ |
| First Day Cover | | | | | 13·00 | | ☐ |
| Presentation Pack (P.O. Pack No. 483) | | | | 13·00 | | ☐ | |
| PHQ Cards (*set of* 10) (375) | | | | 7·00 | 18·00 | ☐ | ☐ |
| *Set of* 2 Gutter Strips of 10 | | | | 25·00 | | ☐ | |

Nos. 3453/7 and 3458/62 were each printed together, *setenant*, as horizontal strips of five stamps in sheets of 50 (2 panes 5×5).

**2632** Jimmy Greaves
(England)

**2633** John Charles
(Wales)

**2634** Gordon Banks
(England)

**2635** George Best
(Northern Ireland)

**2636** John Barnes
(England)

**2637** Kevin Keegan
(England)

**2638** Denis Law
(Scotland)

**2639** Bobby Moore
(England)

**2640** Bryan Robson
(England)

**2641** Dave Mackay
(Scotland)

**2642** Bobby Charlton
(England)

### Football Heroes (1st issue)

**2013** (9 May). 'All-over' phosphor

| | | | (a) Ordinary paper. Perf 14½ | | | | |
|---|---|---|---|---|---|---|---|
| 3463 | **2632** | (1st) | multicoloured | 1·25 | 1·10 | ☐ | ☐ |
| | | a. | Horiz strip of 5. | | | | |
| | | | Nos. 3463/7 | 6·25 | 5·50 | ☐ | ☐ |
| 3464 | **2633** | (1st) | multicoloured | 1·25 | 1·10 | ☐ | ☐ |
| 3465 | **2634** | (1st) | multicoloured | 1·25 | 1·10 | ☐ | ☐ |
| 3466 | **2635** | (1st) | multicoloured | 1·25 | 1·10 | ☐ | ☐ |
| 3467 | **2636** | (1st) | multicoloured | 1·25 | 1·10 | ☐ | ☐ |
| 3468 | **2637** | (1st) | multicoloured | 1·25 | 1·10 | ☐ | ☐ |
| | | a. | Horiz strip of 6. | | | | |
| | | | Nos. 3468/73 | 7·50 | 6·50 | ☐ | ☐ |
| 3469 | **2638** | (1st) | multicoloured | 1·25 | 1·10 | ☐ | ☐ |
| 3470 | **2639** | (1st) | multicoloured | 1·25 | 1·10 | ☐ | ☐ |
| 3471 | **2640** | (1st) | multicoloured | 1·25 | 1·10 | ☐ | ☐ |
| 3472 | **2641** | (1st) | multicoloured | 1·25 | 1·10 | ☐ | ☐ |
| 3473 | **2642** | (1st) | multicoloured | 1·25 | 1·10 | ☐ | ☐ |
| *Set of* 11 | | | | 13·50 | 12·00 | ☐ | ☐ |
| First Day Cover | | | | | 14·00 | | ☐ |

| | | | | |
|---|---|---|---|---|
| Presentation Pack (P.O. Pack No. 484) | 14·00 | | ☐ | ☐ |
| PHQ Cards (*set of* 12) (376) | 8·00 | 20·00 | ☐ | ☐ |
| *Set of* 1 Gutter Strip of 12 and 1 Gutter | | | | |
| Strip of 10 | 27·00 | | ☐ | ☐ |
| **MS**3474 192×74 mm. Nos. 3463/73 | 13·00 | 13·00 | ☐ | ☐ |
| First Day Cover | | 14·00 | | ☐ |

(b) Self-adhesive. Photo Walsall. Die-cut perf 14½

| | | | | | | |
|---|---|---|---|---|---|---|
| 3475 | **2635** | (1st) | multicoloured | 1·25 | 1·10 | ☐ ☐ |
| 3476 | **2639** | (1st) | multicoloured | 1·25 | 1·10 | ☐ ☐ |
| 3477 | **2633** | (1st) | multicoloured (20.2.14) | 1·25 | 1·10 | ☐ ☐ |
| 3478 | **2641** | (1st) | multicoloured (20.2.14) | 1·25 | 1·10 | ☐ ☐ |

Nos. 3463/7 were printed together, *se-tenant*, as horizontal strips of five stamps in sheets of 30 (5×6).

Nos. 3468/73 were printed together, *se-tenant*, as horizontal strips of six stamps in sheets of 30 (6×5).

Nos. 3475/6 were issued in booklets, each containing Nos. 3475/6 and 4× 1st vermilion and originally sold for £3.60.

Nos. 3463/87 commemorate the 150th anniversary of the Football Association and the 140th Anniversary of the Scottish Football Association.

The twelve PHQ cards depict the eleven individual stamps and the complete miniature sheet.

### Football Heroes (2nd issue)

2013 (9 May). Self-adhesive. Litho. 'All-over' phosphor. Die-cut perf 14½×14

| | | | | | | |
|---|---|---|---|---|---|---|
| 3479 | **2632** | (1st) | multicoloured | 1·50 | 1·50 | ☐ ☐ |
| 3480 | **2633** | (1st) | multicoloured | 1·50 | 1·50 | ☐ ☐ |
| 3481 | **2634** | (1st) | multicoloured | 1·50 | 1·50 | ☐ ☐ |
| 3482 | **2635** | (1st) | multicoloured | 1·50 | 1·50 | ☐ ☐ |
| 3483 | **2636** | (1st) | multicoloured | 1·50 | 1·50 | ☐ ☐ |
| 3484 | **2637** | (1st) | multicoloured | 1·50 | 1·50 | ☐ ☐ |
| 3485 | **2638** | (1st) | multicoloured | 1·50 | 1·50 | ☐ ☐ |
| 3486 | **2639** | (1st) | multicoloured | 1·50 | 1·50 | ☐ ☐ |
| 3487 | **2640** | (1st) | multicoloured | 1·50 | 1·50 | ☐ ☐ |
| 3488 | **2641** | (1st) | multicoloured | 1·50 | 1·50 | ☐ ☐ |
| 3489 | **2642** | (1st) | multicoloured | 1·50 | 1·50 | ☐ ☐ |
| *Set of* 11 | | | | 16·50 | 16·50 | ☐ ☐ |

Nos. 3479/89 were only issued in £11.11 Football Heroes premium booklets.

No.3490 is vacant

2646 Preliminary Oil Sketch for The Coronation of Queen Elizabeth II (Terence Cuneo), 1953

2647 Queen Elizabeth II in Garter Robes (Nicky Philipps), 2012

2648 Portrait by Andrew Festing, 1999

2649 Portrait by Pietro Annigoni, 1955

2650 Portrait by Sergei Pavlenko, 2000

2651 Her Majesty Queen Elizabeth II (Richard Stone), 1992

### 60th Anniversary of the Coronation.
### Six Decades of Royal Portraits

2013 (30 May). Phosphor band at left (2nd) or 'all-over' phosphor (others). Perf 14

| | | | | | | |
|---|---|---|---|---|---|---|
| 3491 | **2646** | (2nd) | multicoloured | 1·00 | 90 | ☐ ☐ |
| 3492 | **2647** | (1st) | multicoloured | 1·25 | 1·10 | ☐ ☐ |
| 3493 | **2648** | 78p | multicoloured | 1·75 | 1·75 | ☐ ☐ |
| 3494 | **2649** | 88p | multicoloured | 2·00 | 2·00 | ☐ ☐ |
| 3495 | **2650**£1·28 | | multicoloured | 2·75 | 2·50 | ☐ ☐ |
| 3496 | **2651**£1·88 | | multicoloured | 3·75 | 3·75 | ☐ ☐ |
| *Set of* 6 | | | | 12·50 | 12·00 | ☐ ☐ |
| First Day Cover | | | | | 13·00 | ☐ |
| Presentation Pack (P.O. Pack No. 485) | | | | 13·00 | | ☐ |
| PHQ Cards (*set of* 6) (377) | | | | 4·00 | 15·00 | ☐ ☐ |
| Commemorative Document (Nos. 3491/2) (2 June) | | | | 15·00 | | ☐ ☐ |
| *Set of* 6 Gutter Pairs | | | | 25·00 | | ☐ |
| *Set of* 6 Traffic Light Gutter Blocks of 4 | | | | 50·00 | | ☐ |

2652 UTA W No. 103

2653

### Classic Locomotives (3rd series).
### Northern Ireland

2013 (18 June). 'All-over' phosphor

(a) Self-adhesive. Die-cut perf 14

| | | | | | | |
|---|---|---|---|---|---|---|
| 3497 | **2652** | (1st) | black, grey and gold | 1·25 | 1·10 | ☐ ☐ |

b) Ordinary gum. Sheet 180×74 mm. Perf 14

| | | | | |
|---|---|---|---|---|
| **MS**3498 **2653** (1st) As Type 2652; 78p UTA SG3 No. 35; 88p Peckett No. 2; £1.28 CDRJC Class 5 No. 4 | 7·00 | 7·00 | ☐ | ☐ |
| First Day Cover | | 8·00 | | ☐ |
| Presentation Pack (P.O. Pack No. 486) | 7·50 | | ☐ | |
| PHQ Cards (*set of* 5) (378) | 3·50 | 10·00 | ☐ | ☐ |

No. 3497 was issued in booklets, each containing No. 3497×2 and 4× 1st vermilion and sold for £3.60.

2654 Comma (Polygonia c-album)

2655 Orange-tip (Anthocharis cardamines)

**2656** Small Copper
(*Lycaena phlaeas*)

**2657** Chalkhill Blue
(*Polyommatus coridon*)

**2658** Swallowtail
(*Papilio machaon*)

**2659** Purple Emperor
(*Apatura iris*)

**2660** Marsh Fritillary
(*Euphydrygus awinea*)

**2661** Brimstone
(*Gonepteryx rhamni*)

**2662** Red Admiral
(*Vanessa atalanta*)

**2663** Marbled White
(*Melanargia galathea*)

## Butterflies

**2013** (11 July). 'All-over' phosphor

(a) Ordinary paper. Perf 14×14½

| | | | | | | | |
|---|---|---|---|---|---|---|---|
| 3499 | **2654** | (1st) | multicoloured | 1·25 | 1·10 | ☐ | ☐ |
| | a. | Horiz strip of 5. | | | | | |
| | | Nos. 3499/503 | | 6·25 | 5·50 | ☐ | ☐ |
| 3500 | **2655** | (1st) | multicoloured | 1·25 | 1·10 | ☐ | ☐ |
| 3501 | **2656** | (1st) | multicoloured | 1·25 | 1·10 | ☐ | ☐ |
| 3502 | **2657** | (1st) | multicoloured | 1·25 | 1·10 | ☐ | ☐ |
| 3503 | **2658** | (1st) | multicoloured | 1·25 | 1·10 | ☐ | ☐ |
| 3504 | **2659** | (1st) | multicoloured | 1·25 | 1·10 | ☐ | ☐ |
| | a. | Horiz strip of 5. | | | | | |
| | | Nos. 3504/8 | | 6·25 | 5·50 | ☐ | ☐ |
| 3505 | **2660** | (1st) | multicoloured | 1·25 | 1·10 | ☐ | ☐ |
| 3506 | **2661** | (1st) | multicoloured | 1·25 | 1·10 | ☐ | ☐ |
| 3507 | **2662** | (1st) | multicoloured | 1·25 | 1·10 | ☐ | ☐ |
| 3508 | **2663** | (1st) | multicoloured | 1·25 | 1·10 | ☐ | ☐ |
| Set of 10 | | | | 12·50 | 11·00 | ☐ | ☐ |
| First Day Cover | | | | | 13·00 | ☐ | |
| Presentation Pack (P.O. Pack No. 487) | | | 13·00 | | | ☐ | |
| PHQ Cards (*set of 10*) (379) | | | 6·75 | 18·00 | | ☐ | ☐ |
| Set of 2 Gutter Strips of 10 | | | 25·00 | | | ☐ | |

(b) Self-adhesive. Die-cut perf 14×14½

| | | | | | | | |
|---|---|---|---|---|---|---|---|
| 3509 | **2657** | (1st) | multicoloured | 1·25 | 1·10 | ☐ | ☐ |
| 3510 | **2654** | (1st) | multicoloured | 1·25 | 1·10 | ☐ | ☐ |

Nos. 3499/503 and 3504/8 were each printed together, *se-tenant*, as horizontal strips of five stamps in sheets of 50 (2 panes 5×5).

Nos. 3509/10 were issued in stamp booklets, each containing Nos. 3509/10 and 4× 1st vermilion and sold for £3.60.

**2664** Andy Murray's Wimbledon Victory

**Andy Murray, Men's Singles Champion, Wimbledon**

**2013** (8 Aug). Sheet 192×75 mm. Multicoloured. 'All-over' phosphor. Perf 14½

| | | | | | | |
|---|---|---|---|---|---|---|
| MS**3511** | **2664** | (1st) Andy Murray kissing Wimbledon Trophy; (1st) Andy Murray serving; £1.28 In action; £1.28 Holding Trophy | 7·50 | 7·50 | | |
| First Day Cover | | | | 8·50 | ☐ | ☐ |
| Presentation Pack (P.O. Pack No. M21) | | | 8·00 | | ☐ | ☐ |

**2665** Jaguar E-Type, 1961

**2666** Rolls-Royce Silver Shadow, 1965

**2667** Aston Martin DB5, 1963

**2668** MG MGB, 1962

**2669** Morgan Plus 8, 1968

**2670** Lotus Esprit, 1976

**2671** The Workhorses

## British Auto Legends

**2013** (13 Aug). 'All-over' phosphor. Perf 13½ (3512/17) or 14 (**MS**3518)

| | | | | | | |
|---|---|---|---|---|---|---|
| 3512 | **2665** | (1st) multicoloured | 1·25 | 1·10 | ☐ | ☐ |
| | | a. Horiz strip of 3. Nos. 3512/14 | 3·75 | 3·25 | ☐ | ☐ |
| 3513 | **2666** | (1st) multicoloured | 1·25 | 1·10 | ☐ | ☐ |
| 3514 | **2667** | (1st) multicoloured | 1·25 | 1·10 | ☐ | ☐ |
| 3515 | **2668** | £1·28 multicoloured | 2·75 | 2·50 | ☐ | ☐ |
| | | a. Horiz strip of 3. Nos. 3515/17 | 8·25 | 7·50 | ☐ | ☐ |
| 3516 | **2669** | £1·28 multicoloured | 2·75 | 2·50 | ☐ | ☐ |
| 3517 | **2670** | £1·28 multicoloured | 2·75 | 2·50 | ☐ | ☐ |
| | Set of 6 | | 12·00 | 10·50 | ☐ | ☐ |
| | First Day Cover | | | 12·50 | ☐ | ☐ |
| | Presentation Pack (P.O. Pack No. 488) | | 14·50 | | ☐ | ☐ |
| | PHQ Cards (set of 11) (380) | | 7·50 | 18·00 | ☐ | ☐ |
| | Set of 2 Gutter Strips of 6 | | 24·00 | | ☐ | ☐ |

**MS**3518 180×74 mm. **2671** (1st)×4 Morris Minor Royal Mail van (1953-71); Austin FX4 (1958-97) London taxi; Ford Anglia 105E (1959-67) police car; Coastguard Land Rover Defender 110 (from 1990) 5·00  5·00  ☐ ☐

First Day Cover                                          6·00  ☐

The complete miniature sheet is shown on one of the eleven PHQ cards with the others depicting individual stamps including those from the miniature sheet.

**2672** East Indiaman *Atlas*, 1813

**2673** Royal Mail Ship *Britannia*, 1840

**2674** Tea Clipper *Cutty Sark*, 1870

**2675** Cargo Liner *Clan Matheson*, 1919

**2676** Royal Mail Ship *Queen Elizabeth*, 1940

**2677** Bulk Carrier *Lord Hinton*, 1986

## Merchant Navy (1st issue)

**2013** (19 Sept). 'All-over' phosphor. Perf 14

| | | | | | | |
|---|---|---|---|---|---|---|
| 3519 | **2672** | (1st) multicoloured | 1·25 | 1·10 | ☐ | ☐ |
| 3520 | **2673** | (1st) multicoloured | 1·25 | 1·10 | ☐ | ☐ |
| 3521 | **2674** | (1st) multicoloured | 1·25 | 1·10 | ☐ | ☐ |
| 3522 | **2675** | £1·28 multicoloured | 2·75 | 2·50 | ☐ | ☐ |
| 3523 | **2676** | £1·28 multicoloured | 2·75 | 2·50 | ☐ | ☐ |
| 3524 | **2677** | £1·28 multicoloured | 2·75 | 2·50 | ☐ | ☐ |
| | Set of 6 | | 12·00 | 10·50 | ☐ | ☐ |
| | First Day Cover | | | 12·50 | ☐ | ☐ |
| | Presentation Pack (P.O. Pack No. 489) | | 14·50 | | ☐ | ☐ |
| | PHQ Cards (set of 11) (381) | | 6·75 | 18·00 | ☐ | ☐ |
| | Set of 6 Gutter Pairs | | 24·00 | | ☐ | ☐ |

The complete miniature sheet is shown on one of the eleven PHQ cards with the others depicting individual stamps including those from **MS**3529.

**2678** Destroyer HMS *Vanoc* escorting Atlantic Convoy

**2679** Merchant Ship passing the Naval Control Base in the Thames Estuary

**2680** Sailors clearing Ice from the Decks of HMS *King George V* in Arctic Waters

**2681** Naval Convoy of 24 Merchant Ships in the North Sea

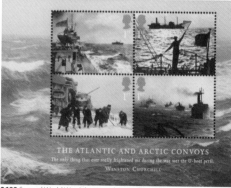

**2682** Second World War Atlantic and Arctic Convoys

## Merchant Navy (2nd issue)

**2013** (19 Sept). 'All-over' phosphor. Perf 14

| | | | | | | |
|---|---|---|---|---|---|---|
| 3525 | **2678** | (1st) multicoloured | 1·40 | 1·40 | ☐ | ☐ |
| 3526 | **2679** | (1st) multicoloured | 1·40 | 1·40 | ☐ | ☐ |
| 3527 | **2680** | (1st) multicoloured | 1·40 | 1·40 | ☐ | ☐ |
| 3528 | **2681** | (1st) multicoloured | 1·40 | 1·40 | ☐ | ☐ |
| | Set of 4 | | 5·50 | 5·50 | ☐ | ☐ |
| | **MS**3529 115×89 mm 2682. Nos. 3525/8 | | 5·50 | 5·50 | | |
| | First Day Cover | | | 6·50 | ☐ | |

Nos. 3525/8 were only issued in the £11.19 Merchant Navy premium booklet and in **MS**3529.

**2683** Royal Mail Van

### Royal Mail Transport: By Land and Sea

**2013** (19 Sept). Self-adhesive booklet stamps. Die-cut perf 14

| | | | | | |
|---|---|---|---|---|---|
| 3530 | **2683** | (1st) | multicoloured | 1·25 | 1·10 |
| 3531 | **2673** | (1st) | multicoloured | 1·25 | 1·10 |

The design of No. 3530 is as the Royal Mail van stamp within **MS**3518.

Nos. 3530/1 were only issued in booklets, each containing Nos. 3530/1 and 4× 1st vermilion and sold for £3.60.

No. 3530 includes the 'EUROPA' emblem.

**2684** Polacanthus

**2685** Ichthyosaurus

**2686** Iguanodon

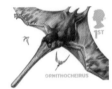

**2687** Ornithocheirus

**2688** Baryonyx

**2689** Dimorphodon

**2690** Hypsilophodon

**2691** Cetiosaurus

**2692** Megalosaurus

**2693** Plesiosaurus

### Dinosaurs

**2013** (10 Oct). Self-adhesive. 'All-over' phosphor. Die-cut perf 13½×14 (with no teeth around protruding parts at top or foot of the designs)

| | | | | | | | |
|---|---|---|---|---|---|---|---|
| 3532 | **2684** | (1st) | multicoloured | 1·25 | 1·10 | ☐ | ☐ |
| | | a. | Horiz strip of 5.  Nos. 3532/6 | 6·25 | | ☐ | ☐ |
| 3533 | **2685** | (1st) | multicoloured | 1·25 | 1·10 | ☐ | ☐ |
| 3534 | **2686** | (1st) | multicoloured | 1·25 | 1·10 | ☐ | ☐ |
| 3535 | **2687** | (1st) | multicoloured | 1·25 | 1·10 | ☐ | ☐ |
| 3536 | **2688** | (1st) | multicoloured | 1·25 | 1·10 | ☐ | ☐ |
| 3537 | **2689** | (1st) | multicoloured | 1·25 | 1·10 | ☐ | ☐ |
| | | a. | Horiz strip of 5.  Nos. 3537/41 | 6·25 | | ☐ | ☐ |
| 3538 | **2690** | (1st) | multicoloured | 1·25 | 1·10 | ☐ | ☐ |
| 3539 | **2691** | (1st) | multicoloured | 1·25 | 1·10 | ☐ | ☐ |
| 3540 | **2692** | (1st) | multicoloured | 1·25 | 1·10 | ☐ | ☐ |
| 3541 | **2693** | (1st) | multicoloured | 1·25 | 1·10 | ☐ | ☐ |
| Set of 10 | | | | 12·50 | 11·00 | ☐ | ☐ |
| First Day Cover | | | | | 13·00 | | ☐ |
| Presentation Pack (P.O. Pack No. 490) | | | | 13·00 | | ☐ | ☐ |
| PHQ Cards (set of 10) (382) | | | | 6·75 | 15·00 | ☐ | |

Nos. 3532/6 and 3537/41 were each printed together as horizontal strips of five stamps in sheets of 50 (2 panes 5×5).

**2694** Madonna and Child (Francesco Granacci)

**2695** Virgin and Child with the Young St. John the Baptist (detail) (Antoniazzo Romano)

**2696** Madonna and Child (Francesco Granacci)

**2697** St. Roch Praying to the Virgin for an End to the Plague (detail) (Jacques-Louis David)

**2698** Virgin and Child with the Young St. John the Baptist (detail) (Antoniazzo Romano)

**2699** La Vierge au Lys (William-Adolphe Bouguereau)

**2700** Theotokos, Mother of God (Fadi Mikhail)

### Christmas. Madonna and Child Paintings

**2013** (5 Nov). One centre band (3542) or two bands (others). Perf 14½×15

**(a) Self-adhesive**

| | | | | | | | |
|---|---|---|---|---|---|---|---|
| 3542 | **2694** | (2nd) | multicoloured | 1·00 | 90 | ☐ | ☐ |
| 3543 | **2695** | (1st) | multicoloured | 1·25 | 1·10 | ☐ | ☐ |

| | | | | | |
|---|---|---|---|---|---|
| 3544 | **2696** (2nd Large) multicoloured | 1·50 | 1·50 | ☐ | ☐ |
| 3545 | **2697** 88p· multicoloured | 2·00 | 2·00 | ☐ | ☐ |
| 3546 | **2698** (1st Large) multicoloured | 2·00 | 2·00 | ☐ | ☐ |
| 3547 | **2699** £1·28 multicoloured | 2·75 | 2·50 | ☐ | ☐ |
| 3548 | **2700** £1·88 multicoloured | 3·75 | 3·75 | ☐ | ☐ |
| *Set of 7* | | 14·00 | 13·50 | ☐ | ☐ |
| First Day Cover | | | 14·50 | | ☐ |
| Presentation Pack (P.O. Pack No. 491) | | 14·50 | | ☐ | |
| PHQ Cards (*set of 8*) | | 5·50 | 18·00 | ☐ | ☐ |

(b) Ordinary gum

| | | | | | |
|---|---|---|---|---|---|
| **MS**3549 146×74 mm. As Nos. 3542/8 | 14·00 | 14·00 | ☐ | ☐ |
| First Day Cover | | 14·50 | | ☐ |

The eight PHQ cards show the seven individual stamps and the complete miniature sheet.

The 2nd class, 1st class, 88p, £1.28 and £1.88 stamps were also issued in sheets of 20 containing eight 2nd class, eight 1st class, two 88p, one £1.28 and one £1.88 stamps , each stamp accompanied by a *se-tenant* label.

Separate sheets of 20 2nd, ten 1st, ten 88p and ten £1.28 were available with personal photographs.

**2701** Angels (Rosie Hargreaves)

**2702** Santa (Molly Robson)

### Children's Christmas

**2013** (5 Nov). One phosphor band at right (2nd) or two phosphor bands (1st). Self-adhesive. Die-cut perf 14½

| | | | | | |
|---|---|---|---|---|---|
| 3550 | **2701** (2nd) multicoloured | 1·00 | 90 | ☐ | ☐ |
| 3551 | **2702** (1st) multicoloured | 1·25 | 1·10 | ☐ | ☐ |
| First Day Cover | | | 3·00 | | ☐ |
| Presentation Pack (P.O. Pack No. M22) | | 3·00 | | ☐ | ☐ |

### Collectors Pack

**2013** (5 Nov). Comprises Nos. 3423/9, 3431/47, **MS**3451, 3453/73, 3491/6, **MS**3498/508, **MS**3511/24, **MS**3529, 3532/48 and 3550/1

| | | | | |
|---|---|---|---|---|
| CP3551a Collectors Pack | £130 | | ☐ | ☐ |

### Post Office Yearbook

**2013** (5 Nov). Comprises Nos. 3423/9, 3431/47, **MS**3451, 3453/73, 3491/6, **MS**3498/508, **MS**3511/24, **MS**3529, 3532/48 and 3550/1

| | | | | |
|---|---|---|---|---|
| YB3551a Yearbook | £135 | | ☐ | ☐ |

### Miniature Sheet Collection

**2013** (5 Nov). Comprises Nos. **MS**3429, **MS**3451, **MS**3474, **MS**3498, **MS**3511, **MS**3518, **MS**3529 and **MS**3549

| | | | | |
|---|---|---|---|---|
| **MS**3551a Miniature Sheet Collection | 50.00 | | ☐ | ☐ |

**2703** Andy Pandy

**2704** Ivor the Engine

**2705** Dougal (*The Magic Roundabout*)

**2706** Windy Miller (*Camberwick Green*)

**2707** Mr. Benn

**2708** Great Uncle Bulgaria (The Wombles)

**2709** Bagpuss

**2710** Paddington Bear

**2711** Postman Pat

**2712** Bob the Builder

**2713** Peppa Pig

**2714** Shaun the Sheep

### Classic Children's TV

**2014** (7 Jan). 'All-over phosphor'. Self-adhesive. Die-cut perf 15

| | | | | | | |
|---|---|---|---|---|---|---|
| 3552 | 2703 | (1st) multicoloured | 1.25 | 1.10 | ☐ | ☐ |
| Horiz strip of 6. Nos. 3552/7 | | | 7.50 | | ☐ | |
| 3553 | **2704** | (1st) multicoloured | 1.25 | 1.10 | ☐ | ☐ |
| 3554 | **2705** | (1st) multicoloured | 1.25 | 1.10 | ☐ | ☐ |
| 3555 | **2706** | (1st) multicoloured | 1.25 | 1.10 | ☐ | ☐ |
| 3556 | **2707** | (1st) multicoloured | 1.25 | 1.10 | ☐ | ☐ |
| 3557 | **2708** | (1st) multicoloured | 1.25 | 1.10 | ☐ | ☐ |
| 3558 | **2709** | (1st) multicoloured | 1.25 | 1.10 | ☐ | ☐ |
| Horiz strip of 6. Nos. 3558/63 | | | 7.50 | | ☐ | |
| 3559 | **2710** | (1st) multicoloured | 1.25 | 1.10 | ☐ | ☐ |
| 3560 | **2711** | (1st) multicoloured | 1.25 | 1.10 | ☐ | ☐ |
| 3561 | **2712** | (1st) multicoloured | 1.25 | 1.10 | ☐ | ☐ |
| 3562 | **2713** | (1st) multicoloured | 1.25 | 1.10 | ☐ | ☐ |
| 3563 | **2714** | (1st) multicoloured | 1.25 | 1.10 | ☐ | ☐ |
| *Set of 12* | | | 15.00 | 13.00 | | ☐ |
| First Day Cover | | | | 18.00 | | ☐ |

| | | |
|---|---|---|
| Presentation Pack (P.O. Pack No. 493) | 15.00 | ☐ ☐ |
| PHQ Cards (*set of* 12) (384) | 8.00  20.00 | ☐ ☐ |
| *Set of* 2 Gutter Strips of 12 | 30.00 | ☐ ☐ |

Nos. 3552/7 and 3558/63 were each printed together in horizontal strips of six stamps in sheets of 60 (6×10).

**2715** Riding for the Disabled Association

**2716** The King's Troop Ceremonial Horses

**2717** Dray Horses

**2718** Royal Mews Carriage Horses

**2719** Police Horses

**2720** Forestry Horse

## Working Horses

**2014** (4 Feb). 'All-over' phosphor. Perf 14

| | | | | | |
|---|---|---|---|---|---|
| 3564 | **2715** | (1st) multicoloured | 1.25 | 1.10 | ☐ ☐ |
| 3565 | **2716** | (1st) multicoloured | 1.25 | 1.10 | ☐ ☐ |
| 3566 | **2717** | 88p multicoloured | 2.00 | 2.00 | ☐ ☐ |
| 3567 | **2718** | 88p multicoloured | 2.00 | 2.00 | ☐ ☐ |
| 3568 | **2719** | £1.28 multicoloured | 2.75 | 2.50 | ☐ ☐ |
| 3569 | **2720** | £1.28 multicoloured | 2.75 | 2.50 | ☐ ☐ |
| *Set of* 6 | | | 12.00 | 11.00 | ☐ ☐ |
| First Day Cover | | | | 14.00 | ☐ |
| Presentation Pack (P.O. Pack No. 494) | | | 14.00 | | ☐ |
| PHQ Cards (*set of* 6) (385) | | | 4.00 | 16.00 | ☐ ☐ |
| | | | | | ☐ ☐ |
| *Set of* 6 Gutter Pairs | | | 24.00 | | ☐ |

**2721** BR Dean Goods No. 2532

**2722** BR D34 Nos. 62471 & 62496

**2723** UTA Class W No. 103 *Thomas Somerset* with Belfast Express, Downhill, near Castlerock, c.1950

**2724** LMS No. 7720

**2725** Peckett R2 *Thor*

**2726** BR D40 No. 62276

**2727** UTA SG3 No. 35

**2728** Hunslet No. 589 *Blanche*

**2729**

## Classic Locomotives (4th and 5th series). Wales (MS3578) and United Kingdom (booklet)

**2014** (20 Feb).. 'All-over' phosphor. Perf 14

| | | | | | |
|---|---|---|---|---|---|
| 3570 | **2721** | (1st) multicoloured | 1.50 | 1.50 | ☐ ☐ |
| 3571 | **2722** | (1st) multicoloured | 1.50 | 1.50 | ☐ ☐ |
| 3572 | **2723** | (1st) multicoloured | 1.50 | 1.50 | ☐ ☐ |
| 3573 | **2724** | (1st) multicoloured | 1.50 | 1.50 | ☐ ☐ |
| 3574 | **2725** | 60p multicoloured | 1.50 | 1.50 | ☐ ☐ |
| 3575 | **2726** | 68p multicoloured | 1.75 | 1.75 | ☐ ☐ |
| 3576 | **2727** | 78p multicoloured | 2.00 | 2.00 | ☐ ☐ |
| 3577 | **2728** | 78p multicoloured | 2.00 | 2.00 | ☐ ☐ |
| *Set of* 8 | | | 13.00 | 13.00 | ☐ ☐ |
| **MS**3578 180×74 mm. 2729 No. 3573; No. 3577; 88p W&LLR No. 822 *The Earl*; £1.28 BR 5600 No. 5652 | | | 7.50 | 7.50 | ☐ ☐ |
| First Day Cover | | | | 9.50 | ☐ |
| Presentation Pack (P.O. Pack No. 495) | | | 9.00 | | ☐ ☐ |
| PHQ Cards (*set of* 5) (386) | | | 3.50 | 11.00 | ☐ ☐ |

Nos. 3570/7 were issued only in £13.97 Classic Locomotives booklets or also in **MS**3578 (Nos. 3573 and 3577).

The five PHQ cards show the four individual stamps and the complete miniature sheet.

**2730** Roy Plomley (1914-85, broadcaster and writer)

**2731** Barbara Ward (1914-81, economist and broadcaster)

**2732** Joe Mercer (1914-90, football player and manager)

**2733** Kenneth More (1914-82, stage and screen actor)

**2734** Dylan Thomas (1914-53, poet and writer)

**2735** Sir Alec Guinness (1914-2000, stage and screen actor)

**2736** Noorunissa Inayat Khan (1914-44, SOE agent in occupied France)

**2737** Max Perutz (1914-2002, molecular biologist and Nobel laureate)

**2738** Joan Littlewood (1914-2002, theatre director and writer)

**2739** Abram Games (1914-96, graphic designer)

### Remarkable Lives

**2014** (25 Mar). 'All-over' phosphor. Perf 14½

| | | | | | | | |
|---|---|---|---|---|---|---|---|
| 3579 | **2730** | (1st) | multicoloured | 1.25 | 1.10 | ☐ | ☐ |
| | | | Horiz strip of 5. Nos. 3579/83 | 6.25 | 5.50 | | |
| 3580 | **2731** | (1st) | multicoloured | 1.25 | 1.10 | ☐ | ☐ |
| 3581 | **2732** | (1st) | multicoloured | 1.25 | 1.10 | ☐ | ☐ |
| 3582 | **2733** | (1st) | multicoloured | 1.25 | 1.10 | ☐ | ☐ |
| 3583 | **2734** | (1st) | multicoloured | 1.25 | 1.10 | ☐ | ☐ |
| 3584 | **2735** | (1st) | multicoloured | 1.25 | 1.10 | ☐ | ☐ |
| | | | Horiz strip of 5. Nos. 3584/8 | 6.25 | 5.50 | | |
| 3585 | **2736** | (1st) | multicoloured | 1.25 | 1.10 | ☐ | ☐ |
| 3586 | **2737** | (1st) | multicoloured | 1.25 | 1.10 | ☐ | ☐ |
| 3587 | **2738** | (1st) | multicoloured | 1.25 | 1.10 | ☐ | ☐ |
| 3588 | **2739** | (1st) | multicoloured | 1.25 | 1.10 | ☐ | ☐ |
| Set of 10 | | | | 12.50 | 11.00 | ☐ | |
| First Day Cover | | | | | 15.50 | | |
| Presentation Pack (P.O. Pack No. 496) | | | | 13.00 | | ☐ | |
| PHQ Cards (set of 10) (387) | | | | 6.75 | 20.00 | ☐ | ☐ |
| Set of 2 Gutter Strips of 10 | | | | 25.00 | | ☐ | |

Nos. 3579/83 and 3584/8 were each printed together, *se-tenant*, as horizontal strips of five stamps in sheets of 50 (2 panes 5×5).

**2740** Buckingham Palace, 2014

**2741** Buckingham Palace, c. 1862

2742 Buckingham Palace, 1846

**2743** Buckingham House, 1819

**2744** Buckingham House, 1714

**2745** Buckingham House, c. 1700

**2746** The Grand Staircase

**2747** The Throne Room

### Buckingham Palace, London (1st issue)

**2014** (15 Apr). 'All-over phosphor' Ordinary gum. Perf 14½

| | | | | | | | |
|---|---|---|---|---|---|---|---|
| 3589 | **2740** | (1st) | multicoloured | 1.25 | 1.10 | ☐ | ☐ |
| | | | Horiz strip of 3. Nos. 3589/91 | 3.75 | 3.25 | ☐ | ☐ |
| 3590 | **2741** | (1st) | multicoloured | 1.25 | 1.10 | ☐ | ☐ |
| 3591 | **2742** | (1st) | multicoloured | 1.25 | 1.10 | ☐ | ☐ |
| 3592 | **2743** | (1st) | multicoloured | 1.25 | 1.10 | ☐ | ☐ |
| | | | Horiz strip of 3. Nos. 3592/4 | 3.75 | 3.25 | ☐ | ☐ |
| 3593 | **2744** | (1st) | multicoloured | 1.25 | 1.10 | ☐ | ☐ |

| 3594 | **2745** | (1st) | multicoloured | 1.25 | 1.10 | ☐ ☐ |
|------|----------|-------|---------------|------|------|-----|
| Set of 6 | | | | 7.50 | 6.50 | ☐ ☐ |
| First Day Cover | | | 9.50 | | | ☐ ☐ |
| Presentation Pack (P.O. Pack No. 497) | | | | 13.00 | | ☐ ☐ |
| PHQ Cards (*set of* 11) | | | | 7.50 | 15.00 | ☐ ☐ |
| Set of 2 Gutter Strips of 6 | | | | 15.00 | | ☐ ☐ |

Self-adhesive. Die-cut perf 14

| 3595 | **2746** | (1st) | multicoloured | 1.25 | 1.10 | ☐ ☐ |
|------|----------|-------|---------------|------|------|-----|
| 3596 | **2747** | (1st) | multicoloured | 1.25 | 1.10 | ☐ ☐ |

Nos. 3589/91 and 3592/4 were each printed together, *se-tenant*, as horizontal strips of three stamps in sheets of 36 (2 panes 3×6).

Nos. 3595/6 were only issued in stamp booklets, each containing Nos. 3595/6 and 4×1st vermilion and originally sold for £3.72.

The complete miniature sheet is shown on one of the eleven PHQ cards with the others depicting individual stamps including those from **MS**3601.

**2748** The Blue Drawing Room

**2749** The Green Drawing Room

**2750**

**Buckingham Palace, London (2nd issue).**

**2014** (15 Apr). 'All-over' phosphor. Perf 14

| 3597 | **2747** | (1st) | multicoloured | 1.50 | 1.50 | ☐ ☐ |
|------|----------|-------|---------------|------|------|-----|
| 3598 | **2746** | (1st) | multicoloured | 1.50 | 1.50 | ☐ ☐ |
| 3599 | **2748** | (1st) | multicoloured | 1.50 | 1.50 | ☐ ☐ |
| 3600 | **2749** | (1st) | multicoloured | 1.50 | 1.50 | ☐ ☐ |
| Set of 4 | | | | 6.00 | 6.00 | ☐ ☐ |
| **MS**3601 146×74 mm. 2750 | | | | | | |
| Nos. 3597/600 | | | | 5.50 | 5.50 | ☐ ☐ |
| First Day Cover | | | | 7.00 | | ☐ ☐ |

Nos. 3597/600 were only issued in the £11.39 Buckingham Palace premium booklet and in **MS**3601.

**2751** A Matter of Life and Death (1946)

**2752** Lawrence of Arabia (1962)

**2753** 2001 A Space Odyssey (1968)

**2754** Chariots of Fire (1981)

**2755** Secrets and Lies (1996)

**2756** Bend It Like Beckham (2002)

**2757** Films by GPO Film Unit

**Great British Films**

**2014** (13 May). 'All-over' phosphor. P 14½ (3602/7) or 14 (**MS**3608)

| 3602 | **2751** | (1st) multicoloured | 1.25 | 1.10 | ☐ ☐ |
|------|----------|---------------------|------|------|-----|
| | | Horiz strip of 3. Nos. 3602/4 | 3.75 | 3.25 | ☐ ☐ |
| 3603 | **2752** | (1st) multicoloured | 1.25 | 1.10 | ☐ ☐ |
| 3604 | **2753** | (1st) multicoloured | 1.25 | 1.10 | ☐ ☐ |
| 3605 | **2754** | £1.28 multicoloured | 2.75 | 2.50 | ☐ ☐ |
| | | Horiz strip of 3. Nos. 3605/7 | 8.25 | 7.50 | ☐ ☐ |
| 3606 | **2755** | £1.28 multicoloured | 2.75 | 2.50 | ☐ ☐ |
| 3607 | **2756** | £1.28 multicoloured | 2.75 | 2.50 | ☐ ☐ |
| Set of 6 | | | 12.00 | 10.50 | ☐ ☐ |
| First Day Cover | | | 14.00 | | ☐ ☐ |
| Presentation Pack (P.O. Pack No. 498) | | | 17.00 | | ☐ ☐ |
| PHQ Cards (*set of* 11) | | | 7.50 | 19.00 | ☐ ☐ |
| Set of 2 Gutter Strips of 6 | | | 24.00 | | ☐ ☐ |

**MS**3608 115×89 mm. **2757** (1st)×4

Night Mail (1936) directed by Harry Watt and Basil Wright; Love on the Wing (1938) directed by Norman McLaren; A Colour Box (1935) directed by Len Lye; Spare Time (1939) directed by Humphrey Jennings ........... 5.50  5.50 ☐ ☐

First Day Cover ....... 7.00 ........................ ☐

Nos. 3602/4 and 3605/7 were each printed together, *se-tenant*, as horizontal strips of three stamps in sheets of 36 (2 panes 3×6).

The complete miniature sheet is shown on one of the eleven PHQ cards with the others depicting individual stamps including those from MS3608.

**2758** Herring

**2759** Red Gurnard

**2760** Dab

**2761** Pouting

**2762** Cornish Sardine

**2763** Common Skate

**2764** Spiny Dogfish

**2765** Wolffish

**2766** Sturgeon

**2767** Conger Eel

**Sustainable Fish (Nos. 3609/13) and Threatened Fish (Nos. 3614/18)**

**2014** (5 June). 'All-over' phosphor. Perf 14×14½

| | | | | | |
|---|---|---|---|---|---|
| 3609 | **2758** | (1st) multicoloured | 1.25 | 1.10 | ☐ ☐ |
| | a. Horiz strip of 5. Nos. 3609/13 | 6.25 | 5.50 | ☐ ☐ |
| 3610 | **2759** | (1st) multicoloured | 1.25 | 1.10 | ☐ ☐ |

| | | | | | |
|---|---|---|---|---|---|
| 3611 | **2760** | (1st) multicoloured | 1.25 | 1.10 | ☐ ☐ |
| 3612 | **2761** | (1st) multicoloured | 1.25 | 1.10 | ☐ ☐ |
| 3613 | **2762** | (1st) multicoloured | 1.25 | 1.10 | ☐ ☐ |
| 3614 | **2763** | (1st) multicoloured | 1.25 | 1.10 | ☐ ☐ |
| | | Horiz strip of 5. Nos. 3614/18 | 6.25 | 5.50 | ☐ ☐ |
| 3615 | **2764** | (1st) multicoloured | 1.25 | 1.10 | ☐ ☐ |
| 3616 | **2765** | (1st) multicoloured | 1.25 | 1.10 | ☐ ☐ |
| 3617 | **2766** | (1st) multicoloured | 1.25 | 1.10 | ☐ ☐ |
| 3618 | **2767** | (1st) multicoloured | 1.25 | 1.10 | ☐ ☐ |
| *Set of 10* | | | 12.50 | 11.00 | ☐ |
| First Day Cover | | | | 15.00 | ☐ |
| Presentation Pack (P.O. Pack No. 499) | | | 13.00 | | ☐ ☐ |
| Stamp Cards (*set of 10*) | | | 6.75 | 19.00 | ☐ ☐ |
| *Set of 2 Gutter Strips of 10* | | | 25.00 | | ☐ |

Nos. 3609/13 and 3614/18 were each printed together, *se-tenant*, as horizontal strips of five in sheets of 50 (2 panes 5×5).

2768 Judo                    2769 Swimming

**2770** Marathon            **2771** Squash

**2772** Netball             **2773** Para-athlete Cycling

**Commonwealth Games, Glasgow**

**2014** (17 July). One phosphor band (3619) or two bands (others) Ordinary gum. Perf 14×14½

| | | | | | |
|---|---|---|---|---|---|
| 3619 | **2768** | (2nd) multicoloured | 1.00 | 90 | ☐ ☐ |
| 3620 | **2769** | (1st) multicoloured | 1.25 | 1.10 | ☐ ☐ |
| 3621 | **2770** | 97p multicoloured | 2.00 | 2.00 | ☐ ☐ |
| 3622 | **2771** | £1.28 multicoloured | 2.75 | 2.50 | ☐ ☐ |
| 3623 | **2772** | £1.47 multicoloured | 3.25 | 3.25 | ☐ ☐ |
| 3624 | **2773** | £2.15 multicoloured | 4.25 | 4.25 | ☐ ☐ |
| *Set of 6* | | | 14.50 | 14.00 | ☐ |
| First Day Cover | | | | 15.00 | ☐ |
| Presentation Pack (P.O. Pack No. 500) | | | 17.00 | | ☐ ☐ |
| PHQ Cards (*set of 6*) | | | 4.00 | 17.00 | ☐ ☐ |
| *Set of 6 Gutter Pairs* | | | 29.00 | | ☐ ☐ |

Self-adhesive. Die-cut perf 14×14½.

| | | | | | |
|---|---|---|---|---|---|
| 3625 | **2769** | (1st) multicoloured | 1.25 | 1.10 | ☐ ☐ |

The phosphor band on No. 3619 is at centre right of the stamps.

No. 3625 was only issued in stamp booklets, each containing No. 3625×2 and 4×1st vermilion and originally sold for £3.72.

**2774** Poppy
(Fiona Strickland)

**2775** Lines from For the Fallen
(Laurence Binyon)

**2776** Private William Cecil Tickle

**2777** A Star Shell (C. R. W. Nevinson)

**2778** The Response (sculpture by
William Goscombe John)

**2779** Princess Mary's Gift Box Fund

(Des Hat-trick Design. Litho International Security Printers or
Enschedé (booklet panes))

**2014** (28 July). Centenary of the First World War (1st issue).
All-over phosphor (3627, 3629) or two bands (others). P 14½.

| | | | | | | |
|---|---|---|---|---|---|---|
| 3626 | **2774** | (1st) multicoloured | 1.25 | 1.10 | | |
| 3627 | **2775** | (1st) multicoloured | 1.25 | 1.10 | | |
| 3628 | **2776** | (1st) multicoloured | 1.25 | 1.10 | | |
| 3629 | **2777** | £1.47 multicoloured | 3.25 | 3.25 | | |
| 3630 | **2778** | £1.47 multicoloured | 3.25 | 3.25 | | |
| 3631 | **2779** | £1.47 multicoloured | 3.25 | 3.25 | | |
| *Set of 6* | | | 13.50 | 13.00 | | |
| First Day Cover | | | | 16.00 | | |
| Presentation Pack (P.O. Pack No. 501) | | | 13.50 | | | |
| PHQ Cards (*set of 6*) | | | 4.00 | 18.00 | | |
| *Set of 6 Gutter Pairs* | | | 27.00 | | | |

**Sustainable Fish and Threatened Fish (2nd issue)**

**2014** (18 Aug). Designs as Nos. 3613/14. Self-adhesive. Die-cut
perf 14×14½

| | | | | | | |
|---|---|---|---|---|---|---|
| 3622 | **2763** | (1st) multicoloured | 1.25 | 1.10 | | |
| 3633 | **2762** | (1st) multicoloured | 1.25 | 1.10 | | |

Nos. 3632/3 were only issued in stamp booklets, each
containing Nos. 3632/3 and 4×1st vermilion and originally
sold for £3.72.

**Classic Locomotives of Wales**

**2014** (18 Sept). Booklet stamp as T 2724. 'All-over' phosphor.
Self-adhesive. Die-cut perf 14

| | | | | | | |
|---|---|---|---|---|---|---|
| 3634 | **2724** | (1st) multicoloured | 1.25 | 1.10 | | |

No. 3634 was only issued in stamp booklets, containing No.
3634×2 and 4×1st vermilion and originally sold for £3.72.

**2780** Eastbourne Bandstand

**2781** Tinside Lido, Plymouth

**2782** Bangor Pier

**2783** Southwold Lighthouse

**2784** Blackpool Pleasure Beach

**2785** Bexhill-on-Sea Shelter

**2786** British Piers

**Seaside Architecture**

**2014** (18 Sept). Two bands (3635/40) or 'All-over' phosphor
(**MS**3641). Perf 14

| | | | | | | |
|---|---|---|---|---|---|---|
| 3635 | **2780** | (1st) multicoloured | 1.25 | 1.10 | | |
| 3636 | **2781** | (1st) multicoloured | 1.25 | 1.10 | | |
| 3637 | **2782** | 97p multicoloured | 2.00 | 2.00 | | |
| 3638 | **2783** | 97p multicoloured | 2.00 | 2.00 | | |
| 3639 | **2784** | £1.28 multicoloured | 2.75 | 2.50 | | |
| 3640 | **2785** | £1.28 multicoloured | 2.75 | 2.50 | | |
| *Set of 6* | | | 12.00 | 11.00 | | |
| First Day Cover | | | | 14.00 | | |
| Presentation Pack (P.O. Pack No. 502) | | | 16.00 | | | |
| PHQ Cards (*set of* 11) | | | 7.50 | 19.00 | | |
| *Set of 6 Gutter Pairs* | | | 24.00 | | | |
| **MS**3641 | 125×89 mm. **2786** (1st) | | | | | |
| | Llandudno Pier; (1st) Worthing | | | | | |
| | Pier; £1.28 Dunoon Pier; £1.28 | | | | | |
| | Brighton Pier | | 7.50 | 7.50 | | |
| First Day Cover | | | | 10.00 | | |

The complete miniature sheet is shown on one of the eleven
PHQ cards with the others depicting individual stamps
including those from the miniature sheet.

**2787** Margaret Thatcher

**2788** Harold Wilson

**2789** Clement Attlee

**2790** Winston Churchill

**2791** William Gladstone

**2792** Robert Peel

**2793** Charles Grey

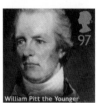

**2794** William Pitt the Younger

## Prime Ministers

**2014** (14 Oct). 'All-over' phosphor. Perf 14½

| | | | | | | |
|---|---|---|---|---|---|---|
| 3642 | **2787** | (1st) | multicoloured | 1.25 | 1.10 | ☐ ☐ |
| | | Horiz strip of 4. Nos. 3642/5 | | 5.00 | 4.25 | ☐ ☐ |
| 3643 | **2788** | (1st) | multicoloured | 1.25 | 1.10 | ☐ ☐ |
| 3644 | **2789** | (1st) | multicoloured | 1.25 | 1.10 | ☐ ☐ |
| 3645 | **2790** | (1st) | multicoloured | 1.25 | 1.10 | ☐ ☐ |
| 3646 | **2791** | 97p | multicoloured | 2.00 | 2.00 | ☐ ☐ |
| | | Horiz strip of 4. Nos. 3646/9 | | 8.00 | 8.00 | ☐ ☐ |
| 3647 | **2792** | 97p | multicoloured | 2.00 | 2.00 | ☐ ☐ |
| 3648 | **2793** | 97p | multicoloured | 2.00 | 2.00 | ☐ ☐ |
| 3649 | **2794** | 97p | multicoloured | 2.00 | 2.00 | ☐ ☐ |
| *Set of 8* | | | | 13.00 | 12.00 | ☐ ☐ |
| First Day Cover | | | | | 16.00 | ☐ |
| Presentation Pack (P.O. Pack No. 503) | | | | 14.00 | | ☐ |
| PHQ Cards (*set of 8*) | | | | 5.50 | 19.00 | ☐ ☐ |

Nos. 3642/5 and 3646/9 were each printed together, *se-tenant*, as horizontal strips of four stamps in sheets of 48 (2 panes 4×6).

**2795** Collecting the Christmas Tree

**2796** Posting Christmas Cards

**2797** Collecting the Christmas Tree

**2798** Posting Christmas Cards

**2799** Building a Snowman

**2800** Carol Singing

**2801** Ice Skating

## Christmas. Illustrations by Andrew Bannecker

**2014** (4 Nov). One centre band (3650) or two bands (others). Perf 14½×15 Self-adhesive

| | | | | | | |
|---|---|---|---|---|---|---|
| 3650 | **2795** | (2nd) multicoloured | 1.00 | 90 | ☐ ☐ |
| 3651 | **2796** | (1st) multicoloured | 1.25 | 1.10 | ☐ ☐ |
| 3652 | **2797** | (2nd Large) multicoloured | 1.50 | 1.50 | ☐ ☐ |
| 3653 | **2798** | (1st Large) multicoloured | 2.00 | 2.00 | ☐ ☐ |
| 3654 | **2799** | £1.28 multicoloured | 2.75 | 2.50 | ☐ ☐ |
| 3655 | **2800** | £1.47 multicoloured | 3.25 | 3.25 | ☐ ☐ |
| 3656 | **2801** | £2.15 multicoloured | 4.25 | 4.25 | ☐ ☐ |
| *Set of 7* | | | 16.00 | 15.50 | ☐ ☐ |
| First Day Cover | | | | 19.00 | ☐ |
| Presentation Pack (P.O. Pack No. 504) | | 16.50 | | ☐ |
| Stamp Cards (*set of 8*) | | 5.25 | 20.00 | ☐ ☐ |
| Ordinary gum | | | | | |
| **MS**3657 146×74 mm. As Nos. 3650/6 | | 16.00 | 16.00 | ☐ ☐ |
| First Day Cover 19.00 | | | | ☐ ☐ |

The eight PHQ cards show the seven individual stamps and the complete miniature sheet.

The 2nd class, 1st class, £1.28 and £1.47 stamps were also issued in sheets of 20 containing eight 2nd class, eight 1st class, two £1.28 and two £1.47 stamps, each stamp accompanied by a *se-tenant* label.

Separate sheets of 20 2nd, 20 1st, 10 1st, 10 £1.28 and ten £1.47 were available with personal photographs.

## Collectors Pack

**2014** (4 Nov). Comprises Nos. 3552/69, **MS**3578/94, **MS**3601/24, 3626/31, 3635/56

| CP3657a Collectors Pack | £130 | ☐ |
|---|---|---|

## Post Office Yearbook

**2014** (4 Nov). Comprises Nos. 3552/69, **MS**3578/94, **MS**3601/24, 3626/31, 3635/56

| YB3657a Yearbook | £160 | ☐ |
|---|---|---|

## Miniature Sheet Collection

**2014** (4 Nov). Comprises Nos. **MS**3578, **MS**3601, **MS**3608, **MS**3641 and **MS**3657 **MS**3657a

| Miniature Sheet Collection | 35.00 | ☐ |
|---|---|---|

# REGIONAL ISSUES

**PERFORATION AND WATERMARK.** All the following Regional stamps are perforated 15 × 14, unless otherwise stated.
For listing of First Day Covers at the end of this section.

## 1 England

EN **1** Three Lions    EN **2** Crowned    EN **3** Oak Tree    EN **4** Tudor Rose
Lion with Shield
of St. George

**2001** (23 Apr.)–02 Printed in photogravure by De La Rue or Questa (Nos. EN1/2), De La Rue (others). One centre phosphor band (2nd) or two phosphor bands (others). Perf 15 × 14 (with one elliptical hole in each vertical side)

| | | | | | | | |
|---|---|---|---|---|---|---|---|
| EN1 | EN **1** | (2nd) | slate-green and silver | 1·00 | 1·00 | ☐ | ☐ |
| EN2 | EN **2** | (1st) | lake-brown and silver | 1·25 | 1·00 | ☐ | ☐ |
| EN3 | EN **3** | (E) | olive-green and silver | 1·75 | 1·75 | ☐ | ☐ |
| EN4 | EN **4** | 65p | deep reddish lilac and silver | 3·00 | 3·00 | ☐ | ☐ |
| EN5 | | 68p | deep reddish lilac and silver (4.7.02) | 3·00 | 3·00 | ☐ | ☐ |

Presentation Pack (P.O. Pack No. 54)
(Nos. EN1/4)    7·50   ☐
PHQ Cards (set of 4) (Nos. EN1/4) (D20)   8·00   14·00   ☐ ☐
Nos. EN1/3 were initially sold at 19p, 27p and 36p, the latter representing the basic European airmail rate.

**Combined Presentation Packs for England, Northern Ireland, Scotland and Wales**
*Presentation Pack* (P.O. Pack No. 59) (contains 68p from England, Northern Ireland, Scotland and Wales (Nos. EN5, NI93, S99, W88)) **9·00**   ☐
*Presentation Pack* (P.O. Pack No. 68) (contains 40p from England, Northern Ireland, Scotland and Wales (Nos. EN9, NI97, S112, W101))   8·00   ☐
*Presentation Pack* (P.O. Pack No. 70) (contains 42p from England, Northern Ireland, Scotland and Wales (Nos. EN10, NI98, S113, W102))   8·00   ☐
*Presentation Pack* (P.O. Pack No. 73) (contains 44p and 72p from England, Northern Ireland, Scotland and Wales (Nos. EN11, EN17, NI99, NI102, S114, S120, W103 and W109)   10·00   ☐
*Presentation Pack* (P.O. Pack No. 76) (contains 48p and 78p from England, Northern Ireland, Scotland and Wales (Nos. EN12, EN18, . NI124, NI128, S115, S121, W104 and W110))   12·50   ☐
*Presentation Pack* (P.O. Pack No. 79) (contains 50p and 81p from England, Northern Ireland, Scotland and Wales (Nos. EN13, EN19, NI125, NI129, S116, S122, W105 and W111))   11·50   ☐

*Presentation Pack* (P.O. Pack No. 81) (contains 2nd, 1st, 50p and 81p from England, Northern Ireland, Scotland and Wales (Nos. EN6/7, EN13, EN19, NI122/3, NI125, NI129, S109/10, S116, S122, W98/9, W105 and W111))   32·00   ☐
*Presentation Pack* (P.O. Pack No. 85) (contains 56p and 90p from England, Northern Ireland, Scotland and Wales (Nos. EN14, EN120, NI126, NI130, S117, S123, W106 and W112   13·50   ☐
*Presentation Pack* (P.O. Pack No. 87) (contains 60p and 97p from England, Northern Ireland, Scotland and Wales (Nos. EN15, EN21, NI127, NI131, S118, S124, W107 and W113))   20·00   ☐
*Presentation Pack* (P.O. Pack No. 91) (contains 68p and £1·10 from England, Northern Ireland, Scotland and Wales (Nos. EN31, EN41, NI103, NI112, S142, W123 and W133))   18·00   ☐
*Presentation Pack* (P.O. Pack No. 95) (contains 87p and £1·28 from England, Northern Ireland, Scotland and Wales (Nos. EN132, EN42, NI103, NI113, S133, S143, W124 and W134))   21·00   ☐
*Presentation Pack* (P.O. Pack No. 98) (contains 88p from England, Northern Ireland, Scotland and Wales (Nos. EN33, NI104, S134, and W125))   9·00   ☐
*Presentation Pack* (P.O. Pack No 100) contains 97p. from England, Northern Ireland, Scotland and Wales (Nos. EN 34, NI105, S135 and W126)   10·00   ☐

**2003** (14 Oct.)–14 As Nos. EN1/3 and EN5 but with white borders. One centre phosphor band (2nd) or two phosphor bands (others). Perf 15 × 14 (with one elliptical hole in each vertical side)

(a) Printed in photogravure by Walsall or De La Rue (2nd), 40p, 42p) or De La Rue (others)

| | | | | | | | |
|---|---|---|---|---|---|---|---|
| EN6 | EN **1** | (2nd) | slate-green and silver | 1·00 | 60 | ☐ | ☐ |
| EN7 | EN **2** | (1st) | lake-brown and silver | 1·25 | 75 | ☐ | ☐ |
| EN8 | EN **3** | (E) | olive-green and silver | 2·00 | 2·00 | ☐ | ☐ |
| EN9 | | 40p | olive-green and silver (11.5.04) | 1·50 | 1·50 | ☐ | ☐ |
| EN10 | | 42p | olive-green and silver (5.4.05) | 1·25 | 1·25 | ☐ | ☐ |
| EN11 | | 44p | olive-green and silver (28.3.06) | 1·50 | 1·50 | ☐ | ☐ |
| EN12 | | 48p | olive-green and silver (27.3.07) | 1·25 | 1·25 | ☐ | ☐ |
| EN13 | | 50p | olive-green and silver (1.4.08) | 90 | 85 | ☐ | ☐ |
| EN14 | | 56p | olive-green and silver (31.3.09) | 1·25 | 1·25 | ☐ | ☐ |
| EN15 | | 60p | olive-green and silver (31.3.10) | 1·40 | 1·40 | ☐ | ☐ |
| EN16 | EN **4** | 68p | deep reddish lilac and silver | 2·50 | 2·50 | ☐ | ☐ |
| EN17 | | 72p | deep reddish lilac and silver (28.3.06) | 2·50 | 2·50 | ☐ | ☐ |
| EN18 | | 78p | deep reddish lilac and silver (27.3.07) | 2·50 | 2·50 | ☐ | ☐ |
| EN19 | | 81p | deep reddish lilac and silver (1.4.08) | 2·00 | 2·00 | ☐ | ☐ |
| EN20 | | 90p | deep reddish lilac and silver (31.3.09) | 2·25 | 2·25 | ☐ | ☐ |
| EN21 | | 97p | deep reddish lilac and silver (31.3.10) | 2·40 | 2·40 | ☐ | ☐ |

(b) Printed in lithography by Enschedé (booklets) (1st) or Cartor (sheets) (1st) or Cartor (others)

| | | | | | | | |
|---|---|---|---|---|---|---|---|
| EN29 | EN **1** | (2nd) | greenish yellow, bright magenta, new blue and black (1.2013) | 1·00 | 1·00 | ☐ | ☐ |
| EN30 | EN **2** | (1st) | lake-brown and silver (20.9.07) | 1·25 | 1·25 | ☐ | ☐ |
| EN31 | EN **3** | 68p | silver, greenish yellow, bright magenta, new blue and black (29.3.11) | 1·50 | 1·50 | ☐ | ☐ |
| EN32 | | 87p | silver, greenish yellow, bright magenta, new blue and black (25.4.12) | 2·50 | 2·50 | ☐ | ☐ |
| EN33 | | 88p | silver, greenish yellow, bright magenta, new blue and black (27.3.13) | 2·00 | 2·00 | ☐ | ☐ |
| EN34 | | 47p. | silver, greenish yellow, bright magenta, new blue and black (26.1.14) | 2.25 | 2.25 | ☐ | ☐ |
| EN41 | EN **4** £1·10 | | deep reddish lilac and silver (29.3.11) | 2·75 | 2·75 | ☐ | ☐ |
| EN42 | | £1·28 | deep reddish lilac and silver (25.4.12) | 3·25 | 3·25 | ☐ | ☐ |

| | | |
|---|---|---|
| Presentation Pack (P.O. Pack No. 63) | | |
| (Nos. EN6/8, EN16) | 6·00 | ☐ |
| PHQ Cards (set of 4) (Nos. EN6/8, EN16) | | |
| (D24) | 4·00 12·00 ☐ ☐ | |

Nos. EN6/8 were initially sold at 20p, 28p and 38p, the latter representing the basic European airmail rate.

Stamps as No. EN30 but self-adhesive were issued on 23 April 2007 in sheets of 20 with *se-tenant* labels. These sheets were printed in lithography by Cartor and perforated 15 × 14 without the elliptical holes. The labels show either English scenes or personal photographs.

No. EN30 was first issued in £7·66 'British Army Uniforms' stamp booklets, but was issued in sheets in January 2013.

Stamps as Nos. EN30, NI95, S131 and W122 but self-adhesive were issued on 29 September 2008 in sheets of 20 containing five of each design with *se-tenant* labels. These sheets were printed in lithograhy by Cartor and perforated 15 × 14 with one elliptical hole in each vertical side.

EN **5**

**Celebrating England**

**2007** (23 Apr.) Sheet 123 × 70 mm. Printed in photogravure by De La Rue. Two phosphor bands. Perf 15 × 14 (with one elliptical hole in each vertical side) (1st) or 15 × 14½ (78p)

| | | |
|---|---|---|
| **MS**EN50 EN **5** (1st) No. EN7; (1st) St. George's flag; 78p St. George; 78p Houses of Parliament, London | 9·00 9·00 | ☐ ☐ |
| First Day Cover | 10·00 | ☐ |
| Presentation Pack (P.O. Pack No. M15) | 11·00 | ☐ |
| PHQ Cards (set of 5) (CGB2) | 4·00 15·00 | ☐ ☐ |

**MS**EN50 was on sale at post offices throughout the UK.

The five PHQ cards show the four individual stamps and the complete miniature sheet.

Stamps as the 1st class St. George's flag stamp within **MS**EN50 but self-adhesive were issued on 23 April 2009 in

sheets of 20 with *se-tenant* labels showing English castles. These sheets were printed in lithography by Cartor.

EN **6** St. George's Flag

**England Flag**

**2013** (9 May) **-14.** Printed in lithography by Cartor or Enschedé. Two phosphor bands. Perf 14½×14 (with one elliptical hole in each vert side)

| | | | | | |
|---|---|---|---|---|---|
| EN51 | EN**6** (1st) | multicoloured | 2·00 | 2·00 | ☐ ☐ |
| | a. Grey Queen's head | | 2·00 | 2·00 | ☐ ☐ |

No. EN 51 were only issued in £11.11 Football Heroes and £13.97 Classic Locomotives booklets.

## 2 Northern Ireland

N **1**     N **2**     N **3**     N **4**

**1958–67** Wmk 179

| | | | | | | |
|---|---|---|---|---|---|---|
| NI1 | N **1** | 3d | lilac (18.8.58) | 15 | 10 | ☐ ☐ |
| | | p. | One centre phosphor band (9.6.67) | 15 | 15 | ☐ ☐ |
| NI2 | | 4d | blue (7.2.66) | 15 | 15 | ☐ ☐ |
| | | p. | Two phosphor bands (10.67) | 15 | 15 | ☐ ☐ |
| NI3 | N **2** | 6d | purple (29.9.58) | 30 | 30 | ☐ ☐ |
| NI4 | | 9d | bronze-green (2 phosphor bands) (1.3.67) | 30 | 70 | ☐ ☐ |
| NI5 | N **3** | 1s3d | green (29.9.58) | 30 | 70 | ☐ ☐ |
| NI6 | | 1s6d | blue (2 phosphor bands) (1.3.67) | 30 | 70 | ☐ ☐ |

**1968–69** One centre phosphor band (Nos. NI8/9) or two phosphor bands (others). No wmk

| | | | | | | |
|---|---|---|---|---|---|---|
| NI7 | N **1** | 4d | blue (27.6.68) | 15 | 15 | ☐ ☐ |
| NI8 | | 4d | sepia (4.9.68) | 15 | 15 | ☐ ☐ |
| NI9 | | 4d | vermilion (26.2.69) | 20 | 20 | ☐ ☐ |
| NI10 | | 5d | blue (4.9.68) | 20 | 20 | ☐ ☐ |
| NI11 | N **3** | 1s6d | blue (20.5.69) | 2·25 | 2·50 | ☐ ☐ |

| | | |
|---|---|---|
| Presentation Pack (comprises Nos. NI1p, NI4/6, NI8/10) (P.O. Pack No. 25) | 3·50 | ☐ |

**Decimal Currency**

**1971–91** Type N **4.** No wmk

(a) Printed in photogravure with phosphor bands

| | | | | | | |
|---|---|---|---|---|---|---|
| NI12 | | 2½p | bright magenta (1 centre band) | 70 | 60 | ☐ ☐ |
| NI13 | | 3p | ultramarine (2 bands) | 30 | 30 | ☐ ☐ |
| NI14 | | 3p | ultramarine (1 centre band) (23.1.74) | 20 | 15 | ☐ ☐ |
| NI15 | | 3½p | olive-grey (2 bands) (23.1.74) | 20 | 25 | ☐ ☐ |
| NI16 | | 3½p | olive-grey (1 centre band) (6.11.74) | 20 | 25 | ☐ ☐ |
| NI17 | | 4½p | grey-blue (2 bands) (6.11.74) | 30 | 25 | ☐ ☐ |
| NI18 | | 5p | reddish violet (2 bands) | 1·00 | 1·00 | ☐ ☐ |

| | | | | | | |
|---|---|---|---|---|---|---|
| NI19 | 5½p | violet (2 bands) *(23.1.74)* | 20 | 20 | ☐ ☐ |
| NI20 | 5½p | violet (1 centre band) *(21.5.75)* | 20 | 25 | ☐ ☐ |
| NI21 | 6½p | greenish blue (1 centre band) *(14.1.76)* | 20 | 20 | ☐ ☐ |
| NI22 | 7p | purple-brown (1 centre band) *(18.1.78)* | 35 | 25 | ☐ ☐ |
| NI23 | 7½p | chestnut (2 bands) | 1·75 | 1·75 | ☐ ☐ |
| NI24 | 8p | rosine (2 bands) *(23.1.74)* | 35 | 35 | ☐ ☐ |
| NI25 | 8½p | yellow-green (2 bands) *(14.1.76)* | 35 | 40 | ☐ ☐ |
| NI26 | 9p | deep violet (2 bands) *(18.1.78)* | 40 | 40 | ☐ ☐ |
| NI27 | 10p | orange-brown (2 bands) *(20.10.76)* | 40 | 50 | ☐ ☐ |
| NI28 | 10p | orange-brown (1 centre band) *(23.7.80)* | 50 | 50 | ☐ ☐ |
| NI29 | 10½p | steel-blue (2 bands) *(18.1.78)* | 40 | 50 | ☐ ☐ |
| NI30 | 11p | scarlet (2 bands) *(20.10.76)* | 50 | 50 | ☐ ☐ |

**(b) Printed in photogravure on phosphorised paper**

| | | | | | | |
|---|---|---|---|---|---|---|
| NI31 | 12p | yellowish green *(23.7.80)* | 50 | 50 | ☐ ☐ |
| NI32 | 13½p | purple-brown *(23.7.80)* | 60 | 70 | ☐ ☐ |
| NI33 | 15p | ultramarine *(23.7.80)* | 60 | 70 | ☐ ☐ |

**(c) Printed in lithography. Perf 14 (11½p, 12½p, 14p (No. NI38), 15½p, 16p, 18p, (No. NI45), 19½p, 20½p, 22p (No. NI53), 26p (No. NI60), 28p (No. NI62)) or 15 × 14 (others)**

| | | | | | | |
|---|---|---|---|---|---|---|
| NI34 | 11½p | drab (1 side band) *(8.4.81)* | 85 | 85 | ☐ ☐ |
| NI35 | 12p | bright emerald (1 side band) *(7.1.86)* | 90 | 90 | ☐ ☐ |
| NI36 | 12½p | light emerald (1 side band) *(24.2.82)* | 60 | 60 | ☐ ☐ |
| | a. | Perf 15 × 14 *(28.2.84)* | 5·25 | 5·25 | ☐ ☐ |
| NI37 | 13p | pale chestnut (1 side band) *(23.10.84)* | 80 | 50 | ☐ ☐ |
| NI38 | 14p | grey-blue (phosphorised paper) *(8.4.81)* | 75 | 75 | ☐ ☐ |
| NI39 | 14p | deep blue (1 centre band) *(8.11.88)* | 75 | 60 | ☐ ☐ |
| NI40 | 15p | bright blue (1 centre band) *(28.11.89)* | 90 | 60 | ☐ ☐ |
| NI41 | 15½p | pale violet (phosphorised paper) *(24.2.82)* | 80 | 80 | ☐ ☐ |
| NI42 | 16p | drab (phosphorised paper) *(27.4.83)* | 1·00 | 1·00 | ☐ ☐ |
| | a. | Perf 15 × 14 *(28.2.84)* | 8·25 | 8·50 | ☐ ☐ |
| NI43 | 17p | grey-blue (phosphorised paper) *(23.10.84)* | 90 | 95 | ☐ ☐ |
| NI44 | 17p | deep blue (1 centre band) *(4.12.90)* | 1·00 | 80 | ☐ ☐ |
| NI45 | 18p | deep violet (phosphorised paper) *(8.4.81)* | 1·00 | 1·00 | ☐ ☐ |
| NI46 | 18p | deep olive-grey (phosphorised paper) *(6.1.87)* | 1·00 | 90 | ☐ ☐ |
| NI47 | 18p | bright green (1 centre band) *(3.12.91)* | 1·00 | 95 | ☐ ☐ |
| | a. | Perf 14 *(31.12.92)** | 5·00 | 5·00 | ☐ ☐ |
| NI48 | 18p | bright green (1 side band) *(10.8.93)* | 2·25 | 2·25 | ☐ ☐ |
| NI49 | 19p | bright orange-red (phosphorised paper) *(8.11.88)* | 1·00 | 1·00 | ☐ ☐ |
| NI50 | 19½p | olive-grey (phosphorised paper) *(24.2.82)* | 1·50 | 1·75 | ☐ ☐ |
| NI51 | 20p | brownish black (phosphorised paper) *(28.11.89)* | 1·00 | 80 | ☐ ☐ |

| | | | | | | |
|---|---|---|---|---|---|---|
| NI52 | 20½p | ultramarine (phosphorised paper) *(27.4.83)* | 4·50 | 4·25 | ☐ ☐ |
| NI53 | 22p | blue (phosphorised paper) *(8.4.81)* | 1·10 | 1·10 | ☐ ☐ |
| NI54 | 22p | yellow-green (phosphorised paper) *(23.10.84)* | 1·10 | 1·10 | ☐ ☐ |
| NI55 | 22p | bright orange-red (phosphorised paper) *(4.12.90)* | 1·25 | 90 | ☐ ☐ |
| NI56 | 23p | bright green (phosphorised paper) *(8.11.88)* | 1·25 | 1·10 | ☐ ☐ |
| NI57 | 24p | Indian red (phosphorised paper) *(28.11.89)* | 1·25 | 1·25 | ☐ ☐ |
| NI58 | 24p | chestnut (phosphorised paper) *(3.12.91)* | 1·10 | 90 | ☐ ☐ |
| NI59 | 24p | chestnut (2 bands) *(10.8.93)* | 2·25 | 2·50 | ☐ ☐ |
| NI60 | 26p | rosine (phosphorised paper) *(24.2.82)* | 1·25 | 1·25 | ☐ ☐ |
| | a. | Perf 15 × 14 *(27.1.87)* | 3·00 | 3·25 | ☐ ☐ |
| NI61 | 26p | drab (phosphorised paper) *(4.12.90)* | 1·75 | 1·75 | ☐ ☐ |
| NI62 | 28p | deep violet-blue (phosphorised paper) *(27.4.83)* | 1·50 | 1·50 | ☐ ☐ |
| | a. | Perf 15 × 14 *(27.1.87)* | 1·25 | 1·25 | ☐ ☐ |
| NI63 | 28p | deep bluish grey (phosphorised paper) *(3.12.91)* | 1·50 | 1·50 | ☐ ☐ |
| NI64 | 31p | bright purple (phosphorised paper) *(23.10.84)* | 1·75 | 2·00 | ☐ ☐ |
| NI65 | 32p | greenish blue (phosphorised paper) *(8.11.88)* | 1·75 | 1·75 | ☐ ☐ |
| NI66 | 34p | deep bluish grey (phosphorised paper) *(28.11.89)* | 1·75 | 1·75 | ☐ ☐ |
| NI67 | 37p | rosine (phosphorised paper) *(4.12.90)* | 2·00 | 2·50 | ☐ ☐ |
| NI68 | 39p | bright mauve (phosphorised paper) *(3.12.91)* | 2·00 | 2·25 | ☐ ☐ |

\* Earliest known date of use.

Nos. NI48 and NI59 were only issued in stamp booklets.

| | | |
|---|---|---|
| *Presentation Pack* (P.O. Pack No. 29) (contains 2½p (NI12), 3p (NI13), 5p (NI18), 7½p (NI23)) | 3·50 | ☐ |
| *Presentation Pack* (P.O. Pack No. 61) (contains 3p (NI14), 3½p (NI15), 5½p (NI19), 8p (NI24) later with 4½p (NI17) added) | 2·75 | ☐ |
| *Presentation Pack* (P.O. Pack No. 84) (contains 6½p (NI21), 8½p (NI25), 10p (NI27), 11p (NI30)) | 2·00 | ☐ |
| *Presentation Pack* (P.O. Pack No. 129d) (contains 7p (NI22), 9p (NI26), 10½p (NI29), 11½p (NI34), 12p (NI31), 13½p (NI32), 14p (NI38), 15p (NI33), 18p (NI45), 22p (NI53)) | 9·00 | ☐ |
| *Presentation Pack* (P.O. Pack No. 4) (contains 10p (NI28), 12½p (NI36), 16p (NI42), 20½p (NI52), 26p (NI60), 28p (NI62)) | 18·00 | ☐ |
| *Presentation Pack* (P.O. Pack No. 8) (contains 10p (NI28), 13p (NI37), 16p (NI42a), 17p (NI43), 22p (NI54), 26p (NI60), 28p (NI62), 31p (NI64)) | 18·00 | ☐ |
| *Presentation Pack* (P.O. Pack No. 12) (contains 12p (NI35), 13p (NI37), 17p (NI43), 18p (NI46), 22p (NI54), 26p (NI60a), 28p (NI62a), 31p (NI64)) | 20·00 | ☐ |

## Combined Presentation Packs for Northern Ireland, Scotland and Wales

*Presentation Pack* (P.O. Pack No. 17) (contains
14p, 19p, 23p, 32p from Northern Ireland,
Scotland and Wales (Nos. NI39, NI49, NI56,
NI65, S54, S62, S67, S77, W40,
W50, W57, W66))        17·00   ☐

*Presentation Pack* (P.O. Pack No. 20) (contains
15p, 20p, 24p, 34p from Northern Ireland,
Scotland and Wales (Nos. NI40, NI5I, NI57,
NI66, S56, S64, S69, S78, W41,
W52, W58, W67))        16·00   ☐

*Presentation Pack* (P.O. Pack No. 23) (contains
17p, 22p, 26p, 37p from Northern Ireland,
Scotland and Wales (Nos. NI44, NI55, NI6I,
NI67, S58, S66, S73, S79, W45,
W56, W62, W68))        16·00   ☐

*Presentation Pack* (P.O. Pack No. 26) (contains
18p, 24p, 28p, 39p from Northern Ireland,
Scotland and Wales (Nos. NI47, NI58,
NI63, NI68, S60, S70, S75, S80, W48,
W59, W64, W69))        16·00   ☐

### 1993 (7 Dec.)–2000

(a) Printed in lithography by Questa. Perf 15 × 14 (with one elliptical hole in each vertical side)

| | | | | | | |
|---|---|---|---|---|---|---|
| NI69 | N **4** | 19p | bistre (1 centre band) | 90 | 80 | ☐ ☐ |
| NI70 | | 19p | bistre (1 side band) | | | |
| | | | *(26.7.94)* | 1·25 | 1·75 | ☐ ☐ |
| NI71 | | 20p | bright green (1 centre band) *(23.7.96)* | 1·50 | 1·50 | ☐ ☐ |
| NI72 | | 25p | red (2 bands) | 75 | 75 | ☐ ☐ |
| NI73 | | 26p | red-brown (2 bands) *(23.7.96)* | 1·75 | 1·75 | ☐ ☐ |
| NI74 | | 30p | deep olive-grey (2 bands) | 1·25 | 1·25 | ☐ ☐ |
| NI75 | | 37p | bright mauve (2 bands) *(23.7.96)* | 2·75 | 3·00 | ☐ ☐ |
| NI76 | | 41p | grey-brown (2 bands) | 1·50 | 1·75 | ☐ ☐ |
| NI77 | | 63p | light emerald (2 bands) *(23.7.96)* | 5·00 | 5·00 | ☐ ☐ |

(b) Printed in photogravure by Walsall (19p, 20p, 26p (No. NI81b), 38p, 40p, 63p, 64p, 65p), Harrison or Walsall (26p (No. NI81), 37p). Perf 14 (No. NI80) or 15 × 14 (others) (both with one elliptical hole in each vertical side)

| | | | | | | |
|---|---|---|---|---|---|---|
| NI78 | N **4** | 19p | bistre (1 centre band) *(8.6.99)* | 3·00 | 3·00 | ☐ ☐ |
| NI79 | | 20p | bright green (1 centre band) *(1.7.97)* | 1·95 | 80 | ☐ ☐ |
| NI80 | | 20p | bright green (1 side band) *(13.10.98)* | 3·00 | 3·00 | ☐ ☐ |
| NI81 | | 26p | chestnut (2 bands) *(1.7.97)* | 1·25 | 1·00 | ☐ ☐ |
| | | | b. Perf 14 *(13.10.98)* | 3·00 | 3·00 | ☐ ☐ |
| NI82 | | 37p | bright mauve (2 bands) *(1.7.97)* | 2·25 | 2·25 | ☐ ☐ |
| NI83 | | 38p | ultramarine (2 bands) *(8.6.99)* | 8·00 | 8·00 | ☐ ☐ |
| NI84 | | 40p | deep azure (2 bands) *(25.4.00)* | 2·50 | 2·50 | ☐ ☐ |
| NI85 | | 63p | light emerald (2 bands) *(1.7.97)* | 5·00 | 5·00 | ☐ ☐ |
| NI86 | | 64p | turquoise-green (2 bands) *(8.6.99)* | 9·00 | 9·00 | ☐ ☐ |
| NI87 | | 65p | greenish blue (2 bands) *(25.4.00)* | 3·25 | 3·25 | ☐ ☐ |

Nos. NI70, NI80 and NI81b were only issued in stamp booklets. No. NI70 exists with the phosphor band at the left or right of the stamp.

*Presentation Pack* (P.O. Pack No. 47)
(contains 19p, 26p, 38p, 64p (Nos. NI78,
NI81, NI83 NI86))        15·00   ☐

*Presentation Pack* (P.O. Pack No. 52)
(contains 1st, 40p, 65p) (Nos. NI84,
NI87, NI88b)        18·00   ☐

### Combined Presentation Packs for Northern Ireland, Scotland and Wales

*Presentation Pack* (P.O. Pack No. 31) (contains
19p, 25p, 30p, 41p from Northern Ireland,
Scotland and Wales (Nos. NI69, NI72, NI74,
NI76, S81, S84, S86, S88, W70,
W73, W75, W77))        16·00   ☐

*Presentation Pack* (P.O. Pack No. 36) (contains
20p, 26p, 37p, 63p from Northern Ireland,
Scotland and Wales (Nos. NI71, NI73, NI75,
NI77, S83, S85, S87, S89, W72,
W74 W76, W78))        23·00   ☐

*Presentation Pack* (P.O. Pack No. 42) (contains
20p (1 centre band), 26p, 37p, 63p from
Northern Ireland, Scotland and Wales
(Nos. NI79, NI81/2, NI85, S90/3, W79/82))  26·00   ☐

N **5**

**2000** (15 Feb.–25 Apr.) Type N **4** redrawn with '1st' face value as Type N **5**. Two phosphor bands. Perf 14 (with one elliptical hole in each vertical side)

| | | | | | | |
|---|---|---|---|---|---|---|
| NI88 | N **5** | (1st) | bright orange-red | 3·00 | 3·00 | ☐ ☐ |
| | | | b. Perf 15 × 14 (25 Apr.) | 12·00 | 12·00 | ☐ ☐ |

No. NI88 was only issued in £7.50 'Special by Design' stamp booklets. No. NI88b was issued in sheets on 25 April.

N **6** Basalt Columns, Giant's Causeway  N **7** Aerial View of Patchwork Fields  N **8** Linen Pattern  N **9** Vase Pattern from Belleck

**2001** (6 Mar.)–**02** Printed in lithography by De La Rue (68p), De La Rue or Walsall (E), Walsall or Enschedé (2nd) or Walsall (others). One centre phosphor band (2nd) or two phosphor bands (others). Perf 15 × 14 (with one elliptical hole in each vertical side)

| | | | | | | |
|---|---|---|---|---|---|---|
| NI89 | N **6** | (2nd) | black, new blue, bright magenta and greenish yellow | 1·00 | 75 | ☐ ☐ |
| NI90 | N **7** | (1st) | black, new blue and greenish yellow | 1·25 | 1·20 | ☐ ☐ |
| NI91 | N **8** | (E) | black, new blue and pale orange | 1·50 | 1·50 | ☐ ☐ |
| NI92 | N **9** | 65p | black, bright magenta and greenish yellow | 3·00 | 3·00 | ☐ ☐ |
| NI93 | | 68p | black, bright magenta and greenish yellow *(4.7.02)* | 3·25 | 3·25 | ☐ ☐ |

| | | | |
|---|---|---|---|
| Presentation Pack (P.O. Pack No. 53) (Nos. NI89/92) | | 8·00 | ☐ |
| PHQ Cards (*set of* 4) (Nos. NI89/92)(D19) | 8·00 | 14·00 | ☐ ☐ |

Nos. NI89, NI90 and NI91 were initially sold at 19p, 27p and 36p, the latter representing the basic European airmail rate.

For combined presentation packs for all four Regions, see under England.

**2003** (14 Oct.)–**14** As Nos. NI89/91 and NI93 but with white borders. One centre phosphor band (2nd) or two phosphor bands (others). Perf 15 × 14 (with one elliptical hole on each vertical side)

(a) Printed in lithography by Walsall (NI98), De La Rue or Enschedé (NI95), Cartor (NI103/4, NI112/13 or De La Rue (others)

| | | | | | | | |
|---|---|---|---|---|---|---|---|
| NI94 | N **6** | (2nd) | black, new blue, bright magenta and greenish yellow | 1·00 | 1·00 | ☐ | ☐ |
| NI95 | N **7** | (1st) | black, new blue and greenish yellow | 1·25 | 1·00 | ☐ | ☐ |
| NI96 | N **8** | (E) | black and new blue | 2·50 | 2·50 | ☐ | ☐ |
| NI97 | | 40p | black and new blue *(11.5.04)* | 1·75 | 1·75 | ☐ | ☐ |
| NI98 | | 42p | black, new blue and orange-yellow *(5.4.05)* | 1·75 | 1·75 | ☐ | ☐ |
| | | a. | Black, new blue and greenish yellow *(26.7.05)* | 2·00 | 2·00 | ☐ | ☐ |
| NI99 | | 44p | black, new blue and greenish yellow *(28.3.06)* | 1·00 | 1·00 | ☐ | ☐ |
| NI100 | N **9** | 68p | black, bright magenta and greenish yellow | 2·75 | 2·75 | ☐ | ☐ |
| NI101 | N **8** | 68p | greenish yellow, bright magenta, new blue and black *(29.3.11)* | 1·50 | 1·50 | ☐ | ☐ |
| NI102 | N **9** | 72p | black, greyish black, bright magenta and greenish yellow *(28.3.06)* | 2·50 | 2·50 | ☐ | ☐ |
| NI103 | N **8** | 87p | greenish yellow, bright magenta, new blue and black *(25.4.12)* | 2·50 | 2·50 | ☐ | ☐ |
| NI104 | | 88p | greenish yellow, bright magenta, new blue and black *(27.3.13)* | 2·00 | 2·00 | ☐ | ☐ |
| NI105 | | 97p. | greenish yellow, bright magenta, new blue and black *(26.3.14)* | 2·25 | 2·25 | ☐ | ☐ |
| NI112 | N **9** | £1·10 | greenish yellow, bright magenta, new blue and black *(29.3.11)* | 2·75 | 2·75 | ☐ | ☐ |
| NI113 | | £1·28 | greenish yellow, bright magenta, new blue and black *(25.4.12)* | 3·25 | 3·25 | ☐ | ☐ |

(b) Printed in photogravure by De La Rue

| | | | | | | | |
|---|---|---|---|---|---|---|---|
| NI122 | N **6** | (2nd) | bright magenta, greenish yellow, new blue and black *(20.9.07)* | 1·00 | 60 | ☐ | ☐ |
| NI123 | N **7** | (1st) | greenish yellow, new blue and black *(20.9.07)* | 1·25 | 75 | ☐ | ☐ |
| NI124 | N **8** | 48p | olive-grey and black *(27.3.07)* | 1·20 | 1·20 | ☐ | ☐ |
| NI125 | | 50p | olive-grey and black *(1.4.08)* | 1·20 | 1·20 | ☐ | ☐ |
| NI126 | | 56p | olive-grey and black *(31.3.09)* | 1·25 | 1·25 | ☐ | ☐ |
| NI127 | | 60p | olive-grey and black *(30.3.10)* | 1·40 | 1·40 | ☐ | ☐ |
| NI128 | N **9** | 78p | bright magenta, greenish yellow and black *(27.3.07)* | 2·00 | 2·00 | ☐ | ☐ |
| NI129 | | 81p | bright magenta, greenish yellow and black *(1.4.08)* | 2·00 | 2·00 | ☐ | ☐ |
| NI130 | | 90p | bright magenta, greenish yellow and black *(31.3.09)* | 2·25 | 2·25 | ☐ | ☐ |
| NI131 | | 97p | bright magenta, greenish yellow and black *(30.3.10)* | 2·40 | 2·40 | ☐ | ☐ |

| | | | | | |
|---|---|---|---|---|---|
| Presentation Pack (P.O. Pack No. 66) (Nos. NI94/6, NI100) | | 7·00 | | ☐ | |
| PHQ Cards (*set of* 4) (Nos. NI94/6, NI100) (D27) | | 2·00 | 10·00 | ☐ | ☐ |

Nos. NI94/6 were initially sold at 20p, 28p and 38p, the latter representing the basic European airmail rate.

The Enschedé printing of No. NI95 comes from £7·66 'British Army Uniforms' stamp booklets.

No. NI98 (Walsall printing) appears bluish grey and No. NI98a (De La Rue printing) appears olive-grey.

Stamps as NI95 but self-adhesive were issued on 11 March 2008 in sheets of 20 with *se-tenant* labels. These sheets were printed in lithography by Cartor and perforated 15 × 14 without the ellipitcal holes. The labels show either Northern Ireland scenes or personal photographs.

Stamps as NI95 but self-adhesive were issued again on 17 March 2009 in sheets of 20 with *se-tenant* labels showing Northern Island castles. These sheets were printed in lithography by Cartor.

Stamps as Nos. EN30, NI95, S131 and W122 but self-adhesive were issued on 29 September 2008 in sheets of 20 containing five of each design with *se-tenant* labels.

N **10**

**Celebrating Northern Ireland**

**2008** (11 Mar.) Sheet 123 × 70 mm. Printed in lithography by De La Rue. Two phosphor bands. Perf 15 × 14½ (with one elliptical hole in each vertical side) (1st) or 15 × 14½ (78p)

| | | | | | |
|---|---|---|---|---|---|
| **MS**NI152 N **10** (1st) Carrickfergus Castle; (1st) Giant's Causeway; 78p St. Patrick; 78p Queen's Bridge and 'Angel of Thanksgiving' sculpture, Belfast | | 7·00 | 7·00 | ☐ | ☐ |
| First Day Cover | | | 8·00 | | ☐ |
| Presentation Pack (P.O. Pack No. 410) | | 9·00 | | ☐ | |
| PHQ Cards (*set of* 5) (CGB3) | | 9·00 | 20·00 | ☐ | ☐ |

**MS**NI152 was on sale at post offices throughout the UK.

The five PHQ cards depict the complete miniature sheet and the four stamps within it.

N **11**

## 50th Anniv of the Country Definitives (1st issue)

**2008** (29 Sept.) Sheet 124 × 70 mm, containing designs as Nos. NI1, NI3, NI5, S1, S3, S5, W1, W3 and W5 (regional definitives of 1958) but inscribed 1st and printed in photogravure by De La Rue on pale cream. Two phosphor bands. Perf 15 × 14 (with one elliptical hole in each vertical side)

**MS**NI153 N **11** (1st) As No. W1; (1st) As
No. S1; (1st) As No. W5; (1st) As No. S5;
(1st) As No. NI1; (1st) As No. W3; (1st)
As No. S3; (1st) As No. NI3; (1st) As No.

| | | | |
|---|---|---|---|
| NI5 | 13·00 | 13·00 | ☐ ☐ |
| First Day Cover | | 14·00 | ☐ |
| Presentation Pack (P.O. Pack No. 80) | 15·00 | | ☐ |
| PHQ Cards (set of 10) (D29) | 9·00 | 20·00 | ☐ ☐ |

**MS**NI153 was on sale at post offices throughout the UK.
The ten PHQ cards show the nine individual stamps and the complete sheet.

## 50th Anniv of the Country Definitives (2nd issue)

**2008** (29 Sept.) As Nos. NI1, NI3 and NI5 (definitives of 1958) but inscribed 1st and printed in lithography by De La Rue. Two phosphor bands. Perf 15 × 14½ (with one elliptical hole in each vertical side)

| | | | | | |
|---|---|---|---|---|---|
| NI154 | N **1** | (1st) | deep lilac | 3·00 | 3·00 ☐ ☐ |
| NI155 | N **3** | (1st) | green | 3·00 | 3·00 ☐ ☐ |
| NI156 | N **2** | (1st) | deep claret | 3·00 | 3·00 ☐ ☐ |
| *Set of 3* | | | | 8.00 | 8.00 ☐ ☐ |

Nos. NI154/6 were only issued in the £9·72 'The Regional Definitives' booklet.

## 3 Scotland

| S **1** |  S **2** |  S **3** |  S **4** |
|---|---|---|---|

**1958–67** Wmk 179

| | | | | | |
|---|---|---|---|---|---|
| S1 | S **1** | 3d | lilac (18.8.58) | 15 | 15 ☐ ☐ |
| | | p. | Two phosphor bands (21.9.63) | 13·00 | 2·75 ☐ ☐ |
| | | pa. | One side band (30.4.65) | 20 | 25 ☐ ☐ |
| | | pd. | One centre phosphor band (9.11.67) | 15 | 15 ☐ ☐ |
| S2 | | 4d | blue (7.7.66) | 15 | 15 ☐ ☐ |
| | | p. | Two phosphor bands | 15 | 15 ☐ ☐ |
| S3 | S **2** | 6d | purple (29.9.58) | 20 | 15 ☐ ☐ |
| | | p. | Two phosphor bands (29.1.63) | 20 | 20 ☐ ☐ |
| S4 | | 9d | bronze-green (2 phosphor bands)(1.3.67) | 35 | 40 ☐ ☐ |
| S5 | S **3** | 1s3d | green (29.9.58) | 40 | 40 ☐ ☐ |
| | | p. | Two phosphor bands (29.1.63) | 40 | 40 ☐ ☐ |
| S6 | | 1s6d | blue (2 phosphor bands) (1.3.67) | 45 | 50 ☐ ☐ |

No. S1pa exists with the phosphor band at the left or right of the stamp.

**1967–70** One centre phosphor band (Nos. S7, S9/10) or two phosphor bands (others). No wmk

| | | | | | |
|---|---|---|---|---|---|
| S7 | S **1** | 3d | lilac (16.5.68) | 10 | 15 ☐ ☐ |
| S8 | | 4d | blue (28.11.67) | 10 | 15 ☐ ☐ |
| S9 | | 4d | sepia (4.9.68) | 10 | 10 ☐ ☐ |
| S10 | | 4d | vermilion (26.2.69) | 10 | 10 ☐ ☐ |
| S11 | | 5d | blue (4.9.68) | 20 | 10 ☐ ☐ |

| | | | | | |
|---|---|---|---|---|---|
| S12 | S **2** | 9d | bronze-green (28.9.70) | 6·00 | 6·00 ☐ ☐ |
| S13 | S **3** | 1s6d | blue (12.12.68) | 1·75 | 1·50 ☐ ☐ |

Presentation Pack (containing Nos. S3,
S5p, S7, S9/13) (P.O. Pack No. 23)    8·00    ☐

**Decimal Currency**

**1971** (7 July)–**93** Type S **4**. No wmk

(a) Printed in photogravure by Harrison and Sons with phosphor bands. Perf 15 × 14

| | | | | |
|---|---|---|---|---|
| S14 | 2½p | bright magenta (1 centre band) | 25 | 20 ☐ ☐ |
| S15 | 3p | ultramarine (2 bands) | 35 | 15 ☐ ☐ |
| S16 | 3p | ultramarine (1 centre band) (23.1.74) | 15 | 15 ☐ ☐ |
| S17 | 3½p | olive-grey (2 bands) (23.1.74) | 20 | 25 ☐ ☐ |
| S18 | 3½p | olive-grey (1 centre band) (6.11.74) | 20 | 25 ☐ ☐ |
| S19 | 4½p | grey-blue (2 bands) (6.11.74) | 30 | 25 ☐ ☐ |
| S20 | 5p | reddish violet (2 bands) | 1·00 | 1·25 ☐ ☐ |
| S21 | 5½p | violet (2 bands) (23.1.74) | 20 | 20 ☐ ☐ |
| S22 | 5½p | violet (1 centre band) (21.5.75) | 20 | 25 ☐ ☐ |
| S23 | 6½p | greenish blue (1 centre band) (14.1.76) | 20 | 20 ☐ ☐ |
| S24 | 7p | purple-brown (1 centre band) (18.11.78) | 30 | 30 ☐ ☐ |
| S25 | 7½p | chestnut (2 bands) | 1·25 | 1·25 ☐ ☐ |
| S26 | 8p | rosine (2 bands) (23.1.74) | 45 | 40 ☐ ☐ |
| S27 | 8½p | yellow-green (2 bands) (14.1.76) | 40 | 40 ☐ ☐ |
| S28 | 9p | deep violet (2 bands) (18.1.78) | 40 | 40 ☐ ☐ |
| S29 | 10p | orange-brown (2 bands) (20.10.76) | 45 | 50 ☐ ☐ |
| S30 | 10p | orange-brown (1 centre band) (23.7.80) | 40 | 50 ☐ ☐ |
| S31 | 10½p | steel-blue (2 bands) (18.1.78) | 45 | 50 ☐ ☐ |
| S32 | 11p | scarlet (2 bands) (20.10.76) | 50 | 50 ☐ ☐ |

(b) Printed in photogravure by Harrison and Sons on phosphorised paper. Perf 15 × 14

| | | | | |
|---|---|---|---|---|
| S33 | 12p | yellowish green (23.7.80) | 50 | 50 ☐ ☐ |
| S34 | 13½p | purple-brown (23.7.80) | 70 | 80 ☐ ☐ |
| S35 | 15p | ultramarine (23.7.80) | 60 | 70 ☐ ☐ |

(c) Printed in lithography by John Waddington. One side phosphor band (11½p, 12p, 12½p, 13p) or phosphorised paper (others). Perf 14

| | | | | |
|---|---|---|---|---|
| S36 | 11½p | drab (8.4.81) | 80 | 80 ☐ ☐ |
| S37 | 12p | bright emerald (7.1.86) | 2·00 | 2·00 ☐ ☐ |
| S38 | 12½p | light emerald (24.2.82) | 60 | 70 ☐ ☐ |
| S39 | 13p | pale chestnut (23.10.84) | 85 | 75 ☐ ☐ |
| S40 | 14p | grey-blue (8.4.81) | 75 | 75 ☐ ☐ |
| S41 | 15½p | pale violet (24.2.82) | 80 | 80 ☐ ☐ |
| S42 | 16p | drab (27.4.83) | 80 | 85 ☐ ☐ |
| S43 | 17p | grey-blue (23.10.84) | 1·50 | 1·50 ☐ ☐ |
| S44 | 18p | deep violet (8.4.81) | 80 | 80 ☐ ☐ |
| S45 | 19½p | olive-grey (24.2.82) | 1·75 | 1·75 ☐ ☐ |
| S46 | 20½p | ultramarine (27.4.83) | 3·50 | 3·50 ☐ ☐ |
| S47 | 22p | blue (8.4.81) | 1·00 | 1·00 ☐ ☐ |
| S48 | 22p | yellow-green (23.10.84) | 4·25 | 4·25 ☐ ☐ |
| S49 | 26p | rosine | 1·25 | 1·25 ☐ ☐ |
| S50 | 28p | deep violet-blue | 1·25 | 1·25 ☐ ☐ |
| S51 | 31p | bright purple | 2·50 | 2·50 ☐ ☐ |

(d) Printed in lithography by Questa. Perf 15 × 14

| | | | | |
|---|---|---|---|---|
| S52 | 12p | bright emerald (1 side band) (29.4.86) | 2·00 | 2·25 ☐ ☐ |

| | | | | | |
|---|---|---|---|---|---|
| S53 | 13p | pale chestnut (1 side band) *(4.11.86)* | 70 | 75 | □ □ |
| S54 | 14p | deep blue (1 centre band) *(8.11.88)* | 60 | 70 | □ □ |
| S55 | 14p | deep blue (1 side band) *(21.3.89)* | 80 | 90 | □ □ |
| S56 | 15p | bright blue (1 centre band) *(28.11.89)* | 70 | 70 | □ □ |
| S57 | 17p | grey-blue (phosphorised paper) *(29.4.86)* | 4·00 | 4·00 | □ □ |
| S58 | 17p | deep blue (1 centre band) *(4.12.90)* | 1·00 | 1·10 | □ □ |
| S59 | 18p | deep olive-grey (phosphorised paper) *(6.1.87)* | 1·10 | 85 | □ □ |
| S60 | 18p | bright green (1 centre band) *(3.12.91)* | 1·25 | 90 | □ □ |
| | a. | Perf 14 *(26.9.92)*\* | 1·00 | 1·00 | □ □ |
| S61 | 18p | bright green (1 side band) *(10.8.93)* | 2·75 | 3·00 | □ □ |
| S62 | 19p | bright orange-red (phosphorised paper) *(8.11.88)* | 70 | 70 | □ □ |
| S63 | 19p | bright orange-red (2 bands) *(21.3.89)* | 2·25 | 2·00 | □ □ |
| S64 | 20p | brownish black (phosphorised paper) *(28.11.89)* | 95 | 95 | □ □ |
| S65 | 22p | yellow-green (phosphorised paper) *(27.1.87)* | 1·25 | 1·50 | □ □ |
| S66 | 22p | bright orange-red (phosphorised paper) *(4.12.90)* | 1·25 | 90 | □ □ |
| S67 | 23p | bright green (phosphorised paper) *(8.11.88)* | 1·25 | 1·10 | □ □ |
| S68 | 23p | bright green (2 bands) *(21.3.89)* | 14·00 | 14·00 | □ □ |
| S69 | 24p | Indian red (phosphorised paper) *(28.11.89)* | 1·25 | 1·25 | □ □ |
| S70 | 24p | chestnut (phosphorised paper) *(3.12.91)* | 1·40 | 1·25 | □ □ |
| | a. | Perf 14 *(10.92)*\* | 6·00 | 6·00 | □ □ |
| S71 | 24p | chestnut (2 bands) *(10.8.93)* | 2·75 | 3·00 | □ □ |
| S72 | 26p | rosine (phosphorised paper) *(27.1.87)* | 3·75 | 4·00 | □ □ |
| S73 | 26p | drab (phosphorised paper) *(4.12.90)* | 1·25 | 1·25 | □ □ |
| S74 | 28p | deep violet-blue (phosphorised paper) *(27.1.87)* | 1·25 | 1·25 | □ □ |
| S75 | 28p | deep bluish grey (phosphorised paper) *(3.12.91)* | 1·25 | 1·50 | □ □ |
| | a. | Perf 14 *(18.12.93)*\* | 8·00 | 8·00 | □ □ |
| S76 | 31p | bright purple (phosphorised paper) *(29.4.86)* | 2·25 | 2·25 | □ □ |
| S77 | 32p | greenish blue (phosphorised paper) *(8.11.88)* | 1·75 | 2·00 | □ □ |
| S78 | 34p | deep bluish grey (phosphorised paper) *(28.11.89)* | 1·75 | 1·75 | □ □ |
| S79 | 37p | rosine (phosphorised paper) *(4.12.90)* | 2·00 | 2·25 | □ □ |
| S80 | 39p | bright mauve (phosphorised paper) *(3.12.91)* | 2·00 | 2·25 | □ □ |
| | a. | Perf 14 *(11.92)* | 7·00 | 7·00 | □ □ |

\* Earliest known date of use.
Nos. S55, S61, S63, S68 and S71 were only issued in stamp booklets.

| | | | |
|---|---|---|---|
| *Presentation Pack* (P.O. Pack No. 27) (contains 2½p (S14), 3p (S15), 5p (S20), 7½p (S25)) | | 3·50 | □ |
| *Presentation Pack* (P.O. Pack No. 62) (contains 3p (S16), 3½p (S17), 5½p (S21), 8p (S26), later with 4½p (S19) added) | | 2·50 | □ |
| *Presentation Pack* (P.O. Pack No. 85) (contains 6½p (S23), 8½p (S27), 10p (S29), 11p (S32)) | | 2·00 | □ |
| *Presentation Pack* (P.O. Pack No. 129b) (contains 7p (S24), 9p (S28), 10½p (S31), 11½p (S36), 12p (S33), 13½p (S34), 14p (S40), 15p (S35), 18p (S44), 22p (S47)) | | 9·00 | □ |
| *Presentation Pack* (P.O. Pack No. 2) (contains 10p (S30), 12½p (S38), 16p (S42), 20½p (S46), 26p (S49), 28p (S50)) | | 18·00 | □ |
| *Presentation Pack* (P.O. Pack No. 6) (contains 10p (S30), 13p (S39), 16p (S42), 17p (S43), 22p (S48), 26p (S49), 28p (S50), 31p (S51)) | | 17·00 | □ |
| *Presentation Pack* (P.O. Pack No. 10) (contains 12p (S52), 13p (S53), 17p (S57), 18p (S59), 22p (S65), 26p (S72), 28p (S74), 31p (S76)) | | 20·00 | □ |

For combined packs containing values from all three Regions see under Northern Ireland.

**1993** (7 Dec.)–**98**

(a) Printed in lithography by Questa. Perf 15 × 14 (with one elliptical hole in each vertical side)

| | | | | | |
|---|---|---|---|---|---|
| S81 | S **4** | 19p bistre (1 centre band) | 80 | 70 | □ □ |
| S82 | | 19p bistre (1 side band) *(25.4.95)* | 3·00 | 3·25 | □ □ |
| S83 | | 20p bright green (1 centre band) *(23.7.96)* | 1·50 | 1·50 | □ □ |
| S84 | | 25p red (2 bands) | 1·10 | 1·00 | □ □ |
| S85 | | 26p red-brown (2 bands) *(23.7.96)* | 1·75 | 2·00 | □ □ |
| S86 | | 30p deep olive-grey (2 bands) | 1·25 | 1·25 | □ □ |
| S87 | | 37p bright mauve (2 bands) *(23.7.96)* | 2·75 | 3·00 | □ □ |
| S88 | | 41p grey-brown (2 bands) | 1·75 | 2·00 | □ □ |
| S89 | | 63p light emerald (2 bands) *(23.7.96)* | 4·00 | 4·25 | □ □ |

(b) Printed in photogravure by Walsall (20p, 26p (No. S91a), 63p), Harrison or Walsall (26p (No. S91), 37p). Perf 14 (No. S90a) or 15 × 14 (others) (both with one elliptical hole in each vertical side)

| | | | | | |
|---|---|---|---|---|---|
| S90 | S **4** | 20p bright green (1 centre band) *(1.7.97)* | 1·00 | 90 | □ □ |
| S90a | | 20p bright green (1 side band) *(13.10.98)* | 3·50 | 3·50 | □ □ |
| S91 | | 26p chestnut (2 bands) *(1.7.97)* | 1·20 | 1·20 | □ □ |
| | a. | Perf 14 *(13.10.98)* | 3·50 | 3·50 | □ □ |
| S92 | | 37p bright mauve (2 bands) *(1.7.97)* | 1·50 | 1·50 | □ □ |
| S93 | | 63p light emerald (2 bands) *(1.7.97)* | 4·00 | 4·00 | □ □ |

Nos. S82, S90a and S91a were only issued in stamp booklets.
For combined presentation packs for all three Regions, see under Northern Ireland.

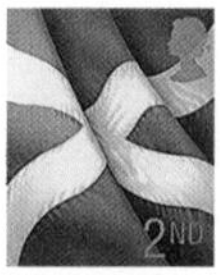

S **5** Scottish Flag     S **6** Scottish Lion     S **7** Thistle     S **8** Tartan

**1999** (8 June)–**2002** Printed in photogravure by De La Rue (68p), De La Rue, Questa or Walsall (2nd, 1st) or Walsall (others). One centre phosphor band (2nd) or two phosphor bands (others). Perf 15 × 14 (with one elliptical hole in each vertical side)

| | | | | | | | |
|---|---|---|---|---|---|---|---|
| S94 | S **5** | (2nd) | new blue, blue and silver | 1·00 | 75 | ☐ | ☐ |
| S95 | S **6** | (1st) | greenish yellow, deep rose-red, rose-red and silver | 1·25 | 1·00 | ☐ | ☐ |
| S96 | S **7** | (E) | bright lilac, deep lilac and silver | 2·00 | 2·00 | ☐ | ☐ |
| S97 | S **8** | 64p | greenish yellow, bright magenta, new blue, grey-black and silver | 9·00 | 9·00 | ☐ | ☐ |
| S98 | | 65p | greenish yellow, bright magenta, new blue, grey-black and silver *(25.4.00)* | 3·00 | 3·25 | ☐ | ☐ |
| S99 | | 68p | greenish yellow, bright magenta, new blue, grey-black and silver *(4.7.02)* | 3·25 | 3·25 | ☐ | ☐ |

| | | |
|---|---|---|
| *Presentation Pack* (P.O. Pack No. 45) (contains 2nd, 1st, E, 64p) (Nos. S94/7) | 14·00 | ☐ |
| *Presentation Pack* (P.O. Pack No. 50) (contains 65p) (No. S98)) | 11·00 | ☐ |
| *Presentation Pack* (P.O. Pack No. 55) (contains 2nd, 1st, E, 65p) (Nos. S94/6, S98) | 15·00 | ☐ |
| PHQ Cards (Nos. S94/7) (D12) | 8·00 | 14·00 ☐ ☐ |

Nos. S94, S95 and S96 were initially sold at 19p, 26p and 30p, the latter representing the basic European airmail rate.

For combined presentation packs for all four Regions, see under England.

S **9**

**2000** (15 Feb.) Type S **4** redrawn with '1st' face value as Type S **9**. Two phosphor bands. Perf 14 (with one elliptical hole in each vertical side)

| | | | | | | | |
|---|---|---|---|---|---|---|---|
| S108 | S **9** | (1st) | bright orange-red | 3·00 | 3·25 | ☐ | ☐ |

No. S108 was only issued in £7.50 'Special by Design' stamp booklets.

**2003** (14 Oct.)–**14** As Nos. S94/6 and S99 but with white borders. One centre phosphor band (2nd) or two phosphor bands (others). Perf 15 × 14 (with one elliptical hole in each vertical side)

(a) Printed in photogravure by Walsall or De La Rue (42p) or De La Rue (others)

| | | | | | | | |
|---|---|---|---|---|---|---|---|
| S109 | S **5** | (2nd) | new blue, blue and silver | 1·00 | 60 | ☐ | ☐ |
| S110 | S **6** | (1st) | rose-red, greenish yellow, deep rose-red and silver | 1·25 | 85 | ☐ | ☐ |
| S111 | S **7** | (E) | bright lilac, deep lilac and silver | 2·50 | 2·50 | ☐ | ☐ |
| S112 | | 40p | bright lilac, deep lilac and silver *(11.5.04)* | 1·75 | 1·75 | ☐ | ☐ |
| S113 | | 42p | bright lilac, deep lilac and silver *(5.4.05)* | 1·75 | 1·75 | ☐ | ☐ |
| S114 | | 44p | bright lilac, deep lilac and silver *(28.3.06)* | 1·50 | 1·50 | ☐ | ☐ |
| S115 | | 48p | bright lilac, deep lilac and silver *(27.3.07)* | 90 | 90 | ☐ | ☐ |
| S116 | | 50p | bright lilac, deep lilac and silver *(1.4.08)* | 80 | 75 | ☐ | ☐ |
| S117 | | 56p | bright lilac, deep lilac and silver *(31.3.09)* | 1·25 | 1·25 | ☐ | ☐ |
| S118 | | 60p | bright lilac, deep lilac and silver *(30.3.10)* | 1·40 | 1·40 | ☐ | ☐ |
| S119 | S **8** | 68p | bright magenta, greenish yellow, new blue, grey-black and silver | 2·00 | 2·00 | ☐ | ☐ |
| S120 | | 72p | bright magenta, greenish yellow, new blue, grey-black and silver *(28.3.06)* | 2·00 | 2·00 | ☐ | ☐ |
| S121 | | 78p | bright magenta, greenish yellow, new blue, grey-black and silver *(27.3.07)* | 2·00 | 2·00 | ☐ | ☐ |
| S122 | | 81p | bright magenta, greenish yellow, new blue, grey-black and silver *(1.4.08)* | 2·00 | 2·00 | ☐ | ☐ |
| S123 | | 90p | bright magenta, greenish yellow, new blue, grey-black and silver *(31.3.09)* | 2·25 | 2·25 | ☐ | ☐ |
| S124 | | 97p | bright magenta, greenish yellow, new blue, grey-black and silver *(30.3.10)* | 2·40 | 2·40 | ☐ | ☐ |

(b) Printed in lithography by Enschedé or Cartor (1st) or Cartor (others)

| | | | | | | | |
|---|---|---|---|---|---|---|---|
| S130 | S **5** | (2nd) | silver, greenish yellow, bright magenta, new blue and black *(27.6.12)* | 75 | 75 | ☐ | ☐ |
| S131 | S **6** | (1st) | silver, greenish yellow, bright magenta, new blue and black *(20.9.07)* | 1·25 | 1·25 | ☐ | ☐ |
| S132 | S **7** | 68p | silver, greenish yellow, bright magenta, new blue and black *(29.3.11)* | 1·50 | 1·50 | ☐ | ☐ |
| S133 | | 87p | silver, greenish yellow, bright magenta, new blue and black *(25.4.12)* | 2·50 | 2·50 | ☐ | ☐ |
| S134 | | 88p | silver, greenish yellow, bright magenta, new blue and black *(27.3.13)* | 2·00 | 2·00 | ☐ | ☐ |
| S135 | | 97p | silver, greenish yellow, bright magenta, new blue and black *(26.3.14)* | 2·25 | 2·25 | ☐ | ☐ |
| S142 | S **8** | £1·10 | silver, greenish yellow, bright magenta, new blue and black *(29.3.11)* | 2·75 | 2·75 | ☐ | ☐ |
| S143 | | £1·28 | silver, greenish yellow, bright magenta, new blue and black *(25.4.12)* | 3·25 | 3·25 | ☐ | ☐ |

| | | |
|---|---|---|
| Presentation Pack (P.O. Pack No. 64) (Nos. S109/11, S119) | 7·00 | ☐ |
| PHQ Cards (*set of* 4) (Nos. S109/11, S119) (D25) | 2·00 | 10·00 ☐ ☐ |

Nos. S109/11 were initially sold at 20p, 28p and 38p, the latter representing the basic European airmail rate.

No. S131 was issued in £7·66 'British Army Uniforms' stamp booklets and also on 27 June 2012 in sheets.

Stamps as No. S131 but self-adhesive were issued on 30 November 2007 in sheets of 20 with *se-tenant* labels. These sheets were printed by Cartor in lithography, and perforated 15 × 14 without the elliptical holes. The labels show either Scottish scenes or personal photographs.

Stamps as Nos. EN30, NI95, S131 and W122 but self-adhesive were issued on 29 September 2008 in sheets of 20 containing five of each design with *se-tenant* labels.

S **9a**

### Opening of New Scottish Parliament Building

**2004** (5 Oct.) Sheet 123 × 70 mm. Printed in photogravure by De La Rue. One centre phosphor band (2nd) or two phosphor bands (others). Perf 15 × 14 (with one elliptical hole in each vertical side)

| | | | |
|---|---|---|---|
| **MS**S152 S **9a** Nos. S109, S110 × 2 and | | | |
| S112 × 2 | 7·00 | 7·00 | ☐ ☐ |
| First Day Cover | | 8·00 | ☐ |

S **10**

### Celebrating Scotland

**2006** (30 Nov.) Sheet 124 × 71 mm. Printed in photogravure by De La Rue. Two phosphor bands. Perf 15 × 14 (with one elliptical hole in each vertical side) (1st) or 14 × 14 (72p)

| | | | |
|---|---|---|---|
| **MS**S153 S **10** (1st) As No. S110; (1st) Scottish | | | |
| Flag; 72p St. Andrew; | | | |
| 72p Edinburgh Castle | 6·50 | 6·50 | ☐ ☐ |
| First Day Cover | | 7·50 | ☐ |
| Presentation Pack (P.O. Pack No. M14) | 8·00 | | ☐ |
| PHQ Cards (*set of* 5) (CGB1) | 4·00 | 17·00 | ☐ ☐ |

**MS**S153 was on sale at post offices throughout the UK. The five PHQ cards depict the complete miniature sheet and the four stamps within it.
Stamps as the 1st class Scottish flag stamp within **MS**S153 but self-adhesive were issued on 30 November 2009 in sheets of 20 with *se-tenant* labels showing Scottish castles. These sheets were printed in lithography by Cartor.

### 50th Anniv of the Country Definitives

**2008** (29 Sept.) As Nos. S1, S3 and S5 (definitives of 1958) but inscribed 1st and printed in lithography by De La Rue. Two phosphor bands. Perf 15 × 14½ (with one elliptical hole in each vertical side)

| | | | | | |
|---|---|---|---|---|---|
| S154 | S **1** | (1st) deep lilac | 2·50 | 2·50 | ☐ ☐ |
| S155 | S **3** | (1st) green | 2·50 | 2·50 | ☐ ☐ |
| S156 | S **2** | (1st) deep claret | 2·50 | 2·50 | ☐ ☐ |

Nos. S154/6 come from £9·72 'The Regional Definitives' stamp booklets.

S **11**

### 250th Birth Anniv of Robert Burns (Scottish poet)

**2009** (22 Jan.) Sheet 145×74 mm. Printed in photogravure by Enschedé. One centre band (2nd) or two phosphor bands (others). Perf 14½ (size 34×34 mm) or 15×14 (with one elliptical hole in each vertical side) (others).

| | | | |
|---|---|---|---|
| **MS**S157 (2nd) No. S109; (1st) 'A Man's | | | |
| a Man for a' that' and Burns | | | |
| ploughing (detail) (James Sargent | | | |
| Storer) (34×34 mm); (1st) No. S110; | | | |
| (1st) Portrait of Burns (Alexander | | | |
| Nasmyth) (34×34 mm); 50p | | | |
| No. S116; 81p No. S122 | 9·00 | 9·00 | ☐ ☐ |
| First Day Cover | | 10·00 | ☐ |
| Presentation Pack (P.O. Pack No. 422) | 11·00 | | ☐ |
| PHQ Cards (*set of* 3) (319) | 3·50 | 12·00 | ☐ ☐ |

**MS**S157 was on sale at post offices throughout the UK. The three PHQ cards show the two 34×34 mm Robert Burns stamps and the complete miniature sheet.

S **12** Saltire

### Scotland Flag

**2013** (9 May) -**14**. Printed in lithography by Cartor or Enschedé. Two phosphor bands. Perf 14½×14 (with one elliptical hole in each vert side)

| | | | | | |
|---|---|---|---|---|---|
| S158 | S **12** | (1st) multicoloured | 2·00 | 2·00 | ☐ ☐ |
| | | a. Grey Queen's head | 2·00 | 2·00 | ☐ ☐ |

No. S 158 were only issued in £11.11 Football Heroes and £13.97 Classic Locomotives booklets.

## 4 Wales

W **1**

W **2**

W **3**

**1958–67** Wmk 179

| | | | | | |
|---|---|---|---|---|---|
| W1 | W **1** | 3d lilac *(18.8.58)* | 15 | 15 | ☐ ☐ |
| | | p. One centre phosphor band *(16.5.67)* | 20 | 15 | ☐ ☐ |
| W2 | | 4d blue *(7.2.66)* | 20 | 15 | ☐ ☐ |
| | | p. Two phosphor bands *(10.67)* | 20 | 15 | ☐ ☐ |
| W3 | W **2** | 6d purple *(29.9.58)* | 35 | 30 | ☐ ☐ |
| W4 | | 9d bronze-green (2 phosphor bands) *(1.3.67)* | 40 | 35 | ☐ ☐ |
| W5 | W **3** | 1s3d green *(29.9.58)* | 40 | 40 | ☐ ☐ |

| | | | | | |
|---|---|---|---|---|---|
| W6 | 1s6d | blue (2 phosphor bands) *(1.3.67)* | 40 | 40 | ☐ ☐ |

**1967–69** One centre phosphor band (Nos. W7, W9/10) or two phosphor bands (others). No wmk

| | | | | | |
|---|---|---|---|---|---|
| W7 | W **1** | 3d lilac *(6.12.67)* | 10 | 15 | ☐ ☐ |
| W8 | | 4d blue *(21.6.68)* | 10 | 15 | ☐ ☐ |
| W9 | | 4d sepia *(4.9.68)* | 15 | 15 | ☐ ☐ |
| W10 | | 4d vermilion *(26.2.69)* | 15 | 15 | ☐ ☐ |
| W11 | | 5d blue *(4.9.68)* | 15 | 15 | ☐ ☐ |
| W12 | W **3** | 1s6d blue *(1.8.69)* | 3·50 | 3·50 | ☐ ☐ |

Presentation Pack (comprises Nos. W4, W6/7, W9/11) (P.O. Pack No. 24)    4·00     ☐

W **4** With 'p'       W **5** Without 'p'

**Decimal Currency**

**1971–92** Type W **4**. No wmk

(a) Printed in photogravure with phosphor bands

| | | | | | |
|---|---|---|---|---|---|
| W13 | 2½p | bright magenta (1 centre band) | 20 | 20 | ☐ ☐ |
| W14 | 3p | ultramarine (2 bands) | 25 | 20 | ☐ ☐ |
| W15 | 3p | ultramarine (1 centre band) *(23.1.74)* | 25 | 25 | ☐. ☐ |
| W16 | 3½p | olive-grey (2 bands) *(23.1.74)* | 20 | 30 | ☐ ☐ |
| W17 | 3½p | olive-grey (1 centre band) *(6.11.74)* | 20 | 30 | ☐ ☐ |
| W18 | 4½p | grey-blue (2 bands) *(6.11.74)* | 30 | 30 | ☐ ☐ |
| W19 | 5p | reddish violet (2 bands) | 1·25 | 1·25 | ☐ ☐ |
| W20 | 5½p | violet (2 bands) *(23.1.74)* | 25 | 30 | ☐ ☐ |
| W21 | 5½p | violet (1 centre band) *(21.5.75)* | 25 | 30 | ☐ ☐ |
| W22 | 6½p | greenish blue (1 centre band) *(14.1.76)* | 20 | 20 | ☐ ☐ |
| W23 | 7p | purple-brown (1 centre band) *(18.1.78)* | 25 | 25 | ☐ ☐ |
| W24 | 7½p | chestnut (2 bands) | 1·75 | 1·75 | ☐ ☐ |
| W25 | 8p | rosine (2 bands) *(23.1.74)* | 30 | 35 | ☐ ☐ |
| W26 | 8½p | yellow-green (2 bands) *(14.1.76)* | 30 | 35 | ☐ ☐ |
| W27 | 9p | deep violet (2 bands) *(18.1.78)* | 40 | 40 | ☐ ☐ |
| W28 | 10p | orange-brown (2 bands) *(20.10.76)* | 40 | 40 | ☐ ☐ |
| W29 | 10p | orange-brown (1 centre band) *(23.7.80)* | 40 | 40 | ☐ ☐ |
| W30 | 10½p | steel-blue (2 bands) *(18.1.78)* | 45 | 45 | ☐ ☐ |
| W31 | 11p | scarlet (2 bands) *(20.10.76)* | 45 | 45 | ☐ ☐ |

(b) Printed in photogravure on phosphorised paper

| | | | | | |
|---|---|---|---|---|---|
| W32 | 12p | yellowish-green *(27.3.80)* | 50 | 50 | ☐ ☐ |
| W33 | 13½p | purple-brown *(27.3.80)* | 60 | 70 | ☐ ☐ |
| W34 | 15p | ultramarine *(27.3.80)* | 60 | 70 | ☐ ☐ |

(c) Printed in lithography. Perf 14 (11½p, 12½p, 14p (No. W39), 15½p. 16p, 18p (No. W46), 19½p, 20½p, 22p (No. W54), 26p (No. W61), 28p (No. W63)) or 15 × 14 (others)

| | | | | | |
|---|---|---|---|---|---|
| W35 | 11½p | drab (1 side band) *(8.4.81)* | 90 | 80 | ☐ ☐ |
| W36 | 12p | bright emerald (1 side band) *(7.1.86)* | 2·00 | 2·00 | ☐ ☐ |
| W37 | 12½p | light emerald | | | |

| | | | | | |
|---|---|---|---|---|---|
| | | (1 side band) *(24.2.82)* | 70 | 70 | ☐ ☐ |
| | a. | Perf 15 × 14 *(10.1.84)* | 4·75 | 4·25 | ☐ ☐ |
| W38 | 13p | pale chestnut (1 side band) *(23.10.84)* | 60 | 60 | ☐ ☐ |
| W39 | 14p | grey-blue (phosphorised paper) *(8.4.81)* | 70 | 70 | ☐ ☐ |
| W40 | 14p | deep blue (1 centre band) *(8.11.88)* | 75 | 75 | ☐ ☐ |
| W41 | 15p | bright blue (1 centre band) *(28.11.89)* | 80 | 75 | ☐ ☐ |
| W42 | 15½p | pale violet (phosphorised paper) *(24.2.82)* | 75 | 75 | ☐ ☐ |
| W43 | 16p | drab (phosphorised paper) *(27.4.83)* | 1·75 | 1·75 | ☐ ☐ |
| | a. | Perf 15 × 14 *(10.1.84)* | 1·75 | 1·75 | ☐ ☐ |
| W44 | 17p | grey-blue (phosphorised paper) *(23.10.84)* | 70 | 80 | ☐ ☐ |
| W45 | 17p | deep blue (1 centre band) *(4.12.90)* | 90 | 80 | ☐ ☐ |
| W46 | 18p | deep violet (phosphorised paper) *(8.4.81)* | 1·00 | 95 | ☐ ☐ |
| W47 | 18p | deep olive-grey (phosphorised paper) *(6.1.87)* | 95 | 90 | ☐ ☐ |
| W48 | 18p | bright green (1 centre band) *(3.12.91)* | 75 | 75 | ☐ ☐ |
| | b. | Perf 14 *(12.1.93)** | 7·50 | 7·50 | ☐ ☐ |
| W49 | 18p | bright green (1 side band) *(25.2.92)* | 2·00 | 2·00 | ☐ ☐ |
| W50 | 19p | bright orange-red (phosphorised paper) *(8.11.88)* | 1·00 | 80 | ☐ ☐ |
| W51 | 19½p | olive-grey (phosphorised paper) *(24.2.82)* | 1·75 | 2·00 | ☐ ☐ |
| W52 | 20p | brownish black (phosphorised paper) *(28.11.89)* | 90 | 90 | ☐ ☐ |
| W53 | 20½p | ultramarine (phosphorised paper) *(27.4.83)* | 3·75 | 3·75 | ☐ ☐ |
| W54 | 22p | blue (phosphorised paper) *(8.4.81)* | 1·10 | 1·10 | ☐ ☐ |
| W55 | 22p | yellow-green (phosphorised paper) *(23.10.84)* | 95 | 1·10 | ☐ ☐ |
| W56 | 22p | bright orange-red (phosphorised paper) *(4.12.90)* | 1·00 | 1·10 | ☐ ☐ |
| W57 | 23p | bright green (phosphorised paper) *(8.11.88)* | 1·00 | 1·10 | ☐ ☐ |
| W58 | 24p | Indian red (phosphorised paper) *(28.11.89)* | 1·25 | 1·25 | ☐ ☐ |
| W59 | 24p | chestnut (phosphorised paper) *(3.12.91)* | 75 | 75 | ☐ ☐ |
| | b. | Perf 14 *(14.9.92)** | 7·50 | 7·50 | ☐ ☐ |
| W60 | 24p | chestnut (2 bands) *(25.2.92)* | 1·25 | 1·50 | ☐ ☐ |
| W61 | 26p | rosine (phosphorised paper) *(24.2.82)* | 1·10 | 1·10 | ☐ ☐ |
| | a. | Perf 15 × 14 *(27.1.87)* | 5·75 | 6·00 | ☐ ☐ |
| W62 | 26p | drab (phosphorised paper) *(4.12.90)* | 1·75 | 1·75 | ☐ ☐ |
| W63 | 28p | deep violet-blue (phosphorised paper) *(27.4.83)* | 1·50 | 1·50 | ☐ ☐ |
| | a. | Perf 15 × 14 *(27.1.87)* | 1·50 | 1·50 | ☐ ☐ |
| W64 | 28p | deep bluish grey (phosphorised paper) *(3.12.91)* | 1·50 | 1·50 | ☐ ☐ |

| | | | | | | |
|---|---|---|---|---|---|---|
| W65 | 31p | bright purple (phosphorised paper) *(23.10.84)* | 1·75 | 1·75 | ☐ | ☐ |
| W66 | 32p | greenish blue (phosphorised paper) *(8.11.88)* | 1·75 | 1·75 | ☐ | ☐ |
| W67 | 34p | deep bluish grey (phosphorised paper) *(28.11.89)* | 1·75 | 1·75 | ☐ | ☐ |
| W68 | 37p | rosine (phosphorised paper) *(4.12.90)* | 2·25 | 2·25 | ☐ | ☐ |
| W69 | 39p | bright mauve (phosphorised paper) *(3.12.91)* | 2·25 | 2·25 | ☐ | ☐ |

\* Earliest known date of use.

Nos. W49 and W60 were only issued in stamp booklets. The former exists with the phosphor band at the left or right of the stamp.

*Presentation Pack* (P.O. Pack No. 28) (contains
  2½p (W13), 3p (W14), 5p (W19), 7½p (W24)) **3·50** ☐

*Presentation Pack* (P.O. Pack No. 63) (contains
  3p (W15), 3½p (W16), 5½p (W20), 8p (W25),
  later with 4½p (W18) added) **2·50** ☐

*Presentation Pack* (P.O. Pack No. 86) (contains
  6½p (W22), 8½p (W26), 10p (W28),
  11p (W31)) **2·00** ☐

*Presentation Pack* (P.O. Pack No. 129c)
  (contains 7p (W23), 9p (W27), 10½p (W30),
  11½p (W35), 12p (W32), 13½p (W33), 14p
  (W39), 15p (W34), 18p (W46), 22p (W54)) **9·00** ☐

*Presentation Pack* (P.O. Pack No. 3) (contains
  10p (W29), 12½p (W37), 16p (W43),
  20½p (W53), 26p (W61), 28p (W63)) **20·00** ☐

*Presentation Pack* (P.O. Pack No. 7) (contains
  10p (W29), 13p (W38), 16p (W43a), 17p
  (W44), 22p (W55), 26p (W61), 28p (W63),
  31p (W65)) **17·00** ☐

*Presentation Pack* (P.O. Pack No. 11) (contains
  12p (W36), 13p (W38), 17p (W44), 18p
  (W47), 22p (W55), 26p (W61a), 28p
  (W63a), 31p (W65)) **20·00** ☐

For combined packs containing values from all three Regions see under Northern Ireland.

**1993** (7 Dec.)–**96** Printed in lithography by Questa. Perf 15 × 14 (with one elliptical hole in each vertical side)

| | | | | | | |
|---|---|---|---|---|---|---|
| W70 | W **4** | 19p bistre (1 centre band) | 80 | 70 | ☐ | ☐ |
| W71 | | 19p bistre (1 side band) *(25.4.95)* | 3·75 | 4·00 | ☐ | ☐ |
| W72 | | 20p bright green (1 centre band) *(23.7.96)* | 1·75 | 2·00 | ☐ | ☐ |
| W73 | | 25p red (2 bands) | 1·25 | 1·00 | ☐ | ☐ |
| W74 | | 26p red-brown (2 bands) *(23.7.96)* | 2·00 | 2·25 | ☐ | ☐ |
| W75 | | 30p deep olive-grey (2 bands) | 1·25 | 1·25 | ☐ | ☐ |
| W76 | | 37p bright mauve (2 bands) *(23.7.96)* | 2·75 | 3·00 | ☐ | ☐ |
| W77 | | 41p grey-brown (2 bands) | 2·00 | 2·00 | ☐ | ☐ |
| W78 | | 63p light emerald (2 bands) *(23.7.96)* | 4·50 | 4·75 | ☐ | ☐ |

No. W71 was only issued in stamp booklets.
For combined presentation packs for all three Regions see under Northern Ireland.

**1997** (1 July)–**98** Printed in photogravure by Walsall (20p, 26p (No. W80a), 63p), Harrison or Walsall (26p (No. W80), 37p) Perf 14 (No. W79a) or 15 × 14 (others) (both with one elliptical hole in each vertical side)

| | | | | | | |
|---|---|---|---|---|---|---|
| W79 | W **5** | 20p bright green (1 centre band) | 80 | 80 | ☐ | ☐ |
| W79a | | 20p bright green (1 side band) *(13.10.98)* | 3·00 | 3·00 | ☐ | ☐ |

| | | | | | | |
|---|---|---|---|---|---|---|
| W80 | 26p | chestnut (2 bands) | 1·00 | 1·00 | ☐ | ☐ |
| | a. | Perf 14 *(13.10.98)* | 3·00 | 3·00 | ☐ | ☐ |
| W81 | 37p | bright mauve (2 bands) | 2·75 | 2·75 | ☐ | ☐ |
| W82 | 63p | light emerald (2 bands) | 5·00 | 5·00 | ☐ | ☐ |

Presentation Pack (P.O. Pack No. 39)
  (Nos. W79 and W80/2) **17·00** ☐

Nos. W79a and W80a were only issued in stamp booklets.

W **6** Leek    W **7** Welsh Dragon    W **8** Daffodil    W **9** Prince of Wales Feathers

**1999** (8 June)–**2002** Printed in photogravure by De La Rue (68p), Walsall or De La Rue (1st), (2nd), (No.W83) or Walsall (others). One phosphor band (2nd) or two phosphor bands (others). Perf 14 (No. W83a) or 15 × 14 (others) (both with one elliptical hole in each vertical side)

| | | | | | | |
|---|---|---|---|---|---|---|
| W83 | W **6** | (2nd) orange-brown, yellow-orange and black (1 centre band) | 1·00 | 50 | ☐ | ☐ |
| W83a | | (2nd) orange-brown, yellow-orange and black (1 side band) *(18.9.00)* | 4·00 | 4·00 | ☐ | ☐ |
| W84 | W **7** | (1st) blue-green, greenish yellow, silver and black | 1·25 | 1·00 | ☐ | ☐ |
| W85 | W **8** | (E) greenish blue, deep greenish blue and grey-black | 1·75 | 1·75 | ☐ | ☐ |
| W86 | W **9** | 64p violet, gold, silver and black | 9·00 | 9·00 | ☐ | ☐ |
| W87 | | 65p violet, gold, silver and black *(25.4.00)* | 3·25 | 3·25 | ☐ | ☐ |
| W88 | | 68p violet, gold, silver and black *(4.7.02)* | 3·25 | 3·25 | ☐ | ☐ |

*Presentation Pack* (P.O. Pack No. 46)
  (contains 2nd, 1st, E, 64p) (Nos. W83,
  W84/6) **14·00** ☐

*Presentation Pack* (P.O. Pack No. 51)
  (contains 65p) (No. W87) **12·00** ☐

*Presentation Pack* (P.O. Pack No. 56)
  (contains 2nd, 1st, E, 65p) (Nos. W83,
  W84/5, W87) **18·00** ☐

*PHQ Cards* (Nos. W83, W84/6) (D13) **8·00** **14·00** ☐ ☐

Nos. W83, W84 and W85 were initially sold at 19p, 26p and 30p, the latter representing the basic European airmail rate.

No. W83a was only issued in £7 'Treasury of Trees' stamp booklets.

For combined presentation packs for all four Regions, see under England.

W **10**

**2000** (15 Feb.) Type W **4** redrawn with '1af/st' face value as Type W **10**. Two phosphor bands. Perf 14 (with one elliptical hole in each vertical side)

| | | | | | | |
|---|---|---|---|---|---|---|
| W97 | W **10** | (1st) bright orange-red | 3·00 | 2·75 | ☐ | ☐ |

No. W97 was only issued in £7.50 'Special by Design' stamp booklets.

**2003** (14 Oct.)–**14** As Nos. W83, W84/5 and W88, but with white borders. One centre phosphor band (2nd) or two phosphor bands (others). Perf 15 × 14 (with one elliptical hole in each vertical side)

(a) Printed in photogravure by Walsall or De La Rue (42p) or De La Rue (others)

| | | | | | | |
|---|---|---|---|---|---|---|
| W98 | W **6** (2nd) | orange-brown, deep orange-brown and black | 1·00 | 75 | ☐ | ☐ |
| W99 | W **7** (1st) | blue-green, greenish yellow, silver and black | 1·25 | 75 | ☐ | ☐ |
| W100 | W **8** (E) | greenish blue, deep greenish blue and grey-black | 2·50 | 2·50 | ☐ | ☐ |
| W101 | 40p | greenish blue, deep greenish blue and grey-black *(11.5.04)* | 1·50 | 1·50 | ☐ | ☐ |
| W102 | 42p | greenish blue, deep greenish blue and grey-black *(5.4.05)* | 1·50 | 1·50 | ☐ | ☐ |
| W103 | 44p | greenish blue, deep greenish blue and grey-black *(28.3.06)* | 1·50 | 1·50 | ☐ | ☐ |
| W104 | 48p | greenish blue, deep greenish blue and grey-black *(27.3.07)* | 90 | 90 | ☐ | ☐ |
| W105 | 50p | greenish blue, deep greenish blue and grey-black *(1.4.08)* | 1·00 | 1·00 | ☐ | ☐ |
| W106 | 56p | greenish blue, deep greenish blue and grey-black *(31.3.09)* | 1·25 | 1·25 | ☐ | ☐ |
| W107 | 60p | greenish blue, deep greenish blue and grey-black *(30.3.10)* | 1·40 | 1·40 | ☐ | ☐ |
| W108 | W **9** 68p | violet, gold, silver and black | 2·00 | 2·00 | ☐ | ☐ |
| W109 | 72p | violet, gold, silver and black *(28.3.06)* | 2·00 | 2·00 | ☐ | ☐ |
| W110 | 78p | violet, gold, silver and black *(27.3.07)* | 2·00 | 2·00 | ☐ | ☐ |
| W111 | 81p | violet, gold, silver and black *(1.4.08)* | 2·00 | 2·00 | ☐ | ☐ |
| W112 | 90p | violet, gold, silver and black *(31.3.09)* | 2·25 | 2·25 | ☐ | ☐ |
| W113 | 97p | violet, gold, silver and black *(30.3.10)* | 2·40 | 2·40 | ☐ | ☐ |

(b) Printed in lithography by Enschedé (booklets) (W122 1st) or Cartor (sheets) (others)

| | | | | | | |
|---|---|---|---|---|---|---|
| W121 | W **6** (2nd) | greenish yellow, bright magenta, new blue and black *(1.2013)* | 1·00 | 1·00 | ☐ | ☐ |
| W122 | W **7** (1st) | greenish yellow, bright magenta, new blue and black *(20.9.07)* | 1·25 | 1·25 | ☐ | ☐ |
| W123 | W **8** 68p | greenish yellow, bright magenta, new blue and black *(29.3.11)* | 1·50 | 1·50 | ☐ | ☐ |
| W124 | 87p | greenish yellow, bright magenta, new blue and black *(25.4.12)* | 2·50 | 2·50 | ☐ | ☐ |
| W125 | 88p | greenish yellow, bright magenta, new blue and black *(27.3.13)* | 2·00 | 2·00 | ☐ | ☐ |
| W126 | 97p | greenish yellow, bright magenta, new blue and black *(26.3.14)* | 2·25 | 2·25 | ☐ | ☐ |
| W133 | W **9** £1·10 | gold, silver, greenish yellow, bright magenta, new blue and black | | | | |

| | | | | | | |
|---|---|---|---|---|---|---|
| | | *(29.3.11)* | 2·75 | 2·75 | ☐ | ☐ |
| W134 | £1·28 | gold, silver, greenish yellow, bright magenta, new blue and black | | | | |
| | | *(25.4.12)* | 3·25 | 3·25 | ☐ | ☐ |

| | | | | |
|---|---|---|---|---|
| Presentation Pack (P.O. Pack No. 65) (Nos. W98/100, W108) | | 7·00 | | ☐ |
| PHQ Cards (*set of* 4) (Nos. W98/100, W108) (D26) | | 2·00 | 6·00 | ☐ ☐ |

Nos. W98/100 were initially sold at 20p, 28p and 38p, the latter representing the basic European airmail rate.

No. W122 was first issued in £7·66 'British Army Uniforms' stamp booklets and **MS**W125. It was issued in sheets in January 2013.

Stamps as W**122** but self-adhesive were issued on 1 March 2007 in sheets of 20 with *se-tenant* labels. These sheets were printed in lithography and perforated 15 × 14 without the elliptical holes. The labels show either Welsh scenes or personal photographs.

Stamps as Nos. EN30, NI95, S131 and W122 but self-adhesive were issued on 29 September 2008 in sheets of 20 containing five of each design with *se-tenant* labels.

### Opening of New Welsh Assembly Building, Cardiff

**2006** (1 Mar.) Sheet 123 × 70 mm. Printed in photogravure by De La Rue. One centre phosphor band (2nd) or two phosphor bands (others). Perf 15 × 14 (with one elliptical hole on each vertical side)

| | | | | |
|---|---|---|---|---|
| **MS**W143 Nos. W98, W99 × 2 and W108 × 2 | | 7·50 | 7·50 | ☐ ☐ |
| First Day Cover | | | 8·50 | ☐ |

### 50th Anniv of the Country Definitives

**2008** (29 Sept.) As Nos. W1, W3 and W5 (definitives of 1958) but inscribed 1st and printed in lithography by De La Rue. Two phosphor bands. Perf 15 × 14½ (with one elliptical hole on each vertical side)

| | | | | | | |
|---|---|---|---|---|---|---|
| W144 | W **1** | (1st) | deep lilac | 3·00 | 3·00 | ☐ ☐ |
| W145 | W **3** | (1st) | green | 3·00 | 3·00 | ☐ ☐ |
| W146 | W **2** | (1st) | deep claret | 3·00 | 3·00 | ☐ ☐ |
| *Set of* 3 | | | | 8.00 | 8.00 | ☐ ☐ |

Nos. W144/6 were only issued in the £9·72 'The Regional Definitives' stamp booklet.

DATHLU CYMRU · CELEBRATING WALES

W **11**

### Celebrating Wales miniature sheet

**2009** (26 Feb.) Sheet 123×70 mm. Printed in lithography by De La Rue. Two phosphor bands. Perf 15×14 (with one elliptical hole on each vertical side (1st) or 14½×14 (81p)

| | | | |
|---|---|---|---|
| **MS**W147 (1st) Red dragon; (1st) No. W120; 81p St. David; 81p National Assembly for Wales, Cardiff | 7·00 | 7·00 | ☐ ☐ |
| First Day Cover | | 8·00 | ☐ |
| Presentation Pack (P.O. Pack No. 424) | 9·00 | | ☐ |
| PHQ Cards (*set of* 5) (CGB4) | 4·00 | 17·00 | ☐ ☐ |

**MS**W125 was on sale at post offices throughout the UK.

The five PHQ cards show the four individual stamps and the complete miniature sheet.

Stamps as the 1st class red dragon stamp from **MS**W147 but self-adhesive were issued on 1 March 2010 in sheets of 20 with *se-tenant* labels showing Welsh castles. These sheets were printed in lithography by Cartor.

**2645** Red
Dragon

**Welsh Flag**

**2013** (9 May) **-14**. Printed in lithography by Cartor or Enschedé. Two phosphor bands. Perf 14½×14 (with one elliptical hole in each vert side)

W148 **W12** (1st) multicoloured          2·00          2·00  ☐ ☐

No. W148 were only issued in £11.11 Football Heroes and £13.97 Classic Locomotives booklets.

## 5 Isle of Man

**Regional Issues**

1                    2                    3

**1958–67** Wmk **179**. Perf 15 × 14

| | | | | | | |
|---|---|---|---|---|---|---|
| 1 | **1** | 2½d red *(8.6.64)* | | 50 | 1·25 | ☐ ☐ |
| 2 | **2** | 3d lilac *(18.8.58)* | | 50 | 20 | ☐ ☐ |
| | | p. | One centre phosphor band *(27.6.68)* | 20 | 50 | ☐ ☐ |
| 3 | | 4d blue *(7.2.66)* | | 1·50 | 1·50 | ☐ ☐ |
| | | p. | Two phosphor bands *(5.7.67)* | 20 | 30 | ☐ ☐ |

**1968–69** One centre phosphor band (Nos. 5/6) or two phosphor bands (others). No wmk

| | | | | | |
|---|---|---|---|---|---|
| 4 | **2** | 4d blue *(24.6.68)* | 25 | 30 | ☐ ☐ |
| 5 | | 4d sepia *(4.9.68)* | 25 | 30 | ☐ ☐ |
| 6 | | 4d vermilion *(26.2.69)* | 45 | 75 | ☐ ☐ |
| 7 | | 5d blue *(4.9.68)* | 45 | 75 | ☐ ☐ |

**Decimal Currency**

**1971** (7 July) One centre phosphor band (2½p) or two phosphor bands (others). No wmk

| | | | | | |
|---|---|---|---|---|---|
| 8 | **3** | 2½p magenta | 20 | 15 | ☐ ☐ |
| 9 | | 3p ultramarine | 20 | 15 | ☐ ☐ |
| 10 | | 5p violet | 80 | 80 | ☐ ☐ |
| 11 | | 7½p chestnut | 90 | 90 | ☐ ☐ |
| Presentation Pack | | | 3·25 | | ☐ |

For comprehensive listings of the Independent Administration issues of the Isle of Man, see Stanley Gibbons *Collect Channel Islands and Isle of Man Stamps.*

## 6 Channel Islands General Issue

C **1** Gathering Vraic          C **2** Islanders gathering Vraic

**Third Anniversary of Liberation**

**1948** (10 May) Wmk Type **127**. Perf 15 × 14

| | | | | | |
|---|---|---|---|---|---|
| C1 | C **1** | 1d red | 25 | 30 | ☐ ☐ |
| C2 | C **2** | 2½d blue | 25 | 30 | ☐ ☐ |
| First Day Cover | | | | 35·00 | ☐ |

## 7 Guernsey

**(a) War Occupation Issues**

Stamps issued under British authority during the German Occupation.

1                    2                    3

**1941–44** Rouletted

| | | (a) White paper. No wmk | | | |
|---|---|---|---|---|---|
| 1d | **1** | ½d green | 4·00 | 2·00 | ☐ ☐ |
| 2 | | 1d red | 3·25 | 2·00 | ☐ ☐ |
| 3a | | 2½d blue | 10·00 | 7·00 | ☐ ☐ |
| | | (b) Bluish French bank-note paper. Wmk loops | | | |
| 4 | **1** | ½d green | 30·00 | 22·00 | ☐ ☐ |
| 5 | | 1d red | 16·00 | 22·00 | ☐ ☐ |

**(b) Regional Issues**

**1958–67** Wmk **179**. Perf 15 × 14

| | | | | | | |
|---|---|---|---|---|---|---|
| 6 | **2** | 2½d red *(8.6.64)* | | 35 | 40 | ☐ ☐ |
| 7 | **3** | 3d lilac *(18.8.58)* | | 30 | 30 | ☐ ☐ |
| | | p. | One centre phosphor band *(24.5.67)* | 15 | 20 | ☐ ☐ |
| 8 | | 4d blue *(7.2.66)* | | 25 | 30 | ☐ ☐ |
| | | p. | Two phosphor bands *(24.10.67)* | 15 | 20 | ☐ ☐ |

**1968–69** One centre phosphor band (Nos. 10/11) or two phosphor bands (others). No wmk

| | | | | | |
|---|---|---|---|---|---|
| 9 | **3** | 4d blue *(16.4.68)* | 10 | 20 | ☐ ☐ |
| 10 | | 4d sepia *(4.9.68)* | 10 | 15 | ☐ ☐ |
| 11 | | 4d vermilion *(26.2.69)* | 20 | 25 | ☐ ☐ |
| 12 | | 5d blue *(4.9.68)* | 20 | 30 | ☐ ☐ |

For comprehensive listings of the Independent Postal Administration issues of Guernsey, see Stanley Gibbons *Collect Channel Islands and Isle of Man Stamps.*

## 8 Jersey

### (a) War Occupation Issues

Stamps issued under British authority during the German Occupation.

5

**6** Old Jersey Farm

**7** Portelet Bay

**8** Corbière Lighthouse

**9** Elizabeth Castle

**10** Mont Orgueil Castle

**11** Gathering Vraic (seaweed)

**1941–42** White paper. No wmk. Perf 11

| | | | | | | |
|---|---|---|---|---|---|---|
| 1 | **5** | ½d green | 8·00 | 6·00 | | |
| 2 | | 1d red | 8·00 | 5·00 | | |

**1943** No wmk. Perf 13½

| | | | | | | |
|---|---|---|---|---|---|---|
| 3 | **6** | ½d green | 12·00 | 12·00 | | |
| 4 | **7** | 1d red | 3·00 | 50 | | |
| 5 | **8** | 1½d brown | 8·00 | 5·75 | | |
| 6 | **9** | 2d orange | 7·50 | 2·00 | | |
| 7a | **10** | 2½d blue | 1·00 | 1·75 | | |
| 8 | **11** | 3d violet | 3·00 | 2·75 | | |
| *Set of 6* | | | 30·00 | 21·00 | | |

### (b) Regional Issues

**12**

**13**

**1958–67** Wmk **179**. Perf 15 × 14

| | | | | | | |
|---|---|---|---|---|---|---|
| 9 | **12** | 2½d red (8.6.64) | 30 | 45 | | |
| 10 | **13** | 3d lilac (18.8.68) | 30 | 25 | | |
| | | p. One centre phosphor band (9.6.67) | 15 | 15 | | |
| 11 | | 4d blue (7.2.66) | 25 | 30 | | |
| | | p. Two phosphor bands (5.9.67) | 15 | 25 | | |

**1968–69** One centre phosphor band (4d values) or two phosphor bands (5d). No wmk

| | | | | | | |
|---|---|---|---|---|---|---|
| 12 | **13** | 4d sepia (4.9.68) | 15 | 25 | | |
| 13 | | 4d vermilion (26.2.69) | 15 | 25 | | |
| 14 | | 5d blue (4.9.68) | 15 | 50 | | |

For comprehensive listings of the Independent Postal Adminstration issues of Jersey, see Stanley Gibbons *Collect Channel Islands and Isle of Man Stamps*.

## REGIONAL FIRST DAY COVERS

PRICES for First Day Covers listed below are for stamps, as indicated, used on illustrated envelopes and postmarked with operational cancellations (before 1964) or with special First Day of Issue cancellations (1964 onwards). First Day postmarks of 8 June 1964 and 7 February 1966 were of the machine cancellation 'envelope' type.

### £sd Issues

**18 Aug. 1958**

| | | |
|---|---|---|
| Guernsey 3d (No. 7) | 20·00 | |
| Isle of Man 3d (No. 2) | 32·00 | |
| Jersey 3d (No. 10) | 20·00 | |
| Northern Ireland 3d (No. NI1) | 30·00 | |
| Scotland 3d (No. S1) | 17·00 | |
| Wales 3d (No. W1) | 12·00 | |

**29 Sept. 1958**

| | | |
|---|---|---|
| Northern Ireland 6d, 1s3d (Nos. NI3, NI5) | 35·00 | |
| Scotland 6d, 1s3d (Nos. S3, S5) | 25·00 | |
| Wales 6d, 1s3d (Nos. W3, W5) | 25·00 | |

**8 June 1964**

| | | |
|---|---|---|
| Guernsey 2½d (No. 6) | 30·00 | |
| Isle of Man 2½d (No. 1) | 45·00 | |
| Jersey 2½d (No. 9) | 30·00 | |

**7 Feb. 1966**

| | | |
|---|---|---|
| Guernsey 4d (No. 8) | 8·00 | |
| Isle of Man 4d (No. 3) | 15·00 | |
| Jersey 4d (No. 11) | 10·00 | |
| Northern Ireland 4d (No. NI2) | 7·00 | |
| Scotland 4d (No. S2) | 7·00 | |
| Wales 4d (No. W2) | 7·00 | |

**1 March 1967**

| | | |
|---|---|---|
| Northern Ireland 9d, 1s6d (Nos. NI4, NI6) | 4·00 | |
| Scotland 9d, 1s6d (Nos. S4, S6) | 6·00 | |
| Wales 9d, 1s6d (Nos. W4, W6) | 4·00 | |

**4 Sept. 1968**

| | | |
|---|---|---|
| Guernsey 4d, 5d (Nos. 10, 12) | 3·00 | |
| Isle of Man 4d, 5d (Nos. 5, 7) | 4·00 | |
| Jersey 4d, 5d (Nos. 12, 14) | 3·00 | |
| Northern Ireland 4d, 5d (Nos. NI8, NI10) | 3·00 | |
| Scotland 4d, 5d (Nos. S9, S11) | 3·00 | |
| Wales 4d, 5d (Nos. W9, W11) | 3·00 | |

### Decimal Issues

**7 July 1971**

| | | |
|---|---|---|
| Isle of Man 2½p, 3p, 5p, 7½p (Nos. 8/11) | 3·00 | |
| Northern Ireland 2½p, 3p, 5p, 7½p (Nos. NI12/13, NI18, NI23) | 3·50 | |
| Scotland 2½p, 3p, 5p, 7½p (Nos. S14/15, S20, S25) | 3·00 | |
| Wales 2½p, 3p, 5p, 7½p (Nos.W13/14, W19, W24) | 3·00 | |

**23 Jan. 1974**

| | | |
|---|---|---|
| Northern Ireland 3p, 3½p, 5½p, 8p (Nos. NI14/15, NI19, NI24) | 2·40 | |
| Scotland 3p, 3½p, 5½p, 8p (Nos. S16/17, S21, S26) | 2·50 | |
| Wales 3p, 3½p, 5½p, 8p (Nos. W15/16, W20, W25) | 2·50 | |

**6 Nov. 1974**

| | | |
|---|---|---|
| Northern Ireland 4½p (No. NI17) | 1·50 | |
| Scotland 4½p (No. S19) | 1·50 | |
| Wales 4½p (No. W18) | 1·50 | |

**14 Jan. 1976**

Northern Ireland 6½p, 8½p
(Nos. NI21, NI25)    1·50 ☐
Scotland 6½p, 8½p
(Nos. S23, S27)    1·50 ☐
Wales 6½p, 8½p
(Nos. W22, W26)    1·50 ☐

**20 Oct. 1976**

Northern Ireland 10p, 11p
(Nos. NI27, NI30)    1·75 ☐
Scotland 10p, 11p (Nos. S29, S32)    1·50 ☐
Wales 10p, 11p (Nos. W28, W31)    1·50 ☐

**18 Jan. 1978**

Northern Ireland 7p, 9p, 10½p
(Nos. NI22, NI26, NI29)    1·75 ☐
Scotland 7p, 9p, 10½p
(Nos. S24, S28, S31)    1·75 ☐
Wales 7p, 9p, 10½p
(Nos. W23, W27, W30)    1·75 ☐

**23 July 1980**

Northern Ireland 12p, 13½p, 15p
(Nos. NI31/3)    3·00 ☐
Scotland 12p, 13½p, 15p
(Nos. S33/5)    2·75 ☐
Wales 12p, 13½p, 15p
(Nos. W32/4)    3·00 ☐

**8 April 1981**

Northern Ireland 11½p, 14p, 18p, 22p
(Nos. NI34, NI38, NI45, NI53)    2·50 ☐
Scotland 11½p, 14p, 18p, 22p
(Nos. S36, S40, S44, S47)    2·50 ☐
Wales 11½p, 14p, 18p, 22p
(Nos. W35, W39, W46, W54)    2·50 ☐

**24 Feb. 1982**

Northern Ireland 12½p, 15½p, 19½p,
26p (Nos. NI36, NI41, NI50, NI60)    4·00 ☐
Scotland 12½p, 15½p, 19½p, 26p
(Nos. S38, S41, S45, S49)    3·50 ☐
Wales 12½p, 15½p, 19½p, 26p
(Nos. W37, W42, W51, W61)    3·50 ☐

**27 April 1983**

Northern Ireland 16p, 20½p, 28p
(Nos. NI42, NI52, NI62)    4·00 ☐
Scotland 16p, 20½p, 28p
(Nos. S42, S46, S50)    4·00 ☐
Wales 16p, 20½p, 28p
(Nos. W43, W53, W63)    3·50 ☐

**23 Oct. 1984**

Northern Ireland 13p, 17p, 22p, 31p
(Nos. NI37, NI43, NI54, NI64)    4·75 ☐
Scotland 13p, 17p, 22p, 31p
(Nos. S39, S43, S48, S51)    4·00 ☐
Wales 13p, 17p, 22p, 31p
(Nos. W38, W44, W55, W65)    4·25 ☐

**7 Jan. 1986**

Northern Ireland 12p (No. NI35)    2·00 ☐
Scotland 12p (No. S37)    2·00 ☐
Wales 12p (No. W36)    2·00 ☐

**6 Jan. 1987**

Northern Ireland 18p (No. NI46)    2·00 ☐
Scotland 18p (No. S59)    1·80 ☐
Wales 18p (No. W47)    2·00 ☐

**8 Nov. 1988**

Northern Ireland 14p, 19p, 23p, 32p
(Nos. NI39, NI49, NI56, NI65)    4·25 ☐
Scotland 14p, 19p, 23p, 32p
(Nos. S54, S62, S67, S77)    4·25 ☐

Wales 14p, 19p, 23p, 32p
(Nos. W40, W50, W57, W66)    4·50 ☐

**28 Nov. 1989**

Northern Ireland 15p, 20p, 24p, 34p
(Nos. NI40, NI51, NI57, NI66)    5·00 ☐
Scotland 15p, 20p, 24p, 34p
(Nos. S56, S64, S69, S78)    5·00 ☐
Wales 15p, 20p, 24p, 34p
(Nos. W41, W52, W58, W67)    5·00 ☐

**4 Dec. 1990**

Northern Ireland 17p, 22p, 26p, 37p
(Nos. NI44, NI55, NI61, NI67)    5·00 ☐
Scotland 17p, 22p, 26p, 37p
(Nos. S58, S66, S73, S79)    5·00 ☐
Wales 17p, 22p, 26p, 37p
(Nos.W45, W56, W62, W68)    5·00 ☐

**3 Dec. 1991**

Northern Ireland 18p, 24p, 28p, 39p
(Nos. NI47, NI58, NI63, NI68)    5·50 ☐
Scotland 18p, 24p, 28p, 39p
(Nos. S60, S70, S75, S80)    5·50 ☐
Wales 18p, 24p, 28p, 39p
(Nos. W48, W59, W64, W69)    5·50 ☐

**7 Dec. 1993**

Northern Ireland 19p, 25p, 30p, 41p
(Nos. NI69, NI72, NI74, NI76)    6·00 ☐
Scotland 19p, 25p, 30p, 41p
(Nos. S81, S84, S86, S88)    6·00 ☐
Wales 19p, 25p, 30p, 41p
(Nos. W70, W73, W75, W77)    6·00 ☐

**23 July 1996**

Northern Ireland 20p (1 centre band),
26p, 37p, 63p (Nos. NI71, NI73,
NI75, NI77)    8·75 ☐
Scotland 20p (1 centre band), 26p, 37p,
63p (Nos. S83, S85, S87, S89)    8·75 ☐
Wales 20p, 26p, 37p, 63p (Nos. W72,
W74, W76, W78)    7·00 ☐

**1 July 1997**

Wales 20p (1 centre band), 26p, 37p,
63p (Nos. W79 and W80/2)    6·00 ☐

**8 June 1999**

Northern Ireland 38p, 64p
(Nos. NI83, NI86)    4·00 ☐
Scotland 2nd, 1st, E, 64p (Nos S94/7)    6·00 ☐
Wales 2nd, 1st, E, 64p (Nos. W83,
W84/6)    6·00 ☐

**25 Apr. 2000**

Northern Ireland 1st, 40p, 65p
(Nos. NI84, NI87, NI88b)    7·00 ☐
Scotland 65p (No. S98)    3·00 ☐
Wales 65p (No. W87)    3·00 ☐

**6 Mar. 2001**

Northern Ireland 2nd, 1st, E, 65p
(Nos. NI89/92)    4·50 ☐

**23 Apr. 2001**

England 2nd, 1st, E, 65p (Nos. EN1/4)    3·25 ☐

**4 July 2002**

England 68p (No. EN5)    3·50 ☐
Northern Ireland 68p (No. NI93)    2·50 ☐
Scotland 68p (No. S99)    1·75 ☐
Wales 68p (No. W88)    1·75 ☐

**14 Oct. 2003**

England 2nd, 1st, E, 68p
(Nos. EN6/8, EN16)    3·25 ☐

Northern Ireland 2nd, 1st, E, 68p
   (Nos. NI94/6, NI100)     3·25 ☐
Scotland 2nd, 1st, E, 68p
   (Nos. S109/11, S119)     3·25 ☐
Wales 2nd, 1st, E, 68p
   (Nos. W98/100, W108)     3·25 ☐

**11 May 2004**
England 40p (No. EN9)     2·75 ☐
Northern Ireland 40p (No. NI97)     2·75 ☐
Scotland 40p (No. S112)     2·75 ☐
Wales 40p (No. W101)     2·75 ☐

**5 Apr. 2005**
England 42p (No. EN10)     1·40 ☐
Northern Ireland 42p (No. NI98)     1·40 ☐
Scotland 42p (No. S113)     1·40 ☐
Wales 42p (No. W102)     1·40 ☐

**28 Mar. 2006**
England 44p, 72p (Nos. EN11, EN17)     2·75 ☐
Northern Ireland 44p, 72p
   (Nos. NI99, NI102)     2·75 ☐
Scotland 44p, 72p (Nos. S114, S120)     2·75 ☐
Wales 44p, 72p (Nos. W103, W109)     2·75 ☐

**27 Mar. 2007**
England 48p, 78p (Nos. EN12, EN18)     4·00 ☐
Northern Ireland 48p, 78p
   (Nos. NI124, NI128)     4·00 ☐
Scotland 48p, 78p (Nos. S115, S121)     4·00 ☐
Wales 48p, 78p (Nos. W104, W110)     3·50 ☐

**1 Apr. 2008**
England 50p, 81p
   (Nos. EN13, EN19)     4·00 ☐
Northern Ireland 50p, 81p
   (Nos. NI125, NI129)     4·00 ☐
Scotland 50p, 81p (Nos. S116, S122)     4·00 ☐
Wales 50p, 81p (Nos. W105, W111)     4·00 ☐

**31 Mar. 2009**
England 56p, 90p (Nos. EN14, EN20)     4·75 ☐
Northern Ireland 56p, 90p
   (Nos. NI126, NI130)     4·75 ☐
Scotland 56p, 90p (Nos. S117, S123)     4·75 ☐
Wales 56p, 90p (Nos. W106, W112)     4·75 ☐

**31 Mar. 2010**
England 60p, 97p (Nos. EN15, EN21)     4·00 ☐
Northern Ireland 60p, 97p
   (Nos. NI127, NI131)     4·00 ☐
Scotland 60p, 97p (Nos. S118, S124)     4·00 ☐
Wales 60p, 97p (Nos. W107, W113)     4·00 ☐

**29 Mar. 2011**
England 68p, £1·10 (Nos. EN31/2)     6·00 ☐
Northern Ireland 68p, £1·10
   (Nos. NI101, NI112)     6·00 ☐
Scotland 68p, £1·10 (Nos. S132/3)     6·00 ☐
Wales 68p, £1·10 (Nos. W123/4)     6·00 ☐

**25 Apr. 2012**
England 87p, £1·28 (Nos. EN32, EN42)     7·25 ☐
Northern Ireland 87p, £1·28
   (Nos. NI103, NI113)     7·25 ☐
Scotland 87p, £1·28 (Nos. S133,
   S143)     7·25 ☐
Wales 87p, £1·28 (Nos. W124, W134)
   7·25 ☐

**27 Mar. 2013**
England 88p (No. EN33,)     3·00 ☐
Northern Ireland 88p, (No. NI104)     3·00 ☐
Scotland 88p, (Nos. S134)     3·00 ☐
Wales 88p, (No. W125)     3·00 ☐

**26 Mar. 2014**
England 97p (No. EN34,)     3·50 ☐
Northern Ireland 97p, (No. NI105)     3·50 ☐
Scotland 97p, (No. S135)     3·50 ☐
Wales 97p, (No. W126)     3·50 ☐

# POSTAGE DUE STAMPS

**PERFORATION.** All postage due stamps to No. D101 are perf 14 × 15.

D 1

D 2

**1914–22** Wmk Type **100** (Royal Cypher ('Simple')) sideways

| | | | | | | |
|---|---|---|---|---|---|---|
| D1 | D **1** | ½d | green | 50 | 25 | |
| D2 | | 1d | red | 50 | 25 | |
| D3 | | 1½d | brown | 48·00 | 20·00 | |
| D4 | | 2d | black | 50 | 25 | |
| D5 | | 3d | violet | 5·00 | 75 | |
| D6wi | | 4d | green | 40·00 | 5·00 | |
| D7 | | 5d | brown | 7·00 | 3·50 | |
| D8 | | 1s | blue | 40·00 | 5·00 | |
| Set of 8 | | | | £120 | 32·00 | |

**1924–31** Wmk Type **111** (Block G v R) sideways

| | | | | | | |
|---|---|---|---|---|---|---|
| D10 | D **1** | ½d | green | 1·25 | 75 | |
| D11 | | 1d | red | 60 | 25 | |
| D12 | | 1½d | brown | 47·00 | 22·00 | |
| D13 | | 2d | black | 1·00 | 25 | |
| D14 | | 3d | violet | 1·50 | 25 | |
| D15 | | 4d | green | 15·00 | 4·25 | |
| D16 | | 5d | brown | 65·00 | 45·00 | |
| D17 | | 1s | blue | 8·50 | 50 | |
| D18 | D **2** | 2s6d | purple/yellow | 85·00 | 1·75 | |
| Set of 9 | | | | £200 | 60·00 | |

**1936–37** Wmk Type **125** (E 8 R) sideways

| | | | | | | |
|---|---|---|---|---|---|---|
| D19 | D **1** | ½d | green | 15·00 | 10·50 | |
| D20 | | 1d | red | 2·00 | 1·75 | |
| D21 | | 2d | black | 15·00 | 12·00 | |
| D22 | | 3d | violet | 2·00 | 2·00 | |
| D23 | | 4d | green | 65·00 | 34·00 | |
| D24a | | 5d | brown | 40·00 | 28·00 | |
| D25 | | 1s | blue | 25·00 | 8·50 | |
| D26 | D **2** | 2s6d | purple/yellow | £350 | 12·00 | |
| Set of 8 | | | | £500 | 90·00 | |

**1937–38** Wmk Type **127** (G vi R) sideways

| | | | | | | |
|---|---|---|---|---|---|---|
| D27 | D **1** | ½d | green | 13·00 | 3·75 | |
| D28 | | 1d | red | 3·00 | 50 | |
| D29 | | 2d | black | 2·75 | 30 | |
| D30 | | 3d | violet | 10·50 | 30 | |
| D31 | | 4d | green | £110 | 10·00 | |
| D32 | | 5d | brown | 16·50 | 75 | |
| D33 | | 1s | blue | 78·00 | 75 | |
| D34 | D **2** | 2s6d | purple/yellow | 85·00 | 1·25 | |
| Set of 8 | | | | £260 | 18·00 | |

**1951–52** Colours changed and new value (1½d). Wmk Type **127** (G vi R) sideways

| | | | | | | |
|---|---|---|---|---|---|---|
| D35 | D **1** | ½d | orange | 3·50 | 3·50 | |
| D36 | | 1d | blue | 1·50 | 75 | |
| D37 | | 1½d | green | 2·00 | 2·00 | |
| D38 | | 4d | blue | 50·00 | 22·00 | |
| D39 | | 1s | brown | 28·00 | 5·25 | |
| Set of 5 | | | | 75·00 | 28·00 | |

**1954–55** Wmk Type **153** (Mult Tudor Crown and E 2 R) sideways

| | | | | | | |
|---|---|---|---|---|---|---|
| D40 | D **1** | ½d | orange | 7·00 | 5·25 | |
| D41 | | 2d | black | 26·00 | 23·00 | |
| D42 | | 3d | violet | 75·00 | 60·00 | |

| | | | | | | |
|---|---|---|---|---|---|---|
| D43 | | 4d | blue | 26·00 | 32·00 | |
| D44 | | 5d | brown | 20·00 | 20·00 | |
| D45 | D **2** | 2s6d | purple/yellow | £150 | 5·75 | |
| Set of 6 | | | | £275 | £120 | |

**1955–57** Wmk Type **165** (Mult St Edward's Crown and E 2 R) sideways

| | | | | | | |
|---|---|---|---|---|---|---|
| D46 | D **1** | ½d | orange | 2·75 | 3·25 | |
| D47 | | 1d | blue | 5·00 | 1·50 | |
| D48 | | 1½d | green | 8·50 | 7·00 | |
| D49 | | 2d | black | 45·00 | 3·50 | |
| D50 | | 3d | violet | 6·00 | 1·50 | |
| D51 | | 4d | blue | 25·00 | 6·00 | |
| D52 | | 5d | brown | 26·00 | 20·00 | |
| D53 | | 1s | brown | 65·00 | 2·25 | |
| D54 | D **2** | 2s6d | purple/yellow | £200 | 8·25 | |
| D55 | | 5s | red/yellow | £150 | 32·00 | |
| Set of 10 | | | | £425 | 65·00 | |

**1959–63** Wmk Type **179** (Mult St Edward's Crown) sideways

| | | | | | | |
|---|---|---|---|---|---|---|
| D56 | D **1** | ½d | orange | 15 | 1·25 | |
| D57 | | 1d | blue | 15 | 50 | |
| D58 | | 1½d | green | 2·50 | 2·50 | |
| D59 | | 2d | black | 1·10 | 50 | |
| D60 | | 3d | violet | 30 | 30 | |
| D61 | | 4d | blue | 30 | 30 | |
| D62 | | 5d | brown | 45 | 60 | |
| D63 | | 6d | purple | 50 | 30 | |
| D64 | | 1s | brown | 90 | 30 | |
| D65 | D **2** | 2s6d | purple/yellow | 3·00 | 50 | |
| D66 | | 5s | red/yellow | 8·25 | 1·00 | |
| D67 | | 10s | blue/yellow | 11·50 | 5·75 | |
| D68 | | £1 | black/yellow | 45·00 | 8·25 | |
| Set of 13 | | | | 70·00 | 20·00 | |

**1968–69** Design size 22½ × 19 mm. No wmk

| | | | | | | |
|---|---|---|---|---|---|---|
| D69 | D **1** | 2d | black | 75 | 1·00 | |
| D70 | | 3d | violet | 1·00 | 1·00 | |
| D71 | | 4d | blue | 1·00 | 1·00 | |
| D72 | | 5d | orange-brown | 8·00 | 11·00 | |
| D73 | | 6d | purple | 2·25 | 1·75 | |
| D74 | | 1s | brown | 4·00 | 2·50 | |
| Set of 6 | | | | 17·00 | 20·00 | |

**1968–69** Design size 21½ × 17½ mm. No wmk

| | | | | | | |
|---|---|---|---|---|---|---|
| D75 | D **1** | 4d | blue | 7·00 | 6·75 | |
| D76 | | 8d | red | 50 | 1·00 | |

D 3

D 4

**Decimal Currency**

**1970–75** No wmk

| | | | | | | |
|---|---|---|---|---|---|---|
| D77 | D **3** | ½p | turquoise-blue | 15 | 2·50 | |
| D78 | | 1p | reddish purple | 15 | 15 | |
| D79 | | 2p | myrtle-green | 20 | 15 | |
| D80 | | 3p | ultramarine | 20 | 15 | |
| D81 | | 4p | yellow-brown | 25 | 15 | |
| D82 | | 5p | violet | 25 | 15 | |
| D83 | | 7p | red-brown | 35 | 1·00 | |
| D84 | D **4** | 10p | red | 30 | 30 | |
| D85 | | 11p | green | 50 | 1·00 | |
| D86 | | 20p | brown | 60 | 25 | |
| D87 | | 50p | ultramarine | 2·00 | 1·25 | |
| D88 | | £1 | black | 4·00 | 1·00 | |
| D89 | | £5 | orange-yellow and black | 36·00 | 1·50 | |
| Set of 13 | | | | 40·00 | 7·75 | |

Presentation Pack (P.O. Pack No. 36)
(Nos. D77/82, D84, D86/8)  32·00 ☐
Presentation Pack (P.O. Pack No. 93)
(Nos. D77/88)  15·00 ☐

D 5          D 6          D 7

**1982** No wmk

| | | | | | | |
|---|---|---|---|---|---|---|
| D90 | D 5 | 1p | lake | 10 | 30 | ☐ ☐ |
| D91 | | 2p | bright blue | 30 | 30 | ☐ ☐ |
| D92 | | 3p | deep mauve | 15 | 30 | ☐ ☐ |
| D93 | | 4p | deep blue | 15 | 25 | ☐ ☐ |
| D94 | | 5p | sepia | 20 | 25 | ☐ ☐ |
| D95 | D 6 | 10p | light brown | 30 | 40 | ☐ ☐ |
| D96 | | 20p | olive-green | 50 | 60 | ☐ ☐ |
| D97 | | 25p | deep greenish blue | 80 | 90 | ☐ ☐ |
| D98 | | 50p | grey-black | 1·75 | 1·75 | ☐ ☐ |
| D99 | | £1 | red | 3·25 | 1·25 | ☐ ☐ |
| D100 | | £2 | turquoise-blue | 7·00 | 4·25 | ☐ ☐ |
| D101 | | £5 | dull orange | 14·00 | 2·25 | ☐ ☐ |
| *Set of* 12 | | | | 24·00 | 10·00 | ☐ ☐ |
| *Set of* 12 Gutter Pairs | | | | 48·00 | | ☐ |
| Presentation Pack (P.O. Pack No. 135) | | | | 48·00 | | ☐ |

**1994** (15 Feb.) Perf 15 × 14 (with one elliptical hole on each vertical side)

| | | | | | | |
|---|---|---|---|---|---|---|
| D102 | D 7 | 1p | red, yellow and black | 10 | 75 | ☐ ☐ |
| D103 | | 2p | magenta, purple and black | 10 | 75 | ☐ ☐ |
| D104 | | 5p | yellow, red-brown and black | 15 | 50 | ☐ ☐ |
| D105 | | 10p | yellow, emerald and black | 30 | 75 | ☐ ☐ |
| D106 | | 20p | blue-green, violet and black | 75 | 1·50 | ☐ ☐ |
| D107 | | 25p | cerise, rosine and black | 1·50 | 2·00 | ☐ ☐ |
| D108 | | £1 | violet, magenta and black | 7·00 | 10·00 | ☐ ☐ |
| D109 | | £1·20 | greenish blue, blue-green and black | 8·00 | 12·00 | ☐ ☐ |
| D110 | | £5 | greenish black, blue-green and black | 30·00 | 20·00 | ☐ ☐ |
| *Set of* 9 | | | | 45·00 | 45·00 | ☐ ☐ |
| First Day Cover | | | | | 45·00 | ☐ |
| Presentation Pack (P.O. Pack No. 32) | | | 60·00 | | | ☐ |

# ROYAL MAIL POSTAGE LABELS

These imperforate labels were issued as an experiment by the Post Office. Special microprocessor-controlled machines were installed at post offices in Cambridge, London, Shirley (Southampton) and Windsor to provide an after-hours sales service to the public. The machines printed and dispensed the labels according to the coins inserted and the buttons operated by the customer. Values were initially available in ½p steps to 16p and in addition, the labels were sold at philatelic counters in two packs containing either 3 values (3½, 12½, 16p) or 32 values (½p to 16p).

From 28 August 1984 the machines were adjusted to provide values up to 17p. After 31 December 1984 labels including ½p values were withdrawn. The machines were taken out of service on 30 April 1985.

Machine postage-paid impression in red on phosphorised paper with grey-green background design. No watermark. Imperforate.

**1984** (1 May–28 Aug.)

| | | | | |
|---|---|---|---|---|
| *Set of* 32 (½p to 16p) | 15·00 | 22·00 | ☐ ☐ |
| *Set of* 3 (3½p, 12½p, 16p) | 2·50 | 3·00 | ☐ ☐ |
| *Set of* 3 on First Day Cover (1 May) | | 6·50 | ☐ |
| *Set of* 2 (16½p, 17p) (28 August) | 4·00 | 3·00 | ☐ ☐ |

# ROYAL MAIL POST & GO STAMPS

Following trials of a number of self-service machines capable of dispensing postage labels, Royal Mail began installing "Post and Go" machines in larger post offices in October 2008. In addition to postage labels, the machines dispense stamps with a pre-printed background and an inkjet printed indicator of the service required, together with a four-part code.

The first machines were sited at the Galleries post office in Bristol and came into use on 8 October 2008. They dispensed five different stamps, dependent on the service; the code at the foot of the stamp referring to the branch in which the machine is sited, the machine number within the branch, and the session and transaction numbers.

The five original stamps were later complemented by values for 40g. and 60g. services. Unused stocks of earlier designs, such as Birds and Farmyard Animals also began to appear carrying the new service indicators and those seen have now been listed, although the set prices shown are generally for the values available at the time each design was released.

> Collectors should note that the listings are for the different *values* available from Post & Go machines, not the different designs provided in the special packs available from Tallents House. These packs are listed as separate items below each set.

FT **1**

(Gravure Walsall, thermally printed service indicator)

**2008** (8 Oct.)**-12** Type FT **1**. Self-adhesive. Olive-brown background. Two phosphor bands. Perf 14×14½

| | | | |
|---|---|---|---|
| FS1a | "1st Class up to 100g" | 2.00 | 2.00 |
| FS2a | "1st Large up to 100g" | 2.50 | 2.50 |
| FS3a | "Europe up to 20g" | 3.50 | 3.50 |
| FS3c | "Europe up to 60g" | 7.50 | 7.50 |
| FS4a | "Worldwide up to 10g" | 4.00 | 4.00 |
| FS5a | "Worldwide up to 20g" | 3.50 | 3.50 |
| FS5c | "Worldwide up to 40g" | 11.00 | 11.00 |
| FS5d | "Worldwide up to 60g" | 8.50 | 8.50 |
| FS1a/3a, 4a/5c *Set of 6* | | 24.00 | 24.00 |
| Special Pack (Nos. FS1/5) *(31.3.09)* | | 70.00 | |

The special pack contains separate stamps. These are reproductions of the first "Post and Go" stamps printed at the Galleries Post Offices, Bristol. They differ from machine printed stamps in having the service indicator and branch code printed in gravure.

It is possible to obtain *se-tenant* strips of mixed values from "Post and Go" machines but we do not list these.

FT **2** Blue Tit

## Birds of Britain (1st series)

**2010** (17 Sept.) Multicoloured. Self-adhesive. Designs printed in gravure by Walsall; thermally printed service indicator. Two phosphor bands. Perf 14×14½

| | | | |
|---|---|---|---|
| FS6 | (1st Class up to 100g) | 7.50 | 7.50 |
| FS7 | (1st Large up to 100g) | 8.00 | 8.00 |
| FS8 | (Europe up to 20g) | 8.00 | 8.00 |
| FS9 | (Worldwide up to 10g) | 15.00 | 15.00 |
| FS10 | (Worldwide up to 20g) | 11.00 | 11.00 |
| FS10a | (Worldwide up to 40g) | 55.00 | 50.00 |
| FS6/10 *Set of 5* | | 45.00 | 45.00 |
| First Day Cover (No. FS6 in 6 designs) | | | 20.00 |
| Special Pack (No. FS6 in 6 designs) | | 22.00 | |

Nos. FS6/10 were each available in six different designs: Type FT **2**, Goldfinch, Wood Pigeon, Robin, House Sparrow and Starling.

Nos. FS6/10 were available from Post and Go terminals in 30 post offices.

Stamps from the special pack and first day cover sold by Tallents House differ from machine printed stamps in having the service indicator and branch code printed in gravure.

No. FS10a resulted from the late use of old stock

FT **3** Blackbird

## Birds of Britain (2nd series)

**2011** (24 Jan.) Multicoloured. Self-adhesive. Two phosphor bands. Designs printed in gravure by Walsall; thermally printed service indicator. Perf 14×14½

| | | | |
|---|---|---|---|
| FS11 | (1st class up to 100g) | 3.00 | 3.00 |
| FS12 | (1st Large up to 100g) | 3.50 | 3.50 |
| FS13 | (Europe up to 20g) | 3.50 | 3.50 |
| FS13a | (Europe up to 60g) | 25.00 | 25.00 |
| FS14 | (Worldwide up to 10g) | 7.50 | 7.50 |
| FS15 | (Worldwide up to 20g) | 4.00 | 4.00 |
| FS15a | (Worldwide up to 40g) | 28.00 | 25.00 |
| FS15b | (Worldwide up to 60g) | 25.00 | 25.00 |
| FS11/13, 14, 15 *Set of 5* | | 20.00 | 20.00 |
| First Day Cover (No. FS11 in 6 designs) | | | 20.00 |
| Special Pack (No. FS11 in 6 designs) | | 40.00 | |

Nos. FS11/15 were each available in 6 different designs: FT **3**, two Magpies, Long-tailed Tit, Chaffinch, Collared Dove and Greenfinch.

Stamps from the special pack and first day cover sold by Tallents House differ from machine printed stamps in having the service indicator and branch code printed in gravure.

No. FS15a resulted from the late use of old stock

FT **4** Mallard

## Birds of Britain (3rd series)

**2011** (19 May) Multicoloured. Self-adhesive. Two phosphor bands. Designs printed in gravure by Walsall; thermally printed service indicator. Perf 14×14½

| | | | |
|---|---|---|---|
| FS16 | (1st Class up to 100g) | 2.75 | 2.75 |
| FS17 | (1st Large up to 100g) | 3.25 | 3.25 |
| FS18 | (Europe up to 20g) | 3.25 | 3.25 |

| | | | | |
|---|---|---|---|---|
| FS18a (Europe up to 60g) | 35·00 | 35·00 | ☐ | ☐ |
| FS19 (Worldwide up to 10g) | 5·00 | 5·00 | ☐ | ☐ |
| FS20 (Worldwide up to 20g) | 3·75 | 3·75 | ☐ | ☐ |
| FS20a (Worldwide up to 40g) | 10·00 | 10·00 | ☐ | ☐ |
| FS20b (Worldwide up to 60g) | 35·00 | 35·00 | ☐ | ☐ |
| FS16/18,19, 20 Set of 5 | 16·00 | 16·00 | ☐ | ☐ |
| First Day Cover (No. FS16 in 6 designs) | | 8·75 | | ☐ |
| Special Pack (No. FS16 in 6 designs) | 10·00 | | | |

Nos. FS16/20 were each available in six different designs: , FT **4**, Greylag Goose and Kingfisher, Moorhen, Mute Swan, Great Crested Grebe.

Stamps from the special pack sold by Tallents House differ from machine printed stamps in having the service indicator and branch code printed in gravure.

No. FS20a resulted from the late use of old stock

FT **5** Puffin

### Birds of Britain (4th series)

**2011** (16 Sept.) Multicoloured. Self-adhesive. Two phosphor bands. Designs printed in gravure by Walsall; thermally printed service indicator. Perf 14x14½

| | | | | |
|---|---|---|---|---|
| FS21 (1st class up to 100g) | 2·50 | 2·50 | ☐ | ☐ |
| FS22 (1st Large up to 100g) | 3·00 | 3·00 | ☐ | ☐ |
| FS23 (Europe up to 20g) | 3·00 | 3·00 | ☐ | ☐ |
| FS23a (Europe up to 60g) | 9·00 | 9·00 | ☐ | ☐ |
| FS24 (Worldwide up to 10g) | 4·50 | 4·50 | ☐ | ☐ |
| FS25 (Worldwide up to 20g) | 4·00 | 4·00 | ☐ | ☐ |
| FS26 (Worldwide up to 40g) | 10·00 | 10·00 | ☐ | ☐ |
| FS26a (Worldwide up to 60g) | 10·00 | 10·00 | ☐ | ☐ |
| FS21/3, 24/6 Set of 6 | 24·00 | 24·00 | ☐ | ☐ |
| First Day Cover (FS21 in 6 designs) | | 7·25 | | ☐ |
| Special Pack (No. FS21 in 6 designs) | 10·00 | | | |

Nos. FS21/5 were each available in six different designs: Type FT **5**, Gannet, Oystercatcher, Ringed Plover, Cormorant and Arctic Tern.

Stamps from the special pack sold by Tallents House differ from machine printed stamps in having the service indicator and branch code printed in gravure.

FT **6** Welsh Mountain Badger Face

### British Farm Animals (1st series). Sheep

**2012** (24 Feb). Multicoloured. Self-adhesive Two phosphor bands. Gravure Walsall, thermally printed service indicator. Perf 14½.

| | | | | |
|---|---|---|---|---|
| FS27 (1st Class up to 100g) | 2·50 | 2·50 | ☐ | ☐ |
| FS28 (1st Large up to 100g) | 3·00 | 3·00 | ☐ | ☐ |
| FS29 (Europe up to 20g) | 3·00 | 3·00 | ☐ | ☐ |
| FS29a (Europe up to 60g) | 10·00 | 10·00 | ☐ | ☐ |
| FS30 (Worldwide up to 10g) | 4·50 | 4·50 | ☐ | ☐ |
| FS31 (Worldwide up to 20g) | 4·00 | 4·00 | ☐ | ☐ |
| FS32 (Worldwide up to 40g) | 5·50 | 5·50 | ☐ | ☐ |
| FS32a (Worldwide up to 60g) | 11·00 | 11·00 | ☐ | ☐ |
| FS27/9, 30/2 Set of 6 | 20·00 | 20·00 | ☐ | ☐ |
| First Day Cover (FS27 in 6 designs) | | 8·75 | | ☐ |
| Special Pack (FS27 in 6 designs) | 8·00 | | | |

Nos. FS27/32 were each available in six different designs: FT **6**; Dalesbred; Jacob; Suffolk; Soay; Leicester Longwool.

FT **7** Berkshire

### British Farm Animals (2nd series). Pigs

**2012** (24 Apr). Multicoloured. Self-adhesive. Two phosphor bands. Designs printed in gravure by Walsall; thermally printed service indicator. Perf. 14x14½.

| | | | | |
|---|---|---|---|---|
| FS33 (1st class up to 100g) | 2·50 | 2·50 | ☐ | ☐ |
| FS34 (1st Large up to 100g) | 3·00 | 3·00 | ☐ | ☐ |
| FS35 (Europe up to 20g) | 3·00 | 3·00 | ☐ | ☐ |
| FS35a (Europe up to 60g) | 11·00 | 11·00 | ☐ | ☐ |
| FS36 (Worldwide up to 10g) | 4·50 | 4·50 | ☐ | ☐ |
| FS37 (Worldwide up to 20g) | 4·00 | 4·00 | ☐ | ☐ |
| FS38 (Worldwide up to 40g) | 5·50 | 5·50 | ☐ | ☐ |
| FS38a (Worldwide up to 60g) | 12·00 | 12·00 | ☐ | ☐ |
| FS33/5, 36/8 Set of 6 | 20·00 | 20·00 | ☐ | ☐ |
| First Day Cover (No. FS33 in 6 designs) | | 8·50 | | ☐ |
| Special Pack (FS33 in 6 designs) | 10·00 | | | ☐ |

Nos. FS33/8 were each available in six different designs: FT **7**; Gloucestershire Old Spot; Oxford Sandy and Black; Welsh; Tamworth; British Saddleback.

FT **8** Union Flag

### Union Flag

**2012** (21 May). Type FT **4**. Multicoloured. Self-adhesive. Two phosphor bands. Designs printed in gravure by Walsall; thermally printed service indicator. Perf 14x14½

| | | | | |
|---|---|---|---|---|
| FS39 (1st Class up to 100g) | 2·50 | 2·50 | ☐ | ☐ |
| FS40 (1st Large up to 100g) | 3·00 | 3·00 | ☐ | ☐ |
| FS41 (Europe up to 20g) | 3·00 | 3·00 | ☐ | ☐ |
| FS41a (Europe up to 60g) | 7·00 | 7·00 | ☐ | ☐ |
| FS42 (Worldwide up to 10g) | 4·50 | 4·50 | ☐ | ☐ |
| FS43 (Worldwide up to 20g) | 4·00 | 4·00 | ☐ | ☐ |
| FS44 (Worldwide up to 40g) | 5·50 | 5·50 | ☐ | ☐ |
| FS44a (Worldwide up to 60g) | 8·00 | 8·00 | ☐ | ☐ |
| FS39/41, 42/4 Set of 6 | 20·00 | 20·00 | ☐ | ☐ |
| First Day Cover (No. FS39 only) | | 2·50 | | ☐ |
| Special Pack (No. FS39 only) | 2·00 | | ☐ | |

FT **9** Irish Moiled

### British Farm Animals (3rd series). Cattle

**2012** (28 Sept.) Multicoloured. Designs printed in gravure by Walsall, thermally printed service indicator. Self-adhesive. Two phosphor bands. Perf 14x14½

| | | | | |
|---|---|---|---|---|
| FS45 (1st Class up to 100g) | 3·25 | 3·25 | ☐ | ☐ |
| FS46 (1st Large up to 100g) | 3·75 | 3·75 | ☐ | ☐ |
| FS47 (Europe up to 20g) | 3·75 | 3·75 | ☐ | ☐ |
| FS47a (Europe up to 60g) | 11·00 | 11·00 | ☐ | ☐ |
| FS48 (Worldwide up to 10g) | 5·00 | 5·00 | • | ☐ |
| FS49 (Worldwide up to 20g) | 4·50 | 4·50 | ☐ | ☐ |

| | | | | |
|---|---|---|---|---|
| FS50 (Worldwide up to 40g) | 6·50 | 6·50 | ☐ | ☐ |
| FS50a (Worldwide up to 60g) | 12·00 | 12·00 | ☐ | ☐ |
| FS45/7, 48/50 Set of 6 | 25·00 | 25·00 | ☐ | ☐ |
| First Day Cover (No. FS45 in 6 designs) | | 8·50 | | ☐ |
| Special Pack (FS45 in 6 designs) | 8·00 | | ☐ | |

Nos. FS45/50 were each available in six different designs: FT9; Welsh Black; Highland; White Park; Red Poll; Aberdeen Angus.

FT **10** Robin

### Christmas Robin

**2012** (6–17 Nov). With date code in background. Type FT 10. Multicoloured. Self-adhesive. Two phosphor bands. Perf 14×14½

| | | | | |
|---|---|---|---|---|
| FS51 (1st Class up to 100g) | 2·50 | 2·50 | ☐ | ☐ |
| FS52 (1st Large up to 100g) | 3·00 | 3·00 | ☐ | ☐ |
| FS53 (Europe up to 20g) | 3·25 | 3·25 | ☐ | ☐ |
| FS53b (Europe up to 60g) | 8·50 | 8·50 | ☐ | ☐ |
| FS54 (Worldwide up to 10g) | 4·00 | 4·00 | ☐ | ☐ |
| FS55 (Worldwide up to 20g) | 4·00 | 4·00 | ☐ | ☐ |
| FS56 (Worldwide up to 40g) | 5·50 | 5·50 | ☐ | ☐ |
| FS56b (Worldwide up to 60g) | 9·50 | 9·50 | ☐ | ☐ |
| FS51/3, 54/6 Set of 6 | 20·00 | 20·00 | ☐ | ☐ |

FT **11** Lesser Silver Water Beetle

### Freshwater Life (1st series). Ponds

**2013** (22 Feb). Multicoloured. Self-adhesive. Two phosphor bands. Perf 14×14½

| | | | | |
|---|---|---|---|---|
| FS59 (1st Class up to 100g) | 2·50 | 2·50 | ☐ | ☐ |
| FS60 (1st Large up to 100g) | 3·00 | 3·00 | ☐ | ☐ |
| FS61 (Europe up to 20g) | 3·00 | 3·00 | ☐ | ☐ |
| FS61a (Europe up to 60g) | 8·50 | 8·50 | ☐ | ☐ |
| FS62 (Worldwide up to 10g) | 4·50 | 4·50 | ☐ | ☐ |
| FS63 (Worldwide up to 20g) | 4·00 | 4·00 | ☐ | ☐ |
| FS64 (Worldwide up to 40g) | 5·50 | 5·50 | ☐ | ☐ |
| FS64a (Worldwide up to 60g) | 9·50 | 9·50 | ☐ | ☐ |
| FS59/61, 62/4 Set of 6 | 20·00 | 20·00 | ☐ | ☐ |
| First Day Cover | | 9·50 | | ☐ |
| Special Pack (FS59 in 6 designs) | 8·00 | | ☐ | |

Nos. FS59/64 were each available in six different designs: Type FT **11**, Three-spined Stickleback, Smooth Newt, Fairy Shrimp, Emperor Dragonfly and Glutinous Snail.

FT **12** Perch

### Freshwater Life (2nd series). Lakes

**2013** (25 June). Self-adhesive. Two phosphor bands. Perf 14×14½

| | | | | |
|---|---|---|---|---|
| FS65 (1st Class up to 100g) | 3·25 | 3·25 | ☐ | ☐ |
| FS66 (1st Large up to 100g) | 3·75 | 3·75 | ☐ | ☐ |
| FS67 (Europe up to 20g) | 3·75 | 3·75 | ☐ | ☐ |
| FS67a (Europe up to 60g) | 11·00 | 11·00 | ☐ | ☐ |
| FS68 (Worldwide up to 10g) | 5·00 | 5·00 | ☐ | ☐ |
| FS69 (Worldwide up to 20g) | 4·50 | 4·50 | ☐ | ☐ |
| FS70 (Worldwide up to 40g) | 6·50 | 6·50 | ☐ | ☐ |
| FS70a (Worldwide up to 60g) | 12·00 | 12·00 | ☐ | ☐ |
| FS65/7 68/70 Set of 6 | 25·00 | 25·00 | ☐ | ☐ |
| First Day Cover | | 9·50 | | ☐ |
| Special Pack (FS65 in 6 designs) | 8·00 | | ☐ | |

Nos. FS65/70 were each available in six different designs: Type FT **12**, European Eel, Crucian Carp, Caddis Fly Larva, Arctic Char and Common Toad.

FT **13** Minnow

### Freshwater Life (3rd series). Rivers

**2013** (20 Sept). Self-adhesive. Two phosphor bands. Perf 14×14½

| | | | | |
|---|---|---|---|---|
| FS71 (1st Class up to 100g) | 2·50 | 2·50 | ☐ | ☐ |
| FS72 (1st Large up to 100g) | 3·00 | 3·00 | ☐ | ☐ |
| FS73 (Europe up to 20g) | 3·00 | 3·00 | ☐ | ☐ |
| FS73a (Europe up to 60g) | 8·00 | 8·00 | ☐ | ☐ |
| FS74 (Worldwide up to 10g) | 4·50 | 4·50 | ☐ | ☐ |
| FS75 (Worldwide up to 20g) | 4·00 | 4·00 | ☐ | ☐ |
| FS76 (Worldwide up to 40g) | 5·50 | 5·50 | ☐ | ☐ |
| FS76a (Worldwide up to 60g) | 9·00 | 9·00 | ☐ | ☐ |
| FS71/3, 74/6 Set of 6 | 20·00 | 20·00 | ☐ | ☐ |
| First Day Cover | | 9·50 | | ☐ |
| Special Pack (FS71 in 6 designs) | 8·00 | | ☐ | |

Nos. FS71/6 were each available in six different designs: Type FT **13**, Atlantic Salmon, White-clawed Crayfish, River Lamprey, Blue-winged Olive Mayfly Larva and Brown Trout.

**2013** (19 Nov.)-**14** Type FT **1**. with date code in background, Self-adhesive. Two phosphor bands. Perf 14×14½

| | | | | |
|---|---|---|---|---|
| FS77a "1st Class up to 100g" | 2.50 | 2.50 | ☐ | ☐ |
| FS78a "1st Large up to 100g" | 3·00 | 3·00 | ☐ | ☐ |
| FS79a "Europe up to 20g" | 7·00 | 7·00 | ☐ | ☐ |
| FS79b "Euro 20g World 10g" | 3·75 | 3·75 | ☐ | ☐ |
| FS80a "Europe up to 60g" | 4·50 | 4·50 | ☐ | ☐ |
| FS81a "Worldwide up to 10g" | — | — | ☐ | ☐ |
| FS82a "Worldwide up to 20g" | 3·75 | 3·75 | ☐ | ☐ |
| FS83a "Worldwide up to 40g" | — | — | ☐ | ☐ |
| FS84a "Worldwide up to 60g" | 5·50 | 5·50 | ☐ | ☐ |
| FS77a, 78a, 79b, 80a, 82a, 84a Set of 6 | 20·00 | 20·00 | ☐ | ☐ |

FS 85/92 are reserved for Union Flag stamps with date codes.

FT **14**

**2013** (20 Nov)-14. Type FT **14** with date code in background. New blue background. Self-adhesive. One phosphor band (over the Queen's head). Perf 14×14½

| | | | | |
|---|---|---|---|---|
| FS93a (2nd Class up to 100g) | 2.50 | 2.50 | ☐ | ☐ |

FS94a (2nd Large up to 100g)    3.00    3.00  ☐  ☐

Post & Go stamps as Type FT **14** were issued by Tallents House on 20 February 2013 in packs and on first day covers (price £7 per pack or first day cover). They were sold at Spring Stampex 2013 but were not made available through post offices until November 2013.

FT **15** Primrose

### British Flora (1st series). Spring Blooms

**2014** (19 Feb-31 Mar). Multicoloured. Self-adhesive. Two phosphor bands. Perf 14×14½

| | | | | |
|---|---|---|---|---|
| FS95 | (1st Class up to 100g) | 2·50 | 2·50 | ☐ ☐ |
| FS96 | (1st Large up to 100g) | 3·00 | 3·00 | ☐ ☐ |
| FS97 | (Europe up to 20g) | 4·00 | 4·00 | ☐ ☐ |
| FS98 | (Europe up to 60g) (31.3) | 7·50 | 7·50 | ☐ ☐ |
| FS99 | (Worldwide up to 10g) | 4·50 | 4·50 | ☐ ☐ |
| FS100 | (Worldwide up to 20g) | 4·00 | 4·00 | ☐ ☐ |
| FS101 | (Worldwide up to 40g) | 6·00 | 6·00 | ☐ ☐ |
| FS102 | (Worldwide up to 60g) (31.3) | 8·50 | 8·50 | ☐ ☐ |
| FS95/7 and FS99/101 *Set of 6* | | 22·00 | 22·00 | ☐ ☐ |
| First Day Cover (FS95 in 6 designs) | | | 9·50 | ☐ |
| Special Pack (FS95 in strip of 6 designs) | | 8·00 | | ☐ |

Nos. FS95/102 were each available in six different designs: Type FT **15**, Snowdrop, Lesser Celandine, Dog Violet, Wild Daffodil and Blackthorn.

**OPEN VALUE LABELS** In February 2014, "Open Value labels", previously dispensed from Post & Go machines printed on white self-adhesive paper began to appear on the same illustrated background labels as Post & Go stamps. These show a service indicator "1L" (1st Letter), "2SP" (2nd Small Parcel), etc and the price. These are outside the scope of this catalogue, but on 7 July 2014 Royal Mail released a special pack containing five such labels in the Machin Head design, as Types FT **1** and FT **14** (Price £8).

FT **17** Forget-me-not

### British Flora (2nd series). Symbolic Flowers

**2014** (17 Sept). Multicoloured. Self-adhesive. Two phosphor bands. Perf 14×14½

| | | | | |
|---|---|---|---|---|
| FS103 | (1st Class up to 100g) | 2·50 | 2·50 | ☐ ☐ |
| FS104 | (1st Large up to 100g) | 3·00 | 3·00 | ☐ ☐ |
| FS105 | (Euro 20g World 10g) | 3·25 | 3·25 | ☐ ☐ |
| FS106 | (Europe up to 60g) | 4·00 | 4·00 | ☐ ☐ |
| FS107 | (Worldwide up to 20g) | 3·75 | 3·75 | ☐ ☐ |
| FS108 | (Worldwide up to 60g) | 5.00 | 5.00 | ☐ ☐ |
| FS103/8 *Set of 6* | | 20.00 | 20.00 | ☐ ☐ |
| First Day Cover (FS103 in 6 designs) | | | 9.50 | ☐ |
| Special Pack (FS103 in 6 designs) | | 8.00 | | ☐ |

Nos. FS103/8 were each available in six different designs: Type FT **17**, Common Poppy, Dog Rose, Spear Thistle, Heather and Cultivated Flax.

FT **18** Common Ivy

### British Flora (2nd series). Winter Greenery

**2014** (17 Sept). Multicoloured. Self-adhesive. Two phosphor bands. Perf 14×14½

| | | | | |
|---|---|---|---|---|
| FS109 | (2nd Class up to 100g) | 2.25 | 2.25 | ☐ ☐ |
| FS110 | (2nd Large up to 100g) | 2.75 | 2.75 | ☐ ☐ |
| FS111 | (1st Class up to 100g) | 2.50 | 2.50 | ☐ ☐ |
| FS112 | (1st Large up to 100g) | 3.00 | 3.00 | ☐ ☐ |
| FS113 | (Euro 20g World 10g) | 3.25 | 3.25 | ☐ ☐ |
| FS114 | (Europe up to 60g) ) | 4.00 | 4.00 | ☐ ☐ |
| FS115 | (Worldwide up to 20g) | 3.75 | 3.75 | ☐ ☐ |
| FS116 | (Worldwide up to 60g) | 5.00 | 5.00 | ☐ ☐ |
| FS109/16 *Set of 8* | | 23.00 | 23.00 | ☐ ☐ |
| First Day Cover (109/12 in 4 designs) | | | 9.50 | ☐ |
| Special Pack (FS109/12 in 4 designs) | | 8.00 | | ☐ |

Nos. FS109/10 were each available as Type FT **18** or Mistletoe. Nos. FS 111/16 were all available as Butcher's Broom or Holly.

# OFFICIAL STAMPS

Various stamps of Queen Victoria and King Edward VII overprinted in Black.

**I.R.**  **I. R.**  **O.W.**

**OFFICIAL**  **OFFICIAL**  **OFFICIAL**
(O **1**)  (O **2**)  (O **3**)

**ARMY**  **ARMY**

**OFFICIAL**  **OFFICIAL**  **GOVᵀ PARCELS**
(O **4**)  (O **5**)  (O **7**)

**BOARD**  **R.H.**  **ADMIRALTY**

**OF**

**EDUCATION**  **OFFICIAL**  **OFFICIAL**
(O **8**)  (O **9**)  (O **10**)

## 1 Inland Revenue
Overprinted with Types O **1** or O **2** (5s, 10s, £1)

**1882–1901** Queen Victoria

| | | | | |
|---|---|---|---|---|
| O2 | 52 | ½d green | 85·00 | 32·00 |
| O5 | | ½d blue | 85·00 | 29·00 |
| O13 | 71 | ½d vermilion | 12·00 | 5·00 |
| O17 | | ½d green | 18·00 | 12·00 |
| O3 | 57 | 1d lilac (Die II) | 7·50 | 5·00 |
| O6 | 64 | 2½d lilac | £500 | £180 |
| O14 | 74 | 2½d purple on blue | £150 | 20·00 |
| O4 | 43 | 6d grey (Plate 18) | £575 | £135 |
| O18 | 79 | 6d purple on red | £450 | £110 |
| O7 | 65 | 1s green | £6000 | £1800 |
| O15 | 82 | 1s green | £900 | £325 |
| O19 | | 1s green and red | £4200 | £1800 |
| O9 | 59 | 5s red | £9500 | £2400 |
| O10 | 60 | 10s blue | £11000 | £3500 |
| O11 | 61 | £1 brown (Wmk Crowns) | £75000 | £30000 |
| O12 | | £1 brown (Wmk Orbs) | £100000 | £40000 |
| O16 | | £1 green | £12000 | £2500 |

**1902–04** King Edward VII

| | | | | |
|---|---|---|---|---|
| O20 | 83 | ½d blue-green | 30·00 | 3·25 |
| O21 | | 1d red | 20·00 | 2·25 |
| O22 | 86 | 2½d blue | £900 | £250 |
| O23 | 83 | 6d purple | £425000 | £190000 |
| O24 | 93 | 1s green and red | £3500 | £700 |
| O25 | 95 | 5s red | £40000 | £10000 |
| O26 | 96 | 10s blue | £120000 | £45000 |
| O27 | 97 | £1 green | £60000 | £24000 |

## 2 Office of Works
Overprinted with Type O **3**

**1896–1902** Queen Victoria

| | | | | |
|---|---|---|---|---|
| O31 | 71 | ½d vermilion | £300 | £130 |
| O32 | | ½d green | £425 | £190 |
| O33 | 57 | 1d lilac (Die II) | £475 | £130 |
| O34 | 78 | 5d dull purple and blue | £3800 | £1200 |
| O35 | 81 | 10d dull purple and red | £6750 | £2000 |

**1902–03** King Edward VII

| | | | | |
|---|---|---|---|---|
| O36 | 83 | ½d blue-green | £550 | £160 |
| O37 | | 1d red | £550 | £160 |
| O38 | 85 | 2d green and red | £1900 | £400 |
| O39 | 86 | 2½d blue | £3250 | £600 |
| O40 | 92 | 10d purple and red | £45000 | £6750 |

## 3 Army
Overprinted with Types O **4** (½d, 1d) or O **5** (2½d, 6d)

**1896–1901** Queen Victoria

| | | | | |
|---|---|---|---|---|
| O41 | 71 | ½d vermilion | 6·00 | 2·75 |
| O42 | | ½d green | 6·00 | 12·00 |
| O43 | 57 | 1d lilac (Die II) | 6·00 | 5·00 |
| O44 | 74 | 2½d purple on blue | 45·00 | 30·00 |
| O45 | 79 | 6d purple on red | £100 | 50·00 |

Overprinted with Type O **4**

**1902** King Edward VII

| | | | | |
|---|---|---|---|---|
| O48 | 83 | ½d blue-green | 5·50 | 2·25 |
| O49 | | 1d red | 5·50 | 2·25 |
| O50 | | 6d purple | £160 | 75·00 |

## 4 Government Parcels
Overprinted with Type O **7**

**1883–1900** Queen Victoria

| | | | | |
|---|---|---|---|---|
| O69 | 57 | 1d lilac (Die II) | 90·00 | 25·00 |
| O61 | 62 | 1½d lilac | £375 | 90·00 |
| O65 | 72 | 1½d purple and green | £140 | 20·00 |
| O70 | 73 | 2d green and red | £225 | 40·00 |
| O71 | 77 | 4½d green and red | £350 | £250 |
| O62 | 63 | 6d green | £3000 | £1200 |
| O66 | 79 | 6d purple on red | £250 | 60·00 |
| O63 | 64 | 9d green | £2500 | £1000 |
| O67 | 80 | 9d purple and blue | £375 | 90·00 |
| O64 | 44 | 1s brown (Plate 13) | £1600 | £275 |
| O64c | | 1s brown (Plate 14) | £3300 | £500 |
| O68 | 82 | 1s green | £650 | £250 |
| O72 | | 1s green and red | £600 | £250 |

**1902** King Edward VII

| | | | | |
|---|---|---|---|---|
| O74 | 83 | 1d red | 55·00 | 13·00 |
| O75 | 85 | 2d green and red | £200 | 38·00 |
| O76 | 83 | 6d purple | £250 | 38·00 |
| O77 | 91 | 9d purple and blue | £600 | £160 |
| O78 | 93 | 1s green and red | £1300 | £275 |

## 5 Board of Education
Overprinted with Type O **8**

**1902** Queen Victoria

| | | | | |
|---|---|---|---|---|
| O81 | 78 | 5d dull purple and blue | £4500 | £1200 |
| O82 | 82 | 1s green and red | £10000 | £5500 |

**1902–04** King Edward VII

| | | | | |
|---|---|---|---|---|
| O83 | 83 | ½d blue-green | £160 | 40·00 |
| O84 | | 1d red | £160 | 40·00 |
| O85 | 86 | 2½d blue | £4700 | £400 |
| O86 | 89 | 5d purple and blue | £32500 | £9500 |
| O87 | 93 | 1s green and red | £185 000 | |

### 6 Royal Household
Overprinted with Type O **9**

**1902** King Edward VII

| | | | | | | |
|---|---|---|---|---|---|---|
| O91 | **83** | ½d | blue-green | £375 | £200 | ☐ ☐ |
| O92 | | 1d | red | £325 | £175 | ☐ ☐ |

### 7 Admiralty
Overprinted with Type O **10**

**1903** King Edward VII

| | | | | | | |
|---|---|---|---|---|---|---|
| O101 | **83** | ½d | blue-green | 27·00 | 13·00 | ☐ ☐ |
| O102 | | 1d | red | 20·00 | 6·50 | ☐ ☐ |
| O103 | **84** | 1½d | purple and green | £300 | £140 | ☐ ☐ |
| O104 | **85** | 2d | green and red | £325 | £150 | ☐ ☐ |
| O105 | **86** | 2½d | blue | £450 | £140 | ☐ ☐ |
| O106 | **87** | 3d | purple on yellow | £400 | £150 | ☐ ☐ |

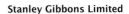

# Prestige and Sponsored Booklets – a Simplified listing

On 1 December 1969 a new style of large-size booklet was issued, entitled "Stamps for Cooks", sponsored by the Milk Marketing Board and containing recipes and stamps to a value of £1. The booklet contained one pane in a *se-tenant* combination that was not available from any other source, ensuring that sales to stamp collectors were high, even if those to cooks were probably rather limited!

In spite of this success, however, it was 1972 before a second sponsored booklet, "The Story of Wedgwood" was issued, providing the only source of the p Machin definitive with one phosphor band at left. Nearly eight years were to pass before the same company sponsored a second "Story of Wedgwood" booklet, followed two years later by Stanley Gibbons with "Story of Stanley Gibbons".

From then on, sponsored large-size booklets became an annual event, generally containing at least one stamp which was not available from any other source. In 1989 Royal Mail themselves became the "sponsors" of each new booklet, which were by then widely known among collectors simply as "Prestige Booklets". Their frequency of issue increased steadily, until in 2009 four such booklets were issued.

In 2011, with the issue of the "Morris & Co" booklet, Royal Mail introduced an additional charge, over and above the face value of the stamps contained in them to cover the costs of manufacturing these booklets and with this change the Stanley Gibbons catalogue number prefix was altered from "DX" to "DY".

This simplified checklist provides a complete listing of the Prestige and Sponsored booklets issued to the end of 2014.

DX**3**

| | | | |
|---|---|---|---|
| ZP1a | £1 Stamps for Cooks *1.2.69* | 13·00 | ☐ |
| DX1 | £1 The Story of Wedgwood *24.5.72* | 75·00 | ☐ |
| DX2 | £3 The Story of Wedgwood *16.4.80* | 8·00 | ☐ |
| DX3 | £4 Story of Stanley Gibbons *19.5.82* | 11·00 | ☐ |
| DX4 | £4 Story of the Royal Mint *14.9.83* | 11·00 | ☐ |
| DX5 | £4 The Story of our Christian Heritage *4.9.84* | 30·00 | ☐ |
| DX6 | £5 The Story of The Times *8.1.85* | 20·00 | ☐ |
| DX7 | £5 The Story of British Rail *18.3.86* | 30·00 | ☐ |
| DX8 | £5 The Story of P&O *3.3.87* | 25·00 | ☐ |
| DX9 | £5 The Story of The Financial Times *9.2.88* | 40·00 | ☐ |

| | | | |
|---|---|---|---|
| DX10 | £5 The Scots Connection *21.3.89* | 22·00 | ☐ |
| DX11 | £5 London Life *20.3.90* | 28·00 | ☐ |
| DX12 | £6 Alias Agatha Christie *19.3.91* | 20·00 | ☐ |
| DX13 | £6 Cymru-Wales *25.2.92* | 20·00 | ☐ |
| DX14 | £6 Tolkien, the Centenary *27.10.92* | 20·00 | ☐ |
| DX15 | £5.64 The Story of Beatrix Potter *10.8.93* | 20·00 | ☐ |
| DX16 | £6.04 Northern Ireland *26.7.94* | 25·00 | ☐ |
| DX17 | £6 The National Trust *25.4.95* | 25·00 | ☐ |
| DX18 | £6.48 European Football Championship *14.5.96* | 20·00 | ☐ |
| DX19 | £6.15 Celebrating 75 years of the BBC *23.9.97* | 20·00 | ☐ |
| DX20 | £7.49 The Wilding Definitives *10.3.98* | 26·00 | ☐ |
| DX21 | £6.16 Breaking Barriers *13.10.98* | 35·00 | ☐ |
| DX22 | £7.54 Profile on Print *16.2.99* | 40·00 | ☐ |
| DX23 | £6.99 World Changers *21.9.99* | 35·00 | ☐ |
| DX24 | £7.50 Special by Design *15.2.00* | 45·00 | ☐ |
| DX25 | £7.03 The Life of the Century *4.8.00* | 32·00 | ☐ |
| DX26 | £7.00 A Treasury of Trees *18.9.00* | 40·00 | ☐ |
| DX27 | £6.76 Unseen & Unheard *22.10.01* | 40·00 | ☐ |
| DX28 | £7.29 A Gracious Ascension *6.2.02* | 45·00 | ☐ |
| DX29 | £6.83 Across the Universe *24.9.02* | 35·00 | ☐ |
| DX30 | £6.99 Microcosmos *25.2.03* | 30·00 | ☐ |
| DX31 | £7.46 A Perfect Coronation *2.6.03* | 70·00 | ☐ |
| DX32 | £7.44 Letters by Night *16.3.04* | 26·00 | ☐ |
| DX33 | £7.23 The Glory of the Garden *25.5.04* | 40·00 | ☐ |
| DX34 | £7.43 The Brontë Sisters *24.2.05* | 28·00 | ☐ |
| DX35 | £7.26 Battle of Trafalgar *18.10.05* | 24·00 | ☐ |
| DX36 | £7.40 Isambard Kingdom Brunel *23.2.06* | 26·00 | ☐ |
| DX37 | £7.44 Victoria Cross *21.9.06* | 35·00 | ☐ |
| DX38 | £7.49 World of Invention *1.3.07* | 24·00 | ☐ |
| DX39 | £7.66 The Machin, the Making of a Masterpiece *5.6.07* | 24·00 | ☐ |
| DX40 | £7.66 British Army Uniforms *20.9.07* | 26·00 | ☐ |
| DX41 | £7.40 Ian Fleming's James Bond *8.1.08* | 30·00 | ☐ |
| DX42 | £7.15 Pilot to Plane, RAF Uniforms *18.9.08* | 20·00 | ☐ |
| DX43 | £9.72 50th Anniversary of Country Definitives *29.9.08* | 28·00 | ☐ |
| DX44 | £7.68 British Design Classics *13.1.09* | 38·00 | ☐ |

| | | | |
|---|---|---|---|
| DX45 | £7.75 | Charles Darwin *12.2.09* | 45·00 ☐ |
| DX46 | £8.18 | Treasures of the Archive *18.8.09* | 22·00 ☐ |
| DX47 | £7.93 | Royal Navy Uniforms *17.9.09* | 20·00 ☐ |
| DX48 | £8.06 | Classic Album Covers *7.1.10* | 30·00 ☐ |
| DX49 | £7.72 | The Royal Society *25.2.10* | 20·00 ☐ |
| DX50 | £11.15 | King George V *8.5.10* | 30·00 ☐ |
| DX51 | £9.76 | Britain Alone *13.5.10* | 25·00 ☐ |
| DX52 | £9.05 | WWF, For a Living Planet *22.3.11* | 25·00 ☐ |
| DY1 | £9.99 | Morris & Co *5.5.11* | 25·00 ☐ |
| DY2 | £9.97 | First United Kingdom Aerial Post *9.9.11* | 40·00 ☐ |
| DY3 | £11.47 | Roald Dahl *10.1.12* | 28·00 ☐ |
| DY4 | £12.77 | The Diamond Jubilee *31.5.12* | 30·00 ☐ |
| DY5 | £10.71 | Olympic and Paralympic Games *27.7.12* | 50·00 ☐ |
| DY6 | £13.77 | 50 Years of Doctor Who *26.3.13* | 30·00 ☐ |
| DY7 | £11.11 | Football Heroes *9.5.13* | 25·00 ☐ |
| DY8 | £11.19 | Merchant Navy *19.9.13* | 25·00 ☐ |
| DY9 | £13.97 | Classic Locomotives *20.2.14* | 32·00 ☐ |
| DY10 | £11.39 | Buckingham Palace *15.4.14* | 25·00 ☐ |
| DY11 | £11.30 | Centenary of the First World War *28.7.14* | 25·00 ☐ |

# Philatelic, Numismatic and Philatelic Medallic Covers

On 2 June 1993 Royal Mail and the Royal Mint prepared a commemorative cover to celebrate the 40th anniversary of the Coronation of Her Majesty The Queen. The cover bore the Royal Mint's Coronation Anniversary Crown and the £10 'Britannia' stamp, issued on 2 March 1993 (No. 1658).

On 1 March 1994 a similar cover was produced for the 25th Anniversary of the Investiture of HRH The Prince of Wales. The cover bore the set of five stamps issued on that date (Nos. 1810/14), showing paintings by Prince Charles, and a commemorative medal struck by the Royal Mint.

So began a series of Philatelic Numismatic Covers (PNC) and Philatelic Medallic Covers (PMC) produced by Royal Mail and the Royal Mint.

This listing comprises only those jointly produced covers sold by the Philatelic Bureau. Privately sponsored covers incorporating coins or medals including those sponsored by the Royal Mint alone, are outside its scope.

| No. | Date | Issue | Stamps | Coin/Medal | Price |
|-----|------|-------|--------|-----------|-------|
| RMC1 | 2.6.93 | Coronation 40th Anniv | 1658 | £5 Coin | 28·00 |
| RMC2 | 1.3.94 | Prince of Wales Investiture 25th Anniv | 1810/14 | Medal | 22·00 |
| RMC3 | 27.7.94 | Bank of England 300th Anniv | 1666×4 + label | £2 Coin | 20·00 |
| RMC4 | 20.5.95 | R. J. Mitchell Birth Cent | 1666×4 + label | Medal | 20·00 |
| RMC5 | 15.8.95 | End of Second World War 50th Anniv | 1873, 1875 | £2 Coin | 20·00 |
| RMC6 | 29.10.95 | William Wyon Birth Bicent | Y1725 | Medal | 20·00 |
| RMC7 | 21.4.96 | Queen's 70th Birthday | 1666×4 + label | £5 Coin | 24·00 |
| RMC8 | 14.5.96 | European Football Championship | 1925/9 | £2 Coin | 20·00 |
| RMC9 | 1.10./3.11.96 | Classic Sports Cars | 1945/9 | Medal | 20·00 |
| RMC10 | 28.1.97 | King Henry VIII 450th Death Anniv | 1965/71 | £1 Coin | 20·00 |
| RMC11 | 30.6.97 | Transfer of Hong Kong to Chinese Rule | 1671×4 + label | Hong Kong $5 Coin | 20·00 |
| RMC12 | 23.8.97 | British Aircraft Designers | 1984/8 | £2 Coin | 20·00 |
| RMC13 | 20.11.97 | Royal Golden Wedding | 2011/14 | £5 Coin | 24·00 |
| RMC14 | 24.2.98 | Order of the Garter 650th Anniv | 2026/30 | £1 Coin | 20·00 |
| RMC15 | 5.7.98 | NHS 50th Anniv | 2046/9 | 50p Coin | 20·00 |
| RMC16 | 25.8.98 | Notting Hill Carnival | 2055/8 | 50p Coin | 20·00 |
| RMC17 | 14.11.98 | HRH Prince of Wales 50th Birthday | 1666×4 + label | £5 Coin | 24·00 |
| RMC18 | 12.5.99 | Berlin Airlift 50th Anniv | 1666×4 + label | Medal | 20·00 |
| RMC19 | 1.7.99 | New Scottish Parliament Building | S94/7 | £1 Coin | 20·00 |
| RMC20 | 1.10.99 | Rugby World Cup, Wales | 1664a×4 + label | £2 Coin | 20·00 |

| No. | Date | Issue | Stamps | Coin/Medal | Price |
|---|---|---|---|---|---|
| RMC21 | 31.12.99 | Millennium | MS2123 | £5 Coin | 34·00 |
| RMC22 | 4.4.00 | National Botanic Garden of Wales | 2124×4 + label | £1 Coin | 20·00 |
| RMC23 | 14.8.00 | 150 Years of Public Libraries | 2116, 2121, 2100 | 50p Coin | 20·00 |
| RMC24 | 4.8.00 | Queen Mother's 100th Birthday | MS2161 | £5 Coin | 24·00 |
| RMC25 | 1.1.01 | Archers Radio Programme 50th Anniv | 2107/8, 2110 | Medal | 20·00 |
| RMC26 | 24.5.01 | RN Submarine Service Cent | 2202/5 | Medal | 20·00 |
| RMC27 | 20.6.01 | Queen Victoria Death Cent | 2133 + label | £5 Coin | 24·00 |
| RMC28 | 2.10.01 | Northern Ireland | NI89/92 | £1 Coin | 20·00 |
| RMC29 | 6.02 | Golden Jubilee | 2253/7 | £5 Coin | 24·00 |
| RMC29a | 6.2.02 | Golden Jubilee | 2258/9 | £5 Coin and £5 note | 28·00 |
| RMC30 | 31.5.02 | World Cup Football, Japan & Korea | 5×1st from MS2292 | £1 Coin | 20·00 |
| RMC31 | 16.7.02 | 17th Commonwealth Games, Manchester | 2299/303 | 4×£2 Coins | 30·00 |
| RMC32 | 11.12.02 | Queen Mother Commemoration | 2280/3 | £5 Coin | 24·00 |
| RMC33 | 25.2.03 | Discovery of DNA 50th Anniv | 2343/7 | £2 Coin | 21·00 |
| RMC34 | 2.6.03 | Coronation 50th Anniv | 2368/77 | £5 Coin | 24·00 |
| RMC35 | 27.8.03 | Extreme Endeavours | 2360/5 | £1 Coin | 20·00 |
| RMC36 | 7.10.03 | British Museum 250th Anniv | 2404/9 | Medal | 20·00 |
| RMC37 | 13.1.04 | Classic Locomotives | 2417/22 | £2 Coin | 21·00 |
| RMC38 | 6.4.04 | Entente Cordiale Cent | 2446/7 + France 50c, 75c | £5 Coin | 25·00 |
| RMC39 | 13.4.04 | Ocean Liners | 2448/53 | Medal | 22·00 |
| RMC40 | 25.5.04 | RHS Bicentenary | 2456/61 | Medal | 21·00 |
| RMC41 | 30.11.04 | Scotland Definitive | S109/10, S112/13 | £1 Coin | 20·00 |
| RMC42 | 24.2.05 | Charlotte Brontë 150th Death Anniv | 2518/23 | 50p Coin | 20·00 |
| RMC43 | 1.3.05 | Wales Definitive | W98/9, W101/2 | £1 Coin | 20·00 |
| RMC44 | 21.4.05 | World Heritage Sites | 2532/5 + Australia 2×50c. & 2×$1 | 50p Coin + Australia 50c. | 24·00 |
| RMC45 | 5.7.05 | End of the War 60th Anniv | MS2547 | Medal and £2 Coin | 24·00 |
| RMC46 | 18.10.05 | Battle of Trafalgar Bicent | 2574/9 | 2×£5 Coins | 37·00 |
| RMC47 | 23.2.06 | Brunel Birth Bicent | 2607/12 | 2×£2 Coins | 24·00 |
| RMC48 | 17.3.06 | Northern Ireland Definitive | NI94/5, NI98, NI100 | £1 Coin | 20·00 |
| RMC49 | 21.4.06 | Queen's 80th Birthday | 2620/7 | £5 Coin | 27·00 |
| RMC50 | 6.6.06 | World Cup Football | 2628/33 | Medal | 22·00 |
| RMC51 | 18.7.06 | National Portrait Gallery 150th Anniv | 2640/9 | Medal | 22·00 |
| RMC52 | 21.9.06 | Victoria Cross 150th Anniv | 2657/62 | 2×50p Coins | 23·00 |
| RMC53 | 16.1.07 | Act of Union 300th Anniv | 6×1st as 2570 but litho | £2 Coin | 23·00 |
| RMC54 | 13.2.07 | 'The Sky at Night' 50th Anniv | 2709/14 | Medal | 22·00 |
| RMC55 | 22.3.07 | Abolition of the Slave Trade Bicent | 2728/33 | £2 Coin | 23·00 |
| RMC56 | 23.4.07 | England Definitive | EN6/8, EN12, EN15 | £1 Coin | 20·00 |
| RMC57 | 5.6.07 | First Machin Stamps 40th Anniv | Type 1984 | Medal | 22·00 |
| RMC58 | 3.7.07 | British Motor Racing | 2744/9 | Medal | 22·00 |
| RMC59 | 26.7.07 | Scouting centenary | 2758/63 | 50p Coin | 23·00 |
| RMC60 | 20.11.07 | Diamond Wedding | 2780/6 | £5 Coin | 35·00 |
| RMC61 | 1.4.08 | Territorial Army Cent | 2774/6 | Medal | 22·00 |
| RMC62 | 13.5.08 | St. Paul's Cathedral 300th Anniv | MS2847 | Medal | 22·00 |
| RMC63 | 5.6.08 | First Machin Coin 40th Anniv | Type 1984 | Medal | 22·00 |
| RMC64 | 17.7.08 | Farnborough 'A Celebration of Aviation' | 2885/60 | Medal | 22·00 |
| RMC65 | 24.7.08 | 1908 Olympic Games, London Cent | 4×1st | £2 Coin | 25·00 |
| RMC66 | 29.9.08 | Country Definitives 50th Anniv and £1 Coin 25th Anniv | MSNI111 | £1 Coin | 20·00 |
| RMC67 | 6.11.08 | Armistice 90th Anniv | 2883/5 | Medal | 22·00 |
| RMC68 | 13.1.09 | Mini car 50th Anniv | 2889×2 | Medal | 22·00 |
| RMC69 | 22.1.09 | Robert Burns 250th Birth Anniv | MSS137 | £2 Coin | 23·00 |
| RMC70 | 12.2.09 | Charles Darwin Birth Bicent | 2898/903 | £2 Coin | 30·00 |
| RMC71 | 2.3.09 | First Concorde Test Flight 40th Anniv | 2891×2 | Medal | 22·00 |
| RMC72 | 23.4.09 | Accession of Henry VIII 500th Anniv and Accession of Elizabeth I 450th Anniv | 2925, 2929 2×£5 | Coins | 35·00 |
| RMC73 | 19.5.09 | Royal Botanic Gardens, Kew 250th Anniv | MS2941 | 50p Coin | 23·00 |
| RMC74 | 1.9.09 | Fire and Rescue Service | 2958/63 | Medal | 22·00 |
| RMC75 | 18.9.09 | Big Ben 150th Anniv | Type 1517 + label | Medal | 22·00 |
| RMC76 | 22.10.09 | Countdown to London 2012 Olympic Games I The countdown begoins... | 2981/90 | £5 Coin | 26·00 |
| RMC77 | 1.12.09 | High value Security Definitives | U2913/16 | £1 Coin | 24·00 |
| RMC78 | 2.2.10 | Girlguiding Cent | MS3025 | 50p Coin | 23·00 |
| RMC79 | 25.2.10 | Royal Society 350th Anniv | 3026/35 | Medal | 22·00 |
| RMC80 | 11.3.10 | Battersea Cats and Dogs Home 150th Anniv | 3036/45 | Medal | 22·00 |
| RMC81 | 21.4.10 | City of London | As 1st St. George's flag stamp from MSEN19 but self-adhesive+label | £1 Coin | 24·00 |
| RMC82 | 13.5.10 | Dunkirk | MS3086 | Medal | 22·00 |
| RMC83 | 27.7.10 | Countdown to London 2012 Olympic Games II The Games spring to life... | 3097/106 | £5 Coin | 26·00 |
| RMC84 | 1.8.10 | Florence Nightingale | 2570 + label | £2 Coin | 24·00 |
| RMC85 | 12.10.10 | Olympic and Paralympic Sports I. Athletics – Track | 2983 | 50p Coin | 15·00 |
| RMC86 | 12.10.10 | Olympic and Paralympic Sports II Cycling | 3101 | 50p Coin | 15·00 |

| No. | Date | Issue | Stamps | Coin/Medal | Price |
|---|---|---|---|---|---|
| RMC87 | 30.11.10 | Olympic and Paralympic Sports III Football | 3104 | 50p Coin | 15·00 |
| RMC88 | 30.11.10 | Olympic and Paralympic Sports IV Boccia | 2985 | 50p Coin | 15·00 |
| RMC89 | 11.1.11 | 'F.A.B. The Genius of Gerry Anderson' | MS3142 | Medal | 22·00 |
| RMC90 | 1.2.11 | Olympic and Paralympic Sports V Weightlifting | 2989 | 50p Coin | 15·00 |
| RMC91 | 1.2.11 | Olympic and Paralympic Sports VI Hockey | 3103 | 50p Coin | 15·00 |
| RMC92 | 17.3.11 | City of Belfast | NI103 | £1 Coin | 24·00 |
| RMC93 | 22.3.11 | WWF 50th Anniv | MS3172 | 50p Coin | 24·00 |
| RMC94 | 24.3.11 | Olympic and Paralympic Sports VII Shooting | 3098 | 50p Coin | 15·00 |
| RMC95 | 24.3.11 | Olympic and Paralympic Sports VIII Goalball | 3105 | 50p Coin | 15·00 |
| RMC96 | 21.4.11 | Royal Wedding | MS3180 | £5 Coin | 26·00 |
| RMC97 | 26.5.11 | Olympic and Paralympic Sports IX Taekwondo | 3100 | 50p Coin | 15·00 |
| RMC98 | 26.5.11 | Olympic and Paralympic Sports X Boxing | 3106 | 50p Coin | 15·00 |
| RMC99 | 14.6.11 | Thomas the Tank Engine | 3187/92 | Medal | 22·00 |
| RMC100 | 27.7.11 | Countdown to London 2012 Olympic Games IV The final push to the line | 3195/204 | £5 Coin | 26·00 |
| RMC101 | 27.7.11 | Olympic and Paralympic Sports XI Wrestling | 3199 | 50p Coin | 15·00 |
| RMC102 | 27.7.11 | Olympic and Paralympic Sports XII Handball | 3204 | 50p Coin | 15·00 |
| RMC103 | 23.8.11 | Restoration of the Monarchy | 3207/14 | £5 Coin | 23·00 |
| RMC104 | 22.9.11 | Olympic and Paralympic Sports XIII Basketball | 2990 | 50p Coin | 15·00 |
| RMC105 | 22.9.11 | Olympic and Paralympic Sports XIV Modern Pentathlon | 3099 | 50p Coin | 15·00 |
| RMC106 | 6.10.11 | 500th Anniv of Launch of *Mary Rose* | 2925 and *Mary Rose* stamp from MS2930 | £2 Coin | 24·00 |
| RMC107 | 8.11.11 | Christmas 400th Anniv of the King James Bible | 3237/43 | £2 coin | 24·00 |
| RMC108 | 29.11.11 | Olympic and Paralympic Sports XV Canoeing | 2981 | 50p coin | 15·00 |
| RMC109 | 29.11.11 | Olympic and Paralympic Sports XVI Archery | 2982 | 50p coin | 15·00 |
| RMC110 | 30.11.11 | City of Edinburgh | S110 + label | £1 coin | 24·00 |
| RMC111 | 5.1.12 | Olympic and Paralympic Games | 3250/3 | £2 coin | 26·00 |
| RMC112 | 12.1.12 | Olympic and Paralympic Sports XVII Aquatics | 2984 | 50p coin | 15·00 |
| RMC113 | 12.1.12 | Olympic and Paralympic Sports XVIII Rowing | 3097 | 50p coin | 15·00 |
| RMC114 | 28.2.12 | Olympic and Paralympic Sports XIX Sailing | 3195 | 50p coin | 15·00 |
| RMC115 | 28.2.12 | Olympic and Paralympic Sports XX Badminton | 2988 | 50p coin | 15·00 |
| RMC116 | 1.3.12 | City of Cardiff | W99+label | £1 coin | 24·00 |
| RMC117 | 1.4.12 | Olympic and Paralympic Sports XXI Judo | 2986 | 50p coin | 15·00 |
| RMC118 | 1.4.12 | Olympic and Paralympic Sports XXII Triathlon | 3203 | 50p coin | 15·00 |
| RMC119 | 6.5.12 | Olympic and Paralympic Sports XXIII Wheelchair rugby | 3198 | 50p coin | 15·00 |
| RMC120 | 6.5.12 | Olympic and Paralympic Sports XXIV Volleyball | 3197 | 50p coin | 15·00 |
| RMC121 | 21.5.12 | Diamond Jubilee | 3319/26 | £5 coin | 26·00 |
| RMC122 | 12.6.12 | Olympic and Paralympic Sports XXV Equestrian | 2987 | 50p coin | 15·00 |
| RMC123 | 12.6.12 | Olympic and Paralympic Sports XXVI Table Tennis | 3102 | 50p coin | 15·00 |
| RMC124 | 19.6.12 | Charles Dickens Birth Bicent | 3330/5 | £2 coin | 24·00 |
| RMC125 | 27.7.12 | Olympic and Paralympic Sports XXVII Wheelchair Tennis | 3200 | 50p coin | 15·00 |
| RMC126 | 27.7.12 | Olympic and Paralympic Sports XXVIII Fencing | 3201 | 50p coin | 15·00 |
| RMC127 | 27.7.12 | Countdown to London 2012 Olympic Games IV. Crossing the Finishing Line | MS3341 | £5 coin and £5 silver proof coin | 26·00 |
| RMC128 | 28.8.12 | Olympic and Paralympic Sports XXIX Gymnastics | 3202 | 50p coin | 15·00 |
| RMC129 | 28.8.12 | Olympic and Paralympic Sports XXX Athletics – Field | 3196 | 50p coin | 15·00 |
| RMC130 | 9.1.13 | 150th Anniv of the London Underground | 3423/8 | 2×£2 Coins | 30·00 |
| RMC131 | 30.5.13 | 60th Anniv of the Coronation. Six Decades of Royal Portraits | 3491/6 | £2 Coin | 26·00 |
| RMC132 | 22.11.13 | Birth Cent of Benjamin Britten | 3459 | 50p. Coin | 24·00 |
| RMC133 | 7.1.14 | Classic Children's TV | 3552/63 | Medal | 30·00 |
| RMC134 | 15.4.14 | Buckingham Palace | 3589/94 | Medal | 22·00 |
| RMC135 | 17.7.14 | Commonwealth Games, Glasgow | 3619/24 | 50p. coin | 26·00 |
| RMC136 | 28.7.14 | Centenary of the First World War | 3626/31 | £2 coin | 26·00 |
| RMC137 | 23.9.14 | Ryder Cup, Gleneagles | S158 | Medal | 22·00 |
| RMC138 | 18.9.14 | 500th Anniversary of Trinity House | 3638 | £2 coin | 24·00 |

# Stanley Gibbons
## 399 Strand

## Unsure how to progress your collection?

Visit 399 Strand to get advice from our experienced and knowledgeable staff. They will help to choose philatelic products that will enhance and develop your collection as well as advising on techniques for the care and storage of your stamps and catalogues.

## We have one of the largest ranges of albums and philatelic accessories in the world.

We pride ourselves in having possibly the most comprehensive range of philatelic accessories and albums available. We strive to cater for every need a collector might have, and if we don't have the exact item you need, we will recommend an equivalent or an alternative.

## Come in, browse our range and choose what's best for you.

Before you commit to a particular album, take the time to talk to our staff who will help you weigh up the pros and cons before you make your decision. We are always happy to demonstrate anything we sell from tweezers to Frank Godden luxury albums.

## OUR PROMISE TO YOU!

If anything is out of stock when you visit, we will ship it to you free of charge.

Scan the QR code for directions to our shop

Please contact Wayne Elliott - **shop@stanleygibbons.com**
399 Strand opening hours **Mon-Fri 9am-5pm  Sat 9:30am-5pm  Sun Closed**

Est 1856
## STANLEY GIBBONS

**Stanley Gibbons Limited**
399 Strand, London, WC2R 0LX
+44 (0)20 7557 4444
www.stanleygibbons.com

# **Collect British Stamps** Order Form

## YOUR ORDER

Stanley Gibbons account number ☐☐☐☐☐☐

| Condition (mint/UM/ used) | Country | SG No. | Description | Price | Office use only |
|---|---|---|---|---|---|
| | | | | | |
| | | | | | |
| | | | | | |
| | | | | | |
| | | | | | |
| | | | | | |
| | | | | | |
| | | | | | |
| | | | | | |
| | | | | | |
| | | | | | |
| | | | POSTAGE & PACKING | £3.60 | |
| | | | TOTAL | | |

The lowest price charged for individual stamps or sets purchased from Stanley Gibbons Ltd, is £1.

## Payment & address details

Name

Address (We cannot deliver to PO Boxes)

Postcode

Tel No.

Email

PLEASE NOTE Overseas customers MUST quote a telephone number or the order cannot be dispatched. Please complete ALL sections of this form to allow us to process the order.

☐ Cheque (made payable to Stanley Gibbons)

☐ I authorise you to charge my

☐ Mastercard  ☐ Visa  ☐ Diners  ☐ Amex  ☐ Maestro

Card No. ☐☐☐☐ ☐☐☐☐ ☐☐☐☐ ☐☐☐☐ ☐☐☐☐ (Maestro only)

Valid from ☐☐☐  Expiry date ☐☐☐  Issue No. (Maestro only) ☐☐  CVC No. (4 if Amex) ☐☐☐☐

CVC No. is the last three digits on the back of your card (4 if Amex)

Signature

Date

## 4 EASY WAYS TO ORDER

**Post to**
Lesley Mourne,
Stamp Mail Order
Department, Stanley
Gibbons Ltd, 399
Strand, London,
WC2R 0LX, England

**Call**
020 7836 8444
+44 (0)20 7836 8444

**Fax**
020 7557 4499
+44 (0)20 7557 4499

**Click**
lmourne@
stanleygibbons.com/
co.uk?

# If YOU Buy at Auction this is How You Can Save £250+ EACH Year

ANDREW PROMOTING PHILATELY ON THE ALAN TITCHMARSH SHOW ITV

## ... I'll Give You £55 OFF to get you started

### *(... some Collectors Save thousands of pounds)*

*By Andrew McGavin, Managing Director, Universal Philatelic Auctions (UPA)*

**In all my 40+ years in the trade I have never seen an introductory offer to new clients like this .. so you may be wondering the reason why my company UPA can afford to make this offer to you?**

In *'plain talk'* most auctions charge 'Buyers Premiums' –YES! You have to pay up to 25% (some charge more) **on top of the *winning price you paid***. That is Simply an Incredible surcharge. Apparently this significant premium is justified by charging the seller a lower fee in order to entice consignments for sale.

My company UPA does not charge any premiums which is one of the reasons why we hold the UK record of 1,750 different bidders in our last auction – an amazing 91% of whom were successful. Fortunately the average bidder spends an average of £250+ per auction...so that with 4 auctions a year offering 80,000+/- lots from £1 to £100,000 for you to choose from ....

**with NO Buyer's Premium You Save up to £250+ <u>EACH YEAR PLUS</u> You take NO RISK with our 28 day unconditional Guarantee**

### So How can UPA offer You £55 OFF too?

1. **Our Business Model is Different.** Fundamentally I believe that if a stamp/philatelic item is not selling then it is too expensive. Compare that with the stamp business whose stock is the same each time you see or hear from them. At the risk of boring you …

2. **Stamp Industry's BIGGEST problem.** … twenty years ago I started to ponder upon what is the biggest problem faced by the average stamp dealer? The answer came back loud and clear. The biggest problem faced by a stamp dealer is not what sells … **but what does not sell**. This is the reason why most stamp dealers have lots of unsold stock you have seen time and time again – worse still this is what prevents that dealer from buying new stock to offer you.

3. **Surface Sell.** There is an actual name for this – it is called 'surface sell' – good material 'floats' on the surface and sells. Less desirable stock sinks so that unless a dealer pays almost nothing to replace his stock then the profit in the business becomes stagnant and bound in less saleable stock. If only that dealer could move this stock he would have more money to invest in new stock to offer to you.

4. **Cover-up.** Twenty years ago almost the entire stamp industry spent its time disguising what did not sell – in those days so pernicious were 'unsolds' that it was common practice for one auction house to sell batches of 'unsolds' to another auction where the new auction could present them to (hopefully) different collectors as new lots. 'Passing the Philatelic Parcel' was common practice.

5. **E-Bay.** Today the philatelic world is almost unrecognisably different. In large part courtesy of the internet. How things have changed. Few 'pass the parcel'. Really active Dealers - these days they **also** sell on eBay - large lots, small lots, all manner of stamps, covers, down to fakes and forgeries – today's equivalent of the Wild West – there's philatelic 'gold' to be mined in those hills … but Boy – you have to work to find it and sadly 'all that glistens is not gold' – you pays your money and you takes your chance often with little support or recourse. UPA too sells surpluses on eBay backed by support and our guarantee – access eBay links via *www.upastampauctions.co.uk*

# If YOU Buy at Auction this is How You Can Save £250+ EACH Year
## ... I'll Give You £55 OFF to get you started

ANDREW PROMOTING PHILATELY ON THE ALAN TITCHMARSH SHOW ITV

## Our Business Model is Different ...

6. **You said that before.** So Just How does UPA differ? We looked for solutions to the 'unsolds' problem – if we could solve that problem we would sell more, utilise stock more efficiently and have funds available for new stock ... and so we created ...

7. **Selling Systems.** It is a 'given' you can order sets / singles in *standard condition* from dealers ... but the moment a stamp becomes used, or even mounted mint it is no longer standard. Is it heavy hinged, is the cancel parcel, wavy or CDS (circular date stamp)? Each stamp requires separate handling and unique pricing so the only way to handle such efficiently is in a selling system.

8. **Integrated Selling Systems.** Avon & Omniphil Approvals - 20 years ago our business sold in 2 different selling systems: individually priced stamps upon home **approval** and **unit priced** 'loose' stamps sent to collectors as **mixtures** (today you can still request either at *www.upastampauctions.co.uk*). A bit like 'Water-Works' and 'Electricity' in monopoly the 2 systems allowed us to buy more, sell more and pay higher prices to obtain better stock ... but we had no outlet for rarer / high value stamps so ...

9. **Universal Philatelic Auctions.** ... 15 years ago we created and added **UPA** to allow us to handle more valuable stamps not suited to Approvals, but we knew that in order to eliminate the 'unsolds' issue we needed to come up with a further unique selling proposition ...

10. **Best of Conventional Auctions.** ... so we scoured the stamp world for best practice ideas and all of the

features that collectors like you love - such as lots unconditionally guaranteed or dislike such as pernicious buyer's premiums. UPA employed all of the best features and then carefully added unique features such as ...

11. **Standardised Airmail Shipping, Insurance Included.** ... so that no matter how much you win you'll know in advance exactly how much delivery will be ... (and we made it modest too) ... finally, and this is the **painful part** we had to recognise that if something was not selling it was too expensive ... so ...

12. **Unique UPA Reducing Estimate System.** ...we created the unique *UPA Reducing Estimate System*. Creating transparency we grabbed the bull by the horns telling you how many times a lot has been previously unsold at the end of each description ... and although we initially set to reduce by 10% each time unsold ... we didn't; in practice we reduce by 11%, then a further12%, 13%, 14% each time re-offered and so on till sold or given away

13. **Today, almost 15 years later.** ... but would it work? ... Today almost 15 years later the *UPA reducing estimate system* **is unique to the trade** and 1,750 different collectors and some dealers bid in our last auction – 91% of whom were successful. Fusing all of the synergies of integrated selling systems combined with the most efficient use of stamps in the industry the system works thanks to loyal support from Collectors like you. Collectors tend to stay with UPA but as clients come and sadly some go ... we need to attract new clients joining to maintain the integrity of the system which is why ...

*... which is Why I'll Give You £55 OFF to get You Started!*

## www.upastampauctions.co.uk        info@upastampauctions.co.uk

## – send the coupon / simply request in any way today!–

## OR VIEW / BID ON-LINE NOW – we'll take your £55 off